MARIANNE M. JENNINGS
...

FOUNDATIONS *of the* LEGAL ENVIRONMENT *of Business*

Marianne Moody Jennings

Arizona State University

SOUTH-WESTERN
CENGAGE Learning™

Australia • Brazil • Japan • Korea • Mexico • Singapore • Spain • United Kingdom • United States

SOUTH-WESTERN
CENGAGE Learning™

Foundations of the Legal Environment of Business
Marianne M. Jennings

VP/Editorial Director: Jack W. Calhoun

Editor-in-Chief: Rob Dewey

Acquisitions Editor: Vicky True

Sr. Developmental Editor:
Laura Bofinger

Marketing Manager: Jennifer Garamy

Sr. Content Project Manager:
Tamborah Moore

Editorial Assistant: Krista Kellman

Managing Media Editor: Pam Wallace

Senior Media Editor: Kristen Meere

Sr. Frontlist Buyer, Manufacturing:
Kevin Kluck

Production Service:
LEAP Publishing Services

Compositor: Macmillan Publishing
Solutions

Rights Acquisitions Account Manager,
Text: Mardell Glinski Schultz

Sr. Art Director: Michelle Kunkler

Internal Designer: Kim Torbeck/
Imbue Design

Cover Designer: Kim Torbeck/
Imbue Design

Cover Images:
Main - © DonovanReese/
PhotoDisc, Inc.

Inset - © Pete Turner/Stone/
Getty Images, Inc.

Photography Manager:
Deanna Ettinger

For product information and technology assistance, contact us at
**Cengage Learning Customer & Sales Support,
1-800-354-9706**

For permission to use material from this text or product,
submit all requests online at **www.cengage.com/permissions**
Further permissions questions can be emailed to
permissionrequest@cengage.com

Library of Congress Control Number: 2008942191
ISBN-13: 978-0-324-56651-2
ISBN-10: 0-324-56651-4

South-Western Cengage Learning
5191 Natorp Boulevard
Mason, OH 45040
USA

Cengage Learning products are represented in Canada by Nelson Education, Ltd.

For your course and learning solutions, visit www.cengage.com

Purchase any of our products at your local college store or at our preferred online store **www.ichapters.com**

Printed in the United States of America
2 3 4 5 6 7   12 11 10

*To my roots, my mother and father, and to my branches, sprouts, gardeners,
and inspiration, my husband and children, Terry, Sarah,
Sam, John, and our beloved Claire*

Brief Contents

Contents

PART 2
BUSINESS: ITS REGULATORY ENVIRONMENT 85

PART 3
THE LEGAL ENVIRONMENT OF BUSINESS OPERATIONS 221

PART 4
THE LEGAL ENVIRONMENT OF BUSINESS RELATIONSHIPS 363

CHAPTER 17
Management and Employee Rights and Laws 384

CHAPTER 18
Employment Discrimination 416

Preface

A World of Daily Legal and Ethical Issues

The business world seems to change on a daily basis. From the way the stock market moves to the litigation between eBay and Tiffany's, there is always business news. Siemens settles bribery charges and AIG agrees to cancel all of its expensive executive retreats because of the taxpayers' concerns about overspending by the company following the government bailout and investment in AIG. Six years ago we were dealing with the collapses of Enron, WorldCom, Adelphia, HealthSouth, Parmalat, Arthur Andersen, Kmart, and others. Just months before going to press with this edition, we lost Bear Stearns, Countrywide Mortgage, New Century Financial, Lehman Brothers, Fannie Mae, and other companies to high-risk investments, too much debt, and too little disclosure. The SEC is investigating stock options backdating at over 200 companies, including a settlement with Apple Computer. The NBA has had a scandal with one of its referees, major league baseball has everything from grand juries to Congressional hearings on player steroid use, and the NFL finds one of its star players entering a guilty plea to federal charges related to dog fighting. Members of Congress have entered guilty pleas to everything from accepting payoffs to wire fraud. One senator was convicted of not reporting substantial gifts and another senator is under investigation for his relationships with a subprime lender. The issues of law and ethics are still at the forefront of business, sports, and government. It has become a tall order just to keep up with all the events!

These companies and organizations and all the individuals working in them certainly could have benefited from understanding and keeping at the forefront of their decision processes the basics of law and ethics! The legal and ethical environments of business are center stage. Congress made massive regulatory reform a reality in 2002 with the passage of the Sarbanes-Oxley legislation on corporate governance, accounting regulation, and criminal penalties. In 2008, Congress reformed everything from mortgage lending to federal deposit insurance at banks. The USA Patriot Act continues to have an effect on businesses in everything from money transfers to hiring employees. Business is even more international, and we are witnessing the need for better regulation of production processes abroad. U.S. toymaker Mattel had to recall 19 million of its made-in-China toys because the factories there had used lead-based paint, something that is legal in China but prohibited in the United States. The world and business continue to change and grow, but law and ethics have retained their role and importance. In fact, now more than ever, we need to understand the legal and ethical issues that affect our businesses and our lives. The knowledge base and even the questions in law and ethics remain the same, but the underlying facts have changed. For example, we still debate the social responsibility role of business. Now we raise that issue in the context of whether Yahoo! should do business in China when the government forces disclosure of customer identity because it believes the Yahoo! customers are using the service for dissident activities. We have new fact patterns with changing events and technology, but we are still debating the same issue of human rights and the role of business in countries in which there are violations of those basic tenets of social responsibility. We still have the question of when a contract is formed, but now we face that question with "point and click" technology rather than faxes and letters. We continue to be concerned about our privacy as consumers, but now we apply the law to our use of the Internet for our purchases and correspondence and wonder whether companies can use the information they find there. Years after the Napster case was settled, we still wonder about the extent of copyright law but now YouTube is the focus of copyright issues and we have plenty of lawsuits and injunctions for the items posted there.

The world is different, but law and ethics remain a constant framework into which we fit the issues of the day. In the materials that follow, you have the chance to understand the marvelous stability of this framework and the ease with which you can apply it to this very different world. Be sure to review this text's unique features, such as the "Consider" tutorials and the ethics issues.

Building the Bridge: Applying Legal and Ethical Reasoning to Business Analysis

My students recently completed their midterm exam—a review of what happened with Mattel and its recalled toys. These students are in the second year of their masters degree studies. They have been trained in economics, marketing, management, and finance. But as they completed their analysis of what went wrong and why with the world's largest toy manufacturer, they had an epiphany. A company can get the finance issues right (Mattel saved 30 percent in production costs by outsourcing to China), have the right brand appeal and great products, and even yield terrific sales figures. However, it can all fall apart over the legal issues. China's standards for paint are different from those of the United States—lead paint is not prohibited there. And the contracts between U.S. companies and Chinese production facilities allowed those factories there to use the paint unless the buyer specified otherwise. The law of contracts and the differing legal standards in international business were at the heart of this major setback for a company, one that would cause a 25 percent drop in its stock. When it comes to problems with safety and toys, my students soon realized there is strict liability for the error and additional financial implications. The students were well trained in economic theory, supply chain management, cash flow issues, and market capitalization. They are very capable *business* students. However, they did not realize until this midterm exam how much of business turns on anticipating the legal issues and getting them resolved correctly. They also realized that all of our discussions of ethics and social responsibility had a critical role in doing busines and in making business decisions. TANSTAAFL—"There ain't no such thing as a free lunch" when it comes to international outsourcing. There are costs associated with using the much cheaper labor and factories in other countries. Those costs come from legal issues, which, if handled poorly, can affect a company's value and tarnish its brand name.

Why couldn't these students see the interconnection and critical roles of law and ethics in business until this case for their midterm? It was not for lack of exposure to the law. I taught my course "by the book," so to speak. Students could recite the components of a valid contract, rattle off the requirements for bankruptcy, recall from memory the antitrust statutes. Yet, I was coming to realize, this rote knowledge was not enough. One of my best former students, who had gone on to medical school, came to me perplexed about her office lease. She said that the complex in which she wanted to open her practice had a "no advertising" policy. In fact, she said that when she toured the premises with a leasing agent, the leasing agent turned to her and said, "You're not one of those doctors who advertises, are you? Because if you are, we can't lease to you. We have a policy against it." One of my best students, who knew the antitrust statutes well, could not apply them to her everyday business. Worse, perhaps, she could not *recognize* when to apply these statutes: She did not see the antitrust implications of the agent's statements nor the problems with the physicians in the complex taking such an approach to screening tenants.

I reached the conclusion that there were shortcomings in the standard approach to teaching business students law and ethics. Students were not ignorant of the law; rather, they simply lacked the necessary skills to recognize legal and ethical issues and to apply their knowledge of law and ethics to business decision making. As instructors, we were not integrating legal and ethical reasoning with business analysis. My conclusion led me to develop my own materials for classroom use and eventually led to the publication of the book, *Business: Its Legal, Ethical, and Global Environment*. But, when I went back to teaching undergraduates at the sophomore level, I realized that book, now in its eighth edition, could be further adapted for the undergraduate level. They need less material, more help with problem solving, and a different way of summarizing the material in the chapters. So, this book was born to serve the needs of this generation of undergraduates.

The same bridge approach is here in this new approach, but the sentences are shorter and complex terms and ideas are explained at a different level. For all areas of law and ethics, this book answers the question: How does this concept affect a business? This book builds a bridge between knowledge of law and ethics and application of both in business. My 32 years of teaching law and ethics finally brought this realization: business ethics is not easily grasped nor practiced in business because we depersonalize ethical issues. If we just allow the company or organization to make the decision, our ethics are not in question; the company's are. The ethical issues in the book require students to bring ethical issues into their lives, their circumstances, their world. This feature also forces them to answer this question in a wide variety of contexts, "If it were you, and you were faced with the dilemma and required to make a decision, what would you do?"

Up-to-Date Content, New Approaches, Business Applications, and Learning Aids

The organizational structure of this text is the result of three rounds of feedback from faculty who teach at the undergraduate level. There are four parts to the text and each part begins with an overview that helps students see the importance of these areas of the law in running a business. Part I offers the student an overview of the legal, ethical, and judicial environments of business. Part II covers the regulatory environments of business. Part III covers the laws involved in business operations, spanning everything from the contracts in the supply chain to the rights of shareholders in a corporation. Part IV covers the legal and ethical issues in business relationships, covering everything from competitors to employees.

ETHICS

Business Ethics and Social Responsibility (Chapter 2) offers up-to-date examples and insights on the application of ethics to business decision making. Chapter 2 is chock full of the examples the last several years have netted—from the MIT dean of admissions' falsified résumé to a "Guess Who?" quiz on the companies that collapsed and the irony of their conduct and statements. Ethics coverage is also integrated throughout all chapters.

Business Applications and Learning Aids

CASE HEADLINES

Every court case has a case headline that summarizes what issues are involved in the case. In Managing Disputes: Alternative Dispute Resolution and Litigation Strategies (Chapter 3), students read *Wal-Mart Stores, Inc. v Johnson*, a case that addresses the issue of our obligations regarding evidence for a potential civil suit. In the case, a customer is injured when a paper mache reindeer falls from an upper shelf and lands on his head and shoulders. The case title is memorable: "'Reining' Deer at the Local Wal-Mart." The vivid one-line description and colorful facts of the case, a common thread throughout the case choices in the text, help students internalize the rules and lessons about not destroying evidence for a potential lawsuit.

CHAPTER OPENERS

Chapters begin with an opening problem, titled *Consider . . .* , which presents a legal dilemma relevant to the chapter's discussion and similar to those business managers need to handle. These are revisited and answered in the body of the chapter. For example, Chapter 15's opening *Consider* presents the case of an adult bookstore with the name, "Victor's Little Secret," and the resulting litigation when Victoria's Secret cried "Foul!" over the use of its good name. Moreover, answers to these opening *Considers* appear in the chapter, generally in the form of the case decision that addressed the teaser issue that the opening *Consider* raises. The student is intrigued by a problem presented as the chapter opens, gets an opportunity to see how a court would resolve that problem, and then has the chance, through additional *Considers* and the chapter problems to solve more problems with the newfound knowledge and skills. These answers provide a step-by-step approach for students to use their new knowledge and skills as they solve the problems, an approach they can also use for solving the chapter problems. Next, opening statements discuss the major topics of the chapter and present the general goals for the chapter in the form of questions to be answered. Finally, quotations, often humorous, pique students' interest and focus the chapter to the major issues.

RED FLAGS FOR MANAGERS

Each chapter concludes with an innovative summary of what the chapter covers. This learning tool evolved after discussions with faculty and students on how learning takes place. Both groups wanted a tool that gave them the chapter's key points and, true to the application focus of the book, why and how those key points mattered. For example, the following is an excerpt from the Red Flags in

Chapter 5, Administrative Law. If you can make administrative law's relevance come alive for a student, think what the Red Flags in Torts and Crimes will do:

> Administrative agencies are also responsible for enforcement of regulations. OSHA, for example, inspects workplaces and issues complaints and levies fines for violations. However, all companies have the right to due process with agencies when those agencies are taking enforcement steps. Those due process rights include the right to a hearing and, eventually, review by a court. However, agencies also have a form of alternative resolution of charges through the use of a consent decree. The consent decree is a settlement between the company and the administrative agency that settles the charges, determines the fine, and usually includes a pledge by the company to change its processes in order to avoid violations in the future.

Thinking, Applying, and Reasoning: Organization and Features

The text is organized in a logical flow for students.

ORGANIZATION

There are four parts in the book, which serve to organize the materials around business operations. Every chapter integrates international and ethical topics.

Part I

In four chapters, Part I offers an introduction to law, an introduction to business ethics and the judicial system, and a discussion of litigation and alternative dispute resolution. Part I provides students with a foundation in law and ethics, as well as legal and ethical reasoning, necessary for the areas of law in the chapters that follow. By being brief (four chapters), Part I offers instructors an early and logical break for exams.

Part II

In five chapters, Part II covers the legal and regulatory environment of business, including the following topics: constitutional law, administrative and international law, business crimes and business torts, and product advertising and liability. At the completion of Parts I and II, students have a grasp of the legal system, ethical boundaries, and the laws that affect business operational decisions. Cyberspace topics are featured throughout the book, but you can find the privacy issues, computer crimes, and even cyber-bullying in these chapters.

Part III

The six chapters in Part III present students with the legal and ethical issues in business operations. Part III includes the following contract topics, areas of law involved in managing the supply chain and distribution: contract and sales law; and financing of sales and leases, including credit disclosure and requirements. Part III also covers the operation of the company itself including how to run a corporation, the law on financing for businesses, and the rights related to intellectual property held by a business. From the negotiation of price to the collection of accounts, this segment of the book covers all aspects of selling business products and services and operating the company itself.

Part IV

The four chapters in Part IV discuss business relationships, from employees to the community. Topics include agency law and employee conduct, management of employee welfare, and employment discrimination. However, the relationship of a business to its community is covered with the placement of environmental law in this section. This new focus on environmental law as part of business inter-action, rather than just a regulatory mass, presents a new way of looking at the importance of environmental law.

FEATURES

Court Cases

Edited court language cases provide in-depth points of law, and many cases include dissenting and concurring opinions. Case questions follow to help students understand the points of law in the case and think critically about the decision. The courts have been active in their business dockets, and there are many 2005–2008 case decisions throughout the book. Students will be able to study the suit brought by a family injured when a "gas-and-dash" driver hit them as he tried to get away without paying, and as the station attendant attempted to write down his license plate. And what happens when employees work so many shifts and are so tired that they have accidents as they return home from work? Are their employers liable? What happens when a young man saves his Pepsi points to claim a Harrier Jet that he sees in a Pepsi spoof ad for "Pepsi stuff"? Does he get his jet?

Consider . . .

Consider problems, along with Ethical Issues and Business Planning Tips, are a part of every chapter. *Considers*, often based on real court cases, ask students to evaluate and analyze the legal and ethical issues discussed in the preceding text. By being integrated into the text, students must address and think critically about these issues as they encounter them. Through interactive problems, students learn to judge case facts and determine the consequences. The *Considers* bring the most current topics into the book and the classroom. This book adds a novel feature for legal environment texts: THINK, APPLY, and ANSWER. At the end of each chapter, students are reminded of what they have just learned in the reading or the case via THINK. In the APPLY section, they are walked through how the case or principles just covered would apply in the circumstances presented in this *Consider*. After they have walked through this system of reasoning, ANSWER gives them the solution. Students are then able to take the chapter problems and solve them using the THINK, APPLY, and ANSWER model on their own. This tool helps students to develop the legal and ethical reasoning skills that will give them a strong foundation for applying legal and ethical principles for the course and eventually in business.

Ethical Issues

The Ethical Issues feature appears in every chapter and presents students with real-world ethical problems to grapple with. Ethical Issues help integrate coverage of ethics into every chapter. The ethical issues also include personal and real-life examples that help students relate to the pervasive nature of ethical dilemmas that they grapple with and will continue to face once the enter the business world.

Business Planning Tips

Students are given sound business and legal advice through Business Planning Tips. With these tips, students who have now mastered the law and legal principles are trained to anticipate issues and ensure compliance.

Cyberlaw

Many chapters also include a segment on cyberlaw. These chapter-by-chapter materials, indicated by an icon in the margin of the text, give students the chance to see how new technology fits into the existing legal framework.

Exhibits

Exhibits include charts, figures, and business and legal documents that help highlight or summarize legal and ethical issues from the chapter. With the UCC revisions and the changes in criminal penalties under Sarbanes-Oxley, many of the charts are either new or updated.

End-of-Chapter Problems

Many end-of-chapter problems have been updated and focus more on actual cases. There are new chapter problems throughout the book with varied length for different instructor needs.

The Informed Manager: Who Should Use This Book?

With its comprehensive treatment of the law, integrated business applications, full-color design, and its clear writing style, *Foundations* is well suited for undergraduate students. This is a text designed to get students reading more than just the chapter summaries. Short paragraphs, thoughtful flow, and non-legalese writing have a way of grabbing students' attention and keeping them focused on the materials.

A Note on AACSB Standards

The strong presence of ethics, social responsibility, international law and issues, and the integration of other business disciplines make the book an ideal fit for meeting AACSB standards and curriculum requirements. The AACSB standards emphasize the need for students to have an understanding of ethical and global issues. The separate chapter on ethics as well as ethical issues and dilemmas for student discussion and resolution in every chapter offer a solid training for students. The separate chapter on international law is complemented by each chapter segment devoted to international law issues in that chapter's area of law. The text offers students insights into more nuanced international issues such as language in contracts, the role of lawyers in other countries, and attitudes outside the United States on insider trading and antitrust laws.

This book provides students with the legal foundation necessary for business operations and sales but also affords the students the opportunities to analyze critically the social and political environments in which the laws are made and in which businesses must operate. Just an examination of the lists of the companies and individuals covered in the text gives an excellent overview of the compelling issues and cases the text covers. All of the materials were chosen to offer students a balanced look at regulation, free enterprise, and the new global economy.

Supplements

Foundations offers a comprehensive and well-crafted supplements package for both students and instructors. Contact your Cengage Learning/South-Western Legal Studies in Business Sales Representative for more details, or visit the Jennings Web site at *www.cengage.com/blaw/jennings.*

Weekly Law Updates. Available to instructors and students is the weekly update on the law at *www.cengage.com/blaw/jennings* (click on any Marianne Jennings book and go to "Author Updates"). The weekly update contributed by the author offers at least 12 current events per month for discussion and analysis. The update features new decisions, new statutes, new regulations, and cites to current periodicals. There are reminders of these updates in each chapter opening.

Instructor's Manual. The Instructor's Manual, written by the author, provides the following for each chapter: a detailed outline; answers to Considers, Ethical Issues, and case problems; briefs of all cases; supplemental readings; and interactive/cooperative learning exercises. Available on both the IRCD and the book's companion Web site.

Test Bank. The Test Bank includes more than 1,500 questions in true-false, multiple-choice, and essay format. Answers to questions provide a subject word for easy identification and a classification indicating if they are intended for review of concepts or for analysis and application of concepts. Available on both the IRCD and the book's companion Web site.

ExamView Testing Software—Computerized Testing Software. This testing software contains all of the questions in the printed test bank. This program is an easy-to-use test creation software compatible with Microsoft Windows. Instructors can add or edit questions, instructions, and answers; and select questions by previewing them on the screen, selecting them randomly, or selecting them by number. Instructors can also create and administer quizzes online, whether over the Internet, a local area network (LAN), or a wide area network (WAN). Available on the IRCD.

Microsoft PowerPoint Lecture Review Slides. Developed by the author, PowerPoint slides are available for use by students as an aid to note-taking, and by instructors for enhancing their lectures. Available on both the IRCD and the book's companion Web site.

Instructor's Resource CD (IRCD). *(ISBN: 0-324-78174-1)* Available for instructors only. An invaluable source of instructor preparation materials, the IRCD stores the complete set of this text's Instructor's Manual, Test Bank with ExamView Testing Software, and PowerPoint Lecture Review Slides.

Lesson Plans and Lectures. Lesson Plans and Lectures, available for download at *www.cengage.com/blaw/jennings*, provides detailed lectures for each semester class period plus sample syllabi, teaching tips, and content and reading quizzes.

Business Law Digital Video Library. Featuring 60+ segments on the most important business law topics, Business Law Digital Video Library helps students make the connection between their textbook and the business world. Access to Business Law's Digital Video Library is free when bundled with a new text, and students with a used book can purchase access to the video clips online. Included with this edition is LawFlix, 12 scenes from Hollywood movies with instructor materials for each film clip. The author chose the clips, and the IM materials were written by the author and include elements such as goals for the clips, questions for students (with answers for the instructor), background on the film and the scene, and fascinating trivia about the film, its actors, and its history. For more information about Business Law Digital Video Library, visit *www.cengage.com/blaw/dvl*.

Court Case Updates from South-Western Legal Studies in Business. Once a month, South-Western provides 10-20 summaries of the most important legal cases happening around the country. Professionally selected and prepared by Roger Meiners, University of Texas–Arlington, these Court Case Updates provide the perfect information source for your legal studies course. To access this material, go to *www.cengage.com/blaw*.

A Handbook of Basic Law Terms, Black's Law Dictionary Series. This paperback dictionary, prepared by the editor of the popular *Black's Law Dictionary*, can be packaged for a small additional cost with any new South-Western Legal Studies in Business text.

Student Guide to the Sarbanes-Oxley Act. This brief overview for undergraduate business students explains the Sarbanes Oxley Act, what is required of whom, and how it might affect students in their business life. This guide is available as an optional package with the text.

WestLaw®. Westlaw® West Group's vast online source of value-added legal and business information, contains over 15,000 databases of information spanning a variety of jurisdictions, practice areas, and disciplines. Qualified instructors who adopt South-Western Legal Studies in Business textbooks may receive ten complimentary hours of Westlaw for their course (certain restrictions apply). Contact your sales representative for more information.

About the Author

Professor Marianne Jennings is a member of the Department of Management in the W.P. Carey School of Business at Arizona State University and is a professor of legal and ethical studies in business. At ASU she teaches graduate courses in the MBA program in business ethics and the legal environment of business. She served as director of the Joan and David Lincoln Center for Applied Ethics from 1995–1999. From 2006–2007, she served as the faculty director for the MBA Executive Program. Professor Jennings earned her undergraduate degree in finance and her J. D. from Brigham Young University. Her internships were with the Federal Public Defender and U.S. Attorney in Nevada, and she has done consulting work for law firms, businesses and professional groups including AES, Boeing, Dial Corporation, Mattel, Motorola, CFA Institute, Southern California Edison, the Arizona Auditor General, the Cities of Phoenix, Mesa, and Tucson, the Institute of Internal Auditors, Coca-Cola, DuPont, Blue Cross Blue Shield, Motorola, Mattel, Pepsi, Hy-Vee Foods, IBM, Bell Helicopter, Amgen, Raytheon, and VIAD.

Professor Jennings has authored hundreds of articles in academic, professional and trade journals. Currently she has six textbooks and monographs in circulation. The sixth edition of her textbook, *Case Studies in Business Ethics*, was published in January 2008 and the eighth editions of her textbooks, *Real Estate Law* and *Business: Its Legal, Ethical and Global Environment* were published in 2008. She was added as a co-author to *Anderson's Business and the Legal Environment* in 1997, a text published in its 20th edition in March 2007. Her book *Business Strategy for the Political Arena* was selected in 1985 by Library Journal as one of its recommended books in business/government relations. Professor Jennings's *A Business Tale: A Story of Ethics, Choices, Success, and a Very Large Rabbit*, a fable about business ethics, was chosen by Library Journal in 2004 as its business book of the year. *A Business Tale* was also a finalist for two other literary awards for 2004. In 2000, her book on corporate governance was published by the New York Times MBA Pocket Series. Her book on long-term success, *Building a Business Through Good Times and Bad: Lessons from Fifteen Companies, Each With a Century of Dividends*, was published in October 2002 and has been used by Booz, Allen, Hamilton for its work on business longevity. Her latest book, *The Seven Signs of Ethical Collapse*, was published by St. Martin's Press in July 2006. Her books have been translated into five languages.

Her columns have been syndicated around the country, and her work has appeared in the *Wall Street Journal, the Chicago Tribune, the New York Times, Washington Post,* and the *Reader's Digest*. A collection of her essays, *Nobody Fixes Real Carrot Sticks Anymore*, first published in 1994 is still being published. She was given an Arizona Press Club award in 1994 for her work as a feature columnist. She has been a commentator on business issues on *All Things Considered* for National Public Radio.

Professor Jennings has conducted more than 300 workshops and seminars in the areas of business, personal, government, legal, academic and professional ethics. She has been named professor of the year in the College of Business in 1981, 1987 and 2000 and was the recipient of a Burlington Northern teaching excellence award in 1985. In 1999, she was given best article awards by the Academy of Legal Studies in Business and the Association for Government Accountants. She was given best article awards by the institute of Internal Auditors and Association of Government Accountants in 2001 and 2004. She has been a Dean's Council of 100 Distinguished Scholar since 1995. In 2000, the Association of Government Accountants inducted her into its Speakers Hall of Fame. In 2005, she was named an All-Star Speaker by the Institute of Internal Auditors. In 2006, her article, "Ethics and Investment Management: True Reform," was selected by the United Kingdom's *Emerald Management Review* from 15,000 articles in 400 journals as one of the top 50 articles in 2005.

Professor Jennings is a contributing editor for the *Real Estate Law Journal*, and the *Corporate Finance Review*. She was appointed to the Board of Editors for the *Financial Analysts Journal* in 2007. She served as editor-in-chief of the *Journal of Legal Studies Education* during 2003–2004. During 1984–85, she served as then–Governor Bruce Babbitt's appointee to the Arizona Corporation Commission. In 1999 she was appointed by Governor Jane Dee Hull to the Arizona Commission on Character. During 1986–1988, she served as Associate Dean in the College of Business. From 1986–87, she served as ASU's faculty athletic representative to the NCAA and PAC-10. In 1999, she was elected president of the Arizona Association of Scholars.

She is a member of twelve professional organizations, including the State Bar of Arizona, and has served on four boards of directors, including Arizona Public Service (now Pinnacle West Capital) (1987–2000), Zealous Capital Corporation, and the Center for Children with Chronic Illness and Disability at the University of Minnesota. She served as chair of the Bonneville International Advisory Board for KHTC/KIDR from 1994–1997 and was a weekly commentator on KGLE during 1998. She was appointed to the board of advisors for the Institute of Nuclear Power Operators in 2004. She has appeared on CNBC, CBS This Morning, the Today Show, and CBS Evening News.

Personal: Married since 1976 to Terry H. Jennings, Maricopa County Attorney's Office Deputy County Attorney; five children: Sarah, Sam, and John, and the late Claire and Hannah Jennings.

Acknowledgments

This book is the product of many fine ideas contributed by colleagues, students, friends, editors, practicing lawyers, and regulators. Listing all those who have engaged with the author in answering the questions, "What do business leaders need to know about law and ethics?" and "How can we best help students to learn?" would be impossible. But, there are those who served as reviewers and those who have provided ideas, cases, and suggestions for improvement and inclusion. For this new effort, the following colleagues offered their seasoned advice:

Steven J. Arsenault, *College of Charleston*
Loretta Beavers, *Southwest Virginia Community College*
Laurel L. Boone, *St. Louis University*
Jerilyn Bowie-Hill, *University of Louisiana – Lafayette*
Peter M. Burrell, *University of Cincinnati*
Val Calvert, *San Antonio College*
Allison A. Cardwell, *University of Tennessee – Chattanooga*
Thomas D. Cavenagh, *North Central College*
Linda Christiansen, *Indiana University Southeast*
Robert H. Doud, *Adelphi University*
David H. Elibol, *SUNY – Buffalo*
Lori K. Harris-Ransom, *Caldwell College*
Johndavid Kerr, *Harris-Stowe State University*
Ernest W. King, *University of Southern Mississippi*
Paul Klein, *Duquesne University*
Paul J. Krazeise, Jr., *Bellarmine University*
Grant L. Learned, *Seattle Pacific University*
Russell W. Lott, *Northwest Mississippi Community College*
Patricia S. Root, *Central Connecticut State University*
Donna Sims, *Central Connecticut State University*
Judith W. Spain, *Eastern Kentucky University*
Alvin Stauber, *Florida State University*
Paulette L. Stenzel, *Michigan State University*
Craig R. Stilwell, *0Michigan State University*
Nicole Forbes Stowell, *University of South Florida – St. Petersburg*
Rizvana Zameeruddin, *University of Wisconsin – Parkside*

Any new book carries the significant imprint of the editors who work to design, refine, market, and produce it. This book began because of thoughtful conversations with my former editor, Steve Silverstein, who was concerned about students and wondered whether we were really helping undergraduate students in learning and their professors in presenting legal environment and ethical issues. When Steve accepted a wonderful opportunity for a different type of editorial work, Laura Bofinger took over the project. She was faced with turning a concept for learning into an actual text. Through focus groups, several rounds of reviews, conference calls, and meetings, Laura provided the guidance and leadership on the book's structure, reading level, and features. Authors cringe when editors say, "Try this," or "How about re-working Part II?" But, editors have a vision and perspective possessive authors lack. The woman is a saint when it comes to nudging me along. Also, not many authors have an editor who responds on the same day the author fires off a question or a whine. Vicky True, Acquisitions Editor, joined us in between the conception and production stages and brought her market and technological savvy as well as her knowledge about students to the features and content. Tamborah Moore, the production editor, has been a steady presence on nearly all of my books, she was here again for this one. When there is an e-mail from "TM," it is a classic "Everyone calm down," one that assures us she can solve whatever production problem has us in a tizzy. She sees every piece of manuscript and every page-proof file and even thanks me for meeting deadlines. Malvine Litten and her production company have also been cursed many times with a Jennings' production. Malvine and her staff are gracious enough to respond to e-mails on weekends and requests for realignments during page proofs. Kris Tabor has been with me for nearly 23 years, continuing her work on IMs, study guides, test banks, PowerPoints, and venting. We have lasted longer together than most marriages. This book also carries the unmistakable liveliness of an author who shares her life with helpful and delightful children and one tolerant husband. They have brought me stories, pop culture, and good sense with their, "Get real, Mom!" They bring me perspective and priorities. I am finally grateful to my parents who taught me through their words and examples the importance and rewards of ethics and hard work.

Marianne Moody Jennings

marianne.jennings@asu.edu

MARIANNE M. JENNINGS
···

FOUNDATIONS *of the* LEGAL ENVIRONMENT *of Business*

Marianne Moody Jennings

Arizona State University

PART 1

BUSINESS: ITS LEGAL, ETHICAL, AND JUDICIAL ENVIRONMENT

Businesses and those who own interests and work in them need to know their rights and obligations. What is legal? Where can I find the laws I need to know? How do I make decisions about legal conduct that, personally, is morally or ethically troublesome to me? What if I have a disagreement with a customer, employee, or shareholder? How can I resolve our differences? What forums are available for airing disputes?

This portion of the book explains what law is, where it can be found, how it is applied, and how legal disputes are resolved. Beyond operating a business within the bounds of the law, is the manager making ethical choices and behaving honorably in the conduct of business? Law and ethics are inextricably intertwined. A commitment to both is necessary and helpful in ensuring smooth operations and successful business performance.

1

Introduction to Law

update ▸

For up-to-date legal news, click on "Author Updates" at

www.cengage.com/blaw/ jennings

You have probably been exposed to law through traffic tickets or because you had a problem with your landlord, your lease, or a roommate who failed to pay the landlord. Or perhaps a company you interviewed with was allowed to look you up on MySpace. Your experiences with law might leave you feeling angry. However, if there were no traffic laws, the roads would be a study in survival of the fittest. In the case of that annoying landlord, the law does give you some help. Each day legislatures and courts are trying to deal with your rights and protections on the Internet. This electronic interaction is terrific, but we have exposed ourselves, literally and figuratively, on YouTube and MySpace. Now what can we do?

Laws exist at every level of government because they are necessary for an orderly society. Laws require us to meet minimum standards of conduct. Traffic laws control not only our conduct when we are driving but also our relationships with other drivers using the roads. In some instances, we owe them a right-of-way and are liable to them for any injuries we cause by not following the traffic laws.

This chapter offers an introduction to law. How is law defined? What types of laws are there? What are the purposes and characteristics of law? Where are laws found, and who enacts them? ■

This country's planted thick with laws from coast to coast . . . and if you cut them down . . . d'you really think you could stand upright in the winds that would blow then?

A Man for All Seasons, Act I

consider...

Shawn Fanning was a young college student when he lost his copyright infringement case for the "peer-to-peer file sharing" technology. His company, Napster, provided millions of computer users and music aficionados with a free program that allowed them to download copyrighted music without paying a fee. The music industry brought a suit that would end Napster as a free service. But along came Grokster and StreamCast to fill the void. They defended their programs because their technology did more than just facilitate student infringement. Colleges, libraries, and government agencies used their technology for perfectly legal purposes. "We only provide the technology," they explained. "How they use our software is your issue with them, not us." The music and film industry sued both Grokster and StreamCast for copyright infringement. Who gets copyright protection? How does the law determine the rights of the parties when there is a technological tidal wave that finds the Internet full of copyrighted materials there for the downloading?

Definition of Law

Philosophers and scholars throughout history have offered definitions of law. Aristotle, the early Greek philosopher, wrote that "the law is reason unaffected by desire" and that "law is a form of order, and good law must necessarily mean good order." *Black's Law Dictionary* defines law as "a body of rules of action or conduct prescribed by the controlling authority, and having legal binding force." Law has been defined at least once by every philosopher, statesman, politician, and police officer.

Law is the body of rules governing individuals and their relationships. Laws give us basic freedoms, rights, and protections. Law also offers a model of conduct for our business and personal lives and provides us with some certainty. Businesses, people with contracts, and property owners rely on the law for consistent protection of rights. Without this consistent framework of law, society would be a mass of chaos, confusion, and uncertainty.

Classifications of Law

PUBLIC VERSUS PRIVATE LAW

Public law includes those laws enacted by some authorized governmental body. State and federal constitutions and statutes are examples of public laws. Public laws govern everything from the sale of stock (federal securities laws) to how tall a building can be (zoning laws).

Private law, on the other hand, is developed by individuals. For example, landlords usually have regulations for their tenants, and these regulations are private laws. Homeowners' associations have developed an important body of private law that regulates everything from the type of landscaping for homes in a subdivision to whether homeowners can install basketball hoops in their driveways. Employer rules in a corporation are also examples of private law. For example, an employer rule that managers cannot have affairs with their direct reports is an example of private law, one that is common in corporations. Private laws are valid so long as they do not infringe any public rights or violate any statutory protections.

CRIMINAL VERSUS CIVIL LAW

A violation of a **criminal law** is a wrong against society. A violation of a **civil law** is a wrong against another person or persons. Criminal violations have penalties such as fines and imprisonment. Running a red light is an example of a criminal violation and generally carries a fine as punishment. Violations of civil laws require restitution: Someone who violates a civil law must compensate those harmed. If you run a red light and strike and injure a pedestrian, you have also committed a civil wrong and may be required to pay damages to that pedestrian if that pedestrian brings a civil suit for the injuries incurred.

SUBSTANTIVE VERSUS PROCEDURAL LAW

Substantive laws are those that give rights and responsibilities. **Procedural laws** provide the means for enforcing substantive rights. For example, if Zeta Corporation breached its contract to buy 3,000 microchips from Yerba Corporation, Yerba has the substantive right to expect performance and may be able to collect damages for breach of contract by bringing suit. The laws governing how Yerba's suit is brought and the trial process are procedural laws. There are also procedural laws for criminal cases, such as grand jury proceedings or arraignments and preliminary hearings.

COMMON VERSUS STATUTORY LAW

The term **common law** has been in existence since 1066, when the Normans conquered England and William the Conqueror sought one common set of laws governing a then-divided England. The judges in each locality developed a body of law common to all localities throughout the country that could be used to settle disputes. They consulted their fellow judges before making decisions. This principle of following other decisions is referred to as *stare decisis*, meaning "let the decision stand" (see pp. 7–9 and also Chapter 3). As a process of legal reasoning, it is still followed today. The courts use the judicial decisions of the past in making their current decisions to provide for consistency.

As much of an improvement as it was, the common law was still just uncodified law. Because of increased trade, population, and complexities, the common law needed to be supplemented. As a result, **statutory law**, which is passed by some governmental body and written in some form, was created.

Today both common law and statutory law exist in the United States. Some of our common law consists of principles from the original English common law. For example, how we own and pass title to real property are two areas of law largely developed from and still controlled by English common law. Our statutory law varies throughout our nation because of the cultural heritages of various regions. For example, the southwestern states have marital property rights statutes—often referred to as community property laws—that were influenced by the Spanish legal system implemented in Mexico. Louisiana's contract laws are based on French principles because of the early French settlements there.

LAW VERSUS EQUITY

Equity is a body of law that attempts to do justice when the law does not provide a remedy, or when the remedy is just not enough, or when the application of the law is terribly unfair. Equity courts originated in England and were given more latitude to get to the heart of a dispute. Over time, they developed remedies not available under common law. Common law, for example, permitted only the recovery of monetary damages. Courts of equity could issue orders, known as **injunctions**, prohibiting certain conduct. Equitable remedies have been gradually combined with legal remedies so that now parties can request that one court determine which remedies are available and appropriate in their case.

For example, in the copyright infringement cases that appear later in this chapter, the recording and motion picture industries asked in their suits for injunctions against the individuals and companies that provided the technological means for the unauthorized copying of movies and songs. The record companies, movie producers, and artists could never be compensated fully with just money for these forms of infringement because the infringement was always ongoing so long as the technology was available.

Purposes of Law

KEEPING ORDER

Laws carry some form of penalty for their violation. Traffic violations carry a fine or imprisonment, or both. Violations of civil laws also carry sanctions. A driver who injures another while driving intoxicated must pay for the damages and the costs of the injuries of the other person. These penalties for violations of laws prevent feuds and other less civilized ways of settling disputes—for example, using force.

In the past five years, Congress has been particularly active in passing legislation that targets terrorist activities as a means of keeping order and safety in the United States. The USA Patriot Act addresses a variety of legal issues from search warrants to reporting requirements for banks and others who handle large-dollar transactions (see Chapters 7 and 15). The purpose of the act was to provide the means to curb terrorist activities through early detection of plots and the control of funds used for terrorist activities.

INFLUENCING CONDUCT

Laws also influence the conduct of society's members. For example, securities laws require certain disclosures about securities before they can be sold to the public. What businesses can and cannot say or promise in ads about their goods is controlled through both federal and state laws that were passed in the early twentieth century to cut back on false and misleading claims in ads. These laws changed the way businesses operated.

HONORING EXPECTATIONS

Businesses commit resources, people, and time with the expectation that the contracts for those commitments will be honored and enforced. Investors buy stock knowing that they have some protection in that investment through securities laws. Knowing we have protections in the law allows us to trust, contract, and invest.

PROMOTING EQUALITY

Laws have been used to achieve equality. For example, the equal opportunity employment acts (see Chapter 18) were passed to bring equality to the job market. The social welfare programs of state and federal governments were created to further the cause of economic justice. The antitrust laws attempt to encourage competition and support the free enterprise system.

LAW AS THE GREAT COMPROMISER

A final and very important purpose of law is to act as the great compromiser. Law serves to mesh different views into one united view so that all parties are at least partially satisfied. When disputes occur, the courts use laws to resolve two opposing views. In the relationship between labor and management, the law serves as the mediator (See Chapter 17).

Characteristics of Law

FLEXIBILITY

cyberlaw

As society changes, the law must change with it. As the United States evolves toward a technological and information-based society, still more areas of law will be created and developed. The fax machine and the Internet have resulted in legislation that allows transmitted and electronic signatures to have the same force and effect as signatures on paper (see Chapter 10). Downloading high-quality music via the Internet meant that there were new issues of copyright protection and infringement. The law had to adapt to technology that made infringement more likely. Changing circumstances found courts using judicial review to resolve issues that resulted because of technology's new ideas.

CONSISTENCY

Although the law must be flexible, it still must be predictable. Law cannot change so suddenly that parties cannot rely on its existence or protection. Being able to predict the outcome allows us to rely on a contract. Businesses make long-term plans because they know the law will remain consistent and give them the rights and remedies they planned on because of their contracts and contract laws.

PERVASIVENESS

The law must be pervasive and cover all necessary areas; but at the same time, it cannot infringe individual freedoms or become so complex that it is difficult to enforce. For example, laws cover the formation, operation, and dissolution of corporations. Laws also cover shareholder rights. Corporations have great flexibility in management, so long as they stay within these legal boundaries.

In the two following cases, the courts struggle as they try to honor law's purposes of keeping order and honoring expectations while also grappling with the unique issues modern technology and its use raise. The principle of *stare decisis* is at work in these two cases (see Chapter 3). Case 1.1, the *Sony* case, is briefed in

Exhibit 1.1. A **brief** is a tool used by lawyers, law students, and judges to help them summarize a case and focus on its facts and the key points of the decision by the court. Case 1.2, the *Grokster* case, provides the answer for the Consider problem posed at the beginning of the chapter.

CASE 1.1

Sony Corporation of America v. Universal City Studios, Inc.
464 U.S. 417 (1984)

TAPE DELAY: CONTRIBUTORY INFRINGEMENT OR FAIR USE?

FACTS

Sony Corporation (petitioner) manufactures millions of Betamax video tape recorders (VTRs) and sells them through retailers (also included as petitioners in the case). The Betamax can record a broadcast off one station while the TV set is tuned to another channel. Tapes can be erased and reused. A timer in the Betamax can be used to turn on the equipment at predetermined times so that programs can be recorded even when no one is at home.

Universal City Studios, Inc. and Walt Disney Productions (respondents) hold the copyrights on a substantial number of motion pictures and other audiovisual works. They can earn additional returns on these works by licensing limited showings on cable and network television, by selling syndicated rights for repeated airings on local TV, and by marketing videotapes or videodiscs.

Universal and Walt Disney brought a copyright infringement action against Sony and its retailers. Universal and Walt Disney claimed that Betamax consumers were using their machines to record copyrighted works from commercially sponsored television.

The District Court found no infringement and denied relief. The Court of Appeals held that Universal and Walt Disney were entitled to enjoin the sales of Betamax VTRs or to collect a royalty on each sale. Sony appealed.

JUDICIAL OPINION

STEVENS, Justice
The Betamax can be used to make authorized or unauthorized uses of copyrighted works, but the range of its potential use is much broader.

The only contact between Sony and the users of the Betamax . . . occurred at the moment of sale.

If vicarious liability is to be imposed on petitioners in this case, it must rest on the fact that they have sold equipment with constructive knowledge of the fact that their customers may use that equipment to make unauthorized copies of copyrighted material. There is no precedent in the law of copyright for the imposition of vicarious liability on such a theory.

The question is thus whether the Betamax is capable of commercially significant noninfringing uses. In this case, there are many important producers of national and local television programs who find nothing objectionable about the enlargement in the size of the television audience that results from the practice of time-shifting (recording a show for later viewing) for private home use. The seller of the equipment that expands those producers' audiences cannot be a contributory infringer if, as is true in this case, it has had no direct involvement with any infringing activity.

If the Betamax were used to make copies for a commercial or profit-making purpose, such use would presumptively be unfair.

Today, the larger the audience for the original telecast, the higher the price plaintiffs can demand from broadcasters from rerun rights.

. . . [We] must conclude that this record amply supports the District Court's conclusion that home time-shifting is fair use.

Reversed.

CASE QUESTIONS

1. What is "time-shifting" and why does the court think this activity is important in the decision?

2. What is the standard for imposing "vicarious liability for infringement"? What does the court examine in determining copyright vicarious infringement liability?

3. What is the difference between Sony selling its Betamax and a company selling bootleg copies of a movie? What is different about these two activities? What is the same?

EXHIBIT   1.1   Sample Case Brief

Name of case:	*Sony Corporation of America* v *Universal City Studios, Inc.*
Court:	U.S. Supreme Court
Citation:	464 U.S. 417 (1984)
Parties and their roles:	*Sony Corporation* (petitioner and defendant); Universal Studios, Inc. and Walt Disney Productions (plaintiffs and respondents)
Facts:	*Sony* manufactures video tape recorders (VTRs) that can record programs in homes. Universal and Walt Disney produce movies. They claimed that *Sony's* VTRs were being used to copy their protected and copyrighted films and that they were therefore entitled to some payment for this type of machine use.
Issues:	Does *Sony's* VTR and its use by its customers infringe on the filmmakers' copyright?
Lower court decision:	The District Court found no infringement. The Court of Appeals found for Universal and Walt Disney and held that they were entitled to either halt the sales of the VTRs or collect a royalty on each.
Decision:	No infringement by *Sony.*
Reasoning:	Congress did not give absolute control over all uses of copyright materials. Some uses (fair uses) are permitted. Consumer uses of the machines for time-shifting to watch shows at another time were not only noncommercial, they were beneficial to those who produced and advertised on the shows because they permitted greater audience exposure. Further, Sony could not be held vicariously liable for infringement using its equipment when it was not a party to such activity and the equipment had valuable uses apart from infringement.

CASE 1.2

Metro–Goldwyn–Mayer Studios Inc. v. Grokster, Ltd.
545 U.S. 913 (2005)

COPYRIGHT INFRINGEMENT? REALLY, IT'S JUST A LITTLE PEER-TO-PEER FILE SHARING

FACTS

Grokster, Ltd., and StreamCast Networks, Inc. (Respondents/defendants) distribute free software products that allow computer users to share electronic files through peer-to-peer networks. Universities, government agencies, corporations, and libraries use this technology.

Grokster and StreamCast do not know when particular files are copied. However, MGM had a statistician do a systematic search of electronic files, and his study showed that nearly 90% of the files available for download on the FastTrack system were copyrighted

works . . . . [T]he probable scope of copyright infringement is staggering.

After Napster was sued by copyright holders for facilitation of copyright infringement, *A & M Records, Inc. v. Napster, Inc.,* 114 F.Supp.2d 896 (N.D.Cal.2000), aff'd in part, rev'd in part, 239 F.3d 1004 (C.A.9 2001), StreamCast gave away a software program of a kind known as OpenNap, designed as compatible with the Napster program and open to Napster users for downloading files from other Napster and OpenNap users' computers. The OpenNap program was engineered "to leverage Napster's 50 million user base."

Grokster and StreamCast receive no revenue from users, who obtain the software itself for nothing.

The District Court held that those who used the Grokster and Morpheus software to download copyrighted media files directly infringed MGM's copyrights, but granted summary judgment in favor of Grokster and StreamCast as to any liability arising from distribution of the then current versions of their software. The Court of Appeals affirmed. MGM appealed.

JUDICIAL OPINION

SOUTER , Justice

The question is under what circumstances the distributor of a product capable of both lawful and unlawful use is liable for acts of copyright infringement by third parties using the product.

When a widely shared service or product is used to commit infringement, it may be impossible to enforce rights in the protected work effectively against all direct infringers, the only practical alternative being to go against the distributor of the copying device for secondary liability on a theory of contributory or vicarious infringement.

[T]his Court has dealt with secondary copyright infringement in only one recent case. In *Sony Corp. v. Universal City Studios*, 464 U.S., at 434, this Court addressed a claim that secondary liability for infringement can arise from the very distribution of a commercial product.

On those facts, with no evidence of stated or indicated intent to promote infringing uses, the only conceivable basis for imposing liability was on a theory of contributory infringement arising from its sale of VCRs to consumers with knowledge that some would use them to infringe. But because the VCR was "capable of commercially significant noninfringing uses," we held the manufacturer could not be faulted solely on the basis of its distribution. Because the Circuit found the StreamCast and Grokster software capable of substantial lawful use, it concluded on the basis of its reading of *Sony* that neither company could be held liable, since

there was no showing that their software, being without any central server, afforded them knowledge of specific unlawful uses.

This view of *Sony*, however, was error, converting the case from one about liability resting on imputed intent to one about liability on any theory.

Here, the summary judgment record is replete with other evidence that Grokster and StreamCast, unlike the manufacturer and distributor in *Sony*, acted with a purpose to cause copyright violations by use of software suitable for illegal use.

[N]either company attempted to develop filtering tools or other mechanisms to diminish the infringing activity using their software. This evidence underscores Grokster's and StreamCast's intentional facilitation of their users' infringement.

StreamCast and Grokster make money by selling advertising space, by directing ads to the screens of computers employing their software. As the record shows, the more the software is used, the more ads are sent out and the greater the advertising revenue becomes. The unlawful objective is unmistakable.

One who distributes a device with the object of promoting its use to infringe copyright, as shown by clear expression or other affirmative steps taken to foster infringement, is liable for the resulting acts of infringement by third parties.

The judgment of the Court of Appeals is vacated, and the case is remanded for further proceedings consistent with this opinion.

CASE QUESTIONS

1. What is the difference between Sony's Betamax and Grokster's software program?

2. What additional grounds for imposing vicarious liability for copyright infringement can be used beyond "other lawful means of use"?

3. List the critical facts that tipped the court's decision against Grokster.

consider 1.1

What if the exchange service, the program developer for the exchange of the music files, developed an encryption device that shielded it from knowing who was using the program, for what, and how often? Could such a server claim immunity from copyright infringement for its development of the exchange program? (Analysis appears at the end of the chapter.)

In re Aimster Copyright Litigation, 334 F.3d 643, (7th Cir. 2003), cert. denied, 540 U.S. 1107 (2004).

. . . .

ethical *issues*

Copyright Infringement or Friendly Sharing?

What do you think of the ethics of peer-to-peer file sharing? Is peer-to-peer file sharing the same as copyright infringement? Who is harmed by the activity? Who is helped? Do you think the users of Napster should have had permission to download the copyrighted music?

Business Planning Tip

Many artists, writers, and inventors with copyrighted works or patented products have lost significant revenues because they did not anticipate technological changes. For example, most actors, writers, and others involved with television shows of the 1950s and 1960s do not enjoy the royalties from their shows running in what seems to be perpetual syndication on networks such as TV Land and Nick at Nite that feature television shows of other generations. Those involved in the production of these shows did not foresee what technology would permit. Walt Disney and Universal did not anticipate the VTR and its capability. Put technology clauses in agreements to cover future means of distribution, written with an open end for evolving technology. Not everyone has heeded this important tip. The Writers Guild strike that ran from 2007–2008 centered on the issue of the writers' rights to royalties on Internet use of programs that they write. Their labor contract did not cover that new technology. The strike was settled when networks and film production companies resolved the internet royalty issues with the writers.

The Theory of Law: Jurisprudence

Many can agree on the definition of law and its purposes but still differ on how those purposes are best accomplished. The incorporation of theories or values into the legal process is, perhaps, what makes each society's laws different and causes law to change as society changes its values. These different theories or value bases for law are found in an area of legal study called **jurisprudence**, a Latin term meaning "wisdom of the law." There are many cases in which how the law should work is unclear. Conflicting philosophical views often come together in litigation. Judges and lawmakers must struggle to do the most good for the most members of society.

There are four basic groups of legal philosophers. There are those who believe in **natural law theory**, or that law's authority comes from a higher and eternal authority and that any law that violates these natural laws is morally wrong. For example, slavery is a violation of natural law and during the time when it was legal in the United States, natural law philosophers maintained that the laws allowing slavery were morally wrong and invalid.

Those who believe in the **power theory** of jurisprudence believe that the law is whatever those who are in charge say the law should be, that law comes from power. Those who follow a **justice theory** of jurisprudence allow only those laws that serve to offer fairness, equality, and opportunity. Laws that deny due process, or the right to be heard, are morally wrong. Finally, there are those who follow the **order theory**, which provides that only those laws that serve to create and preserve order are valid. Order theorists allow laws that control behavior or provide conduct guidelines.

consider 1.2

Maj. Gen. Antonio M. Taguba was the U.S. general who led an investigation of the conduct of U.S. soldiers in the Abu Ghraib prison in Iraq. The 54-page report documented brutal treatment of Iraqi prisoners, torture, and humiliation, all in violation of either the Geneva Convention for the treatment of prisoners of war or the standards of the Red Cross. Gen. Taguba referred to the treatment of the prisoners as consisting of "egregious acts and grave violations of international law."* One of the findings of the report is that the soldiers serving as prison guards had little training. Gen. Taguba recommended training for soldiers in when to disobey orders. A fellow officer said of Gen. Taguba, "If you want the truth; he's going to tell you the truth. He's a stand-up guy."[†]

Gen. Taguba's father was Staff Sgt. Tomas Taguba, a man who fought in the Battle of Bataan and was taken prisoner by the Japanese. He escaped from prison there and joined the fighters in Japan who opposed the government.

Based on these brief descriptions of these two men, what philosophy of law do you think they would follow? (Analysis appears at the end of the chapter.)

[*]Douglas Jehl, "Head of Inquiry on Iraq Abuses Now in Spotlight," *New York Times,* May 11, 2004, A1, A12.
[†]Ibid.

· ·

Sources of Law

Laws exist in different forms at every level of government. Statutory law exists at all levels of government. Statutes are written laws enacted by some governmental body with the proper authority—legislatures, city governments, and counties—and published and made available for public use and knowledge. These written statutes are sometimes referred to as codified law, and their sources, as well as constitutions, are covered in the following sections.

CONSTITUTIONAL LAW

The U.S. Constitution and the constitutions of the various states are unique forms of law. **Constitutions** are unlike statutes in that they cannot be added to, amended, or repealed with the same ease as can statutes. Constitutions are the law of the people and are changed only by lengthier and more demanding procedures, such as ballot propositions.

Constitutions also tend to protect general rights, such as speech, religion, and property (see Chapter 4 for a more complete discussion). They also provide a framework for all other forms of laws. The basic rights and protections afforded in them cannot be abridged or denied by the other sources of law. In other words, a statute's boundaries are formed by constitutionally protected rights. Exhibit 1.2 is an illustration of the sources of law; constitutional law is at the base of the pyramid diagram because of its inviolate status.

STATUTORY LAW AT THE FEDERAL LEVEL

Congressional Law

Congress is responsible for statutory law at the federal level. The laws passed by Congress become part of the **United States Code (U.S.C.).** Examples of such laws are the 1933 and 1934 Securities Acts (see Chapter 14), the Sherman Act and other antitrust laws (see Chapter 16), the Equal Employment Opportunity Act (see Chapter 18), the National Labor Relations Act (see Chapter 17), the Truth-in-Lending Act (see Chapter 15), the USA Patriot Act (see Chapters 8 and 14), and the Internal Revenue Code (see Chapter 13).

Statutes from the U.S.C. are referenced or cited by a standard form of legal shorthand, often referred to as a **cite** or **citation**. The number of the title is put in front of "U.S.C." to tell which volume of the Code to go to. For example, "15 U.S.C." refers to Title 15 of the United States Code (Title 15 happens to cover securities). There may be more than one volume that is numbered "15," however. To enable you to find the volume you need, the reference or cite has a section (§)

EXHIBIT   1.2   Sources of Law

Private
Law

City or Borough
Ordinances

County Ordinances

State Administrative
Regulations

State Legislative Enactments

State Constitutions

Federal Administrative Regulations

Federal Legislative Enactments

U.S. Constitution

Court Decisions

number following it. This section number is the particular statute referenced, and you must look for the volume of Title 15 that contains that section. For example, the first volume of Title 15 contains §§ 1–11. A full reference or cite to a United States Code statute looks like this: 15 U.S.C. § 77.

Federal Administrative Regulations

Another form of codified law exists at the federal level: regulations passed by federal administrative agencies. The **Code of Federal Regulations (C.F.R.)** contains all of the federal agencies regulations such as the rules and forms required for consumer loans.

Executive Orders

Executive orders are laws of the executive branch of the federal government and deal with those matters under the direct control of that branch. For example, George Bush (43) issued one executive order requiring federal agencies to use alternative dispute resolution before going to court and another requiring them to implement recycling programs. On his second day as president, Bill Clinton issued an executive order reversing George H. W. Bush's (41) "gag rule" on abortion counseling. During his first 100 days in office, George W. Bush (43) issued an executive order banning the use of federal funds for abortion in other countries receiving U.S. financial assistance.

STATUTORY LAW AT THE STATE LEVEL

Legislative Law and State Codes

Each state has its own code containing the laws passed by its legislature. **State codes** contain the states' criminal laws, laws for incorporation, laws governing partnerships, and contract laws. Much of the law that affects business is found in these state codes. Some of the laws passed by the states are **uniform laws**, which are drafted by groups of businesspeople, scholars, and lawyers in an effort to make interstate business less complicated. For example, the **Uniform Commercial Code (UCC)**, which has been adopted in 49 states, governs contracts for the sale of goods, commercial paper, security interests, and other types of commercial transactions. Having this uniform law in the various states gives businesses the opportunity to deal across state lines with some certainty. Other uniform acts passed by many state legislatures include the Uniform Partnership Act (Revised), the Uniform Residential Landlord Tenant Act, the Model Business Corporation Act, and the Uniform Probate Code.

State Administrative Law

Just as at the federal level, state governments have administrative agencies with the power to pass regulations dealing with the statutes and powers given by the state legislatures. For example, most states have an agency to handle incorporations and the status of corporations in the state. Most states also have a tax agency to handle income or sales taxes in the state.

Local Laws of Cities, Counties, and Townships

In addition to federal and state statutes, local governments can pass **ordinances** or statutes within their areas of power or control. For example, cities and counties have the authority to handle zoning issues, and the municipal code outlines the zoning system and whatever means of enforcement and specified penalties apply. These local laws govern lesser issues, such as dog licensing, curfews, and loitering.

PRIVATE LAWS

Private laws are a final source of written law and are found in contracts such as a landlord's regulations for tenants that the tenants agree to as part of their lease. These private laws are enforceable provided they are not inconsistent with rights and protections afforded under the other sources of laws (see Chapter 3).

COURT DECISIONS

Looking at Exhibit 1.2, you can see that all of the sources of law just covered are surrounded in the pyramid by the term "court decisions." Often the language in the statute is unclear, or perhaps a new situation, such as a change in technology, requires a court to determine whether a statute applies. When there are new issues, ambiguities, or omissions in the statutory language, a court decision in a dispute brought by one party against another serves to provide an interpretation or clarification of the law. These court decisions are then read along with the statutory language in order to give a complete analysis of the scope and intent of the statute. The *Sony* and *Grokster* cases illustrated the interpretation of copyright laws to cases involving alleged infringement with new technologies.

Introduction to International Law

Businesses now operate in a global market. Companies headquartered in Japan have factories in the United States, and U.S. firms have manufacturing plants in China and call centers in India. Trade and political barriers to economic development have crumbled. An international market requires businesses to understand laws beyond those of the United States. International law is not a neat body of law like contract law or the UCC. Rather, it is a combination of the laws of various countries, varying trade customs, and individual as well as nations' agreements.

CUSTOM

Every country has its boundaries for allowable behavior, and these boundaries are unwritten but recognized laws. Each individual country also has its own customs peculiar to business trade. Businesses operating in various countries must understand those customs in negotiating contracts and conducting operations within those countries. For example, unlike the United States, most countries do not offer a warranty protection on goods and instead follow a philosophy of *caveat emptor*, "Let the buyer beware." Multinational firms must make provisions for protection of shipments in those countries with different standards.

Recently, the customs of China with respect to intellectual property, most particularly computer software, lagged behind those of Europe and the United States. Chinese custom was to separate infringement into two categories: ordinary and serious acts. Ordinary infringement is not regarded as a legal issue and requires only that the party apologize, destroy the software, and not engage in infringement again. Courts were rarely involved in ordinary infringement cases. However, the U.S. government demanded more protection for its copyright holders by imposing trade sanctions, and China eventually agreed to revise its customs and laws to afford protection. In this case, China's customs had to be changed to provide protection similar to that afforded in other countries.

TREATIES

A **treaty** is an agreement between or among nations on a subject of international law signed by the leaders of the nations and ratified by the nations' governing bodies. In the United States, treaties are ratified by the Senate and are included in the pyramid (Exhibit 1.2) as federal legislative enactments.

Treaties can be between two nations—**bilateral treaties**—or among several nations—**multilateral treaties**. There are also treaties recognized by almost all nations, which are called general or **universal treaties**. Universal treaties are a reflection of widely followed standards of behavior. For example, the Geneva Convention, a universal treaty covering the treatment of prisoners of war, has been the focus in the 2004 scandal related to the treatment of Iraqi prisoners of war. The Vienna Convention is a universal treaty covering diplomatic relations. The Warsaw Convention is a treaty that provides international law on the issues of liability for injuries to passengers and property during international air travel.

PRIVATE LAW IN INTERNATIONAL TRANSACTIONS

Even though each country has a different set of laws, all of them recognize the autonomy of parties in an international trade transaction and allow the parties to negotiate contract terms that suit their needs, so long as none of the terms is illegal. **Party autonomy** allows firms to operate uniformly throughout the world if their contracts are recognized as valid in most countries. For example, most international trade contracts have a choice-of-law clause whereby the parties decide which country's law will apply to their disputes under the contract.

INTERNATIONAL ORGANIZATIONS

Some international organizations offer additions to international law. For example, the United Nations General Assembly has the authority to adopt resolutions to govern international relations and to censure companies that create difficulties in the international marketplace because of unfair dealings.

ACT OF STATE DOCTRINE

The **act of state doctrine** is a theory that protects governments from reviews of their actions by courts in other countries. In any action in which the government of a country has taken steps to condemn or confiscate property, the courts of other countries will not interfere. For example, in many cases, foreign countries engage in **expropriation** (also called **appropriation**), or the taking of private property. Also referred to as **confiscation** or **nationalization**, the process is really one of eminent domain, and courts of other countries will not interfere in this governmental process.

TRADE LAW AND POLICIES

The importance of trade laws, tariffs, and policies has increased directly with increases in international business transactions. For example, the U.S. trade representative, once a dignitary position, has been upgraded to a cabinet-level position. Although Congress is responsible for enacting trade laws and various federal agencies are responsible for their administration, the U.S. trade representative assumes responsibility for negotiating trade agreements with foreign countries. Chapter 6 provides additional details on trade laws, tariffs, restrictions, and trade agreements.

The United States has used several treaties to open up markets across borders to allow trade in a more fluid fashion while still protecting the rights of its citizens. The United States used a trade agreement as the means for requiring the Chinese to afford greater intellectual property protections for U.S. businesses. Two additional treaties to which the United States is a party have had a significant effect on our economy. The first is the Geneva-based General Agreement on Tariffs and Trade (GATT). GATT establishes uniform trade policies between the United States and the European Union nations. The goal of GATT has been called "borderless trade."

The second treaty is the North American Free Trade Agreement (NAFTA), which is a trade agreement among the United States, Canada, and Mexico. This lengthy agreement was signed by then-president George H. W. Bush and also approved in the other two countries. The agreement, reaching its 16th year in 2008, has permitted the free flow of goods, services, and capital among the three nations. Some have called the resulting trade from NAFTA a "borderless North America."

A new sort of treaty has arisen that requires those countries ratifying the treaty to change certain internal laws to achieve international uniformity. For example, the Kyoto Treaty requires countries to substantially reduce their carbon dioxide emissions to address what some scientists believe is global warming. Not only do countries ratify the treaty, they also pass new laws within their countries for compliance. The Kyoto Treaty is at varying status in different countries, from signing to ratification. The U.S. Senate, by a vote of 95 to 0, did not ratify the Kyoto Treaty. In 2000, the U.S. Congress passed its E-sign law so that it could become one of many nations recognizing electronic signatures as valid for purposes of contract formation.

UNIFORM INTERNATIONAL LAWS

Not all nations have the same approach to contracts. Indeed, some nations have no contract laws or commercial codes. The UN convention on Contracts for the International Sale of Goods (CISG) has been adopted widely. Similar to the UCC (see Chapter 11), the CISG has provisions on formation, performance, and damages. More information on the CISG can be found in Chapters 6, 10, and 11.

THE EUROPEAN UNION

Once referred to as the Common Market and the European Community (EC), the European Union (EU) is a tariff-free group of European countries that includes Austria, Belgium, Denmark, Finland, France, Germany, Greece, Ireland, Italy, Luxembourg, the Netherlands, Portugal, Spain, Sweden, and the United Kingdom. This group of 25 countries has joined together to enjoy the benefits of barrier-free trade. Formed in 1992, the single economic community requires member nations to subscribe to the same monetary standard, the elimination of immigration and customs controls, universal product and job safety standards, uniform licensing of professionals, and unified taxation schedules. The EU continues to evolve to trade as one country with the introduction of the euro, its single currency. More details on the governance of the EU and its laws can be found in Chapter 6.

Red Flags FOR MANAGERS

Everything a business does involves laws. Before finalizing a contract make sure you have thought through all the possibilities such as how technology might affect your costs and rights under the contract.

Check to be sure you have considered all levels of laws. Zoning laws affect leasing and buying property. Federal laws and the U.S. Constitution provide rights for your employees that you can't take away even with your own private rules.

The law helps businesses through court systems that provide for damages when others fail to honor their promises. The law gives businesses and business people rights, responsibilities, and remedies.

Summary

How is law defined?

- Law is a form of order. Law is the body of rules of society governing individuals and their relationships.

What types of laws are there?

- Public law—codified law; statutes; law by government body
- Private law—rules created by individuals for their contracts, tenancy, and employment
- Civil law—laws regulating harms and carrying damage remedies
- Criminal law—laws regulating wrongful conduct and carrying sentences and fines
- Statutory law—codified law such as the United States Code or municipal ordinances
- Common law—law developed historically and by judicial precedent; began in England
- Substantive laws—laws giving rights and responsibilities
- Procedural laws—laws that provide enforcement rights such as the arraignment or grand jury portions of the criminal judicial process

What are the purposes of law?

- Keep order; influence conduct; honor expectations; promote equality; offer compromises

What are the characteristics of law?

- Flexibility; consistency; pervasiveness

- Jurisprudence—theory of law that addresses the best way to approach the characteristics and role of law

Where are laws found and who enacts them?

- Constitution—document that establishes structure and authority of a government; exists at the state and federal level
- Federal statutes—laws passed by Congress: the United States Code
- State statutes—laws passed by state legislatures, including uniform laws on contracts and business organizations such as the Uniform Commercial Code
- Ordinances—local laws passed by cities, counties, and townships that cover issues such as zoning and licensing for bikes or sales tax

What are the sources of international law?

- Treaties—agreements between and among nations regarding their political and commercial relationships
- Act of state doctrine—immunity of governmental action from discipline by other countries; sanctity of government's right to govern
- European Union—group of 25 nations working collectively for uniform laws and barrier-free trade
- Uniform laws—Contracts for the International Sale of Goods (CISG)

Key Terms

Questions and Problems

1. Bryant Gunderson is a sole proprietor with a successful bungee-jumping business. He is considering incorporating his business. What levels and sources of law would affect and govern the process of incorporation?

2. Jeffrey Stalwart has just been arrested for ticket scalping outside the Great Western Forum in Los Angeles. Jeffrey sold a ticket to a Hannah Montana concert to an intense fan for $1,200; the face value of the ticket was $48. Ticket scalping in Los Angeles is a misdemeanor. Will Jeffrey's court proceedings be civil or criminal?

3. In 1933, Walt Disney Company entered into a contract with Irving Berlin, Inc., assigning musical copyrights in exchange for a share of Berlin revenues. The agreement exempted from copyright protection Disney's use of the assigned music in motion pictures. The music was used in several Disney feature-length cartoons (*Snow White* and *Pinocchio*) that were later made available for sale on videocassette. Mr. Berlin's heirs brought suit, alleging infringement. Was this new technology an infringement? Could videocassettes have been anticipated? (*Bourne* v. *Walt Disney Co.,* 68 F.3d 621 [2d Cir. 1995].)

4. Paris Hilton, a well known celebrity with a ubiquitous presence on television and in *People* magazine, had her driver's license suspended by the state of California because of driving under the influence (DUI) or while intoxicated (DWI). She was then pulled over by officers for DUI while driving with a suspended license.

Following a hearing on the second traffic stop, a judge sentenced Ms. Hilton to 45 days in jail for failure to honor the terms of her DUI probation, including driving while intoxicated. List all the types of laws that apply to Ms. Hilton in her situation and also where the specific California laws would appear on the pyramid of the sources of law. Suppose Ms. Hilton asked for a pardon or commutation of her sentence by the governor of California—would the law allow that?

5. During the 2001 baseball season, Barry Bonds, then a player with the San Francisco Giants, hit 73 home runs in one season, a new record that went beyond the 72 set by Mark McGwire in 2000. Mr. Bonds made his record-breaking home run in San Francisco. When he hit the home run, the ball went into the cheap seats. All agree that Alex Popov had his glove on the home-run ball. However, Patrick Hayashi ended up with the ball.

Mr. Popov filed suit alleging that Mr. Hayashi assaulted Mr. Popov in order to get the ball. A substantial amount of videotape shows Mr. Popov's "gloving" of the ball. Mr. Popov says the ball belongs to him because he held that ball in a "Sno-cone position" and others wrested it from his control.

Mark McGwire's ball from his record-breaking home run sold for $3 million. The Popov/Hayashi battle has high financial stakes. What areas of law will be involved in the judge's determination of who gets the baseball? (Peter Page, "Ownership of historic baseball is in extra innings," *National Law Journal,* November 12, 2001.)

Understanding "Consider" Problems

1.1

THINK: Before answering this problem, review the decisions in the *Sony* and *Grokster* cases. Recall the following.

1. We can record movies and songs for private, noncommercial use, or fair use.

2. Technology that permits copying of copyrighted materials is not an automatic violation of copyright law if:
   a. The technology has other uses.
   b. The developer would have no way to know who was using its product for infringement.

3. It is possible for a company and officers who develop technology that permits recording of copyrighted materials to be "vicariously liable"

for infringement if they are aware that their technology or product is used for infringement, they benefit from the infringement uses, and they take no steps to halt the infringement despite the capability to do so.

APPLY: The use of the Sony Betamax for recording TV programs for individual use was fair use under the copyright laws. The mass sharing of copyrighted music via the Grokster and StreamCast programs was found to be more than fair use. Further, the court determined that Grokster was promoting its programs as a substitute for the original Napster technology that had been outlawed for copyright infringement.

ANSWER: You can answer this Consider by simply reviewing the issues these facts have in common with the facts from the *Sony* and *Grokster* cases. Decide whether the lack of knowledge about who and the extent of downloading is enough to protect the company that provides the software. Then think through the following questions: Does the company still make the copying possible? Will the copying be done for more than personal use? Would consumers not buy DVDs and CDs as a result? How are the programs advertised? Does the company make money from the use of the programs, even though the programs may be provided free of charge? Are there other uses for the technology the company provides? Once you have answered these questions, you have your answer. Lack of knowledge may not be enough to provide copyright infringement liability immunity.

1.2

THINK: There are several theories of law. One theory holds that natural law controls even over existing laws.

Another theory holds that the only valid laws are those that promote equality and justice. Still another theory holds that laws are commands, or orders, that we must follow to maintain a civilized society.

APPLY: The military tends to follow an order philosophy so that it can operate in tense battle situations. However, when soldiers are not in battle, there are questions of fairness and justice that seem to be exceptions to the order theory, especially when human rights are involved.

ANSWER: Gen. and Sgt. Taguba are both military men of order, but they have shown through their actions that they believe there are times when you cannot follow commands and orders. Those times include situations when there is unfairness or human rights are affected.

2 Business Ethics and Social Responsibility

Even after the scandals of Enron, WorldCom, Adelphia, Tyco, and others, and the resulting Sarbanes-Oxley reforms (see Chapters 7, 13, and 14), the scandals keep coming. By 2008, over 200 companies had announced either internal or Securities Exchange Commission (SEC) investigations into whether their executives had back-dated their stock option awards. During 2007, we learned that college and university financial aid officers were accepting consulting fees, stock options, and substantial gifts from student loan companies who then got preferred status on those campuses. By the middle of 2008, the subprime mortgage market and the markets for related financial instruments had collapsed. There are now investigations into fraudulent loan applications, inflated appraisals, and lending cultures in which FOA ("friends of Angelo," the CEO of Countrywide Financial) got fast-track approvals for loans and better rates. Studies released in 2006 found that 75 percent of undergraduate students and 56 percent of graduate business students admitted to cheating during the past year with only 1.5 percent of them indicating that they faced any disciplinary action as a result.[1]

Is business ethical? Or is doing business just a matter of lying and getting away with it? Does anybody really care about ethics in business? Do ethics matter? And what does it mean to be ethical in our lives and in business? This chapter discusses these questions and answers several others: What is ethics? How do they affect me? What is business ethics? Why is business ethics important? What ethical standards should a business adopt? How do employees recognize ethical dilemmas? How are ethical dilemmas resolved? How does a business create an ethical atmosphere? ■

update ▶
For up-to-date legal news, click on "Author Updates" at
www.cengage.com/blaw/ jennings

> **A bad reputation is like a hangover. It takes a while to get rid of, and it makes everything else hurt.**
>
> JAMES PRESTON
>
> *Former CEO, Avon*

> **You can't live in my world and cover stuff up. At some point in time, you will be found out if you don't come clean. It doesn't matter if it was 2 days ago or 20 years ago.**
>
> PETER CRIST
>
> *Expert on checking backgrounds for business hires*

consider...

1. What company's CEO was named *BusinessWeek*'s CEO of the year for 2001?
2. What companies' CFOs were named CFO of the year for 1999, 2000, and 2001 by *CFO* magazine?
3. What company was ranked by *Fortune* among its 100 best companies to work for 2002–2004 and was also named the most ethical company in America by *Business Ethics* magazine for 2005?
4. What CEO said in 2006, "I have the highest ethical standards"?
5. What CEO said, "We are the good guys. We are on the side of angels. We are doing God's work here."?
6. What company had a 64-page, award-winning code of ethics?*

*ANSWERS: 1. Dennis Kozlowski, Tyco, the $6,000-shower-curtain-at-company-expense CEO. 2. WorldCom, Enron, and Tyco. 3. Fannie Mae. 4. Dr. William McGuire, former CEO of UnitedHealth Group, who had stock options worth one-half billion that his board said were backdated to the lowest prices, and not by chance. 5. Jeffrey Skilling, former CEO of Enron. 6. Enron.

The chapter's opening Consider teaches us that often we look at what companies and business executives say and the fact that the companies are doing well and assume that they must be companies with high ethical standards. But all of the companies noted here, which were once recognized and given awards for their business success and for their executives' abilities, have been indicted, are in financial difficulty, or both. The companies and their officers experienced legal and financial problems because they crossed ethical lines. They began with small misdeeds that grew larger until they had created a financial nightmare that ended with guilty pleas, trials, and tremendous losses for shareholders.

We like to think of ourselves as so different from these so-called corporate criminals. But all of them were college graduates, nearly all with business degrees. All of them were respected by their friends and were active in community projects and institutions. These individuals were once good people who lost sight of their personal ethics, business ethics, and the importance of ethics in success. Keeping ethics with us, in life and in business, can help us avoid the kinds of mistakes that so many bright and capable businesspeople have made. But, we wonder, what is ethics? How do we know when we have them? How do we keep them when we face pressures, whether on an important exam or for meeting the quarterly numbers or our sales quota at work? This chapter answers these questions.

What Is Ethics?

When we read about former Congressman Randy Cunningham's acceptance of $2.4 million from defense contractors who were looking for favoritism on government contracts, we label the former representative's conduct "unethical." When we read about Jason Blair, a former reporter with the *New York Times* discovered to have fabricated his stories and lifted large segments from other reporters' work in other papers, we see the term *unethical*. When we read about the multibillion-dollar restatements resulting from correcting to the true dates on stock options, we also read about the "lack of ethics." One analyst noted about the companies facing investigation or undergoing internal inquiries, "People can't seem to keep their worst impulses in check."[2]

We read about these types of situations in the newspaper each day. From politics to journalism to business, ethics runs through the stories. But we also face ethical dilemmas ourselves. Two students purchase admission to see *Hancock*, and when they emerge from the theater they realize they are in an open area with access to other theaters. If they wanted to, they could slip into *Batman: The Dark Knight* or *Wanted* and see another movie without paying for another ticket. "Who's to know?" they might think. "Hollywood makes too much money anyway." "It doesn't really hurt anyone." These thoughts are similar to those running through the minds of the congressman, the reporter, and the executives awarding themselves options. Although we may believe we are different from business executives and others involved in scandals, we all face ethical dilemmas each day. Do I tell the clerk that he gave me too much change? Do I tell the shareholders about the real dates for and cost of these options? Do I go back to pay for the laundry detergent that slipped through on the bottom of my cart? Do I take the extra receipt the cab driver has offered? Do I tell a potential buyer of my car about the hairline crack in the engine block? Do I tell buyers of my shares of stock in a pharmaceutical company that the FDA is about to recall our drug?

We sometimes look at what someone has done and exclaim, "It's just not right!" Priscilla Ceballos's 6-year-old daughter, a fan of Hannah Montana, submitted an essay in a radio contest to win Hannah Montana concert tickets. The essay detailed an account of their husband/father dying in the war in Iraq. Their husband/father was not in Iraq and certainly not dead. When the fake essay was uncovered, Ms. Ceballos said she didn't violate any contest rules and that, "We did the essay, and that's what we did to win . . . We did whatever we could to win."* We know an ethical breach when we see one. What do we mean when we say the mother and daughter acted unethically? Ethical standards are not the standards of the law. In fact, they are a higher standard. Sometimes referred to as

---

*Verbatim, *Time,* Jan. 14, 2008, p. 23.

normative standards in philosophy, ethical standards are the generally accepted rules of conduct that govern society. For example, there is no statute in any state that makes it a crime for someone to cut in line in order to save the waiting time involved by going to the end of the line. But we all view those who "cut in line" with disdain. We sneer at those cars that sneak along the side of the road to get around a line of traffic as we sit and wait our turn. We resent those who march up to the cash register in front of us, ignoring the fact that we were there first and that our time is valuable too.

Waiting your turn in line is a societal expectation. "Waiting your turn" is not an ordinance, a statute, or even a federal regulation. "Waiting your turn" plays a critical role in an orderly society.

So it is with ethics. These unwritten rules are ethics, and they govern us when we are sharing resources or honoring contracts. "Waiting your turn" is a higher standard than the laws passed to maintain order. Assault, battery, and threats are forms of criminal conduct for which the offenders can be prosecuted. But the law does not apply to the stealthy line-cutter who simply sneaks to the front, perhaps using a friend and a conversation as a decoy. No laws are broken, but one individual violated society's unwritten rules.

Ethics consist of standards and norms for behavior that are beyond laws and legal rights. We don't put line-cutters in jail, but we do refer to them as unethical. There are other examples of unethical behavior that carry no legal penalty. Adultery was a crime in the past, but of the few states with statutes prohibiting adultery, it has been two decades since anyone has been prosecuted.[*] But when we describe someone who has committed adultery, we use adjectives such as "unfaithful" and even use a lay term to describe adultery: "cheating."

Speaking of cheating, looking at someone else's paper during an exam is not a criminal violation. If you cheat on a test, your professor may sanction you and your college may impose penalties, but the county attorney will not prosecute you for cheating. But your conduct is unethical because you did not earn your standing and grade under the same set of rules applied to the other students. Just like the line-cutter, your conduct is not fair to those who spent their time studying. Your cheating is unjust because you are getting ahead using someone else's work.

consider 2.1

In the introduction to this chapter, you learned that 75 percent of undergraduates and 56 percent of graduate students admit to cheating in the past year.[†] Why do we worry about ethics in school? What is the point of teaching young people to be honest? Why do we impose penalties for cheating? How does cheating affect those who do not cheat? What are some of the long-term consequences if those who cheat are permitted to pass courses, graduate with honors, and pursue careers in their fields? What happens when the 75 percent figure reaches 100 percent? (Analysis appears at the end of the chapter.)

[†]The data comes from the work of the Center for Academic Integrity. www.academicintegrity.org

. . . .

[*]Alabama, Florida, Idaho, Illinois, Kansas, Michigan, Minnesota, Mississippi, New Hampshire, New York, North Dakota, Utah, and Wisconsin make adultery a crime. Several of these states will not prosecute unless the spouse elects to do so. Massachusetts and Oklahoma have pending legislation to repeal their laws. Georgia, North Carolina, and Virginia statutes prohibiting adultery have been declared unconstitutional.

What Is Business Ethics?

Now that we have an understanding of what ethics are and why we should care and also realize that we are involved in ethical dilemmas nearly every day, we can progress to a discussion of business ethics. What is business ethics?

The term *business ethics* is actually a complex one with many layers of meaning. The first layer consists of basic values (covered in the following section) such as being honest, keeping promises, and not taking things that do not belong to you. Another layer consists of notions of fairness (also covered in the next section) such as how we treat others, including customers and employees who report to us. Still a third layer consists of issues related to how a business interacts with the community, the environment, and its neighbors.

The three layers of business ethics bring in the elements of a fair playing field. Business ethics involve the study of fairness and moral standards amidst the pressure of earning a profit and providing returns to shareholders and others who have invested in the business.

Moral standards can be derived from different sources, and ethicists often debate about the origins of these standards. One theory is that our moral standards are simply the same as actual or **positive law**, that our ethical decisions are made simply upon the basis of whether an activity is legal. But there are ways around laws that may not always be fair. Professor Richard Leftwich has summed up all the misrepresentations in financial reports by saying: "It takes FASB two years to issue a ruling and the investment bankers two weeks to figure out a way around it."[*] There is no violation of the letter of the law, but a violation of the spirit of the law presents an ethical dilemma.

Moral relativism (also called *situational or circumstantial ethics*) establishes moral standards according to the situation in which the dilemma is faced. Violation of the law, for example, is permitted if you are stealing to provide food for your starving family. Under moral relativism, adultery is justified when you are caught in an unhappy marriage. Embezzlement is wrong unless you need the money for medical care for a child.

A final source of moral standards is religious beliefs or divine revelation, sometimes grouped together as **natural law**. This type of law never changes, even though statutes and rules might. The source of natural law standards can be the Bible, the Koran, or any inspired book or writing that is the cornerstone of a religion or faith and believed to have resulted from divine revelation.

What Are the Categories of Ethical Dilemmas?

The following twelve categories were developed and listed in *Exchange*, the magazine of the Brigham Young University School of Business.

TAKING THINGS THAT DON'T BELONG TO YOU

Everything from the unauthorized use of the Pitney-Bowes postage meter at your office for mailing personal letters to exaggerations on travel expenses to the

---

[*]Mark P. Holtzman, Elizabeth Venuti, & Robert Fonfeder, *Enron and the Raptors: SPEs that Flourish in Loopholes*, THE CPA JOURNAL, June 8, 2003, at 7.

downloading of music from the Internet without authorization belongs in this category of ethical violations. A CFO (chief financial officer) of a large electric utility reported that, after taking a cab from LaGuardia International Airport to his midtown Manhattan hotel, he asked for a receipt. The cab driver handed him a full book of blank receipts and drove away. Apparently, the problem of accurately reporting travel expenses involves more than just employees.

SAYING THINGS YOU KNOW ARE NOT TRUE

A salesperson who tells a potential customer that a product carries a "money-back guarantee" when the salesperson knows that only an exchange is possible has said something that is not true, committed an ethical breach and possibly a violation of the law, and misled the customer. A car dealer who assures a customer that a car has not been in an accident when it has, has committed an ethical breach.

ethical *issues*

Marilee Jones, the dean of admissions of MIT, resigned after 28 years as an administrator in the admissions office. The dean for undergraduate education received information questioning Ms. Jones's academic credentials. Her résumé, used when she was hired by MIT, indicated that she had degrees from Albany Medical College, Union College, and Rensselaer Polytechnic Institute. In fact, she had no degrees from any of these schools or from anywhere else. She had attended Rensselaer Polytechnic as a part-time nonmatriculated student during the 1974–75 school year but the other institutions had no record of any attendance at their schools. When Ms. Jones arrived at MIT for her entry-level position in 1979, a degree was probably not required. However, she did progress through the ranks of the admissions office and, in 2007, she was appointed dean of admissions.

At the time she was made dean of admissions, Ms. Jones was promoting her book, *Less Stress, More Success: A New Approach to Guiding Your Teen Through College Admissions and Beyond.* The book advises, "Holding integrity is sometimes very hard to do because temptation may be to cheat or cut corners. But just remember that

'what goes around comes around,' meaning that life has a funny way of giving back what you put out."

Ms. Jones resigned because the chancellor, Philip M. Clay, said, "There are some mistakes people can make for which 'I'm sorry' can be accepted, but this is one of those matters where the lack of integrity is sufficient all by itself."

The résumé exaggeration issue has claimed several other professionals: Joseph Ellis, a Mount Holyoke College, Pulitzer-Prize winning historian, said he fought in Vietnam when he did not; Jeffrey Papow, president of IBM Lotus, who had discrepancies in both his educational and military record; and Denis Waitley, who resigned from the United Health Sciences board after the discovery that he did not have a claimed degree.

Consider Peter Crist's quote in the chapter opening. Is he correct? Why do people falsify their résumés?

Sources: Adapted from Tamar Lewin, "M.I.T.'s Admissions Director Resigns; Ends 28-Year Lie About Degrees," *New York Times*, April 27, 2007, pp. A1, A20; Keith J. Winstein and Daniel Golden, "MIT Admissions Dean Lied on Resume in 1979, Quits," *Wall Street Journal*, April 27, 2007, pp. B1, B2; and JoAnn S. Lublin, "No Easy Solution for Lies on a Resume," *Wall Street Journal*, April 27, 2007, p. B2.

GIVING OR ALLOWING FALSE IMPRESSIONS

An urban legend that has circulated among marketing departments around the country is the story of an infomercial ad that offered two CDs with all the hits of the 1980s on them. The infomercial emphasized over and over again, "All songs by original artists." Even the CDs carried the line, "All songs by original artists." When purchasers read the label with a closer eye and listened to the CDs, they discovered that all the songs were performed by one group, a group called "The Original Artists." While technically true, the advertising left a false impression with customers who assumed they would be buying songs as performed by the recording artists who made the songs popular.

BUYING INFLUENCE OR ENGAGING IN CONFLICT OF INTEREST

A United States Senator receives a mortgage loan with favorable terms while chairing the Sentate Banking Committee. A university researcher fails to disclose that her research on treatments for lung cancer was funded by tobacco company donations.

Those involved in situations such as these often protest, "But I would never allow that to influence me." That they have to insist they are not or would not be influenced is evidence of the conflict. Whether the conflict can or will influence those it touches is not the issue, for neither party can prove conclusively that a *quid pro quo* was not intended. The possibility exists, and it creates suspicion and is a conflict of interest.

consider 2.2

New York Attorney General Andrew Cuomo uncovered some interesting practices in the field of student lenders and college loan officers. The investigation, triggered by a whistle-blower's report to Mr. Cuomo and involving 100 colleges and universities and six student lenders, discovered the following types of activities by the campus financial aid officers:

- David Charlow, dean of student affairs at Columbia, owns 7,500 shares and 2,500 warrants in Educational Lending Group, Inc., the parent company of Student Loan Express. The company did disclose the ownership interest in its SEC filings.*
- Lawrence Burt, VP of student affairs and director of the office of student financial services at UT Austin, owns 1,500 shares and 500 warrants in Educational Lending Group. Mr. Burt said that "his ownership of stock in the company did not influence his decision about whether to place it on the list." "I did not do anything wrong," was Mr. Burt's only comment.**
- Catherine Thomas, associate dean and director of financial aid at USC, is also listed as a stock and warrant owner in the company.
- Ellen Frishberg, financial aid director at Johns Hopkins, took a total of $130,000 in consulting fees, only half of which was disclosed to the university.

Use the following model to analyze the student loan situation.

Steps for Analyzing Ethical Dilemmas and Case Studies in Business

1. Make sure you have a grasp of all the available facts.
2. List any information you would like to have but don't and what assumptions you would have to make, if any, in resolving the dilemma.
3. Take each person involved in the dilemma and list the concerns they face or might have. Be sure to consider the impact on those not specifically mentioned in the case. For example, product safety issues don't involve just engineers' careers and company profits; shareholders, customers, customers' families, and even communities supported by the business are affected by a business decision on what to do about a product and its safety issue.

4. Develop a list of resolutions for the problem. Apply the various models for reaching this resolution. As you apply the various models to the dilemma, you may find additional insights for questions 1, 2, and 3. If the breach has already occurred, consider the possible remedies and develop systemic changes so that such breaches do not occur in the future.
5. Evaluate the resolutions for costs, legalities, and impact. Try to determine how each of the parties will react to and be affected by each of the resolutions you have proposed.
6. Make a recommendation on the actions that should be taken.

(Analysis appears at the end of the chapter.)

*John Hechinger, "Probe Into College-Lender Ties Widens," *Wall Street Journal*, April 5, 2007, pp. D1, D2.
**Jonathan D. Glater, "Student Loans Led to Benefits by College Aides," *New York Times*, April 5, 2007, pp. A1, A13.

. . . .

HIDING OR DIVULGING INFORMATION

Taking your firm's product development or trade secrets to a new place of employment constitutes an ethical violation: divulging proprietary information. Releasing medical information about Britney Spears from your hospital's files on her treatment there would also be an ethical breach.

TAKING UNFAIR ADVANTAGE

Many current consumer protection laws were passed because so many businesses took unfair advantage of customers who were not educated or were unable to discern the nuances of complex contracts. Credit disclosure requirements, truth-in-lending provisions, and regulations on auto leasing all resulted because businesses misled consumers who could not easily follow the jargon of long and complex agreements.

COMMITTING ACTS OF PERSONAL DECADENCE

While many argue about the ethical notion of an employee's right to privacy, it has become increasingly clear that personal conduct outside the job can influence performance and company reputation. A company driver who is a regular substance abuser creates safety issues for all of us.

PERPETRATING INTERPERSONAL ABUSE

A manager sexually harasses an employee. Another manager is verbally abusive to an employee. Still another manager subjects employees to humiliating correction in the presence of customers. In some cases, laws protect employees. However, many situations are simply ethical violations that constitute interpersonal abuse.

PERMITTING ORGANIZATIONAL ABUSE

Many U.S. firms with operations overseas, such as Unocal, Levi Strauss, The Gap, and Nike, have faced issues of organizational abuse. The unfair treatment of workers in international operations appears in the form of child labor, demeaning wages, and excessive working hours. Even though a business cannot change the culture of another country, it can perpetuate—or alleviate—abuse through its operations there.

Violating Rules

Many rules, particularly those in large organizations that tend toward bureaucracy from a need to maintain internal controls or follow lines of authority, seem burdensome to employees trying to serve customers and other employees. Stanford University experienced difficulties in this area of ethics as it used funds from federal grants for miscellaneous university purposes such as yacht depreciation and bed linens. Questions arose not about the legality but about the propriety of the expenditures. Stanford was conducting the research and following federal guidelines in a literal way. But a federal auditor and the public looked at the fringe expenses and concluded, "Just not right." The public outcry resulted in damage to Stanford's reputation and a new president for the university.

Condoning Unethical Actions

In this breach of ethics, the wrong results from the failure to report the wrong. What if you witnessed a fellow employee embezzling company funds by forging his signature on a check that was supposed to be voided? Would you report that violation? A winking tolerance of others' unethical behavior is in itself unethical. Suppose that as a product designer you were aware of a fundamental flaw in your company's new product—a product predicted to catapult your firm to record earnings. Would you pursue the problem to the point of halting the distribution of the product?

Balancing Ethical Dilemmas

In some situations, the answers are neither right nor wrong; rather, the situations present dilemmas to be resolved. For example, Google and Yahoo! struggled with their decision about whether to do business in the People's Republic of China because of known human rights violations by the government there. On the other hand, Google's presence would improve the standard of living for the employees it hires and open up communications channels.

Resolution of Business Ethical Dilemmas

So far you know what business ethics is and you have a list of the areas that cover most ethical dilemmas. But if you were faced with an ethical dilemma, how would you resolve it? The resolution of ethical dilemmas in business is often difficult, even in firms with a code of ethics and a culture committed to compliance with ethical models for decision making. Several prominent scholars in the field of business ethics have developed models for use in difficult situations. This section covers those models.

Blanchard and Peale

The late Dr. Norman Vincent Peale and management expert Kenneth Blanchard offer three questions that managers should ponder in resolving ethical dilemmas: "Is it legal?" "Is it balanced?" "How does it make me feel?" If the answer to the first question, "Is it legal?" is no, for business ethics purposes, your ethical analysis is done. While there is room for conscientious objection on many laws on a moral basis, a manager is not given the authority to break the law and agencies such as the

IRS and SEC are not known for helping companies ease their consciences through refusals to pay taxes or file required securities disclosures and reports. If the answer to the first question is no, a manager should not proceed any further. The Hewlett-Packard board hired private investigators to determine the source of leaks about its board meetings, activities, and decisions. The investigators hired (actually a subcontractor of a contractor) used a technique known as "pretexting" in the trade. They posed as directors in order to obtain access to phone records of directors and reporters to determine who was calling whom, an activity prohibited by a California statute.[3] Eventually, the investigators as well as some within the company, including HP's ethics officer, were charged with violations. These managers failed to stop when the answer to the question of legality was "no."

Answering the second question, "Is it balanced?" requires a manager to step back and view a problem from other perspectives—those of other parties, owners, shareholders, or the community. For example, an M&M/Mars cacao buyer was able to secure a low price on cacao for his company because of pending government takeovers and political disruption. M&M/Mars officers decided to pay more for the cacao than the negotiated figure. Their reason was that someday their company would not have the upper hand, and then they would want to be treated fairly when the price became the seller's choice.

Answering "How does it make me feel?" requires a manager to do a self-examination of the comfort level of a decision. Some decisions, though they may be legal and may appear balanced, can still make a manager uncomfortable. For example, many managers feel uncomfortable about the "management" of earnings when inventory and shipments are controlled to maximize bonuses or to produce a particularly good result for a quarter. Known as the element of conscience, this test for ethics requires businesspeople to find the source of their discomfort in a particular decision.

THE FRONT-PAGE-OF-THE-NEWSPAPER TEST

One very simple ethical model requires only that a decision maker envision how a reporter would describe a decision on the front page of a local or national newspaper.

When Salomon Brothers illegally cornered the U.S. government's bond market, the *Business Week* headline read, "How Bad Will It Get?"; nearly two years later, a follow-up story on Salomon's crisis strategy was headlined, "The Bomb Shelter That Salomon Built." During the aftermath of the bond market scandal, the interim chairman of Salomon, Warren Buffett, told employees, "Contemplating any business act, an employee should ask himself whether he would be willing to see it immediately described by an informed and critical reporter on the front page of his local paper, there to be read by his spouse, children, and friends. At Salomon we simply want no part of any activities that pass legal tests but that we, as citizens, would find offensive."[4]

LAURA NASH AND PERSPECTIVE

Business ethicist Laura Nash has developed a series of questions that business managers should ask themselves as they evaluate their ethical dilemmas. One of the questions is, "How would I view the issue if I stood on the other side of the fence?" For example, in 1993, federal guidelines required meat to be cooked at 140 degrees Fahrenheit. At that time, however, Washington state proposed imposing a higher temperature requirement of 155 degrees. Burger King cooked its hamburgers at 160 degrees and Wendy's, Hardee's, and Taco Bell cooked their meat at 165 degrees.

Health and food industries experts supported a minimum cooking temperature of 155 degrees to be certain *E. coli* bacteria are eliminated. Jack-in-the-Box followed the legal minimum of 140 degrees. Would you want that information as a consumer? Given the trend toward higher temperatures and the pending regulation, would you want your meat cooked at a higher temperature? Although the cooking temperature was legal, there was an ethical issue of continuing to follow only the law when health experts felt there were concerns. Jack-in-the-Box did, in fact, experience an *E. coli* outbreak: One child died and three hundred other customers became ill.[5]

Other questions in the **Nash model** include: "Am I able to discuss my decision with my family, friends, and those closest to me?" "What am I trying to accomplish with my decision?" "Will I feel as comfortable about my decision over time as I do today?" The Nash model forces managers to seek additional perspectives as decisions are evaluated and implemented.

THE *WALL STREET JOURNAL* MODEL

The *Wall Street Journal* **model** for resolution of ethical dilemmas consists of compliance, contribution, and consequences. Like the **Blanchard–Peale model**, any proposed conduct must first be in compliance with the law. The next step requires an evaluation of a decision's contributions to the shareholders, the employees, the community, and the customers.

Finally, managers should envision the consequences of a decision. Mattel made a decision to use Chinese contractors for most of its toy production. While its costs were reduced initially, Mattel learned that it had lost some of the ability to supervise the plants and the workers. The consequences were that the plants had poor labor conditions, and they were using paint with unacceptable lead levels. The result was a Mattel recall of most of its toys, the largest toy recall in history.

OTHER MODELS

Of course, much simpler models for making ethical business decisions are available. One stems from Immanuel Kant's **categorical imperative**, loosely similar to the Golden Rule, "Do unto others as you would have them do unto you." Treating others as we would want to be treated is a powerful evaluation technique in ethical dilemmas.

Why We Fail to Reach Good Decisions in Ethical Dilemmas

Very often, we look at the harmful and wrong conduct of corporate executives and wonder, "Where were their minds and what were they thinking when they decided to engage in such bad behavior?" or as *Fortune* said it, "What were they smoking?" Often those involved did not walk through the steps in resolving ethical dilemmas discussed earlier. But they probably also slipped into **rationalizations** rather than analysis. The following sections provide a list and summary of rationalizations that we use to avoid thinking about ethics (see Exhibit 2.1).

EXHIBIT	2.1	The Language of Rationalization

"Everybody else does it."

"If we don't do it, someone else will."

"That's the way it has always been done."

"We'll wait until the lawyers tell us it's wrong."

"It doesn't really hurt anyone."

"I was just following orders."

"If you think this is bad, you should have seen . . ."

"It's a gray area."

"EVERYBODY ELSE DOES IT"

When 15-year-old Jonathan Lebed was caught using many different screen names to post notices about the value of stocks he had purchased so that he could pump up their value and then sell them, he had made more than $800,000 by taking advantage of others who believed the false notices posted. His father said that he was proud of his son because his son was doing what all the other analysts and investment firms on Wall Street were doing. "Everybody else does it" is a rationalization, but it is not an analysis of the ethical issues involved in conduct.

ethical *issues*

Since the time of his computer scam, Jonathan Lebed finished high school, had a book written about him, appeared on *60 Minutes,* and is negotiating for the movie rights for the book. He also has his own Web site for his favorite stock picks, http://lebed.biz. Mr. Lebed drives a $40,000 Mercedes. Does his experience tell you that adhering to ethics doesn't pay? Are the rewards greater for being unethical?

"IF WE DON'T DO IT, SOMEONE ELSE WILL"

The rationalization of competition is that because someone will do it and make money, it might as well be us. For example, saying, "If we don't go into China, someone else will," may give us some temporary comfort, but it really does not analyze the issues involved.

"THAT'S THE WAY IT HAS ALWAYS BEEN DONE"

Corporate or business history and business practices are not always sound. For example, the fact that so many financial aid officers were involved in conflicts of interest with student lenders was accepted and widespread, but its wide practice did not mean the conduct was fair or ethical.

"We'll Wait until the Lawyers Tell Us It's Wrong"

Lawyers are trained to provide only the parameters of the law. In many situations, they offer an opinion that is correct in that it does not violate the law. For example, lawyers disagreed over whether the downloading of music over the Internet was a violation of copyright law. However, whether the downloading was legal does not answer the question of whether gaining access to and using someone else's intellectual property without permission or compensation is ethical.

"It Doesn't Really Hurt Anyone"

When we are the sole rubbernecker on the freeway, traffic remains unaffected. But if everyone rubbernecks, we have a traffic jam. If all of us made poor ethical choices, we would cause significant harm. A man interviewed after he was arrested for defrauding insurance companies through staged auto accidents remarked, "It didn't really hurt anyone. Insurance companies can afford it." The second part of his statement is accurate. The insurance companies can afford it— but not without cost to someone else. Such fraud harms all of us because we must pay higher premiums to allow insurers to absorb the costs of investigating and paying for fraudulent claims.

"I Was Just Following Orders"

In many criminal trials and disputes over responsibility and liability, managers disclaim their responsibility by stating, "I was just following orders." Values require us to question or depart from orders when others will be harmed or wronged. When the allegations of prisoner abuse in Iraq emerged, along with photos, one of the first defenses raised by lawyers for the soldiers being court-martialed for their role in the abuses was, "I was just following orders." Sometimes following orders is not the ethical thing to do.

"If You Think This Is Bad, You Should Have Seen . . ."

This rationalization finds employees looking back at earlier times and reminding others that the company's safety policies or accounting practices used to be much worse. At one company, when some employees objected to backdating contracts to slip the earnings into the quarter, some employees reassured them by saying, "At least we're not using the 35-day month we used to use to meet targets."

"It's a Gray Area"

The gray area is a comfort level for us when we are in the midst of an ethical dilemma. Once we enter the gray area, we have a fine line that crosses into illegality and also an opportunity to explore an issue beyond just bare, legal requirements. An attorney for former HP general counsel Ann Baskins says that Ms. Baskins now realizes that she should have focused on questioning whether the pretexting was ethical, not just on whether it was legal. "She regrets that she did not do so."[6] Kevin Hunsaker, a deputy general counsel and chief ethics officer, asked internal HP security employees about the legality of the pretexting operations, and one responded, "I think it's on the edge, but aboveboard." Hunsaker responded with what have become the infamous words in the investigation, "I shouldn't have asked." On the edge and in a gray area often lands us into legal difficulty and controversy. Even though many of the charges were dismissed or reduced, five individuals, including Mr. Hunsaker, were charged with criminal misconduct in the HP pretexting case and the company paid a $14 million fine to settle the charges.

Social Responsibility: Another Layer of Business Ethics

So far in this chapter we have covered two layers of business ethics, the basic categories as well as notions of fairness. But a third layer of ethics focuses on relationships and conflicts among relationships.

In some ethical dilemmas in business, the interests of the shareholders might be different from the interests of the employees. In this third layer of business ethics, we look at the interests of those who are affected by business decisions, often called the stakeholders of the business. For example, suppose the business discovers that its air pollution control equipment is not state-of-the-art technology and that, although no laws are being violated, its plants release more pollution than is necessary. To correct the problem, its factory must be shut down for a minimum of three months. The pollution will harm the air and the community, but the shutdown will harm the workers and the shareholders. The business must consider the needs and interests of all its stakeholders in resolving the ethical dilemma it faces. Much discussion and disagreement continues to surround this particular issue. In the following interview excerpt, economist Milton Friedman offers a different perspective on this ethical dilemma.

> *Q: Quite apart from emission standards and effluent taxes, shouldn't corporate officials take action to stop pollution out of a sense of social responsibility?*
>
> **Milton Friedman**: I wouldn't buy stock in a company that hired that kind of leadership. A corporate executive's responsibility is to make as much money for the shareholders as possible, as long as he operates within the rules of the game. When an executive decides to take action for reasons of **social responsibility**, he is taking money from someone else—from the stockholders, in the form of lower dividends; from the employees, in the form of lower wages; or from the consumer, in the form of higher prices. The responsibility of a corporate executive is to fulfill the terms of his contract. If he can't do that in good conscience, then he should quit his job and find another way to do good. He has the right to promote what he regards as desirable moral objectives only with his own money. If, on the other hand, the executives of U.S. Steel undertake to reduce pollution in Gary for the purpose of making the town attractive to employees and thus lowering labor costs, then they are doing the stockholders' bidding. And everyone benefits: The stockholders get higher dividends; the customer gets cheaper steel; the workers get more in return for their labor. That's the beauty of free enterprise. . . . To the extent that pollution caused by the U.S. Steel plant there is confined to that city and the people there are truly concerned about the problem, it's to the company's advantage to do something about it. Why? Because if it doesn't, workers will prefer to live where there is less pollution, and U.S. Steel will have to pay them more to live in Gary, Indiana.[7]

Why Business Ethics?

Now that you have background on the types of ethical issues businesses face, background on social responsibility, and a framework for analysis of ethical issues, you may still be skeptical: "But why should a business worry about these things beyond just complying with the law? Why not just maximize under the system?"

Some compelling reasons promote choosing ethical behavior, as discussed in the following sections.

PERSONAL ACCOUNTABILITY AND COMFORT: BUSINESS ETHICS FOR PERSONAL REASONS

It would be misleading to say that every ethical business is a profitable business. First, not all ethical people are good managers or possess the necessary skills for making a business a success; but many competent businesspeople have suffered for being ethical, and many others seem to survive despite their lack of ethics. Columnist Dave Barry noted that every time an oil spill occurs, the oil companies ready themselves for the higher prices and profits that come because all that oil is lost at sea. Despite his conviction and jail term related to junk bond sales in the 1980s, Michael Milken earned a $50 million fee in 2004 for helping Ted Turner negotiate a merger with Time Warner.[8] Many whistle-blowers, although highly respected, have been unable to find employment in their industries. If ethical behavior does not guarantee success, then why have ethics? The answer has to do with personal ethics applied in a business context. One investment banker who worked on Drexel Burnham's trading desk during the Michael Milken days of that firm and who is now chairman of GoldTree Asset Management said, "Just to be able to sit on the desk and see the calls start at 4:15 in the morning, Boesky and Perelman and Diller and Murdoch. . . ."[9] But Mr. Wagner said that he took not just the memories of the power of Drexel with him but a powerful lesson as well, "There's a difference between being very competitive and can-do, and winning at all costs. All costs is costly."

Some people are ethical because it enables them to sleep better at night. Some people are ethical because of the fear of getting caught. But being personally ethical is a justification for business ethics—it is simply the correct thing to do. *The Parable of the Sadhu* focuses on business ethics for personal reasons.

THE PARABLE OF THE SADHU

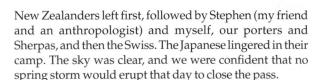

[In 1982], as the first participant in the new six-month sabbatical program that Morgan Stanley has adopted, I enjoyed a rare opportunity to collect my thoughts as well as do some traveling. I spent the first three months in Nepal, walking 600 miles through 200 villages in the Himalayas and climbing some 120,000 vertical feet.

During the Nepal hike, something occurred that has had a powerful impact on my thinking about corporate ethics.

THE SADHU

To get over the steep part of the climb before the sun melted the steps cut in the ice, we departed at 3:30 A.M. The New Zealanders left first, followed by Stephen (my friend and an anthropologist) and myself, our porters and Sherpas, and then the Swiss. The Japanese lingered in their camp. The sky was clear, and we were confident that no spring storm would erupt that day to close the pass.

At 15,500 feet, it looked to me as if Stephen were shuffling and staggering a bit, which are symptoms of altitude sickness. (The initial stage of altitude sickness brings a headache and nausea. As the condition worsens, a climber may encounter difficult breathing, disorientation, aphasia, and paralysis.) I felt strong, my adrenaline was flowing, but I was very concerned about my ultimate ability to get across. A couple of our porters were also suffering from the height, and Pasang, our Sherpa sirdar (leader), was worried.

Just after daybreak, while we rested at 15,500 feet, one of the New Zealanders, who had gone ahead, came staggering down toward us with a body slung across his shoulders. He dumped the almost naked, barefoot body of an Indian holy man—a sadhu—at my feet. He had found the pilgrim lying on the ice, shivering and suffering from hypothermia. I cradled the sadhu's head and laid him out on the rocks. The New Zealander was angry. He wanted to get across the pass before the bright sun melted the snow. He said, "Look, I've done what I can. You have porters and Sherpa guides. You care for him. We're going on!" He turned and went back up the mountain to join his friends.

I took a carotid pulse and found that the sadhu was still alive. We figured he had probably visited the holy shrines at *Muklinath* and was on his way home. It was fruitless to question why he had chosen this desperately high route instead of the safe, heavily traveled caravan route through the kali *Gandaki* gorge. Or why he was almost naked and with no shoes, or how long he had been lying in the pass. The answers were not going to solve our problem.

Stephen and the four Swiss began stripping off outer clothing and opening their packs. The sadhu was soon clothed from head to foot. He was not able to walk, but he was very much alive. I looked down the mountain and spotted below the Japanese climbers marching up with a horse.

Without a great deal of thought, I told Stephen and Pasang that I was concerned about withstanding the heights to come and wanted to get over the pass. I took off after several of our porters who had gone ahead.

On the steep part of the ascent where, if the ice steps had given way, I would have slid down about 3,000 feet, I felt vertigo. I stopped for a breather, allowing the Swiss to catch up with me. I inquired about the sadhu and Stephen. They said that the sadhu was fine and that Stephen was just behind. I set off again for the summit.

Stephen arrived at the summit an hour after I did. Still exhilarated by victory, I ran down the snow slope to congratulate him. He was suffering from altitude sickness, walking fifteen steps, then stopping, walking fifteen steps, then stopping. When I reached them, Stephen glared at me and said: "How do you feel about contributing to the death of a fellow man?"

I did not fully comprehend what he meant.

"Is the sadhu dead?" I inquired.

"No," replied Stephen, "but he surely will be!"

After I had gone, and the Swiss had departed not long after, Stephen had remained with the sadhu.

When the Japanese had arrived, Stephen had asked to use their horse to transport the sadhu down to the hut. They had refused. He had then asked Pasang to have a group of our porters carry the sadhu. Pasang had resisted the idea, saying that the porters would have to exert all their energy to get themselves over the pass. He had thought they could not carry a man down 1,000 feet to the hut, reclimb the slope, and get across safely before the snow melted. Pasang had pressed Stephen not to delay any longer.

The Sherpas had carried the sadhu down to a rock in the sun at about 15,000 feet and had pointed out the hut another 500 feet below. The Japanese had given him food and drink. When they had last seen him he was listlessly throwing rocks at the Japanese party's dog, which had frightened him.

We do not know if the sadhu lived or died.

I defended the larger group, saying, "Look, we all cared. We all stopped and gave aid and comfort. Everyone did his bit. What more could we do?"

THE INDIVIDUAL VERSUS THE GROUP ETHIC

Despite my arguments, I felt and continue to feel guilt about the sadhu. I had literally walked through a classic moral dilemma without fully thinking through the consequences. My excuses for my actions include a high adrenaline flow, a superordinate goal, and a once-in-a-lifetime opportunity—factors in the usual corporate situation, especially when one is under stress.

Real moral dilemmas are ambiguous, and many of us hike right through them, unaware that they exist. When, usually after the fact, someone makes an issue of them, we tend to resent his or her bringing it up.

For each of us the sadhu lives. Should we stop what we are doing and comfort him; or should we keep trudging up toward the high pass? Should I pause to help the derelict I pass on the street each night as I walk by the Yale Club en route to Grand Central Station? Am I his brother? What is the nature of our responsibility if we consider ourselves to be ethical persons? Perhaps it is to change the values of the group so that it can, with all its resources, take the other road.

DISCUSSION QUESTION

Consider the closing questions Mr. McCoy poses. How do they apply to you personally and to businesses?

Source: Reprinted by permission of *Harvard Business Review*. From "The Parable of the Sadhu," by Bowen H. McCoy, May–June 1997. Copyright © 1997 by Harvard Business School Publishing Corporation; all rights reserved.

ethical *issues*

In 2006, David Sharp, 34, from Britain, was not handling the climb to the summit of Mount Everest well (victim of oxygen deprivation) and collapsed on the ground. Forty other climbers passed him by and, unable to move, Mr. Sharp froze to death. Those who passed him by indicated that the conditions are rugged and that climbers know going in that they may have to pay the ultimate price.

Lincoln Hall, 50, from Australia, was discovered by an American guide after he had spent a night on the freezing mountainside. The MyHeroProject describes Mr. Hall's condition as follows, "He was sitting on the trail with his jacket around his waist, wearing no hat or gloves. The group stopped to investigate and found he was suffering from symptoms of edema, frostbite and dehydration. He was alone and hallucinating; and generally incoherent in his responses to their offers of help.

He was without any of the proper equipment for survival in such conditions. Apparently, Mr. Hall had collapsed the previous day on his way down from the summit."

Mr. Dan Mazur and his team abandoned their climb and stayed with Mr. Hall until rescuer sherpas could come to help. Mr. Hall's team assumed that he was dead and had called his wife the evening before to tell her.

In the years since 1953, 3,000 climbers have made it to the Everest summit, but 200 climbers have died. A climb with a guide costs about $60,000. What do you think makes the difference in the decision process between those who stop to help and those who continue their climbs?

Source: Alan Cowell, "Adventurers Change. Danger Does Not.," *New York Times,* June 4, 2006, p. WK 5.

Importance of Values in Business Success

The Tylenol tampering incident of 1982 offers one of the most telling examples of the rewards of being ethical. When Tylenol capsules were discovered to have been tainted with deadly poison, Tylenol's manufacturer, McNeil Consumer Products Company, a subsidiary of Johnson & Johnson, followed its code of ethics, which required it to put the interests of the consumer first. In what many financial analysts and economists considered to be a disastrous decision and a dreadful mistake, McNeil recalled all Tylenol capsules from the market—31 million bottles with a retail value of about $100 million. A new and safer form of a noncapsule Tylenol caplet was developed, and within a few months Tylenol regained its majority share of the market. The recall had turned out to be neither a poor decision nor a financial disaster. Rather, the company's actions enhanced its reputation and served to create a bond between Tylenol and its customers that was based largely on trust and respect for the integrity of the company and the product. (See "Leadership's Role in Ethical Choices" for further discussion of this issue.)

In contrast to the positive nature of ethical behavior is unethical behavior. For example, companies in the defense contracting business who were part of the spending and overcharging scandal several years ago are still reeling from the charges, struggling to regain credibility. Beech-Nut suffered tremendous earnings losses as a result of the discovery that its baby food "apple juice" did not in fact contain any real apple juice. Nestlé endured many consumer boycotts since the early 1970s as a result of its intense—and what came to be perceived by the public as exploitative and unethical—marketing of infant formula in then-Third World nations, where the lack of sanitation, refrigeration, and education led to serious health problems in infants given the formula. In 1989, nearly 20 years after the infant formula crisis, Nestlé's new "Good Start" formula was slow in market infiltration and, because of continuing consumer resistance, did not perform as well as its quality and innovativeness would have predicted. Nestlé has never gained the market share or reputation its quality product deserves. As the Nestlé experience illustrates, a firm's reputation for ethical behavior is the same as an individual's reputation: It takes a long time to gain, but it can be lost instantly as the result of one bad choice.

BP, the oil and natural gas company, was performing well with operations in 100 countries, 96,000 employees, and nearly 24,000 retail service stations around the world. As the second largest oil company in the world and one of the world's 10 largest corporations, BP had been a perennial favorite of NGOs and environmental groups. For example, *Business Ethics* named BP the world's most admired company and one of its top corporate citizens. Green Investors named BP its top company because of BP's continuing commitment to investment in alternative energy sources. In 2005, an explosion at one of BP's refineries, located in Texas City, resulted in the death of 15 employees and injuries to 170 others. Both an internal investigation and a government report indicated that the accident was avoidable if the company had not cut maintenance costs at the expense of safety. The accident followed on the heels of charges that the company's traders were manipulating the price of propane in the markets by holding back on supplies. Also, the company's oil fields at Prudhoe Bay, Alaska, burst in 2006, resulting in a 267,000-gallon oil spill on pristine Alaskan tundra.[10] Industry standards require smart-pigging, or ultrasonic checking of pipelines every five years to detect weaknesses or corrosion. At the time of the March 2006 spill, BP disclosed that it had not done smart-pigging on the Prudhoe Bay line since 1998 and that the pipes had not been cleaned since 1992. The BP field manager at Prudhoe Bay said, following the spill, "If we had it to do over again, we would have been pigging those lines."[11] The line had to be closed down and, again, an internal report revealed that the cost-cutting drive at BP affected the decisions in the oil fields. Following the oil spill, BP's stock price fell more than 15 percent in three months. BP paid a $373 million fine for environmental violations at Prudhoe and has spent $1 billion to fix the Texas refinery. One expert noted that it will take years for BP to recover financially and even longer to restore its credibility with the market and regulators.

By contrast, Goldman Sachs got out of subprime lending well over a year before the subprime market collapsed. Its stock has remained relatively stable because it did not have the multibillion-dollar write-downs the other investment houses had to take for their questionable (in both value and fairness) investments.

ETHICS AS A STRATEGY

Ethical behavior can increase long-term earnings; but it also enables businesses to anticipate and plan for social needs and cultural changes that require the firm or its product to evolve. One of the benefits of a firm's ethical behavior and participation in community concerns is the goodwill that such involvement fosters. Conversely, the absence of that goodwill and consequent loss of trust can mean the destruction of the firm.

When methyl isocyanate gas leaked from the Union Carbide plant in Bhopal, India, in 1984, the deadly gas left over 2,500 dead and 200,000 injured. The follow-up investigations into the accident revealed that there had been problems in the plant with some of the equipment designed to prevent such leaks. While actual liability issues were hotly debated in court, there were clear ethical questions regarding the plant and Union Carbide. Was it a wise decision to build the plant in a country with little expertise in the relevant technology? Did the people in the town know of the potential dangers of the plant? Why were shacks so close to the plant?

The plant had been operated well within legal and regulatory requirements, but the plant did not meet Union Carbide's usual standards. Should Union Carbide have done more than was legally required? Strategically, its decisions affected its financial future. Union Carbide's market capitalization suffered for years following the accident. More than two decades later, Dow Chemical, the company that acquired Union Carbide, is still dealing with issues related to the explosion.

THE VALUE OF A GOOD REPUTATION

A reputation, good or bad, stays with a business or an individual for a long time. Richard Teerlink, the former CEO of Harley-Davidson, has said, "A reputation, good or bad, is tough to shake." Once a company makes poor ethical choices, it carries the baggage of those choices despite successful and sincere efforts to reform. Salt Lake City struggled to regain its credibility as the trials from the bribery allegations surrounding its winning the bid for the 2002 Winter Olympics progressed and companies withdrew sponsorships. Businesses were, at that time, unsure about the reputations and trustworthiness of those running the Salt Lake City Olympic operations. It took new leadership and a commitment to high ethical standards from Mitt Romney, who became a two-term governor of Massachusetts and 2008 presidential candidate, to restore confidence in the 2002 Winter Olympics.

LEADERSHIP'S ROLE IN ETHICAL CHOICES

George Fisher, the former CEO of Motorola and Kodak, has defined leadership as the ability to see around corners. In other words, a leader sees a problem before it becomes a legal issue or liability and fixes it, thus saving company time and money. All social, regulatory, and litigation issues progress along a timeline. As the issue is brought to the public's attention, either by stories or by the sheer magnitude of the problem, the momentum for remedies and reforms continues until behavior is changed and regulated. Ethical choices afford firms opportunities to take positions ahead of the curve. Firms can choose to go beyond the law and perhaps avoid regulation that might be costly or litigation that can be devastating. For example, the issues relating to the problems with asbestos dust in the lungs of asbestos workers and installers were clear in the 1930s. More studies needed to be done, but there was sufficient evidence to justify lung protection for workers and the development of alternative forms of insulation. However, the first litigation relating to asbestos and asbestos workers did not arise until 1968. For that 30-year period, those in the business of producing and selling asbestos insulation products had the opportunity to take preventive actions. They chose to wait out the cycle. The result was a ban on asbestos and litigation at levels that forced the largest producer, Johns-Manville (now Manville), into bankruptcy. Leadership choices were available in the 1930s for offering warnings, providing masks, and developing alternative insulators. Johns-Manville chose to continue its posture of controlling information releases and studies. The liability issue progressed to a point of no choice other than bankruptcy and reorganization.

More recently, the problems resulting from a lack of candor in payday loans and in the so-called subprime loan market have surfaced. "We made so much money, you couldn't believe it. And you didn't have to do anything. You just had to show up,"[12] was the comment of Kal Elsayed, a former executive at New Century Financial, a mortgage brokerage firm based in Irvine, California. With his red Ferrari, Mr. Elsayed enjoyed the benefits of the growth in the subprime mortgage market. However, those risky debtors, whose credit histories spelled trouble, are now defaulting on their loans. New Century Financial is under federal investigation for stock sales and accounting irregularities as it tries to deal with its portfolio of $39.4 billion in subprime loans. "Subprime mortgage lending was easy," is the comment of mortgage brokers and analysts, until the market changes. State and federal regulators have now moved in to curb the most abusive practices of these lenders. In some cases even cities have adopted regulations to limit the interest rates, amounts, or activities of subprime lenders. Their market is now greatly controlled and limited. Known as "Homeowner Security Protection Acts" or "High Cost Home Loan Acts" or "Home Loan Protection Acts," these state laws take various approaches to protecting consumers from predatory lending practices.[13] Ethical choices give businesses the freedom to make choices before regulators mandate them. Breaches of ethics bring about regulation and liability with few opportunities to choose and less flexibility. The notion of choices and leadership are diagrammed in Exhibit 2.2.

Every issue progresses along a cycle that begins with a *latency* phase, in which the industry is aware of a problem. The use of private information about consumers' buying patterns was well known in the marketing industry, but few consumers were aware of that use. The *awareness* stage begins when the popular press reports on an issue and raises questions. Once the public has knowledge of a problem, it responds by demanding assurance that the problem either is resolved or is not really an issue—or by calling for reform. The *activism* stage is one in which members of the public ask for either voluntary or regulatory reform. If voluntary reform is not

EXHIBIT   2.2   Leadership and Ethics: Making Choices Before Liability

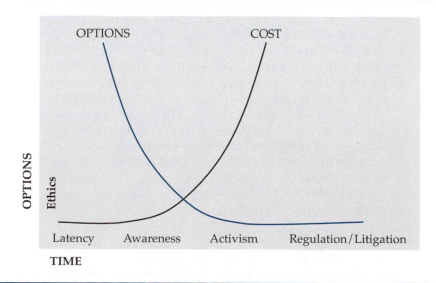

Source: Adapted from James Frierson's "Public Policy Forecasting: A New Approach," *SAM Advanced Management Journal,* Spring 1985, pp. 18–23.

forthcoming, those affected may sue or lobby for reform, or both. For example, a group of parents, police officers, and shareholders protested Time Warner's production of "Cop Killer," a song by the rap music artist Ice-T. The public outcry was strong both in the press and at Time Warner's shareholder meeting. Congress was considering holding hearings on record labels and record content. Time Warner eventually made a choice to voluntarily withdraw the song, later in the regulatory cycle when public outcry was strong but still in time to avert regulation.

During 2004, the public again became active in demanding changes in the content of entertainment when Janet Jackson and Justin Timberlake's performance at the half-time show at the Super Bowl resulted in partial nudity on prime-time television. In 2007, CBS Radio and MSNBC pulled the Don Imus show because of questionable comments he made. Entertainment and television executives undertook voluntary controls to prevent government controls. The televised Academy Awards are on a five-second delay so that any mishaps can be edited out before broadcast. Some artists are not permitted to appear on awards shows because of their past behaviors on similar shows. Voluntary self-control averts government regulation.

Creation of an Ethical Culture in Business

THE TONE AT THE TOP AND AN ETHICAL CULTURE

Employees work under the pressures of meeting quarterly and annual goals and can make poor choices if the company's priority with respect to values and ethics is not made clear. Employees must see that those who evaluate and pay them really do care about ethics. Employees are convinced that ethics is important when they see officers comply with all of the provisions in the company code of ethics. They see the right **tone at the top** when ethical employees are rewarded and unethical conduct is punished. The tone at the top comes from actions by officers and executives that show they "walk the talk" about ethics.

SARBANES-OXLEY, SENTENCING, AND AN ETHICAL CULTURE

Following the collapses of Enron, WorldCom, and other companies noted in the chapter's opening Consider, Congress passed the most extensive reforms of corporate governance and financial reporting since the enactment of the 1933 and 1934 securities laws following the 1929 stock market crash. Although **Sarbanes-Oxley** imposes many requirements on accountants, lawyers, directors, and officers (covered in Chapters 9, 13, and 14), it also mandates the Federal Sentencing Commission to examine the types of things companies could do that would improve the **ethical culture**, thereby reducing the risk of misconduct and earning sentence reductions for companies that attempt to create an ethical culture but still have an ethical or legal lapse.

The Sentencing Commission determined that factors such as the following would be helpful in setting the tone of the company:

- A code of ethics
- Training for employees in the code and in ethics
- A means for employees to report misconduct anonymously
- Follow-up on reports employees make on misconduct

- Action by the board, including follow-up and monitoring, on complaints and reports made by employees
- Self-reporting and investigation of legal and ethical issues
- Sanctions and terminations for those within the company who violate the law and company rules, including officers
- A high-ranking officer, with the ability to communicate with the CEO and board, who is responsible for the code of ethics and ethics training in the company

The guidelines established incorporate the factors most experts agree are critical to setting an ethical culture in a company.

REPORTING LINES: AN ANONYMOUS ETHICS LINE FOR AN ETHICAL CULTURE

Most companies have either an ombudsperson or a **hotline,** or both, to which employees can anonymously report ethical violations. In addition to encouraging employees to discuss issues with their supervisors, most companies now have some means by which employees can raise issues anonymously because of fear and concern that their jobs are at stake. Under the sentencing guidelines, companies that can show they fostered an atmosphere of education and discussion in which employees were encouraged to come forward will fare much better in terms of fines and other punishments if any missteps occur. Many companies have developed ethical news bulletins to offer employees examples of and guidelines on ethical dilemmas. DuPont delivers an ethics bulletin to employees through its e-mail system. Blue Cross Blue Shield has given employees Slinky toys for their desks with the hotline reporting number on them so that as employees think and perhaps use the Slinky to relieve pressure and stress, they will be reminded to report any problems. The federal government has an ethics encyclopedia online for its employees to use. The encyclopedia is filled with examples of government employees' misconduct and the sanctions they received.

Ethical Issues in International Business

The global market presents firms with more complex ethical issues than they would experience if operations were limited to one country and one culture. Moral standards vary across cultures. In some cases, cultures change and evolve to allow conduct that was not previously acceptable. In many executive training seminars for international business, executives are taught to honor customs in other countries and to "Do as the Romans do." Paying a regulatory agency in the United States to expedite a licensing process would be bribery of a public official. Yet many businesses maintain that they cannot obtain such authorizations to do business in other countries unless such payments are made. So-called grease or facilitation payments are permitted under the Foreign Corrupt Practices Act (see Chapter 8), but legality does not necessarily make such payments ethical.

Although the roots of business have been described as primarily economic, this economic system cannot survive without recognition of some fundamental values. Some of these inherent—indeed, universal—values are built into our capitalistic economic system. Exhibit 2.3 depicts this relationship. Everyone in the system

EXHIBIT   2.3   A Possible Uniform Standard for Ethical Choices

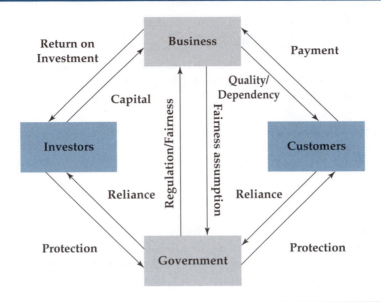

must be ethical. An economic system is like a four-legged stool. If corruption seeps into one leg, the economic system is off balance. In international business, very often the government slips into corruption with bribes controlling which businesses are permitted to enter the country and who is awarded contracts in that country. In the United States, the current wave of reforms at the federal level is the result of perceived corruption by businesses in their economic operations.

To a large extent, all business is based on trust. Economist Douglas Brown has described the differences between the United States and other countries in explaining why capitalism works here and not in all nations. His theory is that capitalism depends on an interdependent system of production. For economic growth to flourish, consumers, risk-takers, and employees must all feel confident about the future, about the concept of a level playing field, and about the absence of corruption.

Perhaps Italy and Brazil provide the best examples of the long-term impact of foreign business corruption. Elaborate connections in Italy between government officials, the Mafia, and business executives were unearthed in the 1990s. As a result, half of Italy's cabinet resigned at one time, and hundreds of business executives were indicted. It has been estimated that the interconnections of these three groups cost the Italian government $200 billion, as well as compromising the completion of government projects.

In Brazil, the level of corruption has led to a climate of murder and espionage. The *Wall Street Journal* offered an example of how Brazil's corruption has damaged the country's economy despite growth and opportunity in surrounding nations. The governor of the northeastern state of Paraiba in Brazil, Ronaldo Cunha Lima, was angry because his predecessor, Tarcisio Burity, had accused Mr. Lima's son of corruption. Mr. Lima shot Mr. Burity twice in the chest while Mr. Burity was having lunch at a restaurant. The speaker of Brazil's Senate praised Mr. Lima for his courage in doing the shooting himself as opposed to sending someone else. Mr. Lima was given a medal by the local city council and granted immunity from prosecution by Paraiba's state legislature.

Economists in Brazil document hyperinflation and systemic corruption. A Saõ Paulo businessman observed, "The fundamental reason we can't get our act together is we're an amoral society." Privatization that has helped the economies of Chile, Argentina, and Mexico cannot take hold in Brazil because government officials enjoy the benefits of generous wages and returns from the businesses they control. The result is that workers are unable to earn enough even to clothe their families, 20 percent of the Brazilian population lives below the poverty line, and crime has reached levels of nightly firefights. Brazil's predicament has occurred over time, as graft, collusion, and fraud have become entrenched in the government-controlled economy.[14]

Red Flags FOR MANAGERS

Managers should always be thinking beyond just the law. A good question to ask in order to keep ethics at the forefront in business is, "Is this fair?" When managers are thinking things such as, "Everybody does this," "That's the way it's always been done," or "This doesn't really hurt anyone," they are in the middle of an ethical dilemma. When they find themselves using these rationalizations, managers should stop and think:

- Will I feel as good about this decision over the long term?
- What if what I am doing right now were reported in the newspaper?
- If I were the customer, the employee, or the vendor, how would I feel about my actions?

- What if everybody acted like me? What would the world look like?

Managers should also be careful when they find themselves saying, "If I don't do this, I'll lose this account," or "If I don't do this, I won't make my numbers for the quarter." Go back to the list of questions and analyze your situation. Be careful of pressures that might blind you to important business concerns as pressure makes you lose sight of the importance of ethics and reputation in business. And remember that employees watch what managers do and use that as a standard for their behavior.

Summary

What is ethics?

- Behavior beyond the law
- A basic question for ethics is, "Is this fair?"
- Day-to-day nature of ethics—we all face ethical dilemmas

What is business ethics?

- Moral standards—standards of behavior set by culture
- Moral obligations—standards of behavior set by natural law
- Moral relativism—moral standards set by situation

What are the categories of ethical dilemmas in business?

- Taking things that don't belong to you
- Saying things you know are not true
- Giving or allowing false impressions
- Buying influence or engaging in conflict of interest
- Hiding or divulging information
- Taking unfair advantage
- Committing acts of personal decadence
- Perpetrating interpersonal abuse
- Permitting organizational abuse
- Violating rules
- Condoning unethical actions
- Balancing ethical dilemmas

How do employees resolve ethical dilemmas?

- Blanchard and Peale
- Front-page-of-the-newspaper test
- *Wall Street Journal* and stakeholders
- Laura Nash and perspective
- Categorical imperative

Why do we fail to reach good ethical decisions?

- "Everybody else does it."
- "If we don't do it, someone else will."
- "That's the way it has always been done."
- "We'll wait until the lawyers tell us it's wrong."
- "It doesn't really hurt anyone."
- "I was just following orders."
- "You think that's bad, you should've seen . . ."
- "It's a gray area."

What is social responsibility and how does a business exercise it?

- Positive law—codified law
- Inherence—serves shareholders' interests
- Enlightened self-interest—serves shareholders' interest by serving larger society
- Invisible hand—serves larger society by serving shareholders' interests
- Social responsibility—serves larger society by serving larger society

Why is business ethics important?

- Can be a means for increasing profit
- When a business acts voluntarily it shows leadership and gains a market position
- Ethical choices influence the reputation of a company
- Ethical choices often give companies a strategic edge

How does a business create an ethical atmosphere?

- Tone at the top—means managers should set a good example
- Sarbanes-Oxley requires companies that are publicly traded to have codes of ethics and ethics training
- The federal sentencing guidelines reduce fines and penalties for companies that work toward an ethical culture
- Companies also need a way, such as a hotline, for employees to report ethical issues and concerns
- Beyond the basics, companies should develop their values and incorporate ethics into their strategy and long-term goals

What are the ethical issues in international business?

- Corruption issues
- Economic systems and ethics

Key Terms

Questions and Problems

1. E.&J. Gallo, the world's largest winery, has just announced that it will stop selling its Thunderbird and Night Train Express wines in the Tenderloin, the skid row of San Francisco, for six months. Gallo took the action after meeting with an activist group called Safe and Sober Streets, which has asked grocers to remove the high-alcohol wine from the district, where citizens say drunks create a menace. One retailer in the district said, "If I don't sell this, I will have to close my doors and go home."

Discuss the actions of Gallo and the dilemma of the retailers in the district. Be sure to discuss the type of philosophy each of them holds with respect to social responsibility and ethical dilemmas.

2. The Association for Competitive Technology (ACT) is a trade group funded largely by Microsoft Corporation. During Microsoft's antitrust trial, ACT was active in public relations.

Lawrence J. Ellison, chairman of Oracle Corporation, a software manufacturer and Microsoft competitor, was concerned that the public might not understand that ACT was funded by Microsoft and was not truly an independent group. Mr. Ellison and Bill Gates, the chairman of Microsoft, were known as fierce competitors and often referred to as each others' nemesis. Through Oracle, Mr. Ellison hired Group International, a private investigation firm headed by Terry Lenzner (who became famous for his work on the Watergate investigation during the Nixon administration and also for his work for President Clinton's lawyers during the Paula Jones civil suit for sexual harassment). Group International was to find information tying Microsoft to ACT. Mr. Ellison described his hiring of Group International as his "civic duty."

Shortly after Group International was hired by Oracle, janitors working the night shift at the offices of ACT were offered $50–$60 each by Blanca Lopez, a woman who worked for Lenzner, if they would turn over ACT's trash to her rather than dumping it. The janitors refused, and Ms. Lopez returned the next evening and offered them $500 each for the trash plus $200 extra to the supervisor if he could convince the janitors to cooperate. All of the staff declined. Ms. Lopez left them her card, explained that she was working on a criminal case, and asked them to call if they changed their minds.

When the janitors disclosed what had happened and the investigator was traced back to Mr. Ellison, he said, "All we did was to try to take information that was hidden and bring it into the light. I don't think that's arrogance. That's a public service."

Mr. Ellison also offered to box up all of Oracle's trash and send it to Mr. Gates in Redmond, Washington, noting, "We believe in full disclosure."

Do you think what Oracle did was legal? Do you think it was ethical? How do you evaluate Mr. Ellison's claim that he was performing a civic responsibility?

3. Paul Wolfowitz has been the head of the World Bank since June 1, 2005. At the time he became president of the bank, Mr. Wolfowitz was romantically involved with an executive at the bank, Shaza Riza. Mr. Wolfowitz went to the board with an ethics question about their relationships and her employment and the bank board advised that Ms. Riza be relocated to a position beyond Mr. Wolfowitz's influence because of their relationship and also because she could no longer be promoted at the bank. On August 11, 2005, Mr. Wolfowitz wrote a memo to Xavier Coll, the bank's vice president of human resources, and suggested the following:

I now direct you to agree to a proposal which includes the following terms and conditions:

The terms and conditions included her future at the bank when Mr. Wolfowitz was no longer heading it as well as an obligation to find her other employment. Ms. Riza now earns $193,590 per year at a nonprofit organization, following a stint at the State Department at World Bank expense. She earned $132,000 at the World Bank (a salary that was tax-free because of diplomatic status). Using the categories of ethical dilemmas that you studied, evaluate Mr. Wolfowitz's conduct. What ethical issues do you see? Did Mr. Wolfowitz act properly? What should the board have done? The overarching goal of Mr. Wolfowitz's tenure as head of the World Bank has been eliminating corruption in all countries that deal with the bank. What effect does his personal conduct have on that goal?

4. Richard M. Scrushy, the former CEO of HealthSouth and now a convicted felon (bribery), was the subject of a probation hearing. Prosecutors said that Mr. Scrushy was trying to leave the country in February via his 92-foot yacht, the *Chez Soiree*. The yacht journey was nixed when bad weather hit the Atlanta coast. Mr. Scrushy protested the allegations, testifying that he had permission to travel to South Florida as part of a vacation that had been approved for him and his family (including going to Disney World). He said he did not tell the probation officer about the trip to Miami because her questions were not specific enough, "I can't answer the question unless she asks me."[15] The federal

magistrate said that Mr. Scrushy was being "coy" with his probation officers. Discuss whether Mr. Scrushy breached any ethical standards with his conduct and interpretation of the terms of his probation.

5. Gerald Grinstein, the CEO of Delta Airlines, indicated that he would not take any bonuses, stock options, or extra compensation and would only take his base salary of $338,000 for 2006. Grinstein arranged to have $1 billion distributed to about 39,000 nonunionized employees and 1,000 managers within 12 to 15 months after the airline emerges from bankruptcy. "I'm the dawning of the old age," was the comment the 74-year-old CEO made when asked why he was

taking such an unprecedented step.[16] Grinstein is giving up an estimated $10 million. He also added, "Corporate pay packages have gotten out of control. It has become a salary derby out there."[17] Grinstein has still arranged to have bonuses for top executives if they hit certain profit targets and explained, "You have got to have a program that attracts executives but at the same time you've got to take care of the relationships with frontline employees."[18] Apply the various schools of social responsibility to Mr. Grinstein and decide which he follows. Think about the regulatory cycle's application to the issue of CEO pay. What do you think regulators will do?

Understanding "Consider" Problems

2.1

THINK: In the discussion of ethical issues you saw that ethical issues cover those areas of conduct that are not violations of the law but are the types of actions that make us think, "Wait! That's not fair."

APPLY: That some students can earn a high grade through cheating, without really learning the course material or having the skills necessary for their fields, means that those who have worked hard and studied cannot show their distinction and ability. Everyone looks the same because we can't measure performance when there is cheating.

ANSWER: When the 75 percent reaches 100 percent, we cannot know who really knows how to build a bridge or treat patients. We don't have tests to make students suffer; we have tests as a measurement of knowledge. Those who have knowledge are treated unfairly when those who don't receive the same recognition and rewards.

2.2

THINK: To help in your analysis, consider the following list of the parties affected by this dilemma.
- The financial aid officials: Their independence and credibility of their recommendations for lenders for students are affected if faced with an actual conflict or the appearance of a conflict.
- Although the colleges and universities may not have known of their employees' conduct, they are affected by the disclosures and they are experiencing a financial impact.
- Students and their families: They lose trust.
- Lenders' credibility is affected by the undisclosed conflict and controversy.

- Lenders who did not participate in the gifts and programs were disadvantaged.
  - Federal government because it underwrites the student loans
  - Taxpayers who subsidize the federal student loan programs

APPLY: To further assist you in your analysis, consider the following categories.
- Conflict of interest: Financial aid officers had an economic interest in the lenders doing well and that interest was at odds with their role of objective evaluation of lenders for their institutions.
- Giving or allowing false impressions: The financial aid officers played the role of objective observers when they were really investors or had a financial interest from the lenders.

ANSWER: Because the conduct has already occurred, your role becomes one of recommendation. You need to provide a recommendation that affords protection to all the parties listed as affected by the conduct. For example, to protect the credibility of the colleges and universities, a policy on accepting gifts will need to be developed, as well as one for disclosures of conflicts of interest, including any investments they hold with the lenders. That policy may require not only disclosure but also prohibitions on certain types of conduct (such as stock ownership) if the conflict seems too difficult to overcome. Conflicts of interest can be managed in two ways: don't do it, or disclose the conflict to those affected. Sometimes disclosure is insufficient and one party must not engage in the conduct. Regulators may force these new standards on colleges and universities.

Notes

1. Donald L. McCabe, Kenneth D. Butterfield, and Linda Klebe Treviño, "Academic Dishonesty in Graduate Business Programs: Prevalence, Causes, and Proposed Action," 5 *Academy of Management Learning and Education* 294 (2006).

2. Jack T. Ciesielski, quoted in David Henry, "How the Options Mess Got So Ugly—and Expensive," *BusinessWeek,* September 11, 2006, p. 40.

3. Steve Stecklow et al., "Sonsini Defended HP's Methods in Leak Inquiry," *Wall Street Journal,* September 8, 2006, p. A1.

4. Leah Nathan Spiro, "The Bomb Shelter Salomon Built," *BusinessWeek,* September 9, 1991, pp. 78–80.

5. Catherine Yang and Amy Barrett, "In a Stew Over Tainted Meat," *BusinessWeek,* April 12, 1993, p. 36.

6. Sue Reisinger, "Runaway Train Hits H-P's GC," *National Law Journal,* December 18–25, 2006, pp. 8–9.

7. From "Interview: Milton Friedman," *Playboy,* February 1973. © 1973 *Playboy.*

8. Mr. Milken was required by the Securities and Exchange Commission to pay a fine for his involvement in the negotiations.

9. Jenny Anderson, "The Drexel Diaspora," *New York Times,* February 6, 2005, pp. 3–1, 3–1, Money & Business.

10. For complete information about BP's presence in Alaska and its contribution to the economic base there, go to http://alaska.bp.com.

11. Chris Woodward, Paul Davidson, and Brad Heath, "BP Spill Highlights Aging Oil Field's Increasing Problems," *USA Today,* August 14, 2006, p. 1B, 2B.

12. Julie Creswell and Vikas Bajas, "A Mortgage Crisis Begins to Spiral, and the Casualties Mount," *New York Times,* March 5, 2007, pp. C1, C4.

13. For a summary of the state legislation on predatory lending practices, see Therese G. Franzén and Leslie M. Howell, "Predatory Lending Legislation in 2004," 60 *Business Lawyer* 677 (2005).

14. This material was adapted from Larry Smeltzer and Marianne M. Jennings, "Why an International Code of Business Ethics Would Be Good for Business," 17 *Journal of Business Ethics* 57 (1998).

15. "Did Anyone Ask About a Yacht?" *New York Times,* April 15, 2007, p. BU2.

16. Corey Dade and Paulo Prada, "Delta CEO to Forgo Extra Payout," *Wall Street Journal,* March 20, 2007, p. A3.

17. Marilyn Adams, "CEO: Give My Bonus Away," *USA Today,* March 20, 2007, p. 1B.

18. Corey Dade and Paulo Prada, "Delta CEO to Forgo Extra Payout," *Wall Street Journal,* March 20, 2007, p. A3.

The Court System and Dispute Resolution

update

For up-to-date legal news, click on "Author Updates" at

www.cengage.com/blaw/ jennings

Our introduction to law included discussions of statutory law and common law. With so many statutes at so many levels, you might think that statutory law is a complete source of law. However, sometimes statutes need interpretation. Someone must determine when, how, and to whom statutes apply. Statutory law is not even half of all the law. The bulk of the law is found in judicial decisions. These decisions have both statutory interpretations and applications of common law. This chapter covers the parties involved in these decisions as well as the courts that make them— what they decide, when they can decide, and how those decisions are made. How do courts proceed with litigation? Is litigation inevitable or are there other ways to resolve disputes? What should a business do when it faces or is bringing a lawsuit? ■

For as thou urgest justice, be assured thou shalt have justice, more than thou desirest.

PORTIA

The Merchant of Venice, Act IV, Scene 1

consider...

A federal judge, faced with two hostile lawyers in a case, found that he was refereeing a dispute between the two over where to hold a witness's deposition. Both wanted neutral territory. The judge proposed the steps of the federal courthouse. One lawyer proposed a conference room in the office building where they both work (four floors apart), while the other proposed holding the deposition at a court reporter's office down the street. Judge Gregory A. Presnell of the district of Orlando ordered the parties to use "rock, paper, scissors" to determine the site, noting that his innovation was "a new form of alternative dispute resolution."

Daniel Pettinato, the lawyer for the plaintiff in the case, said that he had been training with his 5- and 9-year-old daughters for the event. They were encouraging him to open with "rock" because, as they said, "everyone opens with rock," and Mr. Pettinato said his case was "as solid as a rock." The director of the USA Rock Paper Scissors League, the LA-based governing body for the childhood sport, said that opening with paper was better. The lawyer for the defendant, D. Lee Craig, had no comments. Can a judge do this? What is a deposition? Why isn't a deposition held in the courtroom? Why were the parties in federal court?

Source: Adam Liptak, "Lawyers Won't End Squabble, So Judge Turns to Child's Play," *New York Times,* June 9, 2006, p. A20.

© STOCKBYTE/GETTY IMAGES

Introduction

In 2007, the Boeing Company learned that it could not deliver its new Dreamliner Jets on time to its customers because one of its parts suppliers was behind schedule and would be slow in meeting its delivery dates to Boeing. Boeing was in a position that affects many businesses: It was in breach of contract for late delivery to its customers and it had a breach of contract claim against its supplier for late delivery to Boeing. Bringing suit against Boeing would provide Boeing's customers a judicial remedy. Bringing suit against its suppliers would give Boeing its judicial remedies as well. But as Boeing and its customers wait for the suits to make their way through the court system, there is the practical need of getting the parts and the jets rolling. Sometimes the practical side of business demands different ways for resolving business disputes that are outside of the court system. This chapter answers the following questions: What ways can businesses use to resolve disputes? What are the benefits to private resolution versus judicial resolution of a dispute? What happens if a dispute does go to court? What court does it go to? Where will the case be heard? What are the responsibilities of businesses and managers as a case makes it way through the court system? Is a court decision final? Is there any right of appeal?

49

What Are the Ways for Resolving a Business Dispute? Trying Alternatives to Litigation

Managers have an initial choice when there is a dispute or a claim made against the company. The choice is one of going straight to the court system or trying alternative methods for resolution. Before making the choice, managers need to understand all other options, their costs, their benefits, and advantages and disadvantages. You will be able to see the factors a manager must weigh in deciding whether to go to court or to seek some other method for dealing with the business problem, known as **alternative dispute resolution (ADR)**. The following sections describe the types and characteristics of ADR.

ARBITRATION

Arbitration is the oldest form of ADR and provides a means for handling disputes in a less formal setting than a trial. Many contracts have mandatory arbitration clauses that require, in the event of a dispute, that the parties submit to arbitration. The issue of mandatory arbitration, particularly when there are consumers or employees involved, has been resolved. The Federal Arbitration Act (FAA) was passed to stop some of the judicial decisions that were holding arbitration clauses invalid. The U.S. Supreme Court has held that arbitration clauses are binding even in consumer contracts [*Green Tree Financial Corp.* v. *Randolph*, 531 U.S. 79 (2000)].

A contract may also have a voluntary arbitration clause, such as those found in insurance contracts. Finally, the parties may also agree to submit to arbitration after their dispute arises even without a contract clause.

Once the parties agree to arbitrate, they usually notify the American Arbitration Association (AAA) (www.adr.org). For a fee, the AAA will handle all the steps in the arbitration. The AAA is the largest ADR provider in the country, with an annual caseload of 20,711 in 2007, up 46% from the 2006 level of 14,211. However, that caseload is a significant drop from the AAA high of 230,000 in 2002.

Although the atmosphere is more relaxed, an arbitration hearing parallels a trial. The parties are permitted brief opening statements, after which they discuss the remedy that is sought. Each of the parties then has the opportunity to present evidence and witnesses. Some of the emotion of a trial is missing because, although emotional appeal influences juries, an expert arbitrator is not likely to be influenced by it. After the close of the hearing, the arbitrator has 30 days to make a decision.

Recently, businesses have curbed the growth of arbitration because of their concerns that arbitration had grown into such a formal process that its advantages of faster resolution with fewer strict judicial rules have been lost. Some studies confirm that arbitration takes just about as much time as going to court with a dispute.

Arbitration can be binding or nonbinding. **Binding arbitration** means that the decision of the arbitrators is final; there can be no court challenge except on very limited grounds. **Nonbinding arbitration** is a preliminary step to litigation. If one of the parties is not satisfied with the result in the arbitration, the case may still be litigated. In binding arbitration, the courts are strict in their hands-off policy on private arbitration decisions. Businesses do try to find their way out of arbitration decisions, but the following case shows the extent of judicial restraint on arbitration decisions.

CASE 3.1

American Laser Vision, P.A. v. Laser Vision Institute, L.L.C.
487 F.3d 255, (C.A.5 (Tex.) 2007)

ARBITRATORS DON'T NEED LASER PRECISION TO BE RIGHT

FACTS

Ophthalmologists Lewis Frazee and Robert Selkin formed American Laser Vision (ALV), which opened laser vision correction centers in Texas and Oklahoma. ALV signed contracts with The Laser Vision Institute (LVI) to have LVI operate the eye centers by providing management, nonmedical staff, and equipment. ALV would provide the surgeons—Drs. Frazee and Selkin. LVI was to pay ALV a fee for each surgery performed. Their agreement provided that any disputes would be submitted to arbitration. After a few months, Dr. Selkin complained about the LVI staff, quit performing surgeries at LVI, and began doing surgeries at other clinics in other states. Dr. Selkin bought out Frazee's interest in ALV and then filed an arbitration claim against LVI for $4,000,000 in lost surgery fees and other damages. After a three-day hearing, the arbitrator awarded Dr. Selkin $1.8 million. LVI filed suit to have the award set aside because the arbitrator failed to recognize that Dr. Selkin was in breach, was making money elsewhere, and never gave LVI a chance to deal with staff issues. The court granted ALV's motion for judgment and denied LVI's request to vacate the arbitration award. LVI appealed.

PER CURIAM

Judicial review of an arbitration award is "exceedingly deferential."

LVI argues first that the arbitrator disregarded the plain meaning of the contracts by construing them as between Selkin and LVI, not ALV and LVI, and considering the losses of Selkin personally, not those of ALV. We are not persuaded. The record shows that the arbitrator was quite aware of the factual nuances of the case, the identities of the parties, and the flow of money.

LVI next argues that, if the arbitrator correctly analyzed only the losses accruing to ALV, then he completely ignored the notice and cure provisions because Selkin never attempted to provide notice and accept cure and, more importantly, ALV through Frazee provided notice and accepted cure of whatever problems may have existed. As the district court recognized, however, Frazee alone could not bind ALV when Selkin was still the President and co-owner. And the arbitrator heard evidence about Selkin's attempts to provide notice and accept cure—which, if one considers Frazee to have implicitly consented to such acts because he was aware of them, means ALV was attempting to provide notice and accept cure—and there is evidence that those attempts were rebuffed, or at a minimum not satisfied by LVI. In any event, the arbitrator could have found that LVI had notice of the problems forming the basis of this entire dispute.

LVI also urges that, at a minimum, we should remand for the arbitrator to clarify the nature of his award. Remand is rare, appropriate only "when an award is patently ambiguous, when the issues submitted were not fully resolved, or when the language of the award has generated a collateral dispute." None of those situations is present here. Although, as explained above, the exact basis for the award is unclear, the parties agreed that the arbitrator need not state his reasons.

We will not second-guess multiple, implicit findings and conclusions underpinning the award. We do not decide if the award was free from error. We decide only that it is not the kind of extraordinary award that ineluctably leads to the conclusion that the arbitrator was "dispensing his own brand of industrial justice." There are advantages and disadvantages in contracting for private resolution of a dispute announced without explanation of reason. When a party does so and loses, federal courts cannot rewrite the contract and offer review the party contracted away.

AFFIRMED.

CASE QUESTIONS

1. List the areas of arbitrariness LVI raised regarding the arbitrator's decision.

2. How does the court respond to the concerns raised about the arbitrator's decision? Is there something a business could put in a contract to hold the arbitrator for more definite findings of fact?

3. What is the standard for setting aside an arbitration decision?

Many state courts, in order to encourage ADR, now impose mandatory arbitration in all cases involving amounts less than $25,000 or $50,000, for example. In Arizona, these mandatory arbitration proceedings are arbitrated by lawyers in the state, who are required to accept such assignments on a rotating basis either for a fee or as part of their *pro bono* activities. Such mandatory arbitration requirements have reduced the civil caseloads in many states by as much as 50 percent. But that reduction means that court cases do move more quickly than they had in the past. As a result, some businesses are revisiting their mandatory arbitration clauses because they are looking at some of the arbitration decisions and saying, "Maybe the court system isn't so bad—at least you get due process at some point."[1]

MEDIATION

Mediation is a process in which both parties meet with a neutral mediator who listens to each side explain its position. The mediator is trained to get the parties to respond to each other and their concerns. The mediator helps break down impasses and works to have the parties arrive at a mutually agreeable solution. Unlike an arbitrator, the mediator does not issue a decision; the role of the mediator is to try to get the parties to agree on a solution. Mediation is completely confidential. What is said to the mediator cannot be used later by the parties or their lawyers if litigation becomes necessary.

Mediation has been a popular form of dispute resolution among business-to-business (B2B) e-commerce companies. Amazon.com and eBay have used mediation regularly in the resolution of disputes. The Boeing situation, described at the beginning of the chapter, would be an ideal case for mediation.

MEDARB

Mediation arbitration (medarb) is a creation in which the arbitrator begins by attempting to negotiate between the two parties. If the arbitrator is unable to reach a settlement, the case proceeds to arbitration with the same party serving as arbitrator. One percent of the AAA's cases each year are decided by a medarb process.

THE MINITRIAL

In a **minitrial**, the parties have their lawyers present the strongest aspects of their cases to senior officials from both companies in the presence of a neutral advisor or a judge with experience in the field. At the end of the presentations by both parties, the neutral advisor can provide several forms of input, which are controlled by the parties. The advisor may be asked to provide what his or her judgment would be in the case, or the advisor may be asked to prepare a settlement proposal based on the concerns and issues presented by the parties. A minitrial is not binding.

RENT-A-JUDGE

Many companies and individuals are now using a kind of private court system, known as **rent-a-judge**, in which parties may have their case heard before someone with judicial experience without waiting for the slower process of public justice. These private courts are like *The People's Court* or *Judge Judy*, the "syndiccourts," without the television cameras.

SUMMARY JURY TRIALS

Under this method of ADR, the parties are given the opportunity to present summaries of their evidence to a judge and jurors. The jurors then give an advisory verdict to start the settlement process. If the parties are unable to agree on a settlement, a formal trial proceeds. This means of resolution gives the parties an idea of a jury's perception and assists in setting guidelines for settlement. A **summary jury trial** is often a resolution proposed after litigation and discovery (see later in the chapter), so it is a late form of ADR. It can, however, save the expense of a trial.

EARLY NEUTRAL EVALUATION

Early neutral evaluation requires another attorney to meet with the parties, receive an assessment of the case by both sides, and then provide an evaluation of the merits of the case. The attorney, who is either a paid consultant or a volunteer through the state bar association, renders an opinion on the resolution of the case. The idea in this method of resolution is to encourage settlement.

PEER REVIEW

A new form of dispute resolution called **peer review** has become popular, particularly for disputes between employers and employees, and is used by Darden Industries (Red Lobster, Olive Garden), TRW Inc., Rockwell International Corp., and Marriott International, Inc. Peer review, which is generally conducted within three weeks of demand, is a review by coworkers of the action taken against an employee (demotion, termination, discipline). These panels of fellow employees (one chosen by management, one chosen by the employee, and one chosen randomly) can take testimony, review documents, and make decisions that can include an award of damages. The advantage many see in this new form of ADR is that all involved believe it to be a fair process.

What If ADR Didn't Work or Suit the Situation? An Overview of Courts and Their Roles

Sometimes the ADR processes don't work, and sometimes managers just want to use the more controlled atmosphere of the court system. Businesses have the right to file suit and have their case heard in a judicial system. The following sections give the background on the judicial process so that managers can see what courts do, when, why, and how involved the judicial process can be from the start in the trial court through the appellate system.

TRIAL COURTS: FIRST STOP IN THE JUDICIAL SYSTEM

A **trial court** is the place in the judicial system where the facts of a case are presented. This court is where the jury sits if the case is a jury trial. Here the evidence and witnesses are presented and the first decision in the case is made, by either judge or jury. The procedures for trials and trial courts are covered later in the chapter.

APPELLATE COURTS AND JUDICIAL REVIEW

At least one other court, an **appellate court**, reviews a trial court decision to check the conduct of the judge, the trial, the lawyers, and the jury. This process of review helps assure that the lower court applied the law correctly and followed the rules of procedure. Further, this review system provides uniformity. In some appeals, the appellate court issues published opinions, which can then be referred to and used for resources (precedent) in deciding future cases. However, in many cases the appellate court issues unpublished opinions. Unpublished opinions have become a controversial issue; and the cite should always make clear when an opinion is an unpublished one.

The Process of Judicial Review

Appellate courts do not hold trials. Rather, they review what has been done by trial courts to determine whether the trial court, often referred to as the lower court or trial court, made an error in applying the substantive or procedural law in the case. This is the process of **judicial review**.

The appellate court atmosphere is very different from that of the trial court. There are no witnesses, no jury, and no testimony. No new evidence is considered; only the evidence presented at trial is reviewed. The court reviews a transcript of the trial along with all the evidence presented at trial to determine whether an error has been made.

In addition to the transcript and evidence, each of the parties to a case can present the appellate court with a **brief**, which is a summary of the case and the legal issues being challenged on appeal. The appellate brief is each side's summary of why the trial court decision or procedures were correct or incorrect. The parties make their arguments for their positions in the brief and support them with statutes and decisions from other cases. The brief serves as a summary of the major points of error the parties allege occurred during the trial. This type of brief, called an **appellate brief**, is very detailed. In fact, many refer to "briefs" as a misnomer because they are generally quite lengthy. Note that these briefs differ from the case brief presented in Exhibit 1.1.

Many appellate courts permit the attorneys for the opposing parties to make timed oral arguments in their cases. An **oral argument** is a summary of the points that have been made in each party's brief. The appellate judges can also ask questions of the attorneys at that time. At the trial level, one judge makes all decisions. At the appellate level, more than one judge reviews the actions of the lower court in a case. The typical number is three, but, in the case of state supreme courts and the U.S. Supreme Court, the full bench of judges on the court hears each case. For example, in U.S. Supreme Court decisions, all nine justices review the cases before the Court unless they have recused (disqualified) themselves because of some conflict.

The panel of appellate judges reviews the case and the briefs, hears the oral argument, and then renders a decision. The decision in the case could be unanimous or could be a split vote, such as 2 to 1. In the case of a split vote, the justice who is not in the majority will frequently draft a **dissenting opinion**, which is the judge's explanation for a vote different from that of the majority.

The Role of Appellate Courts: Checking for Error

A **reversible error** is one that might have affected the outcome of the case or would have influenced the decision made. Examples of reversible errors include the refusal to allow some evidence to be admitted that should have been admitted, the refusal to allow a particular witness to testify, and misapplication of the law.

When there has been a reversible error, the appellate court **reverses** the lower court's decision. However, in some cases, the appellate court will also **remand** the case, which means the case is sent back to the trial court for further work. For example, if there is a reversal because some evidence should have been admitted that was not, the case is remanded for a new trial with that evidence admitted (i.e., allowed).

If there has not been an error, the appellate court simply **affirms** the decision of the lower court. An affirmed decision does not mean no mistakes were made; it means that none of the mistakes were reversible errors. The decision of the court is written by a member of the court who has voted with the majority. The decision explains the facts and the reasons for the court's reversal, remand, or affirmation.

In some appellate cases, the court will **modify** the decision of a lower court. The full case is neither reversed nor affirmed; instead, a portion or portions of the case are reversed or modified. For example, a trial court verdict finding a defendant negligent might be affirmed, but the appellate court could find that the damages awarded were excessive. In this type of decision, the case would be remanded for a redetermination of damages by the trial court.

The Role of Appellate Courts: Statutory Interpretation, Precedent, and Stare Decisis

In addition to checking for error, appellate courts provide both interpretation of statutes and precedent with their written decisions. Judicial review by appellate courts of lower court decisions provides the database for the doctrine of *stare decisis*, a Latin term meaning "let the decision stand."

Setting Precedent   When a court reviews the decisions of lower courts, that court looks to previous decisions, along with decisions of other courts on the same topic. This process of examining other decisions for help in a new case uses case **precedent**, which is the doctrine of *stare decisis*. Courts examine related cases to determine whether the issue has already been decided and whether the same decision should apply again. Following case precedent does not mean similar cases will be decided identically; several factors influence the weight given to precedent.

The Quality of Precedent   Where a case originated is one of the factors that influences the application of precedent. In federal courts, precedent from other federal courts is strongest when the case involves federal statutes.

In state courts, prior decisions within a particular state's own court system are given greater weight than decisions from courts of other states. One state's courts are not obliged to follow the precedent of another state's courts; they are free to examine it and use it, but, as with all precedent, there is no mandatory requirement to follow another state's decisions.

The Purposes of Precedent   The purposes of precedent are the same as the purposes of law. Law offers some assurance of consistency and reliability. The judiciary recognizes these obligations in applying precedent. There must be stability and predictability in the way law functions.

In addition to consistency, however, judges incorporate the need for flexibility in the law. New twists in facts arise, and new technology develops; the judiciary must be receptive to the need for change. For example, in Chapter 1, the *Sony* and *Napster* cases illustrated the need for a reexamination of the scope of a law based on a newly evolved technology and its role in copyright law and protections.

The Interpretation of Precedent   Every case decision has two parts. One is the actual rule of law, which technically is the precedential part. However, judges never offer just a rule of law in a case. The rule of law is given at the end of the case decision after a full discussion of their reasons and other precedent. This discussion is called the *dicta* of the case, in which case precedent may be cited to the benefit of each party. In some instances, the rule of law may benefit one party while the *dicta* benefits the other party.

A dissenting opinion is *dicta* and is often quoted in subsequent cases to urge a court to change existing precedent. Application of precedent is not a scientific process; there is much room for interpretation and variation.

consider 3.1

The following rule appears in State University's current catalog:

A course in which a grade of C or better has been earned may not be repeated. The second entry will not be counted in earned hours or grade point index for graduation.

Rod took his business math course and earned a C. Not satisfied with his grade but unaware of the catalog regulation, Rod took the math course again and this time earned a D. The registrar has entered the D grade in Rod's cumulative average. Rod objects based on the catalog rule, but the registrar says the rule applies only if a higher grade is earned. What should Rod do? Should the grade count? (Analysis appears at the end of the chapter.)

. . . .

When Precedent Is Not Followed   Precedent may not be followed for several reasons. Some of those reasons have already been given. Precedent is also not followed when the facts of cases can be "distinguished," which means that the context of the facts in one case is different enough from those in other cases that the precedent cannot be applied. For example, suppose that a court decided that using roadblocks to stop motorists to check for drunk drivers is constitutional. Another court then decides that using roadblocks to check for drivers' licenses is not constitutional. The first case can be distinguished because of the purpose of the roadblocks: to prevent a hazardous highway condition. The court may not see the same urgency or safety issue in roadblocks used for checking for drivers' licenses. The precedent is distinguished.

The theories of law discussed in Chapter 1 may also control whether precedent is applied. For example, a court may not follow a precedent because of a moral reason or because of the need to change the law on the basis of what is moral or what is right. A precedent may also be abandoned on an economic theory, in which the court changes the law to do the most good for the most people. For example, a factory may be a nuisance because of the noise and pollution it creates. There is probably ample case law to support shutting down the factory as a nuisance. However, the factory may also be the town's only economic support, and its shutdown will mean unemployment for virtually the whole town. In balancing the economic factors, the nuisance precedent may not be followed or it may be followed in only a modified way.

What Are the Types of Courts and What Determines Which Court Hears What Cases?

Now that you understand ADR and the general role of courts, litigation, and appeals, the next question a business manager would have would be about specific courts. Which court system will be involved? Where will the case be held? You can answer these questions by a brief study of jurisdiction, an area that will also explain the various court systems and the names of the courts in each system. Different types of cases are heard in courts that were created for specific purposes and cases.

THE CONCEPT OF JURISDICTION

There are courts at every level of government, and every court handles a different type of case. In order for a court to decide or try a particular case, both the parties to the case as well as the subject matter of the case must be within the established powers of the court. The established powers of a court make up the court's **jurisdiction**. *Juris* means law, and *diction* means to speak. Jurisdiction is the authority or power of a court to speak the law.

There are two types of jurisdiction. The first is **subject matter jurisdiction**. Some courts handle violations of criminal laws, others deal only with civil suits, and bankruptcy courts handle only bankruptcies. The subject matter of a case controls which court has jurisdiction. For example, a case involving a federal statute belongs in a federal district court by its subject matter. However, there are federal district courts in every state, so what determines which federal court can hear the case? The answer to that question comes from second type of jurisdiction: *in personam* **jurisdiction**, or jurisdiction over the person, which controls the location of the court. Determining which court can be used is a two-step process; subject matter and *in personam* jurisdiction must fit in the same court. The following sections discuss these two parts of jurisdiction.

SUBJECT MATTER JURISDICTION OF COURTS: THE AUTHORITY OVER CONTENT

There are two general court systems in the United States: the federal court system (see Exhibit 3.1) and the state court system.

THE FEDERAL COURT SYSTEM

The Trial Court of the Federal System

The **federal district court** is the general trial court of the federal system. However, federal district courts are limited in the types of cases they can hear. Federal district courts can hear three types of cases: those in which the United States is a party, those that involve a federal question, and those that involve diversity of citizenship.

EXHIBIT   3.1   The Federal Court System

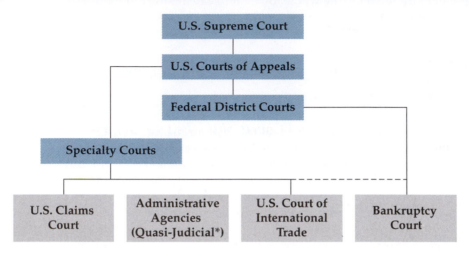

*For example, the Federal Trade Commission (FTC) or the National Labor Relations Bureau (NLRB).**

Federal Jurisdiction When the United States Is a Party

Anytime the U.S. government is a party in a lawsuit, it will want to be tried in its own court system—the federal system. The United States is a party when it brings suit or when it is the defendant named in a suit. If a victim of a plane crash names the Federal Aviation Administration (FAA) in a suit, the United States is a defendant and the federal system again has jurisdiction.

Federal Jurisdiction for a Federal Question

The federal district court also has jurisdiction over cases involving federal questions. For example, if a business is suing for treble damages (a remedy of three times the amount of damages experienced) under the federal antitrust laws (see Chapter 16), there is a federal question and the case may be brought in federal district court. A suit charging a violation of the Equal Protection Clause of the U.S. Constitution (see Chapter 4 for more details) also involves a federal question and can be brought in federal district court. Prosecutions for federal crimes also involve federal questions, and the United States will be a party as the prosecutor; these criminal cases are tried in federal district court.

Federal Jurisdiction by Diversity

Most of the civil cases in federal district court are not there because they are federal questions or because the United States is a party. Most civil cases are in federal district court because the plaintiff and defendant are from different states and their case involves damage claims in excess of $75,000. Cases in which the parties are from different states qualify them for **diversity of citizenship** status, and federal district courts have the authority to hear these diversity cases. That authority is not exclusive; a state court can also hear diversity cases so long as neither party chooses to exercise the right to a federal district court trial. In diversity cases, state and federal courts have **concurrent jurisdiction**. Concurrent jurisdiction means that two courts have the authority to hear a case. By contrast, **exclusive jurisdiction** means that only one court has the authority to hear the case. For example, the earlier example in which the United States had charged an individual or corporation with a federal crime is an example of exclusive jurisdiction.

Federal courts decide controversies among citizens of different states for reasons that go back to fears about state court judges giving preferential or favorable treatment to citizens of their state, as opposed to nonresident parties. If the case is held in one side's state court, that side might have an unfair advantage or built-in prejudice because of the location of the court.

Federal Jurisdiction in the Special Trial Courts of the Federal System

The federal system also has specialized trial courts to handle limited matters. For example, there is a Tax Court in the federal system, the jurisdiction of which is limited to tax issues. If you should decide to challenge the Internal Revenue Service because it would not allow one of your deductions, your case would be heard in Tax Court. The bankruptcy courts make up a well-used limited court system within the federal system that have exclusive jurisdiction over all bankruptcies. No other court can handle a bankruptcy or bankruptcy issues.

The U.S. Claims Court is another specialized federal court: It handles the disputes on government contracts and other claims against the federal government such as eminent domain issues. (See Chapter 4 for more discussion of eminent domain and "takings.")

The U.S. Court of International Trade is a specialized court that focuses on international trade transactions regulated by federal agencies in various ways and also on customs issues.

THE STRUCTURE OF THE FEDERAL COURT SYSTEM

Federal District Court: The Trial Court

There is at least one federal district per state. The number of federal districts in each state is determined by the state's population and caseload. States such as Nevada have only one federal district each, whereas states such as Illinois and New York have many. The number of courts and judges in each federal district is also determined by the district's population and caseload. Even in those states in which there is just one district, there are several judges and multiple courtrooms for federal trials. There are 94 federal districts in the 50 states plus one each in the District of Columbia and Puerto Rico. Three territories of the United States (Guam, the Virgin Islands, and the Northern Mariana Islands) also have district courts, including a bankruptcy court.

Because of the important nature of federal court cases (discussed earlier) and the resulting decisions, the opinions of federal district judges are published in a reporter series called the *Federal Supplement*, which reprints most opinions issued by federal district judges in every federal district. Cases in the *Federal Supplement* provide excellent precedent for interpretation and application of federal statutes. Just as there is a system for citing statutes (see Chapter 1), there is a system for citing case opinions. Such a system is necessary so that precedent can be found easily for use in future cases.

All case cites consist of three elements: an abbreviation for the reporter, the volume number, and the page number. The abbreviation for the *Federal Supplement* is "F.Supp." or, for the second series, after volume 999, "F.Supp.2d." The volume number always appears in front of the abbreviation, and the page number appears after it. A formal cite includes in parentheses the federal district in which the case was decided and the year the case was decided. A sample federal district court cite of a case decided in the Eastern District of Michigan that dealt with the use of race as a criterion for undergraduate and law school admissions looks like this:

Gratz v. *Bollinger*
135 F.Supp.2d 790 (E.D. Mich. 2001)

This method of uniform citation not only helps ease the burden of research but also provides an automatic way to know where a case came from and how it can be used. A number of systems available on the Internet offer copies of court opinions.

The Appellate Level in the Federal System

Cases decided in federal district court and the specialized trial courts of the federal system can be appealed. These cases are appealed to the U.S. courts of appeals (formerly called the U.S. circuit courts of appeals).

All of the federal district courts are grouped into **federal circuits** according to their geographic location. Exhibit 3.2 is a map that shows the 13 federal circuits.

EXHIBIT   3.2   The 13 Federal Judicial Circuits

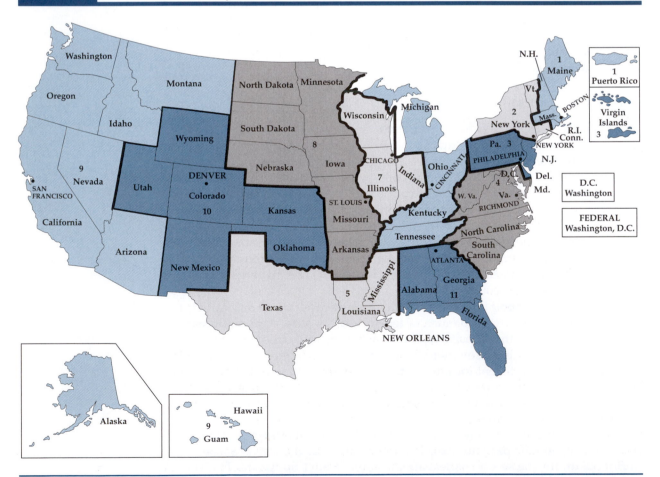

Source: Reprinted with permission and courtesy of West Publishing Company.

Note that 11 of the circuits are geographic groupings of states; the twelfth is the District of Columbia, and the thirteenth is a nongeographic circuit created to handle special cases such as those involving patent disputes and issues, and appeals from the Court of Claims and Court of International Trade. Some scholars and members of Congress have proposed creating a fourteenth circuit by dividing the very large Ninth Circuit.

Each circuit has its own court of appeals. The office of the court's clerk is located in the city named in each of the federal circuits in Exhibit 3.2. The number of judges for each of the federal circuits varies according to caseload. However, most cases are heard by a panel of three of the circuit judges. It is rare for a case to be heard *en banc* (by the whole bench or all the judges in that circuit). One of the more famous cases to be heard *en banc* following a three-judge panel decision involved a father's challenge to his child being required to recite the Pledge of Allegiance because the phrase "under God" was in the pledge (*Elk Grove Unified School Dist.* v. *Newdow,* 292 F.3d 597 (CA9 2002) and 313 F.3d 500 (C.A. 9 2002) with *en banc* rehearing denied, 328 F.3d 466 (C.A. 9 2003).[2]

The U.S. courts of appeals are appellate courts and operate by the same general procedures discussed earlier in the chapter. Their precedential opinions are published in the *Federal Reporter*. The system of citation for these cases is the same as for the federal district court opinions. The abbreviation for the *Federal Reporter* is "F." (or sometimes "F.2d" or "F.3d"; the "2d" means the second series, which was started after the first "F." series reached volume 300, and now there is a third series—"3d"). A formal cite includes in parentheses the federal circuit and date of the decision. A sample U.S. court of appeals cite, the appeal of the *Gratz* case, would look like this:

Gratz v. *Bollinger*
288 F.3d 732, (6th Cir. 2002)

The U.S. Supreme Court

A decision by a U.S. court of appeals is not necessarily the end of a case. There is one more appellate court in the federal system—the **U.S. Supreme Court**. However, the Supreme Court's procedures and jurisdiction are slightly different from those of other appellate courts.

The Supreme Court handles appeals from the U.S. courts of appeals. This appeal process, however, is not an automatic right. The Supreme Court must first decide whether a particular case merits review. That decision is announced when the Court issues a *writ of certiorari* for those cases it will review in full. The Supreme Court, in its writ, actually makes a preliminary determination about the case and whether it should be decided. Only a small number of cases appealed to the Supreme Court are actually heard. In 1945, 1,460 cases were appealed to the court. By 1960, that number had grown to 2,313. Now the number averages about 7,000 each year, with 2006 (the latest year available from the court) having 8,857 cases. The court grants *certiorari* in about 100 cases and hears oral arguments and issues written opinions in about 70 to 80 cases. For example, in the 2008 term, the Supreme Court heard oral arguments in 54 of the 1,972 cases on its docket. In 2006, it issued 67 written opinions. All of the Supreme Court opinions issued in one year total 5,000 pages, including the majority, concurring, and dissenting opinions.

The court grants *writs of certiorari* in cases as a matter of discretion. *Certiorari* may be granted because there is a conflict among the circuits about the law or because the case presents a major constitutional issue. Although the federal appellate workload of the U.S. Supreme Court is great, it is only part of the Court's jurisdictional burden. Decisions from state supreme courts, for example, can be appealed to the U.S. Supreme Court. The Supreme Court also decides whether to review these cases. For example, in 2000, the U.S. Supreme Court granted *certiorari* on George W. Bush's appeal of a Florida Supreme Court decision on recounting the Florida ballots in the November 2000 presidential election.

Because the Court is the highest in the land, its opinions are precedent for every other court in the country. The importance of these opinions has resulted in three different volumes of reporters for U.S. Supreme Court opinions. The first is the *United States Reports* (abbreviated "U.S."). These reports are put out by the U.S. Government Printing Office and are the official reports of the Court. Because these reports are often slow to be published, two private companies publish opinions in the *Supreme Court Reporter* (abbreviated "S.Ct.") and the *Lawyer's Edition* (abbreviated "L.Ed." or "L.Ed.2d"). The three-part cite for *Georgia* v. *Randolph* (the court's decision on a search of a home with the estranged wife's consent) follows:

547 U.S. 103 (2006)
126 S.Ct. 1515 (2006)
164 L.Ed.2d 208 (2006)

THE STATE COURT SYSTEMS

Although each state court has a different structure for its court system and the courts may have different names, there is a basic structure in each state that is similar to the federal system. Exhibit 3.3 is a diagram of a sample state court system.

State Trial Courts
Each state has its own general trial court. This court is usually called a circuit, district, county, or superior court. It is the court in which nondiversity civil cases are heard and state criminal cases are tried.

EXHIBIT   3.3   Typical State Court System

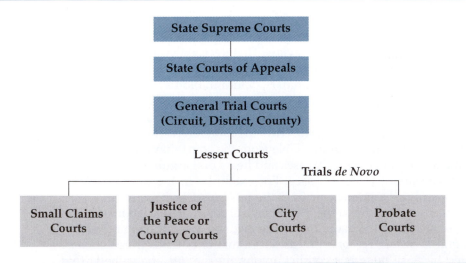

In addition to its general trial court, each state also has its own group of "lesser courts." These are courts with **limited jurisdiction**; they are comparable to the specialty courts of the federal system. For example, most states have a **small claims court** in which civil cases with minimal damage claims are tried. In a true small claims court, there are no attorneys. Parties represent themselves before a judge. Such a setting offers parties the chance to have a judge arrive at a solution without the expense of attorneys. The amount recoverable in small claims court is indeed very small: $200–$5,000 are the typical limits.

Most states also have a lesser court that allows the participation of lawyers but limits the amount that can be recovered. The idea is to take the burden of lesser cases away from the usually overburdened general trial courts. These courts are called **justice of the peace courts** or **county courts**.

Most cities also have their own trial courts, which are limited in their jurisdiction to the trial of lesser crimes, such as violations of city ordinances. Many states call these courts **traffic courts** because city ordinances involve so many traffic regulations.

In addition to these courts, some states have very specialized courts to handle matters that are narrow in their application of law but frequent in occurrence. For example, although probating (processing) a will and an estate involves narrow issues of law, there is a constant supply of this type of case. Many states have a special court to handle this and such related matters as guardianships for incompetent persons.

Many of the lesser courts allow appeals to a general state trial court for a new trial (**trial *de novo***) because not all judges in these lesser courts are lawyers and constitutional protections require a right of *de novo* appeal.

State Appellate Courts

State appellate courts serve the same function as the U.S. courts of appeals. There is an automatic right of review in these courts. Some states have two appellate-level courts to handle the number of cases being appealed. The opinions of these courts are reported in the state's individual reporter, which contains the state's name and some indication that an appellate court decided the case. For example, state appellate decisions in Colorado are reported in *Colorado Appeals Reports* (abbreviated "Colo.App."). These opinions are also reported in a **regional reporter**. All of the states are grouped into regions, and opinions of state appellate courts are grouped into the reporter for that region. Exhibit 3.4 presents the various regions and state groupings. For example, Nevada is part of the Pacific region, and its appellate reports are found in the *Pacific Reporter* (abbreviated "P.," "P.2d," or "P.3d"). The following is a cite from the state appellate court decision that was the same *Randolph* case (the case on the consent search) later appealed to the U.S. Supreme Court:

Randolph v. *State,* 590 S.E.2d 834 (Ga.App. 2003)

State Supreme Courts

State supreme courts are similar in their function and design to the U.S. Supreme Court. These courts do not hear every case because the right of appeal is not automatic. There is some discretion in what these supreme courts will hear. State supreme courts also act as trial courts in certain types of cases and are courts of original as well as appellate jurisdiction. For example, if two counties within

EXHIBIT	3.4	National Reporter System Regions		

Pacific **(P. or P.2d)**	**Northwestern** **(N.W. or N.W.2d)**	**Northeastern** **(N.E. or N.E.2d)**	**Southeastern** **(S.E. or S.E.2d)**
Alaska	Iowa	Illinois	Georgia
Arizona	Michigan	Indiana	North Carolina
(California)	Minnesota	Massachusetts	South Carolina
Colorado	Nebraska	(New York)	Virginia
Hawaii	North Dakota	Ohio	West Virginia
Idaho	South Dakota		
Kansas	Wisconsin	**Atlantic (A. or A.2d)**	**Southern**
Montana		Connecticut	**(So. or So.2d)**
Nevada	**Southwestern**	Delaware	Alabama
New Mexico	**(S.W. or S.W.2d)**	District of Columbia	Florida
Oklahoma	Arkansas	Maine	Louisiana
Oregon	Kentucky	Maryland	Mississippi
Utah	Missouri	New Hampshire	
Washington	Tennessee	New Jersey	
Wyoming	Texas	Pennsylvania	
		Rhode Island	
		Vermont	

Note: California and New York each has its own reporter system.
Source: The national reporter system was developed by West Publishing Company. Reprinted with permission of West Publishing Company.

a state have a dispute, the state supreme court would take the trial to ensure fairness. After a state supreme court decides an issue, it is important to remember that there is still a possibility of appeal to the U.S. Supreme Court if the case involves a federal question or an issue of constitutional rights.

The opinions of state supreme courts are significant and are reported in the regional reporters discussed earlier. Many states also have their own reporters for state supreme court opinions. For example, California has the *California Reporter.* The state supreme court reporters are easily recognized because their abbreviations are the abbreviation of each state's name. The following cite is of the state supreme court decision for the *Randolph* case:

State v. *Randolph,* 604 S.E.2d 835 (Ga. 2004)

Where Would the Court Be Located? In Personam *Jurisdiction of Courts*

Once you know the proper court for subject matter, only half the job is done. For example, the Boeing case would be a multi-million dollar one involving companies headquartered in different states and countries. A federal district court has subject matter jurisdiction, but which of the 94 federal district courts will hear the case? That question can be answered by looking at *in personam* jurisdictions. *In personam* jurisdiction is power over the parties involved in the case.

Exhibit 3.5 and the following sections cover *in personam* jurisdiction.

EXHIBIT   3.5   Personal Jurisdiction

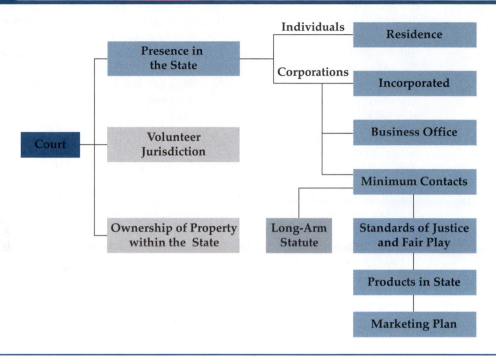

OWNERSHIP OF PROPERTY WITHIN THE STATE

A party who owns real property in a state is subject to the jurisdiction of that state's courts for litigation related to that property. Actually, this type of jurisdiction gives the court authority over the person because the person owns a thing in the state. Technically, this type of jurisdiction is called *in rem* **jurisdiction**.

VOLUNTEER JURISDICTION

A court has jurisdiction over a person who agrees to be subject to that court. In some contracts, for example, the parties agree that any lawsuits will be brought in the seller's state. The seller's state courts then have jurisdiction over that volunteer buyer.

PRESENCE IN THE STATE

The third and final way a state court can take jurisdiction is by the "presence" of a party in the state, which is determined by different factors.

Residence

Individuals are present in a state if they have a residence in that state. There are different definitions of residency for tax and election laws, but the requirement here is simply that the person live in the state some time during any given year.

   Corporations are residents of the states in which they are incorporated. A corporation is also a resident of any state in which it has a business office with employees.

"Minimum Contacts"

Both corporations and residents can be subject to a state court's jurisdiction if they have "minimum contacts" in that state. The standard for **minimum contacts** is a fairness standard, which was established by the U.S. Supreme Court in *International Shoe* v. *Washington,* 326 U.S. 310 (1945). The Court basically required the states to notify out-of-state defendants of a suit and those defendants to have some contact with the state. Fairness does not require an office or an employee in the state. However, undertaking a business plan to get your product into a state is a basis for jurisdiction of that state's courts. These standards for *in personam* jurisdiction are more liberal than the citizenship requirements for diversity actions.

Long-Arm Statutes: The Tools of Minimum Contracts

In order to follow the Supreme Court's ruling on fairness, all of the states have adopted **long-arm statutes**. These statutes give courts the power to extend their arms of jurisdiction into other states. For example, suppose that Zeta Corporation is incorporated in Ohio and has its manufacturing plant there. Zeta ships its glass baking dishes to retail businesses for resale in every state in the country, although it has offices only in Ohio. Joan Berferd, who lives in Alabama, is injured when one of Zeta's baking dishes explodes. Can the Alabama courts allow Berferd to file suit there and require Zeta to come to Alabama to defend the suit? Yes, because a long-arm statute is fair if it covers businesses shipping products to the state. Zeta entered the Alabama market voluntarily and must be subject to the Alabama courts. The following case deals with whether a long-arm statute can be applied to a company that ships its products into a state.

CASE 3.2

Lindgren v. *GDT, LLC*
312 F.SUPP.2D 1125 (S.D. IOWA 2004)

JANGLING JEWELS ON THE INTERNET: CAN THE COURT LOOP THEM IN?

FACTS

Gail Lindgren is an entrepreneur who runs a small business called Moonbeams based in West Des Moines, Iowa. In 1997, Ms. Lindgren designed and began selling JEANJANGLES, jewelry that hangs from the belt loops on jeans. Ms. Lindgren obtained a patent for the trinkets in 2000. JEANJANGLES are designed to hang from the belt loop and are made from sterling silver or gold-filled wire, with pieces incorporating such items as gold nuggets, glass, or abalone. Prices range from $18 to $58. JEANJANGLES may be purchased from Ms. Lindgren's Web site, http://www.jeanjangle.com, or from Teacups and Tiaras in West Des Moines, Iowa, and its online store.

A California company, GDT, began selling "Jeans for the Hip," also called JEAN JEWEL. GDT filed a trademark application for JEAN JEWEL on May 21, 2002. GDT's jewelry is made from sterling silver or gold and may contain semi-precious stones or glass. Prices range from $55 to $835. GDT maintains a Web site, http://www.jeanjewel.com, which began selling JEAN JEWEL merchandise in June 2003. JEAN JEWEL merchandise is also available at foreign and domestic retail outlets, although not in Iowa. GDT's principal place of business is Pacific Palisades, California.

Ms. Lindgren became aware of GDT, its Web site, and its product when *People* magazine did a feature story on the jean trinkets and friends called to congratulate her on her national success. Ms. Lindgren filed suit in federal district court in Iowa against GDT for infringement. GDT filed a motion to dismiss the case for lack of *in personam* jurisdiction.

JUDICIAL OPINION

LONGSTAFF, Chief Judge

The personal jurisdiction issue in this case is a close question. As the Supreme Court has noted, the determination of whether minimum contacts exist "is one in which few answers will be written 'in black or white. The greys are dominant and even among them the shades are innumerable.'"

Prior to the filing of this action, GDT's only conduct directed at Iowa was the state's inclusion on a drop-down menu on the shipping page of GDT's Web site. The shipping page enabled shipment around the world—to Uzbekistan or Palau, if the customer so indicated. Shipments were contracted to FedEx as the third-party carrier, with the costs to be paid by the consumer. While GDT's Web site is both commercial and highly interactive, the site is arguably no more directed at Iowa than at Uzbekistan. As GDT's Web site could be accessed anywhere, including Iowa, its existence does not demonstrate an intent to purposefully target Iowa.

There is no evidence that GDT took any purposeful action towards Iowa—it did not direct any paid advertising to Iowa or solicit Iowa residents to visit its Web site. It merely processed the orders from Iowa customers who visited its site. Furthermore, under both the California and Iowa versions of the U.C.C., the sales were made F.O.B. seller with the carrier acting as the buyer's agent. Title thus passed to the buyer in California when GDT delivered the items to FedEx for shipment. Consequently, the Internet sales were clearly made in California, and are an insufficient basis for personal jurisdiction over GDT in Iowa.

Here, Lindgren asserts that because the alleged confusion occurred in Iowa, and her principal place of business is in Iowa, the "brunt" of the injury is felt here. Additionally, she argues that her registration of the JEANJANGLES name put GDT on constructive notice that infringement of that name would harm her in Iowa.

This Court recognizes that Iowa has a strong interest in providing a forum to protect its citizens from trademark infringement and unfair competition, and that Lindgren would no doubt be inconvenienced if forced to litigate her claim in California. These considerations do not, however, obviate the requirements of due process:

Even if the defendant would suffer minimal or no inconvenience from being forced to litigate before the tribunals of another State; even if the forum State has a strong interest in applying its law to the controversy; even if the forum State is the most convenient location for litigation, the Due Process Clause, acting as an instrument of interstate federalism, may sometimes act to divest the State of its power to render a valid judgment.

GDT lacks minimum contacts with Iowa and considerations of fairness and justice do not warrant an exercise of personal jurisdiction by this Court. Although this Court lacks jurisdiction, it finds that Lindgren's claims may continue in the Central District of California, Western Division. Therefore, GDT's Motion to Dismiss is DENIED.

CASE QUESTIONS

1. Does the fact that a company has a Web site mean that every state with customers has jurisdiction?
2. What would be needed to require GDT to come to Iowa and defend the suit?

ethical *issues*

Now that you know the background of JEANJANGLES and JEAN JEWEL, would you purchase GDT's product? Why or why not? Suppose you were offered a counterfeit Burberry's purse for $25. The purse looks just like the store originals that cost $480. You could give it as a gift or resell it for as much as $75. Would you buy the purse? Why or why not? What difference does it make whether the purse is real or counterfeit? Is it your role to police trademark counterfeiters?

consider 3.2

Since 1980, Richard B. King has run The Blue Note, a jazz club located in Columbia, Missouri. Bensusan Restaurant Corporation runs another jazz club, also called The Blue Note, in New York City. Bensusan applied for and obtained a federal trademark for its club name. In 1993, Bensusan's attorney wrote to Mr. King and asked that Mr. King refrain from using the name. Mr. King and Bensusan simply did not agree and parted ways until 1996, when Mr. King created a Blue Note Web site. The Web site had information about Mr. King's club, special dates of interest, a reference to it being "mid-Missouri's finest jazz club," and a note that it was not connected with The Blue Note of New York City. Bensusan filed suit in New York City for trademark infringement. The district court granted Mr. King's motion to dismiss the complaint for lack of jurisdiction, and Bensusan appealed. Can the New York federal court take jurisdiction over Mr. King and require him to come to New York City to defend the lawsuit? (Analysis appears at the end of the chapter.) [*Bensusan Restaurant Corp.* v. *King*, 126 F.3d 25 (2d Cir. 1997)]

What Would It Be Like If a Business Went to Court?

Now that you understand what the court process looks from a bird's eye view and how precedent is an important part of the judicial process, the next step is understanding the detail of a lawsuit. If your business had to go to court, how would the process go? What are the roles of the parties? How do I work with my lawyer during litigation?

The Parties in Court

PEOPLE WHO BRING SUIT: PLAINTIFFS

Plaintiffs are the parties who initiate a lawsuit and are seeking some type of recovery. In some types of cases, they are called **petitioners** (such as in an action for divorce). The plaintiffs file their suit in the appropriate court, and this filing begins the process.

PEOPLE WHO DEFEND AGAINST SUITS: DEFENDANTS

Defendants are the ones from whom the plaintiffs want recovery. They are the ones charged with some violation of the civil rights of the plaintiff. In some cases, they are referred to as **respondents**.

PEOPLE WHO HELP PEOPLE: LAWYERS

In most cases, each of the parties is represented by a **lawyer**. Lawyers have other functions besides representing clients in a lawsuit. Many lawyers offer "preventive" services. Lawyers draft contracts, wills, and other documents to prevent legal problems from arising. Clients are advised in advance so that they can minimize legal problems and costs.

The attorney-client relationship is a fiduciary one and one that carries privilege. The attorney is expected to act in the best interests of the client and do so without the fear of having to disclose the client's thoughts and decisions. The

attorney-client privilege keeps the relationship confidential and assures that others (even an adversary in a lawsuit) have limited access to lawyer-client conversations. One of the key areas of discussion, debate, and modified reforms under Sarbanes-Oxley has related to imposing upon corporate lawyers the duty to report fraud and other financial misdeeds of their client companies. Lawyers were concerned about the need for client confidentiality, and regulators and investors were concerned that lawyers have remained silent as financial frauds have been ongoing in companies. While the final version of the rules adopted pursuant to Sarbanes-Oxley (as of 2004) does not require lawyers to blow the whistle on their clients, they are required to take steps to notify the audit committee and board about misconduct and eventually resign if the conduct is not changed and rectified.

Because of the privilege, many lawyers know that their clients actually did commit a crime or breach a contract. However, the client's confession to an attorney is confidential. Even with that knowledge, it is the attorney's obligation to represent the client zealously and make certain that the client is given all rights and protections under the law. A criminal defense attorney may know that her client has committed a crime. But committing a crime and the required proof for conviction of that crime are two different things. It is the lawyer's job to see that the other side meets its burdens and responsibilities in proving a case against the client. Lawyers do represent guilty people. Their role is to make sure that the system operates fairly with guilty and innocent people alike. Lawyers are not required to remain silent because of the confidentiality protections if a client is about to commit a crime. A lawyer representing a client accused of murder cannot disclose that the client confessed. However, a lawyer whose client vows to kill someone must make a disclosure in order to prevent a crime.

> ## Business Planning Tip
>
> Businesspeople should exercise caution in the protection of their lawyer-client privilege. Letters and memos to lawyers should be marked as privileged, and limitations should be placed on access to those letters and memos. Revealing to others your communications to your lawyer may cost you your privilege. Holding a conversation or meeting with your lawyer with others present may also cost you your privilege. Privileged communications should be with your lawyer(s) only.

Lawyers and their titles and roles vary from country to country. Great Britain and most of Canada have *solicitors* and *barristers*. Solicitors prepare legal documents, give legal advice, and represent clients in some of the lesser courts. Barristers are the only "lawyers" who can practice before higher courts and administrative agencies. Quebec and France have three types of lawyers: the *avocat*, who can practice before the higher courts and give legal advice; the *notaire*, who can handle real property transactions and estates and can prepare some legal documents; and the *juriste* (legal counselor), who can give advice and prepare legal documents. In Germany, a lawyer who litigates is called *Rechtsanwalt* and a lawyer who advises clients but does not appear in court is called *Rechtsbeistand*. Japan has only one class of lawyers, called *Bengosh*, but does have the *Shiho-Soshi*, a type of advanced notary with the authority to incorporate companies, prepare documents, and create wills. In Italy, the two types of lawyers—whose roles are similar to the dual British system—are *avocati* and *procuratori*.

PEOPLE IN CHARGE: JUDGES

Judges control the proceedings in a case and, in some instances, the outcome. Trial judges control the trial of a case from presiding over the selection of a jury to ruling on evidence questions. Appellate judges, as noted earlier, review the work of trial court judges. They do not actually hear evidence but, rather, review transcripts.

Judges are selected in various ways throughout the country. Some judges are elected to their offices. Some states have merit appointment systems, wherein judges are appointed on the basis of their qualifications. In some states, judges are appointed by elected officials subject to the approval of the legislature. In some states with appointed judges, the judges are put on the ballot every other year (or some other period) for retention; voters in these states do not decide whom they want as judges but do decide whether they want to keep them once they are in office. Federal judges are appointed by the president with Senate approval.

PEOPLE: OTHER NAMES OF PARTIES

The lawyers and the parties stay in the "game" even after a case is appealed. Some states change the name of the case if the party appealing the case is the defendant. For example, suppose that Smith sues Jones for damages in a car accident. The name of the case at trial is *Smith v. Jones.* Smith is the plaintiff, and Jones is the defendant. If Smith wins the case at trial and Jones decides to appeal, Jones is the **appellant** and Smith is the **appellee.** In some courts, the name of the case on appeal becomes *Jones v. Smith.* Other courts leave the case name the same but still label Jones the appellant and Smith the appellee.

The Trial Process

Understanding the trial process helps managers to understand their role in litigation if that path for resolving a dispute is used. If you had to go to court, the following sections provide an overview of how litigation and a trial would proceed. Exhibit 3.6 summarizes the trial process

---

EXHIBIT   3.6   The Trial Process

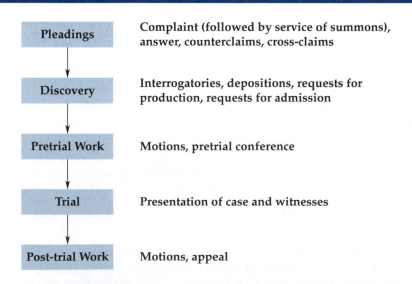

Pleadings	**Complaint (followed by service of summons), answer, counterclaims, cross-claims**
Discovery	**Interrogatories, depositions, requests for production, requests for admission**
Pretrial Work	**Motions, pretrial conference**
Trial	**Presentation of case and witnesses**
Post-trial Work	**Motions, appeal**

THE COMPLAINT (PETITION)

The first step in a lawsuit is filing a document called a **complaint** or **petition**, which must be filed within certain time limits each state has for filing suit. These time limits are called **statutes of limitations**. The typical statute of limitations for personal injuries is two years; the typical limitation for contracts is four years.

A complaint is a general statement of the plaintiff's claim of rights. The final paragraphs of a complaint list the damages or remedies the plaintiff wants (see Exhibit 3.7).

In some cases, a group of plaintiffs who have the same cause of action against one defendant file the complaint. These types of suits are called **class action suits**. Perhaps the most widely publicized type of class action lawsuit is the suit that results when a group of prescription drug patients files suit against a pharmaceutical company for ill side-effects of the company's drug, as when Merck faced multi-billion dollar class suits from Vioxx users. Another form of class action suit is the **derivative suit**, in which shareholders sue a corporation to recover damages for actions taken by the corporation. (See Chapter 13 for more information.)

THE SUMMONS

The defendant will not know of the suit just because it is filed. The second step in a lawsuit is serving the defendant with a copy of the complaint and a **summons**, which is a legal document that tells the defendant of the suit and explains the defendant's rights under the law.

A summons must be delivered to the defendant. Some states require that the defendant be given the papers personally. Other states allow the papers to be given to some member of the defendant's household or, in the case of a business, to an agent of that business. (See Chapter 17 for a discussion of an agent's authority.)

The summons is delivered by an officer of the court (such as a sheriff or magistrate) or by private firms licensed as **process servers**. The server files an affidavit with the court to indicate when and where the service was made.

THE ANSWER

The **pleadings**, which include the complaint or petition, are the basic statement of the case. The defendant's position is found in the **answer**, another pleading in a case. The defendant must file an answer within the time limits allowed by the court. The time limits are typically 20 days for in-state defendants and 30 days for out-of-state defendants. A failure to answer, or a **default**, is like a forfeit in sports: The plaintiff wins because the defendant failed to show up. The plaintiff can then proceed to a judgment to collect damages.

The defendant's answer can admit certain facts. The defendant's answer can also deny the allegations or a statement that the defendant does not know enough to admit or deny the allegations in the complaint. Finally, an answer might also include a **counterclaim**, which is the defendant's suit against the plaintiff, alleging rights and damages against the plaintiff.

EXHIBIT   3.7   Sample Complaint

Reed C. Tolman, Esq. (006502)
TOLMAN & OSBORNE, P.C.
1400 E. Southern, Suite 625
Tempe, Arizona 85282
Attorneys for Plaintiffs

SUPERIOR COURT OF ARIZONA

MARICOPA COUNTY

CRAIG CONNER and KATHY CONNER,) husband and wife, individually) and on behalf of their minor) son, CASEY CONNER,) Plaintiffs,) v.) CARMEN A. CHENAL and THOMAS K.) CHENAL, wife and husband,) Defendants,) _____)	**CV92 - 91319** COMPLAINT (Tort-Motor Vehicle)

For their complaint, plaintiffs allege:

1. Plaintiffs and defendants are residents of Maricopa County, Arizona.

2. This Court has jurisdiction over the subject matter under the Arizona Constitution, Art. 6, § 14.

3. Casey Conner is the minor son of Craig and Kathy Conner.

4. Carmen A. Chenal and Thomas K. Chenal are wife and husband. At all times relevant hereto, Carmen A. Chenal was acting for and on behalf of the marital community of which she is a member.

5. On or about July 20, 1990, defendant Carmen A. Chenal was driving her motor vehicle in the vicinity of Primrose Path and Cave Creek Road in Carefree, Arizona. At the time, Casey Conner was a passenger in the back seat of defendants' vehicle, a 1976 Mercedes, ID No.11603312051326.

6. At all times relevant hereto, defendant Carmen A. Chenal had a duty to care properly for the safety of Casey Conner. That duty included the responsibility to place Casey in an appropriate and functioning seatbelt.

7. Prior to the accident that resulted in injuries to Casey Conner, Carmen A. Chenal knew that the right rear door of her vehicle was damaged and not functioning properly.

8. Despite the duty Carmen A. Chenal had to care properly for the safety of Casey Conner, and despite her knowledge of a malfunctioning right rear door, Carmen A. Chenal negligently failed to place Casey in an appropriate and functioning seatbelt and negligently and carelessly operated her vehicle in such a way that the right rear door opened and allowed Casey to be ejected from the vehicle while the vehicle was in operation.

9. Carmen A. Chenal's failure to exercise reasonable care for the safety of Casey and the failure to operate her vehicle in a careful and safe manner proximately caused Casey to suffer personal injuries.

10. As a result of Casey Conner's injuries, he has experienced physical and psychological suffering, and his parents have incurred medical and other expenses, as well as lost earnings.

WHEREFORE, plaintiffs request judgment against defendants for compensatory damages in an amount to be determined at trial.

DATED: this _____ day of July, 1992.
                    TOLMAN & OSBORNE

By: _____

        Reed C. Tolman
        1400 E. Southern
        Suite 625
        Tempe, Arizona 85282

Source: Complaint appears courtesy of Tolman & Osborne, P.C., Tempe, AZ 85282.

ENDING A CASE EARLY: JUDGES AND MOTIONS

There are several places in litigation where a business might have a chance for an early resolution of the case. For example, once the complaint and answer are filed, a party can make a **motion for judgment on the pleadings**. This motion is granted when the party argues that even if everything the pleadings stated were true, there is still no right of recovery. Another motion is a **motion for summary judgment**. This motion is appropriate when there are no factual issues and the parties just need the court to apply the law. In the Boeing example, there could be a good chance for a motion for summary judgment. The parties do not have a factual issue: the parts were not delivered. Now the parties need the judge to determine whether there was a breach and then perhaps limit the case to hearing evidence on damages. Summary judgments can be a time and money saver for businesses. So, if the parties agree on facts but disagree on what law applies and whether it applies in their circumstances, then a judge can rule on the law without the cost of a full trial.

DISCOVERY

Trials in the United States are not conducted by ambush. Before the trial, the parties engage in a mandatory process of mutual disclosure of all relevant documents and other evidence. This court-supervised process of gathering evidence is called **discovery**. Discovery rules provide for sanctions (penalties) for not turning over relevant documents at the start of a case. Discovery can be long and complicated. Managers play a critical role in discovery because they provide documents and information. The following sections give a brief look at the traditional tools of discovery.

Requests for Admissions

A **request for admissions** asks the other side to admit a certain fact. For example, the parties might have a dispute about the amount due under a contract but should be willing to admit that they signed the contract and that it is authentic. These requests for admission reduce the length of trials because admissions establish facts.

Depositions

Depositions are the oral testimony of parties or witnesses that are taken under oath but outside the courtroom and before the trial. They can be taken long before a trial and help preserve a witness's or party's recollection. Depositions are also helpful in determining just how strong a case is. Managers and executives are often deposed during litigation.

Limitations on Discovery

Discovery has the general limitation of relevance. Only things that are evidence or could lead to the discovery of evidence are discoverable. However, discovery also has a specific limitation. Discovery cannot require the production of **work product**, which consists of the attorney's research, thoughts, analysis, and strategy. Discovery cannot request the production of legal research, trial strategy, or an attorney's comments or reactions to a witness. Communications between lawyers and their clients are protected by a privilege and, except in limited circumstances, are not discoverable.

Requests for Production

A **request for production** requires the other side to produce documents that have not already been given under the new discovery rules. A request for production can include medical records as well as tangible evidence. In *Wal-Mart Stores, Inc.* v. *Johnson* (Case 3.3), the failure to produce physical evidence that was part of an accident resulted in sanctions for that failure.

CASE 3.3

Wal-Mart Stores, Inc. v. *Johnson*
106 S.W.3D 718 (Tx. 2003)

"Reining" Deer at the Local Wal-Mart

Facts

While stocking merchandise, a Wal-Mart employee accidentally knocked one or more decorative reindeer from a high shelf onto Monroe Johnson's head and arm. Mr. Johnson told Phyllis McClane, a Wal-Mart supervisor who had come to investigate, that he was not hurt. After a Wal-Mart employee cleaned and bandaged his cut, Mr. Johnson left the store.

That evening, Mr. Johnson's neck and arm began to hurt, and he could not sleep. The next day, his doctor prescribed muscle relaxers, pain killers, and physical therapy. Still in pain six months later, Mr. Johnson and his wife sued Wal-Mart. While suit was pending, Mr. Johnson consulted three more physicians and tried additional treatments without success. About seventeen months after the accident, a surgeon performed an anterior cervical discectomy and fusion on Mr. Johnson's neck.

During discovery, the Johnsons asked whether Wal-Mart still possessed the reindeer that fell on him. Wal-Mart did not, but the company offered to provide a "reasonable facsimile." The Johnsons did not want the facsimile, and the trial court prohibited Wal-Mart "from introducing into evidence a reasonable facsimile of the reindeer made the basis of this lawsuit."

Only the photograph of the reindeer was introduced in evidence, but its quality was too poor to substantiate or rebut either party's description.

Based on Wal-Mart's failure to keep the reindeer, the Johnsons requested and obtained the following jury instruction (see p. 77 for more information on jury instructions).

You are instructed that, when a party has possession of a piece of evidence at a time he knows or should have known it will be evidence in a controversy, and thereafter he disposes of it, makes it unavailable, or fails to produce it, there is a presumption in law that the piece of evidence, had it been produced, would have been unfavorable to the party who did not produce it. If you find by a preponderance of the evidence that Wal-Mart had possession of the reindeer at a time it knew or should have known they would be evidence in this controversy, then there is a presumption that the reindeer, if produced, would be unfavorable to Wal-Mart.

The jury found for Mr. and Mrs. Johnson and awarded damages. Wal-Mart did not appeal the award or the damages. Rather, Wal-Mart appealed the jury instruction. The court of appeals affirmed, and Wal-Mart appealed again.

Judicial Opinion

PHILLIPS, Chief Justice

In this case, the trial court decided to remedy what it perceived to be Wal-Mart's misconduct by giving a spoliation instruction. The instruction informed the jury that it must presume that the missing reindeer would have harmed Wal-Mart's case if the jury concluded that Wal-Mart disposed of the reindeer after it knew or should have known that they would be evidence in the case. Such an instruction is a common remedy for spoliation, with roots going back to the English common law.

Our courts of appeals have generally limited the use of the spoliation instruction to two circumstances: [1] the deliberate destruction of relevant evidence and [2] the failure of a party to produce relevant evidence or to explain its non-production.

Wal-Mart argues that it had no duty to preserve the reindeer as evidence because it had no notice that they would be relevant to a future claim. Specifically, Wal-Mart contends that it did not learn of the Johnsons' claim until all of the reindeer had been disposed of in the normal course of business. The Johnsons point out that Wal-Mart's extensive investigation on the day of the accident indicates its awareness of both the potential claim and the reindeer's importance to it. Wal-Mart responds that it routinely investigates all accidents on its premises, and this particular investigation revealed that Johnson had not been seriously injured and never indicated that he might seek legal relief. We agree that nothing about the investigation or the circumstances surrounding the accident would have put Wal-Mart on notice that there was a substantial chance that the Johnsons would pursue a claim.

[T]he trial court abused its discretion when it submitted the spoliation instruction to the jury because the Johnsons failed to establish that Wal-Mart had a duty to preserve the reindeer.

While we do not lightly reverse a judgment because of an erroneous instruction, we believe an unnecessary spoliation instruction is particularly likely to cause harm.

Because the instruction itself is given to compensate for the absence of evidence that a party had a duty to preserve, its very purpose is to "nudge" or "tilt" the jury. Thus, if a spoliation instruction should not have been given, the likelihood of harm from the erroneous instruction is substantial, particularly when the case is closely contested.

Accordingly, we reverse the court of appeals' judgment and remand this case to the trial court for further proceedings.

CASE QUESTIONS

1. When does the duty to preserve evidence arise?

2. Why does the court worry about "tilting" or "nudging" the jury in the case?

3. What lessons should a store manager learn from this case?

THE TRIAL ITSELF

The Type of Trial—Jury or Nonjury

Occasionally, the parties agree not to have a jury trial and instead have a trial to the court. In these cases, the judge acts as both judge and jury—both running the trial and determining its outcome.

But there is a right to a jury trial, and managers should be aware of the nature and structure of jurors so that they can weigh the risks of using one as well as going to trial. The size of a jury varies; some states require only six jurors. A jury may have 12 to 18 members, which includes alternates, particularly in long trials, to ensure that a panel of 12 participates fully in the trial.

The pool of potential jurors comes from voting lists alone or combined with other lists (e.g., licensed drivers). People on these lists are randomly notified to report for jury duty. Once a pool is available, the court begins the process of *voir dire*, which determines whether a potential juror is qualified to serve. Most states have jurors complete a questionnaire on general topics so that the selection process can move quickly. The questionnaire covers personal information—age, occupation, and so on. The questionnaire might also ask whether the person has ever been a juror, a party to a lawsuit, or a witness. Exhibit 3.8 provides some sample *voir dire* questions.

A juror can be removed from a jury panel for two reasons. First, a juror can be removed for cause, which means the juror is incapable of making an impartial decision in the case. If a juror is related to one of the attorneys in the case, for example, the juror would be excused for cause. Some jurors reveal their biases or prejudices, like racial prejudice, in the questionnaire they are required to complete. Others may express strong feelings of animosity toward the medical profession.

EXHIBIT   3.8   Sample *Voir Dire* Questions

1. Do you know any of the parties or lawyers in this case? (Asked after the judge introduces all parties and lawyers.)
2. What is your occupation?
3. Are you married?
4. What is your spouse's occupation?
5. Have you ever served on a jury?
6. Are you in favor of compensation for emotional injuries?
7. Do you believe in compensation for victims of police misconduct?
8. Do you support capital punishment?
9. What is your educational background?
10. How old are you?
11. Did you serve in the armed forces?
12. Have you formed an opinion about this case?
13. Do you equate laziness with black people?
14. Do you believe black people commit more crimes than white people?

Sometimes a juror cannot be excused for cause but an attorney feels uncomfortable about the juror or the juror's attitudes. In these circumstances, the lawyer issues a **peremptory challenge**, which excuses the juror. The peremptory challenge is the attorney's private tool. However, the use of peremptory challenges is limited. All states have a statute or court rule limiting the number of peremptory challenges an attorney may use in a trial, with some exceptions for capital crimes.

The Trial Content

The attorney for each party is permitted to make an **opening statement** that summarizes what that party hopes to prove and how it will be proved. Most attorneys also mention the issue of **burden of proof**, which controls who has the responsibility for proving what facts.

Because the plaintiff has the burden of proof, the plaintiff presents his or her case and evidence first. The attorney for the plaintiff decides the order of the witnesses; questioning of these witnesses under oath is called **direct examination**. Although the defense cannot present witnesses during this part of the trial, it can question the plaintiff's witnesses after their direct examination is completed. The defense questioning of plaintiff witnesses is called **cross-examination**, after which the plaintiff may again pose questions to clarify under **redirect examination**.

Once the plaintiff has finished his case, there must be enough evidence to establish a **prima facie case**, one in which the plaintiff has offered some evidence on all the elements required to be established for recovery. Although the evidence may be subjected to credibility questions and challenged by defense evidence, there must be some proof for each part of the claim. If the plaintiff does not meet this standard, the defendant can and may make a motion for a **directed verdict**. This motion for a directed verdict is made outside the jury's hearing and argued to the judge. If it is not granted, the trial proceeds with the defendant's case.

If there is no directed verdict, the defendant has the same opportunity to present witnesses and evidence.

ethical *issues*

Qualcomm was in litigation against a competitor for copyright infringement. Qualcomm did not turn over 200 e-mails that showed that Qualcomm failed to honor an industry agreement to raise infringement issues as the industry worked to develop compatible software and programs. Qualcomm allowed the cooperative project to continue to completion and when the programs were launched, it filed suit against the participants. The e-mails showed that Qualcomm had this plan all along. Evaluate the ethics of Qualcomm and its managers. What risks did Qualcomm run in using this strategy? Given what you have learned about discovery and its purposes, was Qualcomm acting fairly with its conduct? *Qualcomm v. Broadcom*, 539 F.Supp.2d 1214 (S.D.Cal. 2007)

There are restrictions on the forms and types of evidence that can be used at trial. Most people are familiar with the hearsay rule of evidence. **Hearsay** is evidence offered by a witness who does not have personal knowledge of the information being given but just heard it from someone else. For example, suppose that Arkansas Sewing and Fit Fabric are involved in contract litigation. Fit Fabric says there was no contract. Arkansas Sewing has a witness who overheard the president of Fit Fabric talking to someone on a plane saying he had a contract with Arkansas Sewing but had no intention of performing on it. The witness's testimony of the airplane conversation is hearsay and cannot be used to prove the contract existed. The reason for the hearsay rule is to keep evidence as reliable as possible. The person testifying about the hearsay may not know of the circumstances or background of the conversation and is testifying only to what someone else said.

Once the evidence is presented and the parties are finished with their cases, there is one final "go" at the jury. The parties are permitted to make **closing arguments**, which review the presented evidence, highlight the important points for the jurors, and point out the defects in the other side's case. After the cases and closing arguments are presented, the jurors are given their **instructions**. These instructions tell the jurors what the law is and how to apply the law to the facts presented. The instructions are developed by the judge and all the attorneys in the case.

Jury deliberations are done privately; they cannot be recorded, and no one can attend the deliberations except the jurors. The U.S. Supreme Court has ruled that jury verdicts need not be unanimous. A state can adopt a rule that requires only a simple majority or three-fourths of the jury to agree on a verdict. In those states requiring unanimous verdicts, it is not unusual for juries to be unable to agree on a verdict. The jurors have then reached a deadlock, which is called a **hung jury**. If a trial results in a hung jury, the case can be retried. There is, however, the additional expense of retrying the case.

The result of jury deliberations is the **verdict**. The verdict is given to the judge and is usually read by the judge's clerk.

Even after the verdict, the case is not over. The losing party can make several motions to get around the verdict. One such motion is for a new trial, wherein the attorney argues the need and reason for a new trial to the judge.

Another motion after the verdict, one that a judge is less likely to grant, is a motion for a **judgment NOV**. *NOV* stands for *non obstante veredicto,* which means "notwithstanding the verdict." In other words, the moving attorney is asking the trial judge to reverse the decision of the jury. The basis for granting a judgment NOV is that the jury's verdict is clearly against the weight of the evidence. Occasionally, juries are swayed by the emotion of a case and do not apply the law properly. It is, however, a strong show of judicial authority for a judge to issue a judgment NOV, and they are rare.

Even if no motions are granted, the case still may not be over; it can go to an appellate court for review. Such an appeal must be done within a specified time limit in each state. Here the trial has come full circle to the principle of judicial review and *stare decisis* and we can now look at the court systems that have the trial and appellate courts. Exhibit 3.9 summarizes the steps in civil litigation.

Now that you understand ADR, the court system, and the litigation process, you have a set of tools and information that could help you make the decision on how to handle a business dispute. The following chart lists the pros and cons of litigation vs. ADR.

ALTERNATIVE DISPUTE RESOLUTION	LITIGATION
Open lines of communication	Technical discovery rules
Parties can agree to anything	Judicial constraints of precedent
Creative remedies permitted	Remedies limited (by law and precedent)
Parties set timetable	
Privacy	Backlog
Control by parties (or mediator/arbitrator)	Public proceeding
Cheaper (recent growing together of costs of arbitration and trial)	Control by lawyers
	Expensive
More flexibility (some indications arbitration may not be as flexible as once believed)	Strict procedures/timing
	Judge/jury unknowns
Parties select mediator/arbitrator (will often have expertise in the area)	Those who can afford to stay in win
Positions examined for validity	Judicial enforcement tools
Enforcement by good faith	Right of appeal
Appeals restricted	

EXHIBIT 3.9 Steps in Civil Litigation

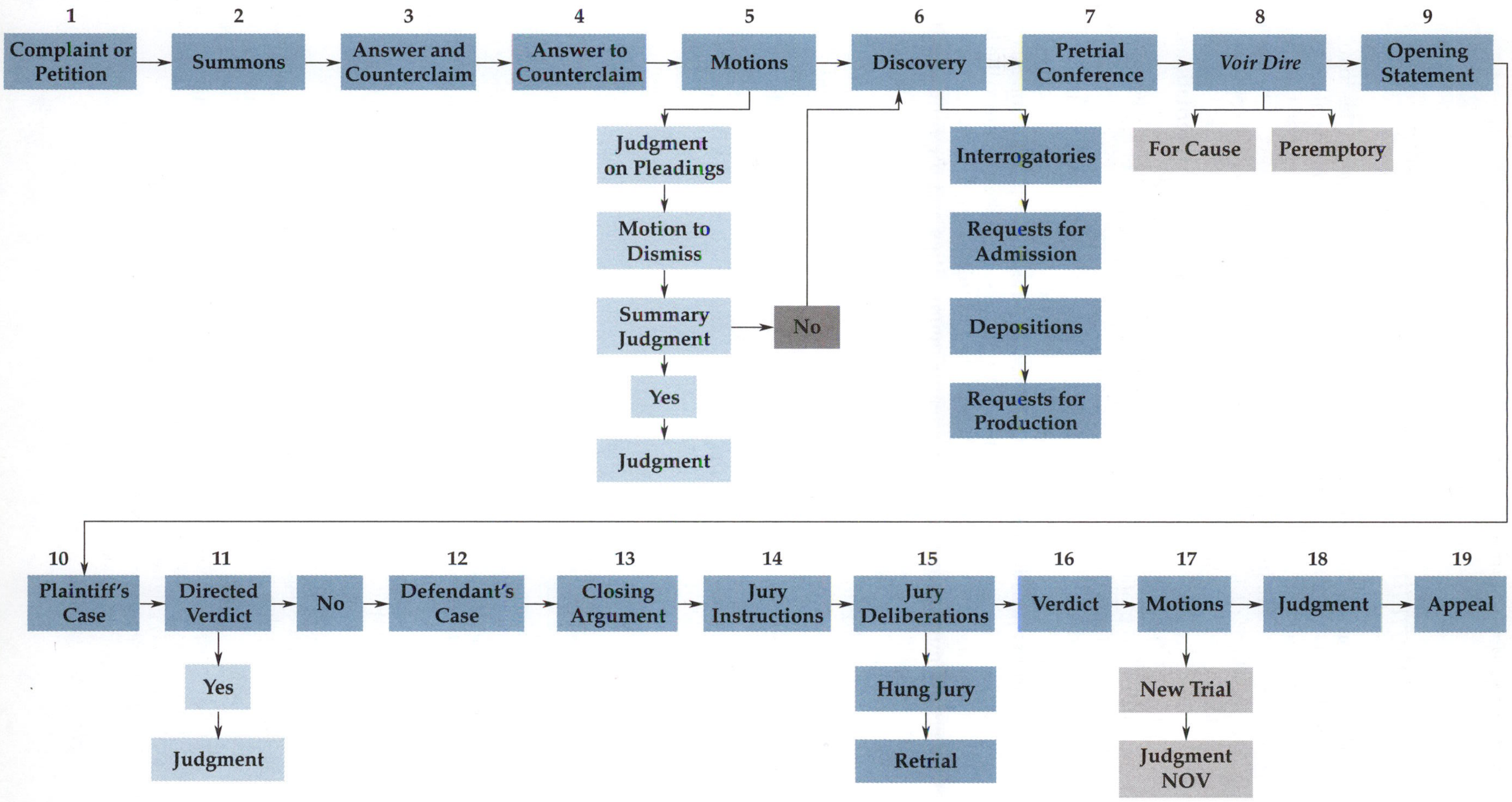

1 Complaint or Petition
2 Summons
3 Answer and Counterclaim
4 Answer to Counterclaim
5 Motions
- Judgment on Pleadings
- Motion to Dismiss
- Summary Judgment → No
- Summary Judgment → Yes → Judgment
6 Discovery
- Interrogatories
- Requests for Admission
- Depositions
- Requests for Production
7 Pretrial Conference
8 Voir Dire
- For Cause
- Peremptory
9 Opening Statement
10 Plaintiff's Case
11 Directed Verdict
- Yes → Judgment
- No
12 Defendant's Case
13 Closing Argument
14 Jury Instructions
15 Jury Deliberations
- Hung Jury → Retrial
16 Verdict
17 Motions
- New Trial
- Judgment NOV
18 Judgment
19 Appeal

The International Courts

The decisions of international courts provide precedent for parties involved in international trade. However, one of the restrictions on international court decisions is that the decision binds only the immediate parties to the suit on the basis of their factual situation. International courts do not carry the enforcement power or authority of courts in the U.S. federal and state systems. They are consensual courts and are used only when the parties agree to use them.

There are several courts of international jurisdiction. The **International Court of Justice** (ICJ) is the most widely known court. It was first established as the Permanent Court of International Justice (PCIJ) in 1920 by the League of Nations. In 1945, the United Nations (UN) changed the name and structure of the court. The ICJ is made up of 15 judges, no more than 2 of whom can be from the same nation, who are elected by the General Assembly of the UN. The court has been described as having **contentious jurisdiction**, which is to say that the court's jurisdiction is consensual: When there is a dispute, the parties can agree to submit the dispute to the ICJ.

There are other international courts in addition to the ICJ. The European Union has its **Court of Justice of European Communities** and the **European Court of Human Rights**. Jurisdiction in these courts is also consensual. Finally, there is the **Inter-American Court of Human Rights**.

In recent years, London's Commercial Court, established over 100 years ago, has become a popular forum for the resolution of international commercial disputes. Over half the cases in this court involve foreign enterprises. Some companies choose London's Commercial Court as the forum for their disputes because it is a neutral forum, uses the English language, has a wide range of experience in international disputes—from shipping contracts to joint trading ventures—has judges who were all once commercial litigators, and moves cases along quickly.

Red Flags FOR MANAGERS

Disputes in business happen. Business managers play a critical role when there is a dispute with a customer, an employee, a supplier, a shareholder, a government agency, and many others who are part of running or working with business. The first critical role a manager plays is determining how the dispute should be resolved. The choices are:

- Alternative dispute resolution methods (ADR) including arbitration, minitrials, mediation, and other non-judicial methods for settling issues.

- Using the court system.

To help make that choice, managers should consider the importance of cost, privacy, timing, and the nature of the evidence. Arbitration is private, but it may not be appealed. The court system applies stricter rules of evidence. Federal courts and cases tried there take longer than state courts to finish a case.

Managers also play a role as a case develops because whether there is ADR or a trial, the other side will be able to obtain information. Managers should be sure that they turn over all the necessary documents and evidence and should always tell the truth in depositions and during the trial.

Managers can also make the business decision to settle litigation or ADR at any time during the process. Early dispositions, such as through summary judgment, can save money and result in a faster resolution in the court system. Managers continue to weigh the costs, the privacy, and how the case unfolds in making the decision to carry on or settle.

Summary

What is the judicial process?

- Judicial review—review of a trial court's decisions and verdict to determine whether any reversible error was made

- Appellate court—court responsible for review of trial court's decisions and verdict; does not hear evidence; only determine whether there was reversible error

- Brief—written summary of basis for appeal of trial court's decisions and verdict

- Reversible error—mistake by trial court that requires a retrial or modification of a trial court's decision

- Options for appellate court:
  - Reverse—change trial court's decision
  - Remand—return case to trial court for retrial or reexamination of issues
  - Affirm—uphold trial court's decisions and verdict
  - Modify—overturn a portion of the trial court's verdict
  - *Stare decisis*—Latin for "let the decision stand"; doctrine of reviewing, applying, and/or distinguishing prior case decisions
  - Case opinion—written court decision used as precedent; contains *dicta* or explanation of reasoning and, often, a minority view or dissenting opinion

Who are the parties in the judicial system?

- Plaintiffs/petitioners—initiators of litigation

- Defendants/respondents—parties named as those from whom plaintiff seeks relief

- Lawyers—officers of the court who speak for plaintiffs and defendants

- Attorney-client privilege—confidential protections for client conversations

- Appellant—party who appeals lower court's decision

- Appellee—party responding in an appeal

What factors decide jurisdiction? The power of the court to hear cases

- Subject matter jurisdiction—authority of court over subject matter

- Jurisdiction over the parties: *in personam* jurisdiction
  - Voluntary
  - Through property
  - Presence in the state: minimum contacts
  - Residence
  - Business office

What are the courts and court systems?

- Federal court system
  - Federal district court—trial court in federal system; hears cases that involve a federal question, the United States as a party, or a plaintiff and defendant from different states (diversity of citizenship), and matters with $75,000 or more at issue; opinions reported in *Federal Supplement*
  - Limited jurisdiction courts—bankruptcy courts, court of claims
  - U.S. Courts of Appeals—federal appellate courts in each of the circuits; opinions reported in *Federal Reporter*
  - U.S. Supreme Court—highest court in United States; requires *writ of certiorari* for review; acts as trial court (original jurisdiction) for suits involving states and diplomats

- State court system
  - Lesser courts—small claims, traffic courts, justice of the peace courts
  - State trial courts—general jurisdiction courts in each state
  - State appellate courts—courts that review trial court decisions
  - State supreme courts—courts that review appellate court decisions

- International courts
  - Voluntary jurisdiction
  - International Court of Justice—UN court; contentious (consensual) jurisdiction; reported in *International Law Reports*
  - London Commercial Court—voluntary court of arbitration

Key Terms

affirms *55*

alternative dispute resolution
   (ADR) *50*

answer *71*

appellant *70*

appellate brief *54*

appellate court *53*

appellee *70*

attorney-client privilege *69*

binding arbitration *50*

brief *54*

burden of proof *76*

class action suits *71*

closing arguments *77*

complaint *71*

concurrent jurisdiction *58*

contentious jurisdiction *80*

counterclaim *71*

county courts *63*

Court of Justice of European
   Communities *80*

cross-examination *76*

default *71*

defendants *68*

depositions *73*

derivative suit *71*

direct examination *76*

directed verdict *77*

discovery *73*

dissenting opinion *54*

diversity of citizenship *58*

European Court of Human
   Rights *80*

exclusive jurisdiction *58*

federal circuits *60*

federal district court *57*

hearsay *77*

hung jury *78*

in personam jurisdiction *57*

in rem jurisdiction *65*

instructions *77*

Inter-American Court of Human
   Rights *80*

International Court of Justice *80*

judges *69*

judgment NOV *78*

judicial review *54*

jurisdiction *57*

justice of the peace courts *63*

lawyer *68*

limited jurisdiction *63*

long-arm statutes *66*

mediation *52*

minimum contacts *66*

minitrial *52*

modify *55*

motion for a summary
   judgment *73*

motion for judgment on the
   pleadings *73*

nonbinding arbitration *50*

opening statement *76*

oral argument *54*

peer review *53*

peremptory challenge *75*

petition *71*

petitioner *68*

plaintiffs *68*

pleadings *71*

precedent *55*

prima facie case *76*

process servers *71*

redirect examination *76*

regional reporter *63*

remand *54*

rent-a-judge *52*

request for admissions *73*

request for production *74*

respondent *68*

reverses *54*

reversible error *54*

small claims court *63*

statutes of limitations *71*

subject matter jurisdiction *57*

summary jury trial *53*

summons *71*

traffic courts *63*

trial court *53*

trial *de novo* *63*

U.S. Supreme Court *61*

verdict *78*

voir dire *75*

work product *73*

Questions and Problems

1. The brokerage firm of E.F. Hutton was charged with federal criminal violations of interstate funds transfers. In reviewing the case, the lawyers for the government discovered internal memorandums from and between branch managers in several states that outline a process for checking-kiting (a literal stringing together of checks and deposits) that enabled E.F. Hutton to earn interest on phantom deposits. Where will the case be tried? Which court system? Which court? Why?

What are the lawyer's obligations with respect to the document? What is the company's obligation? If you were a manager at E.F. Hutton, would you voluntarily disclose the document to the government?

2. Pharmaceutical manufacturer Merck experienced ongoing litigation over its drug Vioxx because of patients who said they had cardiovascular side effects

from taking the antiarthritic pain drug. A jury in a federal court in New Orleans cleared Merck of any responsibility for the death of Richard Irvin, a Florida resident who had a fatal heart attack one month after he began to take Vioxx. The case was the first federal district court verdict for the company that, at one time, faced almost 9,500 lawsuits. In 2005 Merck won one state court verdict in New Jersey and lost another state court trial in Texas. Why would some of the cases be tried in state court and some be tried in federal court? Explain the differing decisions. (Merck has since entered into a class-action settlement on the Vioxx cases.)

3. Centurion Wireless, Inc. is a Nebraska corporation that designs and engineers antennas and power products for telecommunications and information technology purposes. Hop-On is a Nevada corporation, selling, among other products, disposable cellular phones. Hop-On's employee Melyssa Banda contacted Centurion by phone or email in relation to designing an antenna for a cellular phone. The parties then entered into a contract January 22, 2002, entitled "Statement of Work," signed by Steve Bowles, Vice President of Sales in Lincoln, Nebraska, in which Centurion agreed to design, develop, and integrate an antenna design for Hop-On and provide up to 100 prototype antennae. Centurion was to be paid $10,000 by February 15, 2002. Centurion also agreed not to sell the antenna design to any other cellular phone manufacturers.

Centurion completed its work under the Statement of Work and made offers to manufacture up to 3,000,000 antennas, but Hop-On declined. Centurion alleges that Hop-On then offered to buy the design, but the parties could not agree on a price. Centurion's final offer was to sell the antenna design for $45,000.

On April 7, 2003, Centurion was contacted by Banda, the former vice president of Hop-On, and informed that even though Hop-On had not purchased the antenna design, it had copied and used it in their phones. Hop-On's phones, which used the Centurion antenna design, were sold at Walgreens stores in California. Hop-On operates a Web site at Hop-On.com, which provides some information about phones and contact information. Centurion filed suit against Hop-On in Nebraska for copyright infringement, conversion, and unjust enrichment. Hop-On has filed a motion to dismiss because of Nebraska's lack of jurisdiction over it. Does the Nebraska court have jurisdiction? Why or why not? *Centurion Wireless Technologies, Inc. v. Hop-On Communications, Inc.*, 342 F.Supp.2d 832 (D. Neb. 2004)

4. In the Johns-Manville asbestos litigation, Samuel Greenstone, an attorney for 11 asbestos workers, settled their claims for $30,000 and a promise that he would not "directly or indirectly participate in the bringing of new actions against the Corporation." The 1933 case settlement was documented in the minutes of Johns-Manville's board meeting. Could the information in the minutes be used in later litigation against Johns-Manville? How could a plaintiff's attorney obtain the information? Do you feel Mr. Greenstone made an ethical decision in his agreement? Wasn't his loyalty to his 11 clients and his obligation to obtain compensation for them? Would you have agreed to the no-further-participation-in-a-lawsuit clause? Would you, if you had been an executive at Johns-Manville, have supported the clause?

5. After she was found guilty of obstruction of justice and conspiracy (see Chapter 7), lawyers for Martha Stewart filed a motion for a new trial on the grounds that a juror on the case had possible undisclosed bias. The defense lawyers pointed out that juror Chappel Hartridge had checked "No" on the juror questionnaire when asked whether he had been accused of, charged with, or convicted of a crime. The lawyers for Ms. Stewart filed an affidavit from a former girlfriend of Mr. Hartridge's who indicated that he had been arrested and arraigned on charges of assaulting her. Mr. Hartridge's former girlfriend ultimately dropped the charges against him. What bias do you think Ms. Stewart's lawyers alleged? Are they right? Should the juror have been eliminated for cause? *U.S. v. Stewart*, 317 F.Supp.2d 432 (S.D.N.Y.2004)

Understanding "Consider" Problems

3.1

THINK: We use precedent to solve legal issues that are not directly covered by laws and regulations. Those affected by the rules must be able to count on precedent for consistency, stability, and reasonable interpretation of laws and regulations.

APPLY: The purpose of the university regulation was to prevent students from retaking courses to earn a higher grade point average (GPA).

ANSWER: In the factual situation, the student earned a lower grade. The registrar entered the lower grade hoping to create a deterrent for students retaking courses when they had a C or better. However, it is clear that a second grade, whether higher or lower, should not be entered.

If the registrar has always counted the lower grades in the cumulative GPA, does Rod still have an effective argument? Is the registrar using a strained interpretation of the regulation?

3.2

THINK:

1. Determine how much of a presence Mr. King has in New York City.

2. List contacts Mr. King has with residents of New York City.

3. Determine whether Mr. King has tried to infiltrate the New York City jazz market.

4. Determine the only way Mr. King could recruit New York Blue Note customers.

APPLY: Mr. King has no presence in New York City except for individuals who have access to his informational Web site. Mr. King has not targeted New York City customers and has no club in New York City, no office, no employees, and no property. By disclosing his geographic location, Mr. King makes certain that customers are not confused. Mr. King is not recruiting New York customers—only those who travel would be interested in his club.

ANSWER: The facts of this case provide no basis for granting jurisdiction. New York courts cannot require Mr. King to defend a lawsuit in New York.

Notes

1. Michael Orey, "The Vanishing Trial," *BusinessWeek,* April 30, 2007, pp. 38–39.

2. The U.S. Supreme Court ruled that Mr. Newdow lacked standing to challenge the "under God" clause in the pledge of allegiance because he was not the custodial parent of his daughter. 542 U.S. 1 (2004).

PART **2**

Business: Its Regulatory Environment

A business is regulated by everything from the U.S. Constitution to the guidelines of the Consumer Product Safety Commission. Managers must know codified law as well as the law that develops from cases and precedent. The regulatory environment of business covers everything from penalties for criminal conduct to punitive damages for intentional injuries to customers. Part 2 describes the laws that regulate businesses and business operations, the sanctions that are imposed for violation of these laws, and the way for businesses to make compliance with the law a key part of their values.

4

Business and the Constitution

The U.S. Constitution is a remarkable document. It was drafted by a group of independent states more than 200 years ago as a way to unify the states into one national government that still honored rights for individuals and allowed for certain powers to remain in those states. The constitution's survival for so many years with so few changes shows its flexibility and foresight.

This chapter covers the application of the U.S. Constitution to business. It answers these key questions: What are the constitutional limitations on business regulation? Who has more power to regulate business—the states or the federal government? What individual freedoms granted under the Constitution apply to businesses? ■

update ▸
For up-to-date legal news, click on "Author Updates" at

www.cengage.com/blaw/ jennings

Some men look at constitutions with sanctimonious reverence, and deem them like the ark of the covenant, too sacred to be touched. . . . I am certainly not an advocate for frequent and untried changes in laws and constitutions. . . . But . . . laws and institutions must go hand in hand with the progress of the human mind.

THOMAS JEFFERSON

The history of the United States has been written not merely in the halls of Congress, in the Executive offices and on the battlefields, but to a great extent in the chambers of the Supreme Court of the United States.

CHARLES WARREN

consider...

In 1996, Nike responded to negative reports and allegations about its labor practices in overseas factories through a series of press releases, ads, and op-ed pieces in newspapers around the country. Nike had former Atlanta mayor and U.S. ambassador, Andrew Young, visit its factories and then provide a report on their conditions. Nike cited the Young report in a letter to the editor of the *New York Times* in response to a negative op-ed piece that the *Times* had published on Nike's labor practices.

Marc Kasky filed suit against Nike in California alleging that Nike's response in the newspaper violated the False Advertising Law of California. Nike challenged the suit on the grounds that using advertising regulation in such a way violated its rights of free speech. The lower court agreed with Mr. Kasky and held that the advertising statute applied to Nike. Nike appealed to the U.S. Supreme Court. How should the court rule? Were Nike's free speech rights violated?

The U.S. Constitution

AN OVERVIEW OF THE U.S. CONSTITUTION

The **U.S. Constitution** itself is a simple and short document. Contained within it is the entire structure of the federal government, its powers, the powers of the states, and the rights of all citizens. The exact language of the U.S. Constitution appears in Appendix A.

ARTICLES I, II, AND III—THE FRAMEWORK FOR SEPARATION OF POWERS

The first three articles of the U.S. Constitution set up the three branches of the federal government. Article I establishes the **legislative branch**, including the two houses of Congress—the House of Representatives and the Senate—along with the powers they hold and the methods for electing members.

Article II creates the **executive branch** of the federal government, specifying the qualifications, manner of election, term, and powers of the president.

Article III establishes the **judicial branch** of the federal government. Article III actually creates only the U.S. Supreme Court and establishes its jurisdiction, but it authorizes Congress to establish inferior courts, which it has done in the form of federal district courts, specialized federal courts, and U.S. courts of appeals (see Chapter 3, Exhibit 3.1).

The first three articles create a government with **separation of powers**. Each branch of government has unique functions that the other branches cannot perform, but each branch also has powers that can curb overstepping by the other branches. For example, the judicial branch cannot pass laws, but it can prevent a law passed by Congress from taking effect by judicially interpreting the law as unconstitutional. The executive branch does not pass legislation but has veto power over legislation passed by Congress. The executive branch has responsibility for foreign relations and treaty negotiation. However, those treaties do not take effect until the Senate ratifies them. This system of different powers that can be used to curb the other branches' exercise of power is called a system of **checks and balances**.

The drafters of the U.S. Constitution designed the federal government this way to avoid the accumulation of too much power in any one branch of government. For example, in *Clinton v. Jones,* 520 U.S. 681 (1997), the Supreme Court ruled that even the president is subject to the laws of the land and is accountable for civil wrongs alleged by private citizens. In the case, Paula Corbin Jones alleged that Mr. Clinton had sexually harassed her while he was governor of Arkansas. The Court ruled that the president cannot be above the law or judicial process when he has violated the rights of a citizen in his private conduct and wrote, "even the sovereign is subject to God and the law."

OTHER ARTICLES

Article IV deals with states' interrelationships. Article V provides the procedures for constitutional amendments. Article VI is the Supremacy Clause (discussed later in this chapter), and Article VII simply provides the method for state ratification of the U.S. Constitution.

THE BILL OF RIGHTS

In addition to the seven articles, the U.S. Constitution has 27 amendments, the first 10 of which are the **Bill of Rights**. Although these rights originally applied only to federal procedures, the **Fourteenth Amendment** extended them to apply to the states as well. These amendments cover rights from freedom of speech (First Amendment) to the right to a jury trial (Sixth Amendment) to protection of privacy from unlawful searches (Fourth Amendment) to due process before deprivation of property (Fifth Amendment). The amendments as they apply to businesses are covered later in this chapter and in Chapter 7.

The Role of Judicial Review and the Constitution

The Supreme Court and its decisions are often in the news because the cases decided by the Court are generally significant ones that provide interpretations of the U.S. Constitution and also define the rights we have under this foundational document. For example, the Fifth Amendment guarantees that we will not be deprived of our life, liberty, or property without "due process of law." Due process of law, interpreted by the courts many times, includes such rights as the right to a hearing before a mortgage foreclosure or at least the right of notice before property is sold after repossession as a result of a default by the debtor/mortgagor. The U.S. Supreme Court is responsible for determining the extent and scope of the rights and protections afforded by the U.S. Constitution. In addition, the Supreme Court is a crucial part of the system of checks and balances set up in the Constitution.

Constitutional Limitations of Economic Regulations

THE COMMERCE CLAUSE

The **Commerce Clause** is found in Article I, Section 8, Part 3 of the U.S. Constitution and provides Congress with the power "[t]o regulate Commerce with foreign Nations, and among the several States, . . ." Although the language is short and simple, the phrase "among the several states" has created much controversy. The clause limits Congress to the regulation of interstate commerce. Local commerce and intrastate commerce is left to the states for regulation. Defining interstate commerce has been the task of the courts. The standards are defined from two perspectives: federal regulation of state and local commerce, and state and local regulation of interstate commerce.

Standards for Congressional Regulation of State and Local Business Activity

The issue as defined by the U.S. Supreme Court is whether there is sufficient interstate contact or effects for the application of federal standards. The Constitution gives Congress authority to regulate interstate matters and vests all the remaining regulatory authority in the states.

The U.S. Supreme Court initially gave a very narrow interpretation to the scope of the Commerce Clause. For activity to be subject to federal regulation, there had to be a "direct and immediate effect" on interstate commerce. In 1918, the Court ruled that manufacturing was not "commerce" (was solely intrastate) and struck down an act of Congress that attempted to regulate goods manufactured in plants using child labor [*Hammer* v. *Dagenhart*, 247 U.S. 251 (1918)]. During the 1930s, Congress and President Roosevelt bumped heads with the Court many times in their attempts to legislate a recovery from the Depression. The Court consistently refused to validate federal legislation of manufacturing, operations, and labor [*Schechter Poultry* v. *United States*, 295 U.S. 495 (1935); *Carter* v. *Carter Coal*, 298 U.S. 238 (1936)]. Roosevelt refused to accept the roadblock to his legislation and initiated his court-packing plan to increase the number of members of the court with Roosevelt appointees.

The Court responded in *NLRB* v. *Laughlin Steel*, 336 U.S. 460 (1940), by ruling that intrastate activities, even though local in character, may still affect interstate commerce and thus be subject to federal regulation. The "affectation" doctrine thus expanded the authority of the federal government in regulating commerce. In the words of the Court, "If it is interstate commerce that feels the pinch, it does not matter how local the squeeze" (336 U.S. at 464). The Commerce Clause has had a critical role in the elimination of discrimination because the Court's liberal definition of what constitutes interstate commerce has permitted the application of federal civil rights laws to local activities. However, there have been some recent refinements and limits on federal authority. *U.S.* v. *Morrison* (Case 4.1) is a landmark case that limited federal regulation.

CASE 4.1

U.S. v. Morrison
529 U.S. 598 (2000)

ECONOMIC IMPACT IS NOT THE SAME AS COMMERCE: VIOLENCE IS INTRASTATE ACTIVITY

FACTS

Christy Brzonkala (petitioner) enrolled at Virginia Polytechnic Institute (Virginia Tech) in the fall of 1994. In September of that year, Ms. Brzonkala met Antonio Morrison and James Crawford (respondents), who were both students at Virginia Tech and members of its varsity football team. Ms. Brzonkala alleges that, within 30 minutes of meeting Mr. Morrison and Mr. Crawford, they assaulted and repeatedly raped her.

Ms. Brzonkala became severely emotionally disturbed and depressed. She sought assistance from a university psychiatrist, who prescribed antidepressant medication. Shortly after the rape, Ms. Brzonkala stopped attending classes and withdrew from the university.

After a hearing on Ms. Brzonkala's charges, Virginia Tech's Judicial Committee found insufficient evidence to punish Mr. Crawford, but found Mr. Morrison guilty of sexual assault and sentenced him to immediate suspension for two semesters.

Virginia Tech's dean of students upheld the judicial committee's sentence. However, in July 1995, Mr. Morrison took steps to initiate a court challenge to his conviction under the Sexual Assault Policy. University officials held a second hearing and eventually readmitted Mr. Morrison for the Fall 1995 semester.

In December 1995, Ms. Brzonkala filed suit against Virginia Tech in Federal District Court. Her complaint alleged that Mr. Morrison's and Mr. Crawford's attack violated 42 U.S.C. § 13981, the Violence Against Women Act (VAWA). Mr. Morrison and Mr. Crawford moved to dismiss this complaint because § 13981's civil remedy is unconstitutional under the Commerce Clause.

The district court held that Congress lacked authority for the enactment of VAWA and dismissed the complaint against Mr. Morrison and Mr. Crawford. The court of appeals affirmed and Ms. Brzonkala appealed.

JUDICIAL OPINION

REHNQUIST, Chief Justice

Section 13981 was part of the Violence Against Women Act of 1994. It states that "[a]ll persons within the United States shall have the right to be free from crimes of violence motivated by gender" 42 U.S.C. § 13981(b).

Every law enacted by Congress must be based on one or more of its powers enumerated in the Constitution. . . . we turn to the question whether § 13981 falls within Congress' power under Article I, § 8, of the Constitution.

Since *U.S. v. Lopez*, 514 U.S. 564 (1995) most recently canvassed and clarified our case law governing this third category of Commerce Clause regulation, it provides the proper framework for conducting the required analysis of § 13981. In *Lopez*, we held that the Gun-Free School Zones Act of 1990, 18 U.S.C. § 922(q)(1)(A), which made it a federal crime to knowingly possess a firearm in a school zone, exceeded Congress' authority under the Commerce Clause.

First, we observed that § 922(q) was "a criminal statute that by its terms has nothing to do with 'commerce' or any sort of economic enterprise, however broadly one might define those terms." Reviewing our case law, including *Wickard* v. *Filburn*, 317 U.S. 111, 63 S.Ct. 82, 87 L.Ed. 122 (1942); *Katzenbach* v. *McClung*, 379 U.S. 294, 85 S.Ct. 377, 13 L.Ed.2d 290 (1964); and *Heart of Atlanta Motel*, we stated that the pattern of analysis is clear. "Where economic activity substantially affects interstate commerce, legislation regulating that activity will be sustained."

The United States argued that the possession of guns may lead to violent crime, and that violent crime "can be expected to affect the functioning of the national economy. . . ." The Government also argued that the presence of guns at schools poses a threat to the educational process, which in turn threatens to produce a less efficient and productive workforce, which will negatively affect national productivity and thus interstate commerce.

We rejected these "costs of crime" and "national productivity" arguments because they would permit Congress to "regulate not only all violent crime, but all activities that might lead to violent crime, regardless of how tenuously they relate to interstate commerce."

[T]he concern that we expressed in *Lopez* that Congress might use the Commerce Clause to completely obliterate the Constitution's distinction between national and local authority seems well founded. Indeed, if Congress may regulate gender-motivated violence, it would be able to regulate murder or any other type of violence since gender-motivated violence, as a subset of all violent crime, is certain to have lesser economic impacts than the larger class of which it is a part.

Petitioners' reasoning, moreover, will not limit Congress to regulating violence but may, as we suggested in *Lopez*, be applied equally as well to family law and other areas of traditional state regulation since the aggregate effect of marriage, divorce, and childrearing on the national economy is undoubtedly significant.

The Constitution requires a distinction between what is truly national and what is truly local. In recognizing this fact we preserve one of the few principles that has been consistent since the Clause was adopted. The regulation and punishment of intrastate violence that is not directed at the instrumentalities, channels, or goods involved in interstate commerce has always been the province of the States.

Affirmed.

DISSENTING OPINION

Justice SOUTER, with whom Justice STEVENS, Justice GINSBURG, and Justice BREYER join, dissenting

Congress has the power to legislate with regard to activity that, in the aggregate, has a substantial effect on interstate commerce. The fact of such a substantial effect is not an issue for the courts in the first instance, but for the Congress, whose institutional capacity for gathering evidence and taking testimony far exceeds ours.

One obvious difference from *United States* v. *Lopez*, 514 U.S. 549, 115 S.Ct. 1624, 131 L.Ed.2d 626 (1995), is the mountain of data assembled by Congress, here showing the effects of violence against women on interstate commerce. Passage of the Act in 1994 was preceded by four years of hearings, which included testimony from physicians and law professors; from survivors of rape and domestic violence; and from representatives of state law enforcement and private business. The record includes reports on gender bias from task forces in 21 States, and we have the benefit of specific factual findings in the eight separate Reports issued by Congress and its committees over the long course leading to enactment.

The Commerce Clause predicate was simply the effect of the production of wheat for home consumption on supply and demand in interstate commerce. Supply and demand for goods in interstate commerce will also be affected by the deaths of 2,000 to 4,000 women annually at the hands of domestic abusers. . . . Violence against women may be found to affect interstate commerce and affect it substantially.

All of this convinces me that today's ebb of the commerce power rests on error, and at the same time leads me to doubt that the majority's view will prove to be enduring law.

CASE QUESTIONS

1. What did Congress do to establish the connection of VAWA to commerce?

2. What does the dissenting opinion say the test for the constitutionality of federal regulation under the Commerce Clause should be?

3. Name some areas of law that are important but might not involve commerce in the sense defined by the court in this case and that could not, as a result, be regulated by Congress.

4. What rights does Ms. Brzonkala have other than those afforded by VAWA?

consider 4.1

Ollie's Barbecue is a family-owned restaurant in Birmingham, Alabama, specializing in barbecued meats and homemade pies, with a seating capacity of 220 customers. It is located on a state highway 11 blocks from an interstate highway and a somewhat greater distance from railroad and bus stations. The restaurant caters to a family and white-collar trade, with a takeout service for "Negroes." (Note: The court uses this term in the opinion on the case.)

In the 12 months preceding the passage of the Civil Rights Act, the restaurant purchased locally approximately $150,000 worth of food, $69,683 or 46 percent of which was meat that it bought from a local supplier who had procured it from outside the state.

Ollie's has refused to serve Negroes in its dining accommodations since its original opening in 1927, and since July 2, 1964, it has been operating in violation of the Civil Rights Act. A lower court concluded that if it were required to serve Negroes, it would lose a substantial amount of business.

The lower court found that the Civil Rights Act did not apply because Ollie's was not involved in "interstate commerce." Will the Commerce Clause permit application of the Civil Rights Act to Ollie's? (Analysis appears at the end of the chapter.) [*Katzenbach* v. *McClung*, 379 U.S. 294 (1964).]

Standards for State Regulation of Interstate Commerce

The Commerce Clause also deals with issues beyond those of federal power. The interpretation of the clause involves how much commerce the states can regulate without interfering in the congressional domain of interstate commerce. In answering this question, the courts are concerned with two factors: (1) whether federal regulation supersedes state involvement and (2) whether the benefits achieved by the regulation outweigh the burden on interstate commerce. These two factors are meant to prevent states from passing laws that would give local industries and businesses an unfair advantage over interstate businesses. There are, however, some circumstances in which the states can regulate interstate commerce. Those circumstances occur when the state is properly exercising its police power.

What Is Police Power?   **Police power** is the states' power to pass laws that promote the public welfare and protect public health and safety. Regulation of these primary concerns is within each state's domain. It is, however, inevitable that some of the laws dealing with public welfare and health and safety will burden interstate commerce. Many of the statutes that have been challenged constitutionally have regulated highway use. For example, some cases have tested a state's power to regulate the length of trucks on state highways [*Raymond Motor Transportation* v. *Rice,* 434 U.S. 429 (1978)]. In *Bibb* v. *Navajo Freight Lines, Inc.,* 359 US. 520 (1959), the Supreme Court analyzed an Illinois statute requiring all trucks using Illinois roads to be equipped with contour mudguards. These mudguards were supposed to reduce the amount of mud splattering the windshields of other drivers and preventing them from seeing. Both cases revolved around the public safety purpose of the statutes.

The Balancing Test   A statute is not entitled to constitutional protection just because it deals with public health, safety, or welfare. Although the courts try to protect the police power, that protection is not automatic. The police power is upheld only so long as the benefit achieved by the statute does not outweigh the burden imposed on interstate commerce. Each case is decided on its own facts. States present evidence of the safety benefits involved, and the interstate commerce interests present evidence of the costs and effects for interstate commerce. The question courts must answer in these constitutional cases is whether the state interest in public health, welfare, or safety outweighs the federal interest in preventing interstate commerce from being unduly burdened. In performing this balancing test, the courts examine the safety, welfare, and health issues. However, the courts also examine other factors, such as whether the regulation or law provides an unfair advantage to intrastate or local businesses. For example, a prohibition on importing citrus fruits into Florida would give in-state growers an undue advantage.

Courts also examine the degree of the effect on interstate commerce. State statutes limiting the length of commercial vehicles would require commercial truck lines to buy different trucks for certain routes or in some cases to stop at a state's border to remove one of the double trailers being pulled. Such stops can have a substantial effect on interstate travel. On the other hand, a state law that requires travelers to stop at the border for a fruit and plant check is not as burdensome: Only a stop is required, and the traveler would not be required to make any further adjustments. Also, the state's health interest is great; most fruit and plant checks are done to keep harmful insects from entering the state and destroying its crops. In the *Bibb* case, the courts found that the evidence of increased safety was not persuasive enough to outweigh the burden on interstate commerce.

Another question courts answer in their analysis is whether there is any way the state could accomplish its health, welfare, or safety goal with less of a burden on interstate commerce. Suppose a state has a health concern about having milk properly processed. One way to cover the concern is to require all milk to be processed in-state. Such a regulation clearly favors that state's businesses and imposes a great burden on out-of-state milk producers. The same result, however, could be produced by requiring all milk sellers to be licensed. The licensing procedure would allow the state to check the milk-processing procedures of all firms and accomplish the goal without imposing such a burden on out-of-state firms.

In *Granholm* v. *Heald* (Case 4.2), the court dealt with states' regulation of imported wines versus its differing regulation of their domestic wine producers.

CASE 4.2

Granholm v. *Heald*
544 U.S. 460 (2005)

WHINING ABOUT WINE

FACTS

Both the regulations and statutory frameworks in New York and Michigan prohibit out-of-state wine producers from selling their wines directly to consumers there. In-state wineries can sell directly to consumers. Out-of-state wine producers are required to pay wholesaler fees and cannot compete with in-state wine producers on direct-to-consumer sales. The direct-to-consumer sales avenue, especially through the internet, has been a means for small wineries to compete.

Several out-of-state wine producers as well as consumers in both Michigan and New York filed suit in their federal districts challenging these laws that prohibit direct shipment. From different circuit decisions, Michigan and the out-of-state wine producers barred from New York appealed.

JUDICIAL OPINION

KENNEDY, Justice

We consolidated these cases and granted *certiorari* on the following question: "Does a State's regulatory scheme that permits in-state wineries directly to ship alcohol to consumers but restricts the ability of out-of-state wineries to do so violate the . . . Commerce Clause. . .?"

State laws violate the Commerce Clause if they mandate "differential treatment of in-state and out-of-state economic interests that benefits the former and burdens the latter." This rule is essential to the foundations of the Union. The mere fact of nonresidence should not foreclose a producer in one State from access to markets in other States. States may not enact laws that burden out-of-state producers or shippers simply to give a competitive advantage to in-state businesses.

Laws of the type at issue in the instant cases contradict these principles. They deprive citizens of their right to have access to the markets of other States on equal terms. The current patchwork of laws—with some States banning direct shipments altogether, others doing so only for out-of-state wines, and still others requiring reciprocity—is essentially the product of an ongoing, low-level trade war. Allowing States to discriminate against out-of-state wine "invite[s] a multiplication of preferential trade areas destructive of the very purpose of the Commerce Clause."

The discriminatory character of the Michigan system is obvious. Michigan allows in-state wineries to ship directly to consumers, subject only to a licensing requirement. Out-of-state wineries, whether licensed or not, face a complete ban on direct shipment. The differential treatment requires all out-of-state wine, but not all in-state wine, to pass through an in-state wholesaler and retailer before reaching consumers. These two extra layers of overhead increase the cost of out-of-state wines to Michigan consumers.

The New York regulatory scheme differs from Michigan's in that it does not ban direct shipments altogether. Out-of-state wineries are instead required to establish a distribution operation in New York in order to gain the privilege of direct shipment. This, though, is just an indirect way of subjecting out-of-state wineries, but not local ones, to the three-tier system. It comes as no surprise that not a single out-of-state winery has availed itself of New York's direct-shipping privilege.

CONTINUED

We have no difficulty concluding that New York, like Michigan, discriminates against interstate commerce through its direct-shipping laws.

Affirmed as to judgment of the Sixth Circuit Court of Appeals; reversed and remanded as to judgment of the Second Circuit Court of Appeals.

NOTE: There was a strong dissent in the case that indicated that because of the Twenty-First Amendment the federal government (and the court) could not be involved in state liquor regulation.

CASE QUESTIONS

1. What do the Michigan and New York statutes require?

2. Why did the U.S. Supreme Court grant *certiorari* in the cases? Why do you think the court heard and decided the two cases together?

3. What is the economic impact of the statutes on wineries, both in- and out-of-state? On wholesalers? On consumers?

Congressional Regulation of Foreign Commerce

The Commerce Clause also grants Congress the power to regulate foreign commerce. The case of *Gibbons* v. *Ogden,* 9 Wheat. 1 (1824), defined foreign commerce as any "commercial intercourse between the United States and foreign nations." This power to regulate applies regardless of where the activity originates and where it ends. For example, many international trade transactions begin and end in the city of New York. Although the paperwork and delivery of the goods may be solely within one state (here within one city), the foreign commerce power is not restricted by intrastate standards. If there is foreign commerce, there can be congressional regulation regardless of the place of transaction.

CONSTITUTIONAL STANDARDS FOR TAXATION OF BUSINESS

Article I, Section 8, Paragraph 1 of the U.S. Constitution gives Congress its powers of taxation: "The Congress shall have Power To lay and collect Taxes, Duties, Imposts and Excises. . . ." In addition, the Sixteenth Amendment to the Constitution gives this power: "The Congress shall have power to lay and collect taxes on incomes, from whatever source derived, without apportionment among the several States, and without regard to any census or enumeration."

Interstate businesses are not generally exempt from state and local taxes just because they are interstate businesses. However, the taxes imposed on these businesses must meet certain standards.

First, the tax cannot discriminate against interstate commerce. A tax on milk could not be higher for milk that is shipped in from out of state than for milk produced within the state.

Second, the tax cannot unduly burden interstate commerce. For example, a tax on interstate transportation companies that is based on the weight of their trucks as measured upon entering and leaving the states would be a burdensome tax.

Third, there must be some connection—"a sufficient **nexus**"—between the state and the business being taxed. The business must have some activity in the state, such as offices, sales representatives, catalog purchasers, or distribution systems.

Finally, the tax must be apportioned fairly. This standard seeks to avoid having businesses taxed in all 50 states for their property. It also seeks to avoid having businesses pay state income tax on all their income in all 50 states. General Motors does not pay an inventory tax to all 50 states on all of its inventory, but it does pay an inventory tax on the inventory it holds in each state. Perhaps the most significant decision on state taxation in recent years is the U.S. Supreme Court case on catalog sales, *Quill Corporation* v. *North Dakota,* summarized in Case 4.3.

CASE 4.3

Quill Corporation v. North Dakota
504 U.S. 298 (1992)

IS NORTH DAKOTA A TAXING STATE?

FACTS

Quill is a Delaware corporation with offices and warehouses in Illinois, California, and Georgia. None of its employees works or lives in North Dakota, and it owns no property in North Dakota.

Quill sells office equipment and supplies; it solicits business through catalogs and flyers, advertisements in national periodicals, and telephone calls. Its annual national sales exceed $200 million, of which almost $1 million are made to about three thousand customers in North Dakota. The sixth largest vendor of office supplies in the state, it delivers all of its merchandise to its North Dakota customers by mail or common carriers from out-of-state locations.

North Dakota also imposes a use tax upon property purchased for storage, use, or consumption within the state. North Dakota requires every "retailer maintaining a place of business in" the state to collect the tax from the consumer and remit it to the state. In 1987, North Dakota amended its statutory definition of the term "retailer" to include "every person who engages in regular or systematic solicitation of a consumer market in th[e] state." State regulations in turn define "regular or systematic solicitation" to mean three or more advertisements within a 12-month period. Thus, since 1987 mail-order companies that engage in such solicitation have been subject to the tax even if they maintain no property or personnel in North Dakota.

Quill has taken the position that North Dakota does not have the power to compel it to collect a use tax from its North Dakota customers. Consequently, the state, through its tax commissioner, filed an action to require Quill to pay taxes (as well as interest and penalties) on all such sales made after July 1, 1987. The trial court ruled in Quill's favor.

The North Dakota Supreme Court reversed, holding that the state use tax did not violate either the due process clause or the Commerce Clause, and Quill appealed.

JUDICIAL OPINION

STEVENS, Justice

The Due Process Clause "requires some definite link, some minimum connection, between a state and the person, property or transaction it seeks to tax," and that the "income attributed to the State for tax purposes must be rationally related to 'values connected with the taxing State.'" For example, the presence of sales personnel in the State, or the maintenance of local retail stores in the State, justified the exercise of that power.

In this case, there is no question that Quill has purposefully directed its activities at North Dakota residents, that the magnitude of those contacts are more than sufficient for due process purposes, and that the use tax is related to the benefits Quill receives from access to the State. We therefore agree with the North Dakota Supreme Court's conclusion that the Due Process Clause does not bar enforcement of that State's use tax against Quill. . . . [but]while a State may, consistent with the Due Process Clause, have the authority to tax a particular taxpayer, imposition of the tax may nonetheless violate the Commerce Clause. The "substantial nexus" requirement is not, like due process "minimum contacts" requirement, a proxy for notice, but rather a means for limiting state burdens on interstate commerce. Accordingly, contrary to the State's suggestion, a corporation may have the "minimum contacts" with a taxing State as required by the Due Process Clause, and yet lack the "substantial nexus" with that State as required by the Commerce Clause.

The State Supreme Court reviewed our recent Commerce Clause decisions and concluded that those rulings signaled a "retreat from the formalistic constrictions of a stringent physical presence test in favor of a more flexible substantive approach" and thus supported its decision not to apply *Bellas Hess.* 470 N.W.2d, at 214. Although we agree with the state court's assessment of the evolution of our cases, we do not share its conclusion that this evolution indicates that the Commerce Clause ruling of *Bellas Hess* is no longer good law.

Reversed.

CASE QUESTIONS

1. Did Quill Corporation own any property in North Dakota?

2. Were any Quill offices or personnel located in North Dakota? How did Quill come to have customers in North Dakota?

3. What is the difference between the due-process standard for taxation and the Commerce Clause standard?

State Versus Federal Regulation of Business—Constitutional Conflicts: Preemption and the Supremacy Clause

Although the Constitution has sections that deal with the authority of the federal government and some that deal with state and local governments, some crossovers in the two sets of laws still occur. For example, both state and federal governments regulate the sale of securities and both have laws on the sale of real property. Such crossovers create conflicts and a constitutional issue of who has the power to regulate. These conflicts between state and federal laws are governed by Article VI of the Constitution, sometimes called the **Supremacy Clause**, which provides: "This Constitution, and the Laws of the United States which shall be made in Pursuance thereof; and all Treaties made, or which shall be made, under the Authority of the United States, shall be the supreme Law of the Land. . . ."

The Supremacy Clause provides that when state and local laws conflict with federal statutes, regulations, executive orders, or treaties, the federal statute, regulation, executive order, or treaty controls the state or local law. Most statutes, however, do not include the congressional intent on **preemption**. Whether a field has been preempted is a question of fact, of interpretation, and of legislative history. The question of preemption is determined on a case-by-case basis using the following questions:

1. What does the legislative history indicate?
2. How detailed is the federal regulation of the area?
3. What benefits exist from having federal regulation of the area?
4. How much does a state law conflict with federal law? Is there any way that the two laws can coexist?

Geier v. *American Honda Motor Co., Inc.* (Case 4.4) deals with a preemption issue.

CASE 4.4

Geier v. *American Honda Motor Co., Inc.*
529 U.S. 861 (2000)

EXPLOSIVE PREEMPTION ISSUES: HONDA AND AIRBAG LIABILITY

FACTS

In 1992, Alexis Geier (petitioner) collided with a tree while driving a 1987 Honda Accord and was seriously injured. The car was equipped with manual shoulder and lap belts, which Geier had buckled up at the time. The car was not equipped with airbags or other passive restraint devices.

Geier and her parents (also petitioners) sued the car's manufacturer, American Honda Motor Company, Inc., and its affiliates (hereinafter American Honda) under District of Columbia tort law. They claimed, among other things, that American Honda had designed its car negligently and defectively because it lacked a driver's-side airbag. The District Court dismissed the lawsuit. The court noted that Federal Motor Vehicle Safety Standard (FMVSS) 208 gave car manufacturers a choice as to whether to install airbags. The court concluded that the petitioners' lawsuit, because it sought to establish a different safety standard—i.e., an airbag requirement—was expressly preempted by a provision of the act that preempts "any safety standard" that is not identical to a federal safety standard applicable to the same aspect of performance [15 U.S.C. § 1392(d) (1988 ed.)]. The Court of Appeals agreed with the District Court, and Geier appealed.

JUDICIAL OPINION

BREYER, Justice

The basic question, then, is whether a common-law "no airbag" action like the one before us actually conflicts with FMVSS 208. We hold that it does.

Read in light of this history, DOT's own contemporaneous explanation of FMVSS 208 makes clear that the 1984 version of FMVSS 208 reflected . . . why FMVSS 208 sought the mix of devices that it expected its performance standard to produce. DOT wrote that it had rejected a proposed FMVSS 208 "all airbag" standard because of safety concerns (perceived or real) associated with airbags, which concerns threatened a "backlash" more easily overcome "if airbags" were "not the only way of complying." It added that a mix of devices would help develop data on comparative effectiveness, would allow the industry time to overcome the safety problems and the high production costs associated with airbags, and would facilitate the development of alternative, cheaper, and safer passive restraint systems. And it would thereby build public confidence necessary to avoid another interlock-type fiasco.

The 1984 FMVSS 208 standard also deliberately sought a gradual phase-in of passive restraints. And it explained that the phased-in requirement would allow more time for manufacturers to develop airbags or other, better, safer passive restraint systems. It would help develop information about the comparative effectiveness of different systems, would lead to a mix in which airbags and other nonseatbelt passive restraint systems played a more prominent role than would otherwise result, and would promote public acceptance.

Finally FMVSS 208's passive restraint requirement was conditional. DOT believed that ordinary manual lap and shoulder belts would produce about the same amount of safety as passive restraints, and at significantly lower costs—if only auto occupants would buckle up. Thus, FMVSS 208 provided for rescission of its passive restraint requirement if, by September 1, 1989, two-thirds of the States had laws in place that, like those of many other nations, required auto occupants to buckle up.

In effect, . . . a rule of state tort law imposing such a duty—by its terms would have required manufacturers of all similar cars to install airbags rather than other passive restraint systems, such as automatic belts or passive interiors. It thereby would have presented an obstacle to the variety and mix of devices that the federal regulation sought. In addition, it could have made less likely the adoption of a state mandatory buckle-up law. Because the rule of law for which petitioners contend would have stood "as an obstacle to the accomplishment and execution of" the important means-related federal objectives that we have just discussed, it is pre-empted.

The judgment of the Court of Appeals is affirmed.

CASE QUESTIONS

1. Why do you think the Supreme Court decided to grant *certiorari* and hear this case?

2. What in the history of the passive restraint system regulation supports a preemption finding?

3. What would happen if the states were permitted to set their own standards, via tort litigation, for auto safety devices?

4. In an ethical sense, what should a company do when a higher regulatory safety standard is created but the requirement for following it does not go into effect for a few years? Should the company continue with the old standard or make the change as quickly as possible?

Application of the Bill of Rights to Business

Certain of the amendments to the U.S. Constitution have particular significance for business. This is especially true for the First Amendment on freedom of speech and the Fourteenth Amendment for its issues of substantive and procedural due process and equal protection. The Fourth, Fifth, and Sixth Amendments on criminal procedures also have significance for business; those issues are covered in Chapter 7.

COMMERCIAL SPEECH AND THE FIRST AMENDMENT

The area of First Amendment rights and freedom of speech is complicated and full of significant cases. The discussion here is limited to First Amendment rights as they apply to businesses. The speech of business is referred to as **commercial speech**, which is communication used to further the economic interests of the speaker. Advertising is clearly a form of commercial speech.

FIRST AMENDMENT PROTECTION FOR ADVERTISING

Until the early 1970s, the U.S. Supreme Court held that commercial speech was different from the traditional speech afforded protection under the First Amendment. The result was that government regulation of commercial speech was virtually unlimited. The Court's position was refined in the 1970s, however, to a view that commercial speech was entitled to First Amendment protection but not on the same level as noncommercial speech. Commercial speech was not an absolute freedom; rather, the benefits of commercial speech were to be weighed against the benefits achieved by government regulation of that speech. Several factors are examined in performing this balancing test.

1. Is a substantial government interest furthered by restricting the commercial speech?

2. Does the restriction directly accomplish the government interest?

3. Is there any other way to accomplish the government interest? Can it be accomplished without regulating commercial speech? Are the restrictions no more extensive than necessary to serve that interest?

For example, if credit terms are advertised, Regulation Z requires full disclosure of all terms (see Chapter 12 for more details). This regulation is acceptable under the standards just listed. Further, restrictions on where and when advertisements are made are permissible. For example, cigarette ads are not permitted on television, and such a restriction is valid.

Exhibit 4.1 illustrates the degrees of protection afforded business speech.

An evolving area that is part of the overlapping portion of the two circles is that of corporate speech in defense of corporate decisions and policies—speech by corporations that is neither political speech nor advertising, but rather explains and defends corporate policies such as animal testing, outsourcing production to other countries, and environmental policies. The issues the companies are discussing have social and political implications, but they relate directly to the corporation's business and/or operations. Can the government regulate this form of speech? *Nike, Inc.* v. *Kasky* (Case 4.5) addresses such speech and provides the answer to the chapter's opening Consider.

EXHIBIT 4.1 Commercial Speech: First Amendment Protections and Restrictions

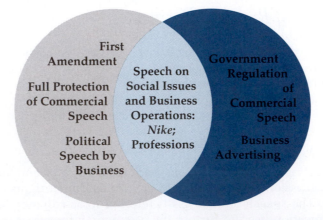

CASE 4.5

Nike, Inc. v. *Kasky*
539 U.S. 654 (2003)

THE SHOE AND MOUTH WRIT OF *CERTIORARI*

FACTS

Beginning in 1996, Nike was besieged with a series of allegations that it was mistreating and underpaying workers at foreign facilities. Nike responded to these charges in numerous ways, such as by sending out press releases, writing letters to the editors of various newspapers around the country, and mailing letters to university presidents and athletic directors. In addition, in 1997, Nike commissioned a report by former Ambassador to the United Nations Andrew Young on the labor conditions at Nike production facilities. After visiting 12 factories, "Young issued a report that commented favorably on working conditions in the factories and found no evidence of widespread abuse or mistreatment of workers."

In April 1998, Marc Kasky (respondent), a California resident, sued Nike for unfair and deceptive practices under California's Unfair Competition Law, Cal. Bus. & Prof. Code Ann. § 17200 *et seq.* (West 1997), and False Advertising Law, § 17500 *et seq.* Mr. Kasky said Nike's statements in its materials and op-ed contained false information.

Nike contended that Mr. Kasky's suit was absolutely barred by the First Amendment. The trial court dismissed the case. Mr. Kasky appealed, and the California Court of Appeal affirmed, holding that Nike's statements "form[ed] part of a public dialogue on a matter of public concern within the core area of expression protected by the First Amendment."

On appeal, the California Supreme Court reversed and remanded for further proceedings. Nike appealed. The Supreme Court granted *certiorari* but later dismissed the case with a ***per curiam*** opinion (an unsigned opinion of the majority of the court) that indicated only that *certiorari* was granted improvidently.

JUDICIAL OPINION

PER CURIAM
The writ of *certiorari* is dismissed as improvidently granted.

Justice STEVENS, with whom Justice GINSBURG joins, and with whom Justice SOUTER joins

This case presents novel First Amendment questions because the speech at issue represents a blending of commercial speech, noncommercial speech and debate on an issue of public importance. On the one hand, if the allegations of the complaint are true, direct communications with customers and potential customers that were intended to generate sales—and possibly to maintain or enhance the market value of Nike's stock—contained significant factual misstatements. The regulatory interest in protecting market participants from being misled by such misstatements is of the highest order. That is why we have broadly (perhaps overbroadly) stated that "there is no constitutional value in false statements of fact." On the other hand, the communications were part of an ongoing discussion and debate about important public issues that was concerned not only with Nike's labor practices, but with similar practices used by other multinational corporations. Knowledgeable persons should be free to participate in such debate without fear of unfair reprisal. The interest in protecting such participants from the chilling effect of the prospect of expensive litigation is therefore also a matter of great importance. That is why we have provided such broad protection for misstatements about public figures that are not animated by malice. See *New York Times Co.* v. *Sullivan,* 376 U.S. 254, 84 S.Ct. 710, 11 L.Ed.2d 686 (1964).

Whether similar protection should extend to cover corporate misstatements made about the corporation itself, or whether we should presume that such a corporate speaker knows where the truth lies, are questions that may have to be decided in this litigation. The correct answer to such questions, however, is more likely to result from the study of a full factual record than from a review of mere unproven allegations in a pleading. Indeed, the development of such a record may actually contribute in a positive way to the public debate. In all events, I am firmly convinced that the Court has wisely decided not to address the constitutional questions presented by the *certiorari* petition at this stage of the litigation.

Accordingly, I concur in the decision to dismiss the writ as improvidently granted.

DISSENTING OPINION

Justice BREYER, with whom Justice O'CONNOR joins
If permitted to stand, the state court's decision may well "chill" the exercise of free speech rights. This concern is not purely theoretical. Nike says without contradiction

CONTINUED

that because of this lawsuit it has decided "to restrict severely all of its communications on social issues that could reach California consumers, including speech in national and international media." It adds that it has not released its annual Corporate Responsibility Report, has decided not to pursue a listing in the Dow Jones Sustainability Index, and has refused "dozens of invitations . . . to speak on corporate responsibility issues." Numerous *amici*—including some who do not believe that Nike has fully and accurately explained its labor practices—argue that California's decision will "chill" speech and thereby limit the supply of relevant information available to those, such as journalists, who seek to keep the public informed about important public issues.

The position of· at least one *amicus*—opposed to Nike on the merits of its labor practice claims but supporting Nike on its free speech claim—echoes a famous sentiment reflected in the writings of Voltaire: "I do not agree with what you say, but I will fight to the end so that you may say it."

I respectfully dissent from the Court's contrary determination.

Case Questions

1. Who is objecting to Nike's speech and how is the objection being voiced?

2. Why does the Supreme Court refuse to decide the case after taking *certiorari*?

3. Why does the dissenting justice believe the court should decide the case?

AFTERMATH: Nike settled the case with terms undisclosed by any of the parties. The case cannot now reach the point of justiciability in order for the Supreme Court to hear it and make a determination on this form of corporate speech. Another case will be required.

First Amendment Rights and Profits from Sensationalism

In the past few years, a number of book publishers and movie producers have pursued criminal figures for the rights to tell the stories of their crimes in books, television programs, and movies. Many of the victims of the crimes and their families have opposed such money-making ventures as benefits that encourage the commission of crimes. The state of New York, for example, passed a statute requiring that earnings from sales of such stories be used first to compensate victims of the crimes. Statutes such as the one in New York create dilemmas between First Amendment rights and public policy issues concerning criminal activities. In *Simon & Schuster, Inc.* v. *Members of the New York State Crime Victims Board*, 502 U.S. 105 (1991), the U.S. Supreme Court addressed the constitutionality of New York's statute. Simon & Schuster had entered into a contract in 1981 with organized crime figure Henry Hill (who was arrested in 1980) and author Nicholas Pileggi for a book about Mr. Hill's life, *Wiseguy*, a book full of colorful details and the day-to-day workings of organized crime, primarily in Mr. Hill's first-person narrative. Throughout *Wiseguy*, Mr. Hill frankly admits to having participated in an astonishing variety of crimes.

The book was also a commercial success: Within 19 months of its publication, more than a million copies were in print. A few years later, the book was converted into a film called *Goodfellas*, which won a host of awards as the best film of 1990.

When the Crime Victims Board requested that Simon & Schuster turn over all monies paid to Mr. Hill and that all future royalties be payable not to Mr. Hill but to the statutorily prescribed escrow account, Simon & Schuster brought suit maintaining that the so-called "Son of Sam law" violated the First Amendment. The U.S. Supreme Court agreed and held that the statute was overly broad, would have a chilling effect on authors and publications, and required a redrafting of the statute to more narrowly tailor its scope so it could still accomplish the public purpose.

ethical *issues*

Orenthal James (O. J.) Simpson was charged with murder in June 1994 in the double homicide of his ex-wife, Nicole Brown Simpson, and her friend Ronald Goldman.

Mr. Simpson was acquitted of the murders. Following his acquittal, prosecutors in the case, Christopher Darden, Marcia Clark, and Hank Goldberg, signed multimillion-dollar book contracts to write about their experiences during the trial. Alan Dershowitz, Johnnie Cochran, and Robert Shapiro, members of the Simpson defense team, signed six-figure contracts to write books about the trial from the defense perspective.

Daniel Petrocelli, the lawyer who represented the Goldmans in their civil suit against Mr. Simpson, also wrote a book, *Triumph of Justice: The Final Judgment on the Simpson Saga*. Mr. Simpson has since written another book, *If I Did It,* and also made a video detailing his side of the story.

Is it ethical to profit from a crime and a trial? Are these contracts a form of making money from the deaths of two people? Many TV stations have refused to carry advertisements for Mr. Simpson's video. Would you have declined this advertising revenue?

FIRST AMENDMENT RIGHTS AND CORPORATE POLITICAL SPEECH

Not all commercial speech is advertising. Some businesses engage in **corporate political speech**. Corporate political speech takes form in three generalized ways:

1. Through financial support such as political candidate donations
2. Through financial support such as party donations
3. Through direct communications and ads about issues, ballot propositions, and funding proposals (such as bond elections)

As the Supreme Court has noted in its opinions on the topic of political donations, "money is like water and it always finds an outlet," and the donations and PAC activity became a concern. As a result, in 1972 and 1974, Congress passed and amended the Federal Election Campaign Act (FECA), which limited individual donations to $2,300 per election cycle (as amended), with an overall annual limitation on donations of $25,000 by any contributor; imposed ceilings on spending by candidates and political parties for national conventions; required reporting and public disclosure of contributions and expenditures exceeding certain limits; and established the Federal Election Commission (FEC) to administer and enforce the legislation [2 U.S.C. § 431(8)(A)(i)].

The limitations in FECA were challenged and the U.S. Supreme Court ruled on their constitutionality in *Buckley* v. *Valeo,* 424 U.S. 1 (1976). The court struck down the expenditure limitations of the law but upheld the dollar donation limitation as being sufficiently narrowly tailored to address the corruption concerns without infringing on the speech elements of donation. Individuals remained free to spend as much as they wanted on their own campaigns.

Under FECA, contributions made with funds that are subject to the act's disclosure requirements and source and amount limitations are called "federal dollars" or "hard dollars." The so-called soft money donations, or the unlimited donations to parties, think tanks, and other groups, became extensive. As a result, Congress passed the Bipartisan Campaign Reform Act of 2002 (BCRA, 2 U.S.C.A. § 431 et seq.). Often referred to as the McCain-Feingold law, Title I of the BCRA regulates the use of soft money by political parties, officeholders, and candidates. The BCRA was immediately challenged by 11 different parties in different federal courts, and the cases were consolidated and eventually heard by the U.S. Supreme Court in *McConnell* v. *Federal Election Comm'n*, 540 U.S. 93 (2003). The Supreme Court concluded the following, in a 500-page opinion (including the dissents) that soft money could be regulated: (1) political parties and candidates could be banned from using soft money for federal election activities; (2) the ban on party donations to tax-exempt entities was generally valid; (3) soft money could not be used for issue ads that clearly identified candidates; (4) the statutory definition of "electioneering communications" was valid; (5) the cost of third-party issue ads coordinated with federal candidates' campaigns could validly be considered as contributions to those campaigns; (6) labor unions and corporations were generally required to pay for issue ads from separately segregated funds; (7) the prohibition on political donations by minors was invalid; and (8) the requirement that broadcasters disclose records of requests for air time for political ads was valid.

However, these Supreme Court decisions and federal legislation do not control activities at the state level and do not infringe on corporations' right to participate in the "public square" debates on issues. For example, many businesses participate in advertising campaigns against certain propositions or resolutions—for example, tax resolutions going before the voters. However, many states once restricted the political advertising allowed corporations and other businesses. The rationale for such a restriction was that corporate assets and funds were great and that corporations might be able to exercise too much power in influencing voters.

In *First National Bank of Boston* v. *Bellotti* 435 U.S. 765 (1978), the U.S. Supreme Court developed what has become known as the *Bellotti* doctrine, which gives corporations the same degree of First Amendment protection for their political speech that individuals enjoy in their political speech. A company can spend as much as it wants on ads and information on ballot propositions.

EMINENT DOMAIN: THE TAKINGS CLAUSE

The right of a governmental body to take title to property for a public use is called **eminent domain**. This right is established in the Fifth Amendment to the Constitution and may also be established in various state constitutions. Private individuals cannot require property owners to sell their property, but governmental entities can require property owners to transfer title for public projects for the public good. The Fifth Amendment provides that "property shall not be taken for a public use without just compensation." For a governmental entity to exercise properly the right of eminent domain, three factors must be present: public purpose, taking (as opposed to regulating), and just compensation.

Public Purpose

To exercise eminent domain, the governmental authority must establish that the taking is necessary for the accomplishment of a government or public purpose. When eminent domain is mentioned, we think of use of property being taken for highways and schools. However, the right of the government to exercise eminent domain extends much further. For example, the following uses have been held to constitute public purposes: the condemnation of slum housing (for purposes of improving city areas), the limitation of mining and excavation within city limits, the declaration of property as a historic landmark, and the taking of property to provide a firm that makes up most of a town's economic base with a large enough tract for expansion.

According to the U.S. Supreme Court, the public purpose requirement for eminent domain is to be interpreted broadly, and "the role of the judiciary in determining whether that power is being exercised for a public purpose is an extremely narrow one" [*United States ex rel. TVA* v. *Welch*, 327 U.S. 546 (1946)]. The *Kelo* v. *City of New London* case was the U.S. Supreme Court decision that changed the eminent domain landscape, as it were.

CASE 4.6

Kelo v. *City of New London*
545 U.S. 469 (2005)

LITTLE PINK HOUSES FOR YOU AND ME

FACTS

In 1978, the city of New London, Connecticut, undertook a redevelopment plan for purposes of creating a redeveloped area in and around the existing park at Fort Trumball. The plan had the goals of achieving all the related ambience a state park should have, including the absence of existing pink cottages and other architecturally eclectic homes that had long been part of the area. Part of the redevelopment plan was the city's deal with Pfizer Corporation for the location of its research facility in the area. The preface to the city's development plan included the following statement of goals and purpose:

to create a development that would complement the facility that Pfizer was planning to build, create jobs, increase tax and other revenues, encourage public access to and use of the city's waterfront, and eventually "build momentum" for the revitalization of the rest of the city, including its downtown area.

Affected property owners, including Susette Kelo, live in homes and pink cottages (15 total) located in and around the area for the proposed new structures that will consist of primarily private land developers and corporations. The central focus of the plan was getting Pfizer to the Fort Trumball area (where the homeowners and their properties were located) with the hope of a resulting economic boost such a major corporate employer can bring to an area.

Kelo and the other landowners whose homes would be razed to make room for Pfizer and the accompanying and resulting economic development plan filed suit challenging New London's legal authority to take their homes. The trial court issued an injunction preventing New London from taking certain of the properties but allowing others to be taken. The appellate court found for New London on all the claims, and the landowners (petitioners) appealed.

JUDICIAL OPINION

STEVENS, Justice

Two polar propositions are perfectly clear. On the one hand, it has long been accepted that the sovereign may not take the property of A for the sole purpose of transferring it to another private party B, even though A is paid just compensation. On the other hand, it is equally clear that a State may transfer property from one private party to another if future "use by the public" is the purpose of the taking; the condemnation of land for a railroad with common-carrier duties is a familiar example. Neither of these propositions, however, determines the disposition of this case.

The disposition of this case therefore turns on the question whether the City's development plan serves a "public purpose." Without exception, our cases have defined that concept broadly, reflecting our longstanding policy of deference to legislative judgments in this field.

Those who govern the City were not confronted with the need to remove blight in the Fort Trumbull area, but their determination that the area was sufficiently distressed to justify a program of economic rejuvenation is entitled to our deference. The City has carefully formulated an economic development plan that it believes will provide appreciable benefits to the community, including—but by no means limited to—new jobs and increased tax revenue. As with other exercises in urban planning and development, the City is endeavoring to coordinate a variety of commercial, residential, and recreational uses of land, with the hope that they will form a whole greater than the sum of its parts. To effectuate this plan, the City has invoked a state statute that specifically authorizes the use of eminent domain to promote economic development. Given the comprehensive character of the plan, the thorough deliberation that preceded its adoption, and the limited

CONTINUED

scope of our review, it is appropriate for us to resolve the challenges of the individual owners, not on a piecemeal basis, but rather in light of the entire plan. Because that plan unquestionably serves a public purpose, the takings challenged here satisfy the public use requirement of the Fifth Amendment.

Petitioners contend that using eminent domain for economic development impermissibly blurs the boundary between public and private takings. We cannot say that public ownership is the sole method of promoting the public purposes of community redevelopment projects. It is further argued that without a bright-line rule nothing would stop a city from transferring citizen A's property to citizen B for the sole reason that citizen B will put the property to a more productive use and thus pay more taxes. Such a one-to-one transfer of property, executed outside the confines of an integrated development plan, is not presented in this case. While such an unusual exercise of government power would certainly raise a suspicion that a private purpose was afoot, the hypothetical cases posited by petitioners can be confronted if and when they arise. They do not warrant the crafting of an artificial restriction on the concept of public use.

Just as we decline to second-guess the City's considered judgments about the efficacy of its development plan, we also decline to second-guess the City's determinations as to what lands it needs to acquire in order to effectuate the project. "It is not for the courts to oversee the choice of the boundary line nor to sit in review on the size of a particular project area. Once the question of the public purpose has been decided, the amount and character of land to be taken for the project and the need for a particular tract to complete the integrated plan rests in the discretion of the legislative branch."

The judgment of the Supreme Court of Connecticut is affirmed.

DISSENTING OPINION

O'CONNOR, Justice, joined by Justices SCALIA, THOMAS, and REHNQUIST

Under the banner of economic development, all private property is now vulnerable to being taken and transferred to another private owner, so long as it might be upgraded—i.e., given to an owner who will use it in a way that the legislature deems more beneficial to the public—in the process. To reason, as the Court does, that the incidental public benefits resulting from the subsequent ordinary use of private property render economic development takings "for public use" is to wash out any distinction between private and public use of property—and thereby effectively to delete the words "for public use" from the Takings Clause of the Fifth Amendment. Accordingly I respectfully dissent.

Where is the line between "public" and "private" property use? Even if there were a practical way to isolate the motives behind a given taking, the gesture toward a purpose test is theoretically flawed. If it is true that incidental public benefits from new private use are enough to ensure the "public purpose" in a taking, why should it matter, as far as the Fifth Amendment is concerned, what inspired the taking in the first place? And whatever the reason for a given condemnation, the effect is the same from the constitutional perspective—private property is forcibly relinquished to new private ownership.

CASE QUESTIONS

1. What is different from this case and a case in which property is taken for a freeway?

2. What is the concern of the dissent about the decision?

3. Why does the majority state that the courts should be reluctant to get involved in local government eminent domain activities?

The impact of the *Kelo* case has been substantial. By the end of 2007, 42 states had passed ballot propositions or legislation that limited the exercise of eminent domain, or restricted economic development justifications for eminent domain.[1] The level of reform varies significantly.

Taking or Regulating

Mere regulation of the property does not constitute a taking [*Village of Euclid, Ohio* v. *Ambler Realty Co.*, 272 U.S. 365 (1926)]. Rather, a taking must go so far as to deprive the landowner of any use of the property. In *Loretto* v. *Teleprompter Manhattan CATV Corp.*, 458 U.S. 100 (1982), the U.S. Supreme Court held that the small invasion of property by the placement of cable boxes and wires did constitute a taking, albeit very small, and required compensation of the property owners for this small but permanent occupation of their land.

The issue of taking arises also because of local zoning restrictions on development. These restrictions focus on beaches, wetlands, and other natural habitats. For example, in *Nollan* v. *California Coastal Commission*, 483 U.S. 825 (1987), the Nollans sought permission from the California Coastal Commission to construct a home on their coastal lot where they currently had only a small bungalow. The commission refused to grant permission to the Nollans for construction of their home unless they agreed to give a public easement across their lot for beach access. The Supreme Court held that the demand for the easement was a taking without compensation and, in effect, prevented the Nollans from using their property until they surrendered their exclusive use.

Yet another taking issue arises when regulations take effect after owners have acquired land but before it is developed. In *Lucas* v. *South Carolina Coastal Council*, 505 U.S. 1003 (1992), the U.S. Supreme Court declared that *ex post facto* legislation that prevents development of previously purchased land is a taking. In *Lucas*, David Lucas purchased for $975,000 two residential lots on the Isle of Palms in Charleston County, South Carolina. In 1988, the South Carolina legislature enacted the Beachfront Management Act, which barred any permanent habitable structures on coastal properties. The court held South Carolina was required to compensate Mr. Lucas because his land was rendered useless.

Just Compensation

The final requirement for the proper exercise by a governmental entity of the right of eminent domain is that the party from whom the property is being taken be given **just compensation**. The issue of just compensation is difficult to determine and is always a question of fact. In *United States ex rel. TVA* v. *Powelson*, 319 U.S. 266 (1943), the Supreme Court defined fair market value to be "what a willing buyer would pay in cash to a willing seller."

PROCEDURAL DUE PROCESS

Both the Fifth and the Fourteenth Amendments require state and federal governments to provide citizens (businesses included) due process under the law. **Procedural due process** is a right that requires notice and the opportunity to be heard before rights or properties are taken away from an individual or business. Most people are familiar with due process as it exists in the criminal justice system: the right to a lawyer, a trial, and so on (Chapter 7). However, procedural due process is also very much a part of civil law. Before an agency can take away a business license, suspend a license, or impose fines for violations, there must be due process. This due process right applies to both state and federal agencies.

Businesses encounter the constitutional protections of due process in their relationships with customers. The Due Process Clause of the U.S. Constitution provides protection for individuals before their property is taken. Property includes land (as in the case of eminent domain, discussed previously), rights of possession (tenants and leases), and even intangible property rights. For example, students cannot be expelled from schools, colleges, or universities without the right to be heard. Students must have some hearing before their property rights with respect to education are taken away.

consider 4.2

When the Crafts moved into their residence in October 1972, they noticed that there were two separate gas and electric meters and only one water meter serving the premises. The residence had been used previously as a duplex. The Crafts assumed, based on information from the seller, that the second set of meters was inoperative.

In 1973, the Crafts began receiving two bills: their regular bill and another with an account number in the name of Willie C. Craft, as opposed to Willie S. Craft. In October 1973, after learning from a Memphis Light, Gas & Water (MLG&W) meter reader that both sets of meters were running in their home, the Crafts hired a private plumber and electrical contractor to combine the meters into one gas and one electric meter. Because the contractor did not combine the meters properly, they continued to receive two bills until January 1974. During this time, the Crafts' utility service was terminated five times for nonpayment.

Mrs. Craft missed work several times to go to MLG&W offices to resolve the "double billing" problem. She sought explanations on each occasion but was never given an answer.

In February 1974, the Crafts and other MLG&W customers filed suit for violation of the Due Process Clause. The district court dismissed the case. The court of appeals reversed, and MLG&W appealed.

Have the Crafts been given due process? (Analysis appears at the end of the chapter.) [*Memphis Light, Gas & Water Div.* v. *Craft*, 436 U.S. 1 (1978).]

. . . .

SUBSTANTIVE DUE PROCESS

Procedural rules deal with how things are done. All rules on the adjudication of agency charges are procedural rules. Similarly, all rules for the trial of a civil case, from discovery to jury instructions, are also procedural. These rules exist to make sure the substantive law is upheld. **Substantive law** consists of rights, obligations, and behavior standards. Criminal laws are substantive laws, and criminal procedure rules are procedural laws. **Substantive due process** is the right to have laws that do not deprive businesses or citizens of property or other rights without justification and reason. The issue of whether a statute was "void for vagueness" and denied due process was a central one in *Gonzales* v. *Carhart*, 455 U.S. 489 (2007), the decision that dealt with a federal statute that prohibited partial birth abortions. The court dealt with the question of the standard for what was a partial birth abortion and held that the standard was so ill-defined that it left too much to the discretion of officials and that there would be a resulting lack of due process.

The Role of Constitutions in International Law

Although the U.S. Constitution is the basis for all law in the United States, not all countries follow a similar system of governance. The incorporation of other systems (such as a constitution or code) depends on a nation's history, including its colonization by other countries and those countries' forms of law. The United States and England (and countries established through English colonization) tend to follow a pattern of establishing a general set of principles, as set forth in a constitution, and of reliance on custom, tradition, and precedent for the establishment of law in particular legal areas.

In countries such as France, Germany, and Spain (and nations colonized through their influences), a system of law that is dependent on code law exists. These countries have very specific codes of law that attempt to be all-inclusive and cover each circumstance that could arise under a particular provision. These nations do not depend on court decisions, and often there are inconsistent results in application of the law because of the lack of dependence on judicial precedent.

Approximately 27 countries follow Islamic law in some way. When Islamic law is the dominant force in a country, it governs all aspects of personal and business life. The constitutions in these lands are the tenets of the nation's religion.

Red Flags FOR MANAGERS

Sometimes constitutional law seems like the last thing someone in business would need to know. But constitutional issues are a part of day-to-day business. The U.S. Constitution is really a document that protects businesses through its simple standards of fairness, notice, and consistency. If Congress, a state legislature, city council, or agency tried to limit your company's involvement in the discussion of a ballot proposition or constitutional amendment, your company would be able to challenge successfully that limitation on its right to free speech. Any state taxes, fees, or registrations that treat your out-of-state business differently from businesses that are located in that state are violations of your business's constitutional rights. For example, if you were required to pay in-state processing companies a higher rate for processing than the rate paid by your in-state company competitors as a requirement for selling your product in that state, you have constitutional protections and rights that can be used to challenge the processing requirements. And if one state tried to collect sales taxes on all of your sales in all states, the Constitution would give you rights

and protections that would require the state to pro rate your taxes. You would have the same protections on your inventory and property taxes. If a state tried to charge additional tariffs beyond those required by our treaties and U.S. Customs on international sales, that state would be required to stop that tariff because the Constitution gives the federal government exclusive control over international trade. Finally, if a state tried to revoke your license or take your warehouse property without giving your company a chance to be heard, your company's constitutional rights have been violated.

The Fifth and Fourteenth Amendment due process protections ensure that your company will have the right to present its side of the story in every type of process from a zoning hearing to an allegation of discrimination to eminent domain. The U.S. Constitution may seem lofty, but it protects day-to-day business operations in everything from tax rates to licensing. If action taken by a government agency or body seems unfair, you probably have a constitutional right that has been violated.

Summary

What is the U.S. Constitution?

- U.S. Constitution—document detailing authority of U.S. government and rights of its citizens

What are the constitutional limitations on business regulations?

- Commerce Clause—portion of the U.S. Constitution that controls federal regulation of business; limits Congress to regulating interstate and international commerce

  - Intrastate commerce—business within state borders

  - Interstate commerce—business across state lines

  - Foreign commerce—business outside U.S. boundaries

Who has more power to regulate business—the states or the federal government?

- Supremacy Clause—portion of the U.S. Constitution that defines the relationship between state and federal laws; the police power or health, safety, and welfare are part of the consideration of this constitutional issue

What individual freedoms granted under the U.S. Constitution apply to businesses?

- Bill of Rights—first ten amendments to the U.S. Constitution, providing individual freedoms and protection of individual rights

- First Amendment—freedom-of-speech protection in U.S. Constitution

- Commercial speech—ads and other speech by businesses
- Corporate political speech—business ads or positions on candidates or referenda
- Due process—constitutional guarantee against the taking of property or other governmental exercise of authority without an opportunity for a hearing

- Equal protection—constitutional protection for U.S. citizens against disparate treatment
- Substantive due process—constitutional protection against taking of rights or property by statute when a statute is so vague that we are unclear when we have violated it

Key Terms

Bill of Rights *88*
checks and balances *88*
Commerce Clause *89*
commercial speech *97*
corporate political speech *101*
eminent domain *102*
executive branch *87*

Fourteenth Amendment *88*
judicial branch *87*
just compensation *105*
legislative branch *87*
nexus *94*
per curiam 99
police power *92*

preemption *96*
procedural due process *105*
separation of powers *87*
substantive due process *106*
substantive law *106*
Supremacy Clause *96*
U.S. Constitution *87*

Questions and Problems

1. The Heart of Atlanta Motel, which has 216 rooms available to transient guests, is located on Courtland Street, two blocks from downtown Peachtree Street in Atlanta, Georgia. It is readily accessible to interstate highways 75 and 85 and state highways 23 and 41. The motel advertises outside Georgia through various national advertising media, including magazines of national circulation; it maintains over 50 billboards and highway signs within the state, soliciting patronage for the motel; it accepts convention trade from outside Georgia; and approximately 75 percent of its registered guests are from out of state.

Prior to passage of Title II of the Civil Rights Act, the motel had followed a practice of refusing to rent rooms to Negroes, and it alleged that it intended to continue to do so. The motel filed suit, challenging Congress for passing this act in excess of its power to regulate commerce under Article I, Section 8, Part 3 of the Constitution of the United States.

Section 201 of Title II provides: "All persons shall be entitled to the full and equal enjoyment of the goods, services, facilities, privileges, advantages, and accommodations of any place of public accommodation, as defined in this section, without discrimination or segregation on the ground of race, color, religion, or national origin."

Is Title II of the Civil Rights Act constitutional? Is this case different from Ollie's Barbecue? from Morrison? [*Heart of Atlanta Motel, Inc.* v. *United States*, 379 U.S. 241 (1964).]

2. Bruce Church, Inc., is a company engaged in extensive commercial farming in Arizona and California. A provision of the Arizona Fruit and Vegetable Standardization Act requires that all cantaloupes grown in Arizona "be packed in regular compact arrangement in closed

standard containers approved by the supervisor." Arizona, through its agent Pike, issued an order prohibiting Bruce Church from transporting uncrated cantaloupes from its ranch in Parker, Arizona, to nearby Blythe, California, for packing and processing.

It would take many months and $200,000 for Bruce Church to construct a processing plant in Parker. Further, Bruce Church had $700,000 worth of cantaloupes ready for transportation. Bruce Church filed suit in federal district court challenging the constitutionality of the Arizona statutory provision on shipping cantaloupes. The court issued an injunction against the enforcement of the act on the grounds that it was an undue hardship on interstate commerce. Will the regulation withstand Commerce Clause scrutiny? [*Pike* v. *Bruce Church, Inc.*, 397 U.S. 137 (1970).] What if a state gave tax-exempt status to its residents for income earned on its own state-issued bonds but required its residents who purchased other states' bond holders to pay taxes on bond income earned from bonds issued by those other states? *Dept. of Revenue of Kentucky v. Davis*, 128 S.Ct. 1801 (2008).

3. For the past 62 years, Pacific Gas & Electric (PG&E) has distributed a newsletter in its monthly billing envelopes. The newsletter, called *Progress*, reaches over 3 million customers and has contained tips on conservation, utility billing information, public interest information, and political editorials.

A group called TURN (Toward Utility Rate Normalization) asked the Public Utility Commission (PUC) of California to declare that the envelope space belonged to the ratepayers and that TURN was entitled to use the *Progress* space four times each year. The PUC ordered TURN's request, and PG&E appealed the order to the California Supreme Court. When the California Supreme Court denied review, PG&E appealed to the U.S. Supreme Court, alleging a violation of its First Amendment rights. Is PG&E correct? [*Pacific Gas & Electric* v. *Public Utility Commission of California*, 475 U.S. 1 (1986).]

4. Amazon.com has now begun collecting sales tax on sales to residents of New York. New York is the first state to pass a law requiring retailers, even those without a physical presence in the state, to collect sales tax from residents of New York. Amazon and Overstock.com have both filed suit challenging the constitutionality of the New York statute. Amazon has only collected taxes in states where it has operations: North Dakota, Kentucky, and Kansas. Amazon.com has no physical facilities in New York. With revenue shortfalls predicted in 29 states for the year 2008, online sales revenue is an untouched pot of money that state legislators and treasurers would like to get their hands on.

What would be the argument against the constitutionality of the tax? What would be the argument upholding its constitutionality?

5. In 1989, the city of Cincinnati authorized Discovery Network, Inc., to place 62 free-standing news racks on public property for distributing free magazines that consisted primarily of advertising for Discovery Network's service. In 1990, the city became concerned about the safety and attractive appearance of its streets and sidewalks and revoked Discovery Network's permit on the ground that the magazines were commercial handbills whose distribution was prohibited on public property by a preexisting ordinance. Discovery Network says the prohibition is an excessive regulation of its commercial speech and a violation of its rights. The city maintains the elimination of the newsracks decreases litter and increases safety. Is the ban on newsracks constitutional? [*City of Cincinnati* v. *Discovery Network, Inc.*, 507 U.S. 410 (1993).]

Understanding "Consider" Problems

4.1

THINK: What did the *Morrison* case require for the Commerce Clause to allow Congressional action on intrastate activities? If Congress was to have the authority to regulate seemingly intrastate activities, there had to be some underlying economic activity and whatever that economic activity was, it had to have some relation to or an impact on interstate activity.

APPLY: What is different about Ollie's Barbecue and the issue of violence against women?

Ollie's Barbecue is a commercial enterprise involved in producing and selling food. This is economic activity, and *Morrison* found that the underlying activity being regulated must be economic in nature before the findings of interstate economic activity can be made.

Ollie's has an impact on interstate commerce because it orders goods in interstate commerce, and it serves travelers who are moving from state to state. The impact may be smaller than that outlined in Congress for VAWA, but it is all pure economic activity.

ANSWER: Congress had the authority under the Commerce Clause to pass the Civil Rights Act and have it apply to intrastate businesses such as Ollie's Barbecue that have an impact on interstate commerce (in an economic way).

4.2

THINK: The U.S. Constitution does not allow someone's property or rights to be taken without due process. Due process includes the right to be heard, the right to tell your side of the story.

APPLY: The Crafts had their property right of receiving electricity taken away without having a chance to tell their side of the story, or explain what had happened on their property.

ANSWER: The Crafts were deprived of their due process rights. The company must give them some right to be heard so that we can be sure that their power was not taken away without justification.

Note

1. There are only 5 states that failed to pass reforms: Arkansas, Hawaii, Mississippi, Oklahoma, and Rhode Island. The remaining states of Massachusetts, New Jersey, and New York had legislation pending. In November 2005, the U.S. House of Representatives passed the Private Property Rights Protection Act of 2005 (also known as House Resolution 4128) by a vote of 376 to 38. The bill died in the Senate.

5

Administrative Law

update

For up-to-date legal news, click on "Author Updates" at

www.cengage.com/blaw/ jennings

The regulations of administrative agencies at the federal and state levels affect the day-to-day operations of all businesses. From permits to labor regulations, every business is affected. Agencies are the enforcement arm of governments. Created by one of the branches of government, they affect the way businesses operate. This chapter answers the following questions: What is an administrative agency? What does it do? What laws govern the operation of administrative agencies? How do agencies pass rules? How do agencies enforce the law? ■

Lord's Prayer	**66 words**
Gettysburg Address	**286 words**
Declaration of Independence	**1,322 words**
Federal regulations on the sale of cabbage	**26,911 words**
Internal Revenue Code	**6,200,000 words**

DO NOT REMOVE UNDER PENALTY OF LAW.

Warning printed on tags required on mattresses sold in the United States

THIS TAG NOT TO BE REMOVED EXCEPT BY THE CONSUMER

Modified warning tag required on mattresses so that agency could reduce the number of calls from citizens about removing their mattress tags

consider...

A. Duda & Sons, Inc., has a plaque posted in the lobby of its company headquarters that reads: "But seek ye first the Kingdom of God, and his righteousness and all these things shall be added unto you." An employee complained to the Equal Employment Opportunity Commission (EEOC) about the plaque, saying the plaque was religious harassment in the workplace.

At the Montgomery County Middle School, the name of its December music event was changed from "Christmas Concert" to "Winter Concert" when a teacher complained that the use of the word "Christmas" was religious harassment.

As a result of these and over 500 other complaints, the EEOC proposed rules that prohibited verbal or physical contact that "denigrates or shows hostility or aversion toward individual because of his/her religion . . . or that of his/her relatives, friends or associates."

An executive in a Florida hospital wondered, "These rules could prevent an employee from wearing a necklace with a crucifix to work. Would I have to control Bible reading by my employees when they're having a break? The rules are unmanageable. Where do I turn? How can I raise my concerns about them?"

What Are Administrative Agencies?

An **administrative agency** is best defined by what it is not: It is not a legislative or judicial body. An administrative agency is a statutory creation within the executive branch with the power to make, interpret, and enforce laws. Such agencies exist at practically every level of government, and their names vary considerably. Exhibit 5.1 is a list of many federal administrative agencies and their acronyms.

States also have administrative agencies that are responsible for such things as the licensing of professions and occupations. Architects, contractors, attorneys, accountants, cosmetologists, doctors, dentists, real estate agents, and nurses are all professionals whose occupations are regulated in most states by some administrative agency. State agencies also handle utility and securities regulation.

These agencies, at every level of government, are given their authority from a legislative body. Congress creates federal agencies; state legislatures create state agencies; and city governments create their cities' administrative agencies.

The structures of agencies may differ significantly, but most will have an organizational chart. Exhibit 5.2 is an organizational chart for the Securities and Exchange Commission (SEC). The SEC consists of 5 commissioners, 6 divisions, and 11 regional offices.

EXHIBIT   5.1   Major Federal Administrative Agencies

EXECUTIVE OFFICE OF THE PRESIDENT

Executive Departments

Department of Agriculture
Department of Commerce
Department of Defense
Office of the Secretary of Defense
Department of the Air Force
Department of the Army
Department of the Navy
Department of Education
Department of Energy
Department of Health and Human Services
Department of Homeland Security
Department of Housing and Urban Development (HUD)
Department of the Interior
Department of Justice
Department of Labor

Department of State
Department of Transportation
Department of the Treasury

Selected Independent Agencies

Civil Aeronautics Board (CAB)
Commodity Futures Trading Commission (CFTC)
Consumer Product Safety Commission (CPSC)
Environmental Protection Agency (EPA)
Equal Employment Opportunity Commission (EEOC)
Federal Aviation Administration (FAA)
Farm Credit Administration (FCA)
Federal Communications Commission (FCC)
Federal Deposit Insurance Corporation (FDIC)

Federal Election Commission (FEC)
Federal Emergency Management Agency (FEMA)
Federal Labor Relations Authority (FLRA)
Federal Maritime Commission (FMC)
Federal Mine Safety and Health Review Commission
Federal Reserve System
Federal Trade Commission (FTC)
General Services Administration (GSA)
Interstate Commerce Commission (ICC)
National Aeronautics and Space Administration (NASA)
National Credit Union Administration (NCUA)
National Highway Traffic Safety Administration (NHTSA)
National Labor Relations Board (NLRB)

National Science Foundation (NSF)
National Transportation Safety Board (NTSB)
Nuclear Regulatory Commission (NRC)
Occupational Safety and Health Administration (OSHA)
Overseas Private Investment Corporation (OPIC)
Patent and Trademark Office
Pension Benefit Guaranty Corporation
Securities and Exchange Commission (SEC)
Selective Service System (SSS)
Small Business Administration (SBA)
Tennessee Valley Authority (TVA)
U.S. Metric Board
U.S. Postal Service (USPS)
Veterans Administration (VA)

Roles of Administrative Agencies

SPECIALIZATION

Administrative agencies are specialists in their particular areas of law, and this type of specialization is needed because both the laws they enforce and the areas they regulate are complex. For example, securities regulation deals with both the complexity of financial reporting as well as the technical accounting rules. In fact, Exhibit 5.2 shows that the SEC has a special division headed by its chief accountant so that it has the expertise to regulate financial reporting and determine valid accounting policies.

DUE PROCESS

Administrative agencies provide the opportunity to be heard, a form of due process before property, rights, or income are taken. *Goldberg v. Kelly*, 397 U.S. 254 (1970), was the seminal judicial decision responsible for creating administrative

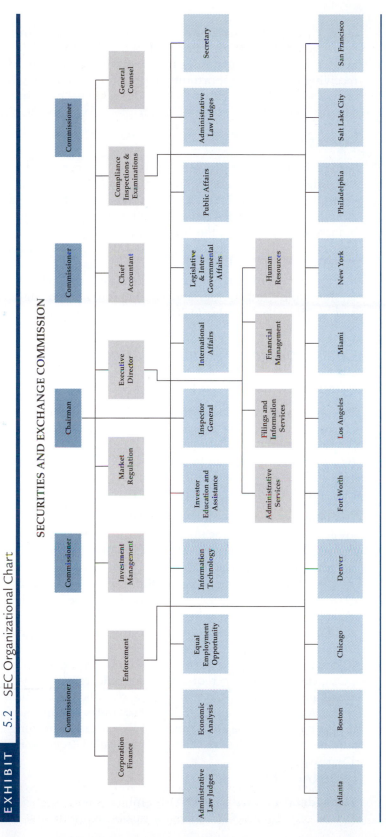

EXHIBIT 5.2 SEC Organizational Chart

SECURITIES AND EXCHANGE COMMISSION

agency procedures that provide timely due process. In *Goldberg,* the Supreme Court ruled that before a benefit (such as aid to dependent children) could be taken away, the agency must present its evidence and allow those who have been receiving the aid an opportunity to respond. Administrative hearings provide citizens and businesses with a process for seeing the evidence against them and presenting their side of the story (see Chapter 4 for more insight on due process).

SOCIAL GOALS

Some experts see administrative agencies as a means for accomplishing social goals that might otherwise be delayed or debated. For example, the Environmental Protection Agency (EPA) is assigned the goal of creating a cleaner environment. Administrative agencies can function independently of the judicial and legislative branches (however, see the *Massachusetts* v. *EPA* case later in the chapter). Often, agencies are created in response to a pressing social issue. For example, the Department of Homeland Security was established to combine several agencies so that the there could be more coordinated responses to terrorism, such as the attacks on the World Trade Center and Washington, D.C., in 2001, and natural disasters, such as Hurricane Katrina in 2005 and Gustav in 2008.

Laws Governing Administrative Agencies

ADMINISTRATIVE PROCEDURES ACT

The **Administrative Procedures Act (APA)** requires agencies to follow certain uniform procedures in making rules (those procedures are covered later in this chapter). The APA includes the Freedom of Information Act, the Federal Privacy Act, and the Government in the Sunshine Act, among others.

FREEDOM OF INFORMATION ACT

The **Freedom of Information Act (FOIA)** allows citizens access to certain agency information and requires that the agencies publicly disclose their procedures and decisions. Agencies must also publish their rules, regulations, procedures, policy statements, and reports.

Unpublished agency information can be obtained by a **FOIA request**. For example, you could request the results of the Federal Trade Commission's study of coaching programs for college entrance exams. The agency can charge for time and for copying costs in processing your request, although agencies can waive fees for nonprofit public interest groups.

Some information is exempt from FOIA requests. There are nine categories of exemptions, including requests that would reveal trade secrets or information about government workers' personnel records. For example, suppose a company requests the government bid contract submitted by another company (its competitor for the bid) to the Department of Defense. The bidding company could bring suit to stop the disclosure. Such suits are called "reverse FOIA suits."

FEDERAL PRIVACY ACT

The **Federal Privacy Act (FPA)** prohibits federal agencies from communicating any records to another agency or person without first obtaining that person's consent. The FPA protects all records about individuals that the agency has, including medical and employment histories.

Because law enforcement agencies would have a difficult time conducting investigations if they had to get permission from the individuals being investigated in order to obtain information, law enforcement agencies are exempt from the FPA. Some routine agency tasks are also exempt from the prior permission requirement. For example, employees of the SEC have constant access to information about stock sales by directors so that they can monitor them for insider trading.

ethical *issues*

In 1997, the Internal Revenue Service (IRS) disciplined employees who, out of curiosity, were looking up tax returns of famous people to see who made how much income. The IRS fired 23 employees, disciplined 349, and provided counseling for 472. During the 2008 election, the director of the Ohio Department of Job and Family Services ordered employees to look up the child support payment record of Samuel Joseph Wurzelbacher, aka, Joe the Plumber, a man who had raised a controversial issue to then-candidate Barack Obama. Helen Jones-Kelley, the director, was a donor to the Obama campaign. Employees in the office complained about the search and the director said, "Our practice is when someone is thrust quickly into the public spotlight, we often take a look." The Ohio Inspector General is investigating the use of state computers for the search.

Is this practice so bad? What is wrong with just looking at data accessible at work? Why are we concerned about selective research about private citizens? Does it matter that the information was not released to the public?

GOVERNMENT IN THE SUNSHINE ACT

The **Government in the Sunshine Act** is often called an **open meeting law**. This open meeting law applies only to meetings between or among agency heads. For example, when the commissioners of the FTC meet together, that meeting must be public and held only after there has been prior notice. Staff members can hold meetings in private without giving notice. Meetings on law enforcement investigations are also exempt.

FEDERAL REGISTER ACT

Although the **Federal Register Act (FRA)** is not a part of the APA, it created the **Federal Register System**, which oversees publication of federal agency information. This system provides the means for Sunshine Act notices and publication of agency rules and procedures.

Three publications make up the Federal Register System. The first is the *U.S. Government Manual*. This publication is reprinted each year and lists all federal agencies and their regional offices along with addresses. The second publication of the Federal Register Act is the *Code of Federal Regulations* (covered in Chapter 1). The *Code of Federal Regulations* contains all the regulations of all the federal agencies. The third publication under the Federal Register System provides a daily update on changes in the regulations. This publication, called the *Federal Register*, is published every government working day and contains proposed regulations, notices of meetings, notices of hearings on proposed regulations, and the final versions of amended or new regulations. The *Federal Register* totals about 70,000 pages a year, or about 250 pages every working day.

The Functions of Administrative Agencies and Business Interaction

Administrative agencies have three functions: promulgating regulations, enforcing rules, and adjudicating rules. Businesses will find themselves interacting with agencies in all three areas of operation.

PROVIDING INPUT WHEN AGENCIES ARE PROMULGATING REGULATIONS

Administrative agencies have a legislative function that takes two forms: **formal rulemaking** and **informal rulemaking**. Some agencies combine these into a type of rulemaking that is a cross between formal and informal—**hybrid rulemaking**. This section explains formal rulemaking.

Formal Rulemaking

Exhibit 5.3 diagrams the steps involved in formal rulemaking.

Enabling Act   Legislators begin the administrative process by passing a law to remedy a problem. The enacted law gives the overview—what the legislature wants to accomplish and the penalties for its violation. The law may also create an administrative agency with the power to adopt rules to enforce the statute. The law, referred to as an **enabling act**, gives the agency the broad power to deal with the issues the act was passed to address.

EXHIBIT   5.3   Steps in Formal Rulemaking by Administrative Agencies

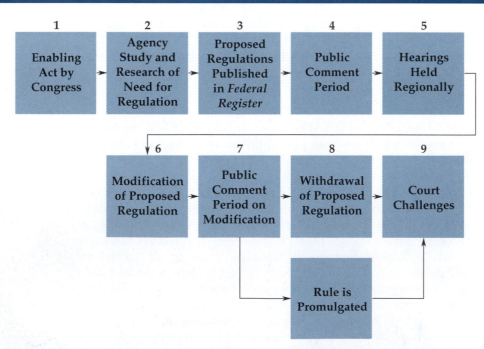

Agency Research of the Problem Agencies must establish a purpose for any new rules proposed and present evidence that the regulation will accomplish the purpose. Agency staff can perform the study, or the agency can hire outside experts to conduct it. The study examines various issues such as whether the regulation will be cost effective. The study focuses on whether the problems the regulation is trying to correct will be corrected as well as the costs if those problems are not corrected.

Proposed Regulations Based on the completed study, the agency will publish its proposed rules or rule changes in the *Federal Register*. In addition to publishing the notice of proposed rules in the *Federal Register*, an agency is required under the **Regulatory Flexibility Act** to publish a notice in trade and industry publications of those businesses that will be affected by the rule. For example, the regulation governing disclosures of sales of used vehicles was published in automobile dealers associations' publications. Exhibit 5.4 is a sample of a proposed rule publication on bunk beds.

The Public Comment Period The time during which the agency accepts comments on the proposed rule is called the **public comment period**. Under the APA, the public comment period cannot be fewer than 30 days, but most comment periods are much longer.

Some agencies hold public hearings on proposed regulations. The purpose of the hearings is to take input on the proposals and consider additional evidence and factors relevant in promulgating the final version of the rule.

Exhibits 5.5, 5.6, and 5.7 are examples of letters sent to the CPSC offering input on the proposed rule on bunk beds. (See the proposal in Exhibit 5.4.)

EXHIBIT   5.4   Sample Proposed CPSC Rule on Bunk Beds

CONSUMER PRODUCT SAFETY COMMISSION

ACTION: Bunk Beds; Advance Notice of Proposed Rulemaking; Request for Comments and Information

15 CFR CHAPTER II

AGENCY: Consumer Product Safety Commission

SUMMARY: The Commission has reason to believe that unreasonable risks of injury and death may be associated with bunk beds constructed so that children can become entrapped in the beds' structure or become wedged between the bed and a wall.

This advance notice of proposed rulemaking (ANPR) initiates a rulemaking proceeding that could result in a rule mandating bunk bed performance requirements to reduce this hazard. This rule could be issued under either the Federal Hazardous Substances Act (FHSA) or the Consumer Product Safety Act (CPSA), or separate rules might be issued under the FHSA and CPSA addressing bunk beds intended for use by children or adults, respectively.

The Commission solicits written comments from interested persons concerning the risks of injury and death associated with bunk beds, the regulatory alternatives discussed in this ANPR, other possible ways to address these risks, and the economic impacts of the various regulatory alternatives. The Commission also invites interested persons to submit an existing standard, or a statement of intent to modify or develop a voluntary standard, to address the risks of injury and death described in this ANPR.

EXHIBIT 5.5 Comments in Favor of the Proposed Rule on Bunk Beds

The CPSC received hundreds of this form letter:

I am writing in regard to the advanced notice of rulemaking pertaining to bunk beds. I truly feel there should be a mandatory standard in the design and construction of bunk beds.

If one child dies due to unsafe bunk bed design and manufacture, this questions whether voluntary standards in the industry are sufficient to protect our children. Due to the fact that there were more than 54 fatalities and over 100,000 injuries from 1990 to 1995, I feel that is overwhelming evidence that mandatory standards **must** be passed to ensure that this tragedy does not strike another American family.

EXHIBIT 5.6 Comments That the Proposed Rules Are Not Enough

From the American Academy of Pediatrics

I am writing to support the creation of a mandatory standard to address children's entrapment in bunk beds.

More than 500,000 bunk beds have been recalled by the U.S. Consumer Product Safety Commission since November 1994, and despite the current voluntary standard, an estimated 50,000 non-conforming bunk beds are sold for residential use in the United States each year. On average, 10 entrapment deaths occur each year, almost all on non-conforming beds.

The Academy supports the requirement for a continuous guardrail along the entire wall side of the bed, and the requirement that all openings of end structures, and not just those within 9 inches of the sleeping surface of the lower mattress, be designed to preclude entrapment.

The Academy also believes that the mandatory standard can be strengthened further. Because bunk beds are often placed in the corner of a room, the end structures of the upper bunk should extend at least 5 inches above the mattress along their entire length to prevent children from slipping between the bed and the wall and becoming entrapped. The proposed rule presumably does not require a 5-inch minimum height along the entire length of the end structures to allow for access to a ladder. This is the same reason the continuous guardrail is not required on the side of the bed. However, closing these gaps may actually decrease the likelihood of falls.

EXHIBIT 5.7 Comments Opposing the Proposed Rule

From the International Mass Retail Association (IRMA)

IRMA urges the CPSC to review alternative measures to reduce bunk bed entrapment hazards, rather than pursuing a mandatory standard that will likely have no significant impact on the high compliance that already exists in the industry with the voluntary bunk bed design.

Product safety is an important concern to the nation's mass retailers, and for that reason, mass retailers actively strive to comply with all industry-recognized product voluntary standards. Potential liability stemming from products that do not meet widely-recognized voluntary standards also serves as an added incentive for retailers to sell compliant products.

Rather than taking the drastic step of implementing a mandatory rule, CPSC would be better advised to seek changes in the standard to address the few entrapment incidents in compliant bunk beds. The agency might also examine conducting a stepped-up education campaign aimed to make consumers, retailers and manufacturers more aware of the voluntary standard.

One of the important distinctions between the legislative process and the regulatory rulemaking process is the nature of the role of those involved. Legislators, such as representatives and senators, can accept campaign contributions and meals from lobbyists. However, those who work in administrative agencies fulfill both a rulemaking and enforcement role and cannot accept such gifts. Case 5.1 illustrates what can happen when businesses and regulators cross the fine line on influence. *U.S. v. Sun-Diamond Growers of California* (Case 5.1) is a criminal prosecution for alleged bribery of officials in order to persuade them to abandon or change proposed regulations before the agency.

Business Planning Tip

When a federal, state, or local agency has proposed a rule that affects your business, be sure to submit a letter or offer to testify about your concerns. For example, those who sold vintage autos to collectors got an exemption for emissions testing for their cars when the rules on testing cars were proposed. Vintage auto sellers simply let the regulators know about the historic nature of their cars, the limited number of cars, and the need for an exemption for cars that are not really driven very much.

CASE 5.1

U.S. v. Sun–Diamond Growers of California
526 U.S. 398 (1999)

GRATITUDE CAN'T BE IN CASH OR KIND

FACTS

Sun-Diamond Growers (Respondent) is a trade association that engaged in marketing and lobbying activities on behalf of its member cooperatives, which were owned by approximately 5,000 individual growers of raisins, figs, walnuts, prunes, and hazelnuts. The United States (Petitioner) charged former Secretary of Agriculture Michael Espy and Sun-Diamond with making illegal gifts to Mr. Espy.

Sun-Diamond was charged with giving Mr. Espy approximately $5,900 in illegal gratuities: tickets to the 1993 U.S. Open Tennis Tournament (worth $2,295), luggage ($2,427), meals ($665), and a framed print and crystal bowl ($524). Sun-Diamond had an interest in favorable treatment from the Secretary at the time it bestowed the gratuities. First, Sun-Diamond's member cooperatives participated in the Market Promotion Plan (MPP), a grant program administered by the Department of Agriculture to promote the sale of U.S. farm commodities in foreign countries. Second, Sun-Diamond had an interest in the federal government's regulation of methyl bromide, a low-cost pesticide used by many individual growers. The jury convicted Sun-Diamond, and the District Court sentenced the company to pay a fine of $400,000. The Court of Appeals reversed the conviction on Count One. The Supreme Court granted *certiorari*.

JUDICIAL OPINION

SCALIA, Justice
Talmudic sages believed that judges who accepted bribes would be punished by eventually losing all knowledge of the divine law.

Bribery requires intent "to influence" an official act or "to be influenced" in an official act, while illegal gratuity requires only that the gratuity be given or accepted "for or because of" an official act. In other words, for bribery there must be a *quid pro quo*—a specific intent to give or receive something of value in exchange for an official act. An illegal gratuity, on the other hand, may constitute merely a reward for some future act that the public official will take (and may already have determined to take), or for a past act that he has already taken. The punishments prescribed for the two offenses reflect their relative seriousness.

[The] Government's . . . reading would . . . criminalize, for example, token gifts to the President based on his official position and not linked to any identifiable act—such as the replica jerseys given by championship sports teams each year during ceremonial White House visits. Similarly, it would criminalize a high school principal's gift of a school baseball cap to the Secretary of Education, by reason of his office, on the occasion of the latter's visit to the school. That these examples are not fanciful is demonstrated by the fact that counsel for the

CONTINUED

United States maintained at oral argument that a group of farmers would violate § 201(c)(1)(A) by providing a complimentary lunch for the Secretary of Agriculture in conjunction with his speech to the farmers concerning various matters of USDA policy—so long as the Secretary had before him, or had in prospect, matters affecting the farmers. Of course the Secretary of Agriculture always has before him or in prospect matters that affect farmers, just as the President always has before him or in prospect matters that affect college and professional sports, and the Secretary of Education matters that affect high schools.

We hold that, in order to establish a violation of 18 U.S.C. § 201(c)(1)(A), the Government must prove a link between a thing of value conferred upon a public official and a specific "official act" for or because of which it was given. We affirm the judgment of the Court of Appeals, which remanded the case to the District Court for a new trial on Count One.

Reversed and remanded.

CASE QUESTIONS

1. What violation is alleged and why?

2. Are administrative agency employees permitted to accept gifts from those affected by their regulations and policies? What types of guidelines would you develop for your employees in their interactions with administrative agency employees?

3. What is required for proof of criminal wrongdoing in making a gift?

ethical *issues*

Three Chippewa Indian tribes submitted applications to the U.S. Department of the Interior seeking approval to convert a greyhound racing facility in Hudson, Wisconsin, to an off-reservation casino.

On June 8, 1995, the Indian Gaming staff in the department issued a draft report recommending approval of the Chippewa application.

While final decision on the application was pending in the agency, Harold Ickes (then White House Deputy Chief of Staff for Policy and Political Affairs) received a letter from Patrick O'Connor, a lobbyist for tribes that opposed the Chippewa application. The O'Connor letter explained the significance of the Chippewa decision, that the opposition tribes were important contributors to the Democratic Party, and that the Chippewa tribes were Republican supporters. In addition, Donald Fowler, the Democratic National Committee chairman, met with

Mr. Ickes and "discussed the basis for the opposition to creating another gaming casino." Further, there were faxes regarding the application between White House staff and Department of the Interior staff.

On June 27, 1995, the Chippewa application was denied. The decision cited "community opposition" but did not incorporate or discuss the lengthy and detailed reports the staff had prepared.

Interior Secretary Bruce Babbitt told Paul Eckstein, a lawyer for the Chippewas and a lifetime friend of Mr. Babbitt, that Mr. Ickes required him to issue the decision on June 27. Following an investigation, Mr. Babbitt was cleared of any violations of the law. However, what ethical issues arise when political activities cross into administrative proceedings? How would the Chippewas perceive this series of events?

Deciding What to Do with the Proposed Regulation   After the comment period is over, the agency has three choices. The first choice is simply to adopt the rules. The second choice is to modify the proposed rules and go through the process of public comment again. If the modification is minor, however, the APA allows the agency to adopt a modified version of the rule without going through the public comment period again. The agency's final choice is to withdraw the rule. This chapter's opening Consider described the EEOC's proposed guidelines on religious harassment in the workplace and the business concerns about those guidelines. The U.S. Senate passed a resolution 94–0 urging the EEOC to drop the guidelines. The general public became actively involved in the rulemaking. Religious and business groups flooded the EEOC with more than 100,000 letters of protest. EEOC attorneys advised that banning such personal expression, a form of speech, would result in a flood of First Amendment suits. The EEOC withdrew the proposed rules. EEOC spokesman Mike Widomski explained that "the public outcry and the number of comments that were received" triggered the reversal. Public comments and input have an impact in the regulatory process.

consider 5.1

Draw on your knowledge of law to this point, including constitutional law, statutory law, and judicial precedent, and discuss why the Senate simply passed a resolution to prevent the promulgation of the proposed EEOC regulations. Explain also how a business might be able to interact with Congress. (Analysis appears at the end of the chapter.)

. . . .

Court and Legislative Challenges to Proposed Rules   Those who made comments on the rules during their proposal stage can challenge the validity of the rules in court. An administrative rule can be challenged on several different grounds. The first ground is to challenge the rule as arbitrary, capricious, an abuse of discretion, or in violation of some other law. The agency must be able to show (usually from its studies) that there is evidence to support the proposed rule. Without such evidence, a court can find that the rule is **arbitrary and capricious**. *Motor Vehicles Manufacturers Ass'n.* v. *State Farm Mutual Insurance Co.* (Case 5.2) addresses the issue of whether an agency's action is arbitrary and capricious.

CASE 5.2

Motor Vehicles Manufacturers Ass'n. v. *State Farm Mutual Insurance Co.*
463 U.S. 29 (1983)

FASTEN YOUR SEATBELTS: RULEMAKING IS A ROUGH RIDE

FACTS

In 1972, after many hearings and comments, the Department of Transportation passed a regulation requiring some type of passive restraint system (Standard 208) on all vehicles manufactured after 1975. The regulation allowed an ignition interlock system, which requires car occupants to have their seatbelts fastened before a car could be started. Congress, however, revoked the requirement of the ignition interlock.

Because of changes in directors of the DOT and the unfavorable economic climate in the auto industry, the requirements for passive restraints were postponed. In 1981, the department proposed a rescission of the passive restraint rule. After receiving written comments and holding public hearings, the agency concluded there was no longer a basis for reliably predicting that passive restraints increased safety levels or decreased accidents. Further, the agency found it would cost $1 billion to implement the rule, and it was unwilling to impose such substantial costs on auto manufacturers.

State Farm filed suit on the rescission of the rule on the basis that it was arbitrary and capricious. The court of appeals held that the rescission was, in fact, arbitrary and capricious. Auto manufacturers appealed.

CONTINUED

JUDICIAL OPINION

WHITE, Justice

Given the effectiveness ascribed to airbag technology by the agency, the mandate of the Safety Act to achieve traffic safety would suggest that the logical response to the faults of detachable seatbelts would be to require the installation of airbags. At the very least this alternative way of achieving objectives of the Act should have been addressed and adequate reasons given for its abandonment. But the agency not only did not require compliance through airbags, it did not even consider the possibility in its 1981 rulemaking. Not one sentence of its rulemaking statement discusses the airbags-only option. We have frequently reiterated that an agency must cogently explain why it had exercised its discretion in a given manner.

For nearly a decade, the automobile industry waged the regulatory equivalent of war against the airbag and lost—the inflatable restraint was proven sufficiently effective. Now the automobile industry has decided to employ a seatbelt system which will not meet the safety objectives of Standard 208. This hardly constitutes cause to revoke the standard itself. Indeed the Motor Vehicle Safety Act was necessary because the industry was not sufficiently responsive to safety concerns. The Act intended that safety standards not depend on current technology and would be "technology-forcing" in the sense of inducing the development of superior safety design.

Since 20 to 50 percent of motorists currently wear seatbelts on some occasions, there would seem to be grounds to believe that seatbelt use by occasional users will be substantially increased by the detachable passive belts. Whether this is the case is a matter for the agency to decide, but it must bring its expertise to bear on the question.

An agency's view of what is in the public interest may change, either with or without a change in circumstances. But an agency changing its course must supply a reasoned analysis. . . . the agency has failed to supply the requisite "reasoned analysis" in this case. Accordingly, we remand the matter to the NHTSA for further consideration consistent with this opinion.

CASE QUESTIONS

1. What regulation is at issue in the case and why was it important to the insurance industry? Name some other businesses that would have an interest in the proposed regulation.

2. What was done with the regulation to result in this judicial decision? Does it matter that this is a withdrawal versus a promulgation? Why or why not?

3. Who challenged the agency's actions, and what were the reasons for this challenge?

A second theory for challenging an agency's regulation is that the agency did not comply with the APA requirements of notice, publication, and public comment or input. Another basis for challenging a regulation is that the regulation is unconstitutional. Many challenges based on constitutional grounds deal with regulations that give an agency authority to search records or that impose discriminatory requirements for licensing professionals.

Another theory for challenging a regulation in court is *ultra vires*, a Latin term meaning "beyond its powers." An *ultra vires* regulation is one that goes beyond the authority given to the agency in its enabling act. Although most agencies stay clearly within their authority, if an agency tries to change the substance and purpose of the enabling act through regulation, the regulations would be *ultra vires*. In *Massachusetts* v. *EPA* (Case 5.3), the court dealt with greenhouse gases and their regulation all within the context of challenges to the EPA based on *ultra vires* (uniquely, the agency's defense was that the actions groups were demanding were *ultra vires*), substantial evidence, and the administrative regulation process.

CASE 5.3

Massachusetts v. EPA
549 U.S. 497 (2007)

WHO HAS JURISDICTION OVER HOT AIR?

FACTS

On October 20, 1999, a group of 19 private organizations (petitioners) filed a rulemaking petition asking EPA to regulate "greenhouse gas emissions from new motor vehicles under § 202 of the Clean Air Act." These organizations argued that greenhouse gas emissions have significantly accelerated climate change; and that "carbon dioxide remains the most important contributor to [man-made] forcing of climate change."

Fifteen months after the petition was filed, the EPA requested public comment on "all the issues raised in [the] petition." The EPA received more than 50,000 comments over the next five months.

On September 8, 2003, EPA entered an order denying the rulemaking petition because (1) the Clean Air Act does not authorize EPA to issue mandatory regulations to address global climate change; and (2) even if the agency had the authority to set greenhouse gas emission standards, it would be unwise to do so at this time. Massachusetts, other states, and private organizations filed suit challenging the EPA denial as arbitrary and capricious, violative of the APA, and *ultra vires* because of statutory mandates for EPA action. The court of appeals dismissed the appeal from the agency denial and the Supreme Court granted *certiorari*.

JUDICIAL OPINION

STEVENS, Justice

In essence, EPA concluded that climate change was so important that unless Congress spoke with exacting specificity, it could not have meant the agency to address it.

While it may be true that regulating motor-vehicle emissions will not by itself *reverse* global warming, it by no means follows that we lack jurisdiction to decide whether EPA has a duty to take steps to *slow* or *reduce* it.

The Clean Air Act's sweeping definition of "air pollutant" includes "*any* air pollution agent or combination of such agents, including *any* physical, chemical . . . substance or matter which is emitted into or otherwise enters the ambient air. . . ." The statute is unambiguous. If EPA makes a finding of endangerment, the Clean Air Act requires the agency to regulate emissions of the deleterious pollutant from new motor vehicles.

EPA finally argues that it cannot regulate carbon dioxide emissions from motor vehicles because doing so would require it to tighten mileage standards, a job (according to EPA) that Congress has assigned to DOT. But that DOT sets mileage standards in no way licenses EPA to shirk its environmental responsibilities. EPA has been charged with protecting the public's "health" and "welfare," a statutory obligation wholly independent of DOT's mandate to promote energy efficiency. The two obligations may overlap, but there is no reason to think the two agencies cannot both administer their obligations and yet avoid inconsistency.

Because greenhouse gases fit well within the Clean Air Act's capacious definition of "air pollutant," we hold that EPA has the statutory authority to regulate the emission of such gases from new motor vehicles.

In short, EPA has offered no reasoned explanation for its refusal to decide whether greenhouse gases cause or contribute to climate change. Its action was therefore "arbitrary, capricious, . . . or otherwise not in accordance with law." We need not and do not reach the question whether on remand EPA must make an endangerment finding, or whether policy concerns can inform EPA's actions in the event that it makes such a finding. We hold only that EPA must ground its reasons for action or inaction in the statute.

The judgment of the Court of Appeals is reversed, and the case is remanded.

DISSENTING OPINION

Chief Justice ROBERTS, with whom Justice SCALIA, Justice THOMAS, and Justice ALITO join, dissenting.

Global warming may be a "crisis," even "the most pressing environmental problem of our time." Indeed, it may ultimately affect nearly everyone on the planet in some potentially adverse way, and it may be that governments have done too little to address it. It is not a problem, however, that has escaped the attention of policymakers in the Executive and Legislative Branches of our Government, who continue to consider regulatory, legislative, and treaty-based means of addressing global climate change.

This Court's standing jurisprudence simply recognizes that redress of grievances of the sort at issue here "is the function of Congress and the Chief Executive," not the federal courts. I would vacate the judgment below and remand for dismissal of the petitions for review.

CONTINUED

Justice SCALIA, with whom THE CHIEF JUSTICE, Justice THOMAS, and Justice ALITO join, dissenting. I simply cannot conceive of what else the Court would like EPA to say.

The Court's alarm over global warming may or may not be justified, but it ought not distort the outcome of this litigation. This is a straightforward administrative-law case, in which Congress has passed a malleable statute giving broad discretion, not to us but to an executive agency. No matter how important the underlying policy issues at stake, this Court has no business substituting its own desired outcome for the reasoned judgment of the responsible agency.

CASE QUESTIONS

1. What authority is given to the EPA by statute? Why does the EPA not want to exercise authority over greenhouse gases?

2. Why does the majority conclude that "greenhouse gases" are included within that authority?

3. List the arguments the dissent makes against requiring the EPA to take action on greenhouse gases. What do you learn about the role of the issue of global warming in the dissent's analysis of the case vs. the analysis of the majority?

consider 5.2

The use of snowmobiles in Yellowstone and Grand Teton National Parks was first permitted in 1963, and their use has been a topic of ongoing concern because of their impact on park resources. In 2003 the National Park Service (NPS), part of the Department of the Interior, groomed over 180 miles of park roads at least every other night. As many as 1,700 snowmobiles enter the parks on peak days.

The Fund for Animals and other environmental groups objected to the snowmobile use, and in December 2000, the NPS issued a proposed rule that capped snowmobile use in the winters of 2001–02 and 2002–03 and completely eliminated snowmobile use by the 2003–04 winter season. The NPS received 5,273 comments during the 30-day public comment period; over 4,300 of these comments supported the proposed phase-out rule. On January 22, 2001, the NPS published the final rule, which allowed snowmobile use to continue but phased out all forms of mechanized snow vehicles, including snowmobiles, by the 2003–04 winter season.

The 2001 Rule, promulgated by the Clinton administration, was published the day after President George W. Bush took office and was immediately stayed pending a review by the new administration. Meanwhile, the International Snowmobiler Manufacturers Association filed suit, challenging the 2001 Rule as an unsupported decision to ban snowmobiling. The lawsuit called for the NPS to set aside the rules. The NPS settled the litigation and agreed to consider data on new snowmobile technologies.

Pursuant to the settlement, in March 2002, the NPS issued another proposed rule. NPS received over 350,000 pieces of correspondence from the public; over 80 percent of the public comments supported the phase-out of snowmobiles. Despite this opposition, on November 18, 2002, one month before the phase-out was scheduled to go into effect, the NPS released a final rule delaying the implementation of the phase-out for an additional year. Snowmobile use was allowed to continue unabated during the 2002–03 winter season.

The Fund for Animals filed suit, challenging the postponement as arbitrary and capricious. Should the Fund win? Is the postponement arbitrary and capricious? In 2007, former National Park Director Fran Mainella called for using science, including studies of their impact, to make the rules on snowmobile use in national parks. Why is her recommendation relevant? (Analysis appears at the end of the chapter.)

Informal Rulemaking

The process for informal rulemaking is the same as that for formal rulemaking, with the exception that no public hearings are held on the rule. The only input from the public comes in the form of comments, using the same procedures discussed earlier.

Business Rights in Agency Enforcement Action

Administrative agencies not only make the rules; they enforce them. In so doing, the agencies are also responsible for adjudicating disputes over the scope or interpretation of the rules. Exhibit 5.8 is a chart of the steps involved in agency enforcement and adjudication.

LICENSING AND INSPECTIONS

Many agencies issue licenses or permits as a way to enforce the law. For example, state administrative agencies may require building contractors to be licensed so that their dues can finance a recovery fund for the victims of bankrupt or negligent contractors. The idea behind the licensing and permit method of enforcement is to curtail illegal activity up front and also to have records in case problems arise.

Agencies also have the authority to conduct inspections, such as when an agency responsible for restaurant licenses inspects restaurant facilities to check for health code violations. The Occupational Safety and Health Administration (OSHA) at the federal level has the authority to inspect plants to check for violations of OSHA standards. This power of inspection at unannounced times is an enforcement tool by itself. There is strong incentive to comply with regulations when an inspection could happen at any time. A business can refuse an inspection, but an agency can obtain a warrant and return for a mandatory inspection.

ENFORCEMENT

Beginning Enforcement Steps

Regardless of the remedy an agency seeks, all action begins when the agency issues a **complaint** against the violating party. The complaint describes when and what the company did and why it is a violation.

Once a complaint is filed, an agency can negotiate with a party for an order or proceed to a hearing to obtain an order from an administrative law judge. The remedies in an order vary according to the type of violation and whether it is ongoing.

EXHIBIT   5.8   Steps for Administrative Agency Enforcement and Adjudication

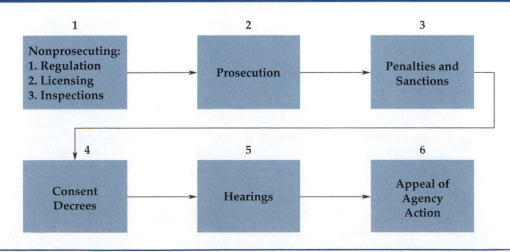

The FTC could, and typically does, order companies running deceptive ads to stop using the ads and promise not to use them again in the future. These sanctions usually come in the form of an **injunction**, which is a court order that prohibits specifically described conduct.

Consent Decrees

Rather than go through a hearing and the expense of the administrative process, some companies agree to penalties proposed by an agency. They do so in a document called a **consent decree**, which is like a *nolo contendere* plea in the criminal system. The party does not admit or deny a violation but simply negotiates a settlement with the administrative agency. The consent decree is a contract between the charged party and the regulatory agency.

Hearings

If the parties cannot reach an agreement through a consent decree, the questions of violations and penalties will go to an administrative hearing, which is quite different from the litigation described in Chapter 3. The defendant is the person or company accused of violating an administrative regulation. The judge is called an **administrative law judge (ALJ)** at the federal level, and in some state-level agencies is called a **hearing examiner** or **hearing officer**.

Administrative hearings can have as participants more than just the agency and the party charged with a violation. Other parties with an interest in the case can intervene. These **intervenors** file motions to intervene and are usually permitted to do so at any time before the start of a hearing. Typical intervenors are industry organizations: Snowmobile manufacturers and the state of Wyoming, because of their economic interests in snowmobile activities, were intervenors in the national park cases mentioned in Consider 5.2.

Administrative Law of Appeals

Once the ALJ has issued a decision, the decision can be appealed. However, the appellate process in administrative law is slightly different. The first step in an appeal of an ALJ decision is not to a court but to the agency itself. This step gives the agency a chance to correct a bad decision before the courts become involved.

The appeal is to the next higher level in the agency. For example, in the FTC an appeal of an ALJ's decision goes to the commissioners of the FTC for reconsideration.

Those appealing an ALJ decision must go through all the required lines of authority in the agency before they can go to court. This process is known as **exhausting administrative remedies**. If an appeal is made before administrative remedies are exhausted, the court will reject the case on those grounds.

A decision of a federal administrative agency is appealed to one of the U.S. courts of appeals (as indicated in Chapter 3). An appellate court can simply affirm an agency action, find that an agency has exceeded its authority, find that an agency has violated the U.S. Constitution, or rule that an agency has acted arbitrarily or that an agency's decision or action is not supported by the evidence. The *State Farm* seatbelt case (see Case 5.2 earlier in the chapter) is an example of a court's reversal of administrative agency action in the area of rulemaking. Exhibit 5.9 is a summary of the roles administrative agencies play.

EXHIBIT	5.9	The Roles of Administrative Agencies

ACTIVITY	STEPS	PARTIES	RESULTS
Passing rules	Rule proposed	Agency	New rules
	Comments	Consumers	Modified rules
	Modification, withdrawal, or promulgation	Business Congress Agency	Withdrawn rules
Enforcement	Licensing	Agency Business	
	Inspections	Agency Courts (if warrant is required) Business	Search and inspection
	Complaints	Agency	Fines Penalties Injunctions Consent decrees Hearings

Red Flags FOR MANAGERS

Administrative law may seem to be a remote and technical area of law, but it affects business in daily and profound ways. Managers should be familiar with the administrative agencies at the federal and state levels that affect their companies. Agencies regulate everything from licensing to professional standards to employee rights.

In addition to knowing which agencies regulate their companies, managers should also stay up-to-date on the actions and proposed rules of administrative agencies. They can learn of proposed agency actions through their trade and professional groups and publications because agencies are required to post notices of rule changes and proposed rules in those publications. Knowing about new rules proposals ensures that managers can exercise their right of input during the agency's rulemaking process. Managers can provide testimony, data, letters, and other relevant information to help the agency understand the issues in their proposed rules.

Administrative agencies are also responsible for enforcement of regulations. OSHA, for example, inspects workplaces and issues complaints and levies fines for violations. However, all companies have the right to due process with agencies when those agencies are taking enforcement steps. Those due process rights include the right to a hearing and, eventually, review by a court. However, agencies also have a form of alternative resolution of charges through the use of a consent decree. The consent decree is a settlement between the company and the administrative agency that settles the charges, determines the fine, and usually includes a pledge by the company to change its processes in order to avoid violations in the future.

Summary

What is an administrative agency?

- Administrative agency—statutory entity with the ability to make, interpret, and enforce laws

What laws govern the operation of administrative agencies?

- Administrative Procedure Act—general federal law governing agency process and operations within agencies
- Government in the Sunshine Act—federal law requiring public hearings by agencies (with limited exceptions)
- Federal Privacy Act—federal law protecting transfer of information among agencies unless done for enforcement reasons
- Freedom of Information Act—federal law providing individuals with access to information held by administrative agencies (with some exemptions such as for trade secrets)

What do administrative agencies do?

- Rulemaking—process of turning proposed regulations into actual regulations; requires public input
- *Federal Register*—daily publication that updates agency proposals, rules, hearing notices, and so forth

- *Code of Federal Regulations*—federal government publication of all agency rules
- Licensing—role in which an agency screens businesses before permitting operation
- Inspections—administrative agency role of checking businesses and business sites for compliance

How do agencies pass rules?

- Enabling legislation creates the agency and/or the general outline of the law and enforcement
  - Agency conducts a study to determine need and basis for a proposed rule
  - Agency publishes proposed rule in *Federal Register* and industry and trade publications
  - Public comment period—period in rulemaking process when any individual or business can provide input on proposed regulations; generally is 30 days
- Promulgation—approval of proposed rules by heads of agencies

How do agencies enforce the law?

- Consent decree—settlement (*nolo contendere* plea) of charges brought by an administrative agency
- Administrative law judge (ALJ)—overseer of hearing on charges brought by administrative agency

Key Terms

administrative agency *111*
administrative law
   judge (ALJ) *126*
Administrative Procedures Act
   (APA) *114*
arbitrary and capricious *121*
Code of Federal Regulations 115
complaint *125*
consent decree *126*
enabling act *116*
exhausting administrative
   remedies *126*

Federal Privacy Act
   (FPA) *114*
Federal Register 115
Federal Register Act
   (FRA) *115*
Federal Register System *115*
FOIA request *114*
formal rulemaking *116*
Freedom of Information Act
   (FOIA) *114*
Government in the Sunshine
   Act *115*

hearing examiner/hearing
   officer *126*
hybrid rulemaking *116*
informal rulemaking *116*
injunction *126*
intervenors *126*
nolo contendere 126
open meeting law *115*
public comment period *117*
Regulatory Flexibility Act *117*
U.S. Government Manual 115
ultra vires 122

Questions and Problems

1. Residents of New York City who were receiving financial aid under the federally assisted program of Aid to Families with Dependent Children (AFDC) brought a class-action suit alleging that the New York officials responsible for the administration of the program were terminating aid to them without notice of the termination or without a hearing prior to the termination. The residents challenged the actions of the state officials as violative of their constitutional right to due process. The procedures for termination changed after the complaints of these residents, and notices and hearings were provided. What types of procedures would be necessary to protect the residents' due process rights? Must a court afford these procedures? [*Goldberg* v. *Kelly*, 397 U.S. 254 (1970).]

2. In 1979, Congress passed the Chrysler Corporation Loan Guarantee Act to keep the Chrysler Corporation in business and out of bankruptcy. The act established the Chrysler Corporation Loan Guarantee Board, made up of top federal officials, to oversee Chrysler's bailout. The meetings of this board necessarily involved sensitive discussions about Chrysler and its status. Would the meetings be covered under the Sunshine Act and thus open to the public? [*Symons* v. *Chrysler Corp. Loan Guarantee*, 670 F.2d 238 (D.C. 1981).]

3. Because of overcrowded conditions at the nation's airports during the late 1960s, the Federal Aviation Administration (FAA) promulgated a regulation to reduce takeoff and landing delays at airports by limiting the number of landing and takeoff slots at five major airports to 60 slots per hour. The airports were Kennedy, LaGuardia, O'Hare, Newark, and National. At National Airport (Washington), 40 of the 60 slots were given to commercial planes, and the commercial carriers allocated the slots among themselves until October 1980. In 1980, New York Air, a new airline, requested some of the 40 slots, but the existing airlines refused to give up any. The secretary of transportation, in response and "to avoid chaos in the skies" during the upcoming holidays, proposed a rule to allocate the slots at National. The allocation rule was proposed on October 16, 1980, and appeared in the *Federal Register* on October 20, 1980. The comment period was seven days starting from the October 16, 1980, proposal date. The airlines and others submitted a total of 37 comments to the secretary. However, Northwest Airlines filed suit on grounds that the APA required a minimum of 30 days for a public comment period. The secretary argued that the 30-day rule was being suspended for good cause (the holiday season was upon them). Who is correct?

Should an exception be made, or should the FAA be required to follow the 30-day rule? [*Northwest Airlines, Inc.* v. *Goldschmidt*, 645 F.2d 1309 (8th Cir. 1981).]

4. Read the following excerpt from the *Wall Street Journal.*

The smell of the greasepaint and the roar of the crowd, indeed.

The circus of yesteryear, loved by children and fondly remembered by older folk, keeps running smack into the modern world. In 1992, tents must fall within local fire codes. If the clown isn't a U.S. citizen, he had better have a valid work visa along with his makeup kit and big false nose. And the kid who wants to run away from home and join the circus? Forget it. . . .

Consider Carson & Barnes, the last of the five-ring road shows. The circus is traveling an 18-state route this year, from March 21 to Nov. 15, doing one-night stands. Each morning, about 200 performers and other employees, 150 animals, 80 trucks roll into town. Roustabouts race to erect the "Biggest Big Top On Earth." The circus performs two shows, packs, goes to sleep, rises at dawn and heads for the next stop.

With scheduling tight, satisfying the local tests is no mean feat. The 237 small towns where the circus is performing this year all usually require about half a dozen permits, with regulations varying from place to place.

This summer, the circus's soft-drink concession got shut down briefly because of bad water. An Illinois inspector found a high bacteria count and sent word to Wisconsin, so the water flunked inspection in Racine and Jefferson. . . .

If a sucker isn't born every minute, it is true that people are easily fooled and that can cause the circus trouble. While his circus was crossing Texas this year, someone complained about the stunt Argentine acrobat Sulliana Montes de Oca does with her French poodle. The dog sits on a platform as Ms. Montes de Oca appears to execute a handstand on the poor dog's head.

It's an illusion, of course, but a local inspector even came out to investigate an abuse complaint, circus officials say. They showed him the steel rod the circus crowd doesn't see that actually supports Ms. Montes de Oca when she does the trick. Dave Brandt, the show's press agent, says, "Who would ever think a nine-pound French poodle can hold up a 90-pound woman?" . . .

Local officials worry about the welfare of children as well as animals. About half a century ago, the Miller family circus actually did hire some young teenagers. And local kids willing to help set up the show got in free. But child-labor laws and insurance policy problems have put a stop to that. Applicants must be 18.

Nevertheless, Carson & Barnes has problems even with the only minors it does employ—those who perform in acts with their parents. Last year, California inspectors demanded that 14-year-old Dulce Vital quit holding target balloons for her father's archery act. Though the act is risky and Ms. Vital is young, she knew the routine. When she was replaced in Desert Hot Springs by a 19-year-old stand-in, Isabel Macias, the new girl caught an arrow in the forehead and today has a scar to show for it.

Then there is the foreign-performer problem. Carson & Barnes employs about 80 Latin Americans a year, and tangles for months with immigration officials to get papers for them. Last year, temporary-visa applications for the Chimals, a Mexican family of acrobats, got lost in the bureaucracy, say circus officials. The up-shot: For 10 days, the circus performed with an empty ring.

Certain towns make it harder on Carson & Barnes than others. "The fire marshall from hell is here today," reads the general manager's journal entry for Ojai, Calif. The fireman was concerned, among other things, that the inspector's ID number wasn't printed on fire extinguishers.

The hang-up forced the gathering afternoon audience to wait in the hot sun while circus officials jumped through hoops. Finally, at showtime, the fireman was willing to let the show go on if one fire extinguisher could be shown to function properly. One was tested, it worked, and the circus started half-an-hour late. . . .

Source: "Bunting & Red Tape: The Modern Circus Walks a High Wire," by Barbara Marsh, *Wall Street Journal*, August 31, 1992, pp. A1, A4. Reprinted by permission of The Wall Street Journal, © 1992 Dow Jones & Company, Inc. via the Copyright Clearance Center.

Is too much regulation exerted upon the circus? Is all the regulation necessary? Why do you think the regulations that apply to circuses resulted?

5. San Diego Air Sports Center (SDAS) operates a sports parachuting business in Otay Mesa, California. SDAS offers training to beginning parachutists and facilitates recreational jumping for experienced

parachutists. Most SDAS jumps occur at altitudes in excess of 5,800 feet.

The jump zone used by SDAS overlaps the San Diego Traffic Control Area (TCA). Although the aircraft carrying the parachutists normally operate outside the TCA, the parachutists themselves are dropped through it. Thus, each jump must be approved by the air traffic controllers.

In July 1987, an air traffic controller in San Diego filed an Unsatisfactory Condition Report complaining of the strain that parachuting was putting on the controllers and raising safety concerns. The report led to a staff study of parachute jumping within the San Diego TCA. In October 1987, representatives of the San Diego Terminal Radar Approach Control (TRACON) facility met with SDAS operators. In December 1987, the San Diego TRACON sent to SDAS a draft letter of agreement outlining agreed-upon procedures and coordination requirements. Nonetheless, the San Diego TRACON conducted another study between January 14, 1988, and February 11, 1988, and about two months after the draft letter was sent, the San Diego TRACON withdrew it.

San Diego TRACON assured SDAS that it would be invited to attend all meetings on parachuting in the San Diego TCA. However, SDAS was not informed of or invited to any meetings.

In March 1988, the Federal Aviation Administration (FAA) sent a letter to SDAS informing SDAS that "[e]ffective immediately parachute jumping within or into the San Diego TCA in the Otay Reservoir Jump Zone will not be authorized." The FAA stated that the letter was final and appealable.

SDAS challenged the letter in federal court on grounds that it constituted rulemaking without compliance with required APA procedures. Evaluate SDAS's challenge to the letter by applying administrative law and procedure. [*San Diego Air Sports Center, Inc.* v. *Federal Aviation Administration*, 887 F.2d 966 (9th Cir. 1989)]

Understanding "Consider" Problems

5.1

THINK: You have learned that there are three branches of government: executive, legislative, and judicial. The administrative agency is part of the executive branch and is granted its authority through the legislation Congress passed. The three-branch structure was created as a means of applying checks and balances.

APPLY: One branch of government (the executive in the form of the agency) was working through its

processes for making laws. The proposed regulations may have their difficulties, but the branches do not reverse each other without following processes.

ANSWER: The Senate passed a resolution because it did not want to revoke an agency's authority in the midst of a rulemaking procedure. The objections could be heard loud and clear from the businesses affected. The resolution was a way of sending a signal without violating the jurisdiction, province, and processes of each of the branches. Businesses, as you learned in

Chapter 4, can have political influence on elected officials by lobbying, donations, and simply by expressing views. The resolution was the result of businesses going to the legislative body that created the agency and asking for some form of action. This situation illustrates how important business and industry involvement is in both the rulemaking and legislative processes.

5.2

THINK: The decision in the *State Farm* case was that pending rules could not be revoked unless an agency followed the same types of processes used for promulgating rules. That process requires public disclosure of the intent to revoke the rule and a public comment period.

APPLY: In this case study, the Department of the Interior has proposed postponing the implementation of a regulation on snowmobiling. While the action taken by the agency is slightly different, a revocation versus a postponement, the agencies in both cases are doing so without notice or comment and without input from those affected.

ANSWER: The NPS cannot simply withdraw a rule. It must consider evidence, propose the withdrawal or postponement, and take comments. An agency cannot reverse a process unilaterally midstream. Ms. Mainella's recommendation is relevant because she is trying to steer the Department of Interior back to the basics of the APA, which requires an agency to base its regulations on studies. [*The Fund for Animals* v. *Norton,* 294 F.Supp.2d 92 (D.C. 2003) (memorandum opinion) and 390 F.Supp.2d 12 (2005). Presently, use of snowmobiles in national parks continues under a 2004 series of regulations promulgated by the Department of the Interior. Objections by environmental groups continue, including calls for greater enforcement of the rules.]

6

International Law

Shakespeare was ahead of his time when he wrote that "the world is your oyster." Today's global business environment is the dream of economists, who have fostered the notion of free trade since the publication of Adam Smith's *The Wealth of Nations* more than two hundred years ago. Trade barriers are down, markets are interconnected, and even the smallest of businesses are involved in international trade. Trade across borders still involves additional issues and laws and carries risks that do not exist in transactions within nations. Businesses must understand the legal environment of international trade to enter into contracts and conduct operations in ways that minimize legal risks. This chapter covers the legal environment of international business. What laws affect businesses in international trade? What international agreements affect global businesses? What contract issues exist in international business? ■

update

For up-to-date legal news, click on "Author Updates" at

www.cengage.com/blaw/jennings

If a foreign country can supply us with a commodity cheaper than we ourselves can make it, better buy it of them with some part of our own industry, employed in a way in which we have some advantage.

ADAM SMITH

The Wealth of Nations

I don't believe you can run a major U.S. company from abroad. George III tried to run the United States from Britain and look what happened to him.

SIR GORDON WHITE

Chairman, Hanson Industries, Inc.

consider...

American Rice, Inc. (ARI), a Houston-based company, exports rice to foreign countries, including Haiti. Rice Corporation of Haiti, a wholly owned subsidiary of ARI, was incorporated in Haiti. Haiti assesses taxes based on the quantity and value of rice imported into the country. David Kay and Douglas Murphy, executives of ARI, were charged with violations of the Foreign Corrupt Practices Act (FCPA) for allegedly bribing Haitian officials to accept false bills of lading that reflected total rice imports to be about one-third of actual levels so that ARI would owe less in taxes. Is this type of an arrangement a bribe? Does it violate the FCPA?

Sources of International Law

"When in Rome, do as the Romans do" is advice that can be modified for business: When in Rome, follow Roman law. In each country where a business has operations, it must comply with the laws of that nation. Just as each U.S. business must comply with all the tax, employment, safety, and environmental laws of each state in which it operates, each international business must comply with the laws of the countries in which it operates.

TYPES OF INTERNATIONAL LAW SYSTEMS

The various systems of laws can be quite different, and businesses are well advised to obtain local legal counsel for advice on the peculiarities of each nation's laws. Generally, a nation's laws are based on one of three types of systems. The United States has a **common law** system. Like England, our laws are built on tradition and precedent (see Chapter 1). Not every possible situation is covered by a statute, or codified; we rely on our courts to interpret and apply our more general statutes.

Other countries rely on civil law or code law. This form of law is found in European nations that are not tied to England, and countries influenced through its colonial activities. France, Germany, Spain, and other countries with code law systems do not rely on court decisions but rely instead on statutes or codes that spell out the law so there is little need for interpretation.

A final system of law is Islamic law, which is followed in some form in 27 countries. Islamic legal systems are based on religious tenets and govern all aspects of life, from appropriate dress in public to remedies for contract breaches. Many Islamic countries have a combination of civil and Islamic systems that result from the influences of both colonization and Islam.

Before its collapse in the former Soviet Union and Eastern Europe, communism was also classified as a legal system. Now the former communist nations struggle within and as well as between each other as they grapple with evolving cultural, market, and governmental systems.

THE ROOTS OF COMMERCE AND LAW: NONSTATUTORY SOURCES OF INTERNATIONAL LAW

Customs and values in a culture affect negotiations, contracts, and performance in international business. The American Bar Association recommends that business-people and their lawyers examine seven cultural factors and do background work in these cultural areas before doing business in a particular country. Referred to as the LESCANT factors, the cultural areas to understand before doing business in a country are language, environment and technology, social organization, contex-ting, authority, nonverbal behavior, and time concept.

Most of the LESCANT factors are self-explanatory, but contexting and time have some nuances for business. Low-context cultures are those that rely on the written word as the controlling factor in their relationship. Low-context cultures give little weight to the circumstances or context in which that agreement is reached. Low-context cultures include the North American countries, Switzerland, Germany, and the Scandinavian countries (although not Finland). Midlevel-context cultures are France, England, and Italy; high-context cultures are the Latin American countries, Arabic nations, and Asian countries, including Japan. In high-context cultures, how and in what setting an agreement is reached are as important as the words in the document itself.

Time concepts differ across countries. The United States is a monochronic nation: Time is everything, and the goal of businesspeople is to get the deal done. Other monochronic nations include Great Britain, Germany, Canada, New Zealand, Australia, the Netherlands, Norway, and Sweden. Countries that operate with great flexibility in time and negotiate with the goal of building a relationship as opposed to completing a deal are called polychronic nations. The remainder of the world operates within this flexible form of time culture.

CONTRACTS FOR THE INTERNATIONAL SALE OF GOODS (CISG)

Sometimes referred to as the Vienna Convention, the United Nations Convention on Contracts for the International Sale of Goods (CISG) began its development in 1964. Following years of discussion and changes, the CISG first became effective in 1988 with its adoption in the United States along with a small group of other countries. Today, CISG has been adopted in 60 countries, with ratification processes under way in many other countries.

The CISG provides for international contracts the convenience and uniformity that the Uniform Commercial Code provides for contracts across state lines in the United States. Although there are some differences (see details in Chapter 10), the CISG is a reflection of the Uniform Commercial Code.

TREATIES, TRADE ORGANIZATIONS, AND CONTROLS ON INTERNATIONAL TRADE

In international trade, a number of treaties, tariffs, and organizations affect inter-national contracts. This section discusses some of the most important ones.

The WTO

In 1994, the General Agreement on Tariffs and Trade (GATT), a **multilateral treaty** (a treaty among more than two nations), was adopted. WTO lists 150 countries as members. GATT established the World Trade Organization (WTO). The WTO is the body charged with the administration and achievement of GATT's objectives. GATT's primary objectives are trade without discrimination and protection through tariffs. Trade without discrimination is achieved through GATT's most-favored-nation clause. The issue of China's membership as a most favored nation was debated extensively, particularly along with the political and social context of human rights issues in that country, prior to its admission in 2001.[1]

Under the most-favored-nation (MFN) clause, subscribing countries treat each other equally in terms of import and export duties and charges. Subscribing countries do not give more favorable treatment to one country as opposed to another. Domestic production is protected by tariffs and not through any other commercial measures.

The WTO has also established a Dispute Settlement Body (DSB), which is an international arbitration body created to bring countries together to resolve trade disputes rather than have those nations resort to trade sanctions. If a WTO panel finds that a country has violated the provisions of GATT, it can impose trade sanctions on that country. The sanctions imposed are generally equal to the amount of economic injury the country caused through its violation of GATT.

European Union (EU)

The European Economic Community (EEC) was created by the Treaty of Rome and was formerly known as the Common Market; it was called the European Community (EC) for a time but is now known as the European Union (EU). The EU 15 members are Austria, Belgium, Denmark, Finland, France, Germany, Greece, Ireland, Italy, Luxembourg, the Netherlands, Portugal, Spain, Sweden, and the United Kingdom. Member states include Bulgaria, Cyprus, Czech Republic, Estonia, Hungary, Latvia, Lithuania, Malta, Poland, Romania, Slovakia, and Slovenia. Candidate countries include Croatia, Macedonia, and Turkey.

Under the Single European Act, the EU, in an effort to provide for the free flow of goods, services, and human and financial capital, eliminated internal barriers to trade. The Maastricht Treaty (treaty on the European Union signed in Maastricht, the Netherlands) set the goals of the EU as single monetary and fiscal policies (including a common currency), common foreign policies, and cooperation in the administration of justice.

In addition, the EU has undertaken the ambitious goals of uniformity in laws, with proposals on product liability and litigation for member countries to ensure uniform costs and results. The EU has progressed to the point of having some enforceable international law. For example, the EU has created the European Commission, which has the authority to issue regulations and decisions that are binding on all EU members. The goal of the EU is to build one market of 340 million consumers. As of January 1999, the EU had its single currency, the euro.

In addition to the European Commission, the EU has created other institutions to assist it in carrying out its goal of unified European commercial operations. The European Council, which consists of the heads of state of the various members, is the policy-making body and establishes the broad directives for the operation of the EU. Beneath the Council is the European Commission, the body charged with implementation of the Council policies. At the third level is the European Parliament, an advisory legislative body with some veto powers. Finally, the European Court of Justice (ECJ) is the judicial body created to handle disputes and any violations of regulations and the EU treaty itself. The EU has nearly 300 directives that govern everything from health and safety standards in the workplace to the sale of mutual funds across national boundaries.

The North American Free Trade Agreement (NAFTA)

The North American Free Trade Agreement (NAFTA) is a treaty among Canada, the United States, and Mexico, effective in 1994, with a goal of eliminating all tariffs among the three countries in their trade over a 15-year period.

Products covered under NAFTA include only those that originate in these countries. All goods traded across the boundaries of these countries must carry a NAFTA certificate of origin, which verifies the original creation of the goods in that country from which they are being exported. NAFTA has eliminated nearly all of the barriers to trade among these three nations. However, NAFTA is unlike EU in that a common labor market, governing body, and currency were not created.

Prohibitions on Trade: Individual Nation Sanctions

In some countries, international tensions have resulted in trade sanctions being imposed so that commerce with certain nations is prohibited. Countries can impose two types of trade sanctions. With primary trade sanctions, companies based in the United States are prohibited from doing business with certain countries. For example, the United States prohibited trade with Iraq at the time of the 1991 Gulf War. The U.S. began lifting those sanctions in 2003, following the UN's lifting of its sanctions. Primary boycotts can be limited to certain categories of goods. The status of "most favored nation" in trade (MFN) means that the country has no restrictions on the types of goods and services that can be imported and exported.

The second form of trade prohibition is the secondary boycott, which is a step beyond the primary boycott in that companies from other nations doing business with a sanctioned country will also experience sanctions for such activity. For example, in 1996, the United States passed the Iran and Libya Sanctions Act (ILSA) as a secondary boycott against two nations against which the United States already had imposed trade restrictions. This law was passed because of active lobbying by the families of those killed when Pan Am Flight 103 exploded over Lockerbie, Scotland, as a result of bombs planted on the flight by Libyan terrorists. Under the secondary boycott trade prohibition, the United States will not grant licenses to, permit its financial institutions to loan money to, award government contracts to, or allow imports from any company that finances, supplies, or constructs oil procurement in Iran or Libya.

The International Monetary Fund (IMF) and the World Bank

Created at Bretton Woods, New Hampshire, the International Monetary Fund (IMF) was established following World War II with the goal of expanding international trade through a bank with a lending system designed to bring stability to national currencies. The IMF created the International Bank for Reconstruction and Development (commonly called the World Bank), which allows signing nations to have Special Drawing Rights (SDR) or the ability to draw on a line of credit in order to maintain the stability of their currency.

The Kyoto Treaty

The Kyoto Protocol, often called the Kyoto Treaty or the global-warming treaty, is a 24-page document that focuses on the reduction of greenhouse gas emissions. The treaty requires signatory countries to reduce emissions "by at least 5% below 1990 levels." The United States, which would be required to reduce its emissions by at least 7 percent below 1990 levels, has not signed the treaty. China, India, and Mexico are excluded from the treaty's coverage. For more information on the Kyoto Treaty, see Chapter 19.

OPEC

The Organization of Petroleum Exporting Countries (OPEC) is a cartel that works together to control oil supplies and production, prices, and taxes. The result of the OPEC cooperation has been increased royalties to those participating countries.

TRUST, CORRUPTION, TRADE, AND ECONOMICS

Perhaps the greatest activity in multilateral agreements among countries has been in the area of curbing bribes because of their devastating impact on trust and the resulting effects on the investment and economic environments of a country. In his departure speech as secretary of the U.S. Treasury, Robert Rubin cautioned government employees to never accept any sort of gift as part of their duties for, he noted, "Corruption and bribery benefit a few at the expense of many."

The Foreign Corrupt Practices Act

U.S. firms that operate internationally are subject to the requirements and prohibitions of the **Foreign Corrupt Practices Act** (FCPA; 15 U.S.C. §§ 78dd-1). The FCPA applies to business concerns that have their principal offices in the United States. It contains antibribery provisions as well as accounting controls for these firms, and it is meant to curb the use of bribery in foreign operations of companies.

The act prohibits making, authorizing, or promising payments or gifts of money or anything of value with the intent to corrupt for the purpose of *obtaining* or *retaining business* for or with, or *directing business*. Under the FCPA, payments designed to influence the official acts of foreign officials, political parties, party officials, candidates for office, any nongovernmental organization (NGO), or any person who will transmit the gift or money to one of the other types of persons are prohibited. Changes in 1998 added the NGO coverage so that foreign officials are now defined to include public international figures, such as officials with the United Nations or the IMF.

First passed in 1977, the FCPA is the result of an SEC investigation that uncovered questionable foreign payments by large stock issuers who were based in the United States. Approximately 435 U.S. corporations had made improper or questionable payments totaling $300 million in Japan, the Netherlands, and Korea. A violation of the FCPA results when there has been payment or something of value given to a foreign official with discretionary authority, a foreign political candidate, or a foreign political party for the purpose of getting the recipient to act or refrain from acting to help business operations or, under the 1998 amendments, to "secure any improper advantage" in doing business in that country. For example, if a U.S. company trying to win a bid on a contract for the construction of highways in a foreign country paid a government official there who was responsible for awarding such construction contracts a "consulting fee" of $25,000, the U.S. company would be in violation of the FCPA. The payment was of money, it was made to a foreign official, and it was made for the purpose of obtaining business within that country.

When the FCPA was first passed, many companies tried to find ways around the bribery prohibitions. Companies would hire foreign agents or consultants to help them gain business in countries and allow these "third parties" to act independently. However, many of these consultants then paid bribers who then bribed the government officials. Under the FCPA, even these types of arrangements can constitute a violation if the consulting fees are high, there are odd payment arrangements, or the company has reason to know of a potential or actual violation. Companies must be able to establish that they have performed "due diligence" in investigating those hired as their agents and consultants in foreign countries. For example, if a U.S. company hired a consultant who charged the company $25,000 in fees and $250,000 in expenses, the U.S. company is, under Justice Department guidelines, on notice that the excessive expenses could signal potential bribes being paid. These types of expenses are known as "red flags" for U.S. companies. The Justice Department uses this information as a means of establishing intent even when the company may not know precisely what was done with the funds and what was paid to whom.

Payments to any foreign official for **facilitation**, often referred to as **grease payments**, are not prohibited under FCPA so long as these payments are made only to get these officials to do their normal jobs that they might not do or would do slowly without some payment. These grease payments can be made for obtaining permits, licenses, or other official documents; processing governmental papers, such as visas and work orders; providing police protection and mail pickup and delivery; providing phone service, power, and water supply; loading and unloading cargo, or protecting perishable products; and scheduling inspections associated with contract performance or transit of goods across the country.

> **Business Planning Tip**
>
> Monitor payments made to agents in other countries. Often their compensation is used to pay government officials in violation of the FCPA. Know your agents and know where and how they spend the money.

Penalties for violations of the FCPA can run up to $250,000 per violation and five years' imprisonment for individuals. Corporate fines are up to $2 million per violation. Also, under the **Alternative Fines Act (AFA)**, the Justice Department can obtain two times the benefit that the bribe attempted to gain, known as disgorgement. For example, if a company paid a bribe to obtain a $100 million contract for computer services for a foreign government, the potential fine, using the AFA, could be $200 million. Penalties for violating the books and records requirements retention of the FCPA are up to $5,000,000 and 20 years for individuals and up to $25,000,000 for corporations. The Justice Department can use the Alternate Fines Act to obtain civil penalties for violation of the FCPA. The largest FCPA penalty was paid by Titan Corporation following its voluntary disclosure of payments to an agent in Benin who then passed the funds along to the reelection campaign of the president of Benin. Titan then received an increase in its management fees for its operation of the telecommunications system in Benin. The payments were uncovered as Lockheed Martin was conducting due diligence for purposes of a merger with Titan. Titan paid a total of $28.5 million as follows: $13 million criminal penalty, $12.6 million disgorgement (benefit), and $2.9 million in interest. Titan had no previous violations.

U.S. v. *Kay* (Case 6.1) answers the chapter's opening Consider and deals with a violation of the FCPA.

CASE 6.1

U.S. v. *Kay*
359 F.3d 738 (5th Cir. 2004)

THROWING THE RICE MARKET AND DODGING TAXES

FACTS

David Kay (defendant) was an American citizen and a vice president for marketing of American Rice, Inc. (ARI), who was responsible for supervising sales and marketing in the Republic of Haiti. Douglas Murphy

(defendant) was an American citizen and president of ARI.

Beginning in 1995 and continuing to about August 1999, Mr. Kay, Mr. Murphy, and other employees and officers of ARI paid bribes and authorized the payment of bribes to induce customs officials in Haiti to accept bills of lading that intentionally understated the true amount of rice that ARI shipped to Haiti for import. With less rice, ARI and RCH had to pay less in customs duties to the Haitian government. ARI reported only approximately 66 percent of the rice it sold in Haiti and saved significant sales taxes.

Mr. Kay directed employees of ARI to prepare two sets of shipping documents for each shipment of rice to Haiti, one that accurately reflected and another that falsely represented the weight and value of the rice being exported to Haiti.

In 2001, a grand jury charged Mr. Kay and Mr. Murphy with 12 counts of FCPA violations. Both Mr. Kay and Mr. Murphy moved to dismiss the indictment for the failure to state an offense, arguing that obtaining favorable tax treatment did not fall within the FCPA definition of payments made to government officials in order to obtain business. The district court dismissed the indictment, and the United States of America ("government") (appellant) appealed.

JUDICIAL OPINION

WIENER, Circuit Judge

[H]ow attenuated can the linkage be between the effects of that which is sought from the foreign official in consideration of a bribe (here, tax minimization) and the briber's goal of finding assistance or obtaining or retaining foreign business with or for some person, and still satisfy the business nexus element of the FCPA?

Obviously, a commercial concern that bribes a foreign government official to award a construction, supply, or services contract violates the statute. Yet, there is little difference between this example and that of a corporation's lawfully obtaining a contract from an honest official or agency by submitting the lowest bid, and—either before or after doing so—bribing a different government official to reduce taxes and thereby ensure that the under-bid venture is nevertheless profitable. Avoiding or lowering taxes reduces operating costs and thus increases profit margins, thereby freeing up funds that the business is otherwise legally obligated to expend. And this, in turn, enables it to take any number of actions to the disadvantage of competitors. Bribing foreign officials to lower taxes and customs duties certainly can provide an unfair advantage over competitors and thereby be of assistance to the payor in obtaining or retaining business.

. . . we cannot hold as a matter of law that Congress meant to limit the FCPA's applicability to cover only bribes that lead directly to the award or renewal of contracts. Instead, we hold that Congress intended for the FCPA to apply broadly to payments intended to assist the payor, either directly or indirectly, in obtaining or retaining business for some person, and that bribes paid to foreign tax officials to secure illegally reduced customs and tax liability constitute a type of payment that can fall within this broad coverage. In 1977, Congress was motivated to prohibit rampant foreign bribery by domestic business entities, but nevertheless understood the pragmatic need to exclude innocuous grease payments from the scope of its proposals. The FCPA's legislative history instructs that Congress was concerned about both the kind of bribery that leads to discrete contractual arrangements and the kind that more generally helps a domestic payor obtain or retain business for some person in a foreign country; and that Congress was aware that this type includes illicit payments made to officials to obtain favorable but unlawful tax treatment.

[W]e conclude that bribes paid to foreign officials in consideration for unlawful evasion of customs duties and sales taxes could fall within the purview of the FCPA's proscription. We hasten to add, however, that this conduct does not automatically constitute a violation of the FCPA: It still must be shown that the bribery was intended to produce an effect—here, through tax savings—that would "assist in obtaining or retaining business."

Reversed and remanded.

CASE QUESTIONS

1. What benefit did ARI obtain and how? Does the payment of money to government officials here meet the spirit and intent of the FCPA?

2. Why do Mr. Kay and Mr. Murphy argue that the FCPA does not apply to their conduct?

3. What does the appellate court look at in order to reach its conclusion?

consider 6.1

A Philip Morris subsidiary, C. A. Tabacalera National, and a B.A.T. subsidiary known as C. A. Cigarrera Bigott entered into a contract with La Fundacion del Nino (the Children's Foundation) of Caracas, Venezuela. The agreement was signed on behalf of the foundation

CONTINUED

by the foundation's president, who also was the wife of the then-president of Venezuela. Under the terms of the agreement, these two tobacco firms were to make periodic donations to the Children's Foundation totaling $12.5 million. In exchange, the two firms would receive price controls on Venezuelan tobacco, elimination of controls on retail cigarette prices in Venezuela, tax deductions for donations, and assurances that the existing tax rates applicable to tobacco companies would not be increased.

Is the donation to the charity a violation of the FCPA? (Analysis appears at the end of the chapter.) [*Lamb* v. *Philip Morris, Inc.*, 915 F.2d 1024 (6th Cir. 1990); *cert. denied*, 498 U.S. 1086 (1995)]

. . . .

A survey by the U.S. Government Accounting Office of the companies affected by the FCPA found that the ability of companies from other countries to bribe officials did not give them a competitive advantage. The survey found that U.S. trade increased in 51 of 56 foreign countries after the FCPA went into effect. The increase was attributed to the position adopted by U.S. companies with respect to their competitors—if they could not bribe government officials, they would disclose publicly any information about bribes made by any of the companies from other nations.

ethical *issues*

PriceWaterhouseCoopers is one of the United States' "Big 4" accounting firms. PwC, as it is known, has had a tax practice in Russia since the time that country changed from Communist rule. One of PwC's clients in Russia was Yukos, a major Russian oil company that is now bankrupt.

Russia's Federal Tax Service, an agency similar to the U.S.'s IRS, has filed suit against PwC, alleging that it concealed tax evasion by Yukos for the years 2002–2004. The Tax Service also announced a criminal probe of PwC's conduct with regard to its tax services for Yukos. Tax Service agents searched PwC's offices in Moscow and questioned PwC employees about the Yukos account. Yukos lost its tax case and has paid $9.2 million in charges for the nonpayment of taxes. However, Yukos and PwC have the case on appeal.

Many see the battle between PwC and the Tax Service as part of the Russian government's ongoing battle to sell of the assets of Yukos and avoid the surrender of the company's assets to investors and creditors who have filed claims. Those suits are pending in courts in The Hague. Some analysts believe that the Russian government is hoping to press PwC into revealing information that would help it take back the Yukos assets.

If PwC is found to have engaged in evasion it loses its license to do business in Russia, and if it turns over information it is likely to lose its clients in Russia.

What issues should a company consider before doing business in an economically developing country? What are the risks? Did this ethical dilemma begin long before the Russian government's demands of PwC? What international law, culture, and ethical issues should a company consider before deciding to do business in another country?

Source: Neil Buckley and Catherine Belton, "Moscow raids PwC ahead of Yukos case," *Financial Times*, March 11, 2007, p. 1.

There are three international bodies that have adopted conventions against bribery. The Council of Europe has its Criminal Law Convention on Corruption. The United Nations has its Convention against Corruption. Finally, the **Organization for Economic Cooperation and Development (OECD)** is the most active supporter of the already existing U.S. position on bribery, and its member countries are enacting legislation for compliance with its international pact against bribery. The OECD's Convention on Combating Bribery of Foreign Public Officials in International Business Transactions has been accepted by its 30 member nations and 6 other countries.[2] The result is that some form of the FCPA that meets OECD standards has been passed in those individual countries.[3]

The convention basically adopts the standards of the United States under the FCPA and requires nations signing the agreement to, among other things: (1) criminalize bribery of foreign public officials, (2) criminalize government officials soliciting requesting bribes, (3) seize or confiscate bribes and bribe proceeds (i.e., net profit), (4) prohibit the establishment of off-the-books accounts and similar practices used to bribe foreign public officials or to hide such bribery, and (5) pledge to work together to provide legal assistance relating to investigations and proceedings and to make bribery of foreign public officials an extraditable offense. In 1998, the United States became the first country to pass implementing procedures and remains active in enforcement with 84 investigations in 2007.

Resolution of International Disputes

As discussed in Chapters 1 and 3, there really is no way to enforce international laws. The International Court of Justice established by the United Nations is a court of voluntary jurisdiction for disputes between nations; it is not a court for the resolution of business disputes between nations. More and more companies and individuals favor arbitration to resolve disputes. The London Commercial Court is viewed as a neutral forum with highly experienced judges who are also experienced commercial litigators.

Principles of International Law

Some principles of international law apply to all countries and people in the international marketplace. The principles of international law affect the decisions and operations of businesses, regardless of the availability of court resolution of rights.

SOVEREIGN IMMUNITY

The concept of **sovereign immunity** is based on the notion that each country is a sovereign nation. Each country is an equal with other countries; each country has exclusive jurisdiction over its internal operations, laws, and people; and no country is subject to the jurisdiction of another country's court system unless it so consents. Our court system cannot be used to right injustices in other countries or to subject other countries to penalties. For example, in *Schooner Exchange* v. *McFaddon*, 7 Cr. 116 (1812), a group of American citizens attempted to seize the vessel *Exchange* when it came into port at Philadelphia because the citizens believed that the ship had been taken improperly on the high seas by the French emperor Napoleon and that the ship rightfully belonged to them. The U.S. Supreme Court held that the ship could not be seized because sovereign immunity applied, and France could not involuntarily be subjected to the jurisdiction of U.S. courts.

The Foreign Sovereign Immunities Act of 1976 clarified the U.S. government's position on sovereign immunity and incorporated the *Schooner Exchange* doctrine. Not only are countries immune, but the act also adds a clarification to the concept of sovereign immunity of sovereign nations for illegal acts. For example, in *Argentine Republic* v. *Amerada Hess Shipping Co.*, 488 U.S. 428 (1989), the Supreme Court dismissed a suit brought in a U.S. federal court by a Liberian-chartered commercial ship company against the government of Argentina for its unprovoked and illegal attack on a company ship that was in neutral waters when the war between Great Britain and Argentina broke out over the Falkland Islands. The attack by the Argentine navy was unprovoked and in clear violation of international law. However, the U.S. Supreme Court clarified that under the Sovereign Immunities Act and principles of international law, all sovereign nations are immune from suits in other countries, even for those acts—like that of Argentina's—that are clear violations of international law.

A distinction has been made, however, by both the Foreign Sovereign Immunities Act and the courts with respect to the commercial transactions of a sovereign nation. For example, the sale of services and goods; loan transactions; and contracts for marketing, public relations, and employment services entered into by a country are, in essence, voluntary agreements that subject that country's government to civil suits in another nation's courts according to the terms of the agreement or according to the basic tenets of judicial jurisdiction (see Chapter 3). *Riedel* v. *Bancam* (Case 6.2) deals with an issue of nation sovereign immunity.

CASE 6.2

Riedel v. *Bancam*
792 F.2d 587 (6th Cir. 1986)

PESOS TO DOLLARS: EXCHANGE RATES CAN KILL INVESTMENTS

FACTS

W. Christian Riedel, a resident of Ohio, had an account with Unibanco, S. A., and asked that it transfer $100,000 to Banca Metropolitana, S. A. (Bamesa) (predecessor to Bancam) for investment in a certificate of deposit (CD). Bamesa merged with another bank to form Bancam, and Mr. Riedel's CD was renewed with the newly merged bank.

Shortly after Mr. Riedel's renewal, the government of Mexico issued new rules governing accounts from foreigners in Mexican banks. The rules required the banks to pay the CDs in pesos at a rate that was substantially below exchange rates. A month after these rules were put into effect, Bancam was nationalized.

When Mr. Riedel's CD came due, the exchange rate was 74.34 pesos to the dollar. He was paid $53,276.23 for his $100,000 investment.

Mr. Riedel brought suit in a U.S. federal district court, alleging that Bancam had violated both federal and Ohio securities laws in selling the CDs in the United States without registration. Bancam filed a motion to dismiss the suit on the ground that the Sovereign Immunities Act of 1976 precluded U.S. courts from taking jurisdiction over the matter. Bancam also claimed protection under the act of state doctrine. The district court dismissed Mr. Riedel's suit on the grounds that it lacked jurisdiction over the claims under Ohio law and also on grounds of sovereign immunity and the act of state doctrine. Mr. Riedel appealed.

JUDICIAL OPINION

KENNEDY, Circuit Judge

Since the Government of Mexico nationalized Bancam on September 1, 1982, Bancam qualifies as an "agency or instrumentality of a foreign state" under 28 U.S.C. § 1603(b)(2). Therefore, this action involves an Ohio citizen and a "foreign state" as a defendant. Consequently, 28 U.S.C. § 1332(a)(4) does not apply. Accordingly, we hold that the District Court properly concluded that it did not have jurisdiction under 28 U.S.C. § 1332 over the breach of contract and Ohio securities law claims.

We conclude, however, that the District Court may have had jurisdiction over the breach of contract and Ohio securities law claims under the [Foreign Sovereign Immunities Act (FSIA) 28 U.S.C. § 1330]. Although the FSIA ordinarily entitles foreign states to immunity from federal jurisdiction, 28 U.S.C. § 1605(a)(2) creates a "commercial activity" exception to this immunity.

The "act of state doctrine" precludes courts in this country from questioning the validity and effect of a sovereign act of a foreign nation performed in its own territory. . . .

Under the "act of state doctrine," courts exercise jurisdiction but prudentially "decline to decide the merits of the case if in doing so we would need to judge the validity of the public acts of a sovereign state performed within its own territory."

Since the District Court may have had the subject matter jurisdiction, we remand the Ohio securities law claim for further proceedings consistent with this opinion. We also note that even if the District Court concludes that it has subject matter jurisdiction, Bancam has also argued that the District Court does not have personal jurisdiction. Assuming that the District Court decides that it has subject matter jurisdiction under the FSIA, the District Court will also have to make findings of fact to determine whether Bancam has sufficient "contacts" with the United States to satisfy due process.

Reversed in part.

CASE QUESTIONS

1. Describe Mr. Riedel's investment and its fate as well as the bases for his suit against Bancam in Ohio.

2. Does the act of state doctrine apply? What is different about this situation from an act of the Mexican government that applies to banks in Mexico?

3. What issues will the court be determining when the case is remanded and why?

PROTECTIONS FOR U.S. PROPERTY AND INVESTMENT ABROAD

The effect of nationalization and expropriation combined with the act of state doctrine and sovereign immunity is to chill U.S. investments in foreign countries. To discourage expropriation, the Foreign Assistance Act of 1962 contained what has been called the Hickenlooper amendment, which requires the president to suspend all forms of assistance to countries that have expropriated the property of U.S. citizens or regulated the property in such a way as to effectively deprive a U.S. citizen of it (through taxation or limits on use).

Many trade treaties that have been negotiated or are being negotiated with other countries contain protections against expropriation. Some treaties provide U.S. companies and investors with the same levels of protection as the citizens of those countries. For example, if a country affords its citizens due process before taking over private property, U.S. citizens and companies must be afforded those same protections prior to expropriation.

Finally, Congress has created a federal insurer for U.S. investments abroad. The Overseas Private Investment Corporation (OPIC) is an insurer for U.S. investment in those countries in which the per capita annual income is $250 or less. OPIC will pay damages for expropriation, for inability to convert the currency of the country, or for losses from war or revolution.

Consumer protections in other countries depend on those countries' laws. For example, many U.S. citizens have constructed luxury homes along the coast near Ensenada in Baja California. They did so because the land and construction were so much cheaper than in the United States that they could afford large, luxurious homes. However, the land on which many of the homes were located was the subject of 14 years of litigation and more than 60 court decisions over disputed ownership rights. With the Mexican Supreme Court's decision on land ownership, most of the current U.S. owners have been told that they must vacate their homes and leave everything behind. While there might be due process and property rights in the United States, the homeowners in Ensenada have no hope so long as the Mexican Supreme Court has declared the law for its country and land there.

REPATRIATION

Repatriation is the process of bringing back to your own country profits earned on investments in another country. In some nations, there are limits on repatriation; businesses can remove only a certain amount of the profits earned from the operations of a business within a country. Repatriation limits are considered acts of state and are immune from litigation in the United States.

Forum Non Conveniens, or "You Have the Wrong Court"

The doctrine of *forum non conveniens* is a principle of U.S. justice under which cases that are brought to the wrong court are dismissed. The doctrine allows judicial discretion whereby such issues as the location of the evidence, the location of the parties, and the location of the property that will be used to satisfy any judgment are examined. For example, when the Union Carbide disaster occurred at its Bhopal, India, plant, victims and families brought suit against Union Carbide in New York City. A U.S. court of appeals dismissed the case and sent it back to India on the grounds of *forum non conveniens* [*In re Union Carbide Corp. Gas Plant Disaster*, 809 F.2d 195 (2d Cir. 1987); *cert. denied*, 484 U.S. 871 (1987)].

Conflicts of Law

No two countries match in terms of the structure of their legal system or in their laws. For example, the law in the United States, codified by the widely adopted Uniform Commercial Code (UCC), is that all contracts and contract relationships are subject to a standard of good faith. In Canada, the good faith exists only if the parties place such a provision in their agreement. Under German law, protections are given not on the basis of good faith but, rather, on the basis of who is the weaker party. Just among three major commercial powers, laws on contracts are significantly different. The rules on conflicts of law in international transactions are as follows: (1) If the parties choose which law applies, that law will apply, and (2) if no provision is made, the law of the country where the contract is performed will be used. Agreeing to and understanding the set of laws to be applied in a contract is a critical part of international transactions.

Protections in International Competition

Although trade barriers are coming down and a global marketplace seems to be a reality, international competition is still subject to much regulation found in the forms of antitrust laws, protections for intellectual property, and trade treaties.

Antitrust Laws in the International Marketplace

All U.S. firms are subject to the antitrust laws of the United States, regardless of where their operations and anticompetitive behavior may occur. Firms from other countries operating in the United States or engaging in trade that has a substantial impact in the United States are also subject to U.S. antitrust laws.

The converse is also true. Firms outside the United States may enjoy the protections and benefits of our antitrust laws and bring suit for violations if it can be established that the violations they are alleging had a substantial impact on trade in the United States.

The Export Trading Company Act of 1982 carved an exception to the antitrust laws for U.S. firms that combine to do business in international markets. Large U.S. firms that would otherwise be prohibited from merging for anticompetitive reasons are permitted to form export trading companies (ETCs) for the purpose of participating in international trade. The Justice Department approves applications for ETCs in advance, provided the applicants can demonstrate that the proposed joint venture will not reduce competition in the United States, increase U.S. prices, or cause unfair competition. For example, Mobil and Exxon worked together to explore Siberian oil fields in a combination that would otherwise be prohibited both under the antitrust laws and for purposes of ongoing operations.

TARIFFS

Tariffs are taxes on goods as they move in and out of countries (import and export tariffs, respectively). Import tariffs are, in effect, a tax on goods coming into a country that increase the cost of those goods, particularly in comparison with domestic goods, and therefore limit the competitiveness of foreign goods within a country.

ethical *issues*

When the Taliban was in power in Afghanistan, it banned watching television. The result of the ban was the creation of a substantial market for smuggling television sets into Afghanistan. For example, a Sony TV set smuggled into Pakistan would cost about $400. The legal cost, paying tariffs, would be $440. The same set smuggled into Afghanistan could bring twice as much. Sony gets the same, or $220, for every set sold, regardless of where it is sold and what happens to it in terms of its final destination.

The Taliban decided to impose tariffs and taxes on TV sets even as it held to the ban because the ban produced the smuggling market from which they could extract substantial sums.

Do you think Sony had an ethical obligation to not sell to the Taliban? Does it have an ethical obligation to police what happens to its products? What happens when a company profits from a government making money from its own ban?

Source: Daniel Pearl and Steve Stecklow, "Taliban Banned TV But Collected Profits on Smuggled Sonys," *Wall Street Journal,* January 9, 2002, pp. A1, A8. (Note that the source for this article was a story coauthored by Daniel Pearl, the U.S. journalist who was kidnapped by terrorists and eventually killed by them with graphic coverage of the execution.)

In the United States, the U.S. Customs Service is responsible for developing the tariffs according to a tariff schedule and for enforcing the tariffs on imported goods. The tariff is based on the computed value of the goods coming into the country. That computed value depends on how the goods are classified under the schedule. For example, if potato chips are classified as bread, they are tariff or duty-free. If they are classified as snacks, they carry a tariff [*Sabritas* v. *U.S.*, 998 F. Supp. 1123 (Ct. Int'l Trade 1998)]. The federal government has created a specialized court to handle the many disputes that arise over the application of the tariffs and the underlying classification of goods.

Competition may also be controlled by import restrictions, a resulting control on trade balance and prices. By limiting the amounts of certain products from certain countries, supply and demand (and, through economic principles, price) are affected. These nontariff regulations also control competition and the flow of goods across borders.

Exhibit 6.1 provides a summary of international law principles and doctrines.

PROTECTIONS FOR INTELLECTUAL PROPERTY

Protections for intellectual property in the international marketplace are constantly undergoing refinements. Worldwide registration for patents, copyrights, and trademarks are goals that are within reach as the mechanisms for administration are being put into place. Details on international protections are found in Chapter 15.

EXHIBIT	6.1	The Treaties, Principles, and Statutes of International Law

NAME	PURPOSE
North Atlantic Treaty North Atlantic Treaty Organization (NATO)	Treaty between U.S. and European nations that establishes a deployment of armed forces and security setup in Europe
Foreign Sovereign Immunities Act of 1976	U.S. statute that clarifies the immunity of foreign countries and officials from prosecution for crimes in the United States
Act of state doctrine (expropriation)	Recognition of foreign government's actions as valid; U.S. courts may not be used to challenge another country's actions, even toward U.S. citizens
Foreign Assistance Act of 1962 (Hickenlooper amendment)	Authorization given to president to cut off aid to countries where U.S. citizens' property has been taken by the government or regulated so as to deprive owner of use
Overseas Private Investment Corporation (OPIC)	Federal insurer for U.S. companies' investments in countries with low per capita income
Repatriation	Bringing back to your own country money earned on investments in other countries
Export Trading Company Act of 1982	Antitrust combination exemption for companies joining to compete in international markets
Maastricht Treaty	Agreement that created European Union
General Agreement on Tariffs and Trade (GATT)	Agreement among 150 countries to increase trade by reducing tariffs
North American Free Trade Agreement (NAFTA)	Agreement among United States, Canada, and Mexico that eliminates 65% of the tariffs across borders now, with the goal of tariff elimination by 2010

CRIMINAL LAW PROTECTIONS

All persons and businesses present within a country are subject to that nation's regulatory scheme for business as well as to the constraints of the country's criminal code. Compliance with the law is a universal principle of international business operations. Expulsion, fines, penalties, and imprisonment are all remedies available to governments when foreign businesses break the law in a particular nation.

consider 6.2

Marc Rich & Co., a commodities trading corporation, was formed in Switzerland by Marc Rich, a U.S. citizen. The company had three members of its board from the United States. A federal grand jury in the United States that was investigating possible violations of U.S. income tax laws issued a subpoena to the company for records related to its crude oil transactions involving U.S. oil and customers. Mr. Rich challenged the subpoena on the grounds that a U.S. court had no jurisdiction over a Swiss corporation. A federal district court held that the company was subject to U.S. laws for its operations here in the U.S. and imposed a $50,000 fine on the company for each day it failed to comply with the subpoena. Could the U.S. federal court enforce the subpoena and the fine? (Analysis appears at the end of the chapter.) [*Marc Rich v. United States*, 707 F.2d 633 (2d Cir. 1983)]

Red Flags FOR MANAGERS

The world has become a very small one when it comes to business because of the Internet and treaties that permit the free flow of goods across countries' borders. But managers need to be careful about their international deals.

- First, know your treaties, duties, and trade rules. For example, shipping goods to Canada and Mexico or between EU countries is a relatively open-trade transaction. For non-GATT, non-EU, and beyond NAFTA transactions, check on tariffs and rules for trade.

- When dealing with government agencies in other countries, use caution. What you may think of as a custom of a tip to a government customs official

may be a violation of the Foreign Corrupt Practices Act, and that tip may find you charged with a felony.

- Decide whether you want the CISG to apply to your contracts and include provisions for arbitration if you want to use that common method for resolving disputes in international contracts. You can choose which law applies and which court you will go to, and it is easier to do that in your contract than later when there is a dispute.

- All businesses, regardless of where they are based, must obey the laws in the countries in which they do business. Learn the tax, antitrust, and securities laws in those countries in which you do business and comply with them.

Summary

What laws affect businesses in international trade?

- Foreign Sovereign Immunities Act of 1976—laws of prosecution of foreign activities

- Foreign Assistance Act of 1962 (Hickenlooper amendment)—allows the U.S. to stop trade with countries that seize U.S. business property

- Overseas Private Investment Corporation (OPIC)—provides protections for U.S. businesses in international trade

- Export Trading Company Act of 1982—allows joint ventures of U.S. companies abroad

- Contracts for the International Sale of Goods (CISG)—a sort of international UCC that is optional

What treaties, agreements, practices, and principles affect international business and trade?

- General Agreement on Tariffs and Trade (GATT)— the MFN treaty

- North American Free Trade Agreement (NAFTA)— Mexico, Canada, and U.S. trade agreement

- International Monetary Fund (IMF)—established World Bank

- Duties, quotas, tariffs—controls on prices and quantities of goods by nations with the goal of balancing imports and exports

- Foreign Corrupt Practices Act (FCPA)—controls on means of accessing governments

What principles of international law affect business?

- Sovereign immunity—freedom of one country from being subject to orders from another country

- Expropriation; act of state doctrine—recognition by U.S. courts of the actions of other governments as valid despite noncompliance with traditional U.S. rights and procedures

- Repatriation—returning profits earned in other countries to one's native land

- Conflict of laws—issue as to which country's law applies in international transactions

- Antitrust issues

- *Forum non conveniens*—doctrine requiring dismissal of cases that should be heard in another country's courts

What protections exist in international competition?

- Antitrust laws

- Protections for intellectual property

- Criminal law protections

Key Terms

Alternative Fines Act (AFA) *138*

common law *133*

facilitation *138*

Foreign Corrupt Practices Act *137*

grease payments *138*

multilateral treaty *134*

Organization for Economic Cooperation
   and Development (OECD) *140*

repatriation *143*

sovereign immunity *141*

Questions and Problems

1. Tom Welch and Dave Johnson, two officials of the Salt Lake City Olympic Committee, were charged with bribery and racketeering for their alleged role in paying money to and giving rather large gifts to members of the International Olympic Committee (IOC) in order to win the bid for holding the Winter Olympics in Salt Lake City in 2002. Salt Lake City did win the bid, but an anonymous letter to the IOC revealed that these types of payments and gifts had been offered. Following an investigation, nine members of the IOC were removed or resigned and others were sanctioned. The Salt Lake City Olympic Committee removed Mr. Welch and Mr. Johnson and replaced them with Mitt Romney as the head of its committee. Utah declined prosecution under state law, and a federal district court judge dismissed the charges against Mr. Welch and Mr. Johnson. The U.S. Attorney for the case filed an appeal with the tenth circuit federal court of appeals asking that the charges be reinstated. He noted that the Olympics were an "international" event and mandated federal jurisdiction. He also argued in the brief that the payments, accommodations, and gifts were more than goodwill and amounted to bribery in violation of federal law.

Applying the cases and law presented in the discussion on the FCPA, determine whether there was or was not a violation of federal law. What jurisdiction do federal courts have over criminal charges? Describe the appellate process and what an appellate court can do in an appeal such as this. [Patrick O'Driscoll, "U.S. appeals in Olympics bribery case," *USA Today,* January 24, 2002, p. 2A.]

2. Royal Dutch/Shell Group is a network of affiliated but formally independent oil and gas companies, many located in the United States. Royal Dutch/Shell also has extensive financial relationships with banks and other investors and shareholders in New York and other parts of the United States. Among these affiliated companies is Shell Petroleum Development Company of Nigeria, Ltd. ("Shell Nigeria"), a wholly-owned Nigerian subsidiary that does extensive oil exploration and development activity in the Ogoni region of Nigeria.

Ken Saro-Wiwa and others were imprisoned, tortured, and killed by the Nigerian government for their political opposition to Shell Nigeria's oil exploration activities. According to a suit filed in New York by surviving activists and their families, and Royal Dutch/Shell investors, Shell Nigeria recruited the Nigerian police and military to attack local villages and suppress the organized opposition to its development activity. Saro-Wiwa and others were repeatedly arrested, detained, and tortured by the Nigerian government because of their leadership roles in the protest movement. In 1995, Saro-Wiwa and others were hanged, along with other Ogoni leaders, after being convicted of murder by a special military tribunal. The suit maintains that while these abuses were carried out by the Nigerian government and military, they were instigated, orchestrated, planned, and facilitated by Shell Nigeria with the Royal Dutch/Shell Group allegedly providing money, weapons, and logistical support to the Nigerian military, including the vehicles and ammunition used in the raids on the villages, procured at least some of these attacks, participated in the fabrication of murder charges against Saro-Wiwa, and bribed witnesses to give false testimony against them. The trial court dismissed the case for *forum non conveniens.* The investors and others appealed. What should the appellate court do and why? [*Wiwa v. Royal Dutch Petroleum Co.*226 F.3d 88 (C.A. 2 2000)]

3. Robert R. King was an executive with Owl Securities and was charged with a violation of the FCPA because of a $1 million payment made to government officials when a land deal in Costa Rica closed. This "kiss" payment was made to secure certain benefits for the property. The payment was made through the bank at the closing and not done by Mr. King himself, but he was charged with a violation of the FCPA. The following is a transcription of conversations recorded when Mr. Kingsley, an undercover agent for federal officials, talked with Mr. King.

June 1 and 2, 2000

King: You see when they walk into the bank, you know, the bank is going to be curious as to what they're putting up a million dollars for . . .

Kingsley: Well do they . . .

King: And we don't, we don't want just a million dollars, we want a hundred thirty-five million.

Kingsley: Yeah. Do they know what the million[']s for though?

King: Ah, probably . . . I think I told them, yeah.

Kingsley: Yeah. Well.

King: They didn't bat an eye. The thing that really worries me is that, uh, if the Justice Department gets a hold of. Finds out how many people we've been paying off down there. Uh, or even if they don't. Are we gonna have to spend the rest of our lives paying off these petty politicians to keep them out of our hair? I can just see us, every, every day some politician on our doorstep down there wanting a hand out for this or that.

Kingsley: Well, I mean.

King: Think we could pay the top people enough, that the rest of the people won't bother us any. That's what I'm hoping this million and a half dollars does. I'm hoping it pays enough top people. . . .

Did King violate the FCPA? Is there enough evidence here to prove intent? [*U.S.* v. *King*, 351 F.3d 859 (8th Cir. 2003)]

4. United Arab Shipping Company (UASC) is a corporation formed under the laws of Kuwait. Its capital stock is wholly owned by the governments of Kuwait, Saudi Arabia, the United Arab Emirates, Qatar, Iraq, and Bahrain. No single government owned more than 19.33 percent of UASC's shares, and the corporation was created by a treaty among the owner nations.

Three seamen who were injured while working for UASC brought suit against it in federal district court in the United States. UASC maintains it enjoys sovereign immunity. The seamen claim it is a commercial enterprise and not entitled to immunity. Who is correct? [*Mangattu* v. *M/V IBN Hayyan*, 35 F.3d 205 (5th Cir. 1994)]

5. When the Barings Bank bankruptcy occurred in 1995, Mr. Nick Leeson, the trader responsible for the immense losses the bank experienced after heavy derivative investments, fled to Germany. He was brought back to Hong Kong, the site of his trades, for trial. He is a British citizen who was arrested in Germany. Describe all the principles and issues of international law involved in his arrest, return, and eventual trial in Hong Kong. (Mr. Leeson has finished his sentence and has written a book about his experiences as a trader.)

Understanding "Consider" Problems

6.1

THINK: The FCPA prohibits payments to government officials for purposes of obtaining contracts/benefits. Third-party payments are also prohibited (i.e., a company cannot get around the FCPA by having someone else make the payment). The *Kay* case indicates that Congress wanted to be as broad as possible to cut back on bribes and corruption.

APPLY: What is different about this situation? The payment here is more indirect and more subtle—the benefit is not to a government official.

ANSWER: If the intent of Congress in passing the FCPA was to stop bribery, both direct and indirect payments should be covered. The *Kay* case covered indirect business benefits, and the statute is clear on the purposes for which payments are made. Here we have an indirect payment with the intent to secure a benefit. The situation is covered under the FCPA.

6.2

THINK: The principle of international law is that businesses must comply with the criminal laws or risk sanctions in those countries in which they do business.

APPLY: Marc Rich had oil supplies and customers located in the United States, so it was doing business in the United States. Marc Rich was subject to the criminal laws of the United States. The federal income tax laws carry both civil and criminal penalties for the failure to pay taxes.

ANSWER: Marc Rich had to comply with the subpoena. Marc Rich cannot do business in the United States and then refuse to comply with its laws or the processes required for enforcement of those laws, including subpoenas. (Mr. Rich was pardoned by President Clinton in 2001, just days before Mr. Clinton left office.)

Notes

1. Russia's status is currently under consideration with concerns about the stability of its legal system, particularly for enforcement of contract rights. The 2008 invasion of Georgia has created further difficulties for Russia because of geopolitical relationships and concerns.

2. The original members are Austria, Belgium, Canada, Denmark, France, Germany, Greece, Iceland, Ireland, Italy, Luxembourg, the Netherlands, Norway, Portugal, Spain, Sweden, Switzerland, Turkey, the United Kingdom, and the United States. The following countries have become members: Japan (1964), Finland (1969), Australia (1971), New Zealand (1973), Mexico (1994), the Czech Republic (1995), Hungary (1996), Poland (1996), Korea (1996), and Slovak Republic (2000). The six additional countries that have adopted the antibribery convention are Argentina, Brazil, Bulgaria, Chile, Estonia, and Slovenia.

3. OECD also has relationships with 70 countries and NGOs.

Business Crime

Business and crime have shared the headlines of newspapers for much of the past decade. Between 2002 and 2007, the Corporate Fraud Task Force of the U.S. Justice Department had 1,236 total corporate fraud convictions, including 214 chief executive officers and presidents, 53 chief financial officers, 23 corporate counsels or attorneys, and 129 vice presidents. White-collar crime, cyber crime, and public corruption are three of the FBI's eight priorities on criminal investigations and prosecutions.

The increase in white-collar crime and law enforcement's focus on it require every businessperson to understand the types and nature of business crimes. This chapter offers that background by answering the following questions: Why does business crime occur? Who is liable for crimes committed by businesses? What penalties are imposed for business crimes? What are the rights of corporate and individual defendants in the criminal justice system? ■

update ▸

For up-to-date legal news, click on "Author Updates" at

www.cengage.com/blaw/ jennings

I do not seek to justify my actions. I did not take these actions for personal financial gain. It was a misguided effort to preserve the company.

SCOTT SULLIVAN, FORMER CFO OF WORLDCOM

On entering his guilty plea to charges of securities fraud, conspiracy, and making false and misleading statements (serving five years)

Embezzlement cannot be condoned in any manner. [N]ot only did he steal from the stockholders . . . but he breached the fiduciary duty placed in him. Wrongdoing of this nature against society is considered a grave matter. . . . [h]e should receive the maximum sentence.

DENNIS KOZLOWSKI, FORMER CEO OF TYCO, CONVICTED OF EMBEZZLEMENT

In a letter, circa 1995, on sentencing of a former Tyco executive who had embezzled (employee did get the maximum sentence as did Kozlowski when he was later convicted of the same crime)

consider...

John Park is the president of Acme Markets, a national retail food chain. Acme operated 16 warehouses that were subject to inspection by the Food and Drug Administration (FDA). During 1970 and 1971, FDA inspectors found rodents in Acme's Philadelphia and Baltimore warehouses. The FDA's chief of compliance wrote to Mr. Park and asked that he direct his attention to cleaning up the warehouses. Mr. Park told a subordinate officer to take care of the problems.

When the FDA inspected the warehouses again, rodents were still there. The FDA charged Acme and Mr. Park with criminal violations of the Federal Food, Drug, and Cosmetic Act. Mr. Park says he tried to clean up the warehouses but his subordinates failed and that he should not be criminally responsible. Is Mr. Park correct?

What Is Business Crime? The Crimes within a Corporation

Many business crimes are committed because companies apply pressure to managers and employees to produce results. Sales goals and quarterly numbers often lead managers to cross ethical and legal lines. Managers also try to meet targets for incentive and bonus plans, so they pass along the pressure they feel to employees. In order to present a good earnings record, employees commit crimes on behalf of their corporations. Although these crimes may not directly line employee pockets, the corporation benefits, and employees benefit indirectly through bonuses or by just being able to keep their jobs.

For example, in January 2004, Andrew Fastow, the former CFO of the collapsed and bankrupt energy company Enron, entered a guilty plea to two counts of conspiracy to commit securities and wire fraud. His wife, Lea Fastow, pleaded guilty to filing a false joint tax return. Mr. Fastow was the mastermind behind the creation of off-the-book partnerships that hid Enron's substantial debt. Because those off-the-book entities did not have to be reported as part of Enron's financial statements, Enron seemed healthy and profitable. Mr. Fastow and other officers, including 26 executives who were indicted, explained that they were simply trying to meet projected earnings statements so that they could preserve shareholder value and share price on the market. As he testified against his former boss, former Enron CEO Jeffrey Skilling, Mr. Fastow said, "I thought I was being a hero for Enron. At the time, I thought I was helping myself and helping Enron to make its numbers."

In addition to company pressure, some employees have personal financial pressures that lead them to embezzlement as a source of pressure-relieving funds.

The Association of Certified Fraud Examiners estimates that total embezzlement from employers for 2008 was 7 percent of total business revenue or $994 billion, an average of about $2.0 million per company. The FBI estimates that the amount lost in financial institution fraud is 100 times the amount taken by bank robbers. The FBI also estimates that the losses attributable to business crimes are 40 times greater than losses from crimes committed on the street. These losses from business crimes do not include the indirect costs businesses now have because of the amount of crime—the costs of security or insurance against internal thefts. The additional emphasis on internal controls because of Sarbanes-Oxley requirements (see pp. 153–163 and Chapter 13) also add to the costs of preventing and detecting embezzlement. Forensic accounting has been labeled "the most secure job in America."

In 2007, the Internet Crime Complaint Center (IC3), a partnership between the FBI and the National White Collar Crime Center, received 206,884 Internet crime complaints. The total losses from Internet fraud topped $239 million in 2007, with most of the complaints generated from Internet auctions. The Justice Department estimates that computer hackers steal $2 billion per year over the Internet, with almost 40 percent of the losses reported topping $100,000.

But businesses still grapple with good old-fashioned theft of hard goods. For example, Aramark, a company specializing in vending machine sales, reported that employees had skimmed millions in revenue by underreporting the sales, ever so slightly over a period of time, in their cash/coin business. Employee theft nearly always carries that hallmark of small amounts taken over a period of time with well-planned and executed schemes. For example, garment workers for apparel manufacturers have gone home with designer label jeans in their purses. And then there are the crimes one business's employee commits against another business. Nine out of every ten purchasing agents take kickbacks. The methods for fraud and stealing are high- and low-tech, but they are all still crimes, prosecuted under federal and state statutes.

These crimes committed for and against a business are often referred to as **white-collar crime.** Exhibit 7.1 provides a partial list of the companies and business executives that have had encounters with laws, regulators, and courts.

EXHIBIT	7.1 A Roster of Wrongdoing

COMPANY/PERSON	ISSUE	STATUS
Adelphia Communications (2002)	Company guaranteed loans to another entity controlled by the Rigas family (John Rigas and his sons held the top executive spots at Adelphia); result was $2.7 billion in guarantees and $1 billion in off-the-balance-sheet debt; overstatement of number of customers and cash	Annual report delayed; shares lost 70% of value from March 2002 to April 2002; Chapter 11 bankruptcy that ended in liquidation; members of the Rigas family indicted and arrested on charges of "looting" the company of more than $1 billion in one of the largest corporate frauds ever; John Rigas and one son convicted; Sentenced to 15 and 20 years
Boeing (2003)	Charges of illicit use of competitor's proprietary documents; charges of recruiting government official	Loss of 7 government contracts worth $250 million; $615 million fine; guilty plea by official who was wooed; 9-month sentence; given right to re-bid in 2008.

COMPANY/PERSON	ISSUE	STATUS
Coca-Cola (2003)	Investigations followed Coke's admissions that product marketing tests for Frozen Coke in Burger King were rigged	Coke settled issue with Burger King, with payments rumored to be $21 million; settled suit with whistleblower
Columbia/HCA Health Care	Overbilling Medicare	$1.7 billion in fines and civil penalties; 53% profit drop; three executives indicted
Computer Associates (2004)	Securities fraud and obstruction following $2.2 billion restatement in sales	Top officers indicted for securities fraud; former CEO Sanjay Kumar enters guilty plea; 12 years
Enron (2001)	Earnings overstated through mark-to-market accounting; off-the-book/ share-special-purpose entities (SPEs) carried significant amounts of Enron debt not reflected in the financial statements; significant offshore SPEs (881 of 3,000 SPEs were offshore, primarily in Cayman Islands)	Company in bankruptcy (touted as the largest bankruptcy in U.S. history); shareholder litigation pending; Congressional hearings held; CEO convicted and serving 24.4 years; numerous indictments, convictions, and guilty pleas
Andrew Fastow, former CFO of Enron (2004)	Multimillion-dollar earnings from serving as principle in SPEs of Enron created to keep debts off the company books; significant sales of shares during the time frame preceding company collapse	Resigned as CFO; appeared before Congress and took the Fifth Amendment; entered guilty plea to securities and wire fraud; 6 years
Lea Fastow (2004)	Filing false income tax return	Guilty plea; 5 months prison; 5 months house arrest
Kenneth Lay, former chairman of Enron (2002)	Significant sales of shares during the time frame preceding Enron collapse; warning memo from one financial executive about possible implosion of company due to accounting improprieties	Resigned as CEO; appeared before chairman of Congress and took the Fifth Amendment; indicted for securities fraud, wire fraud; convicted; died of a massive coronary prior to appeal and sentence; conviction removed
Jeffrey Skilling, former CEO of Enron (2004)	Questions about his role in the Enron fraud; resigned just prior to company's collapse	Testified before Congress; offered assurances that he did not understand what was happening at Enron and that he resigned when he became aware; indicted for securities and wire fraud; found guilty of securities fraud; sentenced to 24.4 years
HealthSouth (2003)	$2.7 billion accounting fraud; overstatement of revenues	16 former executives indicted; 5 guilty pleas
Richard Scrushy, CEO of HealthSouth (2003)	85 federal felony counts, including violations of Sarbanes-Oxley financial certification provisions	Acquitted of financial fraud charges; found guilty of bribery and sentenced to 7 years

CONTINUED

COMPANY/PERSON	ISSUE	STATUS
ImClone (2002)	Questions surrounding the timing of disclosure of FDA action relating to the company's anticancer drug, Erbitux, and its less-than-touted effectiveness	SEC civil suit; shares dropped significantly after announcement of FDA action on December 28, 2001; shares dropped again on revelations of possible insider trading
Dr. Samuel Waksal, former CEO of ImClone (2002)	Sold $50 million in ImClone shares prior to releasing to public information that FDA had rejected marketing for Erbitux	Charged with insider trading; arrested by FBI at his SoHo residence; took the Fifth Amendment before Congress; guilty plea entered; 7 years and $3 million in fines
KMPG (2006)	Tax shelter fraud	Settled with federal regulators by payment of $456 million penalty; some former partners under indictment
Marsh McLennan (2005)	Price-fixing	$850 million in restitution
Joseph P. Nacchio, former CEO of Qwest (2003)	Allocation of IPO shares; friends and family conflicts	Settled with New York attorney general for $400,000; indicted and found guilty of insider trading or, as the blogger Motley Fool says, "guilty of being a moron"
Sotheby's (2003)	Price-fixing	Chairman given 1 year and 1 day in prison and a $7.5 million fine; CEO placed under house arrest for 1 year
Tyco International (2003)	Questions about accounting practices, particularly with regard to the booking of mergers and acquisitions; clandestine deals between CEO and board members for closing deals (one commission to board member was $20 million)	Stock dropped from almost $60 per share to around $20 on announcement of accounting issues; lost 27% value in one day following announcements about CEO; shareholder suits settled; top lawyer for company fired for allegedly impeding probe on board payments
L. Dennis Kozlowski, former CEO of Tyco (2003)	Accused of improper use of company funds	Indicted in New York for failure to pay sales tax on transactions in fine art; found guilty of larceny; sentenced to 15–25 years
WorldCom (2003)	Accounting issues centered on swaps—selling to other telecommunications companies and hiding expenses, thereby overstating revenue	Workforce cut by 17,000 employees; revenues reversed for 2 years to reflect losses; CEO Bernard Ebbers resigned with $366 million in loan forgiveness; share price dropped from over $60 per share in 1999 to less than $10 in 2002; WorldCom emerged from bankruptcy as MCI; four officers and managers entered guilty pleas; Ebbers convicted and sentenced to 25 years
Scott Sullivan, CFO of WorldCom (2004)	Securities fraud	Entered guilty plea to securities fraud and making false filings; sentenced to 5 years

Who Is Liable for Business Crime?

One of the major differences between nonbusiness and business crimes is that more people can be convicted for business crimes. For nonbusiness crimes, those who plan, participate, or are involved in the criminal act or aftermath are criminally responsible. For business crimes, on the other hand, those in the management of firms whose employees actually commit criminal acts can be held criminally responsible if they authorized the conduct, knew about the conduct but did nothing, or failed to act reasonably as managers. Employees who participate with the company and its management in illegal acts are also criminally responsible. For example, employees who help their employers establish fraudulent tax shelters for customers can be held liable along with the company and its officers. The key to liability is personal knowledge of wrongdoing.

United States v. *Park* (Case 7.1), a landmark case, discusses the liability standards for those who are in charge but may not themselves commit a criminal act. It also provides an answer to the chapter's opening Consider.

CASE 7.1

United States v. *Park*
421 U.S. 658 (1975)

Is Chasing Rats from the Warehouse in My Job Description?

Facts

Acme Markets, Inc., was a national food retail chain headquartered in Philadelphia, Pennsylvania. At the time of the government action, John R. Park (respondent) was president of Acme, which employed 36,000 people and operated 16 warehouses.

In 1970, the Food and Drug Administration (FDA) forwarded a letter to Mr. Park describing, in detail, problems with rodent infestation in Acme's Philadelphia warehouse facility. In December 1971, the FDA found the same types of conditions in Acme's Baltimore warehouse facility. In January 1972, the FDA's chief of compliance for its Baltimore office wrote to Mr. Park about the inspection. The letter included the following language:

We note with much concern that the old and new warehouse areas used for food storage were actively and extensively inhabited by live rodents. Of even more concern was the observation that such reprehensible conditions obviously existed for a prolonged period of time without any detection, or were completely ignored.

We trust this letter will serve to direct your attention to the seriousness of the problem and formally advise you of the urgent need to initiate whatever measures are necessary to prevent recurrence and ensure compliance with the law.

After Mr. Park received the letter, he met with the vice president for legal affairs for Acme and was assured that he was "investigating the situation immediately and would be taking corrective action."

When the FDA inspected the Baltimore warehouse in March 1972, there was some improvement in the facility, but there was still rodent infestation. Acme and Mr. Park were both charged with violations of the Federal Food, Drug, and Cosmetic Act. Acme pleaded guilty. Mr. Park was convicted and fined $500.

The court of appeals reversed Mr. Park's conviction, and the government appealed.

Judicial Opinion

BURGER, Chief Justice

The duty imposed by Congress on responsible corporate agents is, we emphasize, one that requires the highest standard of foresight and vigilance, but the Act, in its criminal aspect, does not require that which is objectively impossible. The theory upon which responsible corporate agents are held criminally accountable for "causing" violations of the Act permits a claim that a defendant was "powerless" to prevent or correct the violation to "be raised defensively at a trial on the merits." If such a claim is made, the defendant has the burden of

CONTINUED

coming forward with evidence, but this does not alter the Government's ultimate burden of proving beyond a reasonable doubt the defendant's guilt, including his power, in light of the duty imposed by the Act, to prevent or correct the prohibited condition.

Park testified in his defense that he had employed a system in which he relied upon his subordinates, and that he was ultimately responsible for this system. He testified further that he had found these subordinates to be "dependable" and had "great confidence" in them.

[The rebuttal] evidence [to Park's reliance on his subordinates] was not offered to show that respondent had a propensity to commit criminal acts, that the crime charged had been committed; its purpose was to demonstrate that respondent was on notice that he could not rely on his system of delegation to subordinates to prevent or correct unsanitary conditions at Acme's warehouses, and that he must have been aware

of the deficiencies of this system before the Baltimore violations were discovered. The evidence was therefore relevant since it served to rebut Park's defense that he had justifiably relied upon subordinates to handle sanitation matters.

Reversed.

CASE QUESTIONS

1. What problems did the FDA find in the Acme warehouses and over what period of time did the FDA find the problems?

2. What is the significance of the warnings Mr. Park was given?

3. Is it enough to avoid criminal liability to tell an employee to take care of the problem? What does this case tell you an officer must do to avoid criminal liability?

FEDERAL LAWS TARGETING OFFICERS AND DIRECTORS FOR CRIMINAL ACCOUNTABILITY

With each wave of accounting and fraud scandals, new legislation at the federal level has increased penalties for those who are the masterminds of white-collar crimes. In 1990, Congress enacted what has been called the "white-collar kingpin" law. A response to the 1980s savings and loan scandals, the law imposes minimum mandatory sentences (10 years in most instances) for corporate officers who mastermind financial crimes such as bank and securities fraud. Following the collapses of Enron, WorldCom, Adelphia, and others in the period from 2001 to 2002, Congress passed Sarbanes-Oxley, also known as the White-Collar Criminal Penalty Enhancement Act of 2002. Under SOX, as it is known among businesspeople, penalties for mail and wire fraud increased from their former maximums of 5 years to 20 years in prison. (Refer to Exhibit 7.1 to see the number of wire and fraud charges that have been brought against executives.) Penalties for violation of the trust, reporting, and fiduciary duties under pension laws increased from 1 year to 10 years, with fines increased from $5,000 to $100,000. SOX also provides for the specific crime of false financial statement certification, a crime directed at CEOs and CFOs, who are now required to certify the financial statements issued by their companies. Top officers who certify financials that they know contain false information now face a specific federal crime because of SOX reforms.

The Penalties for Business Crime

Statutes specify penalties for crimes. Some statutes have both business and individual penalties. Exhibit 7.2 provides a summary of the penalties under the major federal statutes.

EXHIBIT 7.2 Penalties for Business Crime under Federal Law

ACT	PENALTIES
Internal Revenue Code 26 U.S.C. 7201	$100,000 ($500,000 for corporations) and/or 5 years for evasion (plus costs of prosecution as well as penalties and assessments: 5–50%)
Sherman Act (antitrust) 15 U.S.C. 1	$350,000 and/or 3 years $10,000,000 for corporations Injunctions Divestiture
Sarbanes-Oxley 15 U.S.C. §1512 (document destruction, concealment, alteration, mutilation during pending civil or criminal investigation)	20 years plus fines
Sarbanes-Oxley (certification of financial statements)	$1,000,000 and/or 10 years If willful: $5,000,000 and 20 years Officers who earn bonuses based on falsified financial statements must forfeit them
1933 Securities Act 15 U.S.C. 77x (as amended by Sarbanes-Oxley)	$100,000 and/or 10 years
Securities and Exchange Act of 1934 15 U.S.C. 78ff	$5,000,000 and/or 20 years $25,000,000 for corporations Civil penalties in addition of up to three times profit made or $1,000,000, whichever is greater
Clean Air Act 42 U.S.C. 7413	$1,000,000 and/or 5 years
Clean Water Act 33 U.S.C. 1319	For negligent violations: $25,000 per day and/or 1 year For knowing violations: $50,000 per day and/or 3 years For second violations: $100,000 per day and/or 6 years For false statements in reports, plans, or records: $10,000 per day and/or 2 years
Occupational Health Safety Act 29 U.S.C. 666	Willful violation causing death: $70,000 and/or 1 year; minimum of $5,000 per willful violation Giving advance notice of inspection: $1,000 and/or 6 months False statements or representations: $10,000 and/or 6 months
Consumer Product Safety Act 15 U.S.C. 2070	$50,000 and/or 1 year Tampering: up to $500,000 and/or 10 years

REFORMING CRIMINAL PENALTIES

Some regulators and legislators argue that the difficulty with most criminal law penalties is that they were instituted with "natural" persons in mind, as opposed to "artificial" corporate persons. Fines may be significant to individuals, but a

$10,000 fine to a corporation with billions in assets and millions in income is simply a cost of doing business.

Criminal penalties have been increased to allow judges to fine the corporation as much as a bad business decision would cost. For example, if a company develops a bad product line, net earnings could decline 10 to 20 percent. Penalties expressed in terms of net earnings, as opposed to set dollar amounts, are more likely to have a deterrent effect on business criminal behavior.

Judges are increasingly assigning monitors to corporations as part of criminal sentences to follow up on corporate activity. For example, as its sentence in an environmental case, ConEd was assigned a Natural Resources Defense Council lawyer as a monitor for its asbestos activity. Even companies that enter into **corporate integrity agreements (CIAs)** that do not include an admission of guilt but provide a way to defer prosecution through the payment of a fine and a period of probation (usually 3 to 5 years) agree to have monitors present in their companies.

Another form of corporate punishment comes from the use of traditional criminal statutes for corporate wrongs. For example, when Ford Motor Company manufactured the Pinto automobile with a design flaw involving the gas tank location, many civil suits were brought for deaths and injuries caused by the exploding gas tank. However, Ford was indicted for a criminal charge of homicide. In 1999, the state of Florida charged ValuJet, Inc., with murder and manslaughter for carelessly handling deadly materials for shipment; their omissions resulted in an airplane crash and the deaths of 110 passengers and the crew.

Another punishment reform came from *United States* v. *Allegheny Bottling Co.*, 695 F.Supp. 856 (E.D. Va. 1988) *cert. denied*, 493 U.S. 817 (1989), in which the court required officers of the corporation to provide community service during the period of the corporate sentence so that nonprofits and community organizations could benefit from the management expertise of executives, expertise that is given free of charge as part of the corporation's penalty. In *Allegheny*, the corporation had to provide one officer for community/nonprofit service for 40 hours per week for three years.

Finally, "shame punishment" has been on the increase in corporate criminal cases. Shame punishment involves public disclosure of an offense. For example, a Delaware federal judge ordered Bachetti Brothers Market to take out an ad for three weeks confessing to its crime of violating federal law by selling meat consisting "in whole or in part of filthy, putrid and contaminated substances."

CORPORATE SENTENCING GUIDELINES: AN OUNCE OF PREVENTION MEANS A REDUCED SENTENCE

The U.S. Sentencing Commission, established by Congress in 1984, has developed both federal sentencing guidelines and a carrot-and-stick approach to fighting white-collar crime. Under the commission's guidelines, companies that take substantial steps to prevent, investigate, and punish wrongdoing and cooperate with federal investigators can be treated less harshly in sentencing. The goal of the commission was to ensure that companies would establish internal crime prevention programs.

The sentencing guidelines use a numeric formula that takes into account the seriousness of the offense, the company's history of violations, its cooperation in the investigation, the effectiveness of its compliance program, and the role of senior management in the wrongdoing. Involvement of top officers in criminal conduct also adds to the score. Prior violations increase a company's score, as do attempts to cover up the conduct (obstruction of justice).

A company's score is decreased by the presence of effective compliance programs designed to prevent and detect violations. If a company comes forward and reports the violations voluntarily, the score is decreased. Cooperation with investigators and acceptance of responsibility also reduce the score.

The guidelines were once a form of mandatory sentencing. However, with the U.S. Supreme Court's decision in *Rita* v. *U.S.*, 127 S. Ct. 2456 (U.S. 2007), the court ruled that the judge's discretion in sentencing cannot be taken away with mandatory time frames. The factors courts can now consider whether a defendant masterminded the corporate crime. In addition, the U.S. Supreme Court has placed some limits on the evidence judges hear before they mete out sentences. In *United States* v. *Booker*, 543 U.S. 220 (2005), the court held that when judges are determining sentences for defendants under the guidelines, any facts, other than the defendant's prior conviction, must be established by a jury beyond a reasonable doubt. In the case, Booker had been convicted of possession of 50 grams of crack cocaine. The sentencing judge considered additional evidence in the sentencing hearing that Booker had 566 additional grams of crack that was not used as evidence at the trial. The result was that Booker was not eligible under the sentencing guidelines for a lesser sentence of 21 years and 10 months, and the judge imposed a sentence of 30 years. The Supreme Court reversed the sentencing portion of the case, remanded the case for resentencing, and held that if the judge was going to consider additional facts that affected the length of sentence, such as the additional crack, those additional facts must be proved in the same way as the crime—before a jury and beyond a reasonable doubt. The impact of the *Booker* and *Rita* case has been widespread with many defendants now in the process of being resentenced, including many of the business executives convicted and sentenced as a result of the Enron-era scandals.

> ## Business Planning Tip
>
> Businesses should follow these basic principles of the sentencing guidelines.
>
> **1.** Have a code of ethics in place.
>
> **2.** Conduct training on the code of ethics.
>
> **3.** Have a company hotline and ombudsperson for employees to report violations anonymously.
>
> **4.** Protect employees who report violations.
>
> **5.** Investigate all allegations regardless of their sources.
>
> **6.** Report all violations immediately and voluntarily.
>
> **7.** Offer restitution to affected parties.
>
> **8.** Cooperate and negotiate with regulators.
>
> **9.** Admit your mistakes and shortcomings.
>
> **10.** Be forthright and public with your code of ethics. Discuss ethics with employees via Web site examples or illustrations of good ethical choices in the news among companies and employees.

Elements of Business Crime

The **elements**, or requirements for proof, of a business crime vary according to type. Crimes are violations of written laws, such as statutes or ordinances. But all crimes' specific elements can be classified into two general components: *mens rea* (or *scienter*) and *actus reus*.

MENS REA

A **crime** implies some voluntary action, which is to say that a criminal wrong is calculated or intentional; this element of criminal intent is the ***mens rea*** of a crime. *Mens rea* is the required state of mind for a crime—the intent to commit the act that is a crime. Concealing income is intentional conduct calculated to avoid paying taxes; it is willful and criminal conduct. An oversight in reporting income is not a crime. *United States* v. *Ahmad* (Case 7.2) discusses the issue of intent in an environmental case.

CASE 7.2

United States v. *Ahmad*
101 F.3d 386 (5th Cir. 1996)

Gasoline, Drains, and Knowledge of the Two Together: A Crime?

FACTS

Mr. Ahmad owns a Spin-N-Market in Conroe, Texas. In 1992 Ahmad discovered a leak in one of the high-octane gasoline tanks at the location. The leak was at the top of the tank, so gasoline did not seep out. However, the leak did allow water to get into the tank and contaminate the gas. Because water is heavier than gas, the water sank to the bottom of the tank, and because the tank was pumped from the bottom, Mr. Ahmad was unable to sell gas from it.

Mr. Ahmad hired CTT Environmental Services to test and examine the tank. Jewel McCoy, a CTT employee, told Mr. Ahmad that the leak could not be repaired until the tank was completely empty, which CTT offered to do for 65 cents per gallon plus $65 per hour of labor. Mr. Ahmad then asked Ms. McCoy whether he could empty the tank himself. Ms. McCoy told him that it would be dangerous and illegal for him to do so. Mr. Ahmad then responded, "Well, if I don't get caught, what then?"

Mr. Ahmad then rented a handheld motorized water pump from a local hardware store, telling a hardware store employee that he was planning to use it to remove water from his backyard. Mr. Ahmad hooked the pump up to his tank at the Spin-N-Market and pumped 5,220 gallons of fluid (4,690 were gasoline) into a manhole near the store and into Lewis Street alongside the store.

The gasoline made its way into both the storm sewer system and Possum Creek. Vacuum trucks had to decontaminate Possum Creek. The town sewage center had to be evacuated, and firefighters and hazardous materials crews had to restore the sewage plant to a safe condition. While the crews worked, two area schools had to be evacuated for safety reasons.

Mr. Ahmad was indicted for three violations of the Clean Water Act (CWA): knowingly discharging a pollutant into navigable waters without a permit, knowingly placing others in imminent danger through a pollutant, and knowingly operating a source in violation of pretreatment requirements. Mr. Ahmad did not dispute the conduct; he said he did not meet the "knowingly" requirements because he believed he was discharging water.

The jury found Mr. Ahmad guilty on two of the three charges and deadlocked on the charge of imminent danger. Mr. Ahmad appealed.

JUDICIAL OPINION

SMITH, Circuit Judge

Ahmad contends that the jury should have been instructed that the statutory *mens rea*—knowledge—was required as to each element of the offenses.

The language of the CWA is less than pellucid. Title 33 U.S.C. § 1319(c)(2)(A) says that "any person who knowingly violates" any of a number of other sections of the CWA commits a felony. The principal issue is to which elements of the offense the modifier "knowingly" applies. Ahmad's main theory at trial was that he thought he was discharging water, not gasoline.

The Supreme Court has spoken to this issue in broad terms. . . . "[T]he presumption in favor of a *scienter* requirement should apply to each of the statutory elements which criminalize otherwise innocent conduct."

The government also protests that CWA violations fall into the judicially created exception for "public welfare offenses," under which some regulatory crimes have been held not to require a showing of *mens rea*.

At best, the jury charge made it uncertain to which elements "knowingly" applied. At worst, and considerably more likely, it indicated that only the element of discharge need be knowingly. The instructions listed each element on a separate line, with the word "knowingly" present only in the line corresponding to the element that something was discharged. That the district court included a one-sentence summary of each count in which "knowingly" was present did not cure the error.

The obvious inference for the jury was that knowledge was required only as to the fact that something was discharged, and not as to any other fact. In effect, with regard to the other elements of the crimes, the instructions implied that the requisite *mens rea* was strict liability rather than knowledge.

There was at least a reasonable likelihood that the jury applied the instructions in this way, so we conclude that the instructions misled the jury as to the elements of the offense. Because the charge effectively withdrew from the jury's consideration facts that it should have been permitted to find or not find, this error requires reversal.

Most of Ahmad's defense, after all, was built around the idea that he thought water, rather than gasoline, was being discharged. A rational jury could so have found, and at the same time could have found that he did not actually know that he was pumping gas.

Reversed and remanded.

CASE QUESTIONS

1. Of what significance is Jewel McCoy's testimony in establishing *mens rea*?

2. What is the difference between knowledge of the law and knowledge of conduct? Why is Mr. Ahmad's testimony that he thought he was discharging water significant?

3. What does the court explain is required for the state of mind under the Clean Water Act?

consider 7.1

Consider the following situation and discuss whether the appropriate *mens rea* is present.

Timothy Sinskey and Wayne Kumm were, respectively, the plant manager and plant engineer at John Morrell & Co. ("Morrell"), a large meat-packing plant in Sioux Falls, South Dakota. The meat-packing process created wastewater, some of which Morrell treated at its own wastewater treatment plant ("WWTP"). After treating wastewater at the WWTP, Morrell would discharge it into the Big Sioux River. Morrell had a permit to discharge the wastewater after its WWTP reduced the ammonia nitrogen in it. The permit had maximum levels of ammonia nitrogen discharge. Morrell had to perform weekly tests to monitor the amounts of ammonia nitrogen and to file those test results monthly with the EPA.

In spring 1991, Morrell doubled the number of hogs that it slaughtered and processed at the Sioux Falls plant. The result was an increased level of ammonia nitrate above that allowed by the permit. Ron Greenwood and Barry Milbauer, the manager and assistant manager, respectively, of the WWTP, manipulated the testing process in three ways. In the first, called "flow manipulation" or the "flow game," Morrell would discharge extremely low levels of water (and thus low levels of ammonia nitrogen) early in the week, when Greenwood and Milbauer would perform the required tests. After the tests had been performed, Morrell would discharge high levels of water (and high levels of ammonia nitrogen) later in the week. The second technique was "selective sampling," in which they did more than the number of tests required by the EPA but reported only the tests in which ammonia nitrogen levels were within range. If these two techniques did not work, the two relied on their third technique of falsifying the test results and the monthly EPA reports. Sinskey signed and sent these monthly reports to the EPA. Morrell submitted false reports for every month but one from August 1991 to December 1992.

Sinskey and Kumm were charged with a variety of CWA violations. What would the government need to show for *mens rea*? Are they criminally responsible? (Analysis appears at the end of the chapter.) [*U.S.* v. *Sinskey*, 119 F.3d 712 (8th Cir. 1997)]

MENS REA, CONSCIOUS AVOIDANCE, AND CORPORATE OFFICERS

The intent element is significant in business crimes because two intents are actually involved when a corporation is prosecuted for a crime: the intent of the corporation to commit the crime and the intent of those in charge of the corporation, the officers and directors, to have the corporation commit the wrong. Individual officers and employees may have intent, but the company as a whole and all officers may not be aware of these pockets of deceit and malfeasance. However, courts have also developed the doctrine of **conscious avoidance** as a means of establishing *mens rea* for officers. Under this theory, executives cannot "consciously try to avoid knowledge" about the actions and activities of those within the company [*United States* v. *Ebbers*, 458 F.3d 110 (2d Cir. 2006), *cert. den.* 127 S.Ct. 1483 (2007).].

The *United States* v. *Park* case has modern application in that top executives are fully accountable for the information in their companies' financial statements. For example, Bernie Ebbers, the former CEO of WorldCom, denied knowing that information in the company's financial statements was false. In fact, he indicated he did not always read the 10-Ks and 10-Qs. However, testimony of witnesses at his trial showed that he attended the "Close the Gap" meetings in which managers discussed how to have actual numbers meet projections. Mr. Ebbers could not avoid criminal culpability and deny *mens rea* by avoiding the final reports when he was aware from those meetings of trouble brewing.

ACTUS REUS

All crimes include, in addition to the mental intent, a requirement of some specific action or conduct, which is the **actus reus** of the crime. For example, in embezzlement the *actus reus* is the taking of an employer's money. Various types of criminal conduct, or *actus reus* examples, are found in subsequent sections on specific crimes.

Examples of Business Crimes

THEFT AND EMBEZZLEMENT

The action of employees who take their employers' property is **theft** or **embezzlement**. Theft requires proof of the following elements: (1) intent to take the property, (2) an actual taking of the property for permanent use, and (3) no authorization to take the property. These three elements are the *actus reus* of the crime. The *mens rea* is the intent of permanently depriving the owner of use and possession.

For embezzlement, the elements are the same as for theft, with the addition of one more element: The person commits the crime while in the employ or position of trust of the property owner. In other words, embezzlement is theft from a specific type of person—an employer. Embezzlement includes theft of funds, inventory, and/or equipment of a business as well as skimming, or receiving payments from customers without entering a sale and even submitting false travel expenses.

OBSTRUCTION OF JUSTICE

Because of the cases involving the destruction of documents, Sarbanes-Oxley amended the federal law on obstruction of justice to make document destruction a specific crime and to increase its penalties. The new obstruction section makes it a felony for anyone, including company employees, auditors, attorneys, and consultants, *to alter, destroy, mutilate, conceal, cover up, falsify, or make a false entry with the "intent to impede, obstruct, or influence the investigation or proper administration of any matter within the jurisdiction of any department or agency of the United States."*[1] Obstruction can be committed by destroying or altering documents that are subject to a subpoena, that are related to a pending investigation, or by encouraging others to alter or destroy those types of documents. Encouraging or giving false testimony is also a form of obstruction of justice. Martha Stewart was convicted of obstruction of justice for her alteration of phone logs, backdating of an order to her broker, and encouraging a broker's assistant to lie to support her backdating story.

The Sarbanes-Oxley provisions on obstruction also cover audit records and require auditors to retain their work papers related to a client's audit for at least five years. Any destruction of these documents prior to the expiration of that period would constitute a felony and carries a penalty of up to 10 years.

ethical *issues*

As the financial performance of the infamous energy company Enron dipped, its audit firm, Arthur Andersen, worried that Enron's accounting and financial statements were doubtful. On October 16, 2001, Enron refused to change its earnings release in response to Andersen's concerns. Andersen was preparing a statement about the release. Nancy Temple, legal counsel for Arthur Andersen, e-mailed back and forth to David Duncan, the audit partner for the Enron account in Houston, about the content of the Andersen statement on Enron.

Later that same day, Temple also sent an e-mail to Andersen's internal team of accounting experts and attached a copy of the company's document policy. On October 20, 2001, the Enron crisis-response team held a conference call, during which Temple instructed everyone to "[m]ake sure to follow the [document] policy." On October 23, 2001, then-Enron CEO Kenneth Lay declined to answer questions during a call with analysts because of "potential lawsuits, as well as the SEC inquiry." After the call, Duncan met with other Andersen partners and told them that they should ensure that team members were complying with the company's document policy. Another meeting for all team members followed, during which Duncan distributed the policy and told everyone to comply. These, and other smaller meetings, were followed by considerable shredding and destruction of both paper and electronic documents.

On October 26, 2001, one of Andersen's senior partners circulated a *New York Times* article discussing the SEC's response to Enron. His e-mail commented that "the problems are just beginning and we will be in the cross hairs. The marketplace is going to keep the pressure on this and is going to force the SEC to be tough." On October 30, the SEC opened a formal investigation and sent Enron a letter that requested accounting documents. The document destruction continued despite reservations by some of Andersen's managers. On November 8, 2001, Enron announced that it would issue a comprehensive restatement of its earnings and assets. Also on November 8, the SEC served Enron and Andersen with subpoenas for records. On November 9, Duncan's secretary sent an e-mail that stated: "Per Dave—No more shredding. . . . We have been officially served for our documents." Enron filed for bankruptcy less than a month later. Duncan was fired and later pleaded guilty to witness tampering.*

Applying the *Park* case, who is criminally liable for the document shredding? The employees who actually did it? The managers who ordered it to begin? The company itself? Were they technically not in violation of the law during the document destruction because there was no formal notice until November 8?
[*Arthur Andersen LLP v U.S.*, 544 U.S. 696 (2005)]

*Mr. Duncan withdrew his plea when the Andersen case was decided by the U.S. Supreme Court. The government has not pursued prosecution against him.

COMPUTER CRIME

What Is a Computer Crime?

The term **computer crime** is used as though it were a completely separate body of law from criminal law. Although certain crimes can only be committed using a computer, the nature of crime, with both *mens rea* and *actus reus,* does not change. The following sections give some examples of types of computer crimes.

Theft of Software   When someone takes software, whether in the form of a program written on paper or a program on a disk or tape, something is taken, but the common-law crime of larceny covers only tangible property. Virtually every state has amended its definition of larceny or theft so that stealing software is a crime.

Unauthorized Access   When someone taps into your computer and gains access to your private information and e-mails, they have committed a computer crime. In 2008, a former Philadelphia TV news anchor was charged with unauthorized access to his co-anchor's computer and e-mail. He leaked the information he obtained from her e-mail to the media to damage her reputation because of an ongoing rivalry between the two over ratings and salary.

Intentional Damage   The computer may be the victim of a crime when it is intentionally destroyed or harmed. Physical destruction is only one small part of the harm. Destruction of the information stored in the computer is also a crime.

Physical destruction can be accomplished without physical contact. For example, interfering with the air-conditioning needs for effective computer operation could result in computer malfunction, the loss of files, and perhaps even the future ability of the computer to process. Intentionally planting a bug or virus in software, causing the program to malfunction, give incorrect output, or affect the hard drive and its content, is also conduct that fits under this intentional damage crime. The Melissa virus and the ILUVYOU virus that spread worldwide in just a day caused an estimated $3 billion in damage to businesses. Those who created and spread the bug committed intentional damage, a crime now updated to cover computers, programs, information, and software.

Using Computers to Commit Economic Espionage

The Economic Espionage Act (EEA) is a federal law[2] passed in response to several cases in which high-level executives were taking downloaded proprietary information from their computers to their new employers. In one case, an executive was accused of taking General Motors' full plan for supply chain management in Europe. The EEA makes it a felony to steal, appropriate, or take a trade secret and also makes it a felony to copy, duplicate, sketch, draw, photograph, download, upload, alter, destroy, replicate, transmit, deliver, send, mail, or communicate a trade secret. When employees take new positions with another company, their former employers are permitted to check the departing employees' computer e-mails and hard drives to determine whether the employees have engaged in computer espionage.

Using Computers to Harass: Cyberbullying

cyberlaw

After Megan Meier hung herself because of humiliating comments about her on a MySpace site, many states passed laws making **cyberbullying** a crime. The nature of the crime of cyberbullying is still evolving but the basic purpose of the laws is to make it illegal to use the Internet to lure or harass a minor.*

Using Computers to Commit Electronic Fund Transfer Crimes

The Electronic Fund Transfers Act (EFTA)[3] makes it a crime to use any counterfeit, stolen, or fraudulently obtained card, code, or other device to obtain money or goods in excess of a specified amount through an electronic fund transfer system. Internet credit card fraud is an EFTA violation.

Using Computers to Circumvent Copyright Protection Devices

The Digital Millennium Copyright Act (DMCA) makes it a federal offense to circumvent or create programs to circumvent encryption devices that copyright owners place on copyrighted material to prevent unauthorized copying. For

---

*Oregon's statute provides that cyberbullying "means the use of any electronic communication device to harass, intimidate or bully." ORS 339.364(1).

example, circumventing the encryption devices on software or CDs would be a violation of the DMCA. Dmitry Sklyarov, a Russian computer programmer, became the first person charged with a violation of DMCA. Mr. Sklyarov was arrested in early 2002 at a computer show after giving a speech on the product he developed that permits the circumvention of security devices on copyrighted materials. Specifically, his program unlocks password-protected e-books and PDF files. He gave his speech in Las Vegas at the Defcon convention, a convention billed as "the largest hacker convention on the planet."

In addition, the No Electronic Theft Act, passed at the end of 1997, makes it a federal criminal offense to willfully infringe copyrighted material worth more than $1,000 using the Internet or other electronic devices even when the infringer does not profit from the use of the material. For example, many Internet users clip articles from subscriber services on the Internet and then send them along via e-mail to nonsubscriber friends. Even though no transaction for profit occurs, the transfer of such copyrighted material still violates this federal law.

Using Computer Access for Unauthorized Advertising: Spamming

Spamming, or the practice of sending out thousands of e-mails at once to many different computer users, is an ever-increasing problem. The issues involved include First Amendment rights, privacy, and theft of property. Congress passed the **Controlling the Assault of Non-Solicited Pornography and Marketing (CAN-SPAM) Act**, which allows private companies to bring suit against spammers for their unauthorized use of ISPs. Microsoft was one of the first companies to use CAN-SPAM when it filed suit against eight spammers under CAN-SPAM in January 2004.

An industry group called the Anti-Spam Technical Alliance has been formed and has endorsed several e-mail authentication technologies. Another of the group's proposals is to have ISPs limit outgoing e-mail traffic for each account. The group also endorses the Register of Known Spam Operations (ROKSO), operated by the Spamhaus Project. Some states have made it a misdemeanor to send out e-mails with a misleading title line; Virginia was the first state to make spamming a criminal act. Under the Virginia statute, spamming becomes a felony when the volume of spam e-mails sent exceeds 10,000 in 24 hours, 100,000 in 30 days, or 1 million in one year.

Using Computers to Commit Fraud

The Counterfeit Access Device and Computer Fraud and Abuse Act (CADCFA) makes it a federal crime to use or access federal or private computers without authorization in several types of situations. The CADCFA was amended in 1994 to cover additional new technologies, such as scanners, handheld computers, and laptops.

CADCFA prohibits unauthorized access to U.S. military or foreign policy information, FDIC financial institutions' data, or any government agency computer. For example, in *Sawyer v. Department of the Air Force*, 31 MPSR 193 (1986), a federal employee was terminated from his position for tampering with Air Force invoices and payments.

The federal Computer Fraud and Abuse Act (CFAA) classifies unauthorized access to a government computer as a felony and trespass into a federal government computer as a misdemeanor. CFAA covers "intentional" and "knowing" acts and includes a section that makes it a felony to cause more than $1,000 damage to a computer or its data through a virus program.

CRIMINAL FRAUD

Criminal fraud elements are the same as those the person defrauded would use to establish a contract defense: A false statement was made; the statement was material—that is, it was the type of information that would affect the buying decision; and the person relied on the statement. The only difference between contract fraud and criminal fraud is that criminal fraud requires proof that the seller intended to mislead the buyer. Forgery of needed documents for a transaction provides proof of intent needed for criminal fraud.

COMMERCIAL BRIBERY

Most states have provisions that govern both the giving and receiving of gifts or funds in exchange for a contract or favor. A supplier offering a purchasing agent of a company $25,000 in cash as an incentive or reward for choosing that supplier has committed commercial bribery. The purchasing agent has betrayed his employer's interest and compromised his judgment by accepting benefits for himself. This condemnation of bribery in commercial transactions dates back to the first eras of business activity because of concerns that quality and pricing would suffer if corruption was introduced into the bargaining process.

RACKETEER INFLUENCED AND CORRUPT ORGANIZATIONS (RICO) ACT

The RICO Act (18 U.S.C. §§ 1961–1968), a complex federal statute, was passed with the intent of curbing organized crime activity. The ease of proof and severity of penalties for RICO violations have made it a popular charge in criminal cases in which organized crime may not actually be involved.

For RICO to apply, a "pattern of racketeering activity" must be established. That pattern is defined as the commission of at least two racketeering acts within a 10-year period. Racketeering acts are defined under the federal statute to include murder; kidnapping; gambling; arson; robbery; bribery; extortion; dealing in pornography or narcotics; counterfeiting; embezzlement of pension, union, or welfare funds; mail fraud; wire fraud; obstruction of justice or criminal investigation; interstate transportation of stolen goods; white slavery; fraud in the sale of securities; and other acts relating to the Currency and Foreign Transactions Reporting Act (an act passed to prevent money laundering). According to the *Journal of Accountancy,* 91 percent of all RICO civil actions have been based on the listed pattern crimes of mail fraud, wire fraud, or fraud in the sale of securities.

RICO provides for both criminal penalties and civil remedies. In a RICO civil suit, injured parties can recover treble damages, the cost of their suit, and reasonable attorney fees.

When RICO charges are brought against corporations, one penalty is seizure of corporate assets. A growing number of states have enacted their own versions of the RICO statute for application at the state level.

BUSINESS CRIME AND THE USA PATRIOT ACT

Prior to September 11, 2001, the federal government had the Money Laundering Control Act, 42 U.S.C. § 5301, that prohibited the knowing and willful participation in any type of financial transaction that was set up in order to conceal or disguise the source of funds. However, investigations into the backgrounds of those who had flown the planes that destroyed the World Trade Center and a portion of the Pentagon revealed intricate financial networks in which the sources of their funds were concealed through various business transactions in different types of industries. As a result, provisions of the USA Patriot Act, passed less than two months after the September 11 destruction, include substantial expansion of the Money Laundering Control Act as well as the Bank Secrecy Act. Under these changes, title and escrow companies; brokerage firms; travel agents; check-cashing firms; auto, plane, and boat dealers; branches of foreign banks located in the United States; and many other businesses are subject to disclosure and reporting requirements for transactions involving cash or transactions of more than $10,000. In addition, the types of accounts covered under the disclosure requirements include not just savings accounts but also money market savings and brokerage accounts.

Under the Federal Sentencing Guidelines, businesses subject to these anti-money laundering provisions must have a "Know Thy Customer" program that trains employees in how to spot money laundering and suspicious activities by customers.

FEDERAL CRIMES

Many of the statutes on business crimes are found at the federal level. Violations of the Securities Exchange Acts (Chapter 14), the Sherman Act (Chapter 16), the Internal Revenue Act, the Pure Food and Drug Act, the environmental statutes (Chapter 19), the Occupational Safety and Health Act (Chapter 17), and Consumer Product Safety statutes (Chapter 9) carry criminal penalties.

STATE CRIMES

Similar criminal statutes at the state level cover such areas as criminal fraud and securities. In addition, states have particular regulations and laws for certain industries. For example, the sale of liquor in most states is strictly regulated.

Procedural Rights for Business Criminals

Business criminals are treated the same procedurally as other criminals. They have the same rights under the criminal justice system. The U.S. Constitution guarantees protection of certain rights. The **Fourth Amendment** protects the individual's privacy and is the basis for requiring warrants for searches of private property. The **Fifth Amendment** provides protection against self-incrimination and is also the "due process" amendment, which guarantees that an accused individual has the right to be heard. The **Sixth Amendment** is meant to ensure a speedy trial; it is the basis for the requirement that criminal proceedings and trials proceed in a timely fashion. These constitutional rights are discussed in the following sections.

FOURTH AMENDMENT RIGHTS FOR BUSINESSES

The Fourth Amendment to the U.S. Constitution provides that "the right of the people to be secure in their persons, houses, papers, and effects, against unreasonable searches and seizures, shall not be violated." This amendment protects individual privacy by preventing unreasonable searches and seizures. Before a government agency can seize the property of individuals or businesses, it must obtain a valid **search warrant**—or have an applicable exception to the warrant requirement—which must be issued by a judge or magistrate and be based on probable cause. In other words, authorities must have good reason to believe that instruments or evidence of a crime are present at the business location to be searched. The Fourth Amendment applies equally to individuals and corporations. In an unauthorized search, a corporation's property is given the same protection. If an improper search is conducted (without a warrant and without meeting an exception), any evidence recovered is inadmissible at trial for the purposes of proving the crime. *Kyllo* v. *United States* (Case 7.3) deals with the issues of privacy, warrants, and evolving technology for observation.

CASE 7.3

Kyllo v. *United States*
533 U.S. 27 (2001)

THERMAL MARIJUANA DYNAMICS

FACTS

In 1991, Agent William Elliott of the United States Department of the Interior suspected that Danny Kyllo (petitioner) was growing marijuana in his home, part of a triplex on Rhododendron Drive in Florence, Oregon. Indoor marijuana growth typically requires high-intensity lamps. In order to determine whether an amount of heat was emanating from the petitioner's home consistent with the use of such lamps, at 3:20 A.M. on January 16, 1992, Agent Elliott and Dan Haas used an Agema Thermovision 210 thermal imager to scan the triplex.

Thermal imagers convert radiation into images based on relative warmth—black is cool, white is hot, shades of gray connote relative differences; in that respect, it operates somewhat like a video camera showing heat images.

The scan of Mr. Kyllo's home was performed from the passenger seat of Agent Elliott's vehicle across the street from the front of the house and also from the street in back of the house. The scan showed that the roof over the garage and a side wall of Mr. Kyllo's home were relatively hot compared to the rest of the home and substantially warmer than neighboring homes in the triplex. Agent Elliott concluded that Mr. Kyllo was using halide lights to grow marijuana in his house, which indeed he was. Based on tips from informants, utility bills, and the thermal imaging, a federal magistrate judge issued a warrant authorizing a search of Mr. Kyllo's home, and the agents found an indoor growing operation involving more than 100 plants. Mr. Kyllo was indicted on one count of manufacturing marijuana. Mr. Kyllo unsuccessfully moved to suppress the evidence seized from his home and then entered a conditional guilty plea.

The Court of Appeals for the Ninth Circuit remanded the case. On remand the District Court upheld the validity of the warrant. A divided Court of Appeals initially reversed, but that opinion was withdrawn and the panel affirmed. Mr. Kyllo appealed.

JUDICIAL OPINION

SCALIA, Justice

This case presents the question whether the use of a thermal-imaging device aimed at a private home from a public street to detect relative amounts of heat within the home constitutes a "search" within the meaning of the Fourth Amendment.

The permissibility of ordinary visual surveillance of a home used to be clear because, well into the 20th century, our Fourth Amendment jurisprudence was tied to common-law trespass. Visual surveillance was unquestionably lawful because "'the eye cannot by the laws of England be guilty of a trespass.'" "[T]he Fourth Amendment protection of the home has never been extended to require law enforcement officers to shield their eyes when passing by a home on public thoroughfares."

The present case involves officers on a public street engaged in more than naked-eye surveillance of a home. We have previously reserved judgment as to how much technological enhancement of ordinary perception from such a vantage point, if any, is too much. While we upheld enhanced aerial photography of an industrial complex in *Dow Chemical* [see Case 7.4], we noted that we found "it important that this is not an area immediately adjacent to a private home, where privacy expectations are most heightened. . . ."

[I]n the case of the search of the interior of homes—the prototypical and hence most commonly litigated area of protected privacy—there is a ready criterion, with roots deep in the common law, of the minimal expectation of privacy that exists, and that is acknowledged to be reasonable. We think that obtaining by sense-enhancing technology any information regarding the interior of the home that could not otherwise have been obtained without physical "intrusion into a constitutionally protected area," constitutes a search—at least where (as here) the technology in question is not in general public use. The fact that equivalent information could sometimes be obtained by other means does not make lawful the use of means that violate the Fourth Amendment. The police might, for example, learn how many people are in a particular house by setting up year-round surveillance; but that does not make breaking and entering to find out the same information lawful. In any event, on the night of January 16, 1992, no outside observer could have discerned the relative heat of Kyllo's home without thermal imaging.

The dissent makes this its leading point, contending that there is a fundamental difference between what it calls "off-the-wall" observations and "through-the-wall surveillance." But just as a thermal imager captures only heat emanating from a house, so also a powerful directional microphone picks up only sound emanating from a house—and a satellite capable of scanning from many miles away would pick up only visible light emanating from a house. We rejected such a mechanical interpretation of the Fourth Amendment. Reversing that approach would leave the homeowner at the mercy of advancing technology—including imaging technology that could discern all human activity in the home. The rule we adopt must take account of more sophisticated systems that are already in use or in development.

We have said that the Fourth Amendment draws "a firm line at the entrance to the house." That line, we think, must be not only firm but also bright—which requires clear specification of those methods of surveillance that require a warrant. While it is certainly possible to conclude from the videotape of the thermal imaging that occurred in this case that no "significant" compromise of the homeowner's privacy has occurred, we must take the long view, from the original meaning of the Fourth Amendment forward.

Where, as here, the Government uses a device that is not in general public use, to explore details of the home that would previously have been unknowable without physical intrusion, the surveillance is a "search" and is presumptively unreasonable without a warrant.

Reversed.

CASE QUESTIONS

1. What would be the difference between thermal scanning and, for example, observing with the human eye patches of snow on a roof with some areas showing more melting than others?

2. Given the development of cell phones and conversation held in public places, what are the rules for warrants and listening to phone conversations?

3. Does the method of invasion of privacy make a difference in determining whether there is a Fourth Amendment violation?

Warrants and ISPs

One of the technological areas that is still evolving deals with the rights of anonymous posters in chat rooms or even the identity of those sending e-mails to others. Must the ISP turn over to law enforcement officials the identity of those who are behind their Internet activities? With a warrant, the answer is clearly yes. And warrants are relatively easy to obtain as law enforcement agencies simply furnish the magistrate or judge with the content of the poster's/e-mailers postings on the Internet. If those postings involve criminal activities or conspiracies, the court can find probable cause. Without a warrant, law enforcement officials would need to have an applicable exception (see the following section) such as an emergency because of a posted threat. In civil cases, the ISP can require a subpoena before disclosing the identity of its customers. Some ISPs have customers sign agreements that provide the ISP will keep their identity private except with regard to law enforcement officials. With this agreement, the ISP can reveal the customer's identity without a warrant.*

---

*The Foreign Intelligence Surveillance Act (FISA) gives telecommunications companies immunity from liability for cooperating with the federal government in releasing information on identity for purposes of national security issues.

Warrants and Exceptions

Exceptions to the warrant requirement are based on emergency grounds. For example, if an office building with relevant records is burning, government agents could enter the property without a warrant to recover the papers. Similarly, if the records are being destroyed, the government need not wait for a warrant. Another exception to the warrant requirement is the "plain view" exception. This exception allows police officers to seize evidence that is within their view. *Dow Chemical Co. v. United States* (Case 7.4) deals with a business issue and this plain view Fourth Amendment exception.

CASE 7.4

Dow Chemical Co. v. United States
476 U.S. 1819 (1986)

LOW–FLYING FEDERAL AGENTS: PHOTOGRAPHIC SEARCHES

FACTS

Dow Chemical (petitioner) operates a two-thousand-acre chemical plant at Midland, Michigan. The facility, with numerous buildings, conduits, and pipes, is visible from the air. Dow has maintained ground security at the facility and has investigated flyovers by other, unauthorized aircraft. However, none of the buildings or manufacturing equipment is concealed.

In 1978, the Environmental Protection Agency (EPA) conducted an inspection of Dow. EPA requested a second inspection, but Dow denied the request. The EPA then employed a commercial aerial photographer to take photos of the plant from 12,000, 3,000, and 1,200 feet. The EPA had no warrant, but the plane was always within navigable air space when the photos were taken.

When Dow became aware of the EPA photographer, it brought suit in federal district court and challenged the action as a violation of its Fourth Amendment rights. The district court found that the EPA had violated Dow's rights and issued an injunction prohibiting the further use of the aircraft. The court of appeals reversed, and Dow appealed.

JUDICIAL OPINION

BURGER, Chief Justice
The photographs at issue in this case are essentially like those used in map-making. Any person with an airplane and an aerial camera could readily duplicate them. In common with much else, the technology of photography has changed in this century. These developments have enhanced industrial processes, and indeed all areas of life; they have also enhanced enforcement techniques. Whether they may be employed by competitors to penetrate trade secrets is not a question presented in this case. Governments do not generally

seek to appropriate trade secrets of the private sector, and the right to be free of appropriation of trade secrets is protected by law.

That such photography might be barred by state law with regard to competitors, however, is irrelevant to the questions presented here. State tort law governing unfair competition does not define the limits of the Fourth Amendment. The Government is seeking these photographs in order to regulate, not compete with, Dow.

Dow claims first the EPA has no authority to use aerial photography to implement its statutory authority of "site inspection" under the Clean Air Act.

Congress has vested in EPA certain investigatory and enforcement authority, without spelling out precisely how this authority was to be exercised in all the myriad circumstances that might arise in monitoring matters relating to clean air and water standards.

Regulatory or enforcement authority generally carries with it all the modes of inquiry and investigation traditionally employed or useful to execute the authority granted. Environmental standards cannot be enforced only in libraries and laboratories, helpful as those institutions may be.

The EPA, as a regulatory and enforcement agency, needs no explicit statutory provisions to employ methods of observation commonly available to the public at large; we hold that the use of aerial photography is within the EPA's statutory authority.

DISSENTING OPINION

POWELL, MARSHALL, BRENNAN, and BLACKMUN, Justices
The Fourth Amendment protects private citizens from arbitrary surveillance by their Government. Today, in the context of administrative aerial photography of

commercial premises, the Court retreats from that standard. It holds that the photography was not a Fourth Amendment "search" because it was not accompanied by a physical trespass and because the equipment used was not the most highly sophisticated form of technology available to the Government. Under this holding the existence of an asserted privacy interest apparently will be decided solely by reference to the manner of surveillance used to intrude on that interest. Such an inquiry will not protect Fourth Amendment rights, but rather will permit their gradual decay as technology advances.

EPA's aerial photography penetrated into a private commercial enclave, an area in which society has recognized that privacy interests may legitimately be claimed. The photographs captured highly confidential information that Dow had taken reasonable and objective steps to preserve as private.

CASE QUESTIONS

1. Of what significance is the fact that Dow's plant could be seen from the air?

2. Did Dow take any steps to protect its privacy? What difference would such steps make?

3. What objections do the dissenting judges raise to the decision?

In many business crimes, the records used to prosecute the defendant are not in the possession of the defendant. The records are, instead, in the hands of a third party, such as an accountant or a bank. Does the Fourth Amendment afford the defendant protection in documents that discuss the defendant or reflect the defendant's finances and transactions when those documents are in the hands of another? In some cases, a privilege exists between the third party and the defendants, and certain documents are protected and need not be turned over. Notes on trial strategy, audit procedures, and other plans and thoughts are not discoverable because such communications are privileged between lawyers and clients. Some states recognize an accountant–client privilege. The priest–parishioner privilege generally exists; however, under certain exceptions, such as in cases of abuse, disclosure of confessions is required under reporting statutes that eliminate the privilege for purposes of stopping, for example, sexual abuse of children.

FIFTH AMENDMENT RIGHTS FOR BUSINESSES

The Fifth Amendment extends several protections to those facing criminal charges.

Self-Incrimination

The statement "I take the Fifth" is used so often that it has made the Fifth Amendment well known for its protection against self-incrimination. For example, former major league baseball (MLB) player Mark McGwire took the Fifth Amendment before a congressional committee investigating MLB's policies on testing players for steroids and suspensions for their use. We cannot be compelled to be witnesses against ourselves. However, this protection applies only to natural persons; corporations are not given this privilege. A corporation cannot prevent the required disclosure of corporate books and records on grounds that they are incriminating.

Corporate officers cannot assert Fifth Amendment protection to prevent compulsory production of corporate records. Nor can corporate officers use the Fifth Amendment to prevent the production of corporate records on grounds that those records incriminate them personally. The rules applicable to corporate officers have been extended to apply to those involved in labor unions, close corporations, and even unincorporated associations. The same rule is applicable to sole shareholders of small corporations as well. This area of the relationships between and among employees, officers, and corporations has been a significant one as corporations have been under investigation by the Department of Justice. The issue of cooperation is important for the corporations because of the implications under the sentencing guidelines for reduced penalties. However, one of the measures of cooperation has been the willingness of the employees and officers to cooperate in the government's investigations. An area of intense litigation is whether a corporation's payment of attorney's fees for officers and employees can be taken as an indicator of an unwillingess to cooperate. [*United States* v. *Stein,* 435 F.Supp.2d 330 (S.D.N.Y.2006), *Stein* v. *KPMG, LLP,* 486 F.3d 753 (2d Cir.2007), and *United States* v. *Stein,* 495 F.Supp.2d 390 (S.D.N.Y. 2007)]

Miranda Rights

The famous *Miranda* doctrine resulted from an interpretation of the Fifth Amendment by the U.S. Supreme Court in *Miranda v Arizona,* 384 U.S. 436 (1966). **Miranda warnings** must be given to all people who are subjected to custodial interrogation. Custody does not necessarily mean "locked in jail," but it is generally based on an individual's perceptions of a situation. If a person feels he is without freedom to leave a place by choice, the level of custody at which *Miranda* rights must be issued has been reached. However, in *Missouri* v. *Seibert,* 542 U.S. 600 (2004), the U.S. Supreme Court held that a law enforcement official cannot coax a confession from an individual and then provide the warnings. The warnings tell those in custody of their Fifth Amendment right to say nothing, as well as their right to an attorney. The failure to give *Miranda* warnings is not fatal to a case if the crime can be proved through evidence other than the statement of the defendant.

Due Process Rights

The Fifth Amendment also contains due process language. The same language is found in the Fourteenth Amendment and made applicable to the states. **Due process** means that no one can be convicted of a crime without the opportunity to be heard, to question witnesses, and to present evidence.

Due process in criminal proceedings guarantees certain procedural protections as a case is investigated, charged, and taken to trial. The Sixth Amendment complements due process rights by requiring that all these procedures be completed in a timely fashion. The following subsections discuss the basic steps in a criminal proceeding as diagrammed in Exhibit 7.3.

Warrant and/or Arrest   A criminal proceeding can begin when a crime is witnessed, as when a police officer attempts to apprehend a person who has just robbed a convenience store. When the convenience store is robbed but the robber escapes, and if the police can establish that a certain individual was probably responsible for the robbery, a **warrant** can be issued and the individual then arrested. Whether with or without a warrant, the due process steps begin with the arrest.

Initial Appearance   Once an arrest has been made, the defendant must have an opportunity to appear before a judicial figure within a short time period (usually 24 hours) to be informed of his charges, rights, and so on. This proceeding is generally referred to as an **initial appearance**. The individual may be required to post a bond to be released; others are held without release terms (release terms generally depend on the nature of the crime and the defendant). The terms *released on his own recognizance* and *released OR* mean the defendant is released without having to post a bond.

EXHIBIT   7.3   Steps in Criminal Proceedings

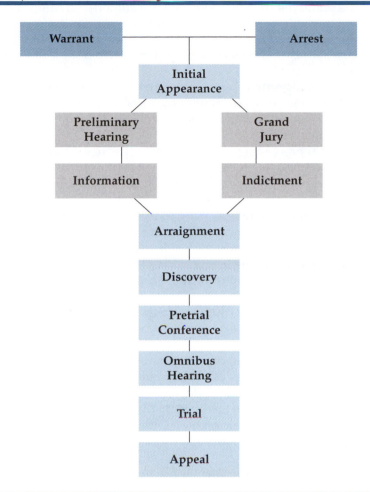

Preliminary Hearing or Grand Jury   Up to this step in the criminal proceedings, the defendant's charges are based on the word of a police officer; there has not yet been any proof brought forth linking the crime and the defendant. The purpose of a preliminary hearing or grand jury proceeding is to require the prosecution to establish that there is some evidence that the defendant committed the crime.

In a **preliminary hearing**, the prosecution presents evidence to a judge to indicate that the accused committed the crime. If the judge finds sufficient proof, an **information** is issued. The information is to a criminal proceeding what a complaint is to a civil proceeding: It establishes what the defendant did and when and what crimes were committed.

In some crimes, the evidence of the crime is presented to a **grand jury**, which is a panel of citizens who serve for a designated period of time (usually six months) and act as the body responsible for the review of evidence of crimes. If the grand jury finds sufficient evidence that a crime was committed, it issues an **indictment**, which is similar to an information and serves the same function.

Grand jury proceedings are conducted secretly, whereas preliminary hearings are public. Grand juries also have the authority to conduct investigations to determine whether crimes were committed and who did so. Perhaps one of the most famous grand juries was the San Francisco grand jury investigating steroid use in baseball. The grand jury heard testimony from some of baseball's biggest stars.

The Arraignment   An **arraignment** is the proceeding at which the defendant enters a plea of guilty, not guilty, or no contest (*nolo contendere*). If a not guilty plea is entered, a date for trial is set. If the defendant enters a guilty or no contest plea, chances are the plea is the result of a **plea bargain**, which is the term used in criminal proceedings for a settlement. The defendant may plead guilty to a lesser offense in exchange for the prosecution's promise to support a lesser sentence, such as probation or minimum jail time.

Discovery   If a case is going to trial, a **discovery** period continues between the time of the arraignment and the trial. Many states have mandatory criminal discovery laws that require each side to turn over certain types of information to the other side, including lists of witnesses they will call and lists of exhibits that will be used at trial. Exhibits include documents, murder weapons, and pictures.

Omnibus Hearing   In some cases, the defense attorney wishes to challenge the prosecution evidence on grounds that it was obtained in violation of any of the constitutional protections discussed earlier. Some documents, for example, may have been seized without a warrant. The **omnibus hearing** is the forum wherein all of these challenges can be presented for the judge's ruling as to the admissibility of evidence. It is held before the trial so the jury is not exposed to evidence that should not have been admitted. In the O. J. Simpson double-homicide trial, an omnibus hearing was held on the admissibility of evidence gathered at Mr. Simpson's estate without a warrant.

Trial   If no plea agreement is reached before trial, the case then proceeds to **trial**.

Red Flags FOR MANAGERS

Follow the law, and when in doubt, ask, before you act. Remember:

- Just because managers did not cook the books themselves does not mean that they could not be held criminally responsible. Managers cannot escape criminal liability because they "did not know" or "it was someone else's job." Managers who close their eyes to numbers that are questionable are still criminally responsible.

- Managers and their companies have due process rights such as the Fourth Amendment protections against warrantless searches of their business records. When asked questions or asked to turn over records, consult with a lawyer to understand your rights and those of your company.

- Managers have their Fifth Amendment right to remain silent when they are questioned.

- Managers who do not have codes of ethics, ethics training, and reporting systems expose their companies to greater fines and liability.

- If your company has violated the law, don't cover it up; report it.

- Ask before you shred documents. Shredding can result in obstruction of justice charges when there is an investigation or litigation pending.

Summary

Who is liable for business crimes?

- Vicarious liability—officers and managers are held accountable for criminal conduct of their employees
- Elements—requirements of proof for crimes
- *Mens rea*—requisite mental state for committing a crime
- *Actus reus*—physical act of committing a crime

What penalties exist for business crimes?

- Penalties—punishments for commission of crimes; include fines and imprisonment
- Corporate sentencing guidelines—federal rules used to determine level of penalties for companies and officers; a system that decreases penalties for effort toward prevention of wrongdoing and cooperation with investigations and increases penalties for lack of effort and other problems in company operations

What is the nature of business crime?

- Obstruction—under Sarbanes-Oxley, prohibits destruction of documents when civil or criminal investigations are pending
- Computer crime—crimes committed while using computer technology
- Counterfeit Access Device and Computer Fraud and Abuse Act (CADCFA)—federal law making it a crime to access computers without authorization
- Controlling the Assault of Non-Solicited Pornography and Marketing (CAN-SPAM) Act—federal law to control unsolicited pornographic and ad materials
- Electronic Espionage Act (EEA)—makes it a crime to take employer's proprietary information
- Criminal fraud—misrepresentation with the intent to take something from another without that person's knowledge; to mislead to obtain funds or property
- Racketeer Influenced and Corrupt Organizations (RICO) Act—federal law designed to prevent racketeering by intensifying the punishments for engaging in certain criminal activities more than once
- USA Patriot Act—federal law that deals with due process rights as well as substantive issues such as money laundering prohibitions and mandatory disclosures by those involved in financial transactions, including banks, escrow, and title companies and other financial institutions
- Money laundering—companies must take care so that transactions are not used to launder money for customers; transactions of $10,000 or more require a report to the federal government

What are the rights of corporate and individual defendants in the criminal justice system?

- Fourth Amendment—provision in U.S. Constitution that protects against invasions of privacy; the search warrant amendment
- Search warrant—judicially issued right to examine home, business, and papers in any area in which there is an expectation of privacy
- Fifth Amendment—the self-incrimination protection of the U.S. Constitution
  - Interrelationships of companies, employees, privilege, and the issues with cooperation with government prosecutors
- Sixth Amendment—the right-to-trial protection of the U.S. Constitution
- *Miranda* warnings—advice required to be given to those taken into custody; details the right to remain silent and the right to have counsel
- Due process—right to trial before conviction
- Warrant—public document authorizing detention of an individual for criminal charges; for searches, a judicial authorization
- Initial appearance—defendant's first appearance in court to have charges explained, bail set, lawyer appointed, and future dates set
- Preliminary hearing—presentation of abbreviated case by prosecution to establish sufficient basis to bind defendant over for trial
- Information—document issued after preliminary hearing requiring defendant to stand trial
- Grand jury—secret body that hears evidence to determine whether charges should be brought and whether defendant should be held for trial
- Indictment—document issued by grand jury requiring defendant to stand trial
- Arraignment—hearing at which trial date is set and plea is entered
- Plea bargain—settlement of criminal charges
- Omnibus hearing—evidentiary hearing outside the presence of the jury
- Trial—presentation of case by each side

Key Terms

actus reus 162
arraignment 174
computer crime 163
conscious avoidance 161
Controlling the Assault of
    Non-Solicited Pornography
    and Marketing (CAN-SPAM)
    Act 165
Corporate integrity agreement
    (CIA) 158
crime 159
criminal fraud 166

cyberbullying 164
discovery 174
due process 172
elements 159
embezzlement 162
Fifth Amendment 167
Fourth Amendment 167
grand jury 173
indictment 173
information 173
initial appearance 172
mens rea 159

Miranda warnings 172
nolo contendere 174
omnibus hearing 174
plea bargain 174
preliminary hearing 173
search warrant 168
Sixth Amendment 167
theft 162
trial 174
warrant 172
white-collar crime 152

Questions and Problems

1. In the summer of 1993, the United States experienced the great, but temporary, Pepsi syringe scare. In several areas throughout the country, "consumers" came forward and claimed they had found medication syringes in cans of Pepsi. The Food and Drug Administration (FDA) and officers of PepsiCo reeled for several days as they attempted to cope with the allegations. Within a short period of time from when the stories on the syringes first appeared, a film taken by a hidden store camera showed one of the "consumers" actually inserting a syringe into a Pepsi drink product prior to purchase.

Assume that a criminal charge of adulteration requires proof of an intentional act. Would the hidden camera film establish the intent element of the crime?

2. Borland International, Inc., and Symantec Corporation are software manufacturers based in Silicon Valley in California. A Borland executive, Eugene Wang, was planning to depart Borland to work for Symantec, considered Borland's archrival. Other Borland executives and its board uncovered evidence, on the evening of Mr. Wang's departure, that Mr. Wang had communicated trade secrets to Gordon Eubanks, Symantec's chief executive. Those secrets included future product specifications, marketing plans through 1993, a confidential proposal for a business transaction, and a memo labeled "attorney/client confidential" summarizing questions asked by the Federal Trade Commission (FTC) in its probe of restraint of trade allegations by Microsoft Corporation.

Mr. Wang allegedly used his computer to communicate the information to Mr. Eubanks. The local police and Borland executives worked through the night, using Symantec's own software that reconstructs computer files after they have been destroyed.

When Mr. Wang reported for his exit interview, he was detained and questioned by investigators. Searches authorized by warrant of Mr. Eubanks's two homes and his office uncovered evidence that he had received Mr. Wang's information. Borland filed a civil suit against the two men.

Later during the day of the exit interview, Mr. Wang's secretary, who was transferring with him to Symantec, returned to copy from her computer what she called "personal files." A company official watched as she copied the files from her computer but became suspicious and notified plainclothes officers in the Borland parking lot. The secretary, Lynn Georganes, was stopped, and the two disks onto which she had copied materials were taken. The disks contained scores of confidential Borland documents, including marketing plans and business forecasts.

Do the actions of Mr. Wang and Mr. Eubanks fit any computer crime statutes? Was theft involved in their actions? Were Ms. Georganes's actions ethical? Can't a competitor always hire an executive away, and wouldn't Mr. Wang have had most of the information in his head anyway? Can Mr. Eubanks be certain Mr. Wang will not do the same thing to him?

3. Emma Mary Ellen Holley and David Holley, an interracial couple, tried to buy a house in Twenty-Nine Palms, California. A real estate corporation, Triad, Inc., had listed the house for sale. Grove Crank, a Triad salesman, prevented the Holleys from obtaining the house for racially discriminatory reasons.

The Holleys brought a lawsuit in federal court against Mr. Crank and Triad. They claimed, among other things, that both were responsible for a fair housing law violation. The Holleys later filed a separate suit against David Meyer, the sole shareholder of Triad and its president and CEO. They claimed that Mr. Meyer was liable for Mr. Crank's unlawful actions, which were a violation of the Fair Housing Act. Are the Holleys correct? [*Meyer* v. *Holley*, 537 U.S. 280 (2003)]

4. The New York City Department of Health is responsible for the inspection of Manhattan restaurants to determine whether they comply with the city's health code. Forty-six of the department's inspectors were inducing restauranteurs to pay money to them for permit approval or for a favorable inspection. Is this activity a basis for a crime? What crime? What would a prosecutor be required to prove? Are the officers and the restaurateurs equally criminally liable? [*United States* v. *Tillem*, 906 F.2d 814 (2d Cir. 1990)]

5. During his trial testimony, Bernie Ebbers, the former CEO of WorldCom, who was charged with, among other things, financial fraud, said that he did not always read the company's 10-K, the annual financial report filed with the SEC (see Chapter 13), from cover to cover. His purpose in testifying was to show that he was not aware of all the financial information that his officers were releasing. However, through the testimony of former officers and employees, a different picture emerged. Scott Sullivan, the former CFO who

testified against Ebbers, said that he learned that line cost expenses would be almost $1 billion greater than expected. He reported that unexpected amount to Mr. Ebbers who emphasized that the company had to hit its quarterly earnings estimates. Mr. Sullivan instructed Controller David Myers and his subordinates Buford Yates, Betty Vinson, and Troy Normand to reduce line cost expense accounts in the general ledger while also reducing reserves in the same amounts, which lowered the reported line costs by about $828 million. As a result, WorldCom's reported earnings were increased by the same amount.

Ms. Vinson and Mr. Normand believed the entries were wrong and considered resigning. When Mr. Sullivan told Mr. Ebbers that the accounting staff might quit, Mr. Ebbers said, "We shouldn't be making adjustments; we've got to get the operations of this company going; we shouldn't be putting people in this position." Mr. Ebbers then spoke to Controller Myers, apologizing for the position that Myers and his staff were put in. Despite Mr. Ebbers's testimony, did the government prove intent to defraud? Is intent still required to be proved for financial fraud charges? Doesn't the act of fraud prove intent? [*U.S. v Ebbers*, 458 F.3d 110 (C.A. 2nd 2006), *cert. den.* 127 S.Ct. 1483 (2007)]

Understanding "Consider" Problem

7.1

THINK: From the *Ahmad* case you learned that for someone to be convicted of an environmental crime that involves unlawful discharges they must be aware that they are actually discharging the substances into the water. From the *Park* case you learned that executives are liable for the conduct of others in running the company if they are aware of violations and continue to allow those violations to occur without taking action.

APPLY: What is different here? The employees in this case were fully aware that they were discharging substances that exceeded their permit amount and that

they were manipulating the tests and the reports to allow the company to continue to discharge the ammonia nitrogen at levels beyond their permitted range so that the company could keep going at higher production levels. Sinskey was not directly involved in the manipulation of the numbers, but he did sign off on the reports while he was aware of higher production.

ANSWER: The court held that Sinskey and other officers, as well as the employees who actually manipulated the numbers and reports, could be held criminally liable for violations of the Clean Water Act.

Notes

1. 15 U.S.C. § 1512.

2. 18 U.S.C. §§ 1831–1839.

3. 41 U.S.C. § 1693.

8

Business Torts

update

For up-to-date legal news, click on "Author Updates" at

www.cengage.com/blaw/ jennings

Torts are civil wrongs that provide remedies. This chapter answers these questions: What are the different types of torts? What must you prove to recover for these torts? What are the business and public policy issues in torts and product liability? ■

One does not seriously attack the expertise of a scientist using the undefined phrase "Butt-head."

JUDGE LOURDES G. BAIRD

In dismissing the late Carl Sagan's lawsuit against Apple Computer for its code name change from "Carl Sagan" to "Butt–Head Astronomer"

consider...

James C. Luedtke, Jr. and his girlfriend, Heather Roberts, drove into the Diamond Shamrock gas station on White Settlement Road in Fort Worth, Texas. The attendant activated the pump, and Roberts pumped gas into the vehicle. Roberts hopped in the vehicle, and Luedtke drove away without paying for the gas. As Luedtke drove off, an employee of the gas station ran outside and attempted to get the license plate number of the vehicle.

In an effort to escape, Luedtke accelerated the vehicle, ran a red light, and collided with a vehicle driven by Alexis

Pichardo, Sr., who had his son Andrew Warren Pichardo with him. Both Alexis and Andrew were injured.

The Pichardos sued Luedtke; Selma Ann Roberts, the owner of the car Luedtke had been driving; and Diamond Shamrock. Diamond Shamrock wants to know how it can be held liable for the reckless driving of a thief? Is there liability here?

What Is a Tort? Roots of Law and Commerce

Tort comes from the Latin term *tortus,* which means "crooked, dubious, twisted." A **tort** is some type of interference with someone or with someone's property that results in injury. For example, using someone else's land without permission interferes with another's property rights and is the tort of trespass. If you held a concert on someone else's land and the concert crowds destroyed the property's vegetation or left litter that had to be removed, then you have committed the tort of trespass. Tort law is the basis for recovering for the damage done by the concertgoers.

TORT VERSUS CRIME

A crime is a public wrong that requires the wrongdoer to pay a debt to society through a fine or by going to prison. For example, the crime of assault results in imprisonment, probation, and/or a fine. However, the assault victim could bring suit against the charged assailant for the tort of assault to recover damages, such as medical bills, lost wages, and pain and suffering.

TYPES OF TORTS

The three types of tort liability include intentional torts, negligence, and strict tort liability. **Intentional torts** are those that involve deliberate actions. For example, a battery, or hitting another person, is an intentional tort. Hitting someone in the nose deliberately is the tort of battery. Suppose that you stretch your arms in a crowd and you hit a man in the nose and hurt him. You have not committed the tort of battery, but you may have committed the tort of **negligence**. You were carelessly swinging your arms in a crowd of people. Such careless conduct, or actions done without thinking through the consequences, is the tort of negligence. We are still responsible for damages to the nose because when we fail to act cautiously and thoughtfully, we are negligent. We have **strict tort liability** for our conduct that carries inherent dangers. For example, when contractors use dynamite to raze a building, they have strict liability because the incendiary devices are so risky and consequences so great that we hold them responsible regardless of the precautions they take. Product liability, discussed in Chapter 9, is a form of strict liability. You will see that a company can be held liable for injuries when a customer has misused its product because even the failure to provide enough warnings results in strict liability.

The Intentional Torts

DEFAMATION

Defamation is an untrue statement made by one party to another about a third party. It consists of either slander or libel; **slander** is oral or spoken defamation, and **libel** is written (or, in some cases, broadcast) defamation. The elements for defamation are:

1. A statement about a person's reputation, honesty, or integrity that is untrue
2. Publication
3. A statement that is directed at a particular person
4. Damages
5. In some cases, proof of malice

Publication

Defamation has not occurred until the untrue statement is said or written (communicated) to a third party. An accountant who addresses a group of lawyers at a luncheon meeting and untruthfully states that another accounting firm has been involved in a securities fraud has met the publication element. So has a supplier who notifies other suppliers that a business is insolvent when it is not. The more folks who hear or read the statement, the greater the defamation damages will be.

Internet messages and blog postings meet the publication requirement. They provide instantaneous and international communication, so damages can be substantial.

consider 8.1

The law firm of Lavely & Singer has become the law firm that celebrities turn to when they are concerned about a pending story in anything from *The National Enquirer* to *The Wall Street Journal*. Lavely & Singer represented Britney Spears against *US Weekly* in a suit for libel for its publication of a story it ran on a sexually explicit home video that she and her now-ex-husband made. A California court dismissed the suit explaining that, given Ms. Spears's reputation, it was difficult to defame her. The court said that because Ms. Spears has "put her modern sexuality squarely, and profitably, before the public eye," the publication of such information could not be considered harmful to her reputation, thereby meaning that one of the elements of defamation could not be established. Is the court correct on the Britney Spears decision? (Analysis appears at the end of the chapter.)

Source: Peter Lattman, "When Celebrities Fear Sting of Publicity, Who Do They Call?" *Wall Street Journal*, December 9, 2006, pp. A1, A6.

Statement about a Particular Person

To qualify as defamation, the statement made must be about an individual or a small enough group that all in the group are affected. For example, the general statement "All accountants are frauds" is too broad to be defamatory. But the statement "All the Andersen audit partners who worked on the Enron accounts were dishonest" is specific enough to meet this requirement.

Product disparagement is defamation of a product. For example, a *Consumer Reports* evaluation of a product that is not truthful about its qualities or abilities would be product disparagement. In *Bose Corporation* v. *Consumers Union of United States, Inc.*, 481 U.S. 1016 (1984), the U.S. Supreme Court dealt with whether product disparagement of the Bose speaker system actually occurred when *Consumer Reports* described individual sounds from the speakers, such as those of violins, as growing to gigantic proportions. The court held that even though Consumers Union had not given the Bose speakers a favorable review, it also did not say anything false about them in its negative review.

Damages

Defamation requires proof of damages, such as lost business, lost profits, lost advertising, lost reputation, or some economic effect that has resulted from the defamatory statements.

Malice

Defamation cases that involve public figures require proof of malice. Public figures are those voluntarily in the public eye, such as elected officials, recording artists, actors, sports figures, and media magnets (think Paris Hilton). However, someone who is injured by Paris Hilton's driving and experiences extensive media coverage as a result is not a public figure simply because Paris watchers brought them into the limelight. They would become public figures only if they used their newfound fame to launch their own careers in the spotlight. Kato Kaelin, for example, was a media hot-spot witness in the O. J. Simpson double-murder trial, but not a public figure. He became a public figure when he followed up his trial testimony with voluntary and paid appearances and interviews.

The malice requirement in public figure cases provides the balance between personal rights and First Amendment protections for the media. Malice exists when the information was published or broadcast knowing that it was false or with reckless disregard for whether it was true or false.

The Defenses to Defamation

Truth   A statement may be damaging, but, if it is the truth, it is not defamation. For example, former Olympic athlete Marion Jones filed a defamation suit against several publications for their statements about her use of steroids. However, Ms. Jones entered a guilty plea to steroid use and began a prison term in 2008. The steroid use was damaging, but it was the truth so there is no defamation. Baseball star Roger Clemens, under a similar cloud of steroid use allegations, has also filed a defamation suit against his former trainer. His trainer, to have a defense, would have to prove that Mr. Clemens did indeed use steroids.

Opinion and Analysis   One current defamation issue is whether the statements made in a columnist's opinion or analysis constitute defamation. Courts are struggling with the right level of protection for viewpoints because the objection is to the conclusions drawn, not any inaccuracies in facts. In business publications, columnist's opinions can be devastating to companies and their stock performance. In *Wilkow v. Forbes, Inc.*, 241 F.3d 552 (7th Cir. 2001), a *Forbes* magazine column stated that a partnership led by Marc Wilkow "stiffed" the bank, paying only $55 million on a $93 million loan while retaining ownership of the building.

The court held that if it is plain that the columnist "is expressing a subjective view, an interpretation, a theory, conjecture, or surmise, rather than claiming to be in possession of objectively verifiable facts, the statement is not actionable." "Stiffing," as the court noted, may "drip of disapproval," but it is an interpretation of values and is not defamation.

Privileged Speech   Some speech is privileged; that is, the speech is protected from defamation claims regardless of whether it is true. For example, members of Congress enjoy an **absolute privilege** when they are speaking on the floor of the Senate or House because of a strong public policy interest in free and open debate. The same is true of judicial proceedings; in order to encourage people to testify, witnesses enjoy an absolute privilege when testifying about the matters at hand, even when they are mistaken about their facts.

In addition to the requirement of proving malice when public figures are involved, the media also have a **qualified privilege**. If the news organization prints a retraction of a published statement, it has a defense to defamation. Perhaps one of the most famous libel cases addressing the defense of the media privilege involved Carol Burnett and a story about her printed by the *National Enquirer*. The case decision on this incident follows in *Burnett v. National Enquirer* (Case 8.1).

CASE 8.1

Burnett v. National Enquirer, Inc.
144 CAL. APP. 3D 991 (1983)

ONLY THE ENQUIRER DIDN'T KNOW FOR SURE: CAROL BURNETT, HENRY KISSINGER, AND DEFAMATION

FACTS

On March 2, 1976, the *National Enquirer* (appellant) published in its weekly publication a "gossip column" headlined "Carol Burnett and Henry K. in Row" that included the following four-sentence item:

In a Washington restaurant, a boisterous Carol Burnett had a loud argument with another diner, Henry Kissinger. Then she traipsed around the place offering everyone a bite of her dessert. But Carol really raised eyebrows when she accidentally knocked a glass of wine over one diner and started giggling instead of apologizing. The guy wasn't amused and "accidentally" spilled a glass of water over Carol's dress.

Ms. Burnett (respondent) filed suit against the *Enquirer* alleging that the item was entirely false and libelous after the *Enquirer* printed the following retraction:

An item in this column on March 2 erroneously reported that Carol Burnett had an argument with Henry Kissinger at

a Washington restaurant and became boisterous, disturbing other guests. We understand these events did not occur and we are sorry for any embarrassment our report may have caused Miss Burnett.

After a jury trial, Ms. Burnett was awarded $300,000 compensatory damages and $1,300,000 punitive damages. The trial court reduced the amounts to $50,000 compensatory and $750,000 punitive damages. The *Enquirer* appealed.

JUDICIAL OPINION

ROTH, Presiding Justice

There was no "row" with Mr. Kissinger, nor any argument between the two, and what conversation they had was not loud or boisterous.

The impetus for what was printed about the dinner was provided to the writer of the item, Brian Walker, by

Couri Hays, a freelance tipster paid by the *National Enquirer* on an ad hoc basis for information supplied by him which was ultimately published by it, who advised Walker he had been informed respondent had taken her Grand Marnier soufflé around the restaurant in a boisterous or flamboyant manner and given bites of it to various other people; that he had further but unverified information respondent had been involved in the wine-water spilling incident; but that, according to his sources, respondent was "specifically, emphatically" not drunk. No mention was made by Hays of anything involving respondent and Henry Kissinger.

Having received this report, Walker spoke with Steve Tinney, whose name appears at the top of the *National Enquirer* gossip column, expressing doubts whether Hays could be trusted. Tinney voiced his accord with those doubts. Walker then asked Gregory Lyon, a *National Enquirer* reporter, to verify what Walker had been told by Hays. Lyon's inquiry resulted only in his verifying respondent had shared dessert with other patrons and that she and Kissinger had carried on a good-natured conversation at the restaurant.

[W]e are of the opinion the award to respondent of $750,000 in order to punish and deter appellant was not justified.

In so concluding, we are persuaded the evidence fairly showed that while appellant's representatives knew that part of the publication complained of was probably false and that the remainder of it in substance might very well be, appellant was nevertheless determined to present to a vast national audience in printed form statements which in their precise import and clear implication were defamatory, thereby exposing respondent to contempt, ridicule and obloquy, and tending to injure her in her occupation. [T]he retraction proffered was evasive, incomplete and by any standard, legally insufficient. [W]e have no doubt the conduct of appellant respecting the libel was reprehensible and was undertaken with the kind of improper motive which supports the imposition of punitive damages.

[T]he penalty award, even when substantially reduced by the trial court based on its conclusion the jury's compensatory verdict was "clearly excessive and . . . not supported by substantial evidence," continued to constitute about 35% of the former and nearly half the latter.

The judgment is affirmed except that the punitive damage award herein is vacated and the matter is remanded for a new trial on that issue only, provided that if respondent shall, within 30 days from the date of our remittitur, file with the clerk of this court and serve upon appellant a written consent to a reduction of the punitive damage award to the sum of $150,000, the judgment will be modified to award respondent punitive damages in that amount, and so as modified affirmed in its entirety. . . .

CASE QUESTIONS

1. What facts establish malice in this case? Why was it necessary to establish malice?

2. What benefits do publications gain through stories such as the Burnett/Kissinger one?

3. Should tabloids like the *National Enquirer* enjoy the protection of the privilege? Are tabloids different from newspapers?

consider 8.2

The *National Enquirer* published a supposed interview with actor Clint Eastwood. The interview had never taken place, and Mr. Eastwood said the publication of such an interview in a sensationalist newspaper made it seem as if he was "washed up as a movie star." Could Mr. Eastwood recover for the publication of the fake interview? What tort has occurred, if any? (Analysis appears at the end of the chapter.)

. . . .

CONTRACT INTERFERENCE

The tort of **contract interference** or **tortious interference with contracts** or tortious interference occurs when parties are not allowed the freedom to contract without interference from third parties.

A basic definition for tortious interference is that someone intentionally persuades another to break a contract already in existence. Bryan A. Garner, the author of *Tortious Interference,* offers the following examples: "Say you had a contract with Joe Blow, and I for some reason tried to get you to break that contract. Or say that Pepsi has an exclusive contract with a hotel chain to carry Pepsi products, and Coke tries to get the hotel to carry Coke despite that contract. That's tortious interference."

One of the most famous cases involving the question of tortious interference involves tortious interference with an inheritance. Former Playmate of the Year, the late Anna Nicole Smith (a.k.a. Vicki Lynn Marshall), married 90-year-old J. Howard Marshall II, an oil magnate. Mr. Marshall died shortly after, leaving a $1.6 billion estate. Mr. Marshall's son was required to pay Ms. Smith $90 million for what Ms. Smith proved was his interference with the execution of a will by the late Mr. Marshall that would have allowed her to be an heir [*In re Marshall,* 253 B.R. 550, 553 (Bankr. C.D. Cal. 2000); 547 U.S. 293 (2006)]. Mr. Marshall's son had interfered with his father's expressed intention that Anna Nicole receive part of his estate.

FALSE IMPRISONMENT

False imprisonment is often referred to as "the shopkeeper's tort" because it generally occurs as a result of a shoplifting accusation in a store. **False imprisonment** is the detention of a person for any period of time (even a few minutes) against his or her will. No physical harm need result; the imprisoned party can collect minimal damages simply for being imprisoned without consent. Because shopkeepers need the opportunity to investigate matters when someone is suspected of shoplifting, the tort of false imprisonment does carry the defense of the **shopkeeper's privilege**. This privilege allows a shopkeeper to detain a suspected shoplifter for a reasonable period of time while the matter or incident is investigated. In most states, the shopkeeper must have a reasonable basis for keeping the person; that is, the shopkeeper must have reason to suspect the individual even if it turns out later that the individual has an explanation or did not do what the shopkeeper suspected.

Business Planning Tip

Invoking the shopkeeper's privilege involves seven key elements.

1. Stop shoppers discreetly.

2. Don't use physical force unless it is in response to the shopper's physical force.

3. Don't question shoppers publicly or make accusations within earshot of others.

4. Call the police quickly to allow them to take over.

5. If you detain shoppers, be certain the physical conditions are appropriate.

6. Don't detain shoppers except for their detention for the police and/or questioning that resolves the matter.

7. Be especially careful in detaining minors; allow them to call their parents or guardians.

INTENTIONAL INFLICTION OF EMOTIONAL DISTRESS

This tort imposes liability for conduct that goes beyond all bounds of decency and results in emotional distress in the harmed individual. To recover, the plaintiff is required to prove outrageous conduct and damages from the emotional distress. Although "pain and suffering" damages have been awarded for some time in negligence actions, awarding damages for emotional distress alone is a relatively new phenomenon. However, the tort of **intentional infliction of emotional distress** has been used quite often by debtors who are harassed beyond standards of decency by creditors and collection agencies in their attempts to collect funds.

INVASION OF PRIVACY

The intentional tort of *invasion of privacy* is actually three different torts.

(1) Intrusion into the plaintiff's private affairs such as in *Galella* v. *Onassis,* 353 F. Supp. 196 (S.D.N.Y. 1972). In the case, the late Mrs. Jacqueline Kennedy Onassis brought suit against Ron Galella, a

photo journalist, for invasion of her privacy. As a result of the case, Mr. Galella was ordered to remain at least 50 yards from Mrs. Onassis and 100 yards from her children. Hollywood stars use this tort to obtain injunctions against paparazzi.

(2) Public disclosure of private facts such as when someone discloses that a CEO was once a meth user. The statement is not defamation but it may well be the tort of invasion of privacy. There are now statutory protections for e-mail and Internet disclosures of private facts. There is ease of access to YouTube and MySpace, but ease of access does not mean that privacy rights are lost.

cyberlaw

There are also statutory protections for computer-stored information One such statute is the **Health Insurance Portability and Accountability Act of 1996** (HIPAA; 42 U.S.C. 1320d-1320d-8). HIPAA controls how medical information is collected, used, and conveyed. For example, doctors must be careful that computer screens of their office personnel are not visible by other patients.

(3) Appropriation of another's name, likeness, or image for commercial advantage. This final form of the privacy tort involves using someone's name, likeness, or voice for commercial advantage without his or her permission and constitutes the tort of **unauthorized appropriation**. For example, if a gas station used your picture in its window to show you as a satisfied customer, you might not be harmed greatly but your privacy is invaded because you have the right to decide when, how, and where your name, face, image, or voice will be used. *Midler* v. *Ford Motor Co.* (Case 8.2) addresses the unauthorized appropriation of a singer's voice.

CASE 8.2

Midler v. *Ford Motor Co.*
849 F.2D 460 (9TH CIR. 1988)

FORD TO BETTE, "DO YOU WANNA DANCE?"; BETTE TO FORD, "NOT REALLY!"

FACTS

In 1985, Ford Motor Company and its advertising agency, Young & Rubicam, Inc., began preparing television commercials for its "The Yuppie Campaign." Young & Rubicam had made its pitch to Ford on the campaign by using Bette Midler (plaintiff/appellant) singing "Do You Want to Dance?"

Ms. Midler refused to grant permission to Young & Rubicam for use of the song. So, Young & Rubicam hired Ula Hedwig, who had been one of the "Harlettes," backup singers for Midler for 10 years, to perform the song. Ms. Hedwig was told by Young & Rubicam that "they wanted someone who could sound like Bette Midler's recording of ['Do You Want to Dance?']." Ms. Hedwig made a record for the commercial after being told to "sound as much as possible like the Bette Midler record."

After the commercial aired, Ms. Midler was told by a number of people that it sounded exactly like her. Ms. Midler filed suit against Ford and Young & Rubicam for appropriation. The district court entered judgment for Ford and Young & Rubicam, and Ms. Midler appealed.

JUDICIAL OPINION

NOONAN, Circuit Judge
At issue in this case is only the protection of Midler's voice.

Bert Lahr once sued Adell Chemical Co. for selling Lestoil by means of a commercial in which an imitation of Lahr's voice accompanied a cartoon of a duck. Lahr alleged that his style of vocal delivery was distinctive in pitch, accent, inflection, and sounds. The First Circuit held that Lahr had stated a cause of action for unfair competition, that it could be found "that defendant's

CONTINUED

conduct saturated plaintiff's audience, curtailing his market."

A voice is as distinctive and personal as a face. The human voice is one of the most palpable ways identity is manifested. We are all aware that a friend is at once known by a few words on the phone. At a philosophical level it has been observed that with the sound of a voice, "the other stands before me." *A fortiori,* these observations hold true of singing, especially singing by a singer of renown. The singer manifests herself in the song. To impersonate her voice is to pirate her identity.

We need not and do not go so far as to hold that every imitation of a voice to advertise merchandise is actionable. We hold only that when a distinctive voice of a professional singer that is widely known is deliberately imitated in order to sell a product, the sellers have

appropriated what is not theirs and have committed a tort in California. Midler has made a showing, sufficient to defeat summary judgment, that the defendants here for their own profit in selling their products did appropriate part of her identity.

CASE QUESTIONS

1. In what context was Ms. Midler's voice sought?
2. Why is the confusion about who was singing in the commercial important for the case?
3. What is the difference between this case and the Bert Lahr case?

Aftermath: Ms. Midler's case was tried, and she recovered $400,000 from the defendants in October 1989.

Negligence

We all have minimal standards of care we are expected to use in driving, in our work, and in the care of our property. The tort of negligence imposes liability when we fall short of those standards. There are five elements of negligence.

ELEMENT ONE: THE DUTY

Each of us has the duty to act like an **ordinary and reasonably prudent person** in all circumstances. The standard of the ordinary and reasonably prudent person is not always what everyone else does or what the law provides. For example, suppose you are driving on a curvy highway late at night and it is raining quite heavily. The posted speed limit is 45 mph. However, the ordinary and reasonably prudent person will not drive 45 mph because the road and the weather conditions dictate that slower driving is more appropriate.

Duties can arise from statutes. Every traffic law carries a criminal penalty (fine and/or imprisonment) for violations, but a violation of that law is also a breach of duty for purposes of proving negligence. When you run a red light, you have not only committed a crime; you have also breached a duty and are liable for injuries and damages resulting from that red light racing.

Professionals such as doctors, lawyers, and dentists have the duty of practicing their professions at the level of a reasonable professional. Failure to do so is a breach of duty and a basis for malpractice (negligence by professionals) lawsuits.

Landowners owe duties to people who enter their property. For example, the duty to trespassers, such as thieves, is not to intentionally injure them. Placing man traps would be a breach of this duty.

Randi W. v. *Muroc Joint Unified School District* (Case 8.3) involves one of the newer issues in whether a duty exists.

CASE 8.3

Randi W. v. Muroc Joint Unified School District
929 P.2D 582 (CAL. 1997)

THE GLOWING LETTER OF RECOMMENDATION THAT FORGOT TO MENTION SEXUAL MISCONDUCT WITH MINORS

FACTS

Randi W. (plaintiff) a 13-year-old minor who attended Livingston Middle School, was molested and sexually touched in 1992 by Mr. Robert Gadams, an assistant principal at the school.

Mr. Gadams had previously been employed at the Mendota Unified School District (from 1985 to 1988). During his time there, Mr. Gadams had been investigated and reprimanded for improper conduct with female junior high students, including giving them back massages, making sexual remarks to them, and being involved in "sexual situations" with them.

Gilbert Rossette, an official with Mendota, provided a letter of recommendation for Mr. Gadams in May 1990. The letter was part of Mr. Gadams's placement file at Fresno Pacific College, where he had received his teaching credentials. The recommendation was extensive and referred to Mr. Gadams's "genuine concern" for students, his "outstanding rapport" with everyone, and concluded, "I wouldn't hesitate to recommend Mr. Gadams for any position."

Mr. Gadams had also previously been employed at the Tranquility High School District and Golden Plains Unified District (1987–1990). Richard Cole, an administrator at Golden Plains, also provided a letter of recommendation for the Fresno placement file that listed Mr. Gadams's "favorable" qualities and concluded that he "would recommend him for almost any administrative position he wishes to pursue." Mr. Cole knew, at the time he provided the recommendation, that Mr. Gadams had been the subject of various parents' complaints, including that he "led a panty raid, made sexual overtures to students, sexual remarks to students." Mr. Cole also knew that Mr. Gadams had resigned under pressure because of these sexual misconduct charges.

Mr. Gadams's last place of employment (1990–1991) before Livingston was Muroc Unified School District, where disciplinary actions were taken against him for sexual harassment. Allegations of "sexual touching" of female students there resulted in Mr. Gadams's forced resignation from Muroc. Nonetheless, Gary Rice and David Malcolm, officials at Muroc, provided a letter of recommendation for Mr. Gadams that described him as "an upbeat, enthusiastic administrator who relates well

to the students," and who was responsible "in large part," for making Boron Junior High School (located in Muroc) "a safe, orderly and clean environment for students and staff." The letter concluded that they recommended Mr. Gadams "for an assistant principalship or equivalent position without reservation."

Randi W. filed suit against the districts for their failure to provide full and accurate information about Mr. Gadams to the placement service. The trial court dismissed the case, and the Court of Appeals reversed. The districts appealed.

JUDICIAL OPINION

CHIN, Associate Justice

Although ordinarily a duty of care analysis is unnecessary in determining liability for intentional misrepresentation or fraud, here we consider liability to *a third person* injured as a result of the alleged fraud, an extension of ordinary tort liability based on fraud.

Did defendants owe plaintiff a duty of care? In defendants' view, absent some special relationship between the parties, or some specific and known threat of harm to plaintiff, defendants had no duty of care toward her, and no obligation to disclose in their letters any facts regarding the charges against Gadams.

[N]o California case has yet held that one who intentionally or negligently provides false information to another owes a duty of care *to a third person* who did not receive the information and who has no special relationship with the provider. Accordingly, the issue before us is one of first impression, and we apply the general analytical principles used to determine the existence of duty in particular cases.

In this state, the general rule is that all persons have a duty to use ordinary care to prevent others from injury.

Although the chain of causation leading from defendants' statements and omissions to Gadams's alleged assault on plaintiff is somewhat attenuated, we think the assault was reasonably foreseeable. Based on the facts alleged in the complaint, defendants could foresee that Livingston's officers would read and rely on defendants' letters in deciding to hire Gadams. Likewise, defendants could foresee that, had they not unqualifiedly recommended Gadams, Livingston would not have hired him. And, finally, defendants could foresee that

CONTINUED

Gadams, after being hired by Livingston, might molest or injure a Livingston student such as plaintiff.

[I]t is certainly arguable that their unreserved recommendations of Gadams, together with their failure to disclose facts reasonably necessary to avoid or minimize the risk of further child molestations or abuse, could be characterized as morally blameworthy.

As for public policy, the law certainly recognizes a *policy of preventing future harm* of the kind alleged here. One of society's highest priorities is to protect children from sexual or physical abuse.

Defendants argue that a rule imposing tort liability on writers of recommendation letters could have one very predictable consequence: employers would seldom write such letters, even in praise of exceptionally qualified employees.

In defendants' view, rather than prepare a recommendation letter stating all "material" facts, positive and negative, an employer would be better advised to decline to write a reference letter or, at most, merely to confirm the former employee's position, salary, and dates of employment. According to defendants, apart from the former employer's difficulty in deciding how much "negative" information to divulge, an employer who disclosed more than minimal employment data would risk a defamation, breach of privacy, or wrongful interference suit from a rejected job seeker.

In a case involving false or fraudulent letters of recommendation sent to prospective employers regarding a potentially dangerous employee, it would be unusual for *the person ultimately injured* by the employee actually to "rely" on such letters, much less even be aware of them.

As previously discussed, plaintiff's complaint alleges that her injury was a "proximate" result of defendants' fraud and misrepresentations. Defendants do not suggest that the complaint fails to state sufficient facts to establish proximate causation, assuming the remaining elements of duty, misrepresentation and reliance are sufficiently pleaded. Based on the facts alleged in the complaint, plaintiff's injury foreseeably and proximately resulted from Livingston's decision to hire Gadams in reliance on defendants' unqualified recommendation of him.

The judgment of the Court of Appeal is affirmed as to counts three and four (negligent misrepresentation and fraud), but reversed as to count five (negligence *per se*).

CASE QUESTIONS

1. Who provided the letters of recommendation for Mr. Gadams? What information was missing from the recommendations?

2. What concerns are raised about imposing liability on those who provide letters of recommendation?

3. What issues should employers address, in light of this case, in providing letters of reference and recommendation?

The majority of the states have some form of law that creates a qualified privilege for employers in providing references. The privilege is designed to allow managers the freedom of candor in their discussions of former employees and their performances as long as those letters are done in good faith and are factually based.

ELEMENT TWO: BREACH OF DUTY

This element requires proof that the defendant fell short of the standard of care or breached that duty. For example, an accountant owes a duty to his client to perform an audit in a competent and professional manner and to conform the audit to the standards and rules established by the American Institute of Certified Public Accounts (AICPA). Failure to comply with these standards would be a breach of duty and would satisfy this second element of negligence.

In many cases, courts try to determine whether the duty was breached to determine whether the defendant's action satisfied the standard of care established in element one.

Pichardo v. *Big Diamond, Inc.* (Case 8.4) focuses on the issues of safety and the liability of businesses and property owners for injuries that result from the acts of third parties. This case provides the answer to the chapter's opening Consider.

CASE 8.4

Pichardo v. Big Diamond, Inc.
215 S.W.3d 479 (Tex. App. 2007)

Pump First, Don't Pay, and Get-Away Liability

Facts

On November 23, 2002, James C. Luedtke, Jr. and his girlfriend, Heather Roberts, drove into the Diamond Shamrock gas station on White Settlement Road, in Forth Worth, Texas. The attendant activated the pump, and Roberts pumped gas into the vehicle. Roberts hopped in the vehicle, and Luedtke drove away without paying for the gas. As Luedtke drove off, an employee of the gas station ran outside and attempted to get the license plate number of the vehicle.

In an effort to escape, Luedtke accelerated the vehicle, ran a red light, and collided with a vehicle driven by Alexis Pichardo, Sr., who had his son Andrew Warren Pichardo with him. Alexis Pichardo, Sr. and Andrew were injured in the collision.

On November 19, 2004, the Pichardos sued Luedtke; Selma Ann Roberts, the owner of the car Luedtke had been driving; and Big Diamond, the believed operator of the gas station. The Pichardos later added Diamond Shamrock, the correct operator of the gas station, as a defendant.

Big Diamond and Diamond Shamrock (Appellees) then filed a joint motion for summary judgment because neither breached a legal duty owed to the Pichardos, that Luedtke's actions were not foreseeable, and that any acts or omissions they committed were not a proximate cause of the Pichardos' injuries. The trial court granted the motion for summary judgment. Big Diamond was not the owner of the property where the gas and dash occurred and therefore was dismissed out of the suit. The Pichardos appealed.

Judicial Opinion

WALKER, Justice
As a general rule, "a person has no legal duty to protect another from the criminal acts of a third person." An exception is that "[o]ne who controls . . . premises does have a duty to use ordinary care to protect invitees from criminal acts of third parties if he knows or has reason to know of an unreasonable and foreseeable risk of harm to the invitee." The exception applies, of course, to a landlord who "retains control over the security and safety of the premises."

Likewise, third-party criminal conduct is a superseding cause of damages arising from a defendant's negligence unless the criminal conduct is a foreseeable result of the defendant's negligence. The defendant must show the third-party criminal conduct rises to the level of a superseding cause.

The Pichardos argue that Diamond Shamrock knew that it was foreseeable that [not requiring] prepayment for gasoline purchases would in all likelihood result in foreseeable criminal activity such as theft of gasoline, and an attempt by the criminal to run away after the commission of the crime, and the possible injury of third persons such as [the Pichardos].

Here, the accident that injured the Pichardos occurred because Luedtke ran a red light after leaving the Diamond Shamrock gas station. The Pichardos were not invitees at the Diamond Shamrock gas station and the accident did not occur on the gas station premises. Consequently, we hold that the factors utilized to determine the scope of the duty owed by "[o]ne who controls . . . premises" to "protect *invitees* from criminal acts of third parties" is not applicable here.

[W]e note at the outset that the Pichardos claim Diamond Shamrock was negligent by not requiring prepayment for the gas before an attendant would activate the gas pump. Diamond Shamrock conclusively established that Luedtke drove away from the gas station and ran a red light, hitting the Pichardos' vehicle. The accident did not occur on the gas station premises.

[T]he "harm"—Alexis Sr.'s and Andrew's injuries—is a harm different in kind from that which would otherwise have resulted from the alleged negligence of not requiring prepayment for gasoline. Luedtke's actions in running a red light and striking the Pichardos' vehicle appear to be extraordinary rather than normal and appear to be independent of any negligence by Diamond Shamrock in not requiring prepayment for gasoline. Luedtke's action in running the red light is clearly due to his own decision to run the red light, and Luedtke is subject to liability to the Pichardos for his action in running the red light. Finally, we cannot see how Diamond Shamrock possesses more than possibly a minute degree of culpability for setting Luedtke's running of the red light in motion; the escape of any criminal following unauthorized criminal conduct could involve the running of a red light. Thus, we hold that Diamond Shamrock negated the foreseeability element of proximate cause by conclusively establishing that Luedtke's act of running the red light was a superseding cause of

CONTINUED

Alexis Sr.'s and Andrew's injuries. The burden then shifted to the Pichardos to raise a genuine issue of fact on foreseeability by presenting controverting evidence that, despite the extraordinary and abnormal nature of the intervening force, there was some indication at the time that this crime—the running of the red light—would be committed.

The Pichardos presented no such controverting evidence. The record is devoid of any evidence showing that similar accidents had occurred, that the Diamond Shamrock gas station was a frequent victim of gas and dashes, or that the area was crime laden. The record contains no evidence that other crimes or gas and dashes had occurred on the property or in its immediate vicinity, or even that individuals committing a gas and dash frequently run red lights or drive recklessly. Because Diamond Shamrock conclusively negated the foreseeability element of the Pichardos' negligence claim, the trial court properly granted summary judgment in favor of Diamond Shamrock.

We affirm the trial court's take-nothing summary judgment.

CASE QUESTIONS

1. What is the connection between Diamond Shamrock and the injuries the Pichardos experienced?

2. What evidence was missing from the Pichardos' case that was necessary?

3. Does the action of the Diamond Shamrock employee in writing down the license number of Luedtke's car have any relevance in determining liability? Why or why not?

ELEMENT THREE: CAUSATION

A negligence suit must also establish that the breach of the duty was the cause of the damages. A test often used to determine **causation** is the **"but for" test**—"but for the action or lack of action of the defendant, the plaintiff would not have been injured." For example, suppose that a guest is enjoying a scenic view of the ocean from a cliff near his hotel. At the edge of the cliff, the hotel had installed a fence, but the hotel does not keep it in good repair. When the guest leans against the fence to take a picture, the fence breaks and the guest falls over the cliff. The hotel breached its duty to keep its premises in reasonably safe condition, and its failure to do so caused the guest's injury. The "but for" test is limited by the so-called zone of danger rule, which requires that the plaintiff be in the zone of danger when the injury occurs. The zone of danger includes all those people who could foreseeably be injured if a duty is breached. For example, the hotel would also be liable to those injured by the guest as he fell through the weak fence because they are in the zone of danger.

ELEMENT FOUR: PROXIMATE CAUSE

There must be some cutoff line between the "but for" causation and events that contribute to the injury of the plaintiff—an element of a negligence case called *proximate cause.* Suppose that you have a tire replaced at a tire store and the technician fails to tighten the wheel sufficiently. As you drive down the street, the tire comes loose, rolls off, and strikes another car. Did the tire store cause the damage to the other car? Yes. Any accidents caused by that car? Yes. Suppose the tire comes off, rolls onto the sidewalk, and strikes a pedestrian. Did the tire store cause that injury? Yes. Suppose the pedestrian sees the tire coming and jumps out of the way but, in so doing, injures another pedestrian. Did the tire store cause that injury? Yes.

Business Planning Tip

All businesses should help create a safe environment for their customers and discourage criminal acts with the following:

1. Good lighting

2. Access to public phones

3. Security patrols

4. Locked gates to parking lots; gate or security access

5. Escorts for customers and employees to their vehicles after closing hours

6. Camera security

7. Assigned parking spaces for tenants and employees

8. Warning signs to use caution and be alert

In all of these accidents, the following statement can be made: "But for the failure to tighten the wheel, the accident would not have occurred." Suppose that the tire injures a pedestrian, although not fatally, but a doctor treating the pedestrian, through malpractice, causes the pedestrian's death. Did the tire store cause the death? No; another's negligence intervened.

Case 8.5, *Palsgraf* v. *Long Island Ry. Co.,* is a landmark case on the element of proximate cause.

CASE 8.5

Palsgraf v. *Long Island Ry. Co.*
162 N.E. 99 (N.Y. 1928)

FIREWORKS IN THE PASSENGER'S PACKAGE AND NEGLIGENCE IN THE AIR

FACTS

Helen Palsgraf (plaintiff) had purchased a ticket to travel to Rockaway Beach on the Long Island Railway (defendant). While she was standing on a platform at the defendant's station waiting for the train, another train stopped at the station. Two men ran to catch the train, which began moving as they were running. One of the men made it onto the train without difficulty, but the other man, who was carrying a package, was unsteady as he tried to jump aboard. Employees of the defendant helped pull the man in and push him onto the train car, but in the process the package was dropped. The package contained fireworks, and when dropped, it exploded. The vibrations from the explosion caused some scales (located at the end of the platform on which Ms. Palsgraf was standing) to fall. As they fell, they hit and injured Ms. Palsgraf. She filed suit against the railroad for negligence.

JUDICIAL OPINION

CARDOZO, Chief Justice
Negligence is not actionable unless it involves the invasion of a legally protected interest, the violation of a right. "Proof of negligence in the air, so to speak, will not do."

One who jostles one's neighbor in a crowd does not invade the rights of others standing at the outer fringe when the unintended contact casts a bomb upon the ground. The wrongdoer as to them is the man who carries the bomb, not the one who explodes it without suspicion of the danger. Life will have to be made over, and human nature transformed, before prevision so extravagant can be accepted as the norm of conduct, the customary standard to which behavior must conform.

The risk reasonably to be perceived defines the duty to be obeyed, and risk imports relation; it is risk to another or to others within the range of apprehension. Here, by concession, there was nothing in the situation to suggest to the most cautious mind that the parcel wrapped in newspaper would spread wreckage through the station. If the guard had thrown it down knowingly and willfully, he would not have threatened the plaintiff's safety, so far as appearances could warn him. His conduct would not have involved, even then, an unreasonable probability of invasion of her bodily security. Liability can be no greater where the act is inadvertent.

DISSENTING OPINION

ANDREWS, Justice
Assisting a passenger to board a train, the defendant's servant negligently knocked a package from his arms.

Where there is the unreasonable act, and some right that may be affected, there is negligence whether damage does or does not result. That is immaterial. Should we drive down Broadway at a reckless speed, we are negligent whether we strike an approaching car or miss it by an inch. The act itself is wrongful. It is a wrong not only to those who happen to be within the radius of danger, but to all who might have been there—a wrong to the public at large.

Negligence does involve a relationship between man and his fellows, but not merely a relationship between man and those whom he might reasonably expect his act would injure; rather, a relationship between him and those whom he does in fact injure. If his act has a tendency to harm some one, it harms him a mile away as surely as it does those on the scene.

CONTINUED

The proposition is this: Every one owes to the world at large the duty of refraining from those acts that may unreasonably threaten the safety of others. Such an act occurs. Not only is he wronged to whom harm might reasonably be expected to result, but he also who is in fact injured, even if he be outside what would generally be thought the danger zone.

What we do mean by the word "proximate" is that, because of convenience, of public policy, of a rough sense of justice, the law arbitrarily declines to trace a series of events beyond a certain point. This is not logic. It is practical politics.

Except for the explosion, she would not have been injured. . . . The only intervening cause was that, instead of blowing her to the ground, the concussion smashed the weighing machine which in turn fell upon her. There was no remoteness in time, little in space. And surely, given such an explosion as here, it needed no great foresight to predict that the natural result would be to injure one on the platform at no greater distance from its scene than was the plaintiff. Just how no one might be able to predict. Whether by flying fragments, by broken glass, by wreckage of machines or structures no one could say. But injury in some form was most probable.

Under these circumstances I cannot say as a matter of law that the plaintiff's injuries were not the proximate result of the negligence.

CASE QUESTIONS

1. Describe the facts. Who was carrying the package? How far away from the incident was Ms. Palsgraf?

2. What does Justice Cardozo find about proximate cause?

3. What point does the dissenting judge make?

ELEMENT FIVE: DAMAGES

Damages from the defendant's negligence could include medical bills, lost wages, and pain and suffering, as well as any property damages. Plaintiffs have also recovered punitive damages. Often referred to as "smart money," punitive damages are like civil penalties that are paid because of the high level of carelessness involved on the defendant's part.

DEFENSES TO NEGLIGENCE

Contributory Negligence

In some cases, an accident results from the combined negligence of two or more people. A plaintiff who is also negligent gives the defendant the opportunity to raise the defense of **contributory negligence**. Contributory negligence is simply negligence by the plaintiff that is part of the cause of an accident. For example, suppose that a boat owner is operating his boat late at night on a lake in which the water is choppy and when he is intoxicated. An intoxicated friend is sitting at the bow of the boat trying to put her feet into the water when the owner takes the boat up to high speed. She falls in and is injured. The issue of causation becomes complicated here because there were breaches of duties by both parties. Did he cause the accident by driving at high speed late at night on a choppy lake while intoxicated? Or did she cause the accident by sitting without protection or restraint on the bow of the boat when the boat was being driven like that? The effect of the defense of contributory negligence is a complete bar to both from recovery.

Comparative Negligence

Many states, in order to eliminate the harsh effect of contributory negligence, have adopted a defense of **comparative negligence**. Under this defense, the jury simply determines the level of fault for both the plaintiff and the defendant and, based on this assessment of fault, determines how much each of the parties will be awarded.

Using our boat example, the jury could find that the boat owner was 75 percent at fault and the passenger was 25 percent at fault. Under comparative negligence, the passenger could recover for her injuries, but the amount recovered would be 25 percent less because of her fault in causing the accident.

Assumption of Risk

Assumption of risk is a defense that requires the defendant to prove that the plaintiff knew there was a risk of injury in the conduct he or she undertook but decided to go forward with it anyway. For example, there are some inherent dangers in activities such as skydiving, skiing, and roller skating. When you ski, you assume the natural risks that exist in skiing, but you do not assume the risk of faulty equipment you rent. If the failure of that equipment causes your injuries, the rental company would be responsible for that injury. To assume the risk, you must be completely aware of the risk and you must assume the risk voluntarily.

Tort Reform

The United States permits greater recovery for torts while requiring less in terms of proof than other nations. Over the past decade, a number of reforms have been proposed, particularly with respect to tort litigation, to limit recovery or place other limitations on the amount of increasing tort litigation. For example, some reform proposals would limit damages. Although nearly all states have adopted some form of limitations in tort recovery, these reforms are a maze of laws differing from state to state, have been subject to judicial challenges (in many cases successful), and have provided little hope for insurers as they try to forecast their risks in insuring businesses and their properties and agents.[1]

In *BMW of North America, Inc. v. Gore* (517 U.S. 559 (1996), the U.S. Supreme Court addressed the issue of large recoveries and concluded that $4,000,000 in damages (reduced to $2 million by the judge on a judgment NOV) for the dealer's failure to disclose to a buyer that his BMW had been refinished was excessive. The actual damages were $4,000, and the court ruled, "In most cases, the ratio will be within a constitutionally acceptable range, and remittitur will not be justified on this basis. When the ratio is a breathtaking 500 to 1, however, the award must surely 'raise a suspicious judicial eyebrow.'" However, the dissent pointed out the problem that tort reform still faces: how much is too much? "As to the ratio of punitive to compensatory damages, we are told that a 'general concern of reasonableness . . . enter[s] into the constitutional calculus,' though even 'a breathtaking 500 to 1' will not necessarily do anything more than 'raise a suspicious judicial eyebrow.'" And as to legislative sanctions provided for comparable misconduct, they should be accorded "substantial deference," One expects the Court to conclude: "To thine own self be true."

In 1998, the Alabama Supreme Court (Alabama was the state in which the *BMW* case arose) placed restrictions on punitive damages. Now, in Alabama, no punitive damages are awarded without a showing of actual damages. Other states have followed with similar statutes. In *State Farm Mutual Auto Insurance Co. v. Campbell,* 538 U.S. 408 (2003), the U.S. Supreme Court held that an award of $145 million in punitive damages and $1 million in compensatory damages against an insurance company for its wrongful refusal to pay a claim violated the due process clause. The court found that the Utah Supreme Court had not applied properly the standards of the *Gore* case. The court also added to the *Gore* case some additional factors for the determination of punitive damages, including the actual harm suffered, how bad the defendant's conduct was, and the comparison of the verdicts in other similar cases.

The U.S. Supreme Court further clarified its *Gore* decision and cited favorably states' statutory damage limitations in its decision in *Exxon Shipping v. Baker*, 128 S.Ct. 2605 (2008). The case was an appeal by Exxon of a punitive damage award against it of $2.5 billion in for the oil spill caused by the crash of the Exxon *Valdez* off the cost of Alaska. The court held that the compensatory damages of $507.5 million should be used in a 1:1 ratio for punitive damages. The damages Exxon is required to pay were reduced by $2 billion with the court noting that when compensatory damages are substantial, punitive damages should be in a 1:1 ratio.

Strict Liability

Strict liability is absolute liability for conduct with few, if any, defenses available. Strict liability can result from violation of a statute. For example, any violation of federal laws on disposal of biomedical waste would result in strict liability. Strict liability can also result because of public policy issues. Public policy has afforded companies few defenses to the strict liability for defective products so that they are careful in the design, production, and packaging of their products. (See Chapter 9 for a full discussion of strict tort product liability.)

Red Flags FOR MANAGERS

- A manager must be careful to provide accurate information about former employees when asked for a reference. If you are providing more information than "She worked here from November 1, 2001 through January 2008," then ask for legal advice.

- Don't use someone's picture, voice, or image in ads without their permission. Posting a bounced check of a customer is invasion of privacy.

- Use a standard of reasonable conduct in collecting bills. Be discreet when you suspect shoplifting.

- Review your operations and the conduct of employees. Keep a record of accidents and make sure you do any needed repairs when accidents occur. Ask yourself, what would a reasonable and prudent person do in this situation? Businesses must inspect, repair, and warn.

Summary

What types of civil wrongs create a right of recovery for harm?

- Tort—a civil wrong; action by another that results in damages that are recoverable

- Intentional tort—civilly wrong conduct that is done deliberately

- Negligence—conduct of omission or neglect that results in damages

- Strict tort liability—imposition of liability because harm results

What are the types and elements of torts?

- Defamation—publication of untrue and damaging statements about an individual or company

- Product disparagement—the tort of defamation for products

- Malice—publication of information knowing it is false or with reckless disregard for whether it is false

- Privilege—a defense to defamation that protects certain statements because of a public interest in having information such as testimony in a trial or media coverage protected from suit

- Interference— asking a party to breach a contract with a third party

- False imprisonment—wrongful detention of an individual; shopkeepers have a privilege to reasonably detain those they have good cause to believe have taken merchandise

- Shopkeeper's privilege—defense to torts of defamation, invasion of privacy, and false imprisonment for merchants who detain shoppers when shopkeepers have reasonable cause to believe merchandise has been taken without payment

- Intentional infliction of emotional distress—bizarre and outrageous conduct that inflicts mental and possible physical harm on another

- Invasion of privacy—disclosing private information, intruding upon another's affairs, or appropriating someone's image or likeness

- Appropriation—the use, without permission, of another's likeness, image, voice, or trademark for commercial gain

- Ordinary and reasonably prudent person—the standard by which the conduct of others is measured; a hypothetical person who behaves with full knowledge and alertness

- Causation—the "but for" reason for an accident

- Proximate cause—the foreseeability requirement of causation

- Contributory negligence—negligence on the part of a plaintiff that was partially responsible for causing injuries

- Comparative negligence—newer negligence defense that assigns liability and damages in accidents on a percentage basis and reduces a plaintiff's recovery by the amount his negligence contributed to the cause of the accident

- Assumption of risk—plaintiff's voluntary subjection to a risk that caused injuries

What are the business issues surrounding torts?

- Tort reform—political and legislative process of limiting damages and changing methods of recovery for civil wrongs

Key Terms

Questions and Problems

1. Douglas Margreiter was severely injured in New Orleans on the night of April 6, 1976. He was the chief of the pharmacy section of the Colorado Department of Social Services and was in New Orleans to attend the annual meeting of the American Pharmaceutical Association.

On Tuesday evening, April 6, Mr. Margreiter had dinner at the Royal Sonesta Hotel with two associates from Colorado who were attending the meeting and were staying in rooms adjacent to Mr. Margreiter's in

the New Hotel Monteleone. Mr. Margreiter returned to his room between 10:30 P.M. and 11:00 P.M.; one of his friends returned to his adjoining room at the same time. Another friend was to come by Mr. Margreiter's room later to discuss what sessions of the meetings each would attend the next day.

About three hours later, Mr. Margreiter was found severely beaten and unconscious in a parking lot three blocks from the Monteleone. The police who found him said they thought he was highly intoxicated, and they took him to Charity Hospital. His friends later had him moved to the Hotel Dieu.

Mr. Margreiter said two men had unlocked his hotel room door and entered his room. He was beaten about the head and shoulders and had only the recollection of being carried to a dark alley. He required a craniotomy and other medical treatment and suffered permanent effects from the incident.

Mr. Margreiter sued the hotel on grounds that the hotel was negligent in not controlling access to elevators and hence to the guests' rooms. The hotel says Mr. Margreiter was intoxicated and met his fate outside the hotel. Is the hotel liable? Any defenses here? [*Margreiter* v *New Hotel Monteleone*, 640 F.2d 508 (5th Cir. 1981)]

2. Carolyn Dolph was shopping at the Dumas, Arkansas, Wal-Mart at 3:00 P.M. on Friday, June 16, 1989. She had just gone through the checkout line and was attempting to leave the store when she was accosted near the exit by the loss-prevention officer for the store, Loretta McNeely. Ms. Dolph testified that Ms. McNeely told her that she knew that Ms. Dolph had been apprehended for shoplifting in the McGehee Wal-Mart the week before, and because of that she was not allowed to shop at any Wal-Mart store. According to Ms. Dolph, Ms. McNeely made the accusation four times. Ms. Dolph countered that Ms. McNeely was mistaken. Ms. McNeely did not believe her; instead, she thought Ms. Dolph was going through typical shoplifter's denial. They were arguing the point, according to Ms. Dolph, where people could overhear, and she felt as if she were on display "right in front of the store."

To resolve the matter, Ms. Dolph and Ms. McNeely moved to a nearby service area, and Ms. McNeely went into a mezzanine office to call the McGehee store. After telephoning McGehee, Ms. McNeely then "hollered down" questions to Ms. Dolph from the office, according to Ms. Dolph. During the time that Ms. McNeely was calling, Ms. Dolph believed that she was being watched by Wal-Mart employees and that she was not free to leave. Ms. McNeely then requested that Ms. Dolph come up to the office, but she refused and asked to see the manager. It turned out that Ms. McNeely was in error and that Ms. Dolph's sister—not Ms. Dolph— had been apprehended in McGehee for shoplifting. Ms. Dolph sued Wal-Mart for slander and was awarded $25,000. Wal-Mart appealed because Ms. Dolph did not produce anyone at the trial who could testify about hearing the "hollered" exchange. Why is this evidence important? Should Wal-Mart win the appeal? [*Wal-Mart Stores, Inc.* v. *Dolph*, 825 S.W.2d 810 (Ark. 1992)]

3. Two disc jockeys at WPYX-FM radio in Albany, New York, were sued for intentional infliction of emotional distress by Annette Esposito-Hilder, who was identified on the air by the two disc jockeys as the "winner" of the "ugliest bride" contest. The two disc jockeys sponsored an ugliest bride contest based on the wedding pictures in the daily newspaper. Viewers were invited to call in with their guesses as to which bride had been chosen. Generally, the disc jockeys did not reveal last names of the brides. However, in Ms. Esposito-Hilder's case, they broke with past practice and revealed her name.

On appeal of the case from an earlier dismissal, the court held that no defamation was involved in their statements because they were "pure, subjective opinion." The court did hold, however, that a suit for intentional infliction of emotional distress could go forward. The court held, "Comedic expression does not receive absolute First Amendment protection."

Is opinion protected by the First Amendment? Does it make any difference that Ms. Esposito-Hilder was employed by a competing radio station in the area at the time she "won" the contest? [*Esposito-Hilder* v. *SFX Broadcasting, Inc.*, 665 N.Y.S.2d 697 (1997)]

4. Mae Tom went to Kresge's store on November 15, 1977, slipped, and fell on a clear substance on the floor. No one ever determined what the substance was, but Kresge's did sell soft drinks in the store, and customers could walk around with their drinks. Ms. Tom wishes to recover for her injuries. Can she do so? [*Tom* v. *S. S. Kresge Co., Inc.*, 633 P.2d 439 (Ariz. App. 1981)]

5. Lawrence Hardesty, a long-haul tractor-trailer driver, picked up a load of stadium seating equipment for delivery to an NFL stadium under construction in Baltimore. While workers were loading the seats and equipment, Mr. Hardesty stayed in the cab of his truck completing the necessary paperwork for the transport. There was a great deal of unused space in the trailer after the seats and equipment were loaded, but Mr. Hardesty did not check the load. When Mr. Hardesty arrived in Baltimore, he opened the truck doors and the shifted boxes fell on him and injured him. Mr. Hardesty filed suit against American Seating for the negligence of its workers in loading the seats and boxes. American Seating defended on the grounds that its workers were not experts in shipping and hauling and that Mr. Hardesty was contributorily negligent for not checking the load before he left. Discuss the issues and decide who should prevail. [*Hardesty* v. *American Seating Co.*, 194 F.Supp. 447 (D. Md. 2002)]

Understanding "Consider" Problems

8.1

THINK: Defamation requires proof of damage to one's honesty, reputation, or integrity. The statement must be untrue and result in harm.

APPLY: The story that *US Weekly* ran stated that Ms. Spears made sexually explicit videos in her home, a statement that would damage the reputation of an upstanding and ordinary person. However, the damage must be tied to the individual bringing suit. Ms. Spears's sexuality is part of her public persona.

ANSWER: The decision of the court was correct. Defamation of Ms. Spears on the basis of sex allegations, particularly those within the confines of her own home, is not possible because there would be no damages, only further attention to her career that is dependent on that component.

8.2

THINK: Recall the elements for defamation: a false statement that impugns the integrity of a specific person.

APPLY: We don't have the content of the interview, but it is false that the interview occurred, and Mr. Eastwood argues that just the suggestion that he would be interviewed by the *National Enquirer* harms his career.

ANSWER: Mr. Eastwood took the case to trial and won, precisely because no interview ever took place and the content and even the suggestion of him granting an interview were false.

Note

1. William Glaberson, "A Study's Verdict: Jury Awards Are Not Out of Control," *New York Times*, August 6, 2001, p. A9.

9

Product Advertising and Liability

The first jury verdict over $1 million in a product liability case was in 1962. Today, the top 10 verdicts each year in the United States exceed $50 million, and more than 400 multimillion-dollar verdicts are returned each year. Business payments to claimants are estimated to be $129–$136 billion per year.[1]

Product liability is a unique area of law. It has social roots in that it attempts to lessen the burden of losses by requiring a manufacturer or manufacturer's insurer to pay for damages and injuries that result from a defective product. It also has contract roots in that if a product does not do what it is supposed to do, a breach of contract has occurred. Finally, it also has roots in tort law because liability can also be based on carelessness. Product liability is a combination of contract law, tort law, and social responsibility.

This chapter answers the following questions: How did product liability law develop? What are the contract theories for recovery? What is required for a tort-based recovery on a defective product? How does advertising create liability for a business? What is strict tort liability for products? What reforms are proposed for cutting back liability? Are international product liability standards different? ■

update ↖

For up-to-date legal news, click on "Author Updates" at

www.cengage.com/blaw/ jennings

Advertising may be described as the science of arresting human intelligence long enough to get money out of it.
STEPHEN LEACOCK

Caution: Cape does not enable user to fly.
INSTRUCTIONS ON KENNER PRODUCTS' BATMAN COSTUME

If you do not understand, or cannot read, all directions, cautions and warnings, do not use this product.

WARNING ON DRAIN CLEANER; WINNER OF LAWSUIT ABUSE WATCH'S ANNUAL "WACKY LABEL CONTEST," 2004

Remove child before folding.

ON A STROLLER

consider...

David DeRienzo and his friends did "extreme" sports. Mr. DeRienzo maintained a Web site, *www.roadgap.com,* which showed the group's sports adventures. Mr. DeRienzo was using a used Trek-brand mountain bike for his jumping. A warning in one of the manuals he received with the used bike from the original owner includes the following, "Avoid jumping. Bicycles are not made for jumping. Doing so may cause your frame to fail. Never ride your bicycle in such a manner as to propel your bicycle airborn [sic], including riding over steps and curbs." Mr. DeRienzo had worked on the bike frame after purchasing it and had substituted parts.

Mr. DeRienzo was injured when the bike frame fell apart after he jumped 5–8 feet off a ledge created by a rock sticking out of the side of a hill. Mr. DeRienzo filed suit against Trek for its defective bike frame as well as its failure to warn him about the dangers of a mountain bike and mountain biking. Can Mr. DeRienzo recover?

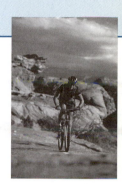

Development of Product Liability

For some time, courts followed the principle of ***caveat emptor***—"Let the buyer beware." *Caveat emptor* means that sellers were not liable for defects in their products and that it was the buyer's responsibility to be on the alert for defects and take the appropriate precautions.

However, the public policy wisdom of *caveat emptor* ended when the *Restatement (Second) of Torts* adopted its now famous Section 402A on strict tort liability (discussed later in this chapter). With this adoption, the area of product liability had gone full swing from no liability (*caveat emptor*) to an almost *per se* standard of liability for defective products (*caveat vendor*).

Advertising as a Contract Basis for Product Liability

EXPRESS WARRANTIES

An **express warranty** under the Uniform Commercial Code (UCC) is an express promise (oral or written) by the seller as to the quality, abilities, or performance of a product (UCC § 2–313). The seller need not use the words *promise* or *guarantee* to make an express warranty. A seller makes a warranty by displaying a sample or model or giving a description of the goods. Promises of how the goods will perform are also express warranties. "These goods are 100% wool," "This tire cannot be punctured," and "These jeans will not shrink," are examples of express warranties.

Although ads are express warranties, they are only one form. The negotiation process can find the seller making express warranties to the buyer. For example, if a seller tells the buyer that a dog is a purebred or that a horse is "disease free," the seller has made an express warranty. Any statements made by the seller to the buyer before the sale that are part of the basis of the sale or bargain are express warranties. Also, information included on product packaging can result in an express warranty: "Will not stain clothing."

Opinions, however, are not considered a basis for transactions and are therefore not express warranties. For example, the statement "These jeans are the best on the market" is sales puffing and not an express warranty. Exhibit 9.1 gives some examples of statements of fact versus opinion.

Castro v. *QVC Network, Inc.* (Case 9.1), deals with an issue of liability for ad statements.

EXHIBIT   9.1   Statements of Fact Versus Opinion

STATEMENT	FACT OR OPINION?
This car gets 20 miles per gallon.	Fact
This car gets great gas mileage.	Opinion
These goods are 100% wool.	Fact
This is the finest wool around.	Opinion
This truck has never been in an accident.	Fact
This truck is solid.	Opinion
This mace stops assailants in their tracks.	Fact (promise of performance)
This mace is very effective.	Opinion
This makeup is hypoallergenic.	Fact
This makeup is good for your skin.	Opinion
This ink will not stain clothes.	Fact
This ink is safe to use.	Opinion
This computer is IBM-compatible.	Fact
This computer is as good as any IBM.	Opinion
This watch is waterproof.	Fact
This watch is durable.	Opinion

CASE 9.1

Castro v. *QVC Network, Inc.*
139 F.3d 114 (2d Cir. 1998)

A Turkey of a Pan: Liability on Thanksgiving Day

Facts

In November 1993, QVC Network (appellee), an operator of a cable television home-shopping channel, advertised, as part of a one-day Thanksgiving promotion, the "T-Fal Jumbo Resistal Roaster." The roaster was manufactured by U.S.A. T-Fal Corporation. The QVC ad described the roaster as suitable for roasting a 25-pound turkey. At the time that T-Fal and QVC entered into an agreement for the sale of the roasting pan, T-Fal did not have a pan in its line large enough to roast a 25-pound turkey. T-Fal asked its parent company in France to provide a suitable roasting pan as soon as possible. The parent company provided a larger pan to which it added two small handles.

Loyda Castro (appellant) ordered the roasting pan and used it for roasting her turkey on Thanksgiving Day, 1993. Mrs. Castro was injured when she tried to remove the turkey from the oven. Using two large insulated oven mitts, Mrs. Castro tried to lift the pan from the oven, placing two fingers on each handle. Two fingers were the maximum grip permitted by the small handles. As the turkey tipped toward her, she lost control of the pan, spilling the hot drippings and fat that had accumulated in the pan during the cooking and basting process. Mrs. Castro suffered second- and third-degree burns to her foot and ankle, which have led to scarring, paresthesia, and swelling.

Mrs. Castro filed suit for strict liability and breach of warranty. The warranty charge was dismissed, and the jury returned a verdict for QVC and T-Fal. Mrs. Castro appealed.

Judicial Opinion

CALABRESI, Circuit Judge

[T]he pan was advertised as suitable for a particular use—cooking a twenty-five pound turkey. Indeed, T-Fal added handles to the pan in order to fill QVC's request for a roasting pan that it could use in its Thanksgiving promotion. The product was, therefore, sold as appropriately used for roasting a twenty-five pound turkey. And it was in that use that allegedly the product failed and injured the appellant.

In such circumstances, the appellants were entitled to a separate breach of warranty charge.

Reversed.

Case Questions

1. How was the turkey pan purchased? Does it make a difference that it was purchased via TV?

2. What type of express warranty was made?

3. Would showing a large turkey being roasted in the pan on QVC be enough to constitute an express warranty or would there need to be statements about its suitability for large birds?

consider 9.1

John R. Klages was employed as a night auditor at Conley's Motel on Route 8 in Hampton Township. He worked from 11 P.M. until 7 A.M., five days a week. On March 30, 1968, at approximately 1:30 A.M., two individuals entered the motel and announced, "This is a stickup. Open the safe." Mr. Klages indicated that he was unable to open the safe because he did not know the combination. One of the individuals then pointed a gun at his head and pulled the trigger. Fortunately for Mr. Klages, the gun was a starter pistol, and he was not seriously injured.

The next day, Mr. Klages and a fellow employee, Bob McVay, decided that they needed something to protect themselves against the possibility of future holdups. After reading an article concerning the effects of mace, Mr. McVay suggested that they consider using mace for their protection and secured from the Mark1 Supply Company four leaflets describing certain mace weapons.

After reading and discussing the literature with their employer, Mr. McVay purchased an MK-II mace weapon from Mark1 Supply Company, which described the mace as follows.

> *Rapidly vaporizes on face of assailant effecting* instantaneous incapacitation. . . . *It will* instantly stop and subdue *entire groups* . . . instantly stops assailants in their tracks. . . . [A]n attacker is subdued instantly, *for a period of 15 to 20 minutes.* . . . Time Magazine *stated the Chemical Mace is* "for police the first, if not the final, answer to a nationwide need—a weapon that *disables as effectively as a gun and yet does no permanent injury.*" . . . *The effectiveness is the result of a unique,* incapacitating formulation (patent pending), *projected in a shotgun-like pattern of heavy liquid droplets that, upon contact with the face, cause extreme tearing, and a stunned, winded condition, often accompanied by dizziness and apathy.*

At approximately 1:40 A.M. on September 22, 1968, while Mr. Klages was on duty, two unknown individuals entered the motel office, requested a room, and announced a stickup. One of the intruders took out a gun and directed Mr. Klages to open the safe. Using the cash register as a shield, Mr. Klages squirted the mace, hitting the intruder "right beside the nose." Mr. Klages immediately ducked below the register, but the intruder followed him down and shot him in the head. The intruders immediately departed, and Mr. Klages called the police. The bullet wound caused complete loss of sight in Mr. Klages's right eye. He claims a breach of an express warranty. Is he right? (Analysis appears at the end of the chapter.) [*Klages* v. *General Ordnance Equipment Corp.,* 19 UCC Rep. Serv. (Callaghan) 22 (Pa. 1976)]

• •

FEDERAL REGULATION OF WARRANTIES AND ADVERTISING

Express warranties are advertisements for goods. Accurate advertising is a basis for full information, and full information is a cornerstone for competitive markets. The federal government works toward full and fair advertising through the 1914 **Federal Trade Commission Act**, in which Congress authorized the **Federal Trade Commission (FTC)** to prevent "unfair and deceptive trade practices." Congress also passed the **Wheeler-Lea Act** of 1938, clarifying and expanding the FTC's power by authorizing it to regulate "unfair and deceptive acts or practices" whenever the public is being deceived, regardless of any effects on competition.

CONTENT CONTROL AND ACCURACY

The FTC has regulated the accuracy of ads in several ways. First, the FTC challenged certain types of price claims. If an ad announces "50% off," the prices must actually be half the original prices charged for the products or services prior to the sale; that price cannot be inflated to cover the markdown. If an ad quotes a "normal" price, that price must reflect what most sellers in the area are charging.

The FTC also challenges ad claims. Claims that goods are "100% wool" are not only the basis for express warranty recovery but, if false, also the basis for an FTC challenge. Sometimes ad claims are true but advertising methods are deceptive. For example, using "marbles" in soup to make it look thicker as it pours is deceptive. The FTC also regulates contract terms and the time for performance. For example, the FTC, through its Mail or Telephone Order Merchandise Rule, requires that catalog merchants disclose delays in delivering ordered goods to consumers and that consumers be informed up front about product delays that result from custom or special orders or because of direct-from-the-manufacturer shipment. The FTC has enforced delay disclosure requirements against Internet merchants as well. In *In the Matter of Macys.com, KBkids.com, and CDnow, Inc.*, the FTC settled charges with these three e-retailers who were alleged to have violated the Mail or Telephone Order Merchandise Rule by failing to provide buyers with adequate notice of shipping delays during the pre-Christmas shopping crunch.

FTC CONTROL OF PERFORMANCE CLAIMS

When an advertising claim cannot be substantiated, the FTC has used **corrective advertising** as a remedy. Corrective advertising requires a seller to explain unsubstantiated claims made in previous ads. The landmark case *Warner-Lambert Co. v. FTC* (Case 9.2) involves an issue of corrective advertising.

CASE 9.2

Warner–Lambert Co. v. *FTC*
562 F.2D 749 (D.C. CIR. 1977), CERT DEN. 435 U.S. 950 (1978)
DOES LISTERINE PREVENT COLDS?

FACTS

Listerine, a product of Warner-Lambert Company (petitioner), has been on the market since 1879 and has been represented through advertising to be beneficial for colds, cold symptoms, and sore throats. After a 1972 complaint about Warner-Lambert advertising for Listerine, the FTC held four months of hearings on the ad issues and then ordered Warner-Lambert to run the following language in its ads, "Contrary to prior advertising, Listerine will not help prevent colds or sore throats or lessen their severity."

Warner-Lambert appealed the order.

JUDICIAL OPINION

WRIGHT, Circuit Judge
[T]he Commission found that Listerine has no significant beneficial effect on the symptoms of sore throat. The Commission recognized that gargling with Listerine could provide temporary relief from a sore throat by removing accumulated debris irritating the throat. But this type of relief can also be obtained by gargling with salt water or even warm water.

Petitioner contends that even if its advertising claims in the past were false, the portion of the Commission's order requiring "corrective advertising" exceeds the Commission's statutory power. The

Commission's position is that the affirmative disclosure that Listerine will not prevent colds or lessen their severity is absolutely necessary to give effect to the prospective cease and desist order; a hundred years of false cold claims have built up a large reservoir of erroneous consumer belief that would persist, unless corrected, long after petitioner ceased making the claims.

If the Commission is to attain the objectives Congress envisioned, it cannot be required to confine its road block to the narrow lane the transgressor has traveled; it must be allowed effectively to close all roads to the prohibited goal, so that its order may not be bypassed with impunity.

[W]e believe the preamble "Contrary to prior advertising" is not necessary. It can serve only two purposes: either to attract attention that a correction follows or to humiliate the advertiser. The Commission claims only the first purpose for it, and this we think is obviated by other terms of the order. The second purpose, if it were intended, might be called for in an egregious case of deliberate deception, but this is not one. While we do not decide whether petitioner proffered its cold claims in good faith or bad, the record compiled could support a finding of good faith. On these facts, the confessional preamble to the disclosure is not warranted.

Accordingly, the order, as modified, is affirmed.

CONTINUED

CASE QUESTIONS

1. What is the difference between the FTC's order for corrective advertising and the court's decision?

2. Explain why the FTC must have corrective advertising as a tool.

3. What is the relationship between the preamble, "Contrary to prior advertising" and good faith?

FTC CONTROL OF CELEBRITY ENDORSEMENTS

Since the 1980s, the FTC has regulated the use of **celebrity endorsements** for products. With a celebrity endorsement, the FTC requires celebrities to be sure that what they claim in their ads is the truth. Second, celebrities cannot make any claims about product use unless they have actually used and experienced the product. Finally, any claims celebrities make about the product or service that are not based on their own experience must also include a disclosure in the ad about the source of their information.

FTC CONTROL OF BAIT AND SWITCH

One of the better-known FTC ad regulations prohibits the use of **bait and switch**, a sales tactic in which a cheaper product than the one in stock is advertised to get customers into a store. The seller has no intention of selling the product and in some cases might not even have the product in stock; but the ad is used as "bait" to get the customers in and present them with a "better," more expensive product. Such ad tactics violate FTC regulations .

FTC CONTROL OF PRODUCT COMPARISONS

The FTC permits and even welcomes comparisons of products, but those comparisons must be fair and accurate. Most litigation over comparative ads is by and against competitors. Federal trademark law permits competitors to recover from companies that run misleading comparative ads. Litigation over comparative ads is somewhat rewarding because plaintiffs can recover treble damages, the defendant company's profits, and, in some cases, attorney fees. Suits that have been filed for competitor misrepresentations include an action by MCI against AT&T for claims that AT&T is cheaper than MCI, and a suit by Gillette against Wilkinson for claims that men preferred Wilkinson's Ultra Glide razor to Gillette's Ultra Plus. *McNeil-PPC, Inc.* v. *Pfizer Inc.* (Case 9.3) involves competitor's litigation over comparisons.

CASE 9.3

McNeil-PPC, Inc. v. *Pfizer Inc.*
351 F.SUPP.2D 226 (S.D.N.Y.2005)

STRINGING THEM ALONG ON NO FLOSS

FACTS

In June 2004, Pfizer Inc. ("Pfizer") launched a consumer advertising campaign for its mouthwash, Listerine Antiseptic Mouthrinse. Print ads and hang tags on the bottles in the stores featured an image of a Listerine bottle balanced on a scale against a white container of dental floss.

The commercial announced that "Listerine's as effective as floss at fighting plaque and gingivitis. Clinical studies prove it." Although the commercial cautioned that "[t]here's no replacement for flossing," the commercial repeats two more times the message that Listerine is "as effective as flossing against plaque and gingivitis."

McNeil-PPC, Inc. ("PPC") (and a division of Johnson & Johnson), the market leader in sales of string dental floss and other interdental cleaning products, brought suit alleging that Pfizer engaged in false advertising and unfair competition. PPC said that Pfizer's advertisements were false and misleading because the ads implicitly claim that Listerine is a replacement for floss—that all the benefits of flossing may be obtained by rinsing with Listerine.

PPC filed a motion for an injunction to stop Pfizer from running the ads.

JUDICIAL OPINION

CHIN, District Judge

Traditionally, the "most widely recommended" mechanical device for removing interproximal plaque is dental floss. The ADA recommends "brushing twice a day and cleaning between the teeth with floss or interdental cleaners once each day to remove plaque from all tooth surfaces." Some 87% of consumers, however, floss either infrequently or not at all. As a consequence, non-flossers are a large consumer market to be tapped. If the 87% of consumers who never or rarely floss can be persuaded to floss more regularly, sales of floss would increase dramatically. PPC has endeavored, with products such as the RADF and the Power Flosser, to reach these consumers by trying to make flossing easier.

Pfizer has come to realize that if it could convince consumers who were reluctant flossers that they could obtain the benefits of flossing by rinsing with Listerine, it would be in a position to see its sales of Listerine increase dramatically. . . . [t]herefore, Pfizer and PPC are competitors.

Pfizer sponsored two clinical studies involving Listerine and floss: the "Sharma Study" and the "Bauroth Study."

The authors (of the Sharma study) concluded that the study provided "additional support for the use of the essential oil mouthrinse as an adjunct to mechanical oral hygiene regimens." They cautioned that "[p]rofessional recommendations to floss daily should continue to be reinforced."

The Bauroth Study authors concluded: "[W]e do not wish to suggest that the mouthrinse should be used instead of dental floss or any other interproximal cleaning device."

Pfizer's ads are comparative ads, and although they do not specifically mention PPC's product by name, PPC is the market leader in sales of floss, with 40% or more of the string floss category. As a PPC marketing executive testified: "[PPC's] brand really is the floss category to many consumers." In addition, the Pfizer ads feature a white floss container similar to if not identical to J&J's white floss container.

Pfizer is directly comparing Listerine to floss, Pfizer and PPC are in head-to-head competition for the same market-non-flossers or reluctant flossers. These individuals would be easily enticed by the notion that they could obtain the benefits of flossing by rinsing with Listerine. Moreover, there may very well be a future impact on regular flossers as well.

I find that Pfizer's false and misleading advertising also poses a public health risk, as the advertisements present a danger of undermining the efforts of dental professionals—and the ADA—to convince consumers to floss on a daily basis.

Injunction granted.

CASE QUESTIONS

1. What are the limitations of the studies on which Pfizer relied?

2. Why are mouthwash and floss competitors?

3. Describe the standards the court uses for stopping a misleading or false ad.

ethical *issues*

Evaluate Pfizer's use of the studies, the ads, and comment on the company's social responsibility posture. Comment on its competitive strategies.

FTC REMEDIES

More often than not, FTC remedies come about through a consent decree. A **consent decree** is a negotiated settlement between the FTC and the advertiser. It is the equivalent of a *nolo contendere* or no contest plea. The FTC and the advertiser, endorser, and/or agency or Web site designer agree to remedies, and the case is disposed of through the decree without further action.

AD REGULATION BY THE FDA

The Food and Drug Administration (FDA) also has authority over some forms of advertising. For example, the FDA has control over direct advertising to the public of prescription medications such as antidepressants. The FDA keeps close watch over the ad claims and makes certain that the ads disclose side effects and tell consumers to see their doctors for advice about the prescription drug being advertised.

PROFESSIONAL ADS

Most states have limitations on the types of ads professionals (such as doctors, lawyers, dentists, and accountants) can use in reaching the public. At one time, states had complete bans on ads by professionals. However, the U.S. Supreme Court held such bans to be too restrictive and violative of First Amendment protections on commercial speech. (See Chapter 4.) Professional ads may be regulated, such as with requirements on fee disclosures, but not eliminated.

Contract Product Liability Theories: Implied Warranties

The UCC's Article 2 also includes sections on implied warranties. The following sections cover the requirements for each of the implied warranties.

THE IMPLIED WARRANTY OF MERCHANTABILITY

The **implied warranty of merchantability** (UCC § 2–314) is given in every sale of goods by a merchant seller. The warranty is given only by merchant sellers. Briefly defined, merchants are those sellers who are engaged in the business of selling the goods that are the subject of the contract. Best Buy is a merchant of electronic goods and appliances. This warranty requires that goods sold by a merchant "© are fit for the ordinary purposes for which goods of that description are used." The warranty means the goods are of fair or average quality and are fit for ordinary purposes. Under this warranty, basketballs must bounce and book bindings must hold together. This is also the "food" warranty, or the warranty that provides a remedy when we find odd items in our purchased or restaurant food. *Mitchell* v. *T.G.I. Friday's* (Case 9.4) deals with one of these "food" cases.

CASE 9.4

Mitchell v. T.G.I. Friday's
748 N.E.2d 89 (Ohio App. 2000)

CLAMMING UP BECAUSE OF SHELL-SHOCK

FACTS

On April 11, 1996, Sandra Mitchell (appellant) was having dinner at Friday's restaurant (appellee). Ms. Mitchell was eating a fried clam strip when she bit into a hard substance that she believed to be a piece of a clam shell. She experienced immediate pain and later sought dental treatment. Some time later, the crown of a tooth came loose. The crown could not be reattached, and an oral surgeon removed the remaining root of the tooth.

Ms. Mitchell filed a product liability action against Friday's, which had served her the meal, and Pro Source Distributing (also appellee), the supplier of the fried clams. Both Friday's and Pro Source filed motions for summary judgment, which the trial court granted without explanation. Ms. Mitchell appealed.

JUDICIAL OPINION

WAITE, Judge
Both Friday's and Pro Source presented essentially the same argument, that regardless of whether the foreign-natural test or reasonable-expectation test was applied, appellant has no claim against appellees.

However, it does not appear necessary to determine which test applies to the present case. Save for reference to the product liability statute, a similar argument was addressed in *Mathews v. Maysville Seafoods, Inc.* (1991), 76 Ohio App.3d 624, 602 N.E.2d 764. In *Mathews*, the plaintiff suffered a bowel injury when he swallowed a fish bone while eating a fish fillet served by the defendant. The trial court granted the defendant's motion for summary judgment. On appeal, the defendant argued for the adoption of the reasonable-expectation test as opposed to the foreign-natural test.

Under the foreign-natural test:

Bones which are natural to the type of meat served cannot legitimately be called a foreign substance, and a consumer who eats meat dishes ought to anticipate and be on his guard against the presence of such bones.

[Q]uoting *Mix v. Ingersoll Candy Co.* (1936), 6 Cal.2d 674, 682, 59 P.2d 144, 148.

The reasonable-expectation test states:

The test should be what is "reasonably expected" by the consumer in the food as served, not what might be natural to the ingredients of that food prior to preparation. . . . As applied to the action for common-law negligence, the test is related to the foreseeability of harm on the part of the defendant. The defendant is not an insurer but has the duty of ordinary care to eliminate or remove in the preparation of the food he serves such harmful substances as the consumer of the food, as served, would not ordinarily anticipate and guard against.

Mathews, 602 N.E.2d at 765.

An occasional piece of clam shell in a bowl of clam chowder is so well known to a consumer that we can say the consumer can reasonably anticipate and guard against it.

Courts cannot and must not ignore the common experience of life and allow rules to develop that would make sellers of food or other consumer goods insurers of the products they sell.

In the present case, it cannot be disputed that the piece of clam shell that caused appellant's injury was natural to the clam strip she consumed. Turning to the question of whether appellant should have reasonably anticipated the presence of the clam shell, we are reminded of the Ohio Supreme Court's holding in *Allen, supra*, that "the possible presence of a piece of oyster shell in or attached to an oyster is so well known to anyone who eats oysters that we can say as a matter of law that one who eats oysters can reasonably anticipate and guard against eating such a piece of shell." We therefore hold that, as a matter of law, one who eats clams can reasonably anticipate and guard against eating a piece of shell.

As appellant's claim fails under both tests, we overrule her assignment of error and affirm the judgment of the trial court.

Judgment affirmed.

CASE QUESTIONS

1. What did Ms. Mitchell eat, and what were her resulting injuries?

2. What test does Ohio follow—the foreign-natural or the reasonable-expectation test?

   And does the court think the Ohio test makes a difference in this case?

3. Is the reasonable-expectation test one that makes the food producer or provider an insurer?

THE IMPLIED WARRANTY OF FITNESS FOR A PARTICULAR PURPOSE

The **implied warranty of fitness for a particular purpose** (UCC § 2–315) arises when the seller promises a buyer that the goods will be suitable for a use the buyer has proposed. For example, the owner of a nursery makes an implied warranty for a particular purpose when telling a buyer that a weed killer will work in the buyer's rose garden without harming the roses. An exercise enthusiast is given this warranty when the seller recommends a particular shoe as appropriate for aerobics.

The requirements for this warranty are:

1. The seller has skill or judgment in use of the goods.
2. The buyer is relying on that skill or judgment.
3. The seller knew or had reason to know of the buyer's reliance.
4. The seller makes a recommendation for the buyer's use and purpose.

consider 9.2

Cynthia Rubin went to Marshall Field's department store on April 5, 1986. While browsing, she got into a conversation with Julianna Reiner, a salesclerk, and told Ms. Reiner that she used Vaseline to remove her eye makeup. Ms. Reiner said Vaseline could clog her eye ducts and cause cataracts or other permanent eye damage, and she recommended Princess Marcella Borghese Instant Eye Make-Up Remover, manufactured by Princess Marcella Borghese, Inc. Ms. Rubin asked if the product was safe. Ms. Reiner showed her the box, which said, "Recommended for all skin types." Ms. Reiner said, "If it wouldn't be safe for you, it wouldn't say this on the box." Relying on Ms. Reiner's representations, Ms. Rubin purchased the product.

That night she used the product to remove her eye makeup. Her eyelids and the skin around her eyes turned red, became taut and rough, and started to sting. She washed her skin repeatedly and kept a cold washrag on her eyes all night. Two days later, when the burning did not subside, she called an ophthalmologist and went to see him the next day. He told her that she had contact dermatitis and prescribed an ointment.

A few weeks later, because the burning and roughness of her eyelids persisted, Ms. Rubin decided to see Dr. Katherine Wier, a dermatologist. Dr. Wier prescribed a similar ointment and told Ms. Rubin that the chemical causing the burning would remain in her system for three or four months. The stinging subsided, but Ms. Rubin could not wear eye makeup again regularly until summer 1987. When she tried to wear makeup again before that, her eyelids turned bright red and began swelling upon removal of the makeup.

Ms. Rubin filed suit for breach of implied warranty of fitness for a particular purpose. Should she recover? (Analysis appears at the end of the chapter.) [*Rubin* v. *Marshall Field & Co.*, 597 N.E.2d 688 (Ill. 1992)]

ELIMINATING WARRANTY LIABILITY BY DISCLAIMERS

Warranties can be eliminated by the use of **disclaimers**. The proper method for disclaiming a warranty depends on the type of warranty. Express warranties, however, cannot be given and then taken back. Basically, an express warranty cannot be disclaimed. Exhibit 9.2 includes a summary of the means for disclaiming warranties.

EXHIBIT   9.2   UCC Warranties: Creation, Restrictions, and Disclaimers

TYPE	CREATION	RESTRICTION	DISCLAIMER
Express	Affirmation of fact or promise of performance (samples, models, descriptions)	Must be part of the basis of the bargain	Cannot make a disclaimer inconsistent with an express warranty
Implied Warranty of Merchantability	Given in every sale of goods by a merchant ("fit for ordinary purposes")	Only given by merchants	(1) Must use disclaimer of quality or use "merchant-ability" or general disclaimer "as is" or "with all faults" (2) if written—(record) must be conspicuous
Implied Warranty of Fitness for a Particular Purpose	Seller knows of buyer's reliance for a particular use (buyer is ignorant)	Seller must have knowledge— Buyer must rely	(1) Must be in writing (record) (2) Must be conspicuous (3) Must be clear there are no warranties (using specific language) or (4) Also disclaimed with "as is" or "with all faults"
Title	Given in every sale	Does not apply in circumstances where apparent warranty is not given	Must state "There is no warranty of title"

The implied warranty of merchantability and the implied warranty of fitness for a particular purpose can be disclaimed by using a phrase such as "WITH ALL FAULTS," or "AS IS." Either warranty alone can be disclaimed by using the name of the warranty: "There is no warranty of merchantability given" or "There is no implied warranty of fitness for a particular purpose." Under Revised Article 2, the disclaimer for the implied warranty of merchantability must include the following language: "The seller undertakes no responsibility for the quality of the goods except as otherwise provided in this contract." Also under the Revised Article 2 provisions, a warranty can be disclaimed in a record. "**Record**" is new to the Revised UCC and expands the definition of writing to include electronic communications such as e-mails and faxes. For those warranty disclaimers required to be in writing, their presence in a record satisfies the writing requirements.

Exhibit 9.2 summarizes the UCC warranty protections and disclaimers.

Business Planning Tip

To disclaim a warranty, follow these guidelines.

1. Use LARGE type.
2. Use a different color for the disclaimer text.
3. Place the disclaimer on the front of the contract.
4. Use proper statutory language.
5. Have buyers initial the disclaimer.
6. On electronic records, get verification of receipt of e-mail or fax with disclaimer.

Strict Tort Liability: Product Liability Under Section 402A

There is liability beyond the statutory, contract, and UCC theories covered so far. A broader focus to product liability is based in tort law. There is both strict liability in tort and liability based on negligence for defective products.

The first tort theory for recovery for defective products is **strict liability** in tort. This tort was created and defined by Section 402A of the *Restatement (Second) of Torts*. Restatements of the law are developed by the American Law Institute, an educational group of professors and practicing attorneys. Restatements are not the law, even though they are adopted and recognized in many states as the controlling statement of law in that state. The adoption of a restatement generally comes in the form of judicial acceptance of the doctrines provided.

Restatement § 402A:

402A. Special Liability of Seller of Product for Physical Harm to User or Consumer

1. One who sells any product in a defective condition unreasonably dangerous to the user or consumer or to his property is subject to liability for physical harm thereby caused to the ultimate user or consumer, or to his property if

   a. the seller is engaged in the business of selling such a product, and

   b. it is expected to and does reach the user or consumer without substantial change in the condition in which it is sold.

2. The rule stated in Subsection (1) applies although

   a. the seller has exercised all possible care in the preparation and sale of his product, and

   b. the user or consumer has not bought the product from or entered into any contractual relations with the seller.

UNREASONABLY DANGEROUS DEFECTIVE CONDITION

The most common types of product liability cases are based on the following types of defects:

1. Design defects
2. Dangers of use due to lack of warnings or unclear use instructions
3. Errors in manufacturing, handling, or packaging of the product

Design Defects

A product with a faulty design exposes its users to unnecessary risks, and products must be designed with all foreseeable uses in mind. Cars must be designed with the probability of accidents in mind. A design that causes a gas tank to explode with the slightest tap of the rear-end bumper is a faulty design example.

One of the evolving product liability issues is whether sellers and manufacturers can be held liable for the dangers inherent in their products, placed there not by design but by nature. For example, eggs that contain a harmful disease or that were injected with a virus would be unreasonably dangerous and subject to product liability recovery claims. However, could there be recovery from egg producers because of the effects of eggs on body cholesterol levels? And is McDonald's liable because its high-calorie, high-fat foods have resulted in weight gains and obesity in those who frequent this restaurant chain? Or can gun and bullet manufacturers be held liable for the crimes, deaths, and injuries that result from the inherently dangerous nature and uses of their products? The courts have been fairly consistent in ruling that the use of a nondefective product that is sold with adequate warnings does not result in liability for the manufacturer. If manufacturers were held liable for the criminal conduct of others, for example, in the case of guns, a result that would be a shift in public policy and accountability.[?]

Improper Warnings and Instructions

Manufacturers have a duty to warn buyers when there is a foreseeably dangerous use of a product that buyers are not likely to realize is dangerous. They also have a duty to supplement the warnings. For example, as defects are discovered in autos, the manufacturers send recall notices to buyers. Similarly, manufacturers of airplanes have sent warnings on problems and proper repair procedures to airlines throughout the life of a particular plane design's use. Manufacturers must also give adequate instructions to buyers on the proper use of the product. Over-the-counter drugs carry instructions about proper dosages and the limitations on dosages.

Errors in Manufacturing, Handling, or Packaging

This breach of duty is the most difficult form of negligence to prove. There are usually so many handlers in the process of manufacturing and packaging a product that it becomes difficult to prove when and how the manufacturer was negligent. One of the issues in drug manufacturing cases is whether the packaging for the materials is sufficient. Does it protect against tampering? Is it childproof? These types of dangers require special duties with regard to packaging drugs.

REACHING THE BUYER IN THE SAME CONDITION

A seller will not be liable for a product that has been modified or changed. Once a product is modified or changed, we can't be sure whether the original product or the modifications caused the unreasonably dangerous condition. This issue arises in airplane crash cases. Did the air carrier follow the manufacturer's repair procedures or did the mechanics take shortcuts? The failure to follow these procedures could eliminate the manufacturer's liability because the aircraft may have been altered.

THE REQUIREMENT OF A SELLER ENGAGED IN A BUSINESS

Section 402A requires the seller to be "engaged in the business of selling the product." This requirement sounds like the merchant requirement for the UCC warranty of merchantability. However, the meaning of "selling the product" is slightly broader under Section 402A than the UCC meaning of merchant. For example, a baseball club is not a merchant of beer, but, if the club sells beer at its games, it is a seller for purposes of Section 402A. Section 402A covers manufacturers, wholesalers, retailers, food sellers, and even those who sell products out of their homes.

Privity Issues in Tort Theories of Product Liability

UCC warranty theories are somewhat limited by the requirement of **privity**, which is a direct contract relationship between parties. Because the warranties are based on contract, it would be difficult for someone who is injured in a plane crash that resulted from a defective bolt in the plane's wing to recover from the bolt manufacturer. There is privity of contract between the bolt manufacturer and the plane manufacturer. But there is not a direct contract relationship between the passenger and the bolt or plane manufacturer or even between the airline and the bolt manufacturer. However, under tort theories of product liability, they meet the standard of a seller with liability and would be responsible to those who are injured by their products, despite the lack of privity. The standard for liability of a manufacturer or seller in tort is the forseeability of their product use.

Negligence: A Second Tort for Product Liability

A suit for product defects can also be based in negligence. The elements for establishing a negligence case are the same as those for a Section 402A case with one addition: establishing that the product seller or manufacturer either knew of the defect before the product was sold or allowed sales to continue with the knowledge that the product had a defect. If a product user proves knowledge, then the court can award punitive damages.

Exhibit 9.3 compares product liability theories, and Exhibit 9.4 details the basis for product liability.

EXHIBIT   9.3   Comparison of Product Liability Theories

TYPE	PRIVITY REQUIRED?	KNOWLEDGE OF PROBLEM REQUIRED?	WARRANTY PROMISE REQUIRED?
Negligence	No	Yes	No
Section 402A/ strict tort liability	No	No	No
Express warranty	Yes	No	Yes
Implied warranty of merchantability	Yes	No	No
Implied warranty of fitness for a particular purpose	Yes	No	Yes

EXHIBIT   9.4   Legal Basis for Product Liability

CONTRACT	TORT
Express warranty	402A—Strict Tort Liability
Implied warranty of merchantability	Elements
Implied warranty of fitness for particular purpose	(1) Defective condition unreasonably dangerous: design; manufacturing defect; or inadequate warning (2) Defendant in business of using, selling, or manufacturing product (3) Condition of product is the same Negligence Same; and add (4) Knowledge of defect

Defenses to Product Liability Torts

Three defenses are available to a defendant in a product liability tort:

1. Misuse or abnormal use of a product
2. Contributory negligence
3. Assumption of risk

MISUSE OR ABNORMAL USE OF A PRODUCT

Any use of a product that the manufacturer has specifically warned against in its instructions is a **misuse**. Using a forklift to lift 25,000 pounds when the instructions limit its capacity to 15,000 pounds is a misuse of the product, and any injuries resulting from such misuse will not be the liability of the manufacturer. Product misuse also occurs when a plaintiff has used the product in a manner that the defendant could not anticipate and warn against.

CONTRIBUTORY NEGLIGENCE

Contributory negligence is traditionally a complete defense to a product liability suit in negligence. For example, although a front loader might have a design failure of no protective netting around the driver, a driver who is injured while using the front loader for recreational purposes is contributorily negligent. Contributory negligence overlaps greatly with product misuse.

Some states, as discussed in Chapter 8, have adopted a standard of **comparative negligence**, under which the plaintiff's negligence is not a complete defense: The negligence of the plaintiff merely serves to reduce the amount the plaintiff is entitled to recover. For example, a jury might find that the defendant is 60 percent at fault and the plaintiff is 40 percent at fault. The plaintiff recovers, but the amount of that recovery is reduced by 40 percent.

ASSUMPTION OF RISK

When a plaintiff is aware of a danger in the product but goes ahead and uses it anyway, **assumption of risk** occurs. If a car manufacturer recalled your car for repair and you failed to have the repair done, despite full opportunity to do so, you have assumed the risk of driving with that problem. Some activities, such as bungee jumping and sky-diving (extreme sports) are inherently dangerous. You assume the risks of these sports but not the risks of a defective bungee cord or a parachute that does not open when you have done everything correctly.

Derienzo v. *Trek Bicycle Corp.* (Case 9.5) involves issues of assumption of risk, provides the answer for the chapter opening Consider, and brings together many of the issues in product liability that you have studied in this chapter.

CASE 9.5

Derienzo v. Trek Bicycle Corp.
376 F.SUPP.2D 537 (S.D.N.Y. 2005)

JUMPING ON A TREK: FRAMING ASSUMPTION OF RISK

FACTS

David DeRienzo (plaintiff) was part of a group of four men who regularly participated in "extreme" sports. The group would videotape themselves riding mountain bikes and watch each other "hit jumps." Mr. DeRienzo maintained a Web site, *www.roadgap.com,* which, at one time, described and showed the group's sports adventures. Mr. DeRienzo was the first of the group to do "lake jumping," in which the goal is to ride one's bike off a jump into a lake. Mr. DeRienzo had done lake jumping 25–30 times.

Mr. DeRienzo bought a used 1998 Trek (defendant) Y5 model (the Bike), which is a "full-suspension" mountain bike. A Trek catalog includes a section entitled, "Off Road," listing the different Y model bikes (the Y5 among them) and their features, showing that the Rock Shox fork is available on certain models. Mr. DeRienzo had worked on the frame when, after purchasing it, it arrived unassembled and wrapped in towels.

The 1999 Trek manual for the Y5 contained the following language:

Jumping your bicycle, performing bicycle stunts, severe off road riding, downhill riding, or any abnormal bike riding can be very dangerous. These activities increase the stress on your frame and components and can lead to premature or sudden failure of your bicycle frame or components. Such failure could cause a loss of control resulting in serious injury or death.

Avoid jumping. Bicycles are not made for jumping. Doing so may cause your frame to fail. Never ride your bicycle in such a manner as to propel your bicycle airborn [sic], including riding over steps and curbs.

This "Avoid jumping" text is the last of five text segments on page 10, the other four being (in order, from top to bottom): *"Wear a helmet," "Know and observe your local bicycle riding laws," "Use special care when off-road riding,"* and *"Use good shifting techniques."* On the opposite (facing) page, there is a text box with the word "CAUTION" and two segments (including bold text) about the dangers of riding at night and in wet conditions.

Mr. DeRienzo did not read the warnings. Mr. DeRienzo was injured when the bike frame fell apart after he jumped 5–8 feet off a ledge created by a rock sticking out of the side of a hill. Mr. DeRienzo filed suit against Trek for its defective bike frame as well as its failure to warn him about the dangers of a mountain bike and mountain biking. Trek moved for summary judgment.

JUDICIAL OPINION

McMAHON, District Judge

Under New York law, a manufacturer who places a defective product on the market that causes injury may be held strictly liable for the ensuing injuries if the product is not accompanied by adequate warnings for the use of the product. The failure to warn must be a proximate cause of plaintiff's injuries.

The adequacy of a warning is generally a question of fact for the jury. A warning that is inconspicuously located and written in small print may be deficient.

[F]ailure to read a warning is not dispositive. While it is true that, in many cases, a plaintiff who admits that he failed to read a warning that was issued with the product will have failed to show that any deficiency in that warning was the proximate cause of his injuries, plaintiff's failure to read an insufficiently conspicuous or prominent warning will not necessarily defeat the causation element of a failure to warn claim.

Plaintiff asserts that his use of the Bike for jumping was typical of aggressive mountain bikers—so, normal and not a misuse—and that Trek was aware that riders such as he would purchase a Trek Y5 bike for jumping. Plaintiff asserts that Trek did not warn of the dangers of jumping at all, and that its buried admonitions in an Owner's Manual to check the frame for damage were inadequate because they were inconspicuous and also because a visual inspection of the frame would not lead to the discovery of the type of damage that caused the frame to fail—namely, fatigue cracks in the head tube/down tube weld.

[The expert witness's] testimony that jumping is an "entirely foreseeable" and "expected" use of a mountain bike is admissible, I find that Plaintiff withstands summary judgment on that issue. Further, [the expert witness] opines that it was foreseeable that a user would modify a bike the way Plaintiff modified this Bike, *i.e.,* by replacing (among other components), the standard fork with a Rock Shox fork, which the parties agree is designed for jumping. This could lead to an inference that Trek knew users would modify Y5 bikes to make them more suitable for jumping.

As for the Owner's Manual, the fact that the parties submitted two different versions with substantially different warnings and graphics is enough to raise triable issues of fact on the failure to warn claim. Moreover, both Manuals contain warnings on almost half of their pages, which could lead a jury to conclude that any warning against jumping was inconspicuous—in either Manual. Thus, it is far from clear whether Trek warned Y5 users not to jump or of the dangers of jumping, and if it did, whether those warnings were conspicuous and/or adequate. There is also a dispute about whether Trek pasted a warning on the Bike itself—and, if so, to which version of the Owner's Manual it referred—which precludes summary judgment.

Plaintiff has supplied admissible evidence sufficient to raise a genuine issue of fact on the question of whether the Y5 was marketed for use in jumping. This,

combined with [expert] testimony, noted above, that taking a Y5 model bike off a 5-foot drop would constitute a "crash," could indicate that jumping was reasonably foreseeable, but that the Y5 was not designed or reasonably safe for such use. Accordingly, Defendant's motion for summary judgment on breach of warranty also must be denied.

Case Questions

1. List all the conduct of Mr. DeRienzo that would work against his winning a product liability suit.

2. What does the court say about not reading the warnings?

3. What is the relevance of Trek being aware of the use of its bikes?

ethical *issues*

In 1994, a group of Chrysler engineers met to review proposals and recommendations for improving their Chrysler Minivan lines in order to make them more competitive. Paul Sheridan, one of the engineers on Chrysler's Minivan Safety Team, raised the number one issue on the lists of proposals and recommendations: The latches on the minivan rear doors appeared to be popping open even in low-speed crashes. The Chrysler Minivan latches did not appear to have the strength of either the Ford Windstar minivan or the Chevy minivan rear door latches. Mr. Sheridan proposed that Chrysler make the latches stronger and use that strength as a marketing tool.

After Mr. Sheridan made his proposal, and according to testimony in a subsequent product liability suit, a top production engineer told Mr. Sheridan, "That ship has sailed. We told you that last time. Next subject."

In *Jimenez* v. *Chrysler Corporation,* the jury deliberated only 2.5 hours before returning a verdict for the Jimenez family of $262.5 million, $250 million of which was punitive damages.

What would you have done if you had been Mr. Sheridan?

Product Liability Reform

"Our product liability system discourages innovation because of unforeseeable potential liability," says Robert Malcott, CEO of FMC Corporation. Mr. Malcott issued this statement as the chair of the Business Roundtable's task force on product liability. This task force and others have proposed several changes, including limiting punitive damages; meeting government standards as a defense; instituting liability shields for drugs, medical devices, and aircraft; and requiring higher standards of proof for recovery of punitive damages.

The American Law Institute (ALI) has proposed the *Restatement (Third) of Torts,* which would change the current strict liability standard to a negligence standard for defective design and informational defect cases. In other words, plaintiffs who bring product liability cases based on defective design and instruction would have to establish negligence to recover. The strict liability standard would be eliminated under this new proposal. Strict liability would still be the standard for manufacturing defects.

Federal Standards for Product Liability

CONSUMER PRODUCT SAFETY COMMISSION

The federal level of government generally is not involved in product liability issues. However, the **Consumer Product Safety Commission (CPSC)** is a regulatory agency set up under the Consumer Product Safety Act to regulate safety standards for consumer products. The commission has several responsibilities in carrying out its purposes.

1. *To protect the public against unreasonable risks of injury from consumer products*—
   To perform this function, the CPSC has been given the authority to recall products and order their repair or correction. The commission also has the power to ban products completely. This ban can apply only if a product cannot be made less dangerous. The ban on asbestos is an example of the commission's powers. In another example, in 1994, the CPSC recalled nearly all types of metal bunk beds.

2. *To develop standards for consumer product safety*—These standards take the form of regulations and minimum requirements for certain products.

3. *To help consumers become more informed about evaluating safety*—Certain regulations require disclosure of the limits of performance and hazards associated with using a particular product.

4. *To fund research in matters of product safety design and in product-caused injuries and illnesses*

The act carries civil penalties of up to a maximum of $500,000. Knowing or willful violations carry a criminal fine of up to $50,000 and/or 1 year imprisonment, and willful repeat violations carry penalties of up to $500,000 and 10 years. In addition, consumers have a right to sue in federal district court for any damages from a violation of a regulation or law.

International Issues in Product Liability

The EU directive on product liability limits liability to "producers"; it is not as inclusive as U.S. law, which holds all sellers liable. A 10-year limit on liability and the "state-of-the-art" defense apply to most member countries: If a product upon its release was as good as any available, it is not subject to product liability.

In addition to the council's guidelines are the International Standards Organization's 9000 Guidelines for Quality Assurance and Quality Management. These directives require products to carry a stamp of compliance with standards and procedures as a means of limiting product defects.

The CISG (see Chapter 6 for more details) contains similar provisions to the UCC warranty protections for goods sold in international transactions. However, disclaimers are made more easily under the CISG, and the notions of consequential damages are limited because the United States' level of damages in product liability cases far exceeds the levels for any other country in the world. Further, the notion of strict liability for products is unique to the United States, and under EU guidelines the notion of knowledge is used as a standard for imposing liability.

Red Flags FOR MANAGERS

Managers should be careful to review the language in ads for their products. They should also take care to be sure that letters, sales presentations, e-mails, and memos do not make representations that are not true or are inconsistent with the manufacturer's warnings and limitations on the product.

What the sales force says, counts. Remind them about representations and promises when selling.

- Be careful when developing product instructions and warnings. Try to anticipate questions and possible misuse by buyers.

- Design your products with product liability in mind: anticipate, have safety precautions, and develop warnings as the product evolves.

- Make sure that when employees are repairing equipment that they follow manufacturer's directions and advice. Make sure employees follow manufacturer directions when using equipment your company buys.

- If a customer has a complaint or injury, follow up to see if you need to correct ads, instructions, or warnings.

Summary

How does advertising create liability for a business?

- Express warranty—contractual promise about the nature or potential of a product that gives right of recovery if the product falls short of a promise that was a basis of the bargain

- Bait and switch—using a cheaper, unavailable product to lure customers to store with a more expensive one then substituted or offered instead

- Federal Trade Commission (FTC)—federal agency responsible for regulating deceptive ads

- Wheeler-Lea Act—federal law that allows FTC to regulate "unfair and deceptive acts or practices"

- Celebrity endorsements—FTC area of regulation wherein products are touted by easily recognized public figures

- Corrective ads—ads the FTC requires to correct any previous misrepresentation the agency has found in ads

- Consent decree—voluntary settlement of FTC complaint

What are the contract theories of product liability?

- Implied warranty of merchantability—warranty of average quality, purity, and adequate packaging given in every sale by a merchant

- Implied warranty of fitness for a particular purpose—warranty given in circumstances in which the buyer relies on the seller's expertise and acts to purchase according to that advice

- Disclaimer—act of negating warranty coverage

- Privity—direct contractual relationship between parties

What is required for tort-based recovery on a defective product? What is strict tort liability for products?

- Strict liability—standard of liability that requires compensation for an injury regardless of fault or prior knowledge

- Restatement (Second) § 402A—American Law Institute's standards for imposing strict liability for defective products

- Negligence—standard of liability that requires compensation for an injury only if the party responsible knew or should have known of its potential to cause such injury

- Punitive damages—damages beyond compensation for knowledge that conduct was wrongful

What defenses exist in product liability?

- Misuse—product liability defense for plaintiff using a product incorrectly

- Contributory negligence—conduct by plaintiff that contributed to plaintiff's injury; serves as a bar to recovery

- Comparative negligence—negligent conduct by plaintiff serves as a partial defense by reducing liability by percentage of fault

- Assumption of risk—defense to negligence available when plaintiff is told of product risk and voluntarily uses the product

What reforms have occurred and are proposed in product liability?

- Consumer Product Safety Commission—federal agency that regulates product safety and has recall power

Key Terms

assumption of risk 213
bait and switch 204
caveat emptor 199
celebrity endorsements 204
comparative negligence 213
consent decree 206
Consumer Product Safety
    Commission (CPSC) 216

contributory negligence 213
corrective advertising 203
disclaimers 208
express warranty 199
Federal Trade Commission (FTC) 202
Federal Trade Commission Act 202
implied warranty of fitness for a
    particular purpose 208

implied warranty of
    merchantability 206
misuse 213
privity 211
record 209
strict liability 210
Wheeler-Lea Act 202

Questions and Problems

1. Lawrence Dorneles purchased a used 1972 Buick GSX from Mr. Carpenito. Mr. Dorneles had seen Mr. Carpenito's ad that contained a picture of the vehicle and that read as follows: "Buick 1972 GSX, not an original, as close as you can get, all new body parts, 5,000 miles on a new rebuilt 455 Stage 1, car show winner, new exhaust system, mint, tires, never seen rain or snow, garage kept, needs minor interior work, 12 bolt posi rear, hood, tachometer, rear spoiler, all replica details, must sell, $4,500.00. . . ."

Mr. Dorneles answered the ad and spoke with Mr. Carpenito, who reiterated the items in the ad and specifically assured Mr. Dorneles that the rebuilt engine had fewer than 5,000 miles and that the car had been "babied," among other things. Mr. Dorneles neither test-drove the vehicle nor had a mechanic inspect the vehicle prior to purchasing it. The seller provided no written warranty.

Mr. Dorneles paid $4,000.00 for the car and drove it from Port Chester to his home in Pelham. He left the car at home until July 17, when he registered it and was going to drive the car to Valhalla to have a mechanic inspect the car. July 17 was a hot summer day; on the way to Valhalla, some 15 miles from Pelham, the car began to overheat. The car's engine apparently seized because of the extreme heat and had to be towed back to Pelham. The engine was removed from the Buick at a

cost of $450.00, and another new rebuilt engine was installed at a cost of $1,152.00. Additional work had to be done on the car, including repairing broken rear suspension springs ($600.00), installing a new transmission ($750.00), and replacing a corroded chain cover ($174.25).

Was an express warranty given that can be the basis of recovery? Do you waive the express warranty when you do not inspect a car? [*Dorneles* v. *Carpenito,* 521 N.Y.S.2d 967 (1987)]

2. Seven-Up Co. began distributing its soft drinks, including its lemon-lime 7UP, in the 1920s, and by the time Coca-Cola introduced its lemon-lime soft drink, Sprite, in 1961, 7UP dominated the market.

Coca-Cola had been trying for years to break 7UP's hold on the market. In 1991, it launched a sales presentation known as "The Future Belongs to Sprite." The sales presentation consisted of charts, graphs, and overhead displays comparing the relative sales performance of Sprite and 7UP during the 1980s. After the sales presentation had been made to 11 bottlers, 5 of them decided to switch their lemon-lime soft drink from 7UP to Sprite.

7UP filed suit, alleging that Coca-Cola had skewed the data in its presentations and misrepresented what was happening with 7UP's market share. Is the presentation a form of advertising for which 7UP has a remedy? Is there damage from a competitor through misleading ads? [*Seven-Up Co. v. Coca-Cola Co.*, 86 F.3d 1379 (5th Cir. 1996)]

3. On August 6, 1998, Mr. Ruvolo purchased two chicken gordita sandwiches from Taco Bell. While eating the second sandwich, he felt a sharp pain in his throat and dislodged a chicken bone. The bone caused a scrape in his throat, and, as a result, he was treated at an emergency room. The following day, Mr. Ruvolo was diagnosed with acute tonsillitis, pharyngitis, sinusitis, and gastritis.

Mr. Ruvolo sued Taco Bell and its food distributors, alleging that the infections were due to the chicken bone scratching his throat and causing an opening where germs and bacteria could enter. He further alleged that Taco Bell and its food distributors were liable because of their failure to properly inspect the chicken. Discuss the theories Mr. Ruvolo might use for recovery and who the defendants might be. [*Ruvolo v. Homovich*, 778 N.E.2d 661 (Ohio App. 2002)]

4. Michael Sanders was a 40-year-old man who made his living as a member of various music bands throughout Fresno. Mr. Sanders graduated from Fresno State University in May 2004 and planned to teach music. On August 20, 2004, Fresno police officers responded to a call made at the Sanders's home. When the police entered, they found Mr. Sanders, who appeared disoriented, standing unclothed behind his wife, Lavette Sanders. The officers decided to subdue Mr. Sanders by firing tasers at his naked body, although Fresno Police Department rules and other instructions require that tasers not come in contact with human skin. The officers fired numerous taser darts into Mr. Sanders's body. The officers then handcuffed Sanders, placed him face down on a gurney, which suffocated him, and then placed him in an ambulance. Sanders stopped

breathing. One of the officers attempted CRP, but Michael Sanders was pronounced dead at 4:30 A.M.

Mrs. Sanders filed suit against the city of Fresno as well as Taser. She based her suit against Taser on, among other things, that Taser expressly warranted that the product was "safe" and "would not cause injuries to police officers or individuals arrested by police officers." Is this the language of an express warranty? [*Sanders v. City of Fresno*, 2006 WL 1883394 (E.D.Cal. 2006), 59 UCC Rep.Serv.2d 1209]

5. Roy E. Farrar Produce Co. ordered a shipment of boxes from International Paper Company that were to be suitable for the packing and storage of tomatoes. The dimensions of the two sizes of boxes were to be such that either 20 or 30 pounds of tomatoes could be packed without the necessity of weighing each box. Mr. Farrar requested that the boxes be the same type as those supplied to Florida packers for shipping tomatoes. Mr. Farrar told Mr. Wilson, an agent for International, to obtain the correct specifications for the Florida-type box.

International shipped Mr. Farrar 21,500 unassembled boxes at a unit price of 64 cents per box. The boxes were not tomato boxes, were not Florida boxes, did not have adequate stacking strength, and would not hold up during shipping. Mr. Farrar had to repack 3,624 boxes (at a cost of $1.92 per box). Substitute boxes were purchased for 10 cents above the International price. The replacement boxes were Florida boxes and did not collapse. Mr. Farrar was also forced to pay growers $6 a box for tomatoes damaged during shipping. He could not use 6,100 boxes, and his sales dropped off, resulting in financial deficiencies in his operation. Can Mr. Farrar recover for his damages? Why or why not? [*International Paper Co. v. Farrar*, 700 P.2d 642 (N.M. 1985)]

Understanding "Consider" Problems

9.1

THINK: The requirements for an express warranty are a statement of fact or a promise of performance.

APPLY: What statements of fact or promises of performance are made in the ad or on the product packaging?

"[I]nstantly stops assailants in their tracks" is a promise of performance; "*subdued instantly, for a period of 15 to 20 minutes*" is also a promise of performance.

ANSWER: The product failed to live up to those promises, so there was a breach of express warranty, and the company is liable for the injury Mr. Klages sustained after using the mace against his attackers.

9.2

THINK: The warranty of fitness for a particular purpose applies when a salesperson make a recommendation to a buyer who asks for advice on a particular product or asks questions about its use.

APPLY: Here, a salesperson at the cosmetics counter was trained to explain and apply cosmetics. A customer with a particular question was relying on the salesperson.

ANSWER: The cosmetic counter salesperson was providing an implied warranty of fitness for a particular purpose—that there would be no allergic reaction to the product, a concern that the customer had.

Notes

1. AEI-Brookings Joint Center for Regulatory Studies, Senior Fellow Judyth W. Pendell with cost analysis conducted by Paul J. Hinton, 2004; White House Study on U.S. Tort System, conducted by the President's Council on Economic Advisors, 2002.

2. See *McCarthy* v. *Olin*, 119 F.3d 148 (2d Cir. 1997). A series of cases dealt with negligent distribution of guns. Those cases too have been dismissed as issues of public policy to be handled by legislatures. See *Hamilton* v. *Beretta U.S.A. Corp.*, 727 N.Y.S.2d 7 (N.Y. App. 2001); *Hamilton* v. *Beretta U.S.A. Corp.*, 264 F.3d 21 (2d Cir. 2001). A new line of cases focuses on public nuisance as a theory for recovery from gun manufacturers. Courts are divided on these cases, with one procedural dismissal for standing, *N.A.A.C.P.* v. *AcuSport, Inc.*, 271 F.Supp.2d 435 (E.D.N.Y.), and one certification for trial, *City of New York* v. *Beretta U.S.A. Corp.*, 315 F.Supp.2d 256 (E.D.N.Y. 2004).

3

THE LEGAL ENVIRONMENT OF BUSINESS OPERATIONS

This section of the book covers the laws and regulations on what a business sells, how it is structured, how it sells its product or securities, how it protects its property rights, and how the sales are set up and financed. How is a business structured? And if the financing comes from others, through securities, what are the responsibilities of the business to those investors? Do you have the right to sell a product, or have you appropriated someone else's idea? What can you say and write in your advertising? When do you have a contract, and what kinds of terms do you need to have in it? In this era of electronic commerce, what exactly is a contract, and when is it formed? When has a contract been performed, and what is a breach? Can you be compensated if the other side fails to perform? How are transactions financed, and what forms do you need? What are a seller's rights for collecting payments due from buyers?

This portion of the text covers all the preliminary aspects of business operation, from formation to financing to contracting. The materials walk through the heart of business formation and operations: sales, property and shareholder rights, advertising, contract formation and performance, and receivables collection.

10

Contracts and Sales: Introduction and Formation

update

For up-to-date legal news, click on "Author Updates" at

www.cengage.com/blaw/ jennings

Contracts have been necessary since business began. They allow businesses to count on money, supplies, and services. Contracts are the private law of business; the parties develop their own private set of laws through their contracts. These private laws can be enforced by the courts in all states. This chapter covers contract basics: What is a contract? What laws govern contracts? What are the types of contracts? How are contracts formed? What contracts must be in writing? ■

A verbal contract isn't worth the paper it's written on.
SAMUEL GOLDWYN

consider...

In the summer of 1996, PepsiCo, Inc., ran a marketing campaign involving Pepsi Points. The Pepsi Points, obtained by drinking Pepsi, could be redeemed for prizes. One television ad promoting Pepsi Points showed a Harrier jet outside a school yard with the campaign's slogan beneath it: DRINK PEPSI—GET STUFF. The jet pictured in the ad was generated by computer. The ad said the jet could be yours for 7 million Pepsi Points. PepsiCo maintains the ad was a spoof. John Leonard, then a 21-year-old business student, saw the ad and delivered to Pepsi 15 original Pepsi Points plus a check for $700,008.50—

sufficient for the cost of a Harrier jet, plus shipping and handling.

Pepsi refused to deliver the jet. Pentagon spokesman Kenneth Bacon indicated that the ad was a joke and not an offer. Mr. Leonard said that the ad induced conduct on his part, as would all Pepsi Points ads, and that Pepsi was required to deliver to him a Harrier jet. Who was correct? Was the ad an offer?

What Is a Contract?

Businesses are dependent upon fulfilled promises. For example, suppose that Aunt Hattie's Bread Company constructs a new wing and buys new equipment to expand production, but when the wing is ready to operate, the wheat supplier backs out of the supply contract with Aunt Hattie's. Aunt Hattie's has relied on that promise, spent money counting on delivery on that promise, and now cannot expand because that promise was broken. The failure to honor a promise is more than just a breach of contract; economic ripple effects occur when businesses cannot rely on contractual promises.

The *Restatement (Second) of Contracts* defines a **contract** as "a promise or set of promises for breach of which the law gives a remedy, or the performance of which the law in some way recognizes as a duty." The remainder of this chapter focuses on the creation, performance, and enforcement of those promises.

Sources of Contract Law

The three general sources of contract law in the United States are common law, the Uniform Commercial Code, and the new sources of law evolving in response to e-commerce—the Uniform Electronic Transactions Act, the Uniform Computer Information Transactions Act, and the Electronic Signatures in Global and National Commerce Act of 2000 (ESIGN).

COMMON LAW

Common law was the first law of contracts. As discussed in Chapter 1, common law consists today of traditional notions of law developed by judicial decisions and often codified by states. Common law contract principles apply to contracts that have land or services as their subject matter. Contracts for the construction of a home or employment are governed by common law. A rental agreement for an apartment may be covered by specific landlord–tenant statutes in addition to common law.

A general treatment of the common law for contracts can be found in the *Restatement (Second) of Contracts.* A group of legal scholars wrote the *Restatement,* and similar groups work together to consider market changes and dynamics and suggest modifications for contract law as necessary.

THE UNIFORM COMMERCIAL CODE

One of the problems with common law is its lack of uniformity. States do not follow the same case decisions on contract law, and some states do not follow the *Restatement;* the result is that different rules apply to contracts in different states.

Consequently, businesses experienced uncertainty when they contracted across state lines because of differences in state contract common law. To address the need for uniformity, the National Conference of Commissioners on Uniform State Laws and the American Law Institute worked to draft a set of commercial laws that all states would find acceptable. The result of their efforts was the **Uniform Commercial Code (UCC).** The final draft of the UCC first appeared in the 1940s. With several revisions and much time and effort, the Code was adopted, at least in part, in all the states.

Article 2 of the UCC governs contracts for the sale of goods and has been adopted in all states except Louisiana. Although sections of Article 2 may have various forms throughout the states, the basic requirements for contracts remain consistent. Under Article 2 contracts can be formed more easily, the standards for performance are more readily defined, and the remedies are more easily determined.

Which contracts are UCC contracts and which are common law contracts is often difficult to determine. Some factors used to determine which are UCC contracts and which are common law contracts are: the cost of the goods versus the cost of services in the contract, the parties' intent, and even some public policy issues. *Cook* v. *Downing* (Case 10.1) addresses an interesting factual issue involving a question of goods and the application of UCC Article 2.

CASE 10.1

Cook v. *Downing*
891 P.2d 611 (Ok. Ct. App. 1995)

THE DENTURES SOLD WERE A "BILL OF GOODS," BUT WERE THEY UCC GOODS?

FACTS

Dr. Cook (appellant) is a licensed dentist who devotes less than 50 percent of his practice to the work of fitting and making dentures. Mrs. Downing (appellee) is a patient of Dr. Cook who was fitted for dentures. Mrs. Downing filed suit against Dr. Cook after she took delivery of her dentures because she said they were ill-fitting and produced sore spots in her mouth. Dr. Cook's

expert witness testified that Mrs. Downing's problems were probably due to candidas, an autoimmune reaction, or an allergy to the dental material. No expert testified that her problems were due to ill-fitting dentures.

The trial court awarded damages to Mrs. Downing on the basis of a breach of UCC Article 2, implied warranty of fitness for a particular purpose. Dr. Cook appealed, maintaining that the dentures were not a sale of goods.

JUDICIAL OPINION

HUNTER, Judge

We agree with Appellant's position that any claim Appellee might have sounds in tort. In Oklahoma, dentists, professionals who are regulated by the state, furnish dentures. In general, dentists must use ordinary skill in treating their patients. We hold that under the laws of Oklahoma, a dentist is not a merchant and dentures, furnished by a dentist, are not goods under the UCC.

A dentist could be sued for breach of contract, if such contract were alleged to exist, but that is not the fact as revealed in the record in our case. Appellee presented evidence of an advertisement guaranteeing dentures to fit, but testified that she did not see this ad until after she had begun her treatment with Appellant. The evidence does not support any breach of contract action.

As a matter of law, Appellee erroneously based her cause of action on the Uniform Commercial Code rather than negligence. The court erred in entering judgment in favor of Appellee based on this law. For this reason, we reverse the judgment of the trial court and remand the matter with directions to enter judgment in favor of Appellant.

Reversed and remanded with directions.

DISSENTING OPINION

JONES, Judge, dissenting

"Dentists" and "dentures" appear to be included in the definitions of merchants and goods.

Whether implied warranties under Article 2 of the U.C.C. apply to such a transaction should depend on whether the predominant element of the transaction is the sale of goods or the rendering of services. If the sale of goods predominates, it would be within the scope of Article 2 and the implied warranties contained therein. However, if the service aspect predominates, there would be no implied warranties.

In contemporary society the old distinctions separating health care professionals from other businessmen are blurring in many respects. This Court's holding that a dentist is not a merchant, and dentures, furnished by a dentist, are not goods ignores the fact that nothing excludes them from the statutory definitions of merchant and goods. It also ignores the fact that health care professionals in some instances are selling goods to their "patients", with the providing of professional services being secondary to the sale. To such transactions there is no reason Article 2 of the UCC should not apply. I respectfully dissent.

CASE QUESTIONS

1. Does classifying the dentures as something other than the sale of goods deprive Mrs. Downing of a remedy?

2. Do you think eyeglasses and contact lenses should be classified as sales of goods? Why or why not?

3. What public policy issues does the dissenting judge raise?

consider 10.1

Jane Pittsley contracted with Hilton Contract Carpet Co. for the installation of carpet in her home. The total contract price was $4,402. Hilton paid the installers $700 to put the carpet in Ms. Pittsley's home. Following installation, Ms. Pittsley complained to Hilton that some seams were visible, that gaps appeared, that the carpet did not lie flat in all areas, and that it failed to reach the wall in certain locations. Although Hilton tried several times to fix the installation by stretching the carpet and other methods, Ms. Pittsley was not satisfied with the work. Eventually, Ms. Pittsley refused to allow Hilton to try to fix the carpet. Ms. Pittsley had paid Hilton $3,500, but she refused to pay the remaining balance of $902.

Ms. Pittsley filed suit, seeking rescission of the contract, return of her $3,500, and incidental damages. Ms. Pittsley argued that the contract was under the UCC and that she was entitled to remedies because the carpet was defective. Hilton also argued that the UCC did not apply. Who is correct? Does the UCC apply to the contract for the carpet sale and installation? Is Ms. Pittsley entitled to the warranty protection of the UCC? (Analysis appears at the end of the chapter.) [*Pittsley* v. *Houser*, 875 P.2d 232 (Idaho 1994)]

. . . .

Article 2A—Leases

The UCC also includes Article 2A Leases, which applies to leases of goods. The long-term auto lease, which appears to be more of a sale than a lease, is governed by Article 2A. Article 2A covers such issues as the statute of frauds (leases in which payments exceed $1,000, for example, must be in writing), contract formation, and warranties in leases. Article 2A Leases has been adopted in most states.

EVOLVING E-COMMERCE CONTRACT LAWS

Uniform Electronic Transactions Act (UETA)

The **Uniform Electronic Transactions Act (UETA)** is a uniform law drafted in 1999. As of the end of 2006, it has been adopted in 46 states and the District of Columbia and is on the agendas of state legislatures in the remaining states.

The UETA was promulgated in response to contracts being formed over the Internet and includes provisions on issues such as electronic signatures. State adoptions of the UETA are not nearly as uniform as those of the UCC, and electronic contract law continues to evolve.

Electronic Signatures in Global and National Commerce Act of 2000

The UETA is state recognition of the **Electronic Signatures in Global and National Commerce Act of 2000 (ESIGN)**, 15 U.S.C. §7001, the federal law that requires that electronic signatures be recognized as valid for purposes of forming contracts. Under ESIGN, states cannot deny legal effect to contracts that are entered into electronically and have electronic signatures. ESIGN is why you can now fax in your signature, sign electronically at stores, and click online a tab that reads, "I accept" and form a valid contract.

Uniform Computer Information Transactions Act (UCITA)

The **Uniform Computer Information Transactions Act (UCITA)** was promulgated in 1999 and has been adopted in two states (Virginia and Maryland) and proposed in others.[1] UCITA allows terms that are not disclosed to the buyer until after payment and delivery to become part of the contract. Typically, these terms are presented in what are often called "shrinkwrap" or "clickwrap" contracts. Once you open the shrinkwrap on the product, you have agreed to the terms, or, once you click "OK" in an electronic transaction, you have agreed to the terms. The UCITA also treats software and digital content contracts as "licenses" rather than sales of goods or sales of copies of software.

Types of Contracts

The following sections cover the various types of contracts and offer an introduction to contract terminology.

BILATERAL VERSUS UNILATERAL CONTRACTS

A contract can result from two parties exchanging promises to perform or from one party exchanging a promise for the other party's actions. A **bilateral contract** is one in which both parties promise to perform certain things. For example, if you sign a contract to buy a used pink Cadillac for $2,000, you have entered into a bilateral contract with the seller. The seller has promised not to sell the car to anyone else and will give you the title to the car when you pay the $2,000. You have promised to buy that pink Cadillac and will turn over the $2,000 to the seller in exchange for the title. The contract consists of two promises: your promise to buy and the seller's promise to sell.

Some contracts have one party issuing a promise and the other party simply performing. This type of contract is called a **unilateral contract.** Unilateral contracts arise when radio listeners rely on offers and promises from radio stations such as concert tickets in exchange for helping at a food kitchen on Thanksgiving Day.

Express Versus Implied Contracts (Quasi Contracts)

Some contracts are written, signed (even notarized), and very formal in appearance. Others are simply verbal agreements between the parties (see p. 239 for a discussion of the types of contracts that can be oral). Still others are electronic contracts entered into via e-mail and the Internet. A contract that is written or orally agreed to is an **express contract**. In still other situations, the parties do not discuss the terms of the contract but nonetheless understand that they have some form of contractual relationship. A contract that arises from circumstances and not from the express agreement of the parties is called an **implied contract**, as when you go to a doctor for treatment of an illness. You and the doctor do not sit down and negotiate the terms of treatment, the manner in which the doctor will conduct the examination, or how much you will pay. You understand that the doctor will do whatever examinations are appropriate to determine the cause of your illness and that you will pay a fee for the doctor's work. The payment and treatment terms are implied from general professional customs. You have an **implied-in-fact contract**.

A second type of implied or enforceable agreement is called an **implied-in-law contract** or a **quasi contract**. The term *quasi* means "as if" and describes the action of a court when it treats parties who do not have a contract "as if" they did. The courts enforce a quasi contract right if one party has conferred a benefit on another, both are aware of the benefit, and the retention of the benefit would be an enrichment of one party at the unjust expense of the other.

The theory of quasi contracts is not used to help "the officious meddler." The officious meddler is someone who performs unrequested work or services and then, based on a quasi contract theory, seeks recovery. For example, you could not be required to compensate a painting contractor who came by and painted your house without your permission because the contractor acted both without your knowledge and without your consent. However, if you are aware the painting is going on and you do nothing to stop it, you would be held liable in quasi contract.

Void and Voidable Contracts

A **void contract** is an agreement to do something that is illegal or against public policy, or one that lacks legal elements (see Chapter 11). For example, a contract to sell weapons to a country under a weapons ban is a void contract. Neither side can enforce the contract, even if the weapons have already been delivered, because allowing the seller to collect payment would encourage further violations of the law banning the weapons sales.

A **voidable contract** is a contract that can be unenforceable at the election of one of the parties. For example, a minor who signs a contract can choose to be bound by the agreement or can choose to disaffirm the contract. Voidable contracts give one party the option disaffirming the contract.

Unenforceable Contracts

An **unenforceable contract** is a contract that cannot be honored judicially because of some procedural problem. A contract that should be in writing or have a record to comply with the statute of frauds but does not is unenforceable.

Formation of Contracts

A contract is formed when two parties with intent to enter into a contract agree to do certain lawful acts in a mutual exchange of detriment. This formation requires the presence of all of these elements; the lack of one element or the presence of a problem, such as illegality, can invalidate the contract. The elements necessary for the formation of a valid contract are outlined in Exhibit 10.1.

OFFER

The **offer** is the first part of a contract. The person who makes the offer is called the **offeror**, and the person to whom the offer is made is called the **offeree**. The requirements for a valid offer are covered in the following sections.

Intent to Contract Versus Negotiation

The intent-to-contract requirement distinguishes offers from negotiations. For example, a letter from a businessperson may read: "I am interested in investing in a franchise. I have heard about your opportunities. Please send me all necessary information." The letter expresses an interest in possibly contracting in the future, but it does not express any present intent to enter into a contract. But suppose this letter of inquiry was followed by another letter with the following language: "I have decided to invest in one of your franchises. Enclosed are the necessary documents, signatures, and a deposit check." Here the parties have passed the negotiation stage and entered into part one of the contract—an offer.

EXHIBIT   10.1 Overview of Contracts

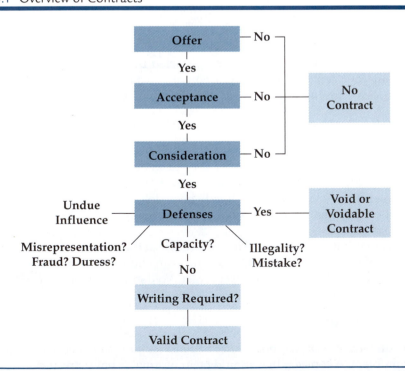

Courts use an objective standard in determining the intent of the parties, which means that courts look at how a reasonable person would perceive the language, the surrounding circumstances, and the actions of the parties in determining whether a contract was formed. For example, a businessperson who is exasperated with the poor financial performance of her firm may say jokingly, "I'd sell this company to anyone willing to take it." If that statement is made in the context of a series of complaints about the firm and the workload, it would not be an offer. That same language used in a luncheon meeting with a prospective buyer would create a different result.

In many situations, one party has simply requested bids or is inviting offers. The frustrated business owner could say, "I am interested in selling my firm. If you run into anyone who is interested, have them call me." The owner has not made an offer to sell but, rather, has made an invitation for an offer.

Ads are simply invitations for offers. *Leonard v. PepsiCo* (Case 10.2) provides the answer for the chapter's opening Consider.

CASE 10.2

Leonard v. PepsiCo
210 F.3d 88 (2d Cir. 2000)*

Does "Pepsi Stuff" Include a Harrier Jet?

FACTS

PepsiCo (defendant/appellee) ran a promotion titled "Pepsi Stuff," which encouraged consumers to collect Pepsi Points from specially marked packages of Pepsi or Diet Pepsi and redeem these points for merchandise featuring the Pepsi logo. John Leonard (plaintiff/appellant) is a resident of Seattle, Washington, who saw a Pepsi Stuff commercial for obtaining a Harrier Jet. The ad featured a teenager and subtitles such as "T-SHIRT 75 PEPSI POINTS," "LEATHER JACKET 1450 PEPSI POINTS," and "SHADES 175 PEPSI POINTS" rolling across the screen. Then a Harrier Jet swings into view and lands by the side of the teen's school building. A military drumroll sounded as the following words appear: "HARRIER FIGHTER 7,000,000 PEPSI POINTS." A few seconds later, "Drink Pepsi—Get Stuff," appeared on the screen.

Inspired by this commercial, Mr. Leonard set out to obtain a Harrier Jet. Mr. Leonard could not collect 7,000,000 Pepsi Points by consuming Pepsi products, fast enough, so through acquaintances, Mr. Leonard raised about $700,000. On March 27, 1996, Mr. Leonard submitted an Order Form, 15 original Pepsi Points, and a check for $700,008.50. At the bottom of the Order Form, Mr. Leonard wrote in "1 Harrier Jet" in the "Item" column and "7,000,000" in the "Total Points" column. On May 7, 1996, PepsiCo rejected Mr. Leonard's submission and returned the check, explaining that:

The item that you have requested is not part of the Pepsi Stuff collection. It is not included in the catalogue or on the order form, and only catalogue merchandise can be redeemed under this program.

The Harrier jet in the Pepsi commercial is fanciful and is simply included to create a humorous and entertaining ad. We apologize for any misunderstanding or confusion that you may have experienced and are enclosing some free product coupons for your use.

Mr. Leonard responded via his lawyer:

Your letter of May 7, 1996 is totally unacceptable. We have reviewed the video tape of the Pepsi Stuff commercial . . . and it clearly offers the new Harrier jet for 7,000,000 Pepsi Points. Our client followed your rules explicitly. . . .

This is a formal demand that you honor your commitment and make immediate arrangements to transfer the new Harrier jet to our client. If we do not receive transfer instructions within ten (10) business days of the date of this letter you will leave us no choice but to file an appropriate action against Pepsi. . . .

Mr. Leonard filed suit, and PepsiCo moved for summary judgment. The court granted summary judgment, and Mr. Leonard appealed.

JUDICIAL OPINION

PER CURIAM

The United States District Court for the Southern District of New York (Wood, J.) [granted] PepsiCo's motion for summary judgment on the grounds (1) that the commercial did not amount to an offer of goods;

CONTINUED

(2) that no objective person could reasonably have concluded that the commercial actually offered consumers a Harrier Jet; and (3) that the alleged contract could not satisfy the New York statute of frauds.

We affirm for substantially the reasons stated in Judge Wood's opinion. See 88 F.Supp.2d 116 (S.D.N.Y. 1999). [To help you understand the issues in the case, portions of Judge Wood's opinion follow.]

WOOD, District Judge
The general rule is that an advertisement does not constitute an offer.

An advertisement is not transformed into an enforceable offer merely by a potential offeree's expression of willingness to accept the offer through, among other means, completion of an order form.

Under these principles, plaintiff's letter of March 27, 1996, with the Order Form and the appropriate number of Pepsi Points, constituted the offer. There would be no enforceable contract until defendant accepted the Order Form and cashed the check.

The exception to the rule that advertisements do not create any power of acceptance in potential offerees is where the advertisement is "clear, definite, and explicit, and leaves nothing open for negotiation," in that circumstance, "it constitutes an offer, acceptance of which will complete the contract." *Lefkowitz* v. *Great Minneapolis Surplus Store,* 251 Minn. 188, 86 N.W.2d 689, 691 (1957). In *Lefkowitz,* defendant had published a newspaper announcement stating: "Saturday 9 A.M. Sharp, 3 Brand New Fur Coats, Worth to $100.00, First Come First Served $1 Each." Mr. Morris Lefkowitz arrived at the store, dollar in hand, but was informed that under defendant's "house rules," the offer was open to ladies, but not gentlemen. The court ruled that because plaintiff had fulfilled all of the terms of the advertisement and the advertisement was specific and left nothing open for negotiation, a contract had been formed.

The present case is distinguishable from *Lefkowitz.* First, the commercial cannot be regarded in itself as sufficiently definite, because it specifically reserved the details of the offer to a separate writing, the Catalog. The commercial itself made no mention of the steps a potential offeree would be required to take to accept the alleged offer of a Harrier Jet. The advertisement in *Lefkowitz,* in contrast, "identified the person who could accept." Second, even if the Catalog had included a Harrier Jet among the items that could be obtained by redemption of Pepsi Points, the advertisement of a Harrier Jet by both television commercial and catalog would still not constitute an offer.

The Court finds, in sum, that the Harrier Jet commercial was merely an advertisement.

Plaintiff's insistence that the commercial appears to be a serious offer requires the Court to explain why the commercial is funny. Explaining why a joke is funny is a daunting task; as the essayist E. B. White has remarked, "Humor can be dissected, as a frog can, but the thing dies in the process. . . ." The commercial is the embodiment of what defendant appropriately characterizes as "zany humor."

CASE QUESTIONS

1. When does the court think an offer was made?

2. Why is whether the ad is funny an important issue?

3. Will Mr. Leonard get his Harrier jet? Why or why not?

*The appellate court affirmed the federal district court opinion in a brief affirmation. The bulk of the facts and discussion presented here are taken from the lower court's decision, 88 F. Supp.2d 116 (S.D.N.Y. 1999).

Certain and Definite Terms

One of the ways to determine whether there is contractual intent is also the second requirement for a valid offer. The offer must contain certain and definite language and cover all the terms necessary for a valid contract, which include the following:

- Parties
- Subject matter of the contract
- Price
- Payment terms
- Delivery terms
- Performance times

Under the UCC, the requirements for an offer are not as stringent as the requirements under common law. So long as the offer identifies the parties and the subject matter, the Code sections can cover the details of price, payment, delivery, and performance (see UCC § 2–204).

Communication of the Offer

An offer must be communicated to the offeree before it is valid. A letter in which an offer is made is not an offer until the letter reaches the offeree. For example, suppose Office Max had prepared an offer letter to be sent to Renco Rental Equipment and other customers. The letter included an offer for a substantial price discount for computers so that Renco and its regular customers might buy computers at that discount. Before the letter is mailed to Renco, Office Max decides that because the computers are in such high demand it will not send the offer and will sell them at their full retail price. The letter to Renco and other Office Max customers is never mailed. Renco, realizing the value of the computers and learning of the unmailed letter, cannot accept the discount computer offer because it was never communicated to them.

Some forms of communication are not treated as offers. For example, as the *Leonard* v. *PepsiCo* case indicates, television ads are generally not offers. Mass communications of information about deals and prices are generally treated as invitations for offers.

Termination of an Offer by Revocation

Because an offer is one-sided, it can be revoked anytime before acceptance by the offeree. **Revocation** occurs when the offeror notifies the offeree that the offer is no longer good.

Revocation is subject to some limitations. Acceptance by the offeree cuts off the right to revoke. Also, under common law, **options** cannot be revoked. An option is a contract in which the offeree pays the offeror for the time needed to consider the offer. For example, suppose that Yolanda's Yogurt is contemplating opening a new restaurant, and Yolanda has a property location in mind but is uncertain about the market potential.

Yolanda does not want the property to be sold to someone else until she can complete a market study. Yolanda could pay the seller (offeror) a sum of money to hold the offer open for 30 days. During that 30-day period, the offeror can neither revoke the offer nor sell to anyone else.

Under the UCC, one form of an option makes an offer irrevocable, even without the offeree's payment. Under a **merchant's firm offer** (see UCC § 2–205), the offer must be made by a merchant, put in some form of record,[2] and signed by the merchant. If these requirements are met, the merchant must hold the offer open for a definite time period (but no longer than three months). A merchant is someone who is in the business of selling the goods that are the subject matter of the contract or who holds particular skills or expertise in dealing with the goods. A rain check for sale merchandise from a store is an example of this type of offer. The firm offer cannot be revoked if the requirements are met, and money or consideration is not one of those requirements.

Termination of an Offer by Rejection

An offer carries no legally binding obligation for the offeree, who is free to accept or reject the offer. Once the offeree rejects the offer, the offer is ended and cannot later be accepted unless the offeror renews the offer.

Rejection by Counteroffer under Common Law   An offer also ends when the offeree does not fully reject the offer but rejects some portion of the offer or modifies it before acceptance. These changes and rejections are called **counteroffers**.

The effect of a counteroffer is that the original offer is no longer valid, and the offeree now becomes the offeror as the counteroffer becomes the new offer. The following dialogue provides an example:

Alice: I will pay you $500 to paint the trim on my house.
Brad: I will do it for $750.

Alice made the first offer. Brad's language is a counteroffer and a rejection at the same time. Alice is now free to accept or reject the $750 offer. If Alice declines the $750 counteroffer, Brad cannot then force Alice to contract for the original $500 because the offer ended.

Rejection by Counteroffer under the UCC   Those who wrote the UCC understood that modification is a necessary part of doing business, and Section 2–207 allows modification flexibility. Under former Section 2–207 (which may still be the law in some states because the adoption of the new UCC has been slow), two separate rules apply for modifications: one governs merchants, and the other governs nonmerchant transactions. Exhibit 10.2 shows a chart of the rules.

For nonmerchants, the addition of terms in the counteroffer does not result in a rejection; there will still be a contract if there is a clear intent to contract, but the additional terms will not be a part of the contract. The following dialogue gives an example:

Joe: I will sell you my pinball machine for $250.
Jan: I'll take it. Include $10 in dimes.

Joe and Jan have a contract, but the $10 in dimes is not a part of the contract. If Jan wanted the dimes, she should have negotiated before formally accepting the offer.

For merchants (both parties must be merchants), former Section 2–207 has more complicated rules and details on additional terms in acceptance. Sometimes

EXHIBIT   10.2 UCC Rules for Additional Terms in Acceptance Under Former Article 2

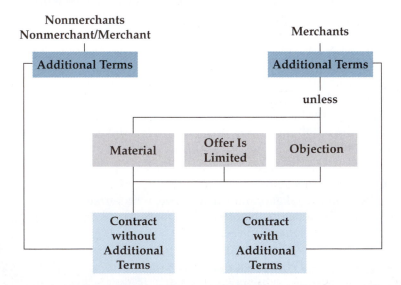

called the **battle of the forms**, Section 2–207 covers situations in which offerors and offerees send purchase orders and invoices back and forth with the understanding that they have a contract. Under Section 2–207, if the parties reach a basic agreement but the offeree has added terms, there will be an enforceable contract; the added terms are not a rejection under Section 2–207. Whether the added terms will become a part of the contract depends on the following questions.

1. Are the terms material?
2. Was the offer limited?
3. Does one side object?

If the terms the offeree adds to the original offer terms are *material,* they do not become a part of the contract. For example, suppose that Alfie sent a purchase order to Bob for 12 dozen red 4-inch balloons at 4 cents each. Bob sends back an invoice that reflects the quantity and price, but Bob's invoice also has a section that states, "There are no warranties express or implied on these goods." Do Alfie and Bob have a contract with or without warranties? The waiver of warranties is a material change in what Alfie gets: now a contract without warranties. Because it is material, Section 2–207 protects Alfie and the warranty waiver is not part of the contract.

Terms that can be added but are not considered material are payment terms such as "30 days same as cash." Shipment terms are generally immaterial unless the method of shipment is unusually costly.

An offeror can avoid the problems of form battles and Section 2–207 by simply *limiting* the offer to the terms stated. The following language could be used: "This offer is limited to these terms." If the offeree attempts to add terms in the acceptance of such a limited offer, there will be a contract, but the added terms will not be part of the contract. For example, suppose Alfie's offer on the balloons was limited and Bob accepted but added that the payment terms were "30 days same as cash." They would still have a contract but without the additional payment term.

A final portion of Section 2–207 allows the parties to take action to eliminate additional terms. They can do so by *objecting* to any added terms within a reasonable time. For example, if Alfie's offer was not limited and Bob accepted the payment terms, Alfie could object to the payment terms and they would then not be a part of the contract. Exhibit 10.2, as already noted, summarizes the UCC's Section 2–207 rules. As noted earlier, the most significant changes under Revised Article 2 deal with Section 2–207.

Because so many confusing circumstances arose under the merchant/nonmerchant rules and the definition of materiality, the effect of the new Section 2–207 is to leave the issues of what is or is not included in a contract to the courts that then determine the intent of the parties. The courts will examine, on a case-by-case basis, what is included as part of the contract, in some cases regardless of what the "record" provides. Revised Section 2–207 applies to merchants and nonmerchants alike and regardless of whether the parties use forms. The new UCC Section 2–207 is often called the "terms later" provision because it permits parties to go forward with contract performance and decide on terms later or resolve any disputes only if they arise during the course of performance. One writer has referred to "terms later" as bad economics because of the inability of parties to rely on definitive laws in making contracts and then performing under them.[3]

Business Planning Tip

The docketing of deadlines is important for businesses. Also, checks that a company receives should be reconciled with the purpose of payment to be certain that accidental overpayments (or acceptances) do not occur through oversight.

EXHIBIT   10.3 Additional Terms Under New UCC Section 2–207

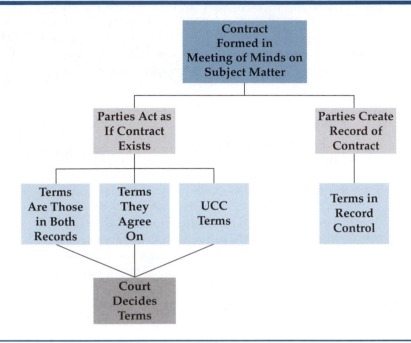

Exhibit 10.3 shows the new way terms added under new Section 2–207 are treated.

Termination by Offer Expiration

An offer can end by expiring and, once expired, can no longer be accepted by the offeree. For example, if an offer states that it will remain open until November 1, it automatically terminates on November 1, and no one has the power to accept the offer after that time. The death of the offeror also ends the offer, unless the offeree holds an option. Even offers without time limits expire after a reasonable time has passed. For example, an offer to buy a home is probably only good for one or two weeks because the offeror needs to know whether to try for another house. The offeror's offer terminates naturally if the offeree fails to timely accept.

ACCEPTANCE: THE OFFEREE'S RESPONSE

An **acceptance** is the offeree's positive response to the offeror's proposed contract, and only persons to whom the offer is made have the power of acceptance. That acceptance must be communicated to the offeror using the proper method of communication, which can be controlled by the offeror or left to the offeree. In either case, the method of communication controls the effective time of the acceptance.

Acceptance by Stipulated Means

Some offerors give a required means of acceptance called a specified or **stipulated means**. If the offeree uses the stipulated means of acceptance, the acceptance is effective sooner than the offeror's receipt; the acceptance is effective when it is properly sent. For example, if the offeror has required a mailed acceptance and the

EXHIBIT	10.4 Timing Rules for Acceptance

TYPE OF OFFER	METHOD OF ACCEPTANCE	ACCEPTANCE EFFECTIVE?
No means given	Same or reasonable method of communication*	When properly mailed, dispatched (mailbox rule)
No means given	Slower or unreasonable method of communication	When received, if offer still open
Means specified (specified or stipulated means)	Stipulated means used	Mailbox rule
Means stipulated (specified or stipulated means)	Stipulated means not used	Counteroffer and rejection

*Some states still follow the common law rule that requires that the same method of communication be used even for UCC subject matter if the offeree wants the protection of the mailbox rule.

offeree properly mails the letter of acceptance, the acceptance is effective when it is sent. This timing rule for acceptance is called the **mailbox rule**, and it applies in stipulated means offers so long as the offeree uses the stipulated means to communicate acceptance.

Acceptance with No Stipulated Means

If the offeror does not stipulate a means of acceptance, the offeree is free to use any method for communication of the acceptance. If the offeree uses the same method of communication or a reasonable means, the mailbox rule also applies. If the offeree uses a slower method of acceptance, the acceptance is not effective until it is received. Exhibit 10.4 summarizes the timing of acceptance rules. *Cantu v. Central Education Agency* (Case 10.3) deals with an issue of timing on offer and acceptance.

CASE 10.3

Cantu v. Central Education Agency
884 S.W.2D 565 (TEX. APP. 1994)

THE TEACHER'S LESSON ON ACCEPTANCE

FACTS

Ms. Cantu had a teaching contract with the San Benito Consolidated Independent School District. She hand-delivered to her supervisor a written offer to resign. Three days later the superintendent of schools mailed her a letter accepting the offer of resignation. Ms. Cantu then changed her mind and the next day hand-delivered a letter withdrawing her resignation. The superintendent refused to recognize the attempted rescission of the resignation. Ms. Cantu appealed to the state district court. It decided against her, and she again appealed.

JUDICIAL OPINION

SMITH, Justice

The sole legal question presented for our review is the proper scope of the "mail-box rule" under Texas law and whether the rule was correctly applied.

As Professor Corbin notes, courts could adopt a rule that no acceptance is effective until received, absent express authorization by the offeror; however, the mailbox rule, which makes acceptance effective on dispatch, closes the deal and enables performance more promptly, and places the risk of inconvenience on the

CONTINUED

party who originally has power to control the manner of acceptance. . . . "Even though the offer was not made by mail and there was no [express] authorization, the existing circumstances may be such as to make it reasonable for the offeree to accept by mail and to give the offeror reason to know that the acceptance will be so made." . . . In short, acceptance by mail is impliedly authorized if reasonable under the circumstances.

The *Restatement* approves and adopts this approach: an acceptance by any medium reasonable under the circumstances is effective on dispatch, absent a contrary indication in the offer. *Restatement (Second) of Contracts* §§ 30(2), 63(a), 65, 66 (1979). In addition, the *Restatement* specifically recognizes that acceptance by mail is ordinarily reasonable if the parties are negotiating at a distance or *even if a written offer is delivered in person to an offeree in the same city.* . . . The same standard, *viz.,* whether the manner of acceptance is reasonable under the circumstances, governs offer and acceptance in commercial transactions under the Texas Business and Commerce Code. (Uniform Commercial Code § 2–206.)

The request or authorization to communicate the acceptance by mail is implied in two cases, namely: (1) Where the post is used to make the offer . . . (2) *Where the circumstances are such that it must have been within the contemplation of the parties that according to the ordinary usages of mankind the post might be used as a means of communicating the acceptance.* . . .

. . . It was reasonable for the superintendent to accept Cantu's offer of resignation by mail. Cantu tendered her resignation shortly before the start of the school year—at a time when both parties could not fail to appreciate the need for immediate action by the district to locate a replacement. In fact, she delivered the letter on a Saturday, when the Superintendent could neither receive nor respond to her offer, further delaying matters by two days. Finally, Cantu's request that her final paycheck be forwarded to an address some fifty miles away indicated that she could no longer be reached in San Benito and that she did not intend to return to the school premises or school-district offices. The Commissioner of Education and district court properly considered that it was reasonable for the school district to accept Cantu's offer by mail. . . .

Judgment affirmed.

Case Questions

1. Who was the offeror? Does the UCC apply in this case?

2. Why did the court refer to the fact that Ms. Cantu's forwarding address was 50 miles away from the place where she delivered her offer to resign?

E-Commerce and Contract Formation

The Internet has provided a means for contracting online. The rules on contract formation in cyberspace require that the parties prove that a click was something more than an accidental action and that the click was made after there had been full disclosure of the terms.

A new section of revised Article 2 deals with electronic communication of acceptance, including the timing issues. Section 2–213 provides that "receipt of an electronic communication has a legal effect, it has that effect even though no individual is aware of its receipt," and that acknowledgment of the receipt of an electronic communication is receipt but, "in itself, does not establish that the content sent corresponds to the content received." So, receipt is required for electronic communication and receipt occurs when the e-mail arrives, even if the receiver does not know it has arrived. Also, the parties are left to use other means of proof to establish that all of the message made it from one party to another because acknowledging receipt does not mean that all terms arrived.

Sellers generally accomplish these two goals by establishing on their Web sites "clickon," "clickthrough," or "clickwrap" agreements. The company or offeror simply lists all the terms of the agreement that the visitor/offeree is about to enter into. The visitor/offeree must click on "I agree" or "I agree to these terms," or he or she cannot proceed to the completion of the contract segments of the site. The terms include cost, payment, warranties, arbitration provisions, and so on, and all applicable terms must be spelled out in advance of the "I agree" click point.

Because this type of contract formation is so new, case law is rare, but *Home Basket Co., LLC. v. Pampered Chef, Ltd.* (Case 10.4) is one example of a contract-formed-on-the-Internet dispute.

CASE 10.4

Home Basket Co., LLC. v. Pampered Chef, Ltd.
2005 WL 82136, 55 UCC Rep. Serv 2d 792 (D. Kan 2005)

MAKING A BASKET CASE

FACTS

The Greenbrier Basket Company (GBC), a goods distributor (plaintiff) (seller), entered into a business relationship in October 2003 to sell woven baskets to The Pampered Chef (TPC) (defendant) (buyer). On October 28, 2003, an executive sales agreement was drafted but never signed by the parties. GBC had, however, accepted purchase orders from TPC.

Cyndee Pollock (a manager at GBC) would receive offers to purchase goods via e-mail from TPC and would tell an employee, Mark Beal, to accept these purchase orders via TPC's Internet site. GBC denies knowing that there were terms and conditions, including a forum selection clause, on TPC's Internet acceptance site. TPC sent Mark Beal an e-mail with an attachment showing him how to use TPC's purchase order management system. The attachment included instructions regarding the use of the purchase order management system, including, in section 4, three paragraphs under the title "Accepting and Rejecting Purchase Orders," the relevant portion of which states:

Clicking on the Accept P.O. button will cause the terms and conditions of the purchase order to pop-up. The user should review these terms and conditions and click the Accept P.O. button at the bottom of the pop-up screen . . . . If the purchase order is not acceptable in it's [sic] current form, the user may click on the Reject and Request Changes button. This causes a pop-up window to appear where the user may enter a free-form text describing the reason for rejecting the purchase order and request changes that would make the purchase order acceptable.

Clause 17 of the Terms and Conditions in TPC's purchase management order system states:

This Purchase Order shall be deemed to have been made in Addison, Illinois USA and shall be governed by and construed in accordance with the laws of State of Illinois [sic]. The sole and exclusive jurisdiction for the purpose of resolving any dispute shall be the United States District Court, Northern District of Illinois, Eastern Division.

When disputes over orders and payments arose, GBC filed suit against TPC in Kansas for breach of contract. TPC moved to dismiss the suit for improper venue (wrong geographic court).

JUDICIAL OPINION

BROWN, Senior J.

TPC's e-mails containing purchase order information constituted an offer to buy baskets. The e-mails consisted of information about the quantity of baskets to be bought, price, shipment information and delivery dates. None of the e-mails had any forum selection clause; however, they did state a specific manner of acceptance:

Plaintiff first argues that the e-mail offers are ambiguous because it did not alert GBC to the forum selection clause that had to be accepted on the website. The TPC e-mails state that the way to acknowledge (i.e. accept) the purchase order was to go to the website. The e-mail is not ambiguous as it also alerted GBC that there were terms and conditions associated with acknowledging the P.O. on the website.

The negligent failure of a party to read the written contract entered into will estop the contracting party from voiding the contract on the ground of ignorance of its contents. Therefore, a party who signs a written contract is bound by its provisions regardless of the failure to read or understand the terms, unless the contract was entered into through fraud, undue influence, or mutual mistake.

Plaintiff was under a duty to read and understand the terms and conditions prior to clicking the "Accept P.O." button as this was the formal acceptance required by TPC's offer to purchase baskets. Failure to read or understand the terms and conditions is not a valid reason to render those provisions nugatory.

Plaintiff next argues that the forum selection clause should not be read into the contract because GBC

CONTINUED

rejected an Exclusive Sales Agreement containing such a clause. Plaintiff claims that the failure to sign this agreement shows that they did not intend that a forum selection clause be part of the contract. The evidence shows that the Exclusive Sales Agreement was discussed on October 28, 2003. The date of the first e-mail inviting GBC to accept a purchase order was October 7, 2003. Plaintiff's subjective reasons for refusing to sign the Exclusive Sales Agreement are irrelevant as GBC consistently agreed, in an objective manner prior to the Exclusive Sales Agreement, to contracts with the terms and conditions on TPC's website. The Court will not alter the plain terms in the parties' contract because GBC refused to sign the Exclusive Sales Agreement.

The Defendant's Motion to Dismiss due to improper venue is denied. The case is transferred to the United States District Court for Northern District of Illinois, Eastern Division.

CASE QUESTIONS

1. Describe the ordering process between the two parties.

2. Does it matter to the court that neither side ever signed a written agreement?

3. What responsibility does the court impose on those who use Web sites for contracting purposes?

CONSIDERATION

Consideration is what distinguishes gifts from contracts and is what each party—offeror and offeree—gives up under the contract; it is sometimes called **bargained-for exchange**. If you sign a contract to buy a 1998 Mercedes for $17,000, your consideration is the $17,000 and is given in exchange for the car. The seller's consideration is giving up the car and is given in exchange for your $17,000. On the other hand, if your grandmother tells you that she will give you her Mercedes, the lack of consideration on your part means your grandmother's promise (unfortunately) is not a contract and is not enforceable.

The courts are not concerned with the amount or nature of consideration as long as it is actually passed from one party to the other. A contract is not unenforceable because a court feels you paid too little under the contract terms. The amount of consideration is left to the discretion of the parties, but one party cannot demand greater consideration once the contract is finalized.

consider. 10.2

In 1977, George Lucas granted Kenner Toys the exclusive right to produce *Star Wars* toys—the action figures and other replicas from the movie—in perpetuity for $100,000 per year. At the time the contract was negotiated, no one understood how valuable the contract rights were.

In 1991, Hasbro Toys purchased Kenner. By this time, the sales of Princess Leia dolls and R2D2 replicas were nonexistent. Because there was no market for the toys, the toys were no longer produced, and an accountant with Kenner decided to save $100,000 and not send the check to Mr. Lucas.

In 1992, an employee of Mr. Lucas saw a line of Galoob toys at a trade show and asked if Galoob was interested in making the *Star Wars* toy line. Galoob jumped at the chance and did quite well marketing the toys. Some executives believe that the popularity of the toys motivated Mr. Lucas to re-release the movies, which turned out to be a money-maker for Mr. Lucas as well as for the Galoob toy line.

In 1996, Mr. Lucas did grant some rights to Hasbro, but it has lost market share and footing to Galoob. Was the failure to make the payment a failure of consideration? Has Hasbro lost its rights? (Analysis appears at the end of the chapter.)

ethical *issues*

Based on a tip from an employee, Bank of America investigated its senior executive at its student-loan operation, Ms. Kathy Cannon, and uncovered that she had exchanged gifts with Daniel M. Meyers, the CEO and chairman of First Marblehead, a company that provides services for 15 of the top 20 student loan originators. Bank of America is one of the top 20 of those lenders. The exchange of the gifts would be a violation of both Bank of America's and First Marblehead's gift policies. Prior to Bank of America's own revelation about its executive, First Marblehead announced Mr. Meyers's resignation following its disclosure that Mr. Meyers had used personal funds to buy $32,000 in gifts for "a major client." Marblehead did not reveal who the client was, but Bank of America acknowledged that it was the client when it announced Ms. Cannon's departure the following day.

First Marblehead was founded in 1991 and issued an IPO in 2003. It had been a NYSE darling until smaller student loan service companies began entering the business and competing with better services. First Marblehead's stock had lost one-half of its value over 2005. The announcement of the gift scandal and Meyers's departure caused a 17 percent drop in First Marblehead's stock by the end of the day of the announcement.

Why do we worry about gifts between vendors and customers? Isn't this common business practice? Isn't it important that Meyers used his own funds for the gifts and not First Marblehead funds?

Sources: http://www.sec.gov; Bank of America and First Marblehead filed 8-K disclosures; John Hechinger and Anne Marie Chaker, "First Marblehead Chief's Exit Tied to Bank of America Official," *Wall Street Journal,* September 29, 2005, p. A11.

Unique Consideration Issues

The concept of consideration and its requirement for contract formation has presented courts with some unique problems. Often an element of fairness and reliance exists in circumstances in which an offer and acceptance are made but no consideration. For example, many nonprofit organizations raise funds through pledges. Such pledges are not supported by consideration, but the nonprofit organizations rely on those pledges. Called **charitable subscriptions**, these agreements are enforced by courts despite the lack of consideration.

The doctrine of **promissory estoppel** is also used as a substitute for consideration in those cases in which someone acts in reliance on a promise that is not supported by consideration. For example, suppose an employer said, "Move to Denver and I'll hire you." There is no detriment on your part until you begin work. The employer has no detriment either. However, if you sold your home in Phoenix and incurred the expense of moving to Denver, it would be unfair to allow the employer to claim the contract did not exist because of no consideration. You have acted in reliance on a promise, and that reliance serves as a consideration substitute.

Contract Form: When Writing or Record Is Required

Some contracts can exist just on the basis of an oral promise. Others, however, must be in writing or be evidence by a record to be enforceable, and these contracts are covered under each state's **statute of frauds**.

Common Law Statute of Frauds

The term *statute of frauds* originated in 1677 when England passed the first rule dealing with written contracts: the Statute for the Prevention of Frauds and Perjuries. The purpose of this original statute and others like it is to have written agreements for the types of contracts that folks are most likely to commit perjury about. The following is a partial list of the types of contracts required to be in writing under most state laws.

1. Contracts for the sale of real property. This requirement includes sales, certain leases, liens, mortgages, and easements.

2. Contracts that cannot be performed within one year. These contracts run for long periods and require the benefit of written terms.

3. Contracts to pay the debt of another. Cosigners' agreements to pay if a debtor defaults must be in writing. A corporate officer's personal guarantee of a corporate note must be in writing to be enforceable.

UCC Statute of Frauds

Under the UCC, a separate statute of frauds applies to contracts covering the sale of goods. Contracts for the sale of goods costing $500 or more must be evidenced by a record to be enforceable. Under Revised Article 2, the amount has been increased from $500 to $5,000.

Exceptions to the Statute of Frauds

Some exceptions to the UCC and common law statute of frauds provisions were created for situations in which the parties have partially or fully performed their unwritten contract. Under both the UCC and common law, if the parties perform the oral contract, courts will enforce the contract for what has already been done. For example, if Alan agreed to sell land to Bertha under an oral contract and Bertha has paid, has the deed, and has moved in, Alan cannot use the statute of frauds to remove Bertha and get the land back.

What Form of Writing/Record Is Required?

Evidence of a written agreement can be pieced together from memos, letters, and electronic communications. Case 10.5 deals with an interesting issue of a different sort of record of a contract.

CASE 10.5

Rosenfeld v. *Basquiat*
78 F.3D 184 (2D CIR. 1996)

THE ARTIST, THE CRAYON, AND THE CONTRACT

FACTS

Michelle Rosenfeld, an art dealer, alleges she contracted with artist Jean-Michel Basquiat to buy three of his paintings. The works that she claims she contracted to buy were entitled *Separation of the K, Atlas,* and *Untitled Head.* Ms. Rosenfeld testified that she went to Mr. Basquiat's apartment on October 25, 1982; while she was there, he agreed to sell her three paintings for $4,000 each, and she picked out three. Mr. Basquiat asked for a cash deposit of 10 percent; she left his loft and later returned with $1,000 in cash, which she paid him. When she asked for a receipt, he insisted on drawing up a contract and got down on the floor and wrote it out in crayon on a large piece of paper, remarking that

some day this contract would be worth money. The handwritten document listed the three paintings, bore Ms. Rosenfeld's signature and Mr. Basquiat's signature, and stated: "$12,000—$1,000 DEPOSIT—Oct 25 82." Ms. Rosenfeld later returned to Mr. Basquiat's loft to discuss delivery, but Mr. Basquiat convinced her to wait for at least two years so that he could show the paintings at exhibitions.

After Mr. Basquiat's death, the estate argued that there was no contract because the statute of frauds made the agreement unenforceable. The estate contended that a written contract for the sale of goods must include the date of delivery. From a judgment in favor of the estate, Ms. Rosenfeld appealed.

Judicial Opinion

CARDAMONE, J.

. . . Because this case involves an alleged contract for the sale of three paintings, any question regarding the Statute of Frauds is governed by the U.C.C. (applicability to "transactions in goods") (contract for $500 or more is unenforceable "unless there is some writing sufficient to indicate that a contract for sale has been made between the parties and signed by the party [charged]"). Under the U.C.C., the only term that *must* appear in the writing is the quantity. See N.Y.U.C.C. § 2–201.

Beyond that, "[a]ll that is required is that the writing afford a basis for believing that the offered oral evidence rests on a real transaction." The writing supplied by the plaintiff indicated the price, the date, the specific paintings involved, and that Rosenfeld paid a deposit. It also bore the signatures of the buyer and seller. Therefore, the writing satisfied the requirements of § 2–201.

. . . Because the writing, allegedly scrawled in crayon by Jean-Michel Basquiat on a large piece of paper, easily satisfied the requirements of § 2–201 of the U.C.C., the estate is not entitled to judgment as a matter of law. It is of no real significance that the jury found Rosenfeld and Basquiat settled on a particular time for delivery and did not commit it to writing. . . . As a consequence, . . . the alleged contract is not invalid on Statute of Frauds grounds. . . .

Judgment reversed.

Case Questions

1. Why was the contract required to be in writing?
2. List the elements that made the writing meet statute of frauds requirements.
3. Does a writing that does not comply with the statute of frauds make the alleged contract void?

E-mails and Web site communications are records that satisfy the statute of frauds requirements. New Section 2–211 of the UCC makes electronic communication and forms of contracts in that mode equal with paper contracts. Under the UCC, merchants can meet the statute of frauds by sending confirmation memos. These **merchants' confirmation memoranda** summarize the oral agreement and are signed, even electronically, by only one party, but they can be used to satisfy the statute of frauds so long as the memo has been sent to the nonsigning party for review and no objection is raised upon that party's receipt. Exhibit 10.5 provides a summary of provisions for contract formation under UCC and common law.

EXHIBIT 10.5 Common Law Versus UCC Rules on Formation

AREA	UCC	COMMON LAW
Application	Sales of goods	Services, real estate, employment contracts
Offers	Need subject matter (quantity); code gives details	Need subject matter, price, terms, full details agreed upon
Options	Merchant's firm offer–no consideration needed	Need consideration
Acceptance	Can have additional terms	Mirror image rule followed
	Mailbox rule works for reasonable means of acceptance	Must use same method to get mailbox rule*
Consideration	Required for contracts but not for modification or firm offers	Always required
Writing requirement	Sale of goods for $500 ($5,000 Revised UCC) or more	Real estate, contracts not to be performed in one year, paying the debt of another
Defenses†	Must be free of all defenses for valid contract	Must be free of all defenses for valid contract

*Some courts have adopted the UCC rule for common law contracts.
†See Chapter 11.

The Effect of the Written Contract: Parol Evidence

Once a contract is reduced to its final form and is complete and unambiguous, the parties to the contract are not permitted to contradict the contract terms with evidence of their negotiations or verbal agreements at the time the contract was executed. This prohibition on extrinsic evidence for fully integrated contracts is called the **parol evidence** rule and is a means for stopping ongoing contradictions to contracts that have been entered into and finalized. It is a protection for the application of the document to the parties' rights as well as a reminder of the need to put the true nature of the agreement into the contract.

Some exceptions apply to the parol evidence rule. If a contract is incomplete or the terms are ambiguous, extrinsic evidence can be used to clarify or complete the contract, as in the case of UCC contracts in which price, delivery, and payment terms can be added (see UCC § 2–202). Also, if one of the parties to the contract is alleging a defense to the contract's formation, evidence of that defense can be used. Evidence that shows lack of capacity or fraud does not violate the parol evidence rule.

Issues in Formation of International Contracts

International contracts carry additional risks and questions about the choice of currency, the impact of culture on contract interpretation and performance, and the stability of the governments of the parties involved in the contract. The **United Nations Convention on Contracts for the International Sale of Goods (CISG)** (introduced in Chapter 6) provides a type of international UCC for those countries that adopt it and when the parties choose to use it.

The CISG, which allows the parties to opt out of its application even in adopting countries, has four parts: Part I: Application; Part II: Formation; Part III: Sale of Goods; and Part IV: Final Provisions. Part II includes provisions for the requirements for offers and acceptance, including a merchant's firm offer provision. Acceptance is effective only upon receipt; and, whenever forms do not match, there is no contract unless the nonmatching terms are immaterial.

Party autonomy continues to remain a priority. The parties can always choose the applicable law, the nation for the location of courts for resolving disputes, and remedies.

Several significant differences distinguish the UCC from the CISG. For example, the CISG follows the common law mirror image rule and not the more liberal UCC "battle of the forms" modification exception. The CISG also requires the presence of a price for an offer to be definite enough to be valid. Merchants' firm offers exist under the CISG, but their validity is not subject to time limitations, as with the UCC three-month limit. Parties in international trade need to be familiar with the hybrid nature of the CISG in order to protect their contract rights.

One of the content and interpretation issues in international contracts focuses on the method of payment. The increase in the number of international transactions will make negotiating the terms of payment under various contracts more of an issue.

In negotiating an international contract, parties should determine which country's laws will govern the transaction. Courts will not interfere with this decision as long as the law chosen has some relation to the transaction. The parties should also agree to submit to the jurisdiction of a particular court so that litigation does not begin with the issue of whether jurisdiction resides with a particular court. If the parties wish to submit to arbitration prior to litigation, the terms and nature of arbitration should be delineated in the contract.

International contracts carry peculiar and additional risks. One of the lessons of the wars in the Middle East, for example, is that international contracts should have provisions for war, interruption of shipping lines, and other political acts. Often referred to as *force majeure* clauses, these provisions in international contracts allow the parties to agree what will happen in the event of sudden changes in government or in the global political climate rather than rely on a court to determine after the fact what rights, if any, the parties had. (See Chapter 11 for more details on *force majeure*.)

Red Flags FOR MANAGERS

- Your negotiations with others are not contracts. But, once you produce a record and you have indicated through your language that you want a contract, you have created legal obligations and also have some rights. Remember, it is your language, including your intent and the level of detail in your communications, that turns the corner from negotiations to forming a contract.

- Remember that, even with detailed negotiations, some contracts have to have a writing or record or you cannot enforce them. Real estate sales and purchases and sales of goods over $5,000 ($500 former UCC) must have some form of a record to be enforceable. Remember, e-mails and Web site clicks count for formation and for records.

- Be sure to get what you want in your contract before you sign it, electronically or otherwise. Once a contract is in its final form, the parol evidence rule will not allow you to change the contract by saying, "I didn't read this," or "I really meant to get this in our contract."

Summary

What are contracts?

- Contract—promise or set of promises for breach of which the law gives a remedy, or the performance of which the law in some way recognizes as a duty

What laws govern contracts?

- Common law—traditional notions of law and the body of law developed in judicial decisions
- *Restatement (Second) of Contracts*—general summary of the common law of contracts
- Uniform Commercial Code (UCC)—set of uniform laws (49 states) governing commercial transactions

What are the types of contracts?

- Bilateral contract—contract of two promises; one from each party
- Unilateral contract—contract made up of a promise for performance
- Express contract—written or verbally agreed-to contract

- Implied contract—contract that arises from parties' voluntary conduct
- Quasi contract—theory for enforcing a contract even though there is no formal contract because the parties behaved as if there were a contract
- Implied-in-fact contract—contract that arises from factual circumstances, professional circumstances, or custom
- Implied-in-law contract—legally implied contract to prevent unjust enrichment
- Void contract—contract with illegal subject matter or against public policy
- Voidable contract—contract that can be avoided legally by one side
- Unenforceable contract—agreement for which the law affords no remedy such as when a contract must be evidenced by a writing or record and is not

How are contracts formed?

- Offer—preliminary to contract; first step in formation
- Offeror—person making the offer

- Offeree—recipient of offer
- Revocation—offeror canceling offer
- Options—offers with considerations; promises to keep offer open
- Merchant's firm offer—written offer signed by a merchant that states it will be kept open
- Counteroffer—counterproposal to offer
- Battle of the forms—UCC description of merchants' tendency to exchange purchase orders, invoices, confirmations, and so on; under Revised UCC, the court determines terms after the fact looking at intent, forms used, and the UCC terms
- Acceptance—offeree's positive response to offer
- Mailbox rule—timing rule for acceptance
- Consideration—something of value exchanged by the parties that distinguishes gifts from contracts
- Charitable subscriptions—enforceable promises to make gifts

- Promissory estoppel—reliance element used to enforce otherwise unenforceable contracts

When must contracts be in writing?

- Statute of frauds—state statutes governing the types of contracts that must be in writing to be enforceable
- Merchants' confirmation memorandum—UCC provision that allows one merchant to bind another based on an oral agreement with one signature
- Parol evidence—extrinsic evidence that is not admissible to dispute an integrated unambiguous contract

What issues for contracting exist in international business?

- CISG—Contracts for the International Sale of Goods; a proposed uniform law for international commercial transactions

Key Terms

acceptance 234
bargained-for exchange 238
battle of the forms 233
bilateral contract 226
charitable subscriptions 239
common law 223
consideration 238
contract 223
counteroffers 231
Electronic Signatories in Global and National Commerce Act of 2000 (ESIGN) 226
express contract 227
force majeure 243
implied contract 227

implied-in-fact contract 227
implied-in-law contract 227
mailbox rule 235
merchant's firm offer 231
merchants' confirmation memoranda 241
offer 228
offeree 228
offeror 228
options 231
parol evidence 242
promissory estoppel 239
quasi contract 227
Restatement (Second) of Contracts 223
revocation 231

statute of frauds 239
stipulated means 234
unenforceable contract 227
Uniform Commercial Code (UCC) 224
Uniform Computer Information Transactions Act (UCITA) 226
Uniform Electronic Transactions Act (UETA) 226
unilateral contract 227
United Nations Convention on Contracts for the International Sale of Goods (CISG) 242
void contract 227
voidable contract 227

Questions and Problems

1. L. A. Becker Co., Inc., sent D. A. Clardy a $100 down payment along with a merchandise order. Clardy deposited the check, as was its usual daily practice for payments. After examining the offer, Clardy sent a rejection letter along with a check for $100 to Becker, which claims Clardy accepted by cashing the check. Is Becker correct? [*L. A. Becker Co. v. Clardy,* 51 So. 211 (Miss. 1910)]

2. Would an arbitration clause added to the reverse side of a buyer's purchase order be a material change for purposes of the merchant's battle of the forms under Section 2–207 of the UCC? [*Berquist Co. v. Sunroc Corp.,* 777 F. Supp. 1236 (E.D. Pa. 1991)]

3. Consider the following sequences of offers and acceptances and determine whether in each case there would be a contract.

a. September 1, 2008:   A mails an offer to B.
   September 2, 2008:   B receives the offer.
   September 3, 2008:   A mails a revocation.
   September 4, 2008:   B mails an acceptance.
   September 5, 2008:   B receives the revocation.
   September 6, 2008:   A receives the acceptance.
   RESULT: _____

b. September 1, 2008:   A mails an offer to B.
   September 2, 2008:   B receives the offer.

September 3, 2008:	B wires an acceptance.
September 4, 2008:	B wires a rejection.
September 4, 2008 (later):	A receives the acceptance.
September 5, 2008:	A receives the rejection.
RESULT: _____

c.

September 1, 2008:	A mails an offer to B.
September 2, 2008:	B receives the offer.
September 3, 2008:	A wires a revocation.
September 3, 2008:	B wires an acceptance.
September 4, 2008:	B receives the revocation.
September 5, 2008:	A receives the acceptance.
RESULT: _____

Would your answers be different under the UCC from those under common law?

4. Procter & Gamble (P&G) began a Pampers catalog promotional offer in 1981. A statement on each box of Pampers explained that by saving the teddy bear proof-of-purchase symbols (Teddy Bears points) on packages of Pampers diapers, a customer could order various baby items from the Pampers Softouches Baby Catalog at a reduced cost. The catalog would be sent free to consumers upon request. Included in the catalog were pictures of the items for sale and the designated amount of Teddy Bears points and cash necessary for purchase. All sale terms, including the dates during which the offer was in effect, were described in each catalog. The only method for ordering merchandise was the use of the specific order form included in each catalog.

About April 1989, P&G sent out its final catalog. On the front of the catalog was a statement that it was the final catalog and that the offer would expire on February 28, 1990.

Ms. Alligood and others had cut out and saved the teddy bear symbols. The diaper purchasers claim that each package of Pampers contained an offer to enter into a unilateral contract, which they accepted by purchasing Pampers and saving the teddy bear proof-of-purchase symbols.

The precise language of the advertisement printed on packages of Pampers states:

> *Save these Teddy Bears points and use them to save money on toys, clothes, furniture, and lots of other baby things when you shop the Pampers Baby Catalog. For your free copy of the Catalog, send your name, complete address and youngest baby's date of birth to:*
> *Pampers Baby Catalog*
> *P.O. Box 8634,*
> *Clinton, Iowa 52736.*

If P&G refused to redeem the Teddy Bears points, would the purchasers have any contract rights to force P&G to deliver the catalog merchandise? [*Alligood* v. *Procter & Gamble Co.,* 594 N.E.2d 668 (Ohio App. 1991)]

Understanding "Consider" Problems

10.1

THINK: The discussion of UCC versus common law has us examine the following:

- The cost of goods versus the cost of service in the contract
- The role of the seller in performing the contract
- The nature of the service component

APPLY: In this case, the cost of the carpet is clearly the largest part of the contract price. Even though the buyer wanted the carpet installed (rather than just delivered to her home), the installation is incidental to the purchase itself. The contract was made for the purchase of the carpet, a good, and the agreement to install the carpet was then tacked onto the contract. Goods such as carpet were intended as part of the UCC to have full warranty protection.

ANSWER: The contract is covered by the UCC.

10.2

THINK: Consideration is required to have a valid contract. The consideration must be paid.

APPLY: The consideration was not paid.

ANSWER: Hasbro lost its rights when it did not pay the consideration due under the contract.

Notes

1. UCITA was formerly Article 2B of the Uniform Commercial Code. It was separated out because reforms for the UCC on Article 2 were pending and the controversy related to Article 2B (now UCITA) was isolated with its separate promulgation as a uniform law. UCITA remains controversial. See Americans for Fair Electronic Commerce at http://www.ucita.com for a summary of the concerns and issues.

2. With the UCC modifications and ESIGN, a writing is no longer required. However, there must be some type of record, which could come in the form of an electronic submission.

3. Roger C. Bern, "'Terms Later' Contracting: Bad Economics, Bad Morals, and a Bad Idea for a Uniform Law, Judge Easterbrook Not Withstanding," 12 *Journal of Law and Policy* 641 (2004).

11

Contracts and Sales: Performance and Remedies

update

For up-to-date legal news, click on "Author Updates" at

www.cengage.com/blaw/ jennings

Once the parties have formed a contract with an offer, acceptance, and considera- tion (as discussed in Chapter 10), it would seem that their troubles are over and that all they need to do is carry through with performance. However, sometimes one party learns new information and challenges the formation; or perhaps what one party believes is performance is just not enough for the other party. Sometimes both sides realize that what they contemplated when they formed the contract just can't happen. This chapter focuses on contract problems and answers the following ques- tions: What if the assumptions made in formation turn out to be untrue? Must the parties go through with the contract? If one party does not perform, is the other excused? When is performance required, and when is it sufficient? What remedies exist? Do third parties have rights in a contract? ■

For want of a nail the shoe was lost;
For want of a shoe the horse was lost;
And for want of a horse the rider was lost;
For the want of a rider the battle was lost;
For the want of the battle the kingdom was lost
And all for the want of a horseshoe-nail.
Poor Richard's Almanac (1758)

consider...

Dorris Reed purchased a home from Robert King for $76,000. After Mrs. Reed moved in, she learned that the house had been the site of the murders of a mother and her four children. Mr. King and the real estate agents were aware of these events but did not disclose them to Mrs. Reed prior to the sale. The neighbors told Mrs. Reed of the murders after she moved into her home. Is Mrs. Reed stuck with the house? Is there any way she can get out of the contract?

Defenses in Contract Formation

Even though a contract may have been formed with the three elements of offer, acceptance, and consideration, one of the elements may be flawed. The result is a contract that may be void, voidable, or unenforceable. When one of the required elements of formation is flawed, the contract is subject to a defense. A **contract defense** is a situation, term, or event that makes an otherwise valid contract invalid. These defenses ensure that the parties enter into contracts voluntarily and on the basis of accurate information. Exhibit 11.1 shows the defenses that are explained in the sections following.

CAPACITY

Both parties to a valid contract must have **capacity**, which includes both age and mental capacity.

EXHIBIT 11.1   Defenses in Contract Formation

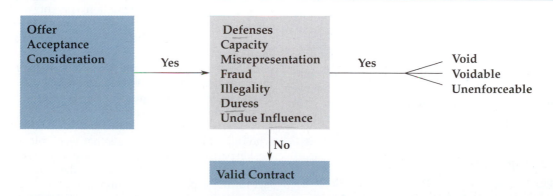

Age Capacity

Age capacity means that the parties to the contract are at least the age of majority. In most states, that age is 18. Before the time a party reaches the age of capacity, his or her contracts are voidable: A **voidable contract** of a minor allows the **minor** (sometimes called an **infant**) to choose not to honor the contract, in which case the other party to the contract will have no remedy. But some exceptions apply to the minors' contracts rules. Some statutes make certain contracts of minors enforceable; for example, student loan agreements are enforceable against minors. Minors' contracts for necessities, called **necessaries**, such as food and clothing, are still voidable, but courts do hold minors liable for the reasonable value of those necessities.

Case 11.1 deals with an issue of a minor's liability under a contract.

CASE 11.1

Yale Diagnostic Radiology v. *Estate of Fountain*
838 A.2D 179 (CONN. 2003)

SHOOTING FOR PAYMENT FROM A MINOR

FACTS

In March 1996, Harun Fountain was shot in the back of the head at point-blank range by a playmate. As a result of his injuries, including the loss of his right eye, Fountain had extensive lifesaving medical services from many providers, including Yale Diagnostic Radiology (Yale/plaintiff). The expenses at Yale totaled $17,694. Yale billed Vernetta Turner-Tucker (Tucker), Fountain's mother, but the bill went unpaid and, in 1999, Yale obtained a judgment against her. In January 2001, all of Tucker's debts were discharged in bankruptcy, including the Yale judgment. None of the cases, from bankruptcy to the present litigation, discussed Fountain's father.

Tucker filed suit against the boy who had shot her son. However, Harun passed away before the case was settled. The settlement from this tort case was placed into probate court as part of Fountain's estate. Tucker was the administrator of her son's estate. When the settlement was deposited, Yale asked the probate court for payment of its $17,694 judgment from the estate. The Probate Court denied the motion, reasoning that parents are liable for medical services rendered to their minor children, and that a parent's refusal or inability to pay for those services does not render the minor child liable. The Probate Court held that Yale could not get payment from the estate. Yale appealed to the trial court, and the trial court held for Yale. Tucker and the estate (defendants) appealed.

JUDICIAL OPINION

BORDEN, Justice
The rule that a minor's contracts are voidable is not absolute. An exception to this rule, eponymously known

as the doctrine of necessaries, is that a minor may not avoid a contract for goods or services necessary for his health and sustenance. Such contracts are binding even if entered into during minority, and a minor, upon reaching majority, may not, as a matter of law, disaffirm them.

. . . [W]e conclude that Connecticut recognizes the doctrine of necessaries. We further conclude that, pursuant to the doctrine, the defendants are liable for payment to the plaintiff for the services rendered to Fountain.

Our common law has long recognized the parents' obligation to provide for their minor child ("[t]here is a law of our universal humanity . . . which impels parents, whether fathers or mothers, to protect and support their helpless children").

The present case illustrates the inequity that would arise if no implied in law contract arose between Fountain and the plaintiff. Although the plaintiff undoubtedly presumed that Fountain's parent would pay for his care and was obligated to make reasonable efforts to collect from Tucker before seeking payment from Fountain, the direct benefit of the services, nonetheless, was conferred upon Fountain. Having received the benefit of necessary services, Fountain should be liable for payment for those necessaries in the event that his parents do not pay.

Fountain received, through a settlement with the boy who caused his injuries, funds that were calculated, at least in part, on the costs of the medical services provided to him by the plaintiff in the wake of those injuries. This fact further supports a determination of an implied-in-law contract under the circumstances of the case.

The judgment is affirmed.

CASE QUESTIONS

1. Describe the series of events that led to Yale requesting that the minor pay for the medical services.

2. What public policy issues and concerns result from this decision?

3. What benefits does the decision provide?

ethical *issues*

Since the time LeAnn Rimes, a country western singer, signed a contract at age 12 with Curb Records, the issues of fairness, accounting practices, and contract length have plagued the recording industry. Curb Records is owned by Mike Curb, a long-standing presence in the music industry who began his career with a group known as The Mike Curb Congregation. Under the terms of that contract as it originally existed, and was signed by Ms. Rimes' guardians, Ms. Rimes would have been 35 before she had delivered the 21 albums required under the terms of the agreement. "At 12, I didn't understand everything in my contract. All I know is that I really wanted to sing," was the explanation Ms. Rimes offered when she later testified before California Senate Select Committee on the Entertainment Industry looking into the labor issues surrounding long-term album requirements contracts. Other artists testified about their lack of health insurance benefits under these contracts. Singer Courtney Love testified, in reference to her minimal insurance coverage, "I can maybe get six days in rehab."

Don Henley, a solo artist also working with The Eagles, testified, "The deck is stacked and has been stacked for sixty years in the recording companies' favor."

Record industry executives testified that the long-term contracts are necessary because of the time, money, and effort required to build young artists. One executive said, "There is one thing that all labels have in common and that's risk."

When she turned 18 (in 2000), Ms. Rimes filed suit against Curb records seeking to get out of the contract she entered into while she was a minor. Part of the suit included litigation against her co-manager who served with her father (who filed a countersuit in the matter) in handling Ms. Rimes' business matters. One year after the suit was filed, Ms. Rimes settled the suit and signed a new contract with Curb Records. However, the precedent was set, and record industry litigation continued. The Dixie Chicks threatened to leave Sony, and Sony filed suit for breach of contract. The Chicks counterclaimed for what they said was "systematic thievery" that "cheated" them out of $4 million through accounting trickery. The group and Sony settled their suit with the Chicks receiving an additional $20 million in royalty payments before their "Home" album was released in 2002. Ms. Love and her band also threatened to leave her label, Vivendi Universal, for what they said were "shoddy" accounting practices. Vivendi filed suit for breach of contract. Love and Vivendi settled after 8 years of litigation in 2008.

Does Ms. Rimes have a possible defense? Are the recording contracts binding, or are they unconscionable? Are the long-term contracts and their requirements ethical?

Mental Capacity

Contracting parties must also have *mental capacity,* which is the ability to understand that contracts are enforceable, that legal documents have significance, and that contracts involve costs and obligations. Contracts of those lacking mental capacity are voidable. The contracts of those who been declared legally incompetent are void. A **void contract** is one the courts will not honor, and neither party is obligated to perform under that agreement.

MISREPRESENTATION

Misrepresentation occurs when one party to a contract is not given full or accurate information by the other party about the contract subject matter. When there has been misrepresentation in the formatiion of a contract, the law allows a <u>**rescission**</u>

of the contract. Rescission means the contract is set aside. For example, failing to disclose that a designer suit you are selling on eBay has a permanent stain on the back of the skirt when you show only a photo view of the front would be misrepresentation. The elements of innocent misrepresentation are:

1. Misstatement of a material fact (or the failure to disclose a material fact)
2. Reliance by the buyer on that material misstatement or omission
3. Resulting damages to the buyer

A **material fact** is the type of information that would affect someone's decision to enter into the contract. For example, if a buyer for your stock in XYZ Corporation failed to disclose that a takeover was pending, it would be considered misrepresentation of a material fact. A takeover affects the price of stock, and the price of stock in the future affects your decision to buy and sell presently.

Misrepresentation cannot be based on sales **puffing**, which is opinion, or "sales hype" about the contract's subject matter. For example, suppose that a cosmetics sales rep told you that a skin exfoliator would make your skin glow. "Glow" is a matter of opinion. By contrast, if the cosmetics rep said the exfoliator would cure acne, there is a promise of performance and measurable factual result, which can be a basis for misrepresentation.

consider 11.1

Analyze the following statements. Are they opinion, or could they be the basis for a misrepresentation claim?

> *This lightbulb will last 200 hours.*
> *These suits are 100 percent wool.*

(Analysis appears at the end of the chapter.)

The buyer must rely on or attach some importance to the statement. A buyer who is buying cars only to take them apart for their used parts does not rely on a misrepresentation that the car has not been in an accident. Whatever information is given must be part of the reason the buyer has agreed to enter into the contract.

Business Planning Tip

When employees and agents are working for commissions as well as salary (or are on commission alone), they are subject to great temptation to engage in misrepresentation. For example, in the Sears Roebuck & Company controversy over the allegations that its auto repair centers overcharged customers, Sears' then-CEO Edward Brennan issued a statement indicating that the presence of incentives for selling parts and services may have contributed to poor decisions by employees in handling customers. Incentive-based pay systems must also have ethical guidelines.

FRAUD OR FRAUDULENT MISREPRESENTATION

Fraud is the knowing and intentional disclosure of false information or the knowing failure to disclose relevant information. Fraud has the same elements of proof as misrepresentation, with the added element of *scienter*, or knowledge that the information given is false. An example of the distinction is a situation in which the seller of a home obtains an exterminator's report that says the house is clear of termites and passes the report along to the buyer. If the house actually has termites, it is a case of misrepresentation but not fraud because the seller was simply passing along the information without knowledge of its accuracy. If, however, that same seller received a report from an exterminator that indicated there were termites and then found another exterminator to report there were no termites, and the seller passed only that second report along to the buyer, there would be fraud because there was knowledge of the false report and the intent to defraud the buyer. If a car dealership that fails to disclose to a customer that the car he is buying was in an accident there has been a misrepresentation. If the car dealership performed the body work on the car in its own body shop, the failure to disclose the accident and repairs would be fraud.

Reed v. *King* (Case 11.2) includes a discussion of the elements of misrepresentation, when misrepresentation becomes fraud, and provides the answer for the chapter's opening Consider.

Most states have passed some form of disclosure statutes for real estate transactions. In some states, the history of criminal activity on a property must be disclosed. In other states, there are prohibitions against certain disclosure such as whether an occupant of the property died of AIDS. However, even in states with protections and immunity from disclosure, the buyer must be told the truth if the buyer asks specifically about the occupants and their health.

CASE 11.2

Reed v. *King*
193 Cal. Rptr. 130 (1983)

Buying Property from the Addams Family: How Scary Must It Be?

Facts

Dorris Reed (plaintiff) purchased a home from Robert King for $76,000. Mr. King and his real estate agents did not disclose to Mrs. Reed that 10 years before, the house had been the site of the murders of a mother and her four children. After Mrs. Reed moved into the home, neighbors disclosed to her the story of the murders and the fact that the house carried a stigma. Because of its history, appraisers evaluated the true worth of the house to be $65,000. Mrs. Reed filed suit on the basis of misrepresentation and sought rescission and damages. Her complaint was dismissed by the trial court, and she appealed.

Judicial Opinion

BLEASE, Associate Justice

In the sale of a house, must the seller disclose it was the site of a multiple murder?

Reed's complaint reveals only nondisclosure despite the allegation King asked a neighbor to hold his peace. There is no allegation the attempt at suppression was a cause in fact of Reed's ignorance. Accordingly, the critical question is: does the seller have duty to disclose here? Resolution of this question depends on the materiality of the fact of the murders.

In general, a seller of real property has a duty to disclose: "where the seller knows of facts *materially* affecting the value or desirability of the property which are known

or accessible only to him and also knows that such facts are not known to, or within the reach of . . . the buyer."

Numerous cases have found nondisclosure of physical defects and legal impediments to use of real property are material. However, to our knowledge, no prior real estate sale case has faced an issue of nondisclosure of the kind presented here. Should this variety of ill-repute be required to be disclosed?

The paramount argument against an affirmative conclusion is it permits the camel's nose of unrestrained irrationality admission to the tent. If such an "irrational" consideration is permitted as a basis of rescission the stability of all conveyances will be seriously undermined. Any fact that might disquiet the enjoyment of some segment of the buying public may be seized upon by a disgruntled purchaser to void a bargain. In our view, keeping this genie in the bottle is not as difficult a task as these arguments assume. We do not view a decision allowing Reed to survive a demurrer in these unusual circumstances as endorsing the materiality of facts predicating peripheral, insubstantial, or fancied harms.

The murder of innocents is highly unusual in its potential for so disturbing buyers they may be unable to reside in a home where it has occurred. This fact may foreseeably deprive a buyer of the intended use of the purchase. Murder is not such a common occurrence that *buyers* should be charged with anticipating and discovering this disquieting possibility. Accordingly, the fact is

CONTINUED

not one for which a duty of inquiry and discovery can sensibly be imposed upon the buyer.

Reed alleges the fact of the murders has a quantifiable effect on the market value of the premises. Reputation and history can have a significant effect on the value of realty. "George Washington slept here" is worth something, however physically inconsequential that consideration may be. Ill-repute or "bad will" conversely may depress the value of property. Failure to disclose such a negative fact where it will have a foreseeably depressing effect on income expected to be generated by a business is tortious. Some cases have held that *unreasonable* fears of the potential buying public that a gas or oil pipeline may rupture may depress the market value of land and entitle the owner to incremental compensation in eminent domain.

Whether Reed will be able to prove her allegation, the decade-old multiple murder has a significant effect on market value we cannot determine. If she is able to do so by competent evidence she is entitled to a favorable ruling on the issues of materiality and duty to disclose. Her demonstration of objective tangible harm would still the concern that permitting her to go forward will open the floodgates to rescission on subjective and idiosyncratic grounds.

CASE QUESTIONS

1. Name the two conflicting public policy concerns the court has about requiring disclosure vs. not requiring disclosure.

2. Why is the ability to quantify the effect of the murders important to the court?

3. Should Mr. King and the real estate agents have disclosed the information to Mrs. Reed? Was there an ethical obligation to do so?

DURESS

Duress occurs when a party is physically forced into a contract or deprived of a meaningful choice when deciding whether to enter into a contract. Requiring employees to sell company stock holdings in order to keep their jobs is an example of duress because of a lack of choice. If duress has occurred, the contract is voidable. The party who experienced the duress has the right to rescind the agreement, but rescission is a choice; the law does not make the contract illegal or unenforceable because duress was present. The choice of enforcement or rescission is left to the party who experienced the duress.

UNDUE INFLUENCE

Undue influence occurs when one party uses a close personal relationship with another party to gain contractual benefits. Before undue influence can be established, a **confidential relationship** of trust and reliance must exist between the parties. Attorneys and clients have a confidential relationship. Elderly parents who rely on a child or children for their care have a confidential relationship with those children. To establish undue influence, abuse of this confidential relationship must occur. For example, conditioning an elderly parent's care upon the signing over of his land to a child is an abuse of the relationship. An attorney who offers advice on property disposition to his benefit is abusing the confidential relationship. Again, contracts subject to undue influence defenses are voidable. They can be honored if the party who experienced the influence chooses to honor the contract.

ILLEGALITY AND PUBLIC POLICY

A contract that violates a statute or the general standards of public policy is void and cannot be enforced by either party. To enforce contracts that violate statutes or public conscience would encourage the commission of these illegal acts.

Contracts in Violation of Criminal Statutes

Contracts that are agreements to commit criminal wrongs are void. For example, the old saying that "there is a contract out on his life" may be descriptive, but it is not legally accurate. There could never be a valid contract to kill someone because the agreement is one to commit a criminal wrong and is therefore void. No one is permitted to benefit from contracts to commit illegal acts. For example, a beneficiary for a life insurance policy will not collect the proceeds from the insured's policy if the beneficiary arranged for the death of the insured (contract for murder).

Contracts in Violation of Licensing Statutes

In some cases, contracts are not contracts to commit illegal acts but are simply contracts for a legal act to be done by one not authorized to perform such services. Every state requires some professionals or technicians to be licensed before they can perform work for the public. For example, a lawyer must be admitted to the bar before representing clients. A lawyer who contracts to represent a client before having been admitted to the practice of law has entered into a void contract. Even if the lawyer successfully represents the client, no fee could be collected because the agreement violated the licensing statute, and to allow the lawyer to collect the fee, even in a quasi contract, would encourage others to violate the licensing requirements.

In some cases, licensing requirements are in place not for competency reasons but to raise revenues. For example, an architect may be required to pass a competency screening to be initially licensed in a state, and after that the license may be renewed simply by paying an annual fee. Suppose that the architect forgot to pay the annual renewal fee and, after the license had lapsed, entered into a $300,000 contract with a developer. The developer discovers the renewal problems after the work is completed and wants to get out of paying the architect. In this case, the issue is not one of competency screening but of financial oversight, and the architect would be permitted to collect the fee.

Contracts in Violation of Usury Laws

These contracts are credit or loan contracts that charge interest in excess of the state's limits for interest or finance charges. These statutes are discussed in detail in Chapter 12.

Contracts in Violation of Public Policy

Some contracts do not violate any criminal laws or statutory provisions but do violate certain standards of fairness or encourage conduct that violates public policy. For example, many firms include **exculpatory clauses** in their contracts that purport to hold the firms completely blameless for any accidents occurring on their premises. Most courts consider trying to hold yourself completely blameless for all accidents, regardless of the degree of care or level of fault, against public policy and do not generally enforce such clauses.

Also grouped into the public policy prohibition are contracts that restrict trade or employment. For example, when a business is sold, part of the purchase price is paid for the business's goodwill. The benefit of that payment is lost if the seller moves down the street and starts another similar business. Courts have permitted **covenants not to compete** to be included in these contracts as long as they are reasonable in time and geographic scope. These covenants are discussed in detail in Chapter 16.

Some contracts are not actually contracts for criminal or illegal activities, but the terms of the contract are grossly unfair to one party. A contract that gives all the benefits to one side and all the burdens to the other is an **unconscionable** contract. The standards for determining whether a contract is unconscionable are the public policy standards for fairness that cover all types of contract provisions and negotiations. Many consumer rental contracts have been declared unconscionable because the consumers were paying more in rent than it would cost to buy the rented appliance outright.

The standards for unconscionability are set on a case-by-case basis. The courts have not given a firm definition of unconscionability. Even the UCC does not specifically define unconscionability, although one section (2–302) prohibits the enforcement of unconscionable contracts.

Contract Performance

Once parties have contracted, they have the obligation of performance. The following subsections cover when performance is due, what constitutes performance, and when performance is excused.

WHEN PERFORMANCE IS DUE

Performance is due according to the times provided in the contract. In some contracts, however, prescribed events must occur before performance is required. These events are called **conditions**. **Conditions precedent** are events that give rise to performance. Suppose that Zelda has agreed to buy Scott's house, and their contract provides that Zelda does not have to pay until she is able to obtain a reasonable loan to finance the purchase. This financing clause is a condition precedent to contract performance. If Zelda is denied financing, she is not required to perform under the contract. Another example of a condition precedent is in a contract for construction of jackets out of a material to be furnished by the seller. Unless the seller gives the manufacturer the fabric to work with, the manufacturer has no obligation to perform. **Conditions concurrent**, or **conditions contemporaneous**, exist in every contract; benefits are exchanged at the same time. One is willing to perform because the other side does.

STANDARDS FOR PERFORMANCE

The contract details what the parties are required to do for complete performance. In some contracts, performance is easily determined. Performance for a contract between an employment agency and a potential employee to find work for the employee is complete once the work is found.

consider. 11.2

High-powered talent presents contract challenges beyond the legal issues. Companies must anticipate several types of issues. One is the morals issue: What happens to contracts when one of the parties is charged with a violation of the law? The contract is not illegal, but the conduct hurts the other party to the contract. For example, Michael Vick, the quarterback for the Atlanta Falcons who had a $130,000,000 contract, was indicted in

July 2007 on charges of running a dog-fighting enterprise. NFL Commissioner Roger Goddell told Mr. Vick, "Don't bother showing up to camp." The owner of the Atlanta Falcons, Arthur Blank, told his $130,000,000 quarterback that he would not be playing until the federal charges of operating a dog-fighting enterprise are resolved. Nike pulled Mr. Vick's endorsement deal on its fifth shoe with the quarterback. Adidas suspended sales of Vick shirts. Coca-Cola and Kraft indicated that there would be no more Vick endorsements for their products. All this happened before Mr. Vick entered his guilty plea and reported to prison. Provisions in contracts on indictments for criminal conduct provide the companies and franchises with the authority to end the relationship. Is this standard for performance clear? When would there be problems with application and interpretation? Does it matter on the endorsement contracts whether there is an indictment?

Another issue arises when the conduct is not illegal, but just offensive.

In 2007, Verizon withdrew its sponsorship of the Gwen Stefani tour when a raunchy video of her opening act, Akon, appeared online. The video shows Akon engaged in questionable on-stage behavior with a fan under the age of 18. The video resulted in considerable coverage and outrage from parents and commentators. Akon issued the following apology, "I want to sincerely apologize for the embarrassment and any pain I've caused to the young woman who joined me on stage, her family, and the Trinidad community for the events at my concert."[1] Under the terms of its sponsorship contracts, Verizon has the right to end its relationships with singers for criminal charges or other misconduct. Ms. Stefani's manager said, "This kid is not getting a fair shake (referring to Akon). I strongly disagree with their take on it. How this has anything to do with Gwen Stefani I have no idea."[2] Who is right under the contract? Verizon will still be required to pay Ms. Stefani the cash due under the contract (estimated at $2 million), but it will no longer have advertisements or other promotional materials as part of the tour. Verizon issued the following statement, "We made a decision, based on what we saw and, in this case, how our own customers, who we listen to, were reacting."[3] What do you learn about celebrity contracts from these examples? (Analysis appears at the end of the chapter.)

[1] Jeff Leeds, "Verizon Drops Pop Singer from Ads," *New York Times*. May 10, 2007, pp. B1, B6.
[2] *Id.*
[3] *Id.*

· ·

In some contracts, performance is complicated, and errors happen. For example, construction contracts are long-term, complicated agreements. During the construction of a building, it is possible that some mistakes might be made. Is an owner allowed to not pay a contractor because of a mistake or two? The doctrine of **substantial performance** applies in construction contracts, and it means that the constructed building is for practical purposes just as good as the one contracted for. For example, a builder might have substituted a different type of copper pipe when the brand name "Reading Copper Pipe" specified in the contract was not available. The substitution is a technical breach of contract, but it is a substitute that is just as good. The builder will be paid for the construction, but the owner will be entitled to damages.

E-Commerce: Payments Have Changed

One aspect of contract performance is payment. Internet and online transactions have changed dramatically how we pay for goods and services. The most common methods for electronic payment include credit cards, digital cash, and person-to-person payment, or PayPal.

WHEN PERFORMANCE IS EXCUSED

Sometimes, all conditions of a valid contract are met but performance of the contract is excused. Under common law, the parties are excused from performance if performance has become impossible. **Impossibility** means that the contract cannot be performed by the parties or anyone else. For example, performance under a contract for the purchase and sale of land that has been washed away into a lake is impossible. Completing a year of dance lessons is impossible for someone who has had a paralyzing accident.

Under the UCC (and under the *Restatement*), performance can be excused in cases of commercial impracticability. **Commercial impracticability** (see UCC § 2–615) excuses performance if the basic assumptions the parties made when they entered into the contract have changed. Although this definition makes it seem that the UCC excuses performance when wars, embargoes, and unusually high price increases occur, courts have been reluctant to apply the excuse of commercial impracticability. In effect, commercial impracticability usually means nothing more or less than the common law standard of impossibility.

Unusual events can be handled through *force majeure* clauses, which excuse the parties from performance in the event of such problems as wars, depression, or embargoes. Following the attacks on the World Trade Center in New York City, many contracts were excused for impossibility. For example, because air traffic was halted, all overnight shipping contract performances were excused.

Sons of Thunder, Inc. v. *Borden, Inc.* (Case 11.3), a case that some experts have labeled a landmark one in terms of imposing a duty of good faith in performance, contains issues of performance and termination of a contract.

Often the obligation to perform is discharged by agreement of the parties. In some cases, the parties substitute someone else for the obligation in an agreement called a **novation**. For example, suppose that before forming a corporation, a business owner had signed a lease for store premises and then incorporates the

---

CASE 11.3

Sons of Thunder, Inc. v. *Borden, Inc.*
690 A.2D 575 (N.J. 1997)

SHIPS AND LIABILITY PASSING IN THE NIGHT?

FACTS

Borden, Inc., owned Snow Food Products Division, a leading producer of clam products. Wayne Booker, a manager for Borden, asked Mr. Donald DeMusz to undertake the Shuck-at-Sea program. Mr. DeMusz submitted a proposal that Mr. Booker and other executives approved.

An internal company memo from Mr. Booker included the following paragraph along with a description of how Mr. DeMusz's purchase of a boat would save money:

[W]e still have a significant mutual interest with DeMuse [sic]. His principal business will still be in chartering the Snow

fleet and in captaining Arlene. He needs a dependable customer for the clams that he catches, either shell stock or meat. If we terminate our agreement with him, he would have a hard time making the payments on his boat.

Mr. DeMusz drafted a one-page contract, and Mr. Booker approved it with one small change. Mr. DeMusz then formed Sons of Thunder, Inc., with Bill Gifford and Bob Dempsey in order to purchase the second boat. The final contract was entered into on January 15, 1985, and included the following provision:

IT IS understood and Agreed to by the parties hereto that Snow Food Products shall purchase shell stock from Sons of

Thunder Corp. for a period of one (1) year, at the market rate that is standardized throughout the industry. The term of this contract shall be for a period of one (1) year, after which this contract shall automatically be renewed for a period up to five years. Either party may cancel this contract by giving prior notice of said cancellation in writing Ninety (90) days prior to the effective cancellation date.

Sons of Thunder Corp. will offer for sale all shell stock that is landed to Snow Food.

In March 1985, Sons of Thunder bought a boat, the *Sons of Thunder.* The cost to rig and purchase the boat was $588,420.26. Sons of Thunder sought financing from First Jersey National Bank but was unable to obtain a loan until Mr. Booker told the bank representative that Mr. DeMusz had a solid relationship with Borden and that although the contract could be terminated within one year, Borden expected the contract to run for five years. Ultimately, Mr. DeMusz obtained a $515,000 loan, which he, Mr. Gifford, Mr. Dempsey, and their spouses personally guaranteed.

For most weeks, the records show that Borden did not buy the minimum amount specified in the contract. Problems continued and the relationship soured. When Borden discovered that a $500,000 accounting error had actually overstated the benefits of the Shuck-at-Sea program, Borden exercised its termination rights under the contract.

Mr. DeMusz, stuck with a boat and a loan and no customer, filed suit. Borden moved for summary judgment on the grounds that it had properly exercised its termination rights. The jury found for Mr. DeMusz, the court of appeals affirmed, and Borden appealed.

Judicial Opinion

GARIBALDI, Justice
The obligation to perform in good faith exists in every contract, including those contracts that contain express and unambiguous provisions permitting either party to terminate the contract without cause.

Borden knew that Sons of Thunder depended on the income from its contract with Borden to pay back the loan. Yet, Borden continuously breached that contract by never buying the required amount of clams from the Sons of Thunder. Borden's failure to honor the contract left Sons of Thunder with insufficient revenue to support its financing for the Sons of Thunder.

Borden was also aware that Sons of Thunder was guaranteeing every loan that Sea Work had taken to finance the rerigging and purchasing costs for the [boat]. Thus, Borden knew that the corporations were dependent on each other, and that if one company failed, the other would most likely fail.

The final issue is whether the jury's assessment of $412,000, approximately one year's worth of additional profits, for the breach of the implied covenant of good faith and fair dealing was a reasonable verdict. Specifically, can a plaintiff recover lost profits for a breach of the implied covenant of good faith and fair dealing? We agree with Judge Humphreys that the jury's award of one year's additional profits "is a reasonable and fair estimate of 'expectation damages.'" Moreover, we agree with the trial court that lost profits are an appropriate remedy when a buyer breaches the implied covenant of good faith and fair dealing.

Case Questions

1. Explain the nature of the relationships between Mr. DeMusz and Borden.

2. What impact does "good faith" have on termination of a contract?

3. What are the damages when there is a lack of good faith in the termination of a contract?

business. The landlord agrees to substitute the new corporation as the tenant. All three parties (landlord, owner, and corporation) sign a novation. The owner is excused from individual liability and performance, and the corporation is substituted. Note that the landlord must agree; the owner cannot discharge his performance obligations by unilaterally substituting the corporation.

In other situations, the parties reach an agreement for payment in full on a contract; such an agreement is called an **accord and satisfaction**. The amount they agree to pay may be less than the original contract amount, but disputes over warranties, repairs, and other issues change the value of the contract. The accord and satisfaction discharges the performance of both parties.

Contract Remedies

If performance is not excused and there is a valid contract, the nonbreaching party can recover for damages from the nonperforming party. The purpose of such **compensatory damages** is to put the nonbreaching party in the same position he or she would have been in had no breach occurred. The law has formulas to calculate the amount of compensatory damages for breach of every type of contract. For example, if a seller has agreed to sell a buyer a used car for $15,000 and the seller breaches, the buyer could collect the extra $1,000 it would cost to buy a substitute car priced at $16,000.

In addition to compensatory damages, nonbreaching parties are entitled to collect the extra damages or **incidental damages** involved because of the breach. If a seller must run an ad in a newspaper to sell a car a buyer has refused to buy, the costs of the ad are incidental damages.

Some parties agree in their contracts on the amounts they will pay in the case of nonperformance. Damages agreed upon in advance are **liquidated damages**, and the liquidated damages clauses are enforceable as long as they are not excessive and compensatory damages have not been paid in addition.

In some cases, the nonbreaching party may be able to collect **consequential damages**. Consequential damages are damages that result because of the breach and generally involve lost business, lost profit, or late penalties. For example, if a contractor must pay a penalty of $2,000 for each day a building is late after the completion date stipulated in the contract and the contractor is late because the steel supplier did not meet its deadline, the $2,000-per-day penalty would be a consequential damage that the steel supplier would be required to pay. Whether a party will be able to collect consequential damages depends on whether the breaching party knew or should have known what the consequences of the breach would be.

consider..11.3

Fingerlakes Aquaculture LLC, an indoor fish hatchery, entered into a contract for Progas Welding Supply to build and deliver a 13,000-gallon oxygen storage tank. The contract required that the tank be delivered during the week of June 21, 1999, with a $400-per-day liquidated damages provision, denoted as a "fine." Throughout the year, Progas delivered smaller tanks, but was never able to deliver the 13,000-gallon tank. In June 2001, Fingerlakes Aquaculture bought a tank from another supplier and filed suit seeking the $400-per-day liquidated damages. Progas says that because of the other tanks, Fingerlakes Aquaculture had no damages and the total of $292,000 (the $400 per day for the 210 days of delay) was void as a penalty. Who is correct? Why? (Analysis appears at the end of the chapter.) [*Fingerlakes Aquaculture LLC* v. *Progas Welding Supply, Inc.*, 825 N.Y.S.2d 559 (2006)]

Third-Party Rights in Contracts

Generally, a contract is a relationship between or among the contracting parties and is not enforceable by others who happen to benefit. For example, suppose a landowner and a commercial developer enter into an agreement for the construction of a shopping mall. Such a project means jobs for the area and additional business for restaurants, hotels, and transportation companies, but these businesses would not have the right to enforce the contract or collect damages for breach if the developer pulled out of the project. However, certain groups of people do have rights in contracts even though they may not have been parties to the contracts. A good example is a beneficiary of a life insurance policy. The beneficiary does not contract with the insurance company and does not pay the premiums, but the beneficiary has contract rights because the purchaser of the policy directed so.

In other types of third-party contract rights, the third parties are not part of the original contract, as is the life insurance beneficiary, but are brought in after the fact. For example, suppose that a homebuilder owes a plumbing contractor $5,000 for work done on homes in the builder's subdivision. In the sales contracts for the homes, the homebuilder is the seller, and the buyer's purchase monies will go to the homebuilder. However, the homebuilder could assign payment rights to the plumber as a means of satisfying the debt. This process, called **assignment**, gives the plumber the right to collect the contract amount from the buyer. The plumber takes the place of the homebuilder in terms of contract rights.

In some cases, the duty or obligation to perform under a contract is transferred to another party. The transfer of contractual duties and obligation is called a **delegation**. Generally, a delegation of duties carries with it an assignment of benefits. For example, suppose that Neptune Fisheries, Inc., has a contract with Tom Tuna, Inc., to sell 30 fresh lobsters each day. Neptune is stopping its lobster line and delegates its duties under the Tom Tuna contract to Louie's Lobsters, Inc. Louie's takes over Neptune's obligation to furnish the 30 lobsters and is assigned the right to benefits (payment for the lobsters) under the contract. Both Louie's and Neptune are liable to Tom Tuna for performance. A delegation, unlike a novation, does not release the original contracting party.

International Issues in Contract Performance

ASSURING PAYMENT

International contract transactions for goods involve extensive shipment requirements. To control access to the goods and payment for them, many sellers use a **bill of lading** for transacting business. The bill of lading is a receipt for shipment issued by the carrier to the seller. It is also a contract for the shipment of the goods and provides evidence of who has title to the goods. If a bill of lading is used, the buyer will not gain access to the goods unless and until the seller provides the necessary documents for release of the goods. Once the seller has the bill of lading, the seller can choose to transfer title to the goods by transferring the bill of lading. The seller could also pledge the bill of lading as security for the payment of a debt. A bill of lading can be made directly to the buyer, or it can be a negotiable bill of lading that can be transferred to anyone.

The bill of lading is often used along with a line of credit in international transactions because the two together offer the seller assurance of payment and the buyer assurance of arrival of the goods. In international transactions, in which resolution of disputes over great distances can be difficult, this means of controlling access to goods and payment is helpful.

In this type of transaction, the seller delivers goods to a carrier for transportation and receives a bill of lading. The seller then sends the bill of lading through its bank to the buyer's bank to give the buyer's bank title to the goods, which will be turned over to the buyer once the funds are deducted from the line of credit established by the bank for the buyer.

The buyer may also arrange for a **letter of credit** that is issued by the buyer's bank and sent to a corresponding bank where the seller is located. The letter of credit lists the terms and conditions under which the seller can be paid. Because banks are involved in these transactions through credit assurances, the seller enjoys more of an assurance of payment prior to shipment because a letter of credit is actually a confirmation of payment.

ASSURING PERFORMANCE: INTERNATIONAL PECULIARITIES

International contracts have a particular need for a *force majeure* clause. Wars, revolutions, and coups are often included in international contracts as justification for noncompletion. The *force majeure* clauses are summaries of potential international events that could hamper production or trade.[1]

One other risk of international contracts is the stability of various currencies and their possible devaluation. The method and means of payment should be specified in the contract, and a clause covering devaluation may also be included so that full payment is ensured.

Red Flags FOR MANAGERS

- Know the customer, or at least know the person you are contracting with. The party must not be a minor and must have the mental capacity to contract. If either of these is lacking, the party has the right to not perform under the contract.

- Trust, but verify. Be sure that the information you share with customers and others you contract with is complete and accurate. And do the same for the information they furnish to you. Be sure to conduct your own investigations of the products, the property, or the service provider you are about to contract with or for so that you have independent information. Although rescission is a remedy for misrepresentation or fraud, you do have the delays in your contract as well as the expense of recovering payments or goods already delivered.

- Be as specific as you can in listing the requirements for performance under your contract. If you want

Reading Copper Pipe as the plumbing pipe in your building, specify that in your contract. And spell out what damages will be. You can use a liquidated damage clause to cover situations in performance when you don't know what damages will be, such as an amount per day.

- If you are aware of circumstances that could prevent you from performing your contract, list those in your contract as grounds for excusing your performance. A *force majeure* clause can give you time or even a defense for non-delivery. For example, if you are shipping goods to Syria, you could spell out in your contract that wars, embargos, and other political events will result in delays or non-delivery. And anytime you have a contract that involves international delivery or performance, be sure to address issues such as currency, payment, and additional precautions such as bills of lading and letters of credit.

Summary

What if the assumptions made and the information given turn out to be untrue? Must the parties still go forward with the contract?

- Contract defense—situation, term, or event that excuses performance
- Capacity—mental and age thresholds for valid contracts
- Voidable contract—one party can choose not to honor the contract
- Puffing—statements of opinion
- Material—fact basis of the bargain
- Void contract—contract that courts will not honor
- Misrepresentation—incomplete or inaccurate information prior to contract execution
- Rescission—setting aside a contract as a remedy for, for example, misrepresentation
- Fraud—intentional misrepresentation
- *Scienter*—knowledge that information given is false
- Duress—physical or mental force that deprives party of a meaningful choice with respect to a proposed contract
- Undue influence—exerting control over another party for purposes of gain
- Confidential relationship—trust, confidence, reliance in a relationship
- Public policy—standards of decency
- Exculpatory clauses—attempt to hold oneself harmless for one's own conduct
- Unconscionable contract—contract that is grossly unfair

If one party does not perform, is the other side excused? When is performance required and when is it excused?

- Conditions precedent—advance events that must occur before performance is due, for example, obtaining financing

- Substantial performance—performance that, for practical purposes, is just as good as full performance
- Commercial impracticability—defense to performance of sales contract based on objective impracticability
- Novation—agreement to change contract among all affected, for example, agreement to substitute parties
- Accord and satisfaction—agreement entered into as settlement of a disputed debt
- Obligation of good faith—must perform in a reasonable fashion; performance must meet commercial standards

What remedies exist?

- Compensatory damages—amount required to place party in as good a position as before breach
- Incidental damages—costs of collecting compensatory damages
- Liquidated damages—agreement clause in contract that preestablishes and limits damages
- Consequential damages—damages owed to third parties from a breach

What are the contract performance issues in international business?

- Bill of lading—title document used to control transfer of goods
- Letter of credit—pledge by bank of availability of funds for a transaction
- Exchange rate and risk issues in contracts

Key Terms

Questions and Problems

1. Robert G. Rawlinson was employed by Germantown Manufacturing in Marple Township as its assistant controller. He embezzled $372,113.21 from the company, which discovered the theft, though not the exact amount, on May 21, 1982. Mr. Rawlinson admitted his wrongdoing and was fired. He did not tell his wife, and it was not until she eavesdropped on a telephone conversation between her husband and Peter Kulaski that she discovered something was amiss. Mr. Rawlinson told her (after his phone conversation) that he had taken $20,000 from the company and was fired. Mrs. Rawlinson testified that her "whole world fell apart" upon hearing the news. She was already depressed and tired because of a miscarriage she had suffered in late April.

The following day, Mr. Kulaski came to the Rawlinson home and asked them to sign two judgment notes. The first note was for $160,000, the amount Mr. Rawlinson admitted taking from the company. The second note was for any amounts above and beyond the $160,000 that would be established by the company president as having been taken by Mr. Rawlinson. Mrs. Rawlinson's name was on the documents, and she asked if they should not have an attorney. Mr. Kulaski told them they did not need an attorney because the company was acting in good faith and that no criminal charges would be brought if the Rawlinsons would cooperate. Mrs. Rawlinson felt that if she signed the notes, her husband would not go to jail.

Mrs. Rawlinson had never before seen a judgment note and cried while trying to read these. She thought she was signing only for $160,000 and, because her husband had a check for $150,000 ready to turn over, that they could easily come up with the remaining $10,000.

In August 1982, the president of the company verified that the total amount taken was $212,113.21 more than the $160,000 already paid. When demand for payment was made, Mrs. Rawlinson requested that the confession of judgment be opened and disallowed on the basis of misrepresentation. The lower court found for Mrs. Rawlinson, and Germantown Manufacturing appealed. Give a list of defenses Mrs. Rawlinson could use. [*Germantown Mfg. Co. v. Rawlinson*, 491 A.2d 138 (Pa. 1985)]

2. Tony Curtis, a respected actor, entered into a contract to write a novel for Doubleday & Company, publishers. Because of complex divorce proceedings and other personal factors, Mr. Curtis was unable to submit a satisfactory manuscript. Doubleday demanded a return of the $50,000 advance Mr. Curtis had received. Is Doubleday entitled to it? [*Doubleday & Co.* v. *Curtis*, 763 F.2d 495 (2d Cir. 1985)]

3. Bernina Sewing Machines imports sewing machines and parts for U.S. distribution. Its contract prices are in francs. Because of the devaluation of the U.S. dollar, Bernina wants to be excused from its contracts. Can it be excused under any contract doctrine? [*Bernina Distributors, Inc.* v. *Bernina Sewing Machines*, 646 F.2d 434 (10th Cir. 1981)]

4. Dan O'Connor paid $125 to have the University of Notre Dame's leprechaun mascot tattooed on his upper arm with the words "Fighting Irish" inscribed above the little gnome. The tattoo parlor inscribed the chosen leprechaun and "Fighing Irish."

Mr. O'Connor's girlfriend pointed out the spelling error, and Mr. O'Connor filed suit against the Tattoo Shoppe in Carlstadt, New Jersey, seeking unspecified damages.

Mr. O'Connor noted, "I was irate, and for a minute or two after I cooled down I kind of giggled. But I can't just live with this. You're not talking about a dented car where you can get another one . . . you're talking about flesh."

What damages should Mr. O'Connor receive? Would a refund of $125 be enough? What if the Tattoo Shoppe had a clause in its contract limiting damages to a refund? Would it be valid?

5. Northland Ford Dealers sponsored a hole-in-one contest at the Moccasin Creek Country Club in South Dakota. The contest winner would receive a new Ford Explorer. Jennifer Harms registered for the contest. She stood at the women's marker for teeing off and hit a hole-in-one. She was denied her car because the dealers' insurance policy for the event indicated the following, "ALL AMATEUR MEN AND WOMEN SHALL UTILIZE THE SAME TEE." That tee was established in the policy as 170 yards. However, the men and women participating in the contest were not told of this rule or restriction. Must the dealers give Ms. Harms her Ford Explorer, or will she remain "tee'd off"? [*Harms v. Northland Ford Dealers*, 602 N.W. 2d 58 (S.D. 1999)]

6. Betty Lobianco had a burglar alarm system installed in her home by Property Protection, Inc. The contract for installing the system provided:

Alarm system equipment installed by Property Protection, Inc. is guaranteed against improper function due to manufacturing defects or workmanship for a period of 12 months. The installation of the above equipment carries a 90-day warranty. The liability of Property Protection, Inc., is limited to repair or replacement of security alarm equipment and does not include loss or damage to possessions, persons, or property.

On November 22, 1975, Ms. Lobianco's home was burglarized and $35,815 in jewelry was taken. The alarm system, which had been installed less than 90 days earlier, included a standby source of power in case the regular source of power failed. On the day of the fateful burglary, the alarm did not go off because the batteries installed in the system had no power.

Ms. Lobianco brought suit to recover the $35,815. She claimed that the liability limitation was unconscionable and unenforceable under the UCC. Property Protection claimed that the UCC did not apply to the installation of a burglar alarm system. Who is correct? [*Lobianco v. Property Protection, Inc.*, 437 A.2d 417 (Pa. 1981)]

Understanding "Consider" Problems

11.1

THINK: Misrepresentation requires a statement of fact or a promise of performance that is a basis for entering into a contract.

APPLY: This statement about the lightbulb is a promise of performance. It is the type of information someone relies on when making a buying decision.

ANSWER: The statement is a basis for claiming misrepresentation if it turns out to be false.

THINK: Misstatement of a material fact that the buyer relies on when making decisions can be the basis for a claim of misrepresentation

APPLY: Saying that the suits are 100 percent wool is a statement of fact about the goods.

ANSWER: If the goods are not 100 percent wool, the statement is a basis for claiming misrepresentation.

Now use this approach to analyze the following statements.

This fabric is the finest money can buy.
This sweater is 50 percent cashmere.
This toothpaste reduces cavities by 20 percent.

11.2

THINK: Performance is not really defined in law, so the courts have to define what is performance according to the parties' contract and their intent.

APPLY: In some contracts, the parties spell out compensation, terms of payment, and work requirements. However, they do not include other factors, such as statements and behavior, that can affect the value of, particularly, endorsement contracts.

ANSWER: These types of behavior issues can be part of the contract requirements for performance, but the parties must spell out their so-called "morals clauses," and provide definitions such as arrest, conviction, or even something such as bringing public disgrace or ridicule. Then the parties should spell out the damages and/or payment due for a breach.

11.3

THINK: The parties can provide for a liquidated damage clause in their contract, something needed when the damages will be difficult to prove but certain.

APPLY: The parties here provided for a $400 per day liquidated damage clause that was automatic.

ANSWER: The court held that the clause was void as a penalty because it applied whether there were damages or not. The liquidated damages clause applied automatically and was void as a penalty.

Note

1. International history has played a role in the development of *force majeure* clauses because wars, trade, and international relations influence contract rights and performance.

12

Financing of Sales and Leases: Credit and Disclosure Requirements

update ➤
For up-to-date legal news, click on "Author Updates" at

www.cengage.com/blaw/ jennings

The English refer to credit sales as "buying on the never never" because you never really pay for everything; there is always some outstanding credit. Credit sales are a way of life in the United States. Nearly all sellers advertise not only their products but also the availability of credit terms for buyers. Credit is used so often that both Congress and state legislatures have enacted statutes regulating credit contracts. This chapter covers those regulations and credit contracts. How is a credit contract set up? What are the requirements? What statutes affect the credit contract? How are credit contracts enforced? ■

**Neither a borrower nor a lender be,
For a loan oft loses both itself and friend
And borrowing dulls the edge of husbandry.**

Hamlet, Act 1, Scene 3

**Consumer Credit Outstanding (per Federal Reserve Bank)
(includes revolving and nonrevolving)**

1993	$8.550 billion
2002	$984 billion
2003	$2,087 billion
2004	$2,201 billion
2005	$2,295 billion
2006	$2,398 billion
2007	$2,492 billion
2008	$2,587 billion

Delinquency Rate of Consumer Loans

Year	Percent of Loans Outstanding
1993	2.60%
2000	2.45%
2001	2.41%
2003	3.93%
2004	3.52%
2005	3.75%
2006	4.00%
2007	4.55%
2008	4.51%

Subprime mortgage delinquency rate (2006)	10.9%
Subprime delinquency rate (June 2008)	23.00%

Upon first exposure to the subject of credit regulation, the impression of the average attorney might be that the field is a maze, if not a mess, and probably both.

CHRISTOPHER L. PETERSON

In "Truth, Understanding, and High–Cost Consumer Credit: The Historical Context of the Truth in Lending Act," 55 Fla. L. Rev. 807 (2003)

consider...

In February 1995, A.B.&S., an auto repair shop owned by Jerry L. Bonner, an African-American, applied for a $230,000 business loan from the South Shore Bank. Mr. Bonner submitted the required Small Business Administration Loan Form 912 on December 27, 1994. In response to the question about arrests and convictions, Mr. Bonner noted the following:

1. Domestic matter between 1982 and 1984
2. Conviction for aggravated battery and assault in 1983 (claims self-defense)
3. Possession of a controlled substance in 1985
4. Disorderly conduct between 1985 and 1990
5. Possession of a controlled substance in 1990
6. Possession of a stolen car in September 1994

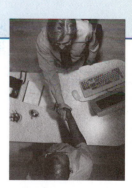

The bank denied the loan.

Mr. Bonner filed suit under the Equal Credit Opportunity Act, alleging that the bank's practice of considering criminal records has an unlawful disparate impact on African American men. Can the bank consider Mr. Bonner's criminal record in making a loan decision?

Establishing a Credit Contract

A credit contract not only needs the usual elements of a contract (as covered in Chapter 10), including offer, acceptance, and consideration, but also requires additional information for the credit agreement to be valid. The following list covers the extra details needed in a credit contract:

1. How much the buyer/debtor is actually carrying on credit or financing
2. The rate of interest the buyer/debtor will pay
3. How many payments will be made, when they will be made, and for how long
4. Penalties and actions for late payments
5. Whether the creditor will have collateral
6. The necessary statutory disclosures on credit transactions

Statutory Requirements for Credit Contracts

The following statutes affect and, in some cases, control the terms in a credit contract. Exhibit 12.1 summarizes the federal statutes.

STATE USURY LAWS

Usury is charging an interest rate higher than the maximum permitted by law. If the maximum rate of interest permitted by statute is 36 percent, a creditor charging 38 percent has violated a statute and created a void contract. The usury rate varies from state to state, and many states have different usury rates for the various types of transactions and what is or is not included in computing that rate also varies.

Penalties for charging a usurious rate also vary. Some states treat the usurious agreement as completely void, and the penalty for the creditor is forfeiture of interest and principal. Other states allow the creditor to recoup the principal but deny any interest. Some states simply require the creditor to forfeit any interest above the maximum; others also impose a penalty on the creditor by allowing the debtor to collect two or three times the amount of excess interest charged as damages.

THE SUBPRIME LENDING MARKET

From 2005–2007 there was a significant increase in the number of high-interest loans. These high-interest loans have often been "do- or-die" loans, or loans secured by titles to cars and homes or by paychecks (sometimes called payday loans). These loans are made instantly, but at high interest rates with title to the car or home or the next paycheck pledged as security for the loan. Subprime mortgages required little or no money down and often began with very low interest rates and payments that escalated with time or if the debtor missed a payment. Referred to as the *subprime lending market*, or *predatory lending*, this type of loan arrangement is now targeted by the Federal Reserve and state and local regulators. By the end of 2007, one-third of U.S. banks had increased their lending requirements because of a then-20 percent default rate in subprime loans. With the problems in the subprime

EXHIBIT 12.1 Summary of Federal Laws on Consumer Credit

CREDIT STATUTE (FEDERAL)	PURPOSE AND SCOPE
Equal Credit Opportunity Act 15 U.S.C. § 1691 (1974)	Prohibits discrimination on the basis of sex, race, age, or national origin in credit extension decision
Consumer Credit Protection Act (CCPA) 15 U.S.C. § 1601 (1968)	Umbrella statute passed to deal with fairness of consumer credit transactions
Truth in Lending Act 15 U.S.C. § 1601 (1968)	Part of CCPA that governs disclosure of credit terms
Amendments (1995) 15 U.S.C. § 1605	Closes loopholes for avoiding loan repayments based on clerical errors in loan documents
Fair Credit and Charge Card Disclosure Act 15 U.S.C. § 1646 (1988)	Provides for disclosure requirements in the solicitation of credit cards
Regulation Z 12 C.F.R. § 226 (1981)	Federal Reserve Board regulations providing details for all disclosure statutes
Home Equity Loan Consumer Protection Act 15 U.S.C. § 1647 (1988)	Disclosure requirements for home equity loans and a rescission period
Home Ownership and Equity Protection Act 15 U.S.C. § 1637 (1994)	Disclosure requirements on payment amounts for home equity loans and cancellation rights (HOEPA)
Fair Credit Billing Act 15 U.S.C. § 1637 (1974)	Rights of debtors on open-end credit billing disputes
Fair Credit Reporting Act 15 U.S.C. § 1681 (1970)	Right of debtors with respect to reports of their credit histories
Consumer Leasing Act 15 U.S.C. § 1667 (1976)	Disclosure requirements for leases of goods by consumers
Fair Debt Collections Practices Act 15 U.S.C. § 1692 (1977)	Regulation of conduct of third-party bill collectors and attorneys
Credit Repair Organization Act (1996) 15 U.S.C. § 1679b	Prohibits misrepresentations by credit repair organizations to consumers seeking help with credit issues
Service Members Civil Relief Act (2003) 50 U.S.C. §§ 501 *et seq*.	Prevents foreclosure while debtor is on active military duty
Defense Authorization Act of 2007 50 U.S.C. §§ 501 *et seq*.	Caps interest on credit to members of military at 36% APR; additional disclosure requirements; administered by Department of Defense

lending market and the resulting impact on the stock market as well as the availability of mortgage funds, Congress and the Federal Reserve Board worked together on additional legislation and regulations to limit and/or regulate the subprime market and resulting foreclosures. The new legislation and regulation includes additional disclosures and waiting periods on subprime loans (defined as loans 3 percentage points or more higher than comparable Treasury securities). From the lending side, there will be new documentation requirements, limits on the **yield spread premium** (the difference between what the mortgage broker charges and the actual interest rate on the loan, which is the broker's fee), and relationships with appraisers. In addition, a new field of lending in response to the high rate of subprime defaults, known as mortgage rescue lending, has emerged. These lenders offer consumers who are near foreclosure yet another lending arrangement to allow them to save their homes from foreclosure. The terms of these rescue loans can include high interest rates, title provisions upon default, and other clauses and covenants that afford little relief from the consumer's debt crisis. Mortgage rescue loans are also under legislative and regulatory scrutiny.

THE EQUAL CREDIT OPPORTUNITY ACT

The **Equal Credit Opportunity Act** (ECOA) was passed to ensure that credit was denied or awarded on the applicant's merits—the ability to pay—and not on such extraneous factors as sex, race, color, religion, national origin, or age. (See Exhibit 12.1 on p. 267.) Creditors may ask about these subject areas for record-keeping purposes, but the decision to extend or deny credit must be based on other factors. The following information also cannot be considered in making the credit decision:

1. Marital status of the applicant
2. Applicant's receipt of public assistance income
3. Applicant's receipt of alimony or child support payments
4. Applicant's plans for having children

Under the ECOA married persons have the right to have individual credit applications, lines, and ratings. Credit applications must specify that a spouse's income need not be disclosed unless the applicant is relying on that income to qualify for credit. Further, even on joint accounts, debtors can require creditors to report credit ratings individually for the spouses.

Violations of the ECOA carry statutory penalties. Debtors can recover their actual damages for embarrassment and emotional distress and also for punitive damages of up to $10,000. If a group of debtors brings a class action against a creditor, they can collect punitive damages of up to the lesser of $500,000 or 1 percent of the creditor's net worth. Punitive damages are recoverable even when no actual damages occur. *A.B.&S. Auto Service, Inc.* v. *South Shore Bank of Chicago* (Case 12.1) involves an issue of an ECOA violation and also provides the answer to the chapter's opening Consider.

CASE 12.1

A.B.&S. Auto Service, Inc. v. *South Shore Bank of Chicago*
962 F.Supp. 1056 (N.D.Ill. 1997)

DO THE CRIME, FORGET THE LOAN

FACTS

A.B.&S. Auto Service, Inc. (AB&S) is an automobile repair shop located in Chicago, Illinois. Jerry L. Bonner is AB&S's president, and he is an African-American. South Shore is a commercial bank that participates in

the Small Business Administration's (SBA) loan guarantee program.

The SBA requires all applicants for the loan guarantee program to fill out an SBA Form 912 Statement of Personal History. SBA Form 912 asks applicants if they have ever been charged with or arrested or convicted for any criminal offense other than a minor motor vehicle violation and, if so, asks applicants to provide details.

In February 1995, AB&S applied for a $230,000 business loan from the bank. Mr. Bonner submitted a Form 912 on December 27, 1994. In response to the question about arrests and convictions, Mr. Bonner noted the following:

1. Domestic matters between 1982 and 1984
2. Conviction for aggravated battery and assault (1983) (claims self-defense)
3. Possession of a controlled substance in 1985
4. Disorderly conduct between 1985 and 1990
5. Possession of a controlled substance in 1990
6. Possession of a stolen car in September 1994

Leslie Davis, an African-American vice president at South Shore Bank, recommended approval of Mr. Bonner's application. However, the loan committee agreed that because of Mr. Bonner's criminal record, the application should be denied. The bank then decided to deny the loan.

During the last 15 years, the South Shore Bank has made at least three business loans to applicants with criminal records. One of these three applicants was an African-American. South Shore evaluates each application on an individual basis and examines criminal record and other information for purposes of determining character.

Mr. Bonner and his company (plaintiffs) filed suit under the ECOA, alleging that the bank's practice of considering criminal record has an unlawful disparate impact on African-American men. South Shore Bank (defendants) moved for summary judgment because Mr. Bonner did not establish a case of discrimination. Mr. Bonner also moved for summary judgment on the grounds that consideration of criminal record without tying it to creditworthiness violated the ECOA.

JUDICIAL OPINION

WILLIAMS, Anne Claire, District Judge
In order to prove discrimination under the disparate impact analysis or "effects" test, an applicant must show how "a policy, procedure, or practice specifically identified by the [applicant] has a significantly greater discriminatory impact on members of a protected class." Plaintiffs traditionally establish this prima facie case by making "a statistical comparison of the representation of the protected class in the applicant pool with representation in

the group actually accepted from the pool. . . . If the statistical disparity is significant, then plaintiff is deemed to have made out a prima facie case."

Once the plaintiff has made the prima facie case, the defendant-lender must demonstrate that any policy, procedure, or practice has a manifest relationship to the creditworthiness of the applicant. In other words, the onus is on the defendant to show that the particular practice makes defendant's credit evaluation system more predictive than it would be otherwise.

Plaintiffs claim that South Shore Bank's practice of considering an applicant's criminal record in making commercial lending decisions has a disparate impact on African-Americans. To make the prima facie case plaintiffs offer the testimony of Dr. Jaslin U. Salmon. Dr. Salmon testified that any decision that is based on arrest records would militate against people of color. He suggests that, based on his research, there are many cases in which the black applicant is qualified, credit worthy, but was not given the loan for other reasons and among those reasons, arrest records had been taken into consideration. However, the bank disputes this point because Dr. Salmon was unable to identify a single study showing that consideration of arrest records has a disproportionate impact on African-American applicants for any type of credit, much less any study addressing the impact on business loan applicants.

Both the statistics and Dr. Salmon's supporting testimony do not answer the following questions: 1) how many African-Americans with convictions or arrests are otherwise qualified for the loan; and 2) how many African-Americans are deterred from applying because of the bank's practice. . . . the bank has made at least three business loans to applicants with criminal records. One of these three applicants with criminal records is African-American.

South Shore Bank's practice of inquiring into a credit applicant's criminal history is legitimately related to its extension of credit for two reasons. First, the regulations require the SBA, in evaluating a loan guarantee application, to consider "the character, reputation, and credit history of the applicant, its associates, and guarantors."

Secondly, the bank's inquiry into an applicant's criminal record provides relevant information about an applicant's creditworthiness, particularly his judgment and character. Plaintiff Bonner admits that several of the incidents described in his completed SBA Form 912: possession of a controlled substance, domestic abuse, and disorderly conduct, reflected negatively on his judgment and character. Specifically, Bonner admits that

CONTINUED

these incidents involved an exercise of bad judgment. Therefore, the court finds that the bank has successfully demonstrated that its practice of inquiring into a credit applicant's criminal record is legitimately related to the extension of credit.

For the foregoing reasons, the court grants defendant South Shore Bank's motion for summary judgment and denies plaintiff Bonner and AB&S's motion for summary judgment.

CASE QUESTIONS

1. What, according to Mr. Bonner's expert, is the impact of considering criminal records of applicants? Did the evidence support the expert's testimony?

2. Is the use of the criminal record in making a decision to extend credit a violation of the ECOA? Explain.

3. Do you think a criminal record is an indication of character?

---

consider 12.1

Lucas Rosa, a biological male, went to Park West Bank & Trust dressed in traditionally feminine attire. He requested a loan application from Norma Brunelle, a bank employee. Ms. Brunelle asked Mr. Rosa for identification. Mr. Rosa produced three forms of photo identification: (1) a Massachusetts Department of Public Welfare Card, (2) a Massachusetts Identification Card, and (3) a Money Stop Check Cashing ID Card. Ms. Brunelle looked at the identification cards and told Mr. Rosa that she would not provide him with a loan application until he "went home and changed." She said that he had to be dressed like one of the identification cards in which he appeared in more traditionally male attire before she would provide him with a loan application and process his loan request. Rosa sued the Bank for violations of the ECOA. The bank moved for summary judgment and the court granted judgment for the bank, finding that there could be no possible theory under the ECOA for discrimination. Did the bank violate ECOA? Be sure to explain your answer. (Analysis appears at the end of the chapter.) [*Rosa* v. *Park West Bank & Trust Co.*, 214 F.3d 213 (C.A. 1 2000)]

. . . .

THE TRUTH IN LENDING ACT

The **Truth in Lending Act** (TILA) is actually part of the **Consumer Credit Protection Act** passed in 1968 by Congress (15 U.S.C. § 1601), which was the first federal statute to deal with credit issues through adequate disclosure of credit terms. The Federal Reserve Board was delegated the responsibility for enforcing the TILA and has promulgated regulations to carry out the details of disclosure. One of them, **Regulation Z** (12 C.F.R. § 226), is perhaps better known than the statute that gave rise to it. Because of the ripple impact of subprime lending, the Federal Reserve made substantial changes in Regulation Z in 2008, including new disclosures and limitations on home-equity loans.

ethical *issues*

Like many companies, Wachovia, Yahoo!, and others sold lists of its customers to various telemarketers and internet companies to give these companies access to their customers. Wachovia, Yahoo! and others follow the FTC "opt-out rule," a rule that requires companies to give their customers the chance to not have their information transferred to third-party companies who are looking to market goods and services. A group of plaintiffs/Wachovia customers filed a class action lawsuit against Wachovia Bank because Wachovia that had sold its customers lists to fraudulent telemarketers that had electronically taken money from their accounts without authorization or in excess of amounts the customers authorized. Wachovia executives insisted that they knew nothing about the unauthorized or excessive funds transfers. However, internal e-mails released during discovery in the case showed that executives were discussing the frauds and providing warnings.

The following was from an email from a Wachovia bank executive to colleagues that the bank had received 4,500 complaints of fraud in two months from customers who had been fleeced of $400 million by marketing firms who paid the bank large fees for access and on returned checks. No action was taken and one executive explained why YIIKES, *"We are making a ton of money from them."*[1]

"YIKES!!!!"
"DOUBLE YIKES!!!!"
"There is more, but nothing more that I want to put into a note."

Wachovia settled charges brought by the Office of the Comptroller of the Currency. Wachovia did not admit or deny any wrongdoing, but it has agreed to pay up to $144 million to consist of the following:

a. $10 million fine
b. $8.9 million for consumer education
c. $125 million for restitution to its customers

Wachovia stated that the situation was "unacceptable" and that "we regret it happened."[2] The settlement with the Comptroller does not cover the lawsuit.

The FTC has also investigated a number of companies, including DoubleClick Inc. for its data-gathering processes, including cookies that give it information about consumer spending habits and allows it to specifically gear marketing and sell target-rich lists to other companies for marketing purposes. One industry analyst said, "DoubleClick is not doing anything that anyone else isn't doing."

Evaluate the ethical implications of that last statement. Analyze the strategic choices of Wachovia and others in waiting for the Comptroller and FTC to take action to protect customers' online privacy as opposed to taking voluntary action themselves.

[1]Charles Duhigg, "Papers Show Wachovia Knew of Thefts," *New York Times,* Feb. 6, 2008, pp. C1 and C8.
[2]Charles Duhigg, "Big Fine Set For Wachovia To End Case," *New York Times,* April 26, 2008, pp. B1 and B2.

TILA Applications

The TILA applies only to consumer credit transactions, which are contracts for goods or services for personal or home use. A computer purchased for use in a law office is not covered by TILA, but a computer purchased for personal use at home is.

The TILA applies to two broad types of consumer credit transactions. **Open-end credit transactions**, like the use of a credit card, are covered under the TILA. **Closed-end transactions**, also covered under the TILA, are those in which the debtor is buying a certain amount and repaying it. A loan to buy a car that will be paid back over a fixed time, such as four years, is a closed-end transaction.

TILA Open-End Disclosure Requirements

In charge card credit arrangements, the creditor has several TILA responsibilities. When a debtor is first sent the credit card, the creditor must include the following information: what the interest (finance) charges and annual percentage rate are for charges on the credit card, when bills will be sent, what to do about questions on the bills, and when payments are due.

The monthly bill that the creditor is required to send must contain the balance from the last statement, payments and credits made during the billing period, new charges made during the billing period, and finance charges and how they were computed.

Other required information on credit card bills includes the following: the dates of the billing period, the free-ride period or the time the debtor has to pay the balance to avoid any finance charges, and where to inquire about billing errors. Any changes in credit terms, billing, or charges must be sent to the debtor at least one month in advance of the change.

The **Fair Credit and Charge Card Disclosure Act of 1988** regulates the solicitation of credit card customers. Credit card solicitations must include up-front disclosure of items such as the fees for issuing the card, the annual percentage rate for the card, any finance or transaction charges, and whether a grace period for payment exists. In addition, the solicitation must include how the average daily balance is computed, when payments are due, whether there is a late payment fee, and whether there are charges for going over the credit limit.

Model forms for all the required disclosures are available at the Federal Reserve's Web site and must be given in writing to a customer at the time of application or solicitation.[1]

Roberts v. *Fleet Bank* (Case 12.2) indicates that creditors and regulators are still thrashing out what constitutes full disclosure in credit card solicitation.

CASE 12.2

Roberts v. *Fleet Bank*
342 F.3D 260 (C.A.3 2003)

THE INTRODUCTORY AND NOT-SO-ANNUAL FEES

FACTS

In May 1999, Fleet Bank sent Denise Roberts a credit card solicitation, encouraging her to apply for its new "Titanium MasterCard."

The solicitation, in the form of a flyer, stated in two places that the credit card would have a "7.99% Fixed APR" for both purchases and balance transfers. The solicitation letter also stated that the card would offer a "7.99% Fixed APR." In two places, the letter claimed that the 7.99% APR was "NOT an introductory rate," promising that "[i]t won't go up in just a few short months."

On the back of the flyer, Fleet included the consumer information section with the so-called Schumer Box, the table of information required by TILA (see Exhibit 12.2 for an example of the Schumer Box). This box contained a column with the headings "Annual Percentage Rate (APR) for Purchases and Balance Transfers." The box beneath that heading stated that "7.99% APR" was the applicable rate. Inside the box, Fleet listed two circumstances under which the rate could change: (1) if the cardholder failed to meet repayment requirements or (2) if the account was closed. Fleet listed no other circumstances that would merit a rate change.

Ms. Roberts completed and returned the invitation and in June 1999, she received her Fleet Titanium MasterCard. The credit card agreement stated that Fleet had "the right to change any terms of this agreement at any time." Thirteen months after she first obtained the card, Fleet sent Ms. Roberts a letter notifying her that Fleet would be increasing the APR on her Titanium MasterCard to 10.5%. Ms. Roberts and others filed a class action suit against Fleet for its violation of the TILA disclosure requirements for solicitation of credit card customers. The lower court entered summary judgment for Fleet, and Ms. Roberts appealed.

JUDICIAL OPINION

FUENTES, Circuit Judge
The TILA requires a credit card provider to disclose certain information in "direct mail applications and solicitations," including "annual percentage rates."

Roberts asserts that Fleet failed to clearly and conspicuously inform consumers that the 7.99% APR was subject to change at any time. The IDS and the Schumer Box included in Fleet's solicitation materials stated only two conditions under which Fleet could raise Roberts' APR. A reasonable consumer could read this list as exhaustive and conclude that the 7.99% APR could be raised only under those two described circumstances. Construing the TILA strictly against the creditor and liberally in favor of the consumer, as we must, we believe that the TILA disclosures in this case, read in conjunction with the solicitation materials, present a material issue of fact as to whether Fleet clearly and conspicuously disclosed its right to change the APR. We therefore conclude that the District Court erred in granting summary judgment to Fleet on Roberts' TILA claim.

Congress created the Schumer Box to assist consumers in accessing such information, not to shield credit card companies from liability for information placed outside of the Schumer Box. In its defense, Fleet relies on Paragraph 24 of the Cardholder Agreement that states "[w]e have the right to change any of the terms of this Agreement at any time." This provision, however, fails to cure any of the TILA defects in the initial mailing. To begin with, Fleet only mails the Cardholder Agreement after a consumer has accepted the invitation. Thus, a consumer will not learn, until after the acceptance of the invitation, that the APR can be changed by Fleet at any time. Indeed, Fleet's practice of mailing the Cardholder Agreement containing important rate change information, after the consumer accepts the card, is contrary to the TILA mandate that credit card solicitations disclose all required information. Nonetheless, Fleet argues that it is prohibited from including "change in terms" information in the Schumer Box. However, as we previously stated, this argument avoids the central issue in this case, which is whether the APR was adequately disclosed. Additionally, we note that the "right to change" language in Paragraph 24 contradicts the statement in the introductory letter that this APR "won't go up in just a few short months."

Accordingly, we reverse the entry of summary judgment and remand for further proceedings.

CASE QUESTIONS

1. Describe the Schumer Box and what was in it in the Fleet solicitation. What is its role in consumer credit disclosure?

2. What was different about the credit terms from what was in the Schumer Box?

3. Were the differing terms disclosed in the solicitation?

TILA Closed-End Disclosure Requirements

In a closed-end contract, in which the amount to be paid is definite from the beginning, the creditor must include in the credit contract the following terms:

1. The amount the debtor is financing

2. The **finance charges**, that is, the rate of interest charged for repayment

3. The **annual percentage rate** (APR), which is the finance charge reflected in a percentage figure

4. The number and amount of payments and when they are due

5. The total cost of financing (a total of the actual price of the goods or services along with all interest charges that will be paid over the scheduled repayment time)

6. Whether any additional penalties such as prepayment penalties or late payment penalties apply

7. Any security interest (lien or collateral) the creditor has in the goods sold by credit

8. The cost of credit insurance if the debtor is paying for credit insurance

Exhibit 12.2 is an example of a closed-end credit contract.

Business Planning Tip

When any question arises as to whether a consumer credit transaction is involved or whether a protective statute applies, the question is resolved in favor of the credit applicant. Many businesses treat all credit applications as consumer credit applications and apply the statutes (even though they are not required to do so) so that they can avoid any issues and questions on consumer credit.

SPECIAL DISCLOSURES AND PROTECTIONS FOR SERVICE MEMBERS

Under the Servicemembers Relief Act of 2005 and the National Defense Act of 2007, Congress updated the credit protections for active service members of the

EXHIBIT   12.2 Sample Closed-End Credit Contract

Credit Sale Model Form   Alice Green

ANNUAL PERCENTAGE RATE	FINANCE CHARGE	Amount Financed	Total of Payments	Total Sale Price
The cost of your credit as a yearly rate.	The dollar amount the credit will cost you.	The amount of credit provided to you or on your behalf.	The amount you will have paid after you have made all payments as scheduled	The total cost of your purchase on credit including your down payment of
14.84%	$ *1496.80*	$ *6107.50*	$ *7604.30*	$ *1500 —* *9129.30*

You have the right to receive at this time an itemization of the Amount Financed.
☐ I want an itemization. ☒ I do not want an itemization.

Your payment schedule will be:

Number of Payments	Amount of Payments	When Payments are Due
36	*$ 211.23*	*Monthly beginning 6-1-95*

Insurance
Credit life insurance and credit disability insurance are not required to obtain credit, and will not be provided unless you sign and agree to pay the additional cost.

Type	Premium*	Signature
Credit Life	*$ 120 —*	I want credit life insurance. *Alice Green* — Signature
Credit Disability		I want credit disability insurance. Signature
Credit Life and Disability		I want credit life and disability insurance. Signature

You may obtain property insurance from anyone you want that is acceptable to (creditor). If you get the insurance from (creditor), you will pay $_____.

Security: You are giving a security interest in: ☒ the goods or property being purchased.
☐ (brief description of other property).

Filing fee $ *12.50*   Non-filing Insurance $_____.
Late charge: If a payment is late, you will be charged $_____/_____ of the payment.

Prepayment: If you pay off early, you
☐ may   ☐ will not   have to pay a penalty.
☒ may   ☐ will not   be entitled to a refund of part of the finance charge.

See your contract documents for any additional information about nonpayment, default, any required repayment in full before the scheduled date, and prepayment refunds and penalties.

Alice Green _____   *5-1-99*
Signature   Date

*Means an estimate

military under the 1940 Soldiers and Sailors Relief Act. The protections now apply to reservists who are called up for active duty and include the following:

- A 6 percent interest limit on ARMs while service members are on active duty
- A maximum of 36 percent interest APR on all debt to all service members (this provision preempts any state law that exceeds 36 percent)
- No delinquency reports on service members to credit agencies while they are on active duty
- No repossession of cars during active duty without a court order
- Continuing protection that prevents foreclosure during active duty

CREDIT ADVERTISING, SOLICITATION, AND DISCLOSURE PROTECTIONS

In addition to ensuring adequate disclosures in credit contracts, Regulation Z covers advertising that includes credit terms. If any part of the credit arrangement is mentioned in an advertisement, all terms must be disclosed. For example, if a creditor advertises payments "as low as $15 per month," the ad must also disclose the APR, the down payment required, and the number of payments.

Credit Card Liabilities Disclosures and Protections

Regulation Z provides protection for credit card holders that are designed to limit the liability of a debtor for unauthorized use of a credit card.

First, a creditor cannot send an unsolicited credit card to a debtor. The debtor must have applied for the card or consented to have one sent. Debtors need to be aware of what cards are coming so that they will know when to report losses or thefts.

Second, even if a credit card is stolen, Regulation Z provides dollar limitations for debtor liability. The maximum amount of liability a debtor can have for the misuse of a credit card is $50, including cases of identity theft. This liability limitation applies only if the debtor takes the steps for notifying the creditor of the theft or loss. The notification procedures are included when the credit card is first sent to the debtor.

Lenders and credit card companies are discovering that credit cards are often not stolen physically, but through electronic surveillance. Whether the credit card is taken physically or the information lifted through cyberspace, consumers have the same liability limitations.

Canceling Credit Contracts: Disclosure of Regulation Z Protections

Certain types of credit contracts must include a **three-day cooling-off period** for the debtor, which is a buyer's protection for "cold feet." The buyer has the right to rescind certain types of credit contracts anytime during the 72 hours that follow the consumer's agreement to enter into the credit contract.

The types of credit contracts covered by the cooling-off period include those in which the creditor takes a security interest in the debtor's home. For example, if Alfie is installing a solar hot water system in his home, has purchased it on credit, and is giving the solar company a lien on his house, the three-day period applies; Alfie has three days to change his mind after he signs the contract. The three-day period also applies to **home solicitation sales**, in which sellers/creditors first approach consumers in the buyers' homes. With this protection, buyers have the chance to step back from sales pressure and revisit their decision on credit.

When there are three-day rescission rights, the creditor must include both a description of the rights in the contract and a full explanation of the procedures the debtor should follow to rescind the contract during the three-day period.

The **Home Equity Loan Consumer Protection Act of 1988** and the **Home Ownership and Equity Protection Act (HOEPA) of 1994** require additional disclosures for those transactions in which consumers use their homes as security for the credit. These additional disclosures must explain that consumers could lose their dwellings, which could be sold if they do not repay the debts. The three-day rescission period also applies to home equity credit lines. If the creditor does not give notice of this three-day rescission right to the homeowner/debtor, the right of rescission runs for three years.

Congress has provided additional rescission rights on home mortgage refinancings. The three-day rescission right applies. If the lender has not made the correct disclosures on the right of rescission, the consumers also have the three-year right of rescission. That right exists even when the consumers have gone on to refinance with another lender. Their remedy would be a refund of any interest paid on the loan as well as the elimination of any security the lender had in the home [*Barrett* v. *JP Morgan Chase Bank, N.A.*, 445 F.3d 874 (C.A. 6 2006)]

Exhibit 12.3 is an example of a three-day cancellation provision.

TILA Penalties for Violations and Failures to Disclose

The TILA makes a creditor is liable to an individual for twice the amount of finance charges and for the debtor's attorney fees for violations. The minimum recovery for an individual is $100 and the maximum, $1,000. A group of debtors bringing a class action against a creditor can collect the lesser of $500,000 or 1 percent of the creditor's net worth as damages.

FAIR CREDIT BILLING ACT

The **Fair Credit Billing Act** allows consumer debtors the opportunity to challenge the figures on an open-end transaction monthly statement. Creditors are required to supply on the monthly statement an address or phone number to write or call in the event a debtor has questions or challenges regarding the bill. The language must read: "IN CASE OF ERRORS, CALL OR WRITE. . . ."

There are specific procedural requirements for challenging a bill. First, a debtor must notify the creditor of any errors within 60 days of the receipt of the statement. The notification must be in writing and if a creditor supplies a phone number for inquiries, the notice must explain that oral protests do not preserve all Regulation Z rights.

The creditor has 30 days from the time of receipt of the written protest to acknowledge to the debtor receipt of the protest. The creditor has 90 days from receipt of the protest to take final action, either giving the debtor's account a credit or reaffirming that the charges are valid.

During the time the creditor is considering the debtor's protest, the debtor is not required to pay the questioned amount or any finance charges on that amount. If the charges are in fact accurate, the debtor will be charged for the finance charges during this time period. If the creditor does not comply with any of the requirements or deadlines on bill protests, the debtor can be excused from payment even if the charges disputed were actually accurate.

EXHIBIT   12.3 Sample Three-Day Cancellation Notice

H-9 Rescission Model Form (Refinancing)

NOTICE OF RIGHT TO CANCEL

Your Right to Cancel

You are entering into a new transaction to increase the amount of credit provided to you. We acquired a [mortgage/lien/security interest] [on/in] your home under the original transaction and will retain that [mortgage/lien/security interest] in the new transaction. You have a legal right under federal law to cancel the new transaction, without cost, within three business days from whichever of the following events occurs last:

(1) the date of the new transaction, which is _____;or

(2) the date you received your new Truth-in-Lending disclosures; or

(3) the date you received this notice of your right of cancel.

If you cancel the new transaction, your cancellation will apply only to the increase in the amount of credit. It will not affect the amount that you presently owe or the [mortgage/lien/security interest] we already have [on/in] your home. If you cancel, the [mortgage/lien/security interest] as it applies to the increased amount is also cancelled. Within 20 calendar days after we receive your notice of cancellation of the new transaction, we must take the steps necessary to reflect the fact that our [mortgage/lien/security interest] [on/in] your home no longer applies to the increase of credit. We must also return any money you have given to us or anyone else in connection with the new transaction.

You may keep any money we have given you in the new transaction until we have done the things mentioned above, but you must then offer to return the money at the address below. If we do not take possession of the money within 20 calendar days of your offer, you may keep it without further obligation.

How to Cancel

If you decide to cancel the new transaction, you may do so by notifying us in writing, at
(creditor's name and business address).

You may use any written statement that is signed and dated by you and states your intention to cancel, or you may use this notice by dating and signing below. Keep one copy of this notice because it contains important information about your rights.

If you cancel by mail or telegram, you must send the notice no later than midnight of _____ (date) _____ (or midnight of the third business day following the latest of the three events listed above). If you send or deliver your written notice to cancel some other way, it must be delivered to the above address no later than that time.

I WISH TO CANCEL

_____   _____
Consumer's Signature   Date

FAIR CREDIT REPORTING ACT

The **Fair Credit Reporting Act** (FCRA) is designed to provide debtors some rights and protections on credit information held by third parties about them. Before the FCRA, many debtors were denied the right to see their credit reports that were often inaccurate. The FCRA brought credit reports out in the open.

When the FCRA Applies

The FCRA applies to consumer reporting agencies, which are third parties (not creditors or debtors) that compile, evaluate, and sell credit information about consumer debt and debtors. Commercial credit reporting agencies and commercial debtors are not subject to FCRA standards.

Limitations on FCRA Disclosures

Under the FCRA, consumer reporting agencies can disclose information only to the following:

1. A debtor who asks for his own report
2. A creditor who has the debtor's signed application for credit
3. A potential employer
4. A court pursuant to a subpoena

When consumers file applications for credit with lenders, they have the right to know where a credit report came from. However, the creditor cannot show the report to the debtor, who must get the report through a credit reporting agency.

Consumer credit agencies also have the following general limitations on debtor disclosures:

1. No disclosure of bankruptcies that occurred more than 10 years ago
2. No disclosure of lawsuits finalized more than 7 years ago
3. No disclosure of criminal convictions and arrests that have been disposed of more than 7 years ago

When a debtor applies for a loan of more than $50,000 or a job that pays more than $20,000, these limitations on disclosures do not apply.

Under the FCRA, debtors also have the right to make corrections of inaccurate information included in those reports. A debtor simply notifies the reporting agency of the alleged error. If the agency acknowledges the error, the debtor's report must be corrected, and anyone who has received a report on that debtor during the previous two years must be notified.

If the agency still stands by the information challenged by the debtor, the debtor has the right to have included in the credit report a 100-word statement explaining his or her position on the matter. This statement is then included with the actual credit report in all future reports sent to third parties.

Stevenson v. *TRW, Inc.* (Case 12.3) deals with a problem of an inaccurate credit report.

CASE 12.3

Stevenson v. *TRW, Inc.*
987 F.2D 288 (5TH CIR. 1993)

THE FATHER WITH THE PRODIGAL SON'S CREDIT RATING

FACTS

TRW, Inc., is one of the nation's largest credit reporting agencies. Subscribing companies report to TRW both the credit information they obtain when they grant credit to a consumer and the payment history of the consumer. TRW then compiles a credit report on that consumer to distribute to other subscribers from whom the consumer has requested credit.

John M. Stevenson is a 78-year-old real estate and securities investor. In late 1988 or early 1989, Mr. Stevenson began receiving numerous phone calls from bill collectors regarding arrearages in accounts that were not his.

Mr. Stevenson first spoke with TRW's predecessor, Chilton's, to try to correct the problem. When TRW purchased Chilton's, Mr. Stevenson began calling TRW's office in Irving, Texas. In August 1989, he wrote TRW and obtained a copy of his credit report dated September 6, 1989. He discovered many errors in the report. Some accounts belonged to another John Stevenson living in Arlington, Texas, and some appeared to belong to his estranged son, John Stevenson, Jr. In all, Mr. Stevenson disputed approximately 16 accounts, 7 inquiries, and much of the identifying information.

Mr. Stevenson wrote to TRW's president and CEO on October 6, 1989, requesting that his credit report be corrected. His letter worked its way to TRW's consumer relations department by October 20, 1989, and on November 1, 1989, that office began its reinvestigation by sending consumer dispute verification forms (CDVs) to subscribers that had reported the disputed accounts. The CDVs ask subscribers to check whether the information they have about a consumer matches the information in TRW's credit report. Subscribers who receive CDVs typically have 20 to 25 working days to respond. If a subscriber fails to respond or indicates that TRW's account information is incorrect, TRW deletes the disputed information. Mr. Stevenson understood from TRW that the entire process should take three to six weeks.

As a result of its initial investigation, TRW removed several of the disputed accounts from Mr. Stevenson's report by November 30, 1989. TRW retained one of the remaining accounts on the report because the subscriber insisted that the account was Mr. Stevenson's. The others were still either pending or contained what TRW called "positive information." It also began to appear that Mr. Stevenson's estranged son had fraudulently obtained some of the disputed accounts by using his father's Social Security number. This information led TRW to add a warning statement in December 1989, advising subscribers that Mr. Stevenson's identifying information had been used without his consent to obtain credit. Meanwhile, Mr. Stevenson paid TRW a fee and joined its Credentials Service, which allowed him to monitor his credit report as each entry was made. TRW finally completed its investigation on February 9, 1990. By then, TRW claimed that all disputed accounts containing "negative" credit information had been removed. Inaccurate information, however, either continued to appear on Mr. Stevenson's reports or was reentered after TRW had deleted it.

Mr. Stevenson filed suit in Texas state court alleging both common law libel and violations of the Fair Credit Reporting Act (FCRA). TRW removed the case to federal court, and on October 2, 1991, the case was tried before a federal court without a jury. The district court

granted judgment for Mr. Stevenson on both the libel and FCRA claims, and TRW appealed.

JUDICIAL OPINION

WILLIAMS, Circuit Judge

Consumers have the right to see their credit information and to dispute the accuracy or completeness of their credit reports. When it receives a complaint, a consumer reporting agency must reinvestigate the disputed information "within a reasonable period of time" and "promptly delete" credit information that has been found to be inaccurate or unverifiable.

The record, however, contains evidence from which the district court could find that TRW did not delete unverifiable or inaccurate information promptly. First, TRW did not complete its reinvestigation until February 9, 1990, although TRW's subscribers were supposed to return the CDVs by December 4, 1989. Second, § 1681i(a) requires prompt deletion if the disputed information is inaccurate or unverifiable. If a subscriber did not return a CDV, TRW claims that it deleted the disputed information as unverifiable. Yet, some disputed accounts continued to appear on Stevenson's credit report for several weeks. One subscriber failed to return the CDV, but its account appeared on the report issued on February 9, 1990. Another subscriber returned its CDV by December 4, 1989, indicating that TRW's information was inaccurate, yet the information was not deleted until after February 9, 1990.

Allowing inaccurate information back onto a credit report after deleting it because it is inaccurate is negligent. Although testimony at trial revealed that TRW sometimes calls subscribers to verify information, it made no calls in Stevenson's case. TRW relied solely on the CDVs despite the number of disputed accounts and the allegations of fraud. TRW also relied on the subscribers to tell TRW whether to delete information from Stevenson's report. In a reinvestigation of the accuracy of credit reports, a credit bureau must bear some responsibility for evaluating the accuracy of information obtained from subscribers.

TRW moved slowly in completing its investigation and was negligent in its compliance with the prompt deletion requirement.

Stevenson testified that it was a "terrific shock" to him to discover his bad credit rating after maintaining a good credit reputation since 1932. Second, Stevenson was denied credit three times during TRW's reinvestigation: by Bloomingdale's, by Bank One, and by Gabbert's Furniture Company. Stevenson testified that he had to go "hat in hand" to the president of Bank One, who was a business associate and friend, to explain his problems with TRW. As a result, he obtained credit at

CONTINUED

Bank One. Third, Stevenson had to explain his credit woes to the president of the First City Bank Colleyville when he opened an account there. With a new president at First City Bank, Stevenson had to explain his situation again. Despite the fact that he was ultimately able to obtain credit, Stevenson testified to experiencing "considerable embarrassment" from having to detail to business associates and creditors his problems with TRW. Finally, Stevenson spent a considerable amount of time since he first disputed his credit report trying to resolve his problems with TRW.

The district court properly found that Stevenson had suffered humiliation and embarrassment from

TRW's violations of FCRA. We affirm the award of $30,000 in actual damages based upon the finding of mental anguish. We also affirm the award of $20,700 in attorney's fees.

CASE QUESTIONS

1. What caused Mr. Stevenson's anguish? Was it the correction process?

2. What suggestions could you offer to TRW to prevent the problems with Mr. Stevenson's credit report?

3. What would you do differently if you were trying to correct your report?

CONSUMER LEASING ACT

The **Consumer Leasing Act** is an amendment to TILA that provides disclosure protection for consumers who lease goods. In 1998, the Federal Trade Commission (FTC) and the Federal Reserve Board developed a disclosure form for consumer leases that require disclosure of the following:

1. The amount due at the lease signing (must be itemized, too)

2. Total of payments

3. Monthly payments and other charges

4. Capitalized cost (shows the actual price of the goods—was previously missing from most lease agreements so as to discourage consumer shopping, especially for cars)

5. Residual value (value at the end of the lease, which helps determine the monthly payments)

6. Rent charge (which really is the interest rate)

7. Trade-ins, rebates, and other credits given at signing

8. Early termination conditions and terms

9. Excessive wear, use, and mileage provisions

Consumer leasing has become an important part of our economy. As noted in Chapter 10, Article 2A of the Uniform Commercial Code covers all aspects of consumer leases. Article 2A covers lease contracts, warranties, and remedies.

Enforcement of Credit Transactions

Although a debtor has the benefit of paying over time, a creditor has the worry of trying to ensure payment. The law affords creditors some protections that can be used to increase their ability to get repayment.

THE USE OF COLLATERAL: THE SECURITY INTEREST

One way a creditor can have additional assurances of repayment is to obtain a pledge of collateral from the debtor. For goods, this collateral pledge is called a

security interest. The creation of security interests is governed by Article 9 of the Uniform Commercial Code.

A security interest is created by a record called a **security agreement**. Once a security interest is created, the creditor is given the right to repossess the pledged goods in the event the debtor defaults on repayment. When a debtor purchases a car on credit, there is nearly always a security interest in that car that allows the lender the right to repossess the car and sell it to satisfy the loan in the event the debtor defaults. This right to sell gives the creditor some additional assurances that the debt will be repaid.

COLLECTION RIGHTS OF THE CREDITOR

If a debtor falls behind on payments, the creditor has the right to proceed with collection tactics. Many creditors refer or sell their delinquent credit accounts to collection agencies. At one time, some of these agencies engaged in questionable conduct in the collection of debts, including harassing debtors with phone calls and embarrassing them by contacting their friends and relatives. To control abuses in the collection process, Congress passed the **Fair Debt Collections Practices Act** (FDCPA) in 1977. The FDCPA controls a great deal of debt collection. About two-thirds of the states have adopted some form of debt collection statutes. If state law, relative to the federal act, provides the same or greater protection for debtors in the collection process, the state law governs. In states without a collection law, the FDCPA applies.

When the FDCPA Applies

The FDCPA applies to consumer debts and debt collectors. Under the FDCPA, debt collectors are third-party collectors. The FDCPA does not apply to original creditors collecting their own debts; for example, Sears collecting Sears' debts is not governed by the FDCPA. However, if Sears referred its collection accounts to Central Credit Collection Agency, Central Credit would be under the FDCPA. If Sears created its own collection agency with a name other than Sears, the FDCPA would apply to that agency as well.

The FDCPA does not apply to the collection of commercial accounts or to banks and the Internal Revenue Service. In a rule revision, attorneys collecting debts for clients were made subject to coverage of the FDCPA.

Collector Restrictions under the FDCPA

Collectors are subject to certain prohibitions under the FDCPA. The following subsections cover the prohibitions.

Debtor Contact   One of the most frequent abuses of collectors prior to the FDCPA was constant debtor contact and harassment. The FDCPA curbs the amount of contact: Debtors cannot be contacted before 8:00 A.M. or after 9:00 P.M., and debtors who work night shifts cannot be disturbed during their sleeping hours in the daytime.

The place of contact is also controlled by the FDCPA: Collectors must avoid contact at inconvenient places. Home contact is permitted, but contact in club, church, or school meetings is prohibited. Collectors can approach debtors at their places of employment unless employers object or have a policy against such contact.

To prevent harassment, the FDCPA gives debtors a chance to "call off" a collector. If a debtor tells the collector that he wants no more contact, the collector must stop and take other steps, such as legal action, to collect the debt. If the debtor is represented by an attorney and gives the name of the attorney to the collector, the collector can contact only the attorney from that point.

Third-Party Contact   The FDCPA also prohibits notifying other parties of the debtor's debts and collection problems. However, the debtor's spouse and parents can be contacted regarding the debt. Other parties can be contacted for information, but the collector cannot disclose the reason for the contact. The only information that can be obtained from these third parties is the address, phone number, and place of employment of the debtor.

The collector must even be careful to use appropriate stationery when writing for information so that the letterhead does not disclose the nature of the collector's business. Postcard contact with the debtor or third parties is prohibited because of the likelihood that others will see the information about the debtor.

Prohibited Acts   Collectors have certain other restrictions on their conduct under the FDCPA. The general prohibition in the FDCPA is that collectors cannot "harass, oppress, or abuse" the debtor. Using abusive language or physical force is prohibited. Misrepresenting the authority of a collector is also prohibited, as is posing as a law enforcement official or producing false legal documents. Debtors cannot be threatened with prison or other actions not authorized by law.

Penalties for FDCPA Violations

The Federal Trade Commission (FTC) is responsible for enforcement of the FDCPA. The FTC can use its cease and desist orders to stop collectors from violating the FDCPA and can also assess penalties for violations. However, the greatest power of enforcement under the FDCPA lies with individual debtors. Debtors who can prove collector violations can collect for actual injuries and mental distress. Debtors can also collect up to $1,000 in addition to actual damages for actions by collectors that are extreme, outrageous, malicious, or repeated. Attorney fees incurred by debtors in bringing their suits are also recoverable.

> **Business Planning Tip**
>
> Generating form collection letters by computer must be carefully monitored. The FDCPA imposes notice and content requirements that must flow in sequence. Threatened actions must be taken, or the threat is a violation.

SUITS FOR ENFORCEMENT OF DEBTS

Occasionally, collection is ineffective and there is no collateral to repossess. The creditor has few options left but to bring suit to enforce collection of the debt. In bringing a successful suit, the creditor will obtain a **judgment**, which is the court's official document stating that the debtor owes the money and the collector is entitled to that money. However, in debt cases, the judgment is only the beginning. Once the creditor has the judgment, it must be executed to obtain funds.

A judgment is executed by having it attach to various forms of the debtor's property. For example, a judgment can attach to real property. A judgment can also attach to funds by **garnishment**, which is the attachment of a judgment to an account, paycheck, or receivables. Once there is attachment, the creditor is entitled to those funds. The third party holding the funds must comply with the terms of the garnishment and release the appropriate amount of funds to the creditor.

Employees are given some protection under the Consumer Credit Protection Act with respect to garnishments. One such protection is the limitation on the employer's ability to fire employees who have their wages garnished by a single creditor.

Under the Consumer Credit Protection Act, the amount that consumer creditors can garnish on debtor wages is limited to 25 percent of the net wages. Garnishment for past-due child support is limited to 50 percent of net wages.

The End of the Line on Enforcement of Debts: Bankruptcy

Bankruptcy is the legal process of having a debtor—individual, partnership, corporation, LLC (see Chapter 13)—turn over all nonexempt assets in exchange for a release from debts following the distribution of those assets to creditors. In October 2005, the **Bankruptcy Abuse Prevention and Consumer Protection Act of 2005** (BAPCPA) took effect.[2] The BAPCPA was passed more than 10 years after the Bankruptcy Reform Commission was created, and the changes in bankruptcy law reflect an expressed congressional desire to curb a 15-year trend of increases in the number of bankruptcies. The changes in the law require consumers who wish to declare bankruptcy to show through a statutory formula that they do not have the means for repaying debts. The ability to declare bankruptcy hinges on disposable income, a figure obtained after the court allows for housing, food, and other necessary expenses. If the consumer has disposable income, then a debt adjustment plan, rather than a bankruptcy, is required.

Bankruptcy takes one of three forms. *Chapter 7* bankruptcy is the liquidation form in which the entity is dissolved or the individual's debts are discharged. *Chapter 11* is the reorganization form in which a business enjoys protection from collection and creditors until a new plan for satisfying the business obligations is approved. *Chapter 13* is the consumer debt adjustment plan under which consumers can be given a new repayment plan for their debts.

Credit repair organizations, or counseling and debt service organizations that, for a fee, help consumers work through debt crises, are subject to additional disclosure requirements under BAPCPA. These CROs, as they are known, must disclose fully their role, their fees, and that bankruptcy may be a result or recommendation from their efforts on behalf of the consumer debtor. CROs are regulated under the Credit Repair Organizations Act (15 U.S.C. §§ 1679-1679j) and are subject to private suit by consumer debtors for misrepresentations and failures to disclose information about fees, payments, bankruptcy, and any affiliations with creditors or credit organizations.

Once an individual or business voluntarily declares bankruptcy, all collection efforts must stop. A voluntary petition in bankruptcy provides the debtor with immediate relief from creditors. A debtor can be involuntarily petitioned into bankruptcy by creditors. In an involuntary petition case, the debtor has the opportunity for a hearing. The standard for creditors petitioning a debtor into involuntary bankruptcy is that the debtor is unable to pay debts as they become due.

Not all debts are discharged in bankruptcy. Alimony, child support, student loans, and taxes are examples of debts that survive bankruptcy.

International Credit Issues

Significant differences distinguish a declaration of bankruptcy in the United States and one in other countries. In Japan, for example:

- Debtors can keep only kitchen utensils and $1,500 in cash.
- A meeting, called *dogeza,* is held wherein the company owner sits on the floor among creditors and begs for forgiveness while the creditors are permitted to yell abusive epithets at the debtor.

Other aspects of Japanese law make a company's failure and the impact on individual businesspeople very different. Japanese creditors routinely require guarantors, even on business debts, and most businesspeople rely on family for such guarantors. As a result, many in-laws find themselves responsible for debt when the business of their son-in-law fails. The divorce rate for executives of bankrupt Japanese businesses is twice that of the national average.

The suicide rate for failed Japanese businesspeople is 50 percent greater than in the general population. Under Japanese law, insurance companies do pay benefits even when death results from suicide as long as the policy has been in effect for at least one year. And the suicide rate for people with insurance policies is 50 percent higher than in the general population.

Red Flags FOR MANAGERS

No matter what type of credit transaction, consumers need full disclosure. No matter what type of consumer credit, there are always forms and federal and state laws you must follow.

- On credit cards, or open-end credit, tell consumers how much they can charge, what the fees are, what the interest rate is, how charges are computed, whether there are late fees, and how they can raise questions or dispute charges and balances.
- If you solicit consumers for credit card applications, you must disclose the same things.
- Consumers have special rights on mortgages, and there are special disclosure forms.

- Consumers also have three-day rights to rescind certain types of agreements such as home equity lines of credit, second mortgages, and refinancing.
- Consumers also have protections on the whens, hows, whys, and whats of use and disclosure of their credit histories.
- When collecting debts from consumers, creditors must be careful about how they contact consumers and what they say and do to collect the debt.
- If a consumer is overwhelmed by collection efforts, bankruptcy is an alternative. The reforms passed in 2005 have created higher thresholds for declaring bankruptcy.

Summary

What statutes affect credit contracts?

- Usury—charging interest in excess of the statutory maximum
- Equal Credit Opportunity Act (ECOA)—federal law prohibiting denial of credit on the basis of sex, race, color, religion, national origin, age, marital status, public assistance income, alimony, or child support income and plans for additional family
- Truth in Lending Act (TILA)—federal law governing disclosures in credit contracts

- Consumer Credit Protection Act (CCPA)—first federal statute on credit disclosure requirements
- Open-end transactions—credit card transactions
- Closed-end transactions—finance contracts for preestablished amounts, as in the financing of a television purchase
- Home Ownership and Equity Protection Act (HOEPA)—a credit disclosure and consumer rights statute directed at second mortgages and home equity lines of credit
- Fair Credit and Charge Card Disclosure Act of 1988—federal law governing solicitation of credit card customers
- Regulation Z—federal regulation governing credit disclosures
- Three-day cooling-off period—right of rescission on credit contracts initiated in the home
- Home Equity Loan Consumer Protection Act of 1988—federal law requiring disclosures for home equity consumer loans
- Fair Credit Billing Act—federal law governing rights of debtors to dispute credit card charge
- Fair Credit Reporting Act (FCRA)—federal law regulating disclosure of credit information to and by third parties

- Consumer Leasing Act—federal law governing consumer lease transactions
- Credit Repair Organizations Act—federal law that provides consumer debtors with disclosures regarding counseling and payment arrangement services
- Bankruptcy Abuse Prevention and Consumer Protection Act of 2005 (BAPCPA)—new bankruptcy law that sets higher requirements for consumer declaration of Chapter 7 bankruptcy

How are credit contracts enforced?

- Security interest—pledge of collateral for credit
- Fair Debt Collections Practices Act (FDCPA)—federal law regulating collection of consumer debt by third parties
- Judgment—court order authorizing collection of money from party
- Garnishment—attachment of account, paycheck, or receivables to collect judgment
- Bankruptcy—federal process of collecting assets to pay creditors and discharge debts
- Chapter 7—liquidation bankruptcy
- Chapter 11—reorganization bankruptcy
- Chapter 13—consumer debt adjustment plan

Key Terms

Questions and Problems

1. In May 1976, TRW (a credit reporting agency) issued a consumer report on Bennie E. Bryant in connection with his application for a federally insured home loan under the Veterans Administration. The consumer report had several inaccuracies, and Mr. Bryant went to TRW to point out the matters needing correction. For unrelated reasons, the mortgage did not close.

In August 1976, Mr. Bryant applied for another mortgage. On September 28, TRW called the mortgage company to let them know his credit report would be unfavorable. When the mortgage company notified Mr. Bryant, he again went to TRW offices and explained that the September report contained new inaccuracies in addition to those that were part of the May report. After this meeting, a memo about possible inaccuracies was placed in Mr. Bryant's file. However, the credit report without corrections was issued to the mortgage company on September 30. No follow-through had been done on the file memo.

Mr. Bryant's August mortgage application was originally denied. After personal efforts on his part, however, the credit report was corrected and the mortgage was eventually given.

Does Mr. Bryant have any rights and protections? [*Bryant v. TRW, Inc.*, 689 F.2d 72 (6th Cir. 1982)]

2. Maurice Miller obtained an American Express credit card in 1966, and his wife, Virginia, was given a supplementary card. Her card had a different number, was issued in her name, and had a separate annual fee. When Mr. Miller died in 1979, American Express canceled both credit cards. Mrs. Miller sued for violation of the ECOA. Has there been a violation? [*Miller v. American Express Co.*, 688 F.2d 1235 (9th Cir. 1982)]

3. In community property states, signatures of both spouses are required on real property transactions. Would a mortgagee that requires both spouses' signatures on a mortgage application be violating the ECOA? [*McKenzie v. U.S. Home Corp.*, 704 F.2d 778 (5th Cir. 1983)]

4. James A. Swanson received a letter from a collection agency, the Southern Oregon Credit Service, indicating that if payment in full or definite arrangements for payment of his account were not made within 48 hours, the agency would begin a complete investigation into his employment and assets. Is the agency's threat a violation of the FDCPA? [*Swanson v. Southern Oregon Credit Service, Inc.*, 869 F.2d 1222 (9th Cir. 1988)]

5. Nash Cooley is a 66-year-old African-American male who lives in Montgomery, Alabama. Since the mid-1980s, Mr. Cooley had earned a living from his ownership of residential rental properties in the Montgomery area. Mr. Cooley owns approximately 15 apartment units and 24 houses.

By the summer of 2000, Mr. Cooley had $100,000 in unsecured lines of credit at two separate banks. Mr. Cooley approached Sterling Bank in September 2000 about another $100,000 unsecured line of credit. He chose Sterling because he had a prior business relationship with Kenny Hill, who had worked at another bank where Mr. Cooley had a line of credit.

In September 2000, Mr. Cooley submitted a credit application and provided Mr. Hill with all of his relevant financial information, including tax returns and a personal financial statement. On September 15, 2000, Mr. Hill conducted a credit check on Mr. Cooley that revealed a "Beacon Score" of 749. Although this score was commensurate with an "excellent credit rating,"

Mr. Hill became concerned because Mr. Cooley's most recent tax return indicated that Mr. Cooley and his wife had a joint pretax income of $106,214. Of this amount, Mr. Hill calculated that the income attributable to Mr. Cooley was $51,483. Because Mr. Cooley was applying for an unsecured line of credit in his name only, Mr. Hill was worried that the income level was insufficient for him to obtain a $100,000 line of credit. Additionally, Mr. Hill was worried about Mr. Cooley's existing $100,000 lines of credit.

Instead of denying Mr. Cooley's request outright, Mr. Cooley's boss suggested making either a secured loan in the same amount or an unsecured loan for $25,000. After these alternatives were agreed to, Mr. Hill told his boss that Mr. Cooley was "African American and might claim racism."

Mr. Hill informed Mr. Cooley of the options of a $25,000 unsecured line of credit or a larger secured line. Mr. Cooley immediately requested a list of the individuals on Sterling's Board of Directors so he could contact them about his loan denial. Mr. Cooley also expressed his belief that Sterling was discriminating against him on the basis of race.

During Sterling's Board of Directors meeting on September 20, 2000, the directors discussed the Cooley loan and, according to Greg Calhoun, an African-American member of Sterling's Board of Directors, the Board "didn't think [Mr. Cooley] could qualify for a hundred thousand dollar line of credit being . . . that he was a retired school teacher." Moreover, Board members "jok[ed] about [Mr. Cooley's application]" and "laughed about Cooley." In response, Mr. Calhoun told the other Board members that he believed they were putting Mr. Cooley down. Mr. Calhoun then "told them they was [*sic*] all Republicans, and they're all members of the Montgomery Country Club. And there's no way that a black man can come in here and get money from the bank." Following this statement, Mr. Calhoun informed the Board that he was resigning. In Mr. Calhoun's opinion, Sterling denied the loan application "because of [Mr. Cooley's] skin color."

Mr. Cooley filed suit for violation of the ECOA. Should he prevail in the suit? [*Cooley v. Sterling Bank*, 280 F.Supp.2d 1331 (M.D. Ala. 2003)]

6. In 1984, Jean Mayes purchased Albert L. Silva, d/b/a Rainbow Motors, a Nantucket car dealership. In May 1985, Mr. Mayes entered into financing arrangements with Chrysler Credit Corporation to finance his car inventory. The borrower was Rainbow Motors, with Mr. Mayes as president and sole shareholder.

Chrysler demanded that Mr. Mayes and his wife, Michele Mayes, sign a "continuing guaranty" before it would extend credit. Mrs. Mayes, a well-compensated corporate attorney, was listed as a director and officer of Rainbow, but she did not participate in managing it. Rainbow defaulted, and Chrysler brought suit against Mrs. Mayes, seeking $750,126.41. Mrs. Mayes said

Chrysler was estopped from collecting the debt because of the ECOA. Is she correct? [*Mayes* v. *Chrysler Credit Corp.,* 37 F.3d 9 (1st Cir. 1994)]

Understanding "Consider" Problems

12.1

THINK: The ECOA requires that the decision to not extend credit be related to creditworthiness and not factors such as race, marital status, age, gender, and so on.

APPLY: In this case, the applicant (Mr. Rosa) applied for credit dressed as a woman but his forms of ID showed him to be a man. There may not be enough evidence in the case. The issue is the basis for the request that he go home and change clothes. If the request for changed clothes was based on the need for proper ID, there was no discrimination. If the request was based on discrimination against gay or transgender individuals, there was no discrimination under the ECOA

because those are not categories. If the request to change was because the bank only wished to make loans to male customers, then there was discrimination.

ANSWER: The bank was not entitled to summary judgment until the court determined the reason for the request that Mr. Rosa change clothes. Some of the reasons for requesting the change could be discriminatory and some are not. The ECOA has specific categories and the action of the bank employee does not meet those categories under some reasons for requesting the change of clothes, but it would so on the basis of other reasons. Determining the reason for the request is key to determining whether there was discrimination.

Note

1. In October 2008, the U.S. House of Representatives passed a new law that amends the TILA and Fair Credit Billing Act. Called The Creditcard Holders' Bill of Rights, the legislation (still in the Senate) would increase the billing statement notice from 14 days to 25, limit changes in terms, reduce late fees, and require same-day posting of consumer payments.

2. Bankruptcy is a universal process that has a deep history. Go to www.cengage.com/blaw/jennings for more background on bankruptcy.

Forms of Doing Business

You can start a business on your own. But, if you need help with management or finances, you may need others. Partnerships, limited partnerships, limited liability companies, and corporations are other ways of doing business. This chapter answers the following questions: How are various business entities formed? What are the advantages and disadvantages of various entities? What are the rights, responsibilities, and liabilities of the individuals involved?

Each of the forms of doing business is examined by reviewing its formation, sources of funding, the personal liability of owners, tax consequences, management and control, and the ease of transferring interest. Exhibit 13.1 presents an overview of the types of business entities. ■

update

For up-to-date legal news, click on "Author Updates" at

www.cengage.com/blaw/ jennings

Please accept my resignation. I don't want to belong to any organization that will accept me as a member.
GROUCHO MARX

Although our form is corporate, our attitude is partnership. We do not view the company itself as the ultimate owner of our business assets but instead view the company as a conduit through which our shareholders own the assets.
WARREN BUFFETT
Chairman, Berkshire Hathaway

consider...

Michael Eisner, then-CEO and chairman of Disney, hired Michael Ovitz as his second-in-command at Disney. Mr. Eisner had a history of not working well with powerful seconds-in-command, and Mr. Ovitz was a powerful Hollywood talent agent and producer. In less than one year, Mr. Ovitz and Mr. Eisner were at such odds that Mr. Eisner and the board agreed to pay Mr. Ovitz more than $38 million in cash compensation and 3 million shares of Disney stock to leave the company. The shareholders brought suit against the Disney board for lax supervision of Eisner, the poor business decision of hiring Ovitz, and waste for the amount paid to Ovitz. The board says it just made a mistake. Can the shareholders recover?

Sole Proprietorships

FORMATION

A **sole proprietorship** is not a true business entity because it consists only of an individual operating a business. According to the U.S. Small Business Association, most small businesses operate as sole proprietorships, with 50 percent operating as home-based businesses. Often, a sole proprietorship is evidenced by the following language: "Homer Lane d/b/a Green Grower's Grocery"; "d/b/a" is an acronym for "doing business as." There are no formal requirements for forming a sole proprietorship—it begins when an individual does business. In some states, a "d/b/a" must be filed or published as a fictitious name for doing business.

SOURCES OF FUNDING

Most sole proprietorships are small businesses, and their small initial capital needs come from loans, either direct loans from banks, through loans from government agencies as the Small Business Administration, or from individuals who are, in effect, investing in the sole proprietor.

LIABILITY

Because financing for a sole proprietorship is based on the sole proprietor's credit rating and assets, the proprietor is personally liable for the business loan, and his or her assets are subject to attachment should a default occur.

TAX CONSEQUENCES

The positive side of a sole proprietor's unlimited personal liability is the right to claim all tax losses associated with the business. The income of the business is the income of the sole proprietor and is reported as Schedule C on the individual's

EXHIBIT 13.1 Comparison of Forms of Conducting Business

FORM	FORMATION	FUNDING	MANAGEMENT	TRANSFER CONTROL	TAXES	DISSOLUTION	LIABILITY
Sole proprietorship	No formal requirements	Individual provides funds	Individual	No transfer restrictions	Individual pays on individual return	Death; voluntary	Individual personally liable
Partnership	Articles of partnership	Capital contributions of partners	All partners or delegated to one	Can transfer interest but not partner status	Partner reports profits and losses on individual return (flow-through)	Dissolution upon death; withdrawal of partner	Partners are personally liable
Limited partnership	Filing of articles of partnership	Capital contributions of general and limited partners	General partner	More easily transferred	Same as partnership (flow-through)	Death of general partner	General partner is personally liable; limited partners liable to extent of contribution
Corporation	Formal filing of articles of incorporation	Debt (bonds)/equity (shareholders)	Board of directors, officers, and/or executive committee	Shares (with reasonable restrictions) are easily transferred	Corporation pays taxes; shareholders pay taxes on dividends	Dissolved only if limited in duration or shareholders vote to dissolve	No shareholder personal liability unless (1) watered or (2) corporate veil
S corporation* or Subchapter S	Same as above (special IRS filings to create special tax [flow-through] status)	Same as above	Same as above	Restrictions on transfers to comply with S corporation rules	Shareholders pay taxes on profits; take losses	Same as above	Same as above
C corporation†	Formal filing of articles of incorporation	Same as above	Same as above	No restrictions	Corporation pays taxes; shareholders pay taxes on dividends	Same as above	Same as above
Limited liability company (LLC)	Formal filing— articles of organization	Capital contributions of members	All members manage or delegate to one member	No admission without consent of majority	Flow-through treatment	Dissolved upon death, bankruptcy	Limited liability (except professional negligence)
Limited liability partnership	Filing of articles of limited liability partnership	Capital contributions partners	All partners or delegated to one	No admission without consent of majority	Flow-through treatment	Dissolved upon death, bankruptcy	Varies by state but liability for acts of partners is limited in some way

*S corporations are formed under state incorporation laws but structured to obtain flow-through or pass-through status for income and losses under IRS regulations.
†C corporation is again a label for tax purpose.

income tax return. Sole proprietors owe all the taxes, but they also get all business deductions.

Management and Control

In many businesses, the sole proprietor is both manager and employee. The proprietor makes all decisions. This form of business operation is truly centralized management.

Transferability of Interest

A sole proprietorship can be transferred only if the owner allows it. When a sole proprietor's business is transferred, the transfer consists of the property, inventory, and goodwill of the business. Upon the owner's death the heirs or devisees of the owner inherit the business property. They could choose to operate the business or liquidate its assets.

> ### Business Planning Tip
>
> Before you decide on the type of business structure you will have, consult your accountant to understand the tax issues, including wage tax expenses. Consult your lawyer to determine what personal assets you can protect and how. If you are married, your spouse has certain property rights that can't be taken away just because you create a new business organization. Spend the time and ask the questions to find out which business form will serve you and your company best.

Partnerships

Partnerships are governed by some version of the **Uniform Partnership Act** (UPA), which was adopted in 49 states. The 1994 **Revised Uniform Partnership Act** (RUPA) has now been adopted in most states. The RUPA defines a partnership as "the association of two or more persons to carry on as co-owners a business for profit forms a partnership, whether or not the persons intend to form a partnership." "Persons" can include corporations as well as natural persons.

Formation

A partnership can be formed voluntarily by direct action of the parties, such as through a partnership agreement or articles of partnership or its formation can be implied by conduct.

Conduct that Forms Partnerships by Implication

In certain circumstances, courts find that a partnership exists even if those involved say they are not partners Simply owning property together does not result in a **partnership by implication**. A cousin to apparent authority (see Chapter 17), a partnership by implication arises because the behavior of the principals leads others to believe there is a partnership. Courts examine a number of factors in finding whether a partnership exists by implication. Section 7 of the RUPA provides that if two or more parties share the profits of a business, it is *prima facie* evidence that a partnership exists. (*Prima facie* evidence means the presumption that a partnership exists.) However, the presumption of partnership by profit sharing can be overcome if someone received profits for any of the following reasons:

1. Profits paid to repay debts
2. Profits paid as wages or rent
3. Profits paid to a widow or estate representative
4. Profits paid for the sale of business goodwill

Many shopping center leases, for example, provide for the payment of both a fixed amount of rent and a percentage of net profits. The owners of the shopping center profit as the stores do, but they profit as landlords, not as partners with the shopping center businesses.

In addition to partnerships by implication, parties can also have partnership liability if the conduct of two or more parties leads others to believe a partnership exists. **Partnerships by estoppel** arise when others are led to believe there is a partnership, such as when two people act as partners.

Byker v. *Mannes* (Case 13.1) addresses the question of whether a partnership is implied by the conduct of two principals.

CASE 13.1

Byker v. *Mannes*
641 N.W.2D 210 (MICH. 2002)*

DUMB AND DUMBFOUNDED

FACTS

In 1985, David Byker (plaintiff) was doing accounting work for Tom Mannes (defendant). The two talked about going into business together because they had complementary business skills. Mr. Mannes could locate certain properties because of his real estate background, and Mr. Byker could raise money for their property purchases.

The two had investment interests in five real estate limited partnerships. They shared equally in the commissions, financing fees, and termination costs of all the partnerships. The two also personally guaranteed loans for these investments from several financial institutions.

The business relationship between the parties began to deteriorate after they created Pier 1000 Ltd. in order to own and manage a marina. The marina had serious financial difficulties, and Byker and Mannes placed their profits from another partnership, the M & B Limited Partnership II, into Pier 1000 Ltd. and borrowed money from several financial institutions.

When Mr. Mannes refused to make any additional monetary contributions, Mr. Byker continued to make loan payments and incurred accounting fees on behalf of Pier 1000 Ltd. Mr. Byker also entered into several individual loans for the benefit of Pier 1000 Ltd. Mr. Mannes had no knowledge of these extra transactions.

The marina was returned to its previous owners in exchange for their assumption of Mr. Byker's and Mr. Mannes's business obligations. Mr. Byker and Mr. Mannes ended their business ventures together.

Mr. Byker then approached Mr. Mannes to obtain his share of the payments of the losses from the various businesses. Mr. Mannes testified that he was "absolutely dumbfounded" by the request for money.

Mr. Byker then filed suit for the payments, saying that the two had a partnership. The court determined that the two had created a general partnership that included all of the business entities. The Court of Appeals reversed that decision. Mr. Byker appealed.

JUDICIAL OPINION

MARKMAN, Justice

"[T]here is no necessity that the parties attach the label 'partnership' to their relationship as long as they in fact both mutually agree to assume a relationship that falls within the definition of a partnership."

[T]he focus is on whether individuals intended to jointly carry on a business for profit regardless of whether they subjectively intended to form a partnership.

Stated more plainly, the statute does not require partners to be aware of their status as "partners" in order to have a legal partnership.

With the language of the statute as our focal point, we conclude that the intent to create a partnership is not required if the acts and conduct of the parties otherwise evidence that the parties carried on as coowners a business for profit. Thus, we believe that, to the extent that the Court of Appeals regarded the absence of subjective intent to create a partnership as dispositive regarding whether the parties carried on as co-owners a business for profit, it incorrectly interpreted the statutory (and the common) law of partnership in Michigan.

Accordingly, we remand this matter to the Court of Appeals for analysis under the proper test for determining the existence of a partnership under the Michigan Uniform Partnership Act.

CASE QUESTIONS

1. What type of relationship did Mr. Byker and Mr. Mannes have?

2. What does the court say about the type of intent the parties must have for a partnership?

3. What lessons should Mr. Mannes learn from his experience in having to pay Mr. Byker when he thought the partnership was through?

*This case created a bit of a tussle between the Michigan Court of Appeals and its Supreme Court. Following this decision and remand, the Court of Appeals found that there was no partnership because the parties had to be aware of it to be liable, thus defying the Michigan Supreme Court. On appeal, the Michigan Supreme Court reversed the Court of Appeals, 668 N.W.2d 909 (Mich. 2003), not offering an opinion but explaining it was reversing for the reasons stated in the dissenting opinion at the Court of Appeals on the second round.

consider 13.1

Richard Chaiken entered into agreements with both Mr. Strazella and Mr. Spitzer to operate a barbershop. Mr. Chaiken was to provide barber chairs, supplies, and licenses. Mr. Strazella and Mr. Spitzer were to bring their tools, and the agreements included work hours and holidays for them. The Delaware Employment Security Commission determined that Mr. Strazella and Mr. Spitzer are employees, not partners, and seeks to collect unemployment compensation for the two barbers. Mr. Chaiken maintains that they are partners and not employees. Who is correct? (Analysis appears at the end of the chapter.) [*Chaiken* v. *Employment Security Comm'n,* 274 A.2d 707 (Del. 1971)]

SOURCES OF FUNDING

Funding for a partnership comes from partners who contribute property, cash, or services to the partnership. Not only are these contributions (the capital) put at the risk of the business, but so also are each of the partners' personal assets: Partners are personally liable for the full amount of the partnership's obligations, even beyond their capital contributions.

consider 13.2

Triangle Chemical Company supplied $671.10 worth of fertilizer and chemicals to France Mathis to produce a cabbage crop. When Mr. Mathis first asked for credit, he was denied. He then told Triangle that he had a new partner, Emory Pope. The company president called Mr. Pope, who said he was backing Mr. Mathis. Mr. Pope had loaned Mr. Mathis money to produce the crop, and Mr. Mathis said Mr. Pope would pay the bills. Mr. Pope said, "We're growing the crop together and I am more or less handling the money." When Mr. Mathis could not pay, Triangle wanted to hold Mr. Pope personally liable. Mr. Pope said his promise to pay another's debt would have to have been in writing. Triangle claimed Mr. Pope was a partner and personally liable. Is he? (Analysis appears at the end of the chapter.) [*Pope* v. *Triangle Chemical Co.,* 277 S.E.2d 758 (Ga. 1981)]

PARTNER LIABILITY

Each partner is both a principal and an agent to the other partners and is liable both for the acts of others and to the others for individual acts. If one partner enters into a contract for partnership business supplies, all the partners are liable. Similarly, if one partner has a motor vehicle accident while on a partnership delivery, the individual partner is liable for his or her own negligence, but because the accident occurred under the scope of partnership business, the partners and the partnership are also liable. Under the RUPA, partners are jointly and severally liable for all obligations.

If partnership assets are exhausted, each partner is individually liable. Creditors can satisfy their claims by looking to the assets of the individual partners after the partnership assets are exhausted.

Vrabel v. *Acri* (Case 13.2) deals with an issue of partnership liability.

CASE 13.2

Vrabel v. *Acri*
103 N.E.2D 564 (OHIO 1952)

SHOT DOWN IN A MA & PA CAFE: IS MA LIABLE WHEN PA GOES TO JAIL?

FACTS

On February 17, 1947, Stephen Vrabel and a companion went into the Acri Cafe in Youngstown, Ohio, to buy alcoholic drinks. While Mr. Vrabel and his companion were sitting at the bar drinking, Michael Acri, without provocation, drew a .38-caliber gun, shot and killed Mr. Vrabel's companion, and shot and seriously injured Mr. Vrabel. Mr. Acri was convicted of murder and sentenced to a life term in the state prison.

Florence and Michael Acri, as partners, had owned and operated the Acri Cafe since 1933. From the time of his marriage to Mrs. Acri in 1931 until 1946, Mr. Acri had been in and out of hospitals, clinics, and sanitariums for the treatment of mental disorders and nervousness. Although he beat Mrs. Acri when they had marital difficulties, he had not attacked, abused, or mistreated anyone else. The Acris separated in September 1946, and Mrs. Acri sued her husband for divorce soon afterward. Before their separation, Mrs. Acri had operated and managed the cafe primarily only when Mr. Acri was ill. Following the marital separation and until the time he shot Mr. Vrabel, Mr. Acri was in exclusive control of the management of the cafe.

Mr. Vrabel brought suit against Mrs. Acri to recover damages for his injuries on the grounds that, as Mr. Acri's partner, she was liable for his tort. The trial court ordered her to pay Mr. Vrabel damages of $7,500. Mrs. Acri appealed.

JUDICIAL OPINION

ZIMMERMAN, Judge

The authorities are in agreement that whether a tort is committed by a partner or a joint adventurer, the principles of law governing the situation are the same. So, where a partnership or a joint enterprise is shown to exist, each member of such project acts both as principal and agent of the others as to those things done within the apparent scope of the business of the project and for its benefit.

However, it is equally true that where one member of a partnership or joint enterprise commits a wrongful and malicious tort not within the actual or apparent scope of the agency, or the common business of the particular venture, to which the other members have not assented, and which has not been concurred in or ratified by them, they are not liable for the harm thereby caused.

Because at the time of Vrabel's injuries and for a long time prior thereto Florence had been excluded from the Acri Cafe and had no voice or control in its management, and because Florence did not know or have good reason to know that Michael was a dangerous individual prone to assault cafe patrons, the theory of negligence urged by Vrabel is hardly tenable.

We cannot escape the conclusion, therefore, that the above rules, relating to the nonliability of a partner or joint adventurer for wrongful and malicious torts committed by an associate outside the purposes and scope of the business, must be applied in the instant case. The willful and malicious attack by Michael Acri upon Vrabel in the Acri Cafe cannot reasonably be said to have come within the scope of the business of operating the cafe, so as to have rendered the absent Florence accountable.

Since the liability of a partner for the acts of his associates is founded upon the principles of agency, the statement is in point that an intentional and willful attack committed by an agent or employee, to vent his own spleen or malevolence against the injured person, is a clear departure from his employment and his principal or employer is not responsible therefore.

Judgment reversed.

CASE QUESTIONS

1. What was the nature of the business and the injury? Why is this information important for liability purposes?

2. Why was Mr. Acri not a defendant?

3. Is Mrs. Acri liable for the injuries? Explain.

TAX CONSEQUENCES IN PARTNERSHIPS

A partnership does not pay taxes. It simply files an informational return. The partners, however, must report their share of partnership income (or losses) and deductions on their individual tax returns and must pay taxes on the reported share.

MANAGEMENT AND CONTROL

Partnership Authority

Unless agreed otherwise, each partner has a duty to contribute time to manage the partnership. Each partner has an equal management say, and each has a right to use partnership property for partnership purposes. No one partner controls the property, funds, or management of the firm unless the partners agree to delegate authority or even delegate the day-to-day management responsibilities to one or more of the partners. Partners are not entitled to compensation for their efforts for their partnership unless they agree to do so.

Each partner is an agent of the other partners (See Chapter 17), and each has the authority given in the agreement or implied by custom. Some partnership matters require unanimous consent of the partners and include: confessing a judgment (settling a lawsuit), transferring all the partnership's assets, or selling its goodwill. Basically, unusual transactions require all the partners' approval.

Partner Fiduciary Duties

Because each partner is an agent for the partnership and the other partners as well, each owes the partnership and the other partners the same fiduciary duties an agent owes a principal. Partners' obligations as fiduciaries are the same as agents' duties to principals.

Partnership Property

Partnership property is property contributed to the firm as a capital contribution or property purchased with partnership funds. Partners are co-owners of partnership property in a form of ownership called *tenancy in partnership*. Tenants in partnership have equal rights in the use and possession of the property for partnership purposes. On the death of one of the partners, rights in the property are transferred to the surviving partner or partners. The partnership interest in the property remains, and the property or a share of the property is not transferred to the estate of the deceased partner. The estate of the deceased partner simply receives the value of the partner's interest, not the property.

Partner Interests

Partners' interests in the partnership are different from partnership property. A partner's interest is a personal property interest that belongs to the partner. It can be sold (transferred) or pledged as collateral to a creditor. Creditors (personal) can attach a partner's interests to collect a debt.

A transfer of a partner's interest does not result in the transferee becoming a new partner because no person can become a partner without the consent of all the existing partners. Further, the transfer does not relieve the transferring partner of personal liability. A transfer of interest will not eliminate individual liability to existing creditors.

TRANSFERABILITY OF INTERESTS

A partner cannot transfer partnership status without the unanimous consent of the other partners. Absent an agreement from creditors, outgoing partners remain personally liable for all partnership debts up to the time they leave. If departing partners give public notice of their disassociation, their personal liability for future contracts and obligations ends once they leave. Incoming partners are liable for all contracts after the date they come into the firm. Incoming partners' liability for existing debts is limited to the amounts of their capital contribution.

The *Byker* case also illustrates that partnership liabilities do not end when the partners no longer do business together. The debts remain and must be satisfied, even from partners no longer involved in running the business.

DISSOLUTION AND TERMINATION OF THE PARTNERSHIP

Dissolution is not necessarily termination. The UPA defines dissolution as one partner's ceasing to be associated with carrying on the business. The RUPA refers to "dissociation" of partners, which may or may not lead to dissolution. When a partner leaves, retires, or dies, the partnership is dissolved, though not terminated. Dissolution is basically a change in the structure of the partnership. The partnership may be reorganized and continue business without the partner who is gone.

Dissolution *can* lead, however, to termination of the partnership. Termination means all business stops, the assets of the firm are liquidated, and the proceeds are distributed to creditors and partners to repay capital contributions and distribute profits (if any). Dissolution occurs by agreement, by operation of law (events such as the death or bankruptcy of a partner result in automatic dissolution), and, finally, by a court order (something a court will order when the partners just cannot work together any longer).

Limited Partnerships

A **limited partnership** is a partnership with a slight variation in the liability of those involved. Limited partnerships must include at least one **general partner** and one **limited partner**. General partners have the same obligations as partners in general partnerships—full liability and full responsibility for the management of the business. Limited partners have liability up to the amount of their contribution to the partnership, provided they are not involved in the management of the firm. General partners run the limited partnership, and the limited partners are the investors.

The Uniform Limited Partnership Act (ULPA) has been the predominant form of business organization for oil exploration and real estate development because of the tax advantages available through limited partnerships. Because of increased use of limited partnerships, the 1916 ULPA proved to be inadequate for governing the creation, structure, and ongoing operations of limited partnerships. The **Revised Uniform Limited Partnership Act** (RULPA) was created in 1985 to update limited partnership law and has been adopted in nearly every state.

FORMATION

A limited partnership is a statutory creature and requires compliance with certain procedures in order to exist. If these procedures are not followed, it is possible that the limited partners could lose their limited liability protection.

The RULPA requires the following information for filing at the appropriate government agency:

1. Name of the limited partnership (cannot be deceptively similar to another corporation's or partnership's name and must contain the words "limited partnership"; no abbreviations permitted)
2. Address of its principal office
3. Name and address of the statutory agent
4. Business address of the general partner
5. Latest date for dissolution of the partnership

The certificate of limited partnership is simply public disclosure of the formation and existence of the limited partnership. The relationships and rights of the partners are then addressed in a much longer document called a **limited partnership agreement** or the **articles of limited partnership**.

SOURCES OF FUNDING

Capital contributions supply the initial funding for a limited partnership. Both the general and limited partners make contributions upon entering the partnership. Under the RULPA, the contribution can be in the form of cash, property, services already performed, or a promissory note or other obligation to pay money or property. The RULPA requires that limited partners' promises to contribute be evidenced by a record to be enforceable.

LIABILITY

The principal advantage of a limited partnership is the limited personal liability. To ensure personal limited liability, several requirements must be met. First, as already discussed, a certificate of limited partnership must be filed, indicating the limited liability status of the limited partners. Second, at least one general partner is required. The general partner can be a corporation. Third, the limited partners must be careful about their activity with and appearances with operations of the partnership. Under the RULPA, a limited partner who participates in the management of the firm in the same way the general partner does is liable only to those persons who are led to believe by the limited partner's conduct that the limited partner is a general partner. The RULPA also provides a list of activities that limited partners can do without losing limited liability status:

1. Being employed by the general partnership as an employee or a contractor
2. Consulting with or advising the general partner
3. Acting as a surety or guarantor for the limited partnership
4. Voting on amendments, dissolution, sale of property, or assumption of debt

If limited partners comply with the rules for limited liability, their liability is limited to the amount of their capital contribution. If they have pledged to pay a certain amount as capital over a period of time, they are liable for the full amount. For example, some real estate syndications that are limited partnerships allow the limited partners to make their investment in installment payments over two to four years. Limited partners in these arrangements are liable for the full amount pledged whenever an obligation to a creditor is not paid.

TAX CONSEQUENCES

Limited partnerships are taxed the same way as general partnerships. The general and limited partners report the income and losses on their individual returns and pay the appropriate taxes. A limited partnership files an information return but does not itself pay any taxes.

Limited partnership interests are closely scrutinized by the IRS to determine whether they are, in reality, corporations as opposed to true limited partnerships. Some of the factors examined in determining whether an organization is a corporation or a limited partnership are (1) the transferability of the interests, (2) the assets of the general partners, and (3) the net worth of the general partners.

MANAGEMENT AND CONTROL

Profits and Distributions

The general partner decides when to distribute funds to limited partners and profits and losses are allocated on the basis of capital contributions. Under the RULPA, the agreement for sharing of profits and losses must be evidenced by a record.

Partner Authority

The authority of the general partner in a limited partnership is the same as the authority of the partners in a general partnership. There are, however, some general activities the general partner cannot perform without the consent of the limited partners, including the following:

1. Admitting a new general partner (also requires consent of other general partners)
2. Admitting a new limited partner unless the partnership agreement allows it
3. Extraordinary transactions, such as selling all the partnership assets

Limited partners can monitor the general partner's activity with the same rights provided to partners in general partnerships: the right to inspect the books and records and the right to an accounting.

TRANSFERABILITY OF INTERESTS

Although the assignment of limited partnership interests is not prohibited by the RULPA, a limited partnership agreement may provide for restrictions on assignment. Limited partnership interests may have been sold without registration as exemptions to the federal securities law (see Chapter 14 for more details on securities registrations). If those exempt interests are readily transferable, the exemption could be lost. Also, for the limited partners to enjoy the tax benefits of limited partner status, the ease of transferability is a critical issue.

The assignment of a partnership interest does not terminate a limited partnership. The RULPA allows limited partners to decide whether they want to transfer their interest or their limited partner status.

DISSOLUTION AND TERMINATION OF A LIMITED PARTNERSHIP

A limited partnership can be dissolved in one of the following ways:

1. Expiration of the time period designated in the agreement or the occurrence of an event causing dissolution, as specified in the agreement

2. Unanimous written consent of all partners

3. Withdrawal of a general partner

4. Court order after application by one of the partners

Upon dissolution, a partnership can continue (assuming a general partner remains); but the partnership can also be terminated after dissolution. If termination occurs, all assets of the partnership are liquidated. The RULPA specifies an order of distribution.

Corporations

Corporations are legal entities in and of themselves. Because they are treated as persons under the law, they can hold title to property, they can sue or be sued in the corporate name, and they are taxed separately. The latest U.S. economic census figures (from 2002; the most recent numbers available) indicate that only 2.13 million partnerships operate in the United States whereas 5.13 million corporations are in operation. Corporations earn nearly 90 percent of all business profits.

TYPES OF CORPORATIONS

Corporations are either **profit corporations** (those seeking to earn a return for investors) or **nonprofit corporations**. There are **domestic corporations** and **foreign corporations**. A corporation is a domestic corporation in the state in which it is incorporated and a foreign corporation in every other state. **Government corporations**, such as TVA, are organized to advance a social interest, such as the development of hydro power. **Professional corporations** are corporations organized by physicians, dentists, attorneys, and accountants; they exist by statute in most states. Professional corporation shareholders have no personal liability for any corporate debts, as in any other corporation, except for professional malpractice claims. The **corporate veil** or shield (explained later) will not give individuals personal immunity for professional negligence despite their general liability limitation through incorporation. **Close corporations** are the opposite of **publicly held corporations**; that is, the former are corporations with few shareholders. Close corporations are governed by specific state statutes and generally have more discretion in their internal operations, with less formality.

The **S corporation** (sometimes called Subchapter S or Sub S corporation) is formed no differently from any other corporation, but it must meet the IRS requirements for an S corporation and must file a special election form with the IRS indicating it wishes to be treated as an S corporation. The benefit of an S corporation is that shareholders' income and losses are treated like those of partners, but the shareholders enjoy the protection of limited liability behind a corporate veil. The income earned and losses incurred by an S corporation are reported on the shareholders' individual returns, but the shareholders' personal assets are protected from creditors of the business.

THE LAW OF CORPORATIONS

The **Model Business Corporation Act** (MBCA), as drafted and revised by the Corporate, Banking and Business Section of the American Bar Association, is the uniform law on corporations. The provisions of the MBCA are quite liberal and give management great latitude in operations. The MBCA tends to follow the principles of corporate law long established in Delaware, a state where many of the country's major companies are incorporated. Delaware boasts a rich body of case law on corporate governance that offers the stability companies want as they incorporate. Despite the ability to draw on the Delaware case law and experience, the MBCA is not adopted as widely as the UPA or the Uniform Commercial Code (UCC). Even those states that have adopted the MBCA have made significant changes in their adopted versions. As a result, each state's law on corporations is quite different. The following sections cover the revised MBCA rules, but each state may have its own variations.

FORMATION

A corporation is a statutory entity. Formal public filing is required to form a corporation. The following procedures for corporate formation are those of the MBCA.

Where to Incorporate

The following factors should be considered when determining in which state to incorporate:

1. The status of the state's corporation laws (See the preceding discussion about Delaware; also, some states' laws and judicial decisions are oriented more toward management than to shareholders.)

2. State tax laws

3. The ability to attract employees to the state

4. The incentives states offer to attract the business (new freeways, office space, attractive urban renewal)

The Formation Document

All states require **articles of incorporation** to be filed in order to create a corporation. Under the MBCA, the articles of incorporation must include the following information:

1. The name of the corporation

2. The names and addresses of all incorporators (In addition, each incorporator must sign the articles of incorporation.)

3. The share structure of the corporation: (a) the common and preferred classes, (b) which shares vote, and (c) the rights of shareholders, or preemptive rights

4. The statutory agent (the party who will be served with any lawsuits against the corporation)

Who Is Incorporating

The **incorporators** (required to be listed in the articles of incorporation) are the parties forming the corporation. Under the MBCA, only one incorporator is required, and that person may be a natural person, a corporation, a partnership, a limited partnership, or an association.

Incorporators are personally liable for any contracts entered into or actions taken during the pre-incorporation stage. After incorporation, the corporation could agree to assume liability through a **novation** of the incorporators' acts. For example, if an incorporator of a lumberyard entered into a contract for the purchase of lumber and the corporate board (after formation) agreed that the contract was a good one, the corporation could ratify it or enter into a novation to assume liability. In novation, the lumberyard agrees to substitute the corporation as the contracting party. In a **ratification**, the corporation assumes primary liability for payment, but the incorporator still remains liable.

Postformation

After the paperwork of incorporating is complete, a corporation must begin its day-to-day operations with an **initial meeting**. At this meeting, the officers of the corporation are elected and **bylaws** are adopted to govern corporate procedures. The bylaws proscribe meeting processes (i.e., quorum numbers and voting numbers) and set the terms of officers and directors. Articles of incorporation give an overview of a corporate entity; the bylaws constitute the operational rules.

CAPITAL AND SOURCES OF CORPORATE FUNDS

A corporation has a variety of sources for funds. It may use short-term financing, which consists of loans from banks or credit lines. The other forms of financing used most frequently by corporations are debt and equity.

Debt Financing: The Bond Market

Long-term debt financing is available to corporations when they issue bonds. Bonds are, in effect, long-term promissory notes from a corporation to the bond buyers. The corporation pays the holders interest on the bonds until the maturity date, which is when the bonds are due or must be paid. The interest is fixed and is a fixed-payment responsibility regardless of the corporation's profitability. The benefits of debt financing include the tax deductibility of interest as an expense. Bondholders have the benefit of first rights in corporate assets in the event of insolvency.

Equity Financing: Shareholders

Equity financing comes through the sale of stock in a corporation. Shareholders are given shares of stock in exchange for their money. To avoid personal liability, the shareholders must pay at least par value for their shares and must honor the terms of their subscription agreement (share purchase agreement). A shareholder who has not paid at least par value holds **watered shares** and is liable to creditors for the amount not paid. For example, if a shareholder paid $500 for shares with a par value of $1,000, the shareholder would be personally liable for the $500 difference. The rights of shareholders depend on the type of stock purchased. A discussion of the various types of stock follows.

Common Stock

Common stock is the typical stock in a corporation and it generally carries voting rights so that common shareholders have a voice in the election of directors, the amendment of articles and bylaws, and other major corporate matters. Common stock dividends depend on both profitability and decisions of the board of directors. If a corporation is dissolved, the common shareholders have a right to a proportionate share of the assets (after creditors and preferred stockholders have been paid).

Preferred Stock

Preferred stock is appropriately named because its owners enjoy preferred status over holders of a corporation's common stock. For example, preferred stockholders have priority in the payment of dividends. Some preferred dividends are even at a fixed rate, and **cumulative preferred stock** guarantees the payment of a dividend so that if a dividend is not paid one year, the holder's right to be paid carries over until funds are available. Preferred shareholders also have priority over common shareholders in the assets in the event the corporation is dissolved.

Shareholder Liability

Shareholders' personal liability is limited to the amount of their investment in the corporation. The personal assets of shareholders are not subject to the claims of corporate creditors. In some circumstances, however, such as watered shares (discussed earlier), a shareholder is personally liable.

In other more serious circumstances, shareholders can be held liable for the full amount of corporate debts. A creditor who successfully pierces the corporate veil can collect from the personal assets of shareholders. The corporate veil can be pierced for several reasons. One is inadequate capitalization. The owners of a corporation are required to place as much capital at risk in the corporation as is necessary to cover reasonably anticipated expenses of the business. The purpose of this requirement is to ensure that someone does not use the corporation to avoid liability without actually transferring assets to the corporation.

Another theory a court can use to pierce the corporate veil is the **alter ego theory**, which means that the owners and managers of the corporation have not treated the corporation as a separate entity but have used the structure more as a personal resource. Personal and corporate assets and debts are mixed, no formality is observed with regard to operations and meetings, and transfers of property are made without explanation or authorization.

U.S. v. Bestfoods (Case 13.3) deals with an issue of piercing the corporate veil in a situation involving CERCLA liability (see Chapter 19).

CASE 13.3

U.S. v. Bestfoods, Inc.
524 U.S. 51 (1998)

LIFTING THE VEIL IS BEST FOR CLEANUP, BUT NOT FOR SHAREHOLDERS

FACTS

In 1957, Ott Chemical Co. manufactured chemicals at its plant near Muskegon, Michigan, and both intentionally and unintentionally dumped hazardous substances in the soil and groundwater near the plant. Ott sold the plant to CPC International, Inc.

In 1965, CPC incorporated a wholly owned subsidiary (Ott II) to buy Ott's assets. Ott II then continued both the chemical production and dumping. Ott II's officers and directors had positions and duties at both CPC and Ott.

In 1972, CPC (now Bestfoods) sold Ott II to Story Chemical, which operated the plant until its bankruptcy in 1977. Aerojet-General Corp. bought the plant from the bankruptcy trustee and manufactured chemicals there until 1986.

In 1989, the EPA filed suit to recover the costs of cleanup on the plant site and named CPC, Aerojet, and the officers of the now defunct Ott and Ott II.

The District Court held both CPC and Aerojet liable. After a divided panel of the Court of Appeals for the Sixth Circuit reversed in part, the court granted a rehearing *en banc* and vacated the panel decision. This time, seven judges to six, the court again reversed the District Court in part. Bestfoods appealed (Ott settled prior to the appeal).

JUDICIAL OPINION

SOUTER, Justice

The issue before us, under the Comprehensive Environmental Response, Compensation, and Liability Act of 1980 (CERCLA), is whether a parent corporation that actively participated in, and exercised control over, the operations of a subsidiary may, without more, be held liable as an operator of a polluting facility owned or operated by the subsidiary. We answer no, unless the corporate veil may be pierced. But a corporate parent that actively participated in, and exercised control over, the operations of the facility itself may be held directly liable in its own right as an operator of the facility.

It is a general principle of corporate law deeply "ingrained in our economic and legal systems" that a parent corporation (so-called because of control through ownership of another corporation's stock) is not liable for the acts of its subsidiary. . . .

But there is an equally fundamental principle of corporate law, applicable to the parent-subsidiary relationship as well as generally, that the corporate veil may be pierced and the shareholder held liable for the corporation's conduct when, inter alia, the corporate form would otherwise be misused to accomplish certain wrongful purposes, most notably fraud, on the shareholder's behalf.

Nothing in CERCLA purports to rewrite this well-settled rule, either. If a subsidiary that operates, but does not own, a facility is so pervasively controlled by its parent for a sufficiently improper purpose to warrant veil piercing, the parent may be held derivatively liable for the subsidiary's acts as an operator.

The fact that a corporate subsidiary happens to own a polluting facility operated by its parent does nothing, then, to displace the rule that the parent "corporation is [itself] responsible for the wrongs committed by its agents in the course of its business." It is this direct liability that is properly seen as being at issue here.

Under the plain language of the statute, any person who operates a polluting facility is directly liable for the costs of cleaning up the pollution. This is so regardless of whether that person is the facility's owner, the owner's parent corporation or business partner, or even a saboteur who sneaks into the facility at night to discharge its poisons out of malice. If any such act of operating a corporate subsidiary's facility is done on behalf of a parent corporation, the existence of the parent-subsidiary relationship under state corporate law is simply irrelevant to the issue of direct liability. . . .

With this understanding, we are satisfied that the Court of Appeals correctly rejected the District Court's analysis of direct liability. But we also think that the appeals court erred in limiting direct liability under the statute to a parent's sole or joint venture operation, so as to eliminate any possible finding that CPC is liable as an operator on the facts of this case.

In sum, the District Court's focus on the relationship between parent and subsidiary (rather than parent and facility), combined with its automatic attribution of the actions of dual officers and directors to the corporate parent, erroneously, even if unintentionally, treated CERCLA as though it displaced or fundamentally altered common-law standards of limited liability. . . .

There is, in fact, some evidence that CPC engaged in just this type and degree of activity at the Muskegon plant. The District Court's opinion speaks of an agent of CPC alone who played a conspicuous part in dealing with the toxic risks emanating from the operation of the plant. G.R.D. Williams worked only for CPC; he was not an employee, officer, or director of Ott, and thus, his actions were of necessity taken only on behalf of CPC. The District Court found that "CPC became directly involved in environmental and regulatory matters through the work of . . . Williams, CPC's governmental and environmental affairs director. Williams . . . became heavily involved in environmental issues at Ott II." He "actively participated in and exerted control over a variety of Ott II environmental matters," and he "issued directives regarding Ott II's responses to regulatory inquiries."

We think that these findings are enough to raise an issue of CPC's operation of the facility through Williams's actions, though we would draw no ultimate conclusion from these findings at this point. Prudence thus counsels us to remand [to determine] who might be said to have had a part in operating the Muskegon facility.

The judgment of the Court of Appeals for the Sixth Circuit is vacated, and the case is remanded.

CASE QUESTIONS

1. Describe the corporate ownership history that surrounds the Muskegon facility.

2. Is there a special CERCLA rule for piercing the corporate veil?

3. What must be shown to hold a parent liable for the actions of the subsidiary? Are joint directors of parent and corporate subsidiaries alone evidence of a need to pierce the corporate veil?

CORPORATE TAX CONSEQUENCES

Although corporations have the benefit of limited liability, they have the detriment of double taxation. Not only does the corporation pay taxes on its earnings, but shareholders must also report their dividend income on their separate returns and pay individual taxes on their dividend income. However, these shareholders pay taxes only if the dividends are paid. Unlike partnerships in which the partners pay taxes on earnings whether they are distributed or not, shareholders pay taxes on corporate earnings only when they are distributed to them. One way to resolve the problem of the cost of double taxation is the S corporation (see p. 299).

CORPORATE MANAGEMENT AND CONTROL: DIRECTORS AND OFFICERS

A corporation might be owned by a million shareholders, but its operation will be controlled by the hands of a few, the **board of directors**. The shareholders elect these directors, who serve as the corporate policy makers and strategic planners for the corporation. They also provide insight and outside perspective on current management practices. They also serve a watchdog role, as with the now mandatory **audit committees** required of all stock exchange companies. Audit committees, made up of independent outside directors and at least one financial expert under Sarbanes-Oxley who have no contracts or former salary ties with the company, are responsible for assuring that the financial reports that management issues are accurate.

Institutional investors and other groups have been placing increasing pressure on boards for accountability. One director responsibility that receives ongoing attention is that of officers' compensation. Directors not only elect the officers of the corporation; they also decide the salaries for these officers and themselves. The issue of officer compensation has received congressional attention with the deductibility of officer compensation limited to $1 million annually and ongoing attention from shareholders in terms of limits on compensation. The issue of executive compensation was front and center in the fall 2008 financial bail-out legislation. Shareholders continue to make proposals to limit executive compensation (see Chapter 14 for more information on such proposals) and exercise their rights of director removal if they feel the board is not responsive to their concerns about compensation.

Director Liability

Officers and directors are **fiduciaries** of the corporation, which means they are to act in the best interests of the corporation and not profit at the corporation's expense. They are subject to the **business judgment rule**, a standard of corporate behavior under which it is understood that officers and directors can make mistakes, but they are required to show that their decisions were made after careful study and discussion. In those decisions, they may consult experts, such as attorneys, accountants, and financial analysts; but again, they need to show that these experts were well-chosen and reliable individuals.

Brehm v. *Eisner* (Case 13.4) deals with the business judgment rule and provides the answer for the chapter's opening Consider.

CASE 13.4

Brehm v Eisner
746 A.2D 244 (DEL. 2000)

KIND OF A MICKEY MOUSE JUDGMENT CALL

FACTS

Michael Eisner, as then-CEO and chairman of Disney, hired Michael Ovitz as Disney's president. Mr. Ovitz was a long-time friend of Mr. Eisner. Mr. Ovitz was also an important talent broker in Hollywood. Although he lacked experience managing a diversified public company, other companies with entertainment operations had been interested in hiring him for high-level executive positions. Mr. Ovitz's employment agreement was unilaterally negotiated by Eisner and approved by the "Old Board." The Old Board felt that Ovitz was a valuable person to hire as president of Disney. Disney agreed to give Ovitz a base salary of $1 million per year, a discretionary bonus, and two sets of stock options.

Disney needed a strong second-in-command because Mr. Eisner's health, due to major heart surgery, was in question, and there really was no succession plan. Mr. Eisner also had a rugged history when it came to working with important or well-known subordinate executives who wanted to position themselves to succeed him. Over the past five years, Disney executives Jeffrey Katzenberg, Richard Frank, and Stephen Bollenbach had all left after short tenures under Eisner.

Following a tumultuous year and legendary battles between the two, Mr. Ovitz and Mr. Eisner negotiated Mr. Ovitz's departure. Mr. Ovitz was given a "Non-Fault Termination" that carried $38,888,230.77 as well as the option to purchase 3 million Disney shares.

The shareholders (plaintiffs) filed suit against the directors for its failure to adequately consider the Ovitz contract initially, for not considering the issues surrounding that hiring as well as the employment package itself, and for committing waste in giving Ovitz what amounted to a $140 million severance package (when the value of the options were included). The Court of Chancery dismissed the suit and the shareholders appealed.

JUDICIAL OPINION

VEASEY, Chief Justice

This is potentially a very troubling case on the merits. On the one hand, it appears from the Complaint that: (a) the compensation and termination payout for Ovitz were exceedingly lucrative, if not luxurious, compared to Ovitz' value to the Company; and (b) the processes of the boards of directors in dealing with the approval and termination of the Ovitz Employment Agreement were casual, if not sloppy and perfunctory. From what we can ferret out of this deficient pleading, the processes of the Old Board and the New Board were hardly paradigms of good corporate governance practices. Moreover, the sheer size of the payout to Ovitz, as alleged, pushes the envelope of judicial respect for the business judgment of directors in making compensation decisions. Therefore, both as to the processes of the two Boards and the waste test, this is a close case.

All good corporate governance practices include compliance with statutory law and case law establishing fiduciary duties. But the law of corporate fiduciary duties and remedies for violation of those duties are distinct from the aspirational goals of ideal corporate governance practices. Aspirational ideals of good corporate governance practices for boards of directors that go beyond the minimal legal requirements of the corporation law are highly desirable, often tend to benefit stockholders, sometimes reduce litigation and can usually help directors avoid liability. But they are not required by the corporation law and do not define standards of liability.

Ovitz' performance as president was disappointing at best. Eisner admitted it had been a mistake to hire him, that Ovitz lacked commitment to the Company, that he performed services for his old company, and that he negotiated for other jobs (some very lucrative) while being required under the contract to devote his full time and energy to Disney.

All this shows is that the Board had arguable grounds to fire Ovitz for cause. But what is alleged is only an argument—perhaps a good one—that Ovitz' conduct constituted gross negligence or malfeasance. The Complaint contends that the Board committed waste by agreeing to the very lucrative payout to Ovitz under the non-fault termination provision because it had no obligation to him, thus taking the Board's decision outside the protection of the business judgment rule.

The Board made a business decision to grant Ovitz a Non-Fault Termination. Plaintiffs may disagree with the Board's judgment as to how this matter should have been handled. But where, as here, there is no reasonable doubt as to the disinterest of or absence of fraud by the

CONTINUED

Board, mere disagreement cannot serve as grounds for imposing liability based on alleged breaches of fiduciary duty and waste. There is no allegation that the Board did not consider the pertinent issues surrounding Ovitz's termination. Plaintiffs' sole argument appears to be that they do not agree with the course of action taken by the Board regarding Ovitz's separation from Disney. This will not suffice to create a reasonable doubt that the Board's decision to grant Ovitz a Non-Fault Termination was the product of an exercise of business judgment.

One can understand why Disney stockholders would be upset with such an extraordinarily lucrative compensation agreement and termination payout awarded a company president who served for only a little over a year and who underperformed to the extent alleged. That said, there is a very large—though not insurmountable—burden on stockholders who believe they should pursue the remedy of a derivative suit instead of selling their stock or seeking to reform or oust these directors from office.

Affirmed.

CASE QUESTIONS

1. What must the shareholders prove to recover?

2. What does the court say is the relationship between good corporate governance, liability, and business judgment?

3. What alternatives do shareholders have to litigation?

consider 13.3

William Shlensky was a minority shareholder of Chicago National League Ball Club, Inc. (the Cubs). In 1966, he brought suit against the directors of the Cubs for violation of the business judgment rule because at the time of the suit the Cubs did not play night games at Wrigley Field, their home field. All of the other 19 teams in the major leagues had some night games with substantially all of their weekday and nonholiday games scheduled under the lights. Between 1961 and 1965, the Cubs had sustained operating losses. Mr. Shlensky filed a derivative suit (a suit on behalf of shareholders) against the Cubs' directors for negligence and mismanagement.

Mr. Shlensky's suit maintained that the Cubs would continue to lose money unless night games were played. The directors' response was that baseball was a "daytime" sport and that holding night games would have a "deteriorating effect upon the surrounding neighborhood."

Why does Mr. Shlensky believe the directors did not use good judgment? Is there a difference between negligence and differing business opinions? Does the business judgment rule allow directors to make mistakes? (Analysis appears at the end of the chapter.) [*Shlensky* v. *Wrigley*, 237 N.W. 2d 776 (Ill. 1968)]

· ·

Officers and directors are also required to follow the **corporate opportunity doctrine**, under which officers and directors may not take an opportunity for themselves that the corporation might be interested in taking. For example, a director of a lumber company who discovers a deal on timberland would be required to present that opportunity to the corporation before taking it. If the director does not first present the idea to the corporation, a constructive trust is put on the profits the director makes, and the corporation is the beneficiary of that trust. If, however, the director presents the opportunity and the corporation is unable or unwilling to take it, the director may go ahead with the opportunity without the problem of a constructive trust.

Officer Liability

Recent prosecutions have demonstrated an increased effort to hold corporate officers criminally responsible for the acts of the corporation. In environmental law, changes in the law and aggressive prosecutions have brought about convictions of officers, particularly concerning the disposal of hazardous waste. The issues of officer liability are covered in Chapters 7 and 14.

Officers, Boards, and Sarbanes-Oxley

Sarbanes-Oxley, the legislation passed following the collapse of companies such as Enron and WorldCom, has imposed dramatic new requirements on boards and officers of publicly traded companies (see Chapter 7 for more details). These reforms are required above and beyond any statutory requirements imposed by state corporation laws such as the MBCA.

Prohibitions on Loans to Officers   Corporations can no longer make loans to officers and directors. This provision is the result of revelations that companies such as WorldCom, Adelphia, and others had made hundreds of millions of dollars in loans to their CEOs and other executives because they had pledged their shares in the company for their personal investments. When those investments did not perform well, their shares needed to be sold to satisfy the loans. A sell-off of their major holdings would have sent the company's stock into a dive. The result was a vicious circle in which more loans were made in order to prevent the sale of shares, with ever-increasing pressure to keep the share price up in order to satisfy the loans the shares secured.

Codes of Ethics for Financial Reporting   Companies must now have codes of ethics in place for the financial officers of their companies. Even though 97 percent of publicly held companies now have codes of ethics, this provision requires specific content about the standards for financial reporting and accounting in the company. These financial officers are also subject to greater federal penalties for certifying false financial statements (see Chapter 7 for more information on their criminal liability).

Role of Legal Counsel for the Company   In many of the collapsed companies, two of the questions that arose were "Where were the auditors?" and "Where were the lawyers?"[1] As Congress and the SEC grappled with these questions, they imposed extensive new legal requirements and disclosure obligations on auditors and accountants (see Chapter 14 for those requirements), but they also imposed reporting requirements on legal counsel for corporations. Under the new requirements, lawyers have several progressive steps in their duties and disclosure requirements.[2]

- A lawyer who suspects material violations must instigate an investigation to determine whether such violations have occurred.
- The lawyer must inform the CEO of the investigation.
- The lawyer must report material violations of the law to the CEO.
- If no action is taken, the lawyer must go "up the ladder" and report the material violations to the audit committee or a group of independent board members.
- Companies must create a legal compliance committee based on the idea of strength in numbers, in that the committee will be told of investigations and findings and can take the matter "up the ladder."

ethical *issues*

Tyco experienced financial setbacks following the indictment and conviction of its CEO, Dennis Kozlowski (best known for his $6,000 shower curtain and Jimmy Buffet birthday party for his wife), and its CFO, Mark Swartz, on state charges of crimes related to larceny and embezzlement. Some of the charges stemmed from Tyco's Key Employee Corporate Loan Program (the KELP), a program established to encourage officers and some employees to own Tyco shares by offering them loans to pay income taxes due when their ownership of shares granted to them under Tyco's restricted share ownership plan vested. This way, instead of selling some of their shares, the officers could pledge their shares in exchange for cash to pay the taxes on this employee benefit.*

The second loan program was a relocation program established to help employees who had to move from New Hampshire to New York. The idea was to provide low-interest loans for employees who had to relocate from one set of company offices to another in order to lessen the impact on their budgets of the move to a much costlier housing market.

The issue of board approval on the loans remains a question, but compensation committee minutes from February 21, 2002, show that the committee was given a list of loans to officers. There was no public disclosure of these developments or the committee's review. In grand jury testimony, Patricia Prue, the Tyco employee in charge of administration of the two loan programs, indicated that board member Joshua Berman pressured her in June 2002 to change the minutes from that February compensation committee meeting. Mr. Berman denies the allegation. However, Ms. Prue did send a memo on June 7, 2002, to John Fort (a Tyco board member), Mr. Swartz, and the board's governance committee with the following included: "As a result of the fact that I was recently pressured by Josh Berman to engage in conduct which I regarded as dishonest—and which I have refused to do— I will decline to have any personal contact with him in the future. In addition, I ask that Josh not go to my staff with any requests for information or directions." Both sides acknowledge that Ms. Prue sent the memo.

Do you think Ms. Prue did the right thing? Should she have done more to stop the loans? Is it a crime if the board authorized the loans and all the paperwork is in place? Did Ms. Prue facilitate abuse of the loan programs? Should she have notified someone? Should she have resigned? What would you have done if you had been in her position? Do you think the officers acted ethically in their use of the loan relocation program?

*This information was obtained from the SEC's press release issued when it filed suit against Mark Swartz, Dennis Kozlowski, and Mark Belnick for the return of the loan amounts. See http://www.sec.gov; click on litigation releases. Mr. Belnick has settled those charges with the SEC.

Because of concerns and objections from the American Bar Association, the SEC did not adopt the so-called noisy withdrawal rule, a process that would have required a lawyer who has found a material violation that the company will not remedy to resign from the company and report the violation to the SEC.

Board Membership Under rules promulgated under Sarbanes-Oxley requirements, boards must consist of a majority of members who are independent. *Independent* is defined as someone who has not been an officer, employee, or manager of the company during any of the past three years; who is not related to anyone who works for the company; who is not under any type of consulting or remuneration arrangement with the company; and who is not a principal or owner of a company that does business with the board or the company. This new definition of independent has caused some shake-ups in boards. For example, Kenneth Chenault, the CEO of American Express, is no longer an independent member of IBM's board because IBM does business with American Express. The chair of the audit committee must be an independent director, and at least one member of the audit committee must meet standards for certification as a financial expert.

CORPORATE MANAGEMENT AND CONTROL: SHAREHOLDERS

Shareholder Rights: Annual Meetings

Shareholders have the opportunity to express their views at the annual meeting by electing directors who represent their interests. Annual meetings also give shareholders the opportunity to vote on critical corporate issues.

Shareholder Rights: Voting

Voting share shareholders have the right to vote. Shareholders may vote their own shares or delegate their votes in a variety of ways.

The Proxy   The most common method of delegating voting authority is the **proxy**, with which shareholders can transfer their right to vote to someone else. Under the MBCA, a proxy is good only for 11 months, which allows a shareholder to decide to give a different proxy before the next annual meeting. Many shareholder groups solicit proxies to obtain control. Those solicitations are subject to the federal securities laws, and certain disclosures are required (see Chapter 14).

Pooling Agreements   Another method of grouping shareholder votes is the **pooling agreement**, which is a contract among shareholders to vote their shares a certain way or for a certain director.

Voting Trust   One last form of shareholder cooperation is the **voting trust**. In this form of group voting, shareholders actually turn their shares over to a trustee and are then issued a trust certificate. The shareholders still have the right to dividends and could sell or pledge the certificate. However, the shares remain in the hands of the trustee, and the trustee votes those shares according to the terms of the trust agreement.

Shareholder Rights in Combinations

Because shareholders' interests are involved, corporations are not free to combine at will or to merge or consolidate without shareholder input. All states have procedures for obtaining shareholder approval for business combinations. Those procedures include a board resolution followed by notice to shareholders and their vote on the proposed merger or consolidation.

Not all shareholders vote in favor of a merger or a consolidation. Under the MBCA and most state statutes, these **dissenting shareholders** are entitled to their appraisal rights. **Appraisal rights** allow shareholders to demand the value of their shares.

Shareholder Rights: Inspection of Books and Records

The MBCA gives shareholders the absolute right to examine shareholder lists. For other records (minutes, accounting), shareholders must give notice of their request. In addition to this mechanical requirement, some courts also require a **proper purpose**, which means a shareholder has a legitimate interest in reviewing corporate progress, financial status, and fiduciary responsibilities. Improper purposes are those related to use of corporate records to advance the shareholders' moral, religious, or political ideas.

Shareholder Rights: Transfer of Shares

Stock shares can have **transfer restrictions**, which are valid as long as the following requirements are met.

1. The restrictions must be necessary. Valid circumstances include family-owned corporations, employee-owned corporations, and corporations that need restrictions to comply with SEC registration exemptions (see Chapter 14).

2. The restrictions must be reasonable. Requiring that the shares first be offered to the board before they can be sold is reasonable; requiring that the shares be offered to all the other shareholders first may be unreasonable if there are more than five to ten shareholders.

3. The restrictions and/or their existence must be conspicuously noted on the stock shares.

THE DISSOLUTION OF A CORPORATION

A corporation can continue indefinitely unless its articles of incorporation limit its duration. Long before perpetuity, however, a corporation can be dissolved voluntarily or involuntarily.

Voluntary dissolution occurs when the shareholders agree to dissolve the corporation. This type of dissolution occurs in smaller corporations when the shareholders no longer get along, the business does not do well, or one of the shareholders is ill or dies. Under the MBCA, all shareholders (voting and nonvoting alike) vote on the issue of dissolution because all of them will be affected by it. Each state also has filing and publication requirements for dissolution.

An involuntary dissolution is one that is forced by some state agency, usually the state-level attorney's office. A dissolution can be forced because of fraud or failure to follow state law regarding reporting requirements for corporations.

Limited Liability Companies

The **limited liability company** (LLC), first created in 1997, is now available in 48 states and the District of Columbia. The LLC has actually been in existence for many years in Europe (known as a GMBH) and South America (*limitada*). The LLC is more of an aggregate form of business organization than an entity such as a corporation. Owners of an LLC are called members. An LLC provides limited liability (members lose only up to their capital contributions) and flow-through tax treatment similar to a partnership in that tax liability is assessed only at the member's level of income and not at the business level. An LLC has limited liability for all its owners, unlike a limited partnership, and all personal owners can participate in management without risking liability.

It has been said that the LLC combines the best of all of the business structures. However, this ideal creation, in order to enjoy the flow-through characteristics necessary for the tax break, must be distinguished from a corporation. The result is that LLCs are limited in duration, with most statutes allowing them to run for periods of 30 to 40 years. The point at which LLCs dissolve by statutory limitations has not yet arrived because LLCs did not exist until 1977. However, when those dissolutions come, the restructuring and recreation should create interesting issues among and between the owners of the LLCs.

FORMATION

An LLC is formed through the filing of a document called the **articles of organization**, which is filed with a centralized state agency. The name of the business formed must contain either "limited liability company," "L.L.C.," or "LLC."

SOURCES OF FUNDING

Members of an LLC make capital contributions in much the same way as partners make capital contributions.

LIABILITY

Members of an LLC have limited liability; the most they can lose is their capital contributions. Debts belong to the LLC, and creditors' rights lie with the LLC's assets, not the personal assets of the members. However, many states require that the nature of the business organization appear on the business cards and stationery of the company.

TAX CONSEQUENCES

The LLC enjoys the so-called flow-through treatment: The LLC does not pay taxes; income and losses are passed through to the members to be reported on their individual returns. LLC agreements must be drafted carefully to enjoy flow-through status.

MANAGEMENT AND CONTROL

Members of an LLC adopt an operating agreement that specifies the voting rights, withdrawal rights and issues, responsibilities of members, and how the LLC is to be managed. The members can agree to manage collectively, delegate authority to one member, or hire an outsider to manage the business.

TRANSFERABILITY OF INTEREST

A member's LLC interest is personal property and is transferable. However, the transferee does not become a member without approval by the majority of members. Members do not hold title to LLC property; the LLC owns the property, and each member has an interest in the LLC that reflects the property's value.

DISSOLUTION AND TERMINATION

Most LLC statutes provide that the LLC dissolves upon the withdrawal, death, or expulsion of a member. Some states permit judicial dissolution, and all states permit voluntary dissolution upon unanimous (usually written) consent of the owners.

Limited Liability Partnerships

A **limited liability partnership** (LLP) is a partnership with unique statutory protection for all its members.

FORMATION

Not all states have LLP statutes, but those with such statutes have strict formal requirements for the creation of an LLP. The failure to comply with these requirements results in a general partnership with full personal liability for all the partners.

The general requirements for LLP registration are filing (1) the name of the LLP (which must include LLP or Reg LLP), (2) the name of the registered agent, (3) the address, (4) the number of partners, and (5) a description of the business.

SOURCES OF FUNDING

As in partnerships and limited partnerships, LLP partners make capital contributions.

LIABILITY

In most of the states with LLP statutes, partners are shielded from liability for the negligence, wrongful acts, or misconduct of their partners. Other states provide more extensive protection, such as limited liability even for debts entered into by other partners. In order to attain this liability limitation, some states require, upon registration, evidence of adequate liability insurance. In some states, professional negligence by partners is not covered by the shield from liability.

TAX CONSEQUENCES

All LLP income is a flow-through or pass-through to partners.

MANAGEMENT AND CONTROL

Partners can manage without risking personal liability exposure because the LLP is identified as such and registered with the state.

TRANSFERABILITY

For tax and security regulation reasons, the transferability must be restricted and is generally governed by the same principles of transfer for limited partnerships.

DISSOLUTION AND TERMINATION

Causes similar to those for the dissolution of limited partnerships and notification to the state are required.

International Issues in Business Structure

Global trade has resulted in global business structures, with many companies discovering the benefits of **joint ventures**. A joint venture is a partnership of existing businesses for a limited time or a limited purpose. The existing businesses are then partners for that limited transaction or line of business. The Justice Department has relaxed antitrust merger rules to permit joint ventures so that U.S. firms can compete more effectively internationally. For example, Mobil and Exxon are involved in a joint oil exploration venture in the West Siberian Basin in Russia. The joint venture allows the combination of their experience and financing so that Russian negotiators can be persuaded to contract for the exploration rights.

In an attempt to break into the Japanese toy market, Toys "R" Us, Inc., entered into a joint venture with McDonald's Co., Ltd., a Japanese toy company with 20 percent of the market. Nestlé and Coca-Cola have formed a joint venture to market ready-to-drink coffees and teas; Nestlé's expertise is in dry goods (instant coffee) and Coca-Cola is a beverage company, so each plans to take advantage of the other's established reputation.

Business structures vary in other countries. In Germany, for example, a public company has both a board of directors and a shareholder advisory committee, which elects the board of directors. It is quite likely, however, that the shareholder advisory committee is composed of shareholders that are large institutional investors (such as banks) or representatives from labor unions.

Red Flags FOR MANAGERS

Even if you just begin doing business, alone or with someone else, and even without any agreements, you have liability, including risking your personal assets.

Before you begin doing business, decide what you want and need. If you want to have the losses and gains flow through to you on your personal income taxes, use a sole proprietorship, general partnership, or be a limited partner or part of an LLC, LLP, or Subchapter S corporation.

If you want to protect your personal assets, then you need to be a limited partner, part of an LLC, LLP, or corporation.

If you need to raise a great deal of capital, then a corporation with shareholders may be necessary.

Regardless of the type of business organization you choose, be sure that you follow all the steps for its creation and then follow the laws and regulations for its operation and filing requirements. When you are sloppy about paper work, fund use, and formalities, creditors can still pierce through that limited liability and get to your personal assets. Hold annual meetings, use resolutions, and honor the funds ownership of the company.

Summary

What are the various forms of business organization?

- Sole proprietorship—individual ownership and operation of a business
- Partnership—voluntary association of two or more persons as co-owners in a business for profit
- Corporation—an entity formed by statute that has the rights of a legal person along with limited liability for its shareholder owners
- Limited liability company—newer form of business organization in which liability is limited except for conduct that is illegal
- Limited liability partnership—newest form of business organization, in which partners' liability is limited

How is a partnership formed and operated?

- Uniform Partnership Act (UPA)—law on partnerships adopted in 49 states

- Revised Uniform Partnership Act (RUPA)—update of partnership law
- Partnership by implication—creation of a partnership by parties' conduct
- Partnership by estoppel—partnership that arises by perception of third parties of its existence
- Dissolution—when partner ceases to be associated with the partnership
- Limited partnership—partnership with two types of partners: general and limited
- General partner—full and personal liability partner
- Limited partner—partner whose personal liability is limited to capital contributions
- Uniform Limited Partnership Act (ULPA)—uniform law adopted in nearly every state
- Revised Uniform Limited Partnership Act (RULPA)—update of limited partnership law

How is a corporation formed and operated?

- Corporation—business organization that is a separate entity with limited liability and full transferability
- Domestic corporation—a corporation is domestic in the state in which its incorporation is filed
- Foreign corporation—category or label for corporation in all states except in state in which it is incorporated
- Professional corporation—entity with limited liability except for malpractice/negligence by its owners
- S corporation—IRS category of corporation with flow-through characteristics
- Model Business Corporation Act (MBCA)—uniform law adopted in approximately one-third of the states
- Articles of incorporation—document filed to organize a corporation
- Common stock—generally most voluminous type of corporate shares and usually allows shareholders to vote
- Preferred stock—ownership interest with priority over common stock
- Corporate veil—liability shield for corporate owners
- Watered shares—failure to pay par value for shares

- Business judgment rule—standard of liability for directors
- Corporate opportunity doctrine—fiduciary responsibility of directors with respect to investments
- Board of directors—policy-setting body of corporations
- Proxy—right to vote for another
- Pooling agreement—shareholder contract to vote a certain way
- Voting trust—separation of legal and equitable title in shares to ensure voting of shares in one way
- Dissenting shareholder—shareholder who objects to merger
- Appraisal rights—value of shares immediately before merger that is paid to dissenting shareholder

How is a limited liability company formed?

- Articles of organization
- Flow-through of income

How is a limited liability partnership formed?

- Register with state
- Flow-through of income
- May need proof of liability insurance

Key Terms

Questions and Problems

1. Gailey, Inc., incorporated in 1980, removed asbestos and mechanical insulation on contract jobs that required union labor. Richard Gailey had been the president, controlling shareholder, and director of Gailey, Inc. from its inception.

Universal Labs, Inc. was incorporated by Mr. Gailey in March 1984 to analyze asbestos samples and air samples and to perform general laboratory work. Mr. Gailey was the sole shareholder of Universal Labs.

As president and director of Gailey, Inc., Mr. Gailey directed Gailey to pay certain debts of Universal Labs. Subsequent to that, $14,500 was provided by Gailey, Inc. to Universal Labs to pay for the latter's start-up expenses and costs.

Gailey, Inc. filed a voluntary petition pursuant to Chapter 11 of the Bankruptcy Code on January 28, 1985. The case was converted to a Chapter 7 proceeding on September 30, 1985.

The trustee in bankruptcy filed suit alleging that Mr. Gailey usurped a corporate business opportunity belonging to Gailey, Inc., when he incorporated Universal Labs. Is the trustee correct? [*In re Gailey, Inc.,* 119 B.R. 504 (Bankr. W.D. Pa. 1990)]

2. Aztec Enterprises, Inc., was incorporated in Washington with a capital contribution of $500. Aztec's incorporator and sole stockholder was H. B. Hunting. Aztec operated a gravel-hauling business and was plagued with persistent working capital problems. Carl Olson, a frequent source of loans for Aztec, eventually acquired the firm. Mr. Olson, who had no corporate minutes or tax returns, personally paid Aztec's lease fees but did not pay when he had Aztec deliver gravel to his personal construction sites. Mr. Olson never had stock certificates issued to him. Despite annual gross sales of more than $800,000, Aztec was unable to pay its debts. Truckweld Equipment Company, a creditor of Aztec, brought suit to pierce the corporate veil and recover its debt from Mr. Olson. Can it pierce the corporate veil? [*Truckweld Equipment Co.* v. *Olson,* 618 P.2d 1017 (Wash. 1980)]

3. The SEC charged HealthSouth with inflating its earnings by $1.4 billion over a three-year period, with total inflated earnings of $2.5 billion over a decade. The case was the first one brought under the new provisions of Sarbanes-Oxley for financial fraud.

In a federal district court hearing in Alabama in which former CEO Richard Scrushy asked for the release of $70 million in his funds in order to pay legal fees and living expenses, the following information emerged:

- Two of the company's CFOs and its current CFO have been indicted for fraud.
- CFO William Owen recorded his conversations with Mr. Scrushy at the request of the FBI.
- Mr. Scrushy said on tape to Mr. Owen, "We just need to get those numbers where we want them to be. You're my guy. You've got the technology and the know-how."
- Mr. Scrushy sold $175 million in HealthSouth shares from the time the accounting fraud began.
- Mr. Scrushy's bookkeeper for his personal companies committed suicide in September 2002. His new bookkeeper, Mary Schabacker, indicated that all of Mr. Scrushy's five corporations owe debts to each other, with no intention to repay them.
- HealthSouth stock was delisted from the NYSE in 2002. It was listed at $15 per share in 2001 and was worth pennies one year later.
- Mr. Owen's wife told him that if he kept signing "phony financial statements" that he might go to jail.
- Mr. Scrushy maintained that he knew nothing about the accounting fraud and that Mr. Owens did it all. Mr. Scrushy was acquitted later of all securities fraud charges but then convicted of bribery and sentenced to 7 years in prison.
- The acting chairman of the HealthSouth board said, "We [directors] really don't know a lot about what has been occurring at the company."
- For seven years, one director was paid a consulting contract of $250,000 per year.
- One director purchased a $395,000 resort property as a partner with Mr. Scrushy.

- One director secured a $5.6 million contract to install glass at a hospital HealthSouth was constructing.

- MedCenterDirect.com had as investors HealthSouth, Mr. Scrushy's private investment company, six of HealthSouth's directors, and the wife of one of the HealthSouth directors.

- HealthSouth directed business to MedCenterDirect .com, almost $174 million last year.

- The audit committee and compensation committee were joint committees made up of the same directors.

- HealthSouth invested $2 million in the Acacia Venture Partners, a venture capital fund founded and run by C. Sage Givens, a director of HealthSouth. When a shareholder questioned her independence as a result, HealthSouth defended her board position.

- Ernst & Young served as HealthSouth's auditor. It earned $1.2 million for financial statement audits and $2.5 million for other services.

Discuss the legal issues that each of these revelations raises. Be sure to cover the changes that Sarbanes-Oxley would impose. Also, refer back to Chapter 7 and determine whether criminal charges could be brought.

4. Allan Jones sold a ski shop franchise to Edward Hamilton. Although Mr. Jones did not contribute equity to the business or share in the profits, he did give Mr. Hamilton advice and share his experience to help him get started. Most of Mr. Hamilton's capital came in the form of a loan from Union Bank. When Mr. Hamilton failed to pay, Union Bank sued Mr. Jones for payment under the theory that Mr. Jones was a partner by implication or estoppel. Was he? [*Union Bank* v. *Jones,* 411 A.2d 1338 (Vt. 1980)]

5. A. W. Ham Jr. served on the board of directors for Golden Nugget, Inc., a Nevada corporation. In 1969, while Mr. Ham was a director and legal counsel for Golden Nugget, he obtained a leasehold interest with an option to purchase in the California Club. The California Club is at 101 Fremont Street, Las Vegas, Nevada, and is located next to a series of properties on which Golden Nugget operates its casinos. Mr. Ham leased the property from his former wife. Golden Nugget was looking for property to expand and had, in fact, been expanding onto other lots in the area. Was there a breach of a corporate opportunity? What if Mr. Ham offers to lease the property to Golden Nugget? [*Ham* v. *Golden Nugget, Inc.,* 589 P.2d 173 (Nev. 1979)]

Understanding "Consider" Problems

13.1

THINK: THE UPA and RUPA require that partners share the profits in a business. A partner can work in the partnership, but a partner also shares in the profits. Partners are managers. Employees have set hours and work for others.

APPLY: Strazella and Spitzer are not sharing profits. They are working in the business, but they are not managing because Chaiken is telling them when they must work.

ANSWER: The court held that the two are not partners. Rather, they are employees. They are managed by another and do not share profits. Chaiken would owe wage taxes on the two.

13.2

THINK: When third parties are led to believe that a partnership exists, those who have created that impression have partnership liability. Partners are personally liable for any debts the partnership cannot pay.

APPLY: Mr. Pope allowed Triangle to believe that he and Mathis were partners. He verified their relationship. The partnership does not have enough money to pay Triangle.

ANSWER: Because Triangle was led to believe there was a partnership and extended credit, there is partnership liability. If the partnership does not have enough money, then the two partners are personally liable for the obligation to Triangle.

13.3

THINK: Under the principles of liability for directors and the protection of the business judgment rule, a director and board can make mistakes. They can make decisions that ultimately prove to be big mistakes, even in judgment. However, courts do not step in and, with hindsight, second-guess the directors. So long as the directors have given their time, thought, and effort to the decision and obtained independent advice, their judgment is protected from liability to shareholders, even if they are proven completely wrong.

APPLY: While the parties disagree over whether to hold day games or night games, the Cubs organization has articulated its reasons, rightly or wrongly.

ANSWER: The reasons show that the Cubs directors have devoted the time, energy, and thought necessary to make the decision and thus enjoy protection from liability under the business judgment rule.

Notes

1. The questions were actually a resurrection of questions asked by Judge Stanley Sporkin when he was dealing with all of the fraud cases from the savings and loan collapses in the early 1990s. [*Lincoln Savings & Loan Ass'n* v. *Wall*, 743 F. Supp. 901, at 920 (D.D.C. 1990)]

2. The final rules can be found at 17 C.F.R. § 205 (2003).

Securities Law

One of the methods for raising the capital needed for a corporation or partnership is to sell interests in them. Corporations sell shares, and partnerships sell limited partnership interests. Investors hope that the business will give them a profit on their investment (dividends on stock and interest income on bonds and other forms of securities) and that the value of their investment will grow as the business in which they have invested increases in value. The investment arrangement in theory is mutually beneficial. However, because people are so eager to have their money grow and because businesses need money for growth, the interests of business and investors are often at odds. Because of this inherent conflict of interest in the investment relationship, laws regulate investments at both state and federal levels. These laws, called securities laws, govern everything from the sale of securities to soliciting proxies from owners of securities. This chapter answers these questions: Why do we have securities laws, and what is their history? What requirements affect primary offerings of securities? How do securities laws regulate the secondary market? How do those laws protect shareholders in share and company acquisitions? ■

update ▶

For up-to-date legal news, click on "Author Updates" at

www.cengage.com/blaw/ jennings

October. This is one of the peculiarly dangerous months to speculate stocks in. The others are July, January, September, April, November, May, March, June, December, August, and February.

MARK TWAIN

Pudd'nhead Wilson

I should have taken off my salesman's hat and tried to be more like an accountant.[1]

MARK KAISER

Former CEO of U.S. Food Service

Sentenced to 7 years for overstating revenues by hundreds of millions

Total Enforcement Actions by the SEC

YEAR	TOTAL ENFORCEMENT ACTIONS INITIATED
1990	300
2000	500
2003	680
2004	897
2005	1039
2006	760
2007	1432

THE SEC'S ANNUAL REPORTS (2007 INCLUDES INVESTIGATIONS, ADMINISTRATIVE, AND CIVIL ACTIONS)

http://www.sec.gov (figures rounded for enforcement actions)

consider...

James Herman O'Hagan was a partner in the law firm of Dorsey & Whitney in Minneapolis, Minnesota. In July 1988, Grand Metropolitan PLC, a company based in London, retained Dorsey & Whitney as local counsel to represent it regarding a potential tender offer for common stock of Pillsbury Company.

Mr. O'Hagan did not work on the Grand Met matter, but on August 18, 1988, he began purchasing call options for Pillsbury stock. Each option gave him the right to purchase 100 shares of Pillsbury stock. By the end of September, Mr. O'Hagan owned more than 2,500 Pillsbury options. Also in September, Mr. O'Hagan purchased 5,000 shares of Pillsbury stock at $39 per share.

Grand Met announced its tender offer in October, and Pillsbury stock rose to $60 per share. Mr. O'Hagan sold his call options and made a profit of $4.3 million.

The SEC indicted Mr. O'Hagan on 57 counts of illegal trading on inside information. He says he did nothing wrong. Who is right?

History of Securities Law

Securities regulation began at the state level. In 1911, Kansas passed the first securities law, which regulated the initial sale of securities to members of the public. Some states followed the lead of Kansas, but state regulation was sparse.[2]

As a result, investors engaged in a great deal of speculation in stocks. Investors traded "on margin," which means they borrowed money to invest in stock and when the stock went up in value, they sold it, paid off the loan, and still made money. On a Friday in 1929, however, stock prices dropped on all the exchanges and continued to drop. Investors defaulted on the margin loans, lenders foreclosed on their properties, and the entire country was thrown into a depression.

Because of the 1929 market crash, Congress passed the **Securities Act of 1933** and the **Securities Exchange Act of 1934**, the former to regulate initial sales of stock by businesses and the latter to regulate the secondary trading of stock on the markets. These statutes and their accompanying regulations still govern the sale of securities today.

Primary Offering Regulation: The 1933 Securities Act

A **primary offering**—an offering by an issuer, which could be its first, known as an initial public offering (IPO)—is a sale of securities by the business itself. The 1933 act regulates these initial sales of securities.

WHAT IS A SECURITY?

The 1933 act applies only to the sale of **securities**. The language of the act itself is broad in the definition of *securities*, and approximately 20 items are considered securities, including notes; stocks; bonds; debentures; warrants; subscriptions; voting-trust certificates; rights to oil, gas, and minerals; and limited partnership interests.

The landmark case on the definition of a security is *SEC v. W. J. Howey Co.*, 328 U.S. 293 (1946). In holding that the sale of interests in Florida citrus groves constituted the sale of securities, the U.S. Supreme Court defined a security as "a contract, transaction, or scheme whereby a person invests his money in a common enterprise and is led to expect profits solely from the efforts of a promoter or a third party." In recent years, the only type of arrangement the U.S. Supreme Court has excluded from this definition is an employer pension plan in which employees are not required to make contributions. The exclusion of these plans from securities laws is probably based on the fact that employees are afforded other statutory protections (see Chapter 17 and the discussion of the Employment Retirement Income Security Act and the Pension Protection Act of 2006).

consider. 14.1

Determine whether general partnership interests would be considered securities for purposes of the 1933 Securities Act. (Analysis appears at the end of the chapter.)

REGULATING PRIMARY OFFERINGS: REGISTRATION

The **Securities and Exchange Commission** (SEC) is the administrative agency responsible for regulating the sale of securities under both the 1933 and 1934 acts. The SEC can issue injunctions, institute criminal proceedings, enter into consent decrees, handle enforcement, and promulgate rules.

The rules promulgated by the SEC provide the details and processes for the registration of securities, financial reporting, and stock exchange operations. The SEC has a complete staff of lawyers, accountants, financial analysts, and other experts for the review of informational filings and the enforcement of the securities laws.

REGULATING PRIMARY OFFERINGS: EXEMPTIONS

Unless an **exemption** applies, anyone selling securities must complete certain filing requirements before the securities can be sold legally. The two types of exemptions are exempt securities and exempt transactions. These exemptions work only for the 1933 act.

Exempt Securities

Certain investments, called **exempt securities**, have been excluded specifically from coverage of the 1933 act. The following is a list of some of the exemptions:

1. Securities (bonds, etc.) issued by federal, state, county, or municipal governments for public purposes
2. Commercial paper (includes notes, checks, and drafts with a maturity date under nine months)
3. Banks, savings and loans, and religious and charitable organizations
4. Insurance policies
5. Annuities
6. Securities of common carriers (those regulated by the Interstate Commerce Commission)
7. Stock dividends and stock splits
8. Charitable bonds

Exempt Transactions

Exempt transactions are more complicated than exempt securities; more details are required to comply with the exempt transaction standards. The following subsections discuss these transaction exemptions, which are summarized in Exhibit 14.1.

The Intrastate Offering Exemption

To qualify for the intrastate exemption, the investors (offerees) and issuer must all be residents of the same state. (If there is one out-of-state offeree, the exemption will not apply.) Further, the issuer must meet the following requirements:

1. Eighty percent of its assets must be located in the state.
2. Eighty percent of its income must be earned from operations within the state.
3. Eighty percent of the proceeds from the sale must be used on operations within the state.

EXHIBIT   14.1   1933 Securities Act Transaction Exemptions

NAME	SIZE LIMITATION	GENERAL SOLICITATION	OFFEREE/ BUYER LIMITATION	RESALE LIMITATION	DISCLOSURE	PUBLIC OFFERING	SEC FILING	TIME
Intrastate exemption, 15 U.S.C. §77(c)(a) (11)	No	No	Buyers must be residents of state of incorporation; triple 80% requirements	Yes, stock transfer restrictions Rule 147— 9 months	No	Yes, in state	No	No restriction
Small-offering or small-issues exemption, 15 U.S.C. §77D, Regulation A	$5,000,000	Yes	Short-form registration required (offering circular)	No	Offering circular	Yes	Short-form	Short-form 12-month period
Rule 504 Regulation D	$1,000,000* or less (in 12-month period)	Yes	None, unlimited accredited and nonaccredited alike	Yes	No†	Yes	Notice of offering within 15 days of first sale	12-month period
Rule 505, Regulation D	Up to $5,000,000	No	No more than 35, excluding accredited investors	Yes—2 years†	Yes, to non-accredited†	No	Notice of offering (15 days)	12-month period
Rule 506, Regulation D	No	No	Unlimited accredited and 35 nonaccredited investors; (nonaccredited must be sophisticated)	Yes, stock restrictions	Yes, to non-accredited†	No	Notice of offering (15 days)	12-month period

*In certain circumstances. $2,000,000 if blue sky registration (504). Up to $7,500,000 if blue sky registration (505).
†Must verify purchaser is buying for himself; must have restrictions on shares.

Under the SEC's Rule 147, some restrictions apply to the transfer of exempt intrastate offerings, including a nine-month transfer restriction to state residents only.

Small-Offering Exemption: Regulation A

Although it is not a true exemption, **Regulation A** is a shortcut method of registration. The lengthy, complicated processes of full registration are simplified in that only a short-form registration statement is filed. Regulation A applies to issues of $5 million or less during any 12-month period.

Small-Offering Exemption: Regulation D

Regulation D creates a three-tiered exemption structure that consists of Rules 504, 505, and 506, which permits sales without registration. Sellers are, however, required to file a Form D informational statement about the sale. Rule 501 of Regulation D lists the definitions of various terms used in the three exemptions. For example, an **accredited investor** is any investor who at the time of the sale is a large company or an individual with substantial assets.

The three tiers of Regulation D exemptions are as follows:

- The **Rule 504** exemption applies to offerings of $1 million or less (within any 12-month period). Sales of stock to directors, officers, and employees are not counted in the $1 million limitation. Recent changes permit the use of the Rule 504 exemption in offerings of up to $2 million, provided the offering is registered under a state **blue sky law**.

- The **Rule 505** exemption covers sales of up to $5 million, provided no more than 35 nonaccredited investors are involved. Again, with state registration, it is possible to take a Rule 505 exemption up to $7.5 million. Issuers qualifying under this exemption cannot engage in public advertising. Also, if the issue is sold to both accredited and nonaccredited investors, the issuer must give all buyers a prospectus.

- The **Rule 506** exemption has no dollar limitation, but the number and type of investors are limited. Any number of accredited investors is allowed, but the number of nonaccredited investors is limited to 35, and these investors must be sophisticated (capable of evaluating the offering and its risk). Under a Rule 506 exemption, the resale of the shares is subject to some restrictions.

Corporate Reorganizations

If a firm is issuing new shares of stock under a Chapter 11 bankruptcy reorganization supervised by a bankruptcy court, registration is not necessary, provided court approval is obtained for the issue.

WHAT MUST BE FILED: DOCUMENTS AND INFORMATION FOR REGISTRATION

If none of the exemptions applies, the offeror of the securities must go through the registration process. The offeror (issuer) must file a **registration statement (S-1)** and sample **prospectus** with the SEC.

The SEC has 20 days to act on the filing, after which the registration statement automatically becomes effective. However, the de facto time period has become

30 days, and the average processing time for the SEC in 2007 was 25.5 days. The SEC takes some form of action within that time period. The SEC need not actually approve or disapprove the offering within that time limit as long as a **comment letter** or **deficiency letter** is issued. A new registration, for a first-time offeror, generally takes about six months to get through the SEC. In 2000, a highpoint for the market in terms of both IPOs and securities issuances, the SEC reviewed 3,970 proposed stock offerings, of which 1,350 were IPOs. In 2003, the SEC reviewed only 370 IPOs, an additional 180 stock offerings, and 30 exempt offerings. However, in 2007, the number of IPOs exceeded the 2000 level of IPOs by 16 percent. The drop-off in 2008 was dramatic, with as few as four IPOs per month.

The SEC's guide in reviewing the registration materials is the **full-disclosure standard**. The SEC does not pass on the merits of the offering or the soundness of the investment; rather, it simply requires that certain information be supplied. The SEC does not verify the accuracy of the information, only that it is on file.

Before the registration statement is filed, the issuer is very much restricted in what can be done to sell the securities. And even after the registration is filed but is not yet effective, the issuer is restricted.

However, the issuer can run a **tombstone ad**, as shown in Exhibit 14.2, which simply announces that securities will be sold and who will have information—but clearly indicates that the ad is not an offer. Also, before the registration statement becomes effective, the issuer can send out a **red herring prospectus**, which has printed in red at the top that the registration is not yet effective. These red herrings are a way to get out information while waiting for SEC approval.

Exhibit 14.3 is a diagram of federal securities registration and exemptions.

VIOLATIONS OF THE 1933 ACT

Section 11 Violations

Section 11 of the 1933 act imposes civil and criminal liability on those who do not comply with the requirements for registration statements. The lack of full disclosures or false material information in the registration statement is a Section 11 violation.

Who Is Liable?

All individuals who signed the registration statement—each director and officer of the issuing corporation and every accountant, engineer, appraiser, attorney, geologist, or other expert whose input was used in the preparation of the statement—is liable under Section 11. Underwriters are also included as potential defendants. Experts (such as accountants, engineers, appraisers, lawyers) are liable only for the information they provided.

Defenses for Section 11 Violations

Because proving that a **material misstatement** or omission was made is part of the investor's case, proving that the statement or omission was immaterial is a valid defense. If the investor knew of the misstatement or omission and purchased the stock anyway, there is no Section 11 liability. The **due diligence** defense is one that allows defendants (nonissuers) to show that they were acting reasonably in preparing and signing the registration statement. This issue of due diligence was at the heart of Sarbanes-Oxley, the legislation that changed both financial reporting and accountability (see the Primer on Sarbanes-Oxley on page 329).

EXHIBIT   14.2 Sample of a Tombstone Ad

This announcement is neither an offer to sell nor a solicitation of offers to buy any of these securities. The offering is made only by the Prospectus, copies of which may be obtained in any State or jurisdiction in which this announcement is circulated only from such of the underwriters as may legally offer these securities in such State.

NEW ISSUE

January 22, 1999

$50,000,000

<allaire>

2,500,000 Shares
Common Stock

NASDAQ Symbol: "ALLR"

Price $20 Per Share

Prior to the offering there had been no public market for these securities. Allaire Corporation develops, markets and supports application development and server software for a wide range of Web development, from building static Web pages to developing high volume, interactive Web applications.

Credit Suisse First Boston

Dain Rauscher Wessels
a division of Dain Rauscher Incorporated
NationsBanc Montgomery Securities LLC

Hambrecht & Quist

Invemed Associates, Inc.

Needham & Company, Inc.

Charles Schwab & Co., Inc.

Tucker Anthony
Incorporated
C.E. Unterberg, Towbin

Wedbush Morgan Securities

CREDIT SUISSE | FIRST BOSTON

EXHIBIT   14.3 Federal Securities Registration and Exemptions

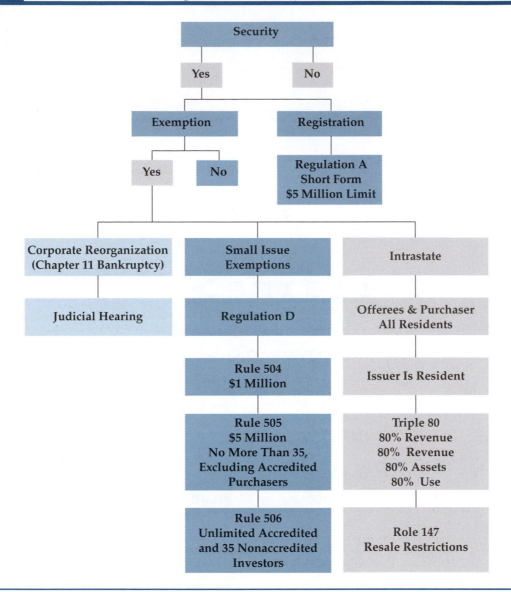

Escott v. *BarChris Constr. Corp.* (Case 14.1) is the leading case on Section 11 liability. Ironically, although the case is from 1968, it remains the classic example of
the type of financial overstatement of a company's performance that SOX was
passed to address.

CASE 14.1

Escott v. BarChris Constr. Corp.
283 F. Supp. 643 (S.D.N.Y. 1968)

BOWLING FOR FRAUD: RIGHT UP OUR ALLEY

FACTS

BarChris was a bowling alley company established in 1946. The bowling industry grew rapidly when automatic pin resetters went on the market in the mid-1950s. BarChris began a program of rapid expansion. BarChris used two methods of financing the construction of these alleys, both of which substantially drained the company's cash flow.

In 1960 BarChris's cash flow picture was troublesome, and it sold debentures. The debenture issue was registered with the SEC, approved, and sold. In spite of the cash boost from the sale, BarChris was still experiencing financial difficulties and declared bankruptcy in October 1962. The debenture holders were not paid their interest; BarChris defaulted.

The purchasers of the BarChris debentures brought suit under Section 11 of the 1933 act. They claimed that the registration statement filed by BarChris contained false information and failed to disclose certain material information. The suit claimed that the audited financial statements prepared by a CPA firm were inaccurate and full of omissions. The following chart summarizes the problems with the financial statements submitted with the registration statements.

1. *1960 Earnings*

  (a) *Sales*

Per prospectus	$9,165,320
Correct figure	8,511,420
Overstatement	$ 653,900

  (b) *Net Operating Income*

Per prospectus	$1,742,801
Correct figure	1,496,196
Overstatement	$ 246,605

  (c) *Earnings per Share*

Per prospectus	$ .75
Correct figure	.65
Overstatement	$ .10

2. *1960 Balance Sheet*

  Current Assets

Per prospectus	$4,524,021
Correct figure	3,914,332
Overstatement	$ 609,689

3. *Contingent Liabilities as of December 31, 1960, on Alternative Method of Financing*

Per prospectus	$ 750,000
Correct figure	1,125,795
Understatement	$ 375,795
Capitol Lanes should have been shown as a direct liability	$ 325,000

4. *Contingent Liabilities as of April 30, 1961*

Per prospectus	$ 825,000
Correct figure	1,443,853
Understatement	$ 618,853
Capitol Lanes should have been shown as a direct liability	$ 314,166

5. *Earnings Figures for Quarter Ending March 31, 1961*

  (a) *Sales*

Per prospectus	$2,138,455
Correct figure	1,618,645
Overstatement	$ 519,810

  (b) *Gross Profit*

Per prospectus	$ 483,121
Correct figure	252,366
Overstatement	$ 230,755

6. *Backlog as of March 31, 1961*

Per prospectus	$6,905,000
Correct figure	2,415,000
Overstatement	$4,490,000

7. *Failure to Disclose Officers' Loans Outstanding and Unpaid on May 16, 1961* $386,615

8. *Failure to Disclose Use of Proceeds in Manner Not Revealed in Prospectus: Approx.* $1,160,000

9. *Failure to Disclose Customers' Delinquencies in May 1961 and BarChris's Potential Liability with Respect Thereto: Over* $1,350,000

The federal district court reviewed each of the defendants' conduct, including officers, directors, attorneys, and the auditors (Peat, Marwick, Mitchell & Co.[3]).

CONTINUED

JUDICIAL OPINION

McLEAN, District Judge

Vitolo and Pugliese. They were the founders of the business who stuck with it to the end. Vitolo and Pugliese are each men of limited education. It is not hard to believe that for them the prospectus was difficult reading, if indeed they read it at all.

But whether it was or not is irrelevant. The liability of a director who signs a registration statement does not depend upon whether or not he read it or, if he did, whether or not he understood what he was reading.

All in all, the position of Vitolo and Pugliese is not significantly different, for present purposes, from Russo's. They could not have believed that the registration statement was wholly true and that no material facts had been omitted. And in any case, there is nothing to show that they made any investigation of anything which they may not have known about or understood. They have not proved their due diligence defenses.

Kircher. Kircher was treasurer of BarChris and its chief financial officer. He is a certified public accountant and an intelligent man. He was thoroughly familiar with BarChris's financial affairs. He knew of the customers' delinquency problems. He knew how the financing proceeds were to be applied and he saw to it that they were so applied. He arranged the officers' loans and he knew all the facts concerning them.

Kircher has not proved his due diligence defenses.

Birnbaum. Birnbaum was a young lawyer, admitted to the bar in 1957, who, after brief periods of employment by two different law firms and an equally brief period of practicing in his own firm, was employed by BarChris as house counsel and assistant secretary in October 1960. Unfortunately for him, he became secretary and director of BarChris on April 17, 1961, after the first version of the registration statement had been filed with the Securities and Exchange Commission. He signed the later amendments, thereby becoming responsible for the accuracy of the prospectus in its final form.

It seems probable that Birnbaum did not know of many of the inaccuracies in the prospectus. He must, however, have appreciated some of them. In any case, he made no investigation and relied on the others to get it right. Having failed to make such an investigation, he did not have reasonable ground to believe that all these statements were true. Birnbaum has not established his due diligence defenses except as to the audited 1960 exhibits.

Auslander. Auslander was an "outside" director, i.e., one who was not an officer of BarChris. Auslander was elected a director on April 17, 1961. The registration statement in its original form had already been filed, of course without his signature. On May 10, 1961, he signed a signature page for the first amendment to the registration statement which was filed on May 11, 1961. This was a separate sheet without any document attached. Auslander did not know that it was a signature page for a registration statement. He vaguely understood that it was something "for the SEC."

Auslander never saw a copy of the registration statement in its final form. It is true that Auslander became a director on the eve of the financing. He had little opportunity to familiarize himself with the company's affairs.

Section 11 imposes liability in the first instance upon a director, no matter how new he is.

Peat, Marwick. Peat, Marwick's work was in general charge of a member of the firm, Cummings, and more immediately in charge of Peat, Marwick's manager, Logan. Most of the actual work was performed by a senior accountant, Berardi, who had junior assistants, one of whom was Kennedy.

Berardi was then about thirty years old. He was not yet a CPA. He had had no previous experience with the bowling industry. This was his first job as a senior accountant. He could hardly have been given a more difficult assignment.

After obtaining a little background information on BarChris by talking to Logan and reviewing Peat, Marwick's work papers on its 1959 audit, Berardi examined the results of test checks of BarChris's accounting procedures which one of the junior accountants had made, and he prepared an "internal control questionnaire" and an "audit program." Thereafter, for a few days subsequent to December 30, 1960, he inspected BarChris's inventories and examined certain alley construction. Finally, on January 13, 1961, he began his auditing work which he carried on substantially continuously until it was completed on February 24, 1961. Toward the close of the work, Logan reviewed it and made various comments and suggestions to Berardi.

Accountants should not be held to a standard higher than that recognized in their profession. I do not do so here. Berardi's review did not come up to that standard. He did not take some of the steps which Peat, Marwick's written program prescribed. He did not spend an adequate amount of time on a task of this magnitude. Most important of all, he was too easily satisfied with glib answers to his inquiries.

This is not to say that he should have made a complete audit. But there were enough danger signals in the materials which he did examine to require some further investigation on his part. Generally accepted accounting standards required such further investigation under these circumstances. It is not always sufficient merely to ask questions.

CASE QUESTIONS

1. How much time transpired between the sale of the debentures and BarChris's bankruptcy?

2. Were all of the errors and omissions material?

3. Make a list of the shortcomings of the defendants in their due diligence.

Penalties for Violations of Section 11

Violations of Section 11 carry maximum penalties of $10,000, and/or five years imprisonment. In addition, the SEC has the authority to bring suit seeking an injunction to stop sales based on false or omitted information in the registration statement. Purchasers harmed by the false or omitted statements have a right of civil suit in federal district court for recovery.

The Private Securities Litigation Reform Act of 1995 (PSLRA) limits attorneys' fees to a reasonable percentage of the amount recovered or the agreed-upon settlement amount.

One important part of PSLRA is the so-called safe-harbor protection. With certain precautions and qualifications, companies can now make forward-looking predictions for company performance in materials given to investors. The company is not held liable for these statements about its future as long as it makes the required SEC disclosures on the nature of forward-looking statements.

Section 12 Violations

Section 12 carries the same criminal penalties as Section 11 and covers selling securities without registration and without an exemption and selling securities before the effective date of the registration statement.

A PRIMER ON SARBANES–OXLEY

On July 30, 2002, PL 107-204 (HR 3763), known as the Sarbanes-Oxley Act of 2002, with several actual names of the Investor Confidence Act, the Public Accounting and Corporate Accountability Act, Public Company Accounting Reform and Investor Protection Act of 2002, became law.

PART I: THE CREATION OF THE PUBLIC COMPANY ACCOUNTING OVERSIGHT BOARD

This section of SOX established a quasi-governmental entity called the **Public Company Accounting Oversight Board (PCAOB,** but called "Peek-a-Boo"**)** under the direction of the SEC to oversee the audit of public companies covered by the federal securities laws (the 1933 and 1934 Acts).

PART II: AUDITOR INDEPENDENCE

This portion of SOX is a bit of a statutory code of ethics for public accounting firms. Accounting firms that audit

publicly traded companies cannot also perform consulting services for those companies.

Another conflicts prohibition is that the audit firm cannot audit, for one year, a company that has one of its former employees as a member of senior management. For example, if a partner from PwC is hired by Xena Corporation as its controller or CFO, PwC cannot be the auditor (for SEC purposes) for Xena for one year.

PART III: CORPORATE RESPONSIBILITY

This section of SOX makes audit committees of publicly traded companies responsible for the hiring, compensation, and oversight of the public accounting firm responsible for conducting the company's audits and certifying its financial statements. All members of the audit committee must be members of the company's board of directors, and must be independent. (See Chapter 13.)

The company's CEO and CFO are required to certify the financial statements the company files with the SEC as

CONTINUED

being fair in their representation of the company's financial condition and accurate "in all material respects." CFOs and CEOs are now required to forfeit any bonuses and compensation that were received based on financial reports that subsequently had to be restated because they were not materially accurate or fair in their disclosures.

Part IV: Enhanced Financial Disclosures

This section of SOX is the accounting section. Again, in direct response to the Enron issues, Congress directed the SEC to do something about accounting practices and take control of accounting and reporting rules.

Also under this section, directors and officers now have only two days, not ten, to report their transactions in the stock of their companies.

Finally, the infamous Section 404 or, simply called, "404," of SOX requires companies to include an internal control report and assessment as part of the 10-K annual reports.

Part V: Analyst Conflicts of Interest

The issue of analysts and their conflicts was one that contributed to the failure of the markets to heed the warning signals at Enron, WorldCom, and other companies. The SEC has promulgated rules that address the supervision, compensation, and evaluation of securities analysts by investment bankers and their conflicts of interest.

Part VIII: Corporate and Criminal Fraud Accountability

This section of SOX is the expansion, clean-up, and criminal law portion that created new crimes, increased

penalties on existing crimes, and elaborated on the elements required to prove already existing crimes. Also known as the Corporate and Criminal Fraud Accountability Act of 2002, most of this SOX section was covered in Chapter 7.

This section extended the time for bringing a civil law suit for securities fraud to not later than the earlier of (1) five years after the date of the alleged violation; or (2) two years after its discovery. This section also prohibits retaliation against employees in publicly traded companies who assist in an investigation of possible federal violations or file or participate in a shareholder suit for fraud against the company (see Chapter 17).

Part IX: White-Collar Criminal Penalty Enhancements

Most of this section was covered in Chapter 7, but it also contains some remarkable grants of authority to the SEC. For example, this section gives the SEC the authority to freeze bonus, incentive, and other payoffs to corporate officers during an ongoing investigation at the company for possible violations of federal securities laws. The SEC has the authority to banish violating officers and directors from the securities markets as well as from working at a publicly traded company in the future.

Source: Adapted from Jennings, *Business Ethics: Case Studies and Selected Readings*, 6th ed., 2009.

The Securities Exchange Act of 1934

The **Securities Exchange Act of 1934** regulates securities and their issuers once they are on the market. Securities sales, brokers, dealers, and exchanges are all regulated under the 1934 act. In addition, the act requires public disclosure of financial information for certain corporations. In effect, the 1934 act is responsible for the regulation of the securities marketplace.

Securities Registration

Under the 1934 act, all securities traded on a national stock exchange must be registered. In addition, any issuer with over $10 million in assets and 500 or more shareholders must register its equity stock (not bonds) under the 1934 act if those shares are traded in interstate commerce. This registration is in addition to all the filing requirements for issuing discussed under the 1933 act.

PERIODIC FILING UNDER THE 1934 ACT: THOSE ALPHABET REPORTS

In addition to the one-time registration required under the 1934 act, those same companies (national stock exchange companies or those with 500 or more shareholders and $10 million in assets) must comply with the periodic reporting requirements imposed by the SEC. Each quarter, these firms must file a **10-Q form**, which is basically a quarterly financial report. An annual report, the **10-K form**, must be filed by the company at the end of its fiscal year. Any unusual events—bankruptcies, spin-offs, takeovers, and other changes in company control—must be reported on the **8-K form**. The 10-Qs and 10-Ks are the reports the CEO and CFO must certify under SOX. The increased penalties for the certifying officers if the financial statements turn out to be false run up to 20 years and $10 million.

THE 1934 ACT ANTIFRAUD PROVISION: 10(B)

In addition to regulating the reporting of information, the 1934 act regulates the propriety of sales in the marketplace. **Section 10(b)** and **Rule 10b-5** (the SEC regulation on 10(b)) are the antifraud provisions of the 1934 act. These sections are statutory versions of common law fraud. If the idea of the free market is to work, all buyers and sellers must have access to the same information. To withhold information is to commit fraud and is a violation of Section 10(b).

Application of Section 10(b)

Of all the provisions of the 1934 act, Section 10(b) has the broadest application. It applies to all sales of securities: exempt, stock-exchange-listed, over-the-counter, public, private, small, and large. Section 10(b) requires only that interstate commerce be involved in the sales transaction.

Proof of Section 10(b) Violation: Corporations Running Afoul

The corporate dissemination violation of 10(b) occurs when a corporation has not been forthcoming with material information, whether positive or negative, about the company, its performance, and its future. In 2000, the SEC promulgated the **"fair-disclosure rule" (Regulation FD)**, which requires that material information about the company be made available to everyone at the same time.

To determine whether an item is material, the question is, "Is this the type of information that would affect the buying or selling decision?" Examples of items that have been held to be material are drops in earnings or lack of approval by the FDA for a new drug.

One of the most famous corporate (and individual) 10(b) cases is *SEC* v. *Texas Gulf Sulphur Co.*, 401 F.2d 833 (2d Cir. 1968). In that case, Texas Gulf Sulphur was involved in test-drilling operations in Canada. Early tests indicated that the company would make a substantial strike. Press releases did not indicate the richness of the strike. Corporate officers, geologists, and relatives bought stock before the richness of the find was finally disclosed, and the price of the stock soared. The court found that the overly pessimistic press release was misleading under 10(b). The company and the individual purchasers both ran afoul of 10(b).

One issue that resulted in 200 SEC investigations in 2007 and 2008 was that of backdating stock options. Stock options were revalued, but the cost of the options, or their strike price, was not reflected accurately in company financial reports and the costs for the options were material.

ethical *issues*

John Mackey, the CEO of Whole Foods, using the name Rahodeb (a scrambled version of his wife's name, Deborah), posted more than 1,000 messages in chat rooms that were dedicated to stock trading. During the period that Mr. Mackey was posting messages, Whole Foods stock quadrupled in value. The messages were flattering to Whole Foods (even to Mackey himself, with one posting reading, "I like Mackey's haircut. I think he looks cute."[a]). The postings were also negative about Wild Oats, a company Whole Foods was trying to acquire, even as the anonymous postings continued. On February 24, 2005, Mackey posted the following about Wild Oats CEO Perry Odak, "Perhaps the OATS Board will wake up and dump Odak and bring in a visionary and highly competent CEO."[b] Mackey was particularly active during that time frame, having posted 17 messages on September 5, 2005, and another 17 on November 11, 2005, with plenty of postings on the days in between.[c] Referred to as "sock-puppeting," it is a common practice for online identities to be concealed in order to praise, defend, garner allies, and engage in a host of other functions accomplished more effectively when identity is concealed.

When his identity was discovered, Mackey apologized and halted the postings. The apology came just six days after the first reports on Rahodeb's identity were reported in the *Wall Street Journal*. The Federal Trade Commission collected the postings he made to show that to allow the merger with Wild Oats would reduce competition in the marketplace. The identity of Rahodeb became public after the FTC filing.

John Coffee, a securities law and corporate governance expert and professor at Columbia law school, said, "This evidence raises more doubts about his sanity than his criminality. The merger is a major business strategy, and he's undercut it with reckless, self-destructive behavior. It's a little weird, like catching him as a Peeping Tom."[d] A crisis communication expert said, "It's more of an embarrassment than an issue of profound ethical and legal consequence."[e] Where do you stand on this issue? Do you think this situation is a case of insider trading? Was this move a fair one on Mackey's part? What about sock-puppeting in general? Is it ethical?

[a] Andrew Martin, "CEO of Whole Foods Extolled His Stock Online," *New York Times*, July 13, 2007, pp. C4.
[b] *Id.*
[c] Greg Farrell and Paul Davidson, "Whole Foods' CEO Was Busy Guy Online," *USA Today*, July 13, 2007, p. 4B.
[d] *Id.*
[e] *Id.*

Proof of a Violation: How Individuals Run Afoul of 10(b)

In simplest form, an individual's 10(b) violation occurs when one side to a securities transaction has information not generally available to the public and the transaction proceeds without disclosure. For example, a seller who knows of a pending merger (something that causes a jump in share price) when the rest of the investing public does not, and who then sells his shares to an unwitting buyer without disclosure of the pending merger, commits a 10(b) violation. If an owner of shares gives a buyer false or misleading information, the owner-seller is liable under 10(b).

Who Runs Afoul: The Extent of Section 10(b) Liability

Anyone who has access to information not readily available to the public is covered under 10(b). Officers, directors, and large shareholders are included in this group. However, 10(b) also applies to employees who know things about their company that are not yet public. Section 10(b) also applies to those who get information from these corporate **insiders**. These people are called **tippees**. For example, relatives of officers, directors, and employees would be considered tippees if they were given nonpublic information.

The scope of Section 10(b) has been a critical question. *United States* v. *O'Hagan* (Case 14.2) is a U.S. Supreme Court ruling on 10(b)'s application. The case answers the chapter's opening Consider.

CASE 14.2

United States v. *O'Hagan*
521 U.S. 657 (1997)

PILLSBURY DOUGH BOY: THE LAWYER/INSIDER WHO CASHED IN

FACTS

James Herman O'Hagan (respondent) was a partner in the law firm of Dorsey & Whitney in Minneapolis, Minnesota. In July 1988, Grand Metropolitan PLC (Grand Met), a company based in London, retained Dorsey & Whitney as local counsel to represent it regarding a potential tender offer for common stock of Pillsbury Company (based in Minneapolis).

Mr. O'Hagan did not work on the Grand Met matter, so on August 18, 1988, he began purchasing call options for Pillsbury stock. Each option gave him the right to purchase 100 shares of Pillsbury stock. By the end of September, Mr. O'Hagan owned more than 2,500 Pillsbury options. Also in September, Mr. O'Hagan purchased 5,000 shares of Pillsbury stock at $39 per share.

Grand Met announced its tender offer in October, and Pillsbury stock rose to $60 per share. Mr. O'Hagan sold his call options and made a profit of $4.3 million.

The SEC indicted Mr. O'Hagan on 57 counts of illegal trading on inside information and other charges. The SEC alleged that Mr. O'Hagan used his profits from the Pillsbury options to conceal his previous embezzlement and conversion of his clients' trust funds. Mr. O'Hagan was convicted by a jury on all 57 counts and sentenced to 41 months in prison. A divided Court of Appeals reversed the conviction, and the SEC appealed.

JUDICIAL OPINION

GINSBURG, Justice

The "misappropriation theory" holds that a person commits fraud "in connection with" a securities transaction, and thereby violates § 10(b) and Rule 10b-5, when he misappropriates confidential information for securities trading purposes, in breach of a duty owed to the source of the information. Under this theory, a fiduciary's undisclosed, self-serving use of a principal's information to purchase or sell securities, in breach of a duty of loyalty and confidentiality, defrauds the principal of the exclusive use of that information.

We agree with the Government that misappropriation, as just defined, satisfies § 10(b)'s requirement that

chargeable conduct involve a "deceptive device or contrivance" used "in connection with" the purchase or sale of securities. We observe, first, that misappropriators, as the Government describes them, deal in deception. A fiduciary who "[pretends] loyalty to the principal while secretly converting the principal's information for personal gain" "dupes" or defrauds the principal.

Although informational disparity is inevitable in the securities markets, investors likely would hesitate to venture their capital in a market where trading based on misappropriated nonpublic information is unchecked by law. An investor's informational disadvantage vis-à-vis a misappropriator with material, nonpublic information stems from contrivance, not luck; it is a disadvantage that cannot be overcome with research or skill.

In sum, considering the inhibiting impact on market participation of trading on misappropriated information, and the congressional purposes underlying § 10(b), it makes scant sense to hold a lawyer like O'Hagan a § 10(b) violator if he works for a law firm representing the target of a tender offer, but not if he works for a law firm representing the bidder.

[W]e emphasize . . . two sturdy safeguards Congress has provided regarding scienter. To establish a criminal violation of Rule 10b-5, the Government must prove that a person "willfully" violated the provision. In addition, the statute's "requirement of the presence of culpable intent as a necessary element of the offense does much to destroy any force in the argument that application of the [statute]" in circumstances such as O'Hagan's is unjust.

Reversed.

CASE QUESTIONS

1. What does the court say the misappropriation theory is?

2. Did Mr. O'Hagan make money from nonpublic information?

3. Could others have done research and obtained the same information Mr. O'Hagan had?

Running Afoul Using the Net: E-Commerce and Insider Trading

One of the trends that has emerged in stock trading is the practice of "pump and dump." This practice uses the rapid communication of the Internet to disperse information about a company so that the market price is affected. Those who have pumped the stock then sell, or dump, their shares when their efforts on the Internet have caused a sufficient jump in the price. If the posted information is false, the pumping is a 10(b) violation.

consider 14.2

The cast of characters:

David Pajacin, a 29-year-old former trader at Goldman Sachs, worked there for 5.5 months after graduating from Notre Dame in 2000 and drifted from job to job

Eugene Plotkin, also a Goldman Sachs employee (until his arrest in April 2006), a Harvard graduate, and 49th in the United States in professional Latin dancing

Stanislav Shpigelman, a 23-year-old analyst at Merrill Lynch

Sonja Anticevic, 63-year-old aunt of Mr. Pajacin and a resident of Croatia, a seamstress retired from her work in an underwear factory

Monica Vujovic, Mr. Pajacin's girlfriend, a stripper he met at a "gentleman's club," who earned between $6,000 and $7,000 per night

The first three, Pajacin, Plotkin, and Shpigelman, met, beginning in 2004, at Spa 88, a Russian day spa in Manhattan. There the three would exchange information about pending deals, such as P&G preparing to buy Gillette. The three also recruited Nickolaus Shuster, a telemarketer from Newark, to move to Wisconsin and get a job as a forklift operator at the company responsible for printing *BusinessWeek*. His job was then to give to the three, prior to release of the magazine, the stocks mentioned favorably in the "Inside Wall Street" column in the magazine.

To disguise the trading, the three used Pajacin's aunt and girlfriend to set up accounts internationally and on Ameritrade. In fact, Ameritrade has a note in its logs from one of its representatives that when a Ms. Vujovic called to change the limits on her account, "The caller does not sound like a female, by no means." The caller was Mr. Pajacin, who upped the trade risk on the account in order to accommodate what would be the trio's undoing.

The three got information that Adidas-Salomon was about to acquire Reebok. The three acquired Reebok stock, and when the acquisition was announced publicly the aunt was able to sell her Reebok shares (through her nephew) for a $2 million gain; the girlfriend made $310,000. All of the cast would net $6.2 million from all their various accounts on the Reebok stock they had purchased in advance of the announcement. However, that kind of trading catches the SEC's eyes, particularly because Pajacin and the others were responsible for 80 percent of the trading in the stock in the days leading up to the announcement. As one government lawyer put it, "They just got greedy."

Who violated 10(b)? (Analysis appears at the end of the chapter.)

Source: http://www.sec.gov; Jenny Anderson and Michael J. De La Merced, "An Insider-Trading Case With a B-Movie Plot," *New York Times*, April 30, 2006, pp. BU1, 7.

. . . .

The Requirement of Scienter Under Section 10(b)

A conviction under 10(b) cannot be based on negligence—that is, the failure to discover financial information. Because 10(b) is a criminal statute, violators must have some intent to defraud or knowledge of wrongdoing, or **scienter**. Convictions are only for knowing the financial information but failing to disclose it. In *Ernst & Ernst v. Hochfelder*, 425 U.S. 185 (1978), the Supreme Court held that an accounting firm that had negligently performed an audit of a business based on a fraud could not be held liable under 10(b) because, although the accounting firm made a mistake, it had no intent to defraud.

Penalties for Running Afoul of Section 10(b)

SOX changes have more than doubled the penalties of those earlier reforms. Violations of 10(b) carry prison terms of up to 25 years plus penalties. The bankruptcy code was amended to prohibit the discharge of these debts in bankruptcy so that repayment becomes a lifetime obligation. In addition to these criminal penalties, the SEC is authorized to bring civil actions against the companies and its officers and collect civil penalties for financial reporting violations, insider trading, and other activities related to 10(b) violations.

To increase the likelihood of corporate employees coming forward with information on fraudulent financial reporting, the SEC can pay bounties of up to 10 percent of the amount recovered to informants who report violations. Sarbanes-Oxley includes protections for company whistle-blowers who report violations to the SEC.

INSIDER TRADING AND SHORT-SWING PROFITS

The 1934 act also has a form of a strict liability statute for insider trading. Officers, directors, and 10 percent or more shareholders have greater access to inside information. They will always have access to information that is not yet available to the public. **Section 16** of the 1934 act is a *per se* liability section designed to deal with stock trading by corporate insiders, who are defined as officers, directors, and 10 percent shareholders of those companies and are required to be registered under the 1934 act.

Under 16(a), officers, directors, and 10 percent shareholders (10 percent of any class of stock) are required to file reports declaring their holdings. In addition, they must file updated reports after any change in ownership (purchase, sale, or transfer). Any changes in ownership must be reported within one day.

Under 16(b), officers, directors, and 10 percent shareholders are required to give to the corporation any **short-swing profits**—that is, profits earned on the sale and purchase or purchase and sale of stock during any six-month period. For example, suppose Director Cadigan of a New York Stock Exchange company engaged in the following transactions:

April 11, 2009—Ms. Cadigan buys 200 shares of her corporation's stock at $50 each.

April 30, 2009—Ms. Cadigan sells 200 shares at $30 each.

May 15, 2009—Ms. Cadigan buys 200 shares at $20 each.

The SEC will match the highest sale with the lowest purchase. Ms. Cadigan has a profit of $10 per share even though she has a net loss. This profit must be returned to the corporation. It is irrelevant whether the officer, director, or 10 percent shareholder actually used inside information.

These rules also apply to stock options. To minimize or eliminate the incentives for making the financial picture brighter for purposes of increasing the value of stock options, some companies, such as GE and Coca-Cola, have changed their compensation plans to eliminate options and offer employees special classes of stock that have predetermined values or that are awarded only after a period of years following the release of earnings.

REGULATING VOTING INFORMATION

At one time, shareholders could give their proxies to the company just by endorsing the backs of their dividend checks; proxies then were obtained easily and without much disclosure. The 1934 act changed the way proxies were solicited. With the same philosophy used for registration, the SEC required full disclosure to be the goal of all **proxy solicitations**. To achieve that goal, the SEC now requires prior filing and adequate representation of shareholder interests.

The Proxy Statement

Under Section 14 of the 1934 act, all companies required to register under the act must file their proxy materials with the SEC at least 10 days before those materials are to be sent. Proxy materials include the proxy statement and all other solicitation materials that will be sent to shareholders. Exhibit 14.4 shows a sample proxy.

Shareholder Proposals

Because the purpose of Section 14 is full disclosure, the representation of views other than those of corporate management is important in proxy solicitations. Shareholders can submit proposals to be included in proxy solicitation materials. The proposing shareholder has the right of a 200-word statement on the proposal in the materials. These proposals must be related to business operations, as opposed to social, moral, religious, and political views. During the Vietnam era, many shareholders wanted to include proposals in proxy materials for companies that were war suppliers. Their proposals centered on the political opposition to the war and not the business practices of the company. Through 2003, shareholders focused on social issues such as human rights initiatives for companies' international operations. However, as shown in Exhibit 14.5, attention has shifted back to corporate governance proposals.

Remedies for Violations of Section 14

If proxies are solicited without following the Section 14 guidelines, the proxies are invalid. They must then be resolicited, and if the meeting has been held in which the invalid proxies were used, the action taken at the meeting can be set aside.

The Foreign Corrupt Practices Act

The **Foreign Corrupt Practices Act** (FCPA) was passed in 1977 as an amendment to the 1934 Securities Exchange Act. (See Chapter 6 for more details.)

State Securities Laws

Today all states have their own securities laws. In addition to federal laws, all issuers are required to follow state **blue sky laws** in all states in which their securities are sold. Two types of state securities laws govern registration: those that follow the SEC standards for full disclosure and those that follow a merit review standard. Under SEC standards a filing is required, and as long as all the required information is there the offering will be approved for public sale. Under a **merit review** standard the regulatory agency responsible for securities enforcement can actually examine a filed offering for its merits as to adequate capitalization, excessive stock ownership by the promoters, and penny-stock problems. These agencies apply a general standard that the offering must be "fair, just, and equitable."

Exhibit 14.6 provides a summary of securities regulation under state and federal law.

EXHIBIT 14.4 Sample Proxy

P **ARIZONA PUBLIC SERVICE COMPANY**   PROXY CARD
P.O. Box 53999
Phoenix, Arizona 85072-3999

R **THIS PROXY IS SOLICITED ON BEHALF OF THE BOARD OF DIRECTORS FOR THE ANNUAL MEETING ON MAY 21, 1996.**

O The undersigned hereby appoints O. Mark DeMichele and Nancy C. Loftin, and each of them, proxies for the undersigned, each with full power of substitution, to attend the annual meeting of shareholders of Arizona Public Service Company to be held May 21, 1996, at 10:00a.m., Phoenix time, and at any adjournment thereof, and to vote as specified in this Proxy all the shares of stock of the company which the undersigned would be entitled to vote if personally present.

X

Voting with respect to the election of directors and the proposals may be indicated on the reverse of this card. Nominees for director are: O. Mark Demichele, Martha O. Hesse, Marianne Moody Jennings, Robert G. Matlock, Jaron B. Norberg, John R. Norton III, William J. Post, Donald M. Riley, **Y** Henry B. Sargent, Wilma W. Schwada, Richard Snell, Dianne C. Walker, Ben F. Williams Jr., and Thomas G. Woods, Jr.

Your vote is important! Please sign, date, and mail promptly in the enclosed postage-paid envelope.

This proxy, when properly executed, will be voted in the manner directed herein. If no direction is made, it will be voted FOR the election of directors and FOR the proposals.

The board of Directors recommends a vote FOR the election of directors.

The board of Directors recommends a vote FOR the proposal to amend Article Sixth of the Company's Articles of Incorporation.

The board of Directors recommends a vote FOR the proposal to amend Article Fifth of the Company's Articles of Incorporation.

1. Election of Directors (see other side)

FOR*   WITHHELD
☐   ☐
*For all nominees, except withhold vote for the following:
_____

2. Proposal to amend Article Sixth of the Company's Articles of Incorporation.

FOR AGAINST ABSTAIN
☐   ☐   ☐

3. Proposal to amend article Fifth of the Company's Articles of Incorporation.

FOR AGAINST ABSTAIN
☐   ☐   ☐

4.   In their discretion, the proxies are to vote upon such other business as may properly come before the meeting.

_____   _____
Signature   date
_____   _____
Signature   date
Please sign as your name(s) appear to the left. Joint owners should both sign. Fiduciaries, attorneys, corporate officers, etc., should state their capacities.

Source: Reprinted with permission of the Arizona Public Service Company.

EXHIBIT	14.5 Shareholder Focus in Business Strategy

TOPICS IN SHAREHOLDER PROPOSALS FOR 2007–2008 ANNUAL MEETINGS	PERCENTAGE OF TOTAL PROPOSALS
Social and environmental	31%
Structure and election of board	28%
Advisory vote on compensation	25%
Independent board chairperson	6.2%
Other director related	7.1%
Cumulate voting	3%
Miscellaneous	Remaining

EXHIBIT	14.6 State and Federal Securities Law

1933 ACT	1934 ACT	BLUE SKY
S1—Registration statement Financial information Officers/directors Prospectus 20-day effective date, deficiency letter *Section 11—Filing false registration statement* Liability: Anyone named in prospectus or offering expert materials for it Material, false statement; privity not required unless longer than one year Defenses; due diligence; buyer's knowledge *Section 12—Failure to file; selling before effective date; False prospectus* Materials; false statement; privity required Defenses; due diligence; buyer's knowledge *Penalties* $100,000 and/or five years (criminal/civil suit)	*Application* 500 or more shareholders with $10 million or more in assets or listed on national exchange Sec. 10b—insider trading/fraud *10K* Annual reports *10Q* Quarterly report *Foreign Corrupt Practices Act* Financial reports Internal controls Applies to 1933 and 1934 act registrants *Section 14* Proxy registration Compensation disclosure *Section 16A* Officers, directors, 10% shareholders Sales registration *Section 16B* Short-swing profit *Penalties* Penalties plus up to 25 years	Separate financial certification penalties under Sarbanes-Oxley State securities registration Merit vs. disclosure standards Federally exempt securities may still need to register at state level

International Issues in Securities Laws

The following policy statement from the State Department summarizes the nature of international capital markets today: "The United States Government is committed to an international system which provides for a high degree of freedom in the movement of trade and investment flows."

The United States has ten stock exchanges; Germany, eight; France, seven; and Switzerland, seven. The United Kingdom, Japan, Canada, the Netherlands, Belgium, Luxembourg, Norway, Kuwait, Australia, and many other countries have at least one stock exchange each.

A directive from the European Union has developed uniform requirements for disclosure in primary offering. Often called a "listing of particulars" instead of a "prospectus," uniform information is given to shareholders prior to their purchases. One difficulty that must be resolved is that accounting practices outside the United States are not uniform. Often these practices create different financial pictures for investors.

Insider trading has been prosecuted vigorously in the United States for the past 30 years. European enforcement has been limited. In addition to the lack of enforcement, little regulatory structure for investigation and prosecution is in place.

The United States is the only country with proxy disclosure requirements. Although Japan regulates solicitations, Germany requires only advance notice of meetings.

Red Flags FOR MANAGERS

- Before you sell investment interests, be sure that you look at state and federal laws on securities (1933 Securities Act and state blue sky laws).

- When you are preparing financial statements, remember your company must make full disclosures in those reports.

- Under the 1934 Securities Exchange Act, you cannot trade in your company's stock when you have information not available to the public. You can't pass that information along. For example, telling your father about a merger at your company makes your father a tippee. Even if your father gets a friend to buy your company's stock, there is still a 10(b) violation.

- SOX requires auditors and companies to follow best practices rules on independence of auditors and board members. You can't have a consultant to your company as a member of the audit committee.

- Stock options are covered under insider trading rules and are tricky, in everything from their exercise to carrying their costs in financial reports.

- Remember, when in doubt, ask because the SEC wins most of the time.

Summary

What requirements affect primary offerings?

- Primary offering—sale of securities by the business in which interests are offered
- Security—investment in a common enterprise with profits to come from efforts of others

Why do we have securities laws, and what is their history?

- Securities Act of 1933—federal law regulating initial sales of securities
- Securities Exchange Act of 1934—federal law regulating securities and companies in the secondary market
  - Amendments include SOX and PSLRA

How do securities laws regulate the secondary market?

- 10-Q—periodic reporting forms required of 1934 act companies
- SOX and certification of financial reports by CEO and CFO
- 10-K—periodic reporting forms required of 1934 act companies
- 8-K—periodic reporting forms required of 1934 act companies
- Section 10(b)—antifraud provision of Securities Exchange Act
- Rule 10b-5—SEC regulation on antifraud provision of Securities Exchange Act
- Insider—person with access to nonpublic information about a company
- Tippee—person who gains nonpublic information from an insider
- "Fair-disclosure rule" (Regulation FD)—SEC regulation on disclosure to analysts
- Section 16—portion of 1934 act regulating short-swing profits by officers, directors, or 10 percent shareholders
- Short-swing profits—gain on sale and purchase or purchase and sale of securities within a six-month period
- Proxy solicitations—formal paperwork requesting authority to vote on behalf of another

- Blue sky laws—state securities registration regulations
- Merit review—regulation of merits of an offering as opposed to disclosure
- SEC—federal agency responsible for enforcing federal securities laws
- Exemption—security not required to be registered
- Exempt transaction—offering not required to be registered
- Regulation D—small offering exemption rules
- Accredited investor—investor who meets threshold standards for assets and income
- Rules 504, 505, 506—portion of Regulation D affording exemptions for variously structured offerings
- Registration statement—disclosure statement filed by the offeror with the SEC
- Prospectus—formal document explaining offering or any ad or written materials describing offering
- Comment letter—request by SEC for more information
- Deficiency letter—request by SEC for more information
- Full-disclosure standard—review for information, not a review on the merits
- Tombstone ad—ad announcing offering that can be run prior to effective date of registration statement
- Red herring prospectus—redlined prospectus that can be given to potential purchasers prior to effective date of registration statement
- Material misstatement—false information that would affect the decision to buy or sell
- Section 11—portion of 1933 act that provides for liability for false statements or omissions in registration statements
- Due diligence—defense of good faith and full effort to Section 11 charges
- Section 12—portion of 1933 act that provides for liability for selling without registration or exemption before effective date or with a false prospectus
- SOX—numerous protections on certifications and disclosures

Key Terms

8-K form *331*
10-K form *331*
10-Q form *331*
accredited investor *323*
blue sky laws *323*
comment letter *324*
deficiency letter *324*
due diligence *324*
exempt securities *321*
exempt transactions *321*
exemption *321*
"fair-disclosure rule"
   (Regulation FD) *331*
Foreign Corrupt Practice Act *336*
full-disclosure standard *324*

insiders *332*
material misstatement *324*
merit review *336*
per se 335
primary offering *320*
prospectus *323*
proxy solicitations *336*
Public Company Accounting
   Oversight Board (PCAOB, but
   called "Peek-a-Boo") *329*
red herring prospectus *324*
registration statement (S-1) *323*
Regulation A *323*
Regulation D *323*
Rule 10b-5 *331*

Rule 504 *323*
Rule 505 *323*
Rule 506 *323*
scienter 334
Section 10(b) *331*
Section 16 *335*
securities *320*
Securities Act of 1933 *320*
Securities Exchange
   Act of 1934 *320*
Securities Exchange
   Commission *321*
short-swing profits *335*
tippees *332*
tombstone ad *324*

Questions and Problems

1. The Farmer's Cooperative of Arkansas (Co-Op) was an agricultural cooperative that had approximately 23,000 members. In order to raise money to support its general business operations, the Co-Op sold promissory notes payable on demand by the holder. The notes were uncollateralized and uninsured and paid a variable rate of interest that was adjusted to make it higher than the rate paid by local financial institutions. The notes were offered to members and nonmembers and were marketed as an "investment program." Advertisements for the notes, which appeared in the Co-Op newsletter, read in part: "YOUR CO-OP has more than $11,000,000 in assets to stand behind your investments. The Investment is not Federal [*sic*] insured but it is . . . Safe."

Despite the assurance, the Co-Op filed for bankruptcy in 1984. At the time of the bankruptcy filing, over 1,600 people held notes worth a total of $10 million.

After the bankruptcy filing, a class of note holders filed suit against Arthur Young & Co., alleging that Young had failed to follow generally accepted accounting principles in its audit, specifically with respect to the valuation of the Co-Op's major asset, a gasohol plant. The note holders claimed that if Young had properly treated the plant in its audited financials, they would not have purchased the notes. The petitioners were awarded $6.1 million in damages by the federal district court. Are the notes securities? [*Reves* v. *Ernst & Young,* 494 U.S. 56 (1990)]

2. In August 1994, Mervyn Cooper, a psychotherapist, was providing marriage counseling to a Lockheed executive. The executive had been assigned to conduct the due diligence (review of the accuracy of the books and records) of Martin Marietta, a company with which Lockheed was going to merge.

At his August 22, 1994, session with Mr. Cooper, the executive revealed to him the pending, but nonpublic, merger. Following his session with the executive, Mr. Cooper contacted a friend, Kenneth Rottenberg, and told him about the pending merger. They agreed that Mr. Rottenberg would open a brokerage account so they could buy Lockheed call options and common stocks and then share in the profits.

When Mr. Rottenberg went to some brokerage offices to set up an account, he was warned by a broker about the risks of call options. Mr. Rottenberg told the broker that Lockheed would announce a major business combination shortly and that he would not lose his money.

Did Mr. Rottenberg and Mr. Cooper violate Section 10(b)? What about the broker? [*SEC* v. *Mervyn Cooper and Kenneth E. Rottenberg,* No. 95–8535 (C.D. Cal. 1995)]

3. Steve Hindi is an animal rights activist who owns $5,000 in Pepsi stock. He discovered that Pepsi advertises in bull rings in Spain and Mexico, and he has attended annual shareholder meetings and put forward shareholder proposals to have the company halt the practice. His proposal did not pass, but he did not give up easily and started a Web site to increase pressure on the company.

Pepsi has withdrawn from bullfighting ads in Mexico but continues with them in Spain. Mr. Hindi continues his quest. Should the proposal have been approved? Does Mr. Hindi run any risk with his Web site activism?

4. Beginning in March 1981, R. Foster Winans was a *Wall Street Journal* reporter and one of the writers of the "Heard on the Street" column (the "Heard" column), a widely read and influential column in the *Journal*. David Carpenter worked as a news clerk at the *Journal* from December 1981 through May 1983. Kenneth Felis, who was a stockbroker at the brokerage house of Kidder Peabody, had been brought to that firm by another Kidder Peabody stockbroker, Peter Brant, Mr. Felis's longtime friend who later became the government's key witness in this case.

Mr. Winans participated in a scheme with Mr. Brant and later Mr. Felis and Mr. Carpenter in which he agreed to provide the two stockbrokers (Mr. Brant and Mr. Felis) with securities-related information that was scheduled to appear in "Heard" columns; based on this advance information, the two brokers would buy or sell the subject securities. Mr. Carpenter, who was involved in a private, personal, nonbusiness relationship with Mr. Winans, served primarily as a messenger for the conspirators. During 1983 and early 1984, these defen-dants made prepublication trades on the basis of their advance knowledge of approximately 27 *Wall Street Journal* "Heard" columns, although not all of those columns were written by Mr. Winans. Generally, he would inform Mr. Brant of an article's subject the day before its scheduled publication, usually by calls from a pay phone and often using a fictitious name. The net profits from the scheme approached $690,000. Was this scheme a 10(b) violation? [*United States* v. *Carpenter,* 791 F.2d 1024 (2d Cir. 1986); *affirmed, Carpenter v United States,* 484 U.S. 19 (1987)]

5. Vincent Chiarella was employed as a printer in a financial printing firm that handled the printing for takeover bids. Although the firm names were left out of the financial materials and inserted at the last moment, Mr. Chiarella was able to deduce who was being taken over and by whom from other information in the reports being printed. Using this information, Mr. Chiarella was able to dabble in the stock market over a 14-month period for a net gain of $30,000. After an SEC investigation, he signed a consent decree that required him to return all of his profits to the sellers he purchased from during that 14-month period. He was then indicted for violation of 10(b) of the 1934 act and the SEC's Rule 10b-5. Did Mr. Chiarella violate 10b-5? [*Chiarella* v. *United States,* 445 U.S. 222 (1980)]

Understanding "Consider" Problems

14.1

THINK: The *Howey* definition is that securities are investments in a common enterprise with profits to come from the efforts of others.

APPLY: Even though partnerships are investments in a common enterprise, we learned in Chapter 13 that each partner is required to contribute work and effort to the partnership. General partners, unless otherwise speci-fied, are not paid salaries for their work and effort in making the partnership work. Because of this obligation to work and the full liability exposure, the results from investing in a partnership do not come primarily from the efforts of others but through the partnership itself.

ANSWER: A general partnership interest is not a secu-rity for purposes of the 1933 act.

Now determine whether the following are securi-ties under the 1933 Securities Act.

- Limited partnership interests
- Limited liability company interests
- Limited liability partnership interests
- Oil and gas leases

- Limited partnership in an oil field
- Options to buy tickets for the World Series if your team makes it to that point

14.2

THINK: Section 10(b) prohibits trading on information that is not yet available publicly. Section 10(b) requires some breach of a duty by the person who acquires the information. That employee can be anyone who has ac-cess to nonpublic information. Tippees of insiders are also covered.

APPLY: The use of advance information on a merger by an employee is insider trading. The use of information not yet available to the public is insider trading.

ANSWER: The cast of characters included insiders (Goldman employees) and anyone to whom they dis-closed the information: friends and family were tippees in this case. Also, the forklift driver was an employee who breached a duty to his employer by releasing non-public information.

Notes

1. "Ahold Ex-Official Sentenced," *New York Times,* May 18, 2007, p. C2.

2. For more on the history of securities law, see the Web site and the *Instructor's Manual*.

3. Peat, Marwick, Mitchell was one of the Big 8 accounting firms that existed during the 1960s and 1970s. These firms did all the audits on publicly traded companies. During the 1980s, the firms merged down to the Big 5. With the demise of Andersen following Enron, the Big 4 accounting firms remain.

15

Business Property

The Vatican Library. The House of Windsor. The estate of Princess Diana. Barney. NASCAR. *Shrek*. The common thread? They all have lucrative arrangements for the licensing of their images and symbols. The law affords protection for these images and symbols even though the property right is a bundle of images and feelings about a person, business, or logo. According to the *National Law Journal*, intellectual property, particularly with the rise of Internet commerce, remains the fastest-growing legal specialty.

This chapter covers the rights of businesses and their property. Property comes in different forms: personal, intellectual, and real. The rights and protections differ for each type. What does a business own? What are the types of business property? What are the rights and issues in personal property owned by a business? What statutory protections exist for intellectual property? What issues of property protection exist in international business operations? Protecting the goodwill that symbols, names, and motifs provide for a business is an important part of the ongoing success of a business.[1]

update

For up-to-date legal news, click on "Author Updates" at

www.cengage.com/blaw/ jennings

Possession is nine points of the law. No, it's not. Paperwork is.

Harvard Business Review, September/October 1995

We must take care to guard against two extremes equally prejudicial: the one, that men of ability, who have employed their time for the service of the community, may not be deprived of their just merits, and the reward for their ingenuity and labour; the other, that the world may not be deprived of improvements, nor the progress of the arts retarded.

Sayre v. Moore, 102 Eng. Rep. 138, 140 (1785)

consider...

Victor and Cathy Moseley owned and operated an adult toy, gag gift, and lingerie shop that they called Victor's Little Secret near Elizabethtown, Kentucky. The store advertised its grand opening in a publication for the Fort Knox base, and an army colonel notified Victoria's Secret of the shop's name and merchandise. Victoria's Secret owns 750 stores around the country and distributes 400 million catalogs each year via U.S. mail. Two of Victoria's Secret's stores were located in Louisville, Kentucky, a short drive from Elizabethtown and Fort Knox.

Legal counsel for Victoria's Secret asked the Moseleys to stop using the name Victor's Secret because of possible confusion over the trademark. Are the Moseleys infringing the trademark, image, and name of Victoria's Secret?

What Can a Business Own? Personal Property: The Tangible Kind

When we see a Dreyer's or Edy's Ice Cream truck driving along beside us, we understand that Dreyer's or Edy's Ice Cream owns that truck; it is a part of the Dreyer/Edy fleet and is carried as business equipment on the books of the Dreyer/Edy corporation. If someone took that truck, it would be theft, and Dreyer's or Edy's would be entitled to compensation if the truck were damaged or destroyed by the theft. Dreyer's or Edy's would also be entitled to compensation if someone hit the truck in an accident and damaged it. Owning a truck gives you certain rights of ownership. The delivery truck is **tangible property**. Tangible property is the type of property we can see and touch. Delivery trucks, desks, computers, inventory, and the building and land in which a business is located are all forms of tangible property. We have specific laws governing real and personal property rights for tangible property. We have laws to protect us against theft of our property and laws that provide remedies if someone harms or destroys that property.

TYPES OF PERSONAL PROPERTY

An ice cream truck is one example of a form of business personal property—equipment. Everything from the laser printer in the office to the Thermos brand water coolers that construction crews have attached to their company trucks is business equipment. Businesses also have personal property interests in their inventory or the goods they hold for sale to customers.

TRANSFER OF PERSONAL PROPERTY

Business property that is equipment or inventory may or may not have **documents of title**. Vehicles in a company's fleet have the standard title documents for motor vehicles. Other types of tangible personal property that would have title documents include the corporate jet and even purebred animals. Title to these forms of personal property is transferred when the document of title passes.

Other forms of business property do not have any formal documents of title. Computers, desks, and file cabinets are typical forms of business property that do not have title documents. These forms of personal property are transferred by a **bill of sale**. A bill of sale provides all the proof necessary to establish ownership of personal property that does not have a title document.

What Can a Business Own? Personal Property: The Intangible or Intellectual Kind

On the ice cream trucks referred to earlier, you see painted the signature brown and white stripes that are part of the ice cream's packaging. You recognize the distinctive writing, "Dreyer's" or "Edy's Grand Ice Cream." You know the truck from its distinctive paint and writing probably before you even read the name "Dreyer's" or "Edy's." That distinctive color scheme, name, and writing are also business property. The recognition and goodwill that come from those brown stripes and the name are **intangible property** that are also protected. These protections include Dreyer's/Edy's right to prevent others from using their distinctive names and colors, which represent the goodwill and reputation of the companies. The name, colors, stripes, and symbols represent a bundle of valuable rights for the business.

Forms of intangible property, also called **intellectual property**, include patents, copyrights, trademarks, trade names, and trade dress. Intellectual property is protected by federal, international, and common law.

PROTECTION FOR BUSINESS INTELLECTUAL PROPERTY

This section of the chapter covers the statutory protections for intellectual property.

Patents
Patents provide exclusive use rights when registered with the U.S. Patent Office. So fundamental is the protection of new products and processes that the protection for inventors is found in Article 1, Section 8, of the U.S. Constitution.

Patents come in three basic types. *Utility or function patents* cover machines, processes, and improvements to existing devices. For example, a computerized method for tracking a dry cleaner's inventory of clothing is protected by a patent. Prior to 1995, this type of patent was valid for 17 years. However, with GATT (see Chapter 6 for more information on this treaty) provisions, the U.S. protection was extended to 20 years in 1995. *Design patents* are those that protect the features of a product. The lace configuration on Eve of Milady bridal gowns and Procter & Gamble's method for elasticized legs on its disposable diapers are examples of product designs protected by patent. Design patents are granted for 14 years. Finally, *plant patents* protect new forms of plants and hybrids. Plant patents also carry a 20-year protection.

During these exclusive rights periods of 14 and 20 years, the patent holder has the sole rights for profits on sales. Anyone who sells or uses a patented product or process without the consent of the patent holder has committed patent infringement. **Infringement** entitles the patent holder to a statutory action for damages.

Copyrights

Patents protect inventors. **Copyrights** protect authors of books, magazine articles, plays, movies, songs, dances, recordings, and so on, as well as the creators of photographs. A copyright protects the expression of ideas. A copyright gives the holder of the copyright the exclusive right to sell, control, or license the copyrighted work. A copyright exists automatically for works created after 1989. Although the placement of the traditional copyright symbol (©) is not required, it is recommended. Further, the existence of a copyright in the United States is recognized in all nations that have signed the Berne Convention. Under the terms of the Berne Convention and U.S. law, copyright registration is not required, but it is recommended. Registration is a means of preventing someone violating the copyright from claiming a lack of knowledge about the work's protection. In order to register a copyright, the creator need only file two copies of the work with the Copyright Office in Washington, D.C. Without copyright registration, the owner cannot bring a suit for copyright infringement.

A copyright runs for the life of the creator plus 70 years. If the work produced was done by an employee of a business, the business then registers the copyright. These employer copyrights run for 120 years from the time of creation or 95 years from publication of the work, whichever is shorter. Mattel just won a verdict against one of its former employees for taking the Bratz doll design, developed while he still worked for the company, to competitor MGA. MGA will be required to pay royalties to Mattel for infringement as well as for the decline in sales of Mattel's Barbie dolls as a result of the Bratz doll development. These time limits for protection have been expanding over the years with the most recent extension, from 50 to 70 years, passed with the **Sonny Bono Copyright Term Extension Act** (CTEA). The late Representative Bono was concerned because copyrights he held and those held by many others, such as the copyright on the cartoon character Mickey Mouse, were about to expire. Even though the Constitution prohibits granting copyrights in perpetuity, a clear trend in congressional actions favors extending that protection period.

A copyright holder has control over the use of the created work. Control covers reproduction, distribution, public performances, derivative works, and public displays. Some copyright holders assign or license these rights to others in exchange for royalties. For example, most songwriters assign their rights for public performances of their songs to the American Society of Composers, Authors, and Publishers (ASCAP) and Broadcast Music, Inc. (BMI), who then pay the writers each time their song is used, according to a previously determined schedule of fees. An international fee schedule for payment for tapes, CDs, and records is also in place; it could be a flat fee, a per-minute fee, a per-record fee, or a per-song fee. The rates of the Copyright Royalty Tribunal are the greater of 9.1 cents or 1.75 cents per minute. Iron Butterfly's *In-a-Gadda-Da-Vida* will cost you $38 to play, but the BoxTops, *The Letter*, at only 2 minutes, will run you 9.1 cents.

Damages for copyright infringement include the profits made by the infringer, actual costs, attorney fees, and any other expenses associated with the infringement action. A court can order all illegal copies destroyed and issue an injunction that halts distribution of the illegal copies. In addition to civil recovery for the damages from infringement, federal criminal penalties for copyright infringement can be imposed when the infringement was willful and for "commercial advantage or private financial gain."

Technology has created new issues in copyright infringement, particularly in the areas of copyrighted software and music, with the availability of digital technology. For example, an MIT student uploaded and downloaded copyrighted software programs and then gave fellow students passwords for access. The result was that students at MIT enjoyed free access to the Internet at a cost of $1 million to the system's owners. However, the student did not charge for the access and thus realized no personal financial gain from the project. Technically, no violation of the copyright laws occurred.

As a result of this case, music producers and software developers added protection technology to their copyrighted products and lobbied for a change in copyright law, which came with the **Digital Millennium Copyright Act** in 1998. This act criminalizes the circumvention of protection technology in order to make copies of copyrighted materials as well as assisting others, providing expertise, or manufacturing products to circumvent protection technology. Circumvention and facilitating circumvention are now violations of copyright laws. The liability has also been extended to those who facilitate the infringement via downloading programs. Individuals who maneuver around encryption devices and those who hire them to avoid those devices, as in the case of industrial espionage, may face criminal sanctions.

Under the **Computer Software Copyright Act of 1980**, all software can be copyrighted, whether it is written in ordinary language (source code) or machine language (object code). Although software copyrights do not cover methods of operation (such as menus), they do cover the underlying programs themselves.

Fair Use and Copyrights

When the copyright laws were amended in 1976, one change permitted "fair use" of copyrighted materials. **Fair use** is occasional and spontaneous use of copyrighted materials for limited purposes—for example, a short quote from a copyrighted work. Fair use also allows instructors to reproduce a page or chart from a copyrighted work to use in the classroom; and copies of book pages can be made for research purposes. The three key questions for fair use are:

1. Is the use for commercial or nonprofit/educational use?
2. Is the work large, small, song, poem, book? Using a sentence from a book is different from using a sentence from a poem.
3. What is the effect of the use on the copyrighted work? If you copy a book, the author and publisher lose sales. If you use a clip from a film, folks may rent or buy the film and you may actually increase sales.

One interesting question that has arisen is the relationship between the notion of fair use and the prohibitions under the Digital Millennium Copyright Act. Can a professor circumvent protection technology for fair use in the classroom? Some feel the professor can do so if he has purchased the work. In other words, the professor can use an excerpt from the Beatles' *White Album* if the professor owns that album.

Fair use does run into First Amendment issues. For example, satirical works use the lyrics and speech of others as a form of social commentary such as those found in *Mad Magazine* and *Saturday Night Live.* The First Amendment protects social commentary, and the copyright laws protect original work. *Campbell* v. *Acuff-Rose Music, Inc.* (Case 15.1) involves an issue of a parody of copyrighted material and balancing First Amendment rights with copyright protection.

CASE 15.1

Campbell v. *Acuff–Rose Music, Inc.*
510 U.S. 569 (1994)

JUSTICE SOUTER DOES THE PRETTY WOMAN RAP

FACTS

2 Live Crew, a popular rap musical group, recorded and performed "Pretty Woman," a rap music version of Roy Orbison's famed 1964 "Oh, Pretty Woman" rock ballad. The song was written by Mr. Orbison and William Dees, and the rights to the song were assigned to Acuff-Rose Music, Inc. (respondent). 2 Live Crew's manager had written to Acuff-Rose for permission to do the parody and offered to pay for rights to do so. Acuff-Rose's response: "I am aware of the success enjoyed by the '2 Live Crew,' but I must inform you that we cannot permit the use of a parody of 'Oh, Pretty Woman.'"

2 Live Crew recorded the parody anyway and named Mr. Orbison and Mr. Dees as the songwriters and Acuff-Rose as the publisher on the CD cover. After over 250,000 copies of the CD had been sold and over one year later, Acuff-Rose filed suit against Luther Campbell (also known as Luke Skywalker), Christopher Wongwon, Mark Ross, and David Hobbs, members of the 2 Live Crew group, for infringement. 2 Live Crew maintained that its song was a parody and fell into a fair use exception of the copyright laws. The district court granted summary judgment for 2 Live Crew. The court of appeals held that the commercial nature made the parody a presumptively unfair use. 2 Live Crew (petitioners) appealed.

JUDICIAL OPINION

SOUTER, Justice

2 Live Crew's song would be an infringement of Acuff-Rose's rights in "Oh, Pretty Woman," under the Copyright Act of 1976, 17 U.S.C. § 106 (1988 ed. and Supp. IV), but for a finding of fair use through parody.

Parody needs to mimic an original to make its point, and so has some claim to use the creation of its victim's (or collective victims') imagination, whereas satire can stand on its own two feet and so requires justification for the very act of borrowing.

The fact that parody can claim legitimacy for some appropriation does not, of course, tell either parodist or judge much about where to draw the line. Like a book review quoting the copyrighted material criticized, parody may or may not be fair use, and petitioner's suggestion that any periodic use is presumptively fair has no more justification in law or fact than the equally hopeful claim that any use for news reporting should be presumed fair.

. . . we think it fair to say that 2 Live Crew's song reasonably could be perceived as commenting on the original or criticizing it, to some degree. 2 Live Crew juxtaposes the romantic musings of a man whose fantasy comes true, with degrading taunts, a bawdy demand for sex, and a sigh of relief from paternal responsibility. The later words can be taken as a comment on the naivete of the original of an earlier day, as a rejection of its sentiment that ignores the ugliness of street life and the debasement that it signifies. It is this joinder of reference and ridicule that marks off the author's choice of parody from the other types of comment and criticism that traditionally have had a claim to fair use protection as transformative works.

This is not, of course, to say that anyone who calls himself a parodist can skim the cream and get away scot free. In parody, as in news reporting, context is everything, and the question of fairness asks what else the parodist did besides go to the heart of the original. It is significant that 2 Live Crew not only copied the first line of the original, but thereafter departed markedly from the Orbison lyrics for its own ends. 2 Live Crew not only copied the bass riff and repeated it, but also produced otherwise distinctive sounds, interposing "scraper" noise, overlaying the music with solos in different keys, and altering the drum beat. This is not a case, then, where "a substantial portion" of the parody itself is composed of a "verbatim" copying of the original.

It was error for the Court of Appeals to conclude that the commercial nature of 2 Live Crew's parody of

CONTINUED

"Oh, Pretty Woman" rendered it presumptively unfair. The court also erred in holding that 2 Live Crew had necessarily copied excessively from the Orbison original, considering the parodic purpose of the use. We therefore reverse the judgment of the Court of Appeals.

The case was remanded for trial.

APPENDIX A

"Oh, Pretty Woman," by Roy Orbison and William Dees
Pretty Woman, walking down the street,
Pretty Woman, the kind I like to meet,
Pretty Woman, I don't believe you,
you're not the truth,
No one could look as good as you
Mercy
Pretty Woman, won't you pardon me,
Pretty Woman, I couldn't help but see,
Pretty Woman, that you look lovely as can be
Are you lonely just like me?
Pretty Woman, stop a while,
Pretty Woman, talk a while,
Pretty Woman give your smile to me
Pretty Woman, yeah, yeah, yeah
Pretty Woman, look my way,
Pretty Woman, say you'll stay with me
'Cause I need you, I'll treat you right
Come to me baby, Be mine tonight
Pretty Woman, don't walk on by,
Pretty Woman, don't make me cry,
Pretty Woman, don't walk away,
Hey, O.K.
If that's the way it must be, O.K.
I guess I'll go on home, it's late
There'll be tomorrow night, but wait!
What do I see
Is she walking back to me!
Oh, Pretty Woman.

APPENDIX B

"Pretty Woman," as recorded by 2 Live Crew
Pretty woman walkin' down the street
Pretty woman girl you look so sweet
Pretty woman you bring me down to that knee

Pretty woman you make me wanna beg please
Oh, pretty woman
Big hairy woman you need to shave that stuff
Big hairy woman you know I bet it's tough
Big hairy woman all that hair it ain't legit
'Cause you look like "Cousin It"
Big hairy woman
Bald headed woman girl your hair won't grow
Bald headed woman you got a teeny weeny afro
Bald headed woman you know your hair could look nice
Bald headed woman first you got to roll it with rice
Bald headed woman here, let me get this hunk of biz for ya
Ya know what I'm saying you look better than rice a roni
Oh bald headed woman
Big hairy woman come on in
And don't forget your bald headed friend
Hey pretty woman let the boys
Jump in
Two timin' woman girl you know you ain't right
Two timin' woman you's out with my boy last night
Two timin' woman that takes a load off my mind
Two timin' woman now I know the baby ain't mine
Oh, two timin' woman
Oh pretty woman

CASE QUESTIONS

1. What is the significance of 2 Live Crew's commercial gain from the parody?

2. Why did 2 Live Crew's manager seek permission first?

3. Should the owner of the rights be allowed to decide how a song will be parodied for commercial gain?

Aftermath: The 2 Live Crew case began a trend in the music parody industry, based on what has become known as "Footnote 10." In Footnote 10 in the Supreme Court opinion, the Court noted its concern for the use of injunctions in parody cases. The footnote indicates that automatic injunctive relief when the parody goes beyond fair use is wrong because there may be a strong public interest in the publication of the secondary work, as in the 2 Live Crew parody, in which social commentary is present.

consider................................15.1

The San Diego Chicken, a mascot at professional baseball games, has a portion of his act in which he grabs a purple dinosaur and stomps it, stamps it, pounds it, and pummels it. Lyons Partnership, L.P. produces the *Barney & Friends* television show, which features a purple dinosaur, and holds all its product licenses. Lyons filed suit against Ted Giannoulas (the man beneath the San Diego Chicken costume) for copyright infringement.

A Texas court classified the portion of Mr. Giannoulas's act that involved a purple dinosaur as a form of parody or satire that was thereby protected by the First Amendment. Kenneth Fitzgerald, the lawyer for Mr. Giannoulas, said Mr. Giannoulas will seek to recover his attorney's fees in the case.

Mr. Fitzgerald noted during the case that Barney has been spoofed by Jay Leno as well as on the television show *Saturday Night Live,* but Lyons chose only to pursue Mr. Giannoulas.

What is wrong with selective enforcement of one's copyright protections? Is Barney the Dinosaur something that can be copyrighted? (Analysis appears at the end of the chapter.) *Lyons Partnership* v. *Giannoulas,* 14 F.Supp.2d 947 (N.D.Tex.1998).

· ·

ethical *issues*

In the summer of 1996, the dance song "Macarena" hit the pop music scene and charts in the United States. The line-type dance inspired by the song is called the Macarena. At camps around the country, the song was played and children were taught the dance.

The American Society of Composers, Authors, and Publishers (ASCAP) serves as a clearinghouse for fee payments for use of copyrighted materials belonging to its members. ASCAP sent a letter to the directors of camps and nonprofit organizations sponsoring camps (Girl Scouts, Boy Scouts, Camp Fire Girls, American Cancer Association, and so forth) that warned them that licensed songs should not be used without paying ASCAP the licensing fees and that violators would be pursued. ASCAP's prices for songs are, for example, $591 for the camp season for "Edelweiss" (from *The Sound of Music*) or "This Land Is Your Land."

Some of the nonprofit-sponsored camps charge only $44 per week per camper. The directors could not afford the fees, and the camps eliminated their oldies dances and dance classes. ASCAP declined to offer discounted licensing fees for the camps.

Why did ASCAP work so diligently to protect its rights? What ethical and social responsibility issues do you see with respect to the nonprofit camps? Some of these camps are summer retreats for children who suffer from cancer, AIDS, and other terminal illnesses. Does this information change your feelings about ASCAP's fees?

Irving Berlin (now his estate), the author of "God Bless America," earns royalties each time the song is played or performed. The song became a standard at memorial services for the September 11, 2001, victims. Mr. Berlin's estate always gives the royalties from the song to the Boy Scouts of America. What would you do if you were an ASCAP member and owned the rights to a song a camp wished to use?

Trademarks

Trademarks are words, pictures, designs, or symbols that businesses place on goods to identify those goods as their product. "Xerox," the Mercedes-Benz triangle, and "M&M's" are all examples of trademarks. Owens-Corning has the color pink for its insulation trademarked. No other insulation company can have pink insulation, and the use of the Pink Panther reminds us of the company's unique product. If the symbol is one for a service, such as the symbol for "Martinizing" at the dry cleaners, it is a service mark. The **Lanham Act** of 1946 is the foundation of federal law on trademarks. Trademarks protect a company's goodwill. A trademark becomes associated with that company and is used as a means of identifying that company's goods or services.

A trademark is registered on the *Principal Register*. The trademark must be unique and nongeneric. For example, "cola" is a generic term; "Coca-Cola" is a trademark. Before recent changes in the law, a trademark must have been in use before registration, but a recent amendment to the Lanham Act allows preregistration, a practice followed in Europe for many years.[2] Once a trademark is registered, its registration can be challenged for five years. If there is no challenge, the trademark becomes incontestable and is protected if its owner enforces it.

Once a trademark is registered, the holder must self-enforce the unique nature of that trademark. The owner must take care so that the trademark does not fall into common use by the public as a descriptive or generic term. For example, there are "Band-Aid brand adhesive strips" instead of "Band-Aids." There is "Jell-O brand gelatin dessert" instead of "Jell-O." There are "Formica brand kitchen countertops" instead of "Formica" and "Rollerblade in-line skates" instead of "Rollerblades." Parker Brothers lost its "Monopoly" trademark because there is no generic term for the type of board game it was. Hasbro recently won an injunction to stop the online knock-off game of "Scrabulous," developed by two brothers in India, as a trademark infringement of its Scrabble game. If Hasbro had allowed even the partial use of its game's name along with the game's similarities to continue, its Scrabble trademark was at risk.

Harley-Davidson, Inc. v. *Grottanelli* (Case 15.2) deals with an issue of generic or protectable use.

CASE 15.2

Harley–Davidson, Inc. v. Grottanelli
164 F.3D 806 (2D CIR. 1999) CERT. DENIED 531 U.S. 1103 (2001)

WHEN IS A HOG GENERIC?

FACTS

Harley-Davidson (Harley-Davidson, Harley, or the company), a corporation based in Milwaukee, Wisconsin, manufactures and sells motorcycles, motorcycle parts and accessories, apparel, and other motorcycle-related merchandise. It brought suit against The Hog Farm, owned by Ronald Grottanelli (Grottanelli), for its use of the word "hog" in its business name and in reference to other products. Harley maintains that "hog" is a trademark associated with its motorcycles.

The lower court enjoined Mr. Grottanelli from using the term "hog" in his store except as to his store's name, which he could keep so long as confined to a narrow geographic area. Mr. Grottanelli appealed, as did Harley-Davidson (the latter to request a more narrow geographic scope for use of "The Hog Farm" name by Mr. Grottanelli).

JUDICIAL OPINION

NEWMAN, Circuit Judge
In the late 1960s and early 1970s, the word "hog" was used by motorcycle enthusiasts to refer to motorcycles

generally and to large motorcycles in particular. The October 1975 issue of *Street Chopper* contained an article entitled "Honda Hog," indicating that the word "hog" was generic as to motorcycles and needed a trade name adjective.

Beginning around the early 1970s and into the early 1980s, motorcyclists came to use the word "hog" when referring to Harley-Davidson motorcycles. However, for several years, as Harley-Davidson's Manager of Trademark Enforcement acknowledged, the company attempted to disassociate itself from the word "hog." The Magistrate Judge drew the reasonable inference that the company wished to distance itself from the connection between "hog" as applied to motorcycles and unsavory elements of the population, such as Hell's Angels, who were among those applying the term to Harley-Davidson motorcycles.

In 1981, Harley-Davidson's new owners recognized that the term "hog" had financial value and began using the term in connection with its merchandise, accessories, advertising, and promotions. In 1983, it formed the Harley Owners' Group, pointedly using the acronym "H.O.G." In 1987, it registered the acronym in conjunction with various logos. It subsequently registered the mark "HOG" for motorcycles.

Grottanelli opened a motorcycle repair shop under the name "The Hog Farm" in 1969. At some point after 1981, Grottanelli also began using the word "hog" in connection with events and merchandise. He has sponsored an event alternatively known as "Hog Holidays" and "Hog Farm Holidays," and sold products such as "Hog Wash" engine degreaser and a "Hog Trivia" board game. . . .

Harley's Manager of Trademark Enforcement acknowledged that in the past Harley had attempted to disassociate itself from the term "hog." As the Magistrate Judge noted, Harley's own history of the company, "The Big Book of Harley-Davidson," makes no reference to "hog" as relating to its products before the early 1980s.

Harley-Davidson suggests, albeit in a footnote, that it is entitled to trademark use of "HOG" as applied to motorcycles because a substantial segment of the relevant consumers began to use the term specifically to refer to Harley-Davidson motorcycles before the company made trademark use of the term. . . . The public has no more right than a manufacturer to withdraw from the language a generic term, already applicable to the relevant category of products, and accord it trademark significance, at least as long as the term retains some generic meaning.

The public may also take a trademark and give it a generic meaning that is new. See *Lucasfilm, Ltd.* v. *High Frontier,* 622 F. Supp. 931 (D.D.C.1985) ("Strategic Defense Initiative" referred to as "Star Wars Program" without infringing movie trademark STAR WARS).

For all of these reasons, Harley-Davidson may not prohibit Grottanelli from using "hog" to identify his motorcycle products and services. Like any other manufacturer with a product identified by a word that is generic, Harley-Davidson will have to rely on all or a portion of its trade name (or other protectable marks) to identify its brand of motorcycles, e.g., "Harley Hogs."

Reversed.

CASE QUESTIONS

1. Who used the term *hog* first among the two parties?

2. What was the effect of Harley-Davidson trying to distance itself from "hog" for a time?

3. Can Harley-Davidson reclaim the term *hog* from its generic standing?

consider 15.2

Wordspy.com is a site that specializes in noting newly coined words. The site noted that the popularity of the search engine, Google, has netted a verb, such as when someone says, "I went in and googled it." A lawyer from Google has asked that the new term be deleted from Wordspy's site. Why does Google want to stop its use as a verb? (Analysis appears at the end of the chapter.)

Trade Names

Not all commonly used terms, however, are generic because they may be trade names. In *San Francisco Arts & Athletics, Inc.* v. *United States Olympic Committee,* 483 U.S. 522 (1987), the Supreme Court held that the term *Olympic* belongs to the U.S. Olympic Committee and could not be used by San Francisco Arts & Athletics, Inc. (SFAA) in promoting its "Gay Olympic Games." The SFAA did not have permission to use the term *Olympic.* Use of a **trade name** without the registered owner's permission is infringement.

If the plaintiff can show a willful infringement, the Lanham Act allows the plaintiff to recover treble damages. An injunction is also available for using a trademark or trade name without authorization. Recent changes in the law allow a competitor to seek treble damages when its product is used deceptively in a comparative ad.

Business Planning Tip

Before you use a song, a symbol, or part of a written work, be sure to check on the intellectual property rights related to the song. For example, you can use an excerpt from Beethoven without stepping on anyone's IP rights. But playing "How to Save a Life" by the Fray, a 2006 song, would require permission and fees. Stores play fees for even the generic Muzak background music that is piped over their PA systems.

Federal Trademark Dilution Act and Confused Consumers

In 1995, Congress passed the **Federal Trademark Dilution Act**, a statute that permits recovery and injunctions for "dilution" of distinctive trademarks. Dilution results when others use a trademark or trade name to capitalize on the recognition, familiarity, and reputation of a distinctive trademark or name. Dilution results in blurring or creating confusion among consumers about the source of a product and tarnishes the product's or company's image or portrays a product in an unsavory manner.*

Moseley, dba Victor's Little Secret, v. *Secret Catalogue, Inc.* (Case 15.3) deals with a trademark dilution issue and also provides the answer to the chapter's opening Consider.

CASE 15.3

Moseley, dba Victor's Little Secret, v. *V Secret Catalogue, Inc.*
537 U.S. 418 (2003)

THE BARE ESSENTIALS ON TRADEMARK LAW:
VICTOR OR VICTORIA'S SECRET?

FACTS

Victor and Cathy Moseley (petitioners) owned and operated an adult toy, gag gift, and lingerie shop that they called Victor's Little Secret near Elizabethtown, Kentucky. In the February 12, 1998, edition of a weekly publication distributed to residents of the military installation at Fort Knox, Kentucky, the Moseleys advertised the "GRAND OPENING Just in time for Valentine's Day!" of their store "VICTOR'S SECRET" in Elizabethtown. The ad featured "Intimate Lingerie for every woman"; "Romantic Lighting"; "Lycra Dresses"; "Pagers"; and "Adult Novelties/Gifts."

An army colonel, who saw the ad and was offended by what he perceived to be an attempt to use a reputable company's trademark to promote the sale of "unwholesome, tawdry merchandise," sent a copy to Victoria's Secret, Inc. (respondents).

Victoria's Secret owns 750 stores around the country and distributes 400 million catalogs each year via U.S. mail. Victoria's Secret spends $55 million annually on advertising "the VICTORIA'S SECRET brand—one of moderately priced, high quality, attractively designed lingerie sold in a store setting designed to look like a wom[a]n's bedroom." Legal counsel for Victoria's Secret asked the Moseleys to stop using the name Victor's Secret because of possible confusion over the trademark and resulting

dilution. The Moseleys changed the name of their store to Victor's Little Secret. Not satisfied, Victoria's Secret filed suit for dilution of its trademark under the Federal Trademark Dilution Act (FTDA).

The District Court granted summary judgment for Victoria's Secret under the FTDA, and the Sixth Circuit affirmed, finding that the respondents' mark was "distinctive" and that the evidence established "dilution" even though no actual harm had been proved. The Moseleys appealed.

JUDICIAL OPINION

STEVENS, Justice

Respondents described their business as follows: "Victoria's Secret stores sell a complete line of lingerie, women's undergarments and nightwear, robes, caftans and kimonos, slippers, sachets, lingerie bags, hanging bags, candles, soaps, cosmetic brushes, atomizers, bath products and fragrances." Petitioners sell a wide variety of items, including adult videos, "adult novelties," and lingerie. In answer to an interrogatory, petitioners stated that they "sell novelty action clocks, patches, temporary tattoos, stuffed animals, coffee mugs, leather biker wallets, zippo lighters, diet formula, diet supplements, jigsaw puzzles, whips, handcufs [sic], hosiery

---

* Tiffany's was responsible for bringing the first cases to have courts determine whether third parties could be held liable for trademark dilution and infringement. In *Tiffany, Inc.* v. *eBay, Inc.*, 2008 WL 2755787 (S.D.N.Y. 2008), a federal court held that eBay cannot be held vicariously responsible for the infringing goods being sold on eBay. However, Tiffany's did win a case in the EU, and eBay was ordered to pay millions in damages, a decision it is appealing.

bubble machines, greeting cards, calendars, incense burners, car air fresheners, sunglasses, ball caps, jewelry, candles, lava lamps, blacklights, fiber optic lights, rock and roll prints, lingerie, pagers, candy, adult video tapes, adult novelties, t-shirts, etc."

"The term 'dilution' means the lessening of the capacity of a famous mark to identify and distinguish goods or services, regardless of the presence or absence of—

"(1) competition between the owner of the famous mark and other parties, or

"(2) likelihood of confusion, mistake, or deception"

The record in this case establishes that an army officer who saw the advertisement of the opening of a store named "Victor's Secret" did make the mental association with "Victoria's Secret," but it also shows that he did not therefore form any different impression of the store that his wife and daughter had patronized. There is a complete absence of evidence of any lessening of the capacity of the VICTORIA'S SECRET mark to identify and distinguish

goods or services sold in Victoria's Secret stores or advertised in its catalogs. The officer was offended by the ad, but it did not change his conception of Victoria's Secret. His offense was directed entirely at petitioners, not at respondents. Moreover, the expert retained by respondents had nothing to say about the impact of petitioners' name on the strength of respondents' mark.

The evidence in the present record is not sufficient to support the summary judgment on the dilution count. The judgment is therefore reversed.

CASE QUESTIONS

1. Why was the connection that the Army officer made between the two companies not enough for dilution?

2. What is Victoria's Secret concerned about?

3. What does Victoria's Secret have to prove to get an injunction under the FTDA?

Trade Dress

The Lanham Act also protects **trade dress**. Trade dress is the colors, designs, and shapes associated with a product. If someone copies the color schemes and shapes, they are likely to benefit from the goodwill of the owner and developer of the trade dress. The subtle copying of trade dress dilutes the value of the company's goodwill and reputation. In *Two Pesos, Inc. v. Taco Cabana, Inc.,* 505 U.S. 763 (1992), the U.S. Supreme Court resolved issues related to trade dress infringement. In the case, Taco Cabana, Inc., which operated a chain of fast-food restaurants in Texas that serve Mexican food, had opened in San Antonio and had distinctive trade dress that Two Pesos used as its motif when it opened its restaurants in Houston. With expansion around Texas, the two chains ended up in head-to-head competition in Dallas, and a trade dress infringement suit resulted. The U.S. Supreme Court held that a claim of trade dress infringement requires proof of the same elements as trademark infringement. That is, a company must show that its trade dress is distinctive and that consumers are likely to be confused by the similarity.

In *Wal-Mart v. Samara,* 529 U.S. 205 (2000), the U.S. Supreme Court limited its ruling in *Two Pesos.* In the case, Samara designed, produced, and sold a line of seersucker children's clothes with bold appliqués and large collars. Wal-Mart had introduced its own line of clothing that was similar. Product design trade dress enjoys no inherent protection. Product packaging, which the court noted was involved in *Two Pesos,* does enjoy protection, as in the shape of a Coca-Cola bottle. However, absent some other statutory protection, product design, with the exception of famous designers such as Tommy Hilfiger, Ralph Lauren, and Izod, requires legislative change for protection.

CYBER INFRINGEMENT

What are the rights of search engines such as Google to use the symbols and trademarks of companies to direct Internet users to sites that are not affiliated with the trademark owners? Playboy Enterprises filed suit against Netscape to stop that search engine's use of the Playboy Bunny symbol in ads that directed Internet users to sites oriented toward sexual content. Netscape benefits when users click onto those sites. However, the use of the Playboy symbol allows Netscape and the sites to capitalize on Playboy's name, advertising, and goodwill. In *Playboy Enterprise, Inc.* v. *Netscape Communications,* 354 F.3d 1020 (9th Cir. 2004), a unanimous Ninth Circuit ruled that such use was an infringement.

Companies also have the right to stop Internet sales that are not by authorized distributors. For example, in *Australian Gold, Inc.* v. *Hatfield,* 436 F.3d 1228 (10th Cir. 2006), ETS Inc., like most beauty supply companies, sold its tanning products primarily through tanning salons. ETS, like most beauty suppliers, has distribution contracts that limit sales to beauty and tanning salons. ETS does not want its products available in stores because of the need for in-person consultation on their use and application. The Hatfields used a series of fictitious names to purchase ETS products through distributors and then made the products available on the Internet through seven different Web sites. The seven Web sites used the ETS trademark, product pictures, and metatags. ETS recovered $3.7 million for infringement because of the unauthorized use of the trademark and the resulting diversion of Internet traffic and sales to the Hatfields. Use of a trademark on the Internet without permission brings the resulting profits back to the owner.

Cybersquatting

Cybersquatting is registering sites and domain names that are deceptively or confusingly similar to existing trademarks that belong to others. Although the Federal Trademark Dilution Act had been used to halt cybersquatting, Congress enacted the Federal Anticybersquatting Consumer Protection Act (ACPA) in 1999 to prohibit cybersquatting and to offer clear standards of proof as well as remedies for this activity. The remedies available include injunctions to stop use of the name, forfeiture of the name, and recovery of money damages and costs of litigation. Although a defense of good faith can be used, cybersquatters may not use the intent to compete in good faith as a defense to using a deceptively similar name. For example, in *Victoria's Secret Stores Inc.* v. *Artco,* 194 F. Supp.2d 704 (S.D. Ohio 2002), the court held that the use of the name www.victoriassecrets.net was too confusing with www.victoriassecret.com, and the cybersquatter must halt its use even though his stated intention was simply to get people to come to his site and look at competitive lingerie.

The **Internet Corporation for Assigned Names and Numbers** (ICANN) has been the provider of arbitration services for disputes between trademark owners and Internet sites.

consider 15.3

They can be spotted from a distance. The classic Ferrari design with its lined side panels and hidden headlights is unique. Although the Ferrari name is a registered trademark, the design of the Ferrari is not. Roberts Motor Company designed a car with a look similar to the Ferrari, but the Roberts car would sell for a much lower price. Ferrari brought suit against Roberts, alleging infringement. Is Ferrari correct? Can a non-patented, noncopyrighted design belong exclusively to Ferrari? (Analysis appears at the end of the chapter.) [*Ferrari* v. *Roberts Motor Co.,* 944 F.2d 1235 (6th Cir. 1991), *cert. denied,* 505 U.S. 1219 (1992)]

Exhibit 15.1 provides a summary of intellectual property rights and protections.

EXHIBIT   15.1 Summary of Intellectual Property Rights

TYPE OF INTELLECTUAL PROPERTY	TRADEMARKS	COPYRIGHTS	PATENTS	TRADE SECRETS
Protection	Words, names, symbols, or devices used to identify a product or service	Original creative works of authorship, such as writings, movies, records, and computer software	Utility, design, and plant patents	Advantageous formulas, devices, or compilation of information
Applicable standard	Identifies and distinguishes a product or service	Original creative works in writing or in another format	New and non-obvious advances in the art	Not readily ascertainable, not disclosed to the public
Where to apply	Patent and Trademark Office	Register of Copyrights	Patent and Trademark Office	No public registration necessary
Duration	Indefinite so long as it continues to be used	Life of author plus 70 years; corporate is 120 years from creation or 95 years from publication of the work	Utility and plant patents, 20 years from date of application; design patents, 14 years	Indefinite so long as secret is not disclosed to public

Source: Adapted from *Anderson's Business Law,* © 2007 by David Twomey and Marianne Jennings.

International Intellectual Property Issues

Companies must be ever vigilant in protecting intellectual property in countries that may have standards and requirements that are different from those in the United States.

PATENT PROTECTION

The period for patent protection varies from country to country. The United States does not permit patent protection for products until the patent is granted, whereas other countries afford protection from the time application is made. Procedures for obtaining patents also vary significantly from country to country. For example, many countries hold **opposition proceedings** as part of the patent process. Much like the federal regulatory promulgation steps (see Chapter 5), the process includes publishing the description of the patent and inviting the public to study the description and possibly oppose the granting of a patent.

Some countries impose **working requirements** on the patent holder, which means that the idea or product must be produced commercially within a certain period of time or the patent protection is revoked.

TRADEMARK PROTECTION

U.S. trademark registration is effective only in the United States. For protection in other countries, a trademark must be registered (if the country affords the protection of registration). In some countries, known as common law countries, trademark protection is established through use in that country and through the recognition by others of the use and distinction provided by the trademark.

Several international registries attempt to offer international protection. For example, the 1891 **Madrid Agreement** (updated in 1989) provides for the Madrid System of International Registration of Marks (the Madrid Protocol), which is central registration through the International Bureau, which is part of the World Intellectual Property Organization (WIPO) in Geneva, Switzerland. Registrations with the bureau are effective for five years in all member countries unless one of the members objects to the trademark registration, in which case the registration is not effective in that country. The United States became one of 60 signatory countries to that protocol in 2003.

In 1996, the European Union began its one-stop trademark registration known as Community Trademark (CTM). Under the provisions of this program, U.S. companies register their trademarks once and enjoy protection in all countries that are part of the European Union. The trademark and backup materials are filed with the Office of Harmonization of the Internal Market (OHIM). The OHIM will then notify the trademark offices in each of the member states of the European Union.

Many countries have permitted the unauthorized use of trademarks in an effort to develop local economies. These countries permit the production of **knock-off goods**, which are goods that carry the trademark or trade name of a firm's product but are not actually produced by that firm. A costly problem for trademark holders is the **gray market**. Manufacturers in foreign countries are authorized to produce a certain amount of goods, but many foreign manufacturers exceed their licensed quota and dump the goods into the market at a much lower price and thereby reduce the trademark owner's market. Both knock-off and gray market goods are forms of infringement.

COPYRIGHTS IN INTERNATIONAL BUSINESS

The United States was a party to the 1986 Berne Convention agreement and made it a part of U.S. copyright law through the **Berne Convention Implementation Act of 1988**. The purpose of the Berne Convention, called the Convention for the Protection of Literary and Artistic Works, was to establish international uniformity in copyright protection. The convention was signed on September 9, 1986, and became effective in the United States on March 1, 1989. The convention is administered by WIPO and covers member countries. However, the Berne Convention gives backdoor copyright protection to works originating in non-Berne member countries if the work is simultaneously published in a Berne member country.

Enforcing Business Property Rights

PRODUCT DISPARAGEMENT

When an untrue statement is made about a business product or service, the defamation is referred to as **disparagement** and is either **trade libel** (written) or **slander of title** (oral). These business torts occur when one business makes untrue statements about another business, its product, or its abilities. The elements for disparagement are the same as those for defamation covered in Chapter 8.

PALMING OFF

Palming off, one of the oldest unfair methods of competition, occurs when one company sells its product by leading buyers to believe it is really another company's product. For example, many cases of palming off took place during the 1980s, when Cabbage Patch dolls were popular, in demand, and scarce. Many replicas were made and called "Cabbage Patch dolls" even though they were not manufactured by Coleco, the original creator. Coleco can halt those sales of "fake" dolls.

MISAPPROPRIATION

Some businesses have **trade secrets**—chemical formulas, procedures, customer lists, data, or devices unique to them. Generally, these types of secrets should be given patent or copyright protection. However, those that do not qualify for these federal statutory protections have the tort of **misappropriation** as protection. Misappropriation is conversion of a trade secret, such as a customer list, a proposed marketing plan, or new strategy to personal use, including use for self-benefit or the benefit of a new employer. For example, an employee who takes proprietary information from her employer and uses it, such as a customer list, to start a competing business is guilty of misappropriation. Most companies put non-compete clauses in their employment contracts that address the issue of taking trade secrets to a new company or forming a competing company. Those clauses are covered in Chapter 16.

Red Flags FOR MANAGERS

When you have a name, a jingle, a logo, a process, or a product that is unique, take the steps necessary to protect you unique competitive advantage:

- Get patents for your processes and products, and remember to develop new ideas because your exclusive rights last only 20 years.
- Get copyrights for songs, books, poems, articles, and your business materials such as employee handbooks and advertising copy.
- Register your trade name and trademark so that others can't use these to draw on your goodwill.

- If a competitor is untruthful about your product in an ad, you have the right to bring suit for their deception about your products and name.
- If a competitor makes its product look just like yours through its colors and packaging, then you have rights for preventing dilution and misappropriation.
- Be sure that your employees are not using songs, articles, logos, and patents without authorization and without paying royalties required.

Summary

What does a business own? What are the types of business property?

- Tangible property—physical: real and personal property

- Intangible property—bundles of rights with respect to goodwill, trade names, copyrights, patents, trade dress, and trade secrets

What are the rights and issues in personal property owned by a business?

- Documents of title—formal legal document that serves to prove and transfer title to tangible personal property

- Bill of sale—informal document or contract that serves to prove and transfer title to tangible personal property

What statutory protections exist for intellectual property?

- Patents—statutory protection for products and processes

- Copyrights—statutory protection for words, thoughts, ideas, music

- Trademarks—statutory protection for product symbols

- Trade names—statutory protection for unique product labels and names

- Trade dress—statutory protection for product colors and motifs

- Trade secrets—criminal sanctions for unauthorized transfer or use

What issues of intellectual property protection exist in international operations?

- Issue of copyright protection afforded only in Berne signatory countries

- WIPO—World Intellectual Property Organization

What private remedies exist for property protections?

- Product disparagement—false and damaging statements

- Misappropriation—use of another's ideas or trade secrets

- Palming off—causing deception about the maker or source of a product

Key Terms

Berne Convention Implementation
    Act of 1988 *358*
bill of sale *346*
Computer Software Copyright
    Act of 1980 *348*
copyrights *347*
cybersquatting *356*
Digital Millennium Copyright Act *348*
disparagement *359*
documents of title *346*
fair use *348*
Federal Trademark Dilution Act *354*

gray market *358*
infringement *347*
intangible property *346*
intellectual property *346*
Internet Corporation for Assigned
    Names and Numbers *356*
knock-off goods *358*
Lanham Act *351*
Madrid Agreement *358*
misappropriation *359*
opposition proceedings *357*
palming off *359*

patents *346*
slander of title *359*
Sonny Bono Copyright
    Term Extension Act *347*
tangible property *345*
trade dress *355*
trade libel *359*
trade name *353*
trade secrets *359*
trademarks *351*
working requirements *358*

Questions and Problems

1. Storck Candy manufactures Werther's Original Butter Toffee Candy. The toffee is sold in an eight-ounce bag with a brown background, a picture of a mound of unwrapped candy, an Alpine village, and an old-fashioned container pouring white liquid.

Farley Candy Company introduced its butter toffee candy in a bag the same size and shape as Werther's, with a pair of containers pouring liquid.

Storck says that Farley is using its trade dress to sell the Farley candy. Has Farley done anything that is a tort? Do federal laws offer protection? [*Storck USA, L.P. v. Farley Candy Co., Inc.*, 785 F. Supp. 730 (N.D. Ill. 1992)]

2. Tommy Hilfiger Licensing, Inc. ("Hilfiger") is the owner of the world-famous TOMMY HILFIGER and flag design trademarks used in connection with the sale of numerous high-end products, including fragrances. The flag design mark is comprised of a combination of red, white, and blue geometric shapes. These marks are federally registered trademarks. Nature Labs, LLC manufactures, markets, and sells a line of pet perfumes whose names parody elegant brands sold for human consumption—Timmy Holedigger (Tommy Hilfiger), CK-9 (Calvin Klein's cK-1), Pucci (Gucci), Bono Sports (Ralph Lauren's Polo Sports), Miss Claybone (Liz Claiborne), and White Dalmations (Elizabeth Taylor's White Diamonds). Nature Labs' initial spoof of Hilfiger was called Tommy Holedigger and had a flag-shaped label with side-by-side red and white squares bordered on top and bottom by a blue stripe with white letters. Hilfiger complained that this use infringed its marks. Nature Labs then changed the name to Timmy Holedigger and changed the label to its present form: inverted side-by-side yellow and red triangles bordered on top and bottom by a blue stripe with white letters. Beneath the new logo design, the following phrase appears: "If You Like Tommy Hilfiger Your Pet Will Love Timmy Holedigger." Neither party performed a disciplined olfactory comparison or chemical analysis, but John Harris, the general partner of Nature Labs, testified at his deposition that the two scents are similar, based on his recollection of Hilfiger cologne. An asterisk following the words "Tommy Hilfiger" references a disclaimer in red type on the back label, which states, "This imitation fragrance is not related to Tommy Hilfiger Licensing, Inc." Another current version of the product, a two-ounce bottle being marketed primarily to PetCo, changes the flag-shape label to a bone with red and yellow triangles and a thick blue border. Tommy Hilfiger Licensing, Inc. brought suit for trademark infringement, trademark dilution, false designation of origin, and false advertising. Can Tommy Hilfiger stop the production and sale of the Nature Labs' Timmy Holedigger? [*Tommy Hilfiger Licensing, Inc.* v. *Nature Labs, LLC* 221 F.Supp.2d 410 (S.D. N.Y. 2002)]

3. Roger Burten submitted his "Triumph" electronic game to Milton Bradley for possible mass production, but it was rejected twice after review. One year later, however, Milton Bradley began marketing a new electronic board game under the name of "Dark Tower." There were structural and design similarities between "Triumph" and "Dark Tower." Mr. Burten brought suit for fraud, breach of contract, and trade secret misappropriation. Can Mr. Burten recover under any of these theories? [*Burten* v. *Milton Bradley Co.*, 763 F.2d 461 (1st Cir. 1985)]

4. Vanna White is the hostess of *Wheel of Fortune,* one of the most popular game shows in television history. Capitalizing on the fame that her participation in the show has bestowed on her, Ms. White markets her identity to various advertisers.

Samsung Electronics ran a series of ads in at least six publications with widespread, and in some cases national, circulation. Each of the advertisements in the series followed the same theme: Each depicted a current item from popular culture and a Samsung electronic product. Each was set in the twenty-first century and conveyed the message that the Samsung product would still be in use at that future time.

The advertisement that prompted a dispute was for Samsung video cassette recorders (VCRs). The ad depicted a robot dressed in a wig, gown, and jewelry that was consciously selected to resemble Ms. White's hair and dresses. The robot was posed next to a game board instantly recognizable as the *Wheel of Fortune* game show set in a stance for which Ms. White is famous. The caption of the ad read: "Longest-running game show. 2012 A.D." Samsung executives referred to the ad as the "Vanna White ad." Unlike the other celebrities used in the campaign, Ms. White neither consented to the ads nor was paid. Have Ms. White's rights been violated? Did Samsung violate federal law? [*White* v. *Samsung Elect. Am., Inc.*, 971 F.2d 1395 (9th Cir. 1992)]

5. Charles Atlas has been in the business of selling bodybuilding courses for more than 70 years. Advertisements for Atlas's bodybuilding courses, which have appeared in DC Comic books, have included a one-page comic strip story titled "The Insult that Made a Man out of Mac." In the storyline: (1) a bully kicks sand in Mac's face at the beach; (2) after taking the Atlas course, the skinny Mac develops a muscular physique; (3) Mac finds the bully, again on the beach, and punches him, for which he receives newfound respect, particularly from his female companion; (4) in the final panel, the phrase "HERO OF THE BEACH" appears as a halo-like formation hovering over Mac's head. Mr. Atlas registered Mac with the Principal Register as the before and after characters of "Skinny" and "Joe." "Joe" is Mac in his muscular form with the leopard-skin trunks.

DC Comics created a character known as Flex Mentallo, who like Mac, came to be imbued with extraordinary strength. Flex Mentallo, once a scrawny weakling who has sand kicked in his face by a bully, returns to the beach with his muscular physique, and like Mac in the Atlas comic ad, he beats up the bully and becomes "the Hero of the beach."

However, after Flex Mentallo acquires his powers, the Charles Atlas tale changes a bit and Flex beats up the woman he had been with by smashing her in the face and proclaims "I don't need a tramp like you anymore!" Mr. Atlas sued for infringement saying that the depiction tarnished the image of Mac and thus, the Atlas product line. DC defends its new character and storyline as parody. Determine what the court should do with the Atlas infringement suit. [*Charles Atlas, Ltd. v. DC Comics, Inc.* 112 F.Supp.2d 330 (S.D.N.Y. 2000)]

Understanding "Consider" Problems

15.1

THINK: Copyright laws protect images and characters. The owner has exclusive rights to use, with the exception of fair use. The First Amendment permits the use of copyrighted property for purposes of satire and parody. Fair use applies to balancing copyright protections with First Amendment satire and parody.

APPLY: Barney is a character that is protected by copyright; its owner has the right to control its use. The actions of Mr. Giannoulas are a form of satire, but they are for commercial purposes.

ANSWER: The court held that the skit was parody, humorous, and protected by the First Amendment.

15.2

THINK: Trademarks and trade names allow their owners exclusive use. Allowing generic use of the term can cause the loss of trademark/trade name exclusivity.

APPLY: Google is a trade name. Its use as a verb is a generic use.

ANSWER: Google has the right to stop the generic use. If Google does not stop the generic use, the term will become a verb and the company will lose its exclusivity as well as its brand identity.

15.3

THINK: The protections for design require proof that consumers would be confused about the product, that they would likely think the Roberts car was a Ferrari. Also, where the products are the same and one company seeks to draw upon the advertising and goodwill of the other, the confusion and damages are more easily established.

APPLY: If Ferrari is able to show confusion, it can halt the design and seek damages. But proof of that confusion is necessary to seek a remedy for design infringement. Would your answer be the same if Avanti Motor Corporation designed and built a new vehicle that looks like General Motors' Hummer?

ANSWER: The court held that (1) the automobile designs had acquired secondary meaning; (2) there was likelihood of confusion between plaintiff's cars and defendant's replicas; and that (3) injunction granted by district court was proper.

Notes

1. The protection of intellectual property has been important to commercial development both here and in other countries for centuries. See the course Web site and the *Instructor's Manual* for more information.

2. Some states do have provisions for registration of trade names for businesses, such as when a company is named Carla's Hair Salon, DBA (doing business as) "The Mane Place."

PART 4

The Legal Environment
of Business Relationships

16

Trade Practices: Antitrust

update

For up-to-date legal news, click on "Author Updates" at

www.cengage.com/blaw/ jennings

Economic power is an inevitable result of the free enterprise system. Building a better mousetrap should result in attracting more customers and developing economic power. But gaining economic power through means other than "superior skill, foresight, and industry" destroys the free enterprise system and often means that buyers don't get a better mousetrap. They are stuck with a mediocre mousetrap built by a firm with ill-gained economic power and resulting market control.

Antitrust law exists to prevent the growth of economic or market power through means other than superior skill, foresight, and industry. Making sure that the free enterprise system has its necessary fuel of competition is the purpose of antitrust laws. This chapter answers the following questions: What interferes with competition? Or, in other words, what are restraints of trade? What forms do they take? What antitrust laws apply when concerns about competition arise? What penalties can be imposed for violations of these laws? ■

People of the same trade seldom meet together, even for merriment and diversion, but the conversation ends in some contrivance to raise prices. It is impossible indeed to prevent such meetings, by any law which would be consistent with liberty and justice. But though the law cannot hinder people of the same trade from sometimes assembling together, it ought to do nothing to facilitate such assemblies.

ADAM SMITH

The Wealth of Nations

While the law of competition may be sometimes hard for the individual, it is best for the race, because it ensures the survival of the fittest in every department.

ANDREW CARNEGIE

consider...

Leegin Creative Leather Products, Inc., designs, manufactures, and distributes leather goods and accessories under the brand name "Brighton." The Brighton brand, often known as the brand with the silver heart, has a full line of women's fashion accessories and is sold across the United States in more than 5,000 retail stores. In 1997, Leegin notified its retailers that it was going to continue focusing on its strong customer service, so readily available in its smaller outlets, but not in places such as Wal-Mart or Costco. To prevent the Brighton brand from being sold at warehouses and over the Internet, Leegin required its retailers to follow a minimum price policy or be terminated as a Brighton retailer. Kay's Kloset was terminated for holding sales on Brighton items in order to compete with local retailers. Kay's Kloset wants to know, "Can Leegin do that to us because we sold at a cheaper price? Isn't this anticompetitive?"

What Interferes with Competition? Covenants Not to Compete

As early as the sixteenth century, businesspeople developed agreements or covenants not to compete. The initial reaction to those agreements was not positive, with the courts issuing a resounding "No!" to those who came seeking to keep others from competing. However, by the seventeenth and eighteenth centuries, the courts began to see that some circumstances required trade restraint if competition was to flourish. As odd as it may sound, covenants not to compete can ensure competition. Through careful review of the covenants that resulted in judicial disputes, the courts began to carve out permissible types of restraints, such as protections for the buyer of a business. In these purchase agreements, the seller agreed not to open a competing business. This trade restraint, called a **covenant not to compete**, was necessary to preserve competition. A buyer purchasing a business meant someone else was entering the market. If the seller dropped down a few doors and opened the same business again, the seller would take customers and put the new buyer out of business.

So, covenants that were part of business purchase agreements are valid as long as they are reasonable in length and scope. For example, in *Mitchell* v. *Reynolds*, 24 Eng. Rep. 347 (1711), a baker who sold his bakery agreed not to compete in the immediate area for five years, and a court held the covenant valid because it was limited in time and geographic scope.

Contracts and covenants that restrain trade are not illegal *per se,* meaning prohibited all the time no matter what. Courts continue to examine the scope of covenants and contracts that restrain trade to make sure that they are necessary for protection and not too broad in scope. For example, a covenant in a contract for the sale of a dry cleaning business that prohibits the seller from opening another dry cleaning business anywhere in the state is unreasonably broad, but a similar covenant limited to the town where the business is located is probably reasonable. The goodwill of the business must be preserved if competition is to take hold. The extent of the protection for the goodwill is determined by the economic base of the area: How many dry cleaners can the area support?

Competition restraints in leases for commercial property are another example of covenants not to compete that are also generally valid. For example, a restriction in a shopping center lease that prohibits a lessee from operating a business that competes with other tenants is valid as long as the purpose of the restriction is to obtain a proper mix in the shopping center with the idea of attracting more business.

What Interferes with Competition? An Overview of the Federal Statutory Scheme on Restraint of Trade

During the last half of the nineteenth century, the United States experienced a tremendous change in its economy. A primarily agricultural economy changed to an industrial economy. Law on business combinations was largely undeveloped and unsuitable for the types of predatory business practices this new industrial age brought. The common law standards discussed in the first section resulted in inconsistencies in the law. Congress addressed anticompetitive behavior with a series of antitrust statutes passed in the late nineteenth and early twentieth centuries. With some amendments and changes, this scheme still exists and applies today. Exhibit 16.1 summarizes the general federal statutory antitrust statutes.

Federal antitrust laws apply to business conduct in interstate commerce. Even if an activity is purely intrastate, it is subject to federal laws if the activity has a substantial economic effect on interstate commerce. Interstate commerce is easily established. In *McClain* v. *Real Estate Board of New Orleans,* 441 U.S. 942 (1980), for example, an antitrust action against real estate brokers who worked only in the New Orleans area was permitted under the Sherman Act because the U.S. Supreme Court found that the brokers facilitated the loans and insurance for the properties they sold. The loans and insurance were provided by national firms, and funding came from outside the state. Interstate commerce, even if indirect, is still sufficient for Sherman Act jurisdiction.

The **Clayton Act** and the **Robinson-Patman Act** have more detailed requirements for federal application such as having sales across state lines or two businesses involved in interstate commerce.

Even if the federal laws do not apply to a particular transaction, states will also have their own laws on anticompetitive behavior, with some states regulating different sorts of activities such as price-gouging, which is charging a price that produces a gross or net profit above a certain percentage determined by the statute or regulation. These statutes go into effect in situations such as in post-hurricane areas when clean water is not readily available but willing sellers are offering it at prices up to five times higher than normal.

| EXHIBIT | 16.1 | Federal Antitrust Statutes |

STATUTE	ORIGINAL DATE	JURISDICTION	COVERAGE	PENALTIES
Sherman Act 15 U.S.C. § 1	1890	Commerce Clause	Monopolies; attempts to monopolize; boycotts; refusals to deal; price fixing; resale price maintenance; division of markets	Criminal; $100,000,000 if a corporation, or, individual, $1,000,000, or by imprisonment not exceeding 10 years, $10,000,000, for individuals if intentional or by both private suits
Clayton Act 1914 15 U.S.C. § 12	1914	Persons engaged in commerce	Tying; treble damages; mergers; interlocking directorates	Private suits
Federal Trade Commission Act 15 U.S.C. § 41	1914	Commerce Clause	Unfair methods of FTC competition	
Robinson-Patman Act 15 U.S.C. § 13	1936	Persons engaged in commerce and selling goods across state lines	Price discrimination	Private suits and criminal for international acts
Celler-Kefauver (part of Clayton Act) 15 U.S.C. § 18	1950		Asset acquisitions	
Hart-Scott Rodino Antitrust Improvements Act 15 U.S.C. § 1311	1976 amended 1980, 1994	Gives greater authority to Justice Department for prosecution; requires premerger notification to Justice Department		
Antitrust Modernization Commission	2002	Gives authority to study antitrust laws and their impact and to provide proposals for updating the statutes; commission finished its work and issued its report on May 31, 2007		

What Types of Activities Do the Federal Laws Regulate?

The federal antitrust laws can be broken down into a chart overview that will help you to understand what anticompetitive behavior is and where the federal antitrust laws apply. Exhibit 16.2 is a diagram of the types of activities and what laws apply.

Anticompetitive behavior breaks down first into two large chunks: horizontal and vertical. Horizontal behaviors are those between and among competitors, and federal law takes any activities here seriously. In horizontal activities, the statutes and courts often find *per se* **illegal** behavior, which means that courts do not analyze what the competitors did; their behavior is just plain illegal. Fixing prices and/or monopolizing are *per se* illegal. Vertical behaviors are those along the supply chain, between manufacturer and distributor, or between manufacturer and retailer. Because other manufacturers and retailers are competing with the parties in the

EXHIBIT 16.2 A Look at Markets, Competition, and Antitrust Laws	
HORIZONTAL MARKETS	**VERTICAL MARKETS**
Monopolization (Sherman Act)	Tying Monopsony (Sherman Act)
Price-Fixing (Sherman Act) Refusals to deal Group Boycotts (Sherman Act)	Price Discrimination (Robinson-Patman Act) Resale Price Maintenance Exclusive Dealing, Sole Outlets, Customer and Territory Restrictions (Sherman Act; FTC)
Mergers Among Competitors Interlocking Directorates (Clayton Act)	Mergers Along the Supply Chain Interlocking Directorates (Clayton Act)

supply chain for the same customers, arrangements that these parties make could actually help competition. Although some vertical behaviors are *per se* illegal, the courts have been chipping away to make more of the vertical activities subject to a **rule of reason** standard, which means that the courts do not classify the conduct as illegal *per se*. Rather, the courts examine whether the activities help or hinder competition.

Horizontal Restraints of Trade

Horizontal restraints of trade lessen competition among a firm's competitors. For example, the 2007 collusion on fuel surcharges between Virgin Airlines and British Airways would be a horizontal restraint because the two airlines are competitors and the collusion fixes prices. The Sherman Act covers the horizontal restraints of **price fixing**, market division, **group boycotts** and refusals to deal, and monopolization. The Clayton Act also covers the problem of anticompetitive horizontal mergers or mergers with competitors.

MONOPOLIZATION

Section 2 of the Sherman Act prohibits the act of **monopolization**. A Sherman Act monopolization charge requires proof of (1) market power in the relevant market, and (2) some intentional or willful abuse of that power.

Market power is the power to control prices or exclude competition in a relevant market. Market power is an economic term that means the firm has a relatively inelastic demand curve. An elastic demand curve means that the firm's products have competition from other firms or from firms with substitute products. For example, cosmetic firms have an elastic demand; buyers can switch to other products when prices increase in one line or they can even give up the use of cosmetics. On the other hand, the demand curve for gasoline is less elastic. Although substitute means of transportation are available, those who need to use their cars need gasoline.

The factors that courts examine to determine market power include the firm's market share. No set percentage figure translates into a final determination of power. However, most monopolization cases were directed at firms with market shares greater than 50 percent.

Market share is measured after we determine the **relevant market**; including a look at the relevant **geographic market**. For example, a beer producer may have 50 percent of all nationwide beer sales, but, in a suit involving a local competitor, the producer's share might be only 20 percent because of the local beer's popularity. This local or **submarket** could be used as the relevant geographic market. A product may have an international market but may have only 10 percent market share in a particular area.

Each firm also has its own relevant **product market**, which is determined by consumers' preferences and their willingness to substitute other products for the product at issue. For example, a market could be defined as plastic wrapping materials, or it could be defined as food storage materials and include such wraps as wax paper, aluminum foil, and plastic storage bags. A company may have 90 percent of the plastic wrap market, but if buyers use plastic wrap interchangeably with foil, storage bags, plastic containers, and Press-n-Seal, then that share may only be 20 percent. The product market is determined by the **cross-elasticity** of demand, explained earlier.

However, the Sherman Act does not prohibit market power or even all monopolies—certain types of monopolies are recognized as lawful exceptions. For example, a small town usually only has an economic base large enough to support one newspaper; such an operation is a lawful monopoly. Some businesses are monopolies because they make a product or provide a service that is superior or unique. When a business has obtained a large market share by **superior skill, foresight, and industry**, it has simply put its product in the market in a superior way and is entitled to its market share. A second requirement for a Sherman Act charge is that the firm acquired or is maintaining monopoly power by some purposeful or deliberate act that is not "superior skill, foresight, and industry" (which, in short, is the ability to build a better mousetrap). Those who bring suit against a company alleging monopolization must have some proof of conspiratorial or nefarious activity, and not just market power. In *Bell Atlantic* v. *Twombly*, 550 U.S. 544 (2007), the U.S. Supreme Court held that companies can't be required to figure out on their own, as defendants in an antitrust suit, what exactly they did that was monopolistic. Plaintiffs must allege enough facts to give the alleged monopolist notice of what they are defending against.

Some examples of prohibited purposeful conduct are **predatory pricing** and **exclusionary conduct**. Predatory pricing is pricing below actual cost for a temporary period to drive a potential competitor out of business. Exclusionary conduct is conduct that prevents a potential competitor from entering the market. For example, interfering with the purchase of a factory by a competitor would be improper exclusionary conduct. The landmark case *U.S.* v. *Microsoft* 253 F.3d 34 (C.A. D.C. 2001) held that Microsoft was a monopolist because of its 90 percent market share as well as its refusal to sell its products to customers who also sold Microsoft's competitors' products. The Justice Department and Microsoft settled the case. Microsoft did not have to be broken up, but it did agree to pay penalties, including a donations of $180 million in software to school districts.

consider. 16.1

Penny Stafford, the owner of Stafford's Coffee Shop, Belvi Coffee and Tea Exchange, located in Bellevue, Washington, has brought an antitrust suit against Starbucks. She alleges that through its exclusive leases, Starbucks bans other coffee shops from competing.

Starbucks currently has a 73 percent market share, $8.4 billion in annual sales in the United States, and owns 7,551 of the 21,400 coffee houses located in the United States. However, if Dunkin' Donuts and Krispy Kreme and Tim Hortons are included in the gourmet coffee market, then Starbucks holds only 43 percent of the coffee market. Starbucks purchased Seattle's Best Coffee (SBC) in 2003 and Torrefazione Italia in the same year. Starbucks then closed one-half of all the SBC stores and all of the Torrefazione outlets. Starbucks runs 59 stores within a 2-mile radius of downtown Seattle.

Stafford said that Starbucks has exclusive leases with landlords so that the landlords cannot lease space in the same building to another coffee shop. Does such an exclusive lease violate any antitrust laws or are such clauses permitted under the law? (Analysis appears at the end of the chapter.)

. . . .

PRICE FIXING

Any agreement or collaboration among competitors "for the purpose and with the effect of raising, depressing, fixing, pegging, or stabilizing the price of a commodity" is price fixing, a *per se* violation of Section 1 of the Sherman Act.

Price fixing can take many forms, but all of them are illegal. A minimum fee or price schedule discourages competition, puts an artificial restriction on the market, and provides a shield from market forces. Even proof that the minimum price is a reasonable price is irrelevant once there is proof of an agreement. Although establishing maximum prices sounds like an excellent benefit for consumers, the effect is to stabilize prices, which translates into a restriction on free-market forces.

Some competitors have tried to use list prices as a guideline, but circulating such lists is still an antitrust violation. Just the exchange of price information has an effect on the market and interferes with competition.

Often price can be controlled through competitors' actions that affect supply. An agreement among competitors to limit production is an agreement to fix prices because the parties are controlling the supply, which in turn controls the right to demand the resulting price. Likewise, an agreement to limit or eliminate bidding, a form of a group boycott, has an effect on price because the supply is constrained. In *National Society of Professional Engineers* v. *United States*, 435 U.S. 679 (1978), a professional society agreed to ban bidding on engineering projects because the bidding process encouraged cost cutting and posed resulting shortcuts and safety risks in construction. Although the Society's motives were well intentioned, it was still price fixing and a *per se* violation of the Sherman Act.

Business Planning Tip

The following tips can help keep trade associations free of anticompetitive behavior.

1. Do not exchange price information, including disclosures about credit terms, shipping fees, and so on.

2. Do not reveal future plans with respect to customers (e.g., "I'm not going to deal with that company anymore").

3. Do not define or reveal territories (e.g., "I'm not interested in the Yuma region anymore").

4. Do not agree to uniform pricing, commissions, or refusals to deal.

consider 16.2

British Airways and Virgin Airlines discussed fuel surcharges at least six times during an 18-month period from 2005 through 2006. As a result, the two companies' fuel surcharges rose in tandem from 5 pounds (about $10) to 60 pounds (about $120). Would Britain's Office of Fair Trading be able to establish an antitrust violation? (Analysis appears at the end of the chapter.)

. . . .

DIVVYING UP THE MARKETS

Any agreement between competitors to divide up an available market is a *per se* violation under the Sherman Act because such an agreement gives the participants monopolies in their particular area. For example, office product supply companies that agree to operate only in certain cities throughout a state would be a division of markets and a *per se* violation.

GROUP BOYCOTTS AND REFUSALS TO DEAL

A group of competitors that agrees not to deal with buyers unless those buyers agree to standard credit or arbitration clauses has committed a *per se* violation.

Some group boycotts appear to have the best intentions. Many garment manufacturers once agreed not to sell to buyers who sold discount or pirated designer clothing. Certainly their intentions were good, but the result still has the anticompetitive effect of controlling the marketplace. Other avenues of relief for violations of the law are available. The American Medical Association's rules that prohibited salaried medical practices and prepaid medical plans are illegal boycotts in spite of the good intentions. In *FTC v. Superior Court Trial Lawyers Ass'n*, 493 U.S. 411 (1990), the U.S. Supreme Court held that a group of well-intentioned defense lawyers who went on strike to get a higher hourly rate for public defenders was noble and perhaps in the interest of justice, but it was still an illegal boycott by horizontal market participants.

MERGING COMPETITORS AND THE EFFECT ON COMPETITION

To determine the legality of mergers among horizontal competitors, courts have applied a test of "presumptive illegality": Any merger that produces an undue percentage share of the market or significantly increases market concentration is a violation. Courts examine market share and the relevant markets to determine whether undue concentration is a factor.

Not all horizontal mergers are prohibited. The **failing-company doctrine** allows the acquisition of a competitor that is teetering on insolvency, shut-down, or bankruptcy if it is an asset or inventory acquisition. Under the **small-company doctrine**, two small companies are permitted to merge because the hope is that they will be better able to compete with the larger businesses in that market.

The trend in mergers has been to approve larger and larger combinations. In *United States v. Von's Grocery Co.*, 384 U.S. 270 (1966), the Supreme Court held that a merger between Von's Grocery Company and Shopping Bag Food Stores, which would have given the two companies together a 7.5 percent share of the retail grocery market in Los Angeles, was an anticompetitive violation of the Clayton Act. However, by 1988, the Justice Department approved the merger of Von's and Safeway in southern California. The merger made the new Von's the largest competitor in terms of market percentage as well as in the number of stores. Justice Department attitudes and guidelines on mergers have changed and geographic markets are now defined in light of international trade.

Vertical Trade Restraints

Various steps are involved in getting a product from its creation to its ultimate consumer. For example, producing packaged sandwich meats requires the manufacturer to obtain bulk-butchered meat (originally from a ranch) through a distributor and turn it into packaged sandwich meat that is sold to another distributor. This distributor sells to a grocery wholesaler, who sells to grocery stores, where consumers buy the packaged meat. This entire process has different levels of production and distribution, but it is one vertical chain from start to finish.

The types of vertical restraints are:

- Resale price maintenance
- Monopsony
- Sole outlets and exclusive distributorships
- Customer and territorial restrictions
- Tying arrangements
- Price discrimination

RESALE PRICE MAINTENANCE

Resale price maintenance is an attempt by a manufacturer to control the price that retailers charge for the manufacturer's product. Resale price maintenance is a rule-of-reason violation of Section 1 of the Sherman Act. Resale price maintenance includes either minimum or maximum prices, or both.

State Oil v. *Khan* (Case 16.1) deals with the issue of resale price maintenance and the *per se* violation vs. rule-of-reason standard.

CASE 16.1

State Oil v. *Khan*
522 U.S. 3 (1997)

FILL IT UP, BUT ONLY AT MY PRICE

FACTS

Barkat U. Khan and his corporation (respondents) entered into an agreement with State Oil (petitioner) to lease and operate a gas station and convenience store owned by State Oil. The agreement provided that Mr. Khan would obtain the gasoline supply for the station from State Oil at a suggested retail price set by State Oil, less a margin of 3.25 cents per gallon. Mr. Khan could charge any price he wanted, but if he charged more than State Oil's suggested retail price, the excess was rebated to State Oil. Mr. Khan could sell the gasoline for less than State Oil's suggested retail price, but the difference came out of his allowed margin.

After a year, Mr. Khan fell behind on his lease payments, and State Oil began proceedings for eviction. The court had Mr. Khan removed and appointed a receiver to operate the station. The receiver operated the gas station without the price constraints and received an overall profit margin above the 3.25 cents imposed on Mr. Khan.

Mr. Khan filed suit, alleging that the State Oil agreement was a violation of Section 1 of the Sherman Act because State Oil was controlling prices. The district court held that there was no *per se* violation and that Mr. Khan had failed to demonstrate antitrust injury. The Court of Appeals reversed, and State Oil appealed.

JUDICIAL OPINION

O'CONNOR, Justice

Although the Sherman Act, by its terms, prohibits every agreement "in restraint of trade," this Court has long recognized that Congress intended to outlaw only unreasonable restraints.

As a consequence, most antitrust claims are analyzed under a "rule of reason," according to which the finder of fact must decide whether the questioned practice imposes an unreasonable restraint on competition, taking into account a variety of factors, including specific information about the relevant business, its condition before and after the restraint was imposed, and the restraint's history, nature, and effect.

Some types of restraints, however, have such predictable and pernicious anticompetitive effect, and such limited potential for procompetitive benefit, that they are deemed unlawful per se. . . .

"Low prices," we have explained, "benefit consumers regardless of how those prices are set, and so long as they are above predatory levels, they do not threaten competition." Our interpretation of the Sherman Act also incorporates the notion that condemnation of practices resulting in lower prices to consumers is "especially costly" because "cutting prices in order to increase business often is the very essence of competition." *Matsushita Elec. Industrial Co. v. Zenith Radio Corp.,* 475 U.S. 574, 594, 106 S.Ct. 1348, 1360, 89 L.Ed.2d 538 (1986).

So informed, we find it difficult to maintain that vertically-imposed maximum prices could harm consumers or competition to the extent necessary to justify their per se invalidation.

Further, although vertical maximum price fixing might limit the viability of inefficient dealers, that consequence is not necessarily harmful to competition and consumers.

[W]e of course do not hold that all vertical maximum price fixing is per se lawful. Instead, vertical maximum price fixing, like the majority of commercial arrangements subject to the antitrust laws, should be evaluated under the rule of reason. In our view, rule-of-reason analysis will effectively identify those situations in which vertical maximum price fixing amounts to anticompetitive conduct. . . .

We therefore vacate the judgment of the Court of Appeals and remand the case for further proceedings consistent with this opinion.

Remanded.

CASE QUESTIONS

1. What were the terms of Mr. Khan's lease?

2. What happened when a receiver operated the station without the State Oil lease constraints? Why is this information important for the case?

3. Is vertical price fixing a *per se* violation? Why or why not?

A minimum price encourages a retailer to carry a certain product because its profit margin will be higher. One explanation offered to justify minimum prices is that, without them, dealers who advertise and offer service may be used by consumers for information only, after which these consumers actually buy at discount houses.

The "suggested retail price" has been tolerated under the rule-of-reason standard as long as manufacturers and distributors did not enforce that suggested price through refusals to sell. A 1975 federal law eliminated state laws that protected these enforcement arrangements, often called **fair trade contracts**. However, in 2007, the U.S. Supreme Court reversed a long-standing precedent with the *Leegin* case (Case 16.2) that has changed the nature of distribution agreements by allowing sellers to enforce their suggested prices.[1]

CASE 16.2

Leegin Creative Leather Products, Inc. v. PSKS, Inc.
127 S.Ct. 2705 (2007)

It's Not in the Bag; It's in the Service

FACTS

Leegin Creative Leather Products, Inc. (Leegin) (petitioner), designs, manufactures, and distributes leather goods and accessories under the brand name "Brighton." The Brighton brand has now expanded into a full line of women's fashion accessories and is sold across the United States in over 5,000 retail stores. PSKS, Inc., (PSKS) (respondent) runs Kay's Kloset, a Brighton retailer in Lewisville, Texas, that carried about 75 different product lines, but was known as the place in that area to go for Brighton. Kay's ran Brighton ads and had Brighton days in its store.

Leegin's president, Jerry Kohl, who also has an interest in about 70 stores that sell Brighton products, released a new strategic refocus for Brighton by explaining: "[W]e want the consumers to get a different experience than they get in Sam's Club or in Wal-Mart. And you can't get that kind of experience or support or customer service from a store like Wal-Mart." As a result, Leegin instituted the "Brighton Retail Pricing and Promotion Policy," which banished retailers that discounted Brighton goods below suggested prices. The policy had an exception for products not selling well that the retailer did not plan on reordering. The established prices gave its retailers sufficient margins to provide customers with the quality service central to Brighton's strategy.

In December 2002, Leegin discovered Kay's Kloset had been marking down Brighton's entire line by 20 percent. Kay's Kloset said it did so to compete with nearby retailers who also were undercutting Leegin's suggested prices. Leegin, nonetheless, requested that Kay's Kloset cease discounting. Its request refused, Leegin stopped selling to the store. The loss of the Brighton brand had a considerable negative impact on the store's revenue from sales (about 40–50% of its profits were from Brighton).

PSKS sued Leegin for violation of the antitrust laws. Leegin asked to introduce expert testimony describing the procompetitive effects of its pricing policy. The District Court excluded the testimony, relying on Leegin's conduct to be a *per se* violation of federal antitrust laws. The jury awarded PSKS $1.2 million in damages, and the judge trebled the damages and reimbursed PSKS for its attorney's fees and costs, for a total judgment against Leegin of $3,975,000.80. The Court of Appeals affirmed. Leegin appealed. The U.S. Supreme Court granted *certiorari*.

JUDICIAL OPINION

KENNEDY, Justice

[T]he per se rule is appropriate only after courts have had considerable experience with the type of restraint at issue, and only if courts can predict with confidence that it would be invalidated in all or almost all instances under the rule of reason.

The justifications for vertical price restraints are similar to those for other vertical restraints. Minimum resale price maintenance can stimulate interbrand competition—the competition among manufacturers selling different brands of the same type of product—by reducing intrabrand competition—the competition among retailers selling the same brand. Resale price maintenance also has the potential to give consumers more options so that they can choose among low-price, low-service brands; high-price, high-service brands; and brands that fall in between.

If the consumer can then buy the product from a retailer that discounts because it has not spent capital providing services or developing a quality reputation, the high-service retailer will lose sales to the discounter, forcing it to cut back its services to a level lower than consumers would otherwise prefer. With price competition decreased, the manufacturer's retailers compete among themselves over services.

Resale price maintenance, in addition, can increase interbrand competition by facilitating market entry for new firms and brands. "[N]ew manufacturers and manufacturers entering new markets can use the restrictions in order to induce competent and aggressive retailers to make the kind of investment of capital and labor that is often required in the distribution of products unknown to the consumer."

Resale price maintenance can also increase interbrand competition by encouraging retailer services that would not be provided even absent free riding. It may be difficult and inefficient for a manufacturer to make and enforce a contract with a retailer specifying the different services the retailer must perform. Offering the retailer a guaranteed margin and threatening termination if it does not live up to expectations may be the most efficient way to expand the manufacturer's market share by inducing the retailer's performance and allowing it to use its own initiative and experience in providing valuable services.

While vertical agreements setting minimum resale prices can have procompetitive justifications, they may have anticompetitive effects in other circumstances. Vertical price restraints also "might be used to organize cartels at the retailer level." A group of retailers might collude to fix prices to consumers and then compel a manufacturer to aid the unlawful arrangement with resale price maintenance. In that instance the manufacturer does not establish the practice to stimulate services or to promote its brand but to give inefficient retailers higher profits. Retailers with better distribution systems and lower cost structures would be prevented from charging lower prices by the agreement.

Vertical agreements establishing minimum resale prices can have either procompetitive or anticompetitive effects, depending upon the circumstances in which they are formed.

Resale price maintenance, it is true, does have economic dangers. If the rule of reason were to apply to vertical price restraints, courts would have to be diligent in eliminating their anticompetitive uses from the market.

Reversed.

DISCUSSION QUESTIONS

1. What reasons did Leegin give for wanting the minimum price established for its retailers?

2. What points does the court make about not having minimum prices in terms of reducing competition?

3. What risks are there in allowing minimum price requirements?

MONOPSONY

A **monopsony** exists when the buyer, rather than the seller, has the ability to control market prices. In *Weyerhaeuser* v. *Ross-Simons*, 549 U.S. 312 (2007), the U.S. Supreme Court held that antitrust laws apply to both predatory pricing and **predatory bidding**. In the case, Ross-Simons Hardware Lumber alleged that Weyerhaeuser tried to drive it out of business by bidding up the price of sawlogs to a level that prevented Ross-Simons from being profitable. Although the lower courts found for Ross-Simons, the U.S. Supreme Court held that a plaintiff in a predatory bidding case must be able to show what a plaintiff in a predatory pricing case must show—that the bids were at such a level that below-cost pricing resulted.

Weyerhaeuser was able to show that its investment in equipment and advanced processes allowed it to process more timber and that its huge demand was driving up the price. Ross-Simons was not able to establish that the price increases were actually sought by Weyerhaeuser. The demand drove up the price, but the demand came through Weyerhaeuser's superior processing, not through nefarious means.

SOLE OUTLETS AND EXCLUSIVE DISTRIBUTORSHIPS

A **sole outlet** or **exclusive distributorship** agreement is one in which a manufacturer appoints a distributor or retailer as the sole or exclusive outlet for the manufacturer's product. This type of arrangement can be a violation of Section 1 but is subject to a rule of reason analysis. In a rule of reason analysis of sole outlets or exclusive distributorships, courts examine a manufacturer's freedom to pick and choose outlets or distributors. However, the extent of the **interbrand competition**, which is the competition available for the manufacturer's product, is critical. For example, in the case of the sandwich-meat manufacturer, as long as other manufacturers are selling their products in the area, the manufacturer could agree to sell to only one chain of grocery stores. But without interbrand competition, the antitrust laws require more **intrabrand competition**. If a manufacturer were the only one distributing sandwich meats in the area, dealing with only one grocery chain might not survive an antitrust challenge under the rule of reason.

ethical *issues*

Department 56 is a company that manufactures and sells collectible Christmas village houses and other replica items to allow collectors to create the whimsical "Snow Village" town or "Dickens Christmas." Department 56 has only authorized dealers. Sam's Club, a division of Wal-Mart Stores, Inc., began selling Department 56 pieces from The Heritage Village Collection.

Susan Engel, president and CEO of Department 56, attempted to contact Wal-Mart because it is not an authorized Department 56 dealer. Wal-Mart did not respond, and Ms. Engel sent by FedEx to National Collector clubs a letter that contained the following language:

Sam's Club should not have any Department 56 merchandise. In a marketing environment where most companies are fighting to get their merchandise into the Wal-Marts of the world, we are fighting to get our merchandise out. While we recognize there is surely a place for mass market and warehouse stores, Department 56 Villages enjoy a strong heritage of dealer sales and service support. Our products simply do not fit the warehouse-style selling environment of Sam's Club.

Of strong importance to us—and we hope to you too—is the tradition of selling our villages through an exclusive dealer network made up almost entirely of independent retailers. Wal-Mart Stores, Inc., and its subsidiaries are predators on these hard-working individuals. Sales of our products mean virtually nothing to the bottom line of a company the size of Wal-Mart. But to many of our loyal dealers, healthy Department 56 product sales mean survival.

Do you really need to shop at Sam's Club or Wal-Mart? Let's refuse to purchase villages or any other products from local Wal-Mart owned stores.

The letter asked collector club members to write Wal-Mart executives and local store managers. Names, mailing addresses, and telephone and fax numbers were offered.

Has Ms. Engel violated any laws? How do you think Sam's Club obtained the Department 56 products? Evaluate Ms. Engel's conduct in sending out the letter. Were her statements about Wal-Mart and calls to action fair? Ethical? Should Wal-Mart respond? How?

CUSTOMER AND TERRITORIAL RESTRICTIONS

Sole outlets allow manufacturers to decide (within limitations) to whom they will sell goods. However, manufacturers are not given the right to control what the buyer does with goods and how those goods are sold. The restrictions are subject to the rule of reason because interbrand competition may be increased even though intrabrand competition is reduced. For **customer and territorial restrictions** to be valid, enough interbrand competition must balance out decreased intrabrand competition.

TYING ARRANGEMENTS

Tying sales require buyers to take an additional product in order to buy a needed product. For example, requiring the buyer of a copier machine to buy the seller's paper when other brands of paper are equally suitable for use in the machine is a tying arrangement. The copier machine is the tying product or the desired product, and the paper is the tied product or the required product. Tying is usually an illegal *per se* violation of Section 3 of the Clayton Act (for goods contracts) and Section 1 of the Sherman Act (for services, real property, and intangibles). The presence of market power is the key to whether tying is a violation. For example, requiring the purchase of inferior movie films in order to buy copyrighted quality films is an example of the presence of market power. Because the seller is the only one with the copyrighted films, market power is being used to sell another unnecessary, low-demand product.

Two defenses have been recognized in tying cases. The first is the *new industry defense.* Under this defense, the manufacturer of the tying product is permitted to have a tied product to protect initially the quality control in the start-up of a business. For example, a cable television antenna manufacturer required purchasers to take a service contract also. The tying was upheld during the outset of the business so that the system could begin functioning properly and this new cable television industry could catch hold.

A second defense is *quality control for the protection of goodwill.* This defense is rarely supportable. The defense applies if the specifications for the tied goods were so detailed that they could not possibly be supplied by anyone other than the manufacturer of the tying product or there are issues of branding and goodwill.

consider 16.3

David Ungar holds a Dunkin' Donuts franchise. The terms of his franchise agreement require him to use only those ingredients furnished by Dunkin' Donuts. He is also required to buy their napkins, cups, and so on with the Dunkin' Donuts trademark on them. Is this an illegal tying arrangement? What if Dunkin' Donuts maintains that it needs these requirements to maintain its quality levels on a nationwide basis? (Analysis appears at the end of the chapter.) [*Ungar* v. *Dunkin' Donuts of Am., Inc.,* 531 F.2d 1211 (3d Cir. 1976)]

. . . .

Price Discrimination

The Robinson-Patman Act prohibits **price discrimination**, which is selling goods at prices that have different ratios to the marginal cost of producing them. If two goods have the same marginal cost and are sold to different people at different prices, it is a case of price discrimination. Price discrimination is an example of the use of vertical restraints to lessen horizontal competition. Predatory pricing or pricing below cost is an example of conduct that will injure or destroy competition.

Price discrimination can come in the form of the actual price charged but can also come from indirect charges. For example, offering different credit terms to equally qualified buyers can constitute price discrimination. The products sold must be of **like grade or quality**, which means no physical differences in the product. Label differences do not make the products different. For example, the sandwich-meat manufacturer that makes a private-label meat cannot discriminate in price for the sale of that meat if the contents are the same as the manufacturer's advertised label meat and only the label is different. However, if the private-label meat has lower-quality meat in it, a price difference can be justified because the products are not the same. In *Utah Pie Co.* v. *Continental Baking Co.,* 386 U.S. 685 (1967), the U.S. Supreme Court held that a company that prices differently in different markets to eliminate competition, particularly when that pricing is below cost, has engaged in price discrimination. In the case, an out-of-state pie manufacturer priced its pies below cost in Utah so that it could eliminate competition from a local pie manufacturer. The mark of price discrimination is that once the competition is eliminated, prices return to a much higher level. The larger out-of-state company sustains the losses on the sales until the competitor is driven out of business. The result is less competition.

Defenses to Price Discrimination

Legitimate cost differences in the manufacture or handling of a product mean price discrimination is not the issue. Additional costs of delivery or of adding specifications to a product can increase the price without violating the Robinson-Patman Act.

For example, if a sandwich-meat manufacturer produces a special low-fat bologna, the price for that product can be different. If the manufacturer uses different shipping companies for its customers, a price differential may be acceptable.

Quantity discounts are permitted as long as the seller can show actual cost savings are realized in the sale of increased quantities and not just an assumption that larger sales are more economical. Limiting the number of buyers who qualify for quantity discounts is some proof that the actual cost savings are not present.

Prices for products also can change according to market, inflation, material costs, and other variable factors. The seller must simply establish that a price change was initiated in response to one of these factors.

Another defense to a charge of price discrimination is **meeting the competition**. This defense must establish that a price change was made in a certain market to meet the competition there. Also, the seller must charge the same as its competitors and not a lower price. Finally, the price differences must be limited to an area or individuals. For example, a national firm may have a different price in one state because of more competition within that particular state.

VERTICAL MERGERS

Vertical mergers are between firms that have a buyer–seller relationship. For example, if a sandwich-meat manufacturer merged with its meat supplier, it would be a vertical merger. In determining whether a vertical merger violates the Clayton Act, the courts determine the relevant geographic and product markets and then determine whether the effect of the merger will be to foreclose or lessen competition.

What Are the Penalties and Remedies for Anticompetitive Behavior?

The federal antitrust laws have powerful incentives for compliance that include substantial penalties and remedies. The penalties and remedies are summarized in the following text and in Exhibit 16.3.

EXHIBIT   16.3   Antitrust Remedies

	SHERMAN ACT	CLAYTON ACT	ROBINSON-PATMAN ACT	FTC ACT
Criminal	$350,000 and/or three years in prison for individuals; $100 million for corporations; directors and officers also liable as to intent and knowledge	None	Section 4 for intentional price discrimination	None
Civil	Treble damages plus costs and attorney fees	Same	Same	None
Equitable	Injunctions, divestitures, asset distributions, sales	Same	Same	Same
Enforcers	Justice Department; U.S. attorney; state attorneys general; private persons	Same	Same	FTC

CRIMINAL PENALTIES

The Sherman Act carries felony criminal penalties. For individuals, the penalties are fines of up to $10 million and/or up to 10 years in prison. Corporations may be assessed fines of up to $100 million. These criminal penalties require proof that the violator intended the anticompetitive conduct and realized the consequences of the action taken.

The FTC and Clayton Acts do not carry criminal penalties. However, Section 4 of the Robinson-Patman Act makes criminal certain forms of intentional price discrimination. Officers and directors of violating corporations can also be held criminally liable for antitrust violations, depending upon their level of knowledge and involvement. For example, in the Archer Daniels Midland price-fixing case, officers were held responsible for the violations because of their direct knowledge of the price-fixing activities. The Antitrust Division of the Department of Justice or the local U.S. attorney's office is responsible for bringing criminal actions under the antitrust laws.

EQUITABLE REMEDIES

Equitable remedies consist of court orders that restrain or prevent anticompetitive conduct. Equitable remedies are available in both private and government enforcement actions. An **injunction** is a frequent form of antitrust relief; it is a court order prohibiting a violating party from engaging in anticompetitive conduct. For example, a firm can be ordered to divest itself of an acquired firm or, in an unlawful asset acquisition, a court order can require that the assets be divided with a competing firm. Contracts whose terms violate the antitrust laws can be canceled by court order. Equitable remedies give the courts discretion to fashion remedies that will eliminate the results of anticompetitive behavior.

PRIVATE ACTIONS FOR DAMAGES

Section 4 of the Clayton Act allows any person whose business or property is injured as a result of an antitrust violation to recover "threefold the damages by him sustained"—commonly referred to as **treble damages**—along with the costs of the suit and reasonable attorney fees. This section, with its substantial recovery provisions, is strong incentive for private enforcement of antitrust laws. Consumers, businesses, and state attorneys general can all bring private damage actions under Section 4. These treble damages have found plaintiffs looking for ways to tap into the antitrust statutes, but the U.S. Supreme Court has been cautious in extending the remedies. In *Credit Suisse Securities (USA) LLC v. Billing,* 127 S.Ct. 2383 (2007), the Court held that securities investors who were bringing suit for IPO (initial primary offerings, see Chapter 14) pricing and allocation needed to turn to the securities laws for their remedies, not the antitrust laws and their treble damages. The court held that securities regulation is so extensive and investor protections so readily available that the antitrust laws did not apply to the conduct of investment bankers and brokers for purposes of investor relief.

Types of damages include lost profits, increased costs, and decreased value in property. These damage suits have a four-year statute of limitations; that is, suit must be brought within four years of the alleged violation. Those who bring private damage suits enjoy a proof benefit: They can use the government's judgment in its suit as *prima facie* evidence against the violating defendant. A ***prima facie* case** allows a plaintiff to survive a directed verdict and entitles the plaintiff to a judgment if the defendant offers no contradictory evidence (see Chapter 3 for more discussion).

What Lies Ahead in Anticompetitive Behavior: The Antitrust Modernization Commission

The Antitrust Modernization Commission (AMC), created in 2002, finished its work and completed its report on May 31, 2007. The AMC had the following general findings and recommendations:

1. Courts have been taking the correct approach in their reasoning and analyses of cases involving antitrust issues by carefully examining markets, economic systems, and individual companies and products. That approach should continue.

2. Congress does not need to change either Section 2 of the Sherman Act or Section 7 of the Clayton Act. The case law has evolved in a consistent and understandable manner.

3. The AMC also noted that change in the antitrust laws was unnecessary because, as many argued, the reality is now a "new economy" of technology-driven business rather than an old economy of traditional businesses. The AMC noted that the laws of economics are the same and if applied to cases with consistency, the issues of the "new economy" were resolved correctly through judicial interpretation and application.

4. The AMC did find some issues with regard to the interaction of patent protections with competition and that certain provisions and protections in the patent laws may actually be serving as blockades for competition. Also, the AMC noted that holding a patent does not automatically translate into monopolistic behavior. The AMC felt that Congress should address the patent law issues but not the antitrust laws.

   What lies ahead is now up to Congress and its response to the findings.

Antitrust Issues in International Competition

As the level of international trade has increased, so also has the number of competitors. For example, three domestic manufacturers produce cars in the United States. However, the availability of international trade markets has resulted in the importing of cars from Japan, Great Britain, Germany, Sweden, and Yugoslavia; and international competition changes the market perspective because the relevant market is not the United States, but the world. In fact, in 2007, Toyota became the number one seller of autos in the United States because of open international competition.

As a result of increased levels of international competition, more joint ventures of competitors and large companies that once would have seemed unthinkable under antitrust protections will be permitted. For example, American Telephone and Telegraph (AT&T) has entered into a joint venture agreement with the Economic Ministry of Taiwan to improve that nation's telecommunications systems. General Mills, Inc., was permitted to acquire RJR Nabisco's cold-cereal business in both the United Kingdom and the United States so that it could compete more effectively in the large North American and European markets.

The EU has developed its own antitrust guidelines and has challenged a number of proposed U.S. firm mergers in the EU. As these large mergers are proposed, the EU and other countries are taking a closer look at their anticompetitive effects. In 2001, General Electric was handed one of the few management setbacks legendary and then-CEO Jack Welch ever experienced. The proposed acquisition of Honeywell International by General Electric was opposed by EU antitrust enforcers. The EU's Merger Task Force recommended that the $41 billion proposed merger not be permitted.

The U.S. Supreme Court has held that companies from other countries that engage in commerce in the United States will be subject to U.S. antitrust laws. Foreign corporations doing business here are subject to the same rules of competition required of U.S. corporations.

Red Flags FOR MANAGERS

Antitrust laws help keep the playing field for competitors level. Businesses can capture all the market they can through superior skill, foresight, and industry. If a company has built a better mousetrap and customers flock to it for that mousetrap and the company then dominates the mousetrap market, there is no antitrust violation.

If you exchange price lists with your competitors and agree to charge the same prices for your products, you have violated the Sherman Act. Even meetings among competitors to discuss their market, pricing, or credit terms are violations.

Buyers also have to have a level playing field. You cannot charge higher prices to some customers when those prices are not tied to marginal costs (volume).

You also cannot require customers to purchase unwanted products or services to get one of your products that they want.

The vertical distribution of goods is also covered by antitrust laws. Use caution on requiring your retailers to sell at a certain price. Be careful when you make a decision to refuse to deal with a retailer. Retail price maintenance and refusals to deal in the vertical chain may also be antitrust violations.

There is risk in not complying with federal antitrust laws. Beyond civil and criminal penalties, customers and competitors can recover treble damages. When you create a monopoly unlawfully, the Justice Department can require a break-up of your company.

Summary

What restraints of trade are permissible?

- Covenant not to compete—clause in employment or business sale contracts that restricts competition by one of the parties; must be reasonable in scope and time

What antitrust laws exist?

- Sherman Act—first federal antitrust law; prohibits monopolization and horizontal trade restraints such as price fixing, boycotts, and refusals to deal

- Clayton Act—federal antitrust statute that prohibits tying and interlocking directorates; controls mergers

- Federal Trade Commission Act—federal law that allows the FTC to regulate unfair competition

- Robinson-Patman Act—anti–price discrimination federal statute

- Celler-Kefauver Act—regulates asset acquisitions

- Hart-Scott-Rodino Antitrust Improvements Act—antitrust law that broadened Justice Department authority and provided new merger guidelines

What are the forms of horizontal trade restraint and defenses?

- Horizontal restraints of trade—anticompetitive behavior among a firm's competitors
- Price fixing—controlling price of goods through agreement, limiting supply, controlling credit
- Group boycotts—agreement among competitors to exclude competition
- Joint ventures—temporary combinations that may restrain trade
- *Per se* violation—violation of antitrust laws that has no defense or justification
- Monopolization—possession of monopoly power in the relevant market by willful acquisition
- Market power—power to control prices or exclude competition
- Relevant market—geographic and product market used to determine market power
- Predatory pricing—pricing below actual cost to monopolize

What are the forms of vertical trade restraints and defenses?

- Resale price maintenance—requiring prices be set in vertical distribution
- Exclusive distributorship—limited dealership rights; not an antitrust violation as long as horizontal competition exists
- Tying—requiring buyers to take an additional product in order to purchase the product they wish
- Price discrimination—selling goods across state lines at prices that have different ratios to marginal costs

What penalties can be imposed for restraints of trade?

- Equitable remedies—nonmonetary remedies such as injunctions
- Treble damages—three times actual damages available in antitrust cases

Key Terms

Clayton Act 366
covenant not to compete 365
cross-elasticity 369
customer and territorial restrictions 376
equitable remedies 379
exclusionary conduct 369
exclusive distributorship 375
failing-company doctrine 371
fair trade contracts 373
geographic market 369
group boycotts 368
horizontal restraints of trade 368
injunction 379

interbrand competition 375
intrabrand competition 375
like grade or quality 377
market power 368
meeting the competition 378
monopolization 368
monopsony 373
per se illegal 367
predatory bidding 373
predatory pricing 369
price discrimination 377
price fixing 368
prima facie case 379
product market 369

relevant market 369
resale price maintenance 372
Robinson-Patman Act 366
rule of reason 368
small-company doctrine 371
sole outlet 375
submarket 369
superior skill, foresight, and industry 369
treble damages 379
tying sales 376
vertical mergers 378

Questions and Problems

1. Amanda Reiss had completed her residency in ophthalmology in Portland, Oregon, and was moving to Phoenix, Arizona, to start her practice. She began looking for office space and met with a leasing agent who showed her several complexes of medical suites. Dr. Reiss was ready to sign for one of them when the leasing agent turned to her and said, "Oh, by the way, you're not one of those advertising doctors, are you? Because they don't want that kind in any of my complexes." Has there been a violation of the antitrust laws?

2. Budget Rent-a-Car and Aloha Airlines have developed a "fly-drive" program. Under their agreement, customers of Aloha receive a $7 first-day rental rate for car rentals (the usual rate is $14). Robert's Waikiki U-Drive has brought suit, challenging the agreement as a tying arrangement and unlawful. Is Robert's correct? [*Robert's Waikiki U-Drive v. Budget Rent-a-Car*, 732 F.2d 1403 (9th Cir. 1984)]

3. In April 1965, Berkeley Heights Shopping Center leased 11,514 square feet of space to A&P Supermarkets. Under the terms of the lease, Berkeley agreed not to lease any other shopping center space to another grocery store. On April 16, 1977, A&P informed Berkeley that it was ceasing operations and subleasing the premises to Drug Fair, a modern drug store chain that sells foodstuffs. In 1985, Berkeley sought to lease other space in the center to another grocery store, and Drug Fair objected on the grounds of the covenant not to compete. Berkeley maintains the covenant only applies when the premises Drug Fair occupies are used as a grocery store operation. Who is correct? [*Berkeley Dev. Co. v. Great Atlantic & Pacific Tea Co.,* 518 A.2d 790 (N.J. 1986)]

4. Russell Stover is a candy manufacturer that ships its products to 18,000 retailers nationwide. Stover designates resale prices for its dealers but does not request assurances from them that they are honoring the prices. It has, however, refused to sell to those retailers it believes will sell below the prices suggested. Is there an antitrust violation in this conduct? [*Russell Stover Candies, Inc. v. FTC,* 718 F.2d 256 (8th Cir. 1982)]

5. Systems and Software, Inc. (SAS), located in Colchester, Vermont, designs, develops, sells, and services software that allows utility providers to organize their data, including customer information, billing, work management, asset management, and finance and accounting. In August 2002, SAS hired Randy Barnes as an at-will employee to become a regional vice president of sales. At the time he commenced work for SAS, Barnes signed a noncompetition agreement that, among other things, prohibited him—during his employment and for six months thereafter—from becoming associated with any business that competes with SAS. In April 2004, Barnes voluntarily left his position with SAS and started a partnership with his wife called Spirit Technologies Consulting Group. Spirit Technologies' only customer was Utility Solutions, Inc., which, like SAS, services municipalities and utilities nationwide with respect to customer-information-systems software. Shortly after Barnes left SAS, he represented Utility Solutions at a trade fair in a booth near SAS's booth and identified himself as Utility Solution's sales director.

SAS filed suit requesting for injunctive relief and enforcement of the parties' noncompetition agreement. Barnes says that the effect of enforcement of the clause is to prevent him from working for six months and stopping competition in Vermont. Who is correct on the noncompetition agreement? Is it valid? Why or why not? [*Systems and Software, Inc. v. Barnes,* 886 A.2d 762, (Vt. 2005)]

Understanding "Consider" Problems

16.1

THINK: A monopolist has market power or the ability to control prices and exclude competition. Market share is an indicator of market power, and defining the market controls how great the market share will be. There must also be some act that puts the monopolist ahead in the market by some means other than skill, insight, and industry.

APPLY: Starbucks has a 73 percent market share in coffee shops, but if the combination donut and coffee houses are included, its share is less than 50%. However, Starbucks does dominate certain geographic areas.

ANSWER: The situation presents a potential monopolist situation because of Starbuck's market power and its deal with landlords. On the other hand, covenants in leases in which landlords agree not to lease to competitors are protected as a need for product mix. The outcome will depend on the findings of Starbucks' market power and acts other than the leases. Stafford's case survived a motion to dismiss in 2007 and was headed to trial in 2008.

Source: Edward Iwata, "Owner of small coffee shop takes on java titan Starbucks," *USA Today,* December 20, 2006, p. 1B.

16.2

THINK: The elements for price fixing are that competitors act together to keep prices at a certain level or agree to charge a certain price or even to discuss the components of price. The statute does require an agreement between the parties.

APPLY: There must be evidence of an agreement to fix prices.

ANSWER: Britain's Office of Fair Trade found that the peculiar parallel movement of fares throughout the period was evidence that the airlines were fixing pricing by sharing information about costs. The airlines settled the case.

16.3

THINK: Tying is illegal unless the tied product is something required to maintain quality, such as in a franchise for purposes of quality or goodwill.

APPLY: Dunkin' Donuts is a franchise organization that has a brand to protect and wants uniform quality.

ANSWER: This tying arrangement was not a violation of federal antitrust laws because the paper goods help to endure uniformity, brand recognition, and quality. Consumers are drawn to uniformity, so the requirement enhances Dunkin' Donuts ability to compete with other donut shops.

Notes

1. The author is grateful to Professor Sue Mota of Bowling Green State University for her insights on this case and the new trends in antitrust law. See Sue Mota, "Antitrust Limited: The Supreme Court Reins In Antitrust Enforcement," 7 *Fla. State U. Bus. Rev.* 1 (2007).

17

Management and Employee Rights and Laws

update

For up-to-date legal news, click on "Author Updates" at

www.cengage.com/blaw/ jennings

All businesses have a common thread: employees. They need them, rely on them, pay them, and give them authority to perform certain business tasks. This chapter focuses on that delegation of authority and these questions: When does an employee act on behalf of an employer? How much authority does an employee have? What are the statutory duties and obligations between employers and employees? What is the law on safety, termination, and the right to form a union? When is a business liable for an employee's acts? ■

Fatal occupational injuries in 2007: 5,488
Females killed in the workplace: 417 (8%)
Percentage of workforce who are women: 46%
Industry with highest fatality rate: Agriculture
Industry with second highest fatality rate: Mining
Industry with third highest fatality rate: Transportation
Deaths on the job in 2007 from vehicle accidents: 1,311
Homicides in the workplace in 2007: 610
Accident rate in the workplace in 1992: 8.3 per 100
Accident rate in the workplace in 2007: 3.7 per 100
U.S. DEPARTMENT OF LABOR STATISTICS, 2007

OSHA violations found in 2007 in the workplace: 83,913
OCCUPATIONAL SAFETY AND HEALTH ADMINISTRATION
http://www.osha.gov (2007 is the most recent data available in 2008)

How to Fire Someone Without Being Sued

1. Do not fire anyone.

2. Fire everyone.

3. Fire everyone in the same division.

4. Fire only those employees with well-documented and written performance problems.

5. Fire only those employees for whom managers can articulate a legitimate business justification.

6. Do not violate any internal company procedures when selecting employees for termination.

7. Offer terminated employees a severance package in exchange for signing a release not to sue the company.

8. Do not threaten the employee.

9. Give the employee a brief but specific reason for the termination.

10. Be kind.

From Cameron Stracher, "How to Fire Someone Without Being Sued"
New York Times Magazine, *April 8, 2001, p. 54*

---

consider...

Jerome Lange was the manager of a small grocery store that carried Nabisco products. Ronnell Lynch was Nabisco's cookie salesman-trainee. On May 1, 1969, Mr. Lynch came to Mr. Lange's store to place previously delivered Nabisco products on the shelves. An argument developed between the two over Mr. Lynch's service to the store. Mr. Lynch became very angry and started swearing. Mr. Lange told him to either stop swearing or leave the store because children were present. Mr. Lynch then became uncontrollably angry and said, "I ought to break your neck." He then went behind the counter and dared Mr. Lange to fight. When Mr. Lange refused, Mr. Lynch viciously assaulted him, after which he threw merchandise around the store and left.

Is Nabisco liable for Mr. Lynch's actions?

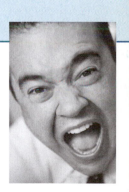

The Common Law Issues in the Employment Relationship: Agency

NAMES AND ROLES: AGENCY TERMINOLOGY

A principal–agent relationship is one in which one party acts on behalf of another. A clerk who helps you to the dressing room and takes your payment in a department store is an agent. Michael Phelps has an agent who negotiates his endorsement and appearance contracts for him. A **power of attorney** is a form of agency relationship that grants to another the authority to enter into transactions, such as when a landowner gives another the authority to close a particular land transaction or when a person hires an adviser to manage his or her financial affairs, including everything from handling checking accounts to entering into contracts. The common thread in all of these relationships is that one party acts on behalf of another.

Agency

In an agency relationship, one party agrees to act on behalf of another party according to directions. Agency is a consensual relationship—both sides agree to it—and a fiduciary relationship with duties and responsibilities on both sides.

Principals

In the employer–employee relationship, the employers are referred to as the **principals**. The term *principal* is used because some agents are not truly employees. A literary agent, for example, represents many authors who are the agent's principals, but the principals are not "employers," in the usual sense, of the agent.

Agents

Agents are people hired by a principal to do a task on behalf of the principal. The agent represents the principal in such a way that if the agent negotiates a contract, the principal, but not the agent, is bound by and a party to the contract. A president of a corporation is an agent of the corporation. When the president negotiates a contract, the corporation, not the president, is bound to perform that contract.

All employees are agents of the principal employer, but not all agents are employees. A corporation might hire an architect to design a new office building and obtain bids for the construction of the building. The architect would be an agent for limited purposes but not an employee of the company.

Employers and Employees: Master–Servant Relationships

A **master–servant relationship** is one in which the principal (master) exercises a great deal of control over the agent (servant).[1] An employer–employee relationship for a production line worker is an example of a master–servant relationship. Among the various factors considered are whether an employee works regular hours, is paid a regular wage, and is subject to complete supervision and control by the employer during work hours. The factors used to determine whether a master–servant relationship exists are as follows:

- Level of supervision of the agent
- Level of control of the agent
- Nature of the agent's work

- Regularity of hours and pay
- Length of employment

Independent Contractors

An **independent contractor** is a person who is hired by another to perform a task but is not under the direct control of the hiring party. For example, a corporation's attorney is an agent of the corporation only for purposes of legal representation and court appearances. The attorney is not a corporate employee, and the corporation has no control over the attorney's office operations. The attorney is an independent contractor. A subcontractor hired to perform partial work on a construction site is also an example of an independent contractor.

Principals have less responsibility for independent contractors than for servants because they have little control over a contractor's conduct.

Agency Law

Agency law is not statutory; rather, its source is common law. Common law regarding agency is found in the ***Restatement of Agency***, which is a summary of the majority view of agency law in the United States that is followed by many courts in handling agency cases.

Studying agency law actually involves examining three different components: creation of the agency relationship, the relationship between principals and agents, and the relationship of the agents and principals to third parties.

CREATION OF THE AGENCY RELATIONSHIP

Agency relationships can be created in different ways.

Express Authority

An employee who is hired by agreement (oral or written) is an agent and has been given **express authority** to act on behalf of the business.

The Record

An agency relationship is created by agreement, which need not be evidenced by a record, although it is best for both employer and employee to have a record. Some form of a record, electronic or written, that specifies the agent's authority is required only if the agent will enter into contracts required to have a record or if a state statute requires an agent's authority to be in some record form. For example, many states require that real estate agents' commission contracts be evidenced by a record. That record could be a written, faxed, or PDF document that is signed by the principal.

Capacity

Because agents will enter into contracts for their principals, the principals must have the **capacity** to contract. *Capacity* here means capacity in the traditional contract sense: age and mental capacity (as covered in Chapter 11).

An agency capacity issue that comes up frequently in sole proprietor, general partnership, and other smaller businesses that are dependent on key individual personalities is the stalemate that results when mental incapacity (through accident or illness frequently) in one of these key individuals becomes a factor. Under the **Uniform Durable Power of Attorney Act** (a uniform law that has been adopted in most states), these key individuals can execute a type of power of attorney that comes into existence in the event of disability or incapacity of the principal. This authority then "kicks in" when needed. The UDPAA has also been helpful for children who are trying to manage their parents' financial affairs when their parents become mentally or physically disabled.

The contractual capacity of the agent is not an issue in the agency relationship for purposes of the agent's authority to enter into contracts. However, the capacity of the agent to drive, operate equipment, or work with the public is an issue that affects the employer's liability to third parties. Because of this liability, many employers conduct background checks, polygraph and psychological tests, and drug screening as a precondition to hiring employees. Many firms also have ongoing drug-testing programs.

One of the most controversial issues in agency law concerns the **unincorporated association**, which is a group that acts as an entity but has no legal existence. Some charitable organizations—churches, for example—have an ongoing existence and have probably built buildings, had fund-raising drives, and entered into many contracts. However, because these organizations are not incorporated and do not have any legal existence, those who sign contracts for these groups are not agents, and as a result they have personal liability under contract. For example, suppose that a Little League coach signs a credit contract for the purchase of Little League equipment. The Little League organization is nonprofit and is not incorporated. In the event the league does not raise enough money to pay for the sporting equipment, the signing coach is liable because the league is not a principal with capacity.

The National Conference of Commissioners on Uniform State Laws proposed the *Uniform Unincorporated Nonprofit Association Act* (UUNAA) in 1996, and it has been adopted in 10 states. Under the UUNAA, the contract and tort liability of individual members of a nonprofit association would be eliminated if they were acting on behalf of their nonprofit unincorporated association.

Business Planning Tip

Before you sign on behalf of an organization, be sure you understand your liability. For example, if you sign a contract with a hotel for a group's meeting, you will have personal liability if your group is not incorporated and if the hotel is not paid. If your group is incorporated, be sure to sign so that the corporation, not you, is personally liable. You can use the following format:

(Your Group Name)

By: (Your Name)

(Your Title)

Here is an example:

Weaving Through the Maze, a nonprofit corporation

By: Marianne M. Jennings

President

Implied Authority

An agent under contract not only has the authority given expressly but also has certain **implied authority**. Implied authority is the extension of express authority by custom. For example, presidents of a corporation probably do not have their exact duties specified. However, this president will likely have the same type of authority customarily held by corporate presidents: to sign contracts, to authorize personnel changes, to conduct salary reviews and changes, and to institute operational changes.

Apparent Authority

In many cases an agency relationship arises not by express or implied contracts but because of the way a principal presents himself to third parties. This theory of agency law, called **apparent authority** or **agency by estoppel**, holds a principal liable if the principal makes someone else think he has an agent.

Apparent authority exists by appearance. A third party is led to believe that an agent, although not actually holding express and accompanying implied authority, had the proper authority to deal with the third party. *Montoya* v. *Grease Monkey Holding Corp.* (Case 17.1) is a landmark case in agency and corporation law that deals with issues of apparent authority.

CASE 17.1

Montoya v. Grease Monkey Holding Corp.
904 P.2D 468 (COLO. 1995)

A GREASE MONKEY'S UNCLE, ER, AGENT

FACTS

From 1983 through 1991, Arthur Sensenig was Grease Monkey's President, COO (chief operating officer), and Chairman of the Board. During that time, Mr. Sensenig ran Grease Monkey and had authority to raise capital from banks and other lenders.

Nick and Aver Montoya (respondents) were married for over 50 years. Aver Montoya was a factory worker for approximately 17 years, and she left financial matters primarily to her husband.

Nick Montoya met Mr. Sensenig in the mid-1960s when Mr. Sensenig was a teller at a bank where Mr. Montoya was a customer. During the 1960s and 1970s, Mr. Sensenig gave Mr. Montoya investment advice. Mr. Montoya was impressed by Mr. Sensenig, who ultimately became vice president of the bank before leaving. Mr. Montoya also knew Mr. Sensenig through a church connection.

From 1983 through 1991, Mr. Sensenig got payments from the Montoyas under the guise that the payments were investments in Grease Monkey. Mr. Sensenig told the Montoyas that because Grease Monkey was a new company, it did not have its own account, and that as President and Chairman of the Board, Mr. Sensenig used his personal account as the corporate account. Mr. Sensenig took Mr. Montoya to the Grease Monkey offices and showed him a promotional slide show presentation used by Grease Monkey to solicit franchise business. However, none of the payments were invested in Grease Monkey, and Grease Monkey did not receive any of the funds. Rather, Mr. Sensenig used the Montoyas' money for his own personal benefit.

Dreams turned to dust, and the Montoyas sought to put the monkey on the back of the corporation and filed suit against Grease Monkey, as Mr. Sensenig's employer, for breach of contract, fraud, misrepresentation, breach of duty of good faith and fair dealing, promissory estoppel, extreme and outrageous conduct, and negligent hiring and supervision.

After a trial to the court, the trial court entered judgment against Grease Monkey for the outstanding balance due on the promissory notes. The court of appeals affirmed the trial court judgment. Grease Monkey appealed.

JUDICIAL OPINION

ERICKSON, Justice

[I]f an agent acts with apparent authority, a principal may be liable even though the agent acts solely for his own purposes. Applying an apparent authority theory, "[l]iability is based upon the fact that the agent's position facilitates the consummation of the fraud, in that from the point of view of the third person the transaction seems regular on its face and the agent appears to be acting in the ordinary course of the business confided to him." In both state and federal misrepresentation cases, "[c]ourts have commonly imposed liability based on 'apparent authority' . . . particularly when the person making the misrepresentation is an important corporate official." . . .

[A] plaintiff must establish that the servant or other agent was put in a position which enabled the agent to commit fraud, the agent acted within his apparent authority, and the agent committed fraud. First, the trial court found that Sensenig was the highest authority at Grease Monkey. He had authority to raise up to $500,000 without Board approval, and as general officer and agent for Grease Monkey, he had broad authority to act without corporate restrictions. The findings of the trial court support a conclusion that Grease Monkey put Sensenig in a position where he could commit fraud if he had a mind to.

Second, the trial court found that Sensenig acted within his apparent authority when he raised capital from individuals such as respondents. We also note that "the theory of apparent authority . . . the agent's conduct is seen through the eyes of the third party." . . .

Third, the trial court found that Sensenig made false representations to respondents. Sensenig made these representations with the awareness they were false and with intent to induce respondents to rely on the representations. The representations were material, and respondents reasonably relied on the representations to their detriment. The trial court found for respondents on their claim of fraud and misrepresentation, and we are unwilling to disturb that finding on review.

. . . "few doctrines of the law are more firmly established or more in harmony with accepted notions of

CONTINUED

social policy than that of the liability of the principal without fault of his own." Our decision recognizes the legal principle that "when one of two innocent persons must suffer from the acts of a third, he must suffer who put it in the power of the wrongdoer to inflict the injury." This policy motivates organizations to see that their agents abide by the law.

Affirmed.

CASE QUESTIONS

1. What is the purpose of the apparent authority doctrine?

2. What duties does apparent authority impose on principals?

3. What should Grease Monkey have done to avoid being liable to the Montoyas?

consider 17.1

Suppose that a bar owner has employed a bouncer and the bouncer injures someone while removing him from the premises. Is the employer liable for the conduct of the bouncer? (Analysis appears at the end of the chapter.) [*Byrd* v. *Faber,* 57 Ohio St.3d 56, 565 N.E.2d 584, 587 (1991)]

Ratification

On occasion, an agent without proper authority enters into a contract. **Ratification** occurs when the principal reviews a contract and voluntarily decides that, even though the agent did not have proper authority, the contract will be honored as if the agent had full authority. Once a contract is ratified, it is effective from the time the agent entered into it even though the agent had no authority until after the fact. Ratification gives an agent authority retroactively.

For example, suppose that an apartment manager does not have the authority to contract for any type of construction work except routine maintenance. Because the fence around the apartment complex is deteriorated, the manager contracts for the construction of a completely new fence at a cost that exceeds by six times any maintenance work he has had done in the past. The contractor begins work on the fence, and the apartment owner drives by, sees the work, and says nothing. By her inaction in allowing the contractor to continue building the fence, the apartment complex owner ratifies the contract.

THE PRINCIPAL–AGENT RELATIONSHIP

There is a contractual relationship between the agent and the principal, so that each has certain obligations and rights. This section of the chapter covers that relationship.

The Agent's Responsibilities

Principals and agents have a **fiduciary** relationship, which is one of loyalty, trust, care, and obedience. An agent in the role of fiduciary must act in the principal's best interests.

Duty of Loyalty: General   An agent is required to act only for the benefit of the principal, and an agent cannot represent both parties in a transaction unless each knows and consents. Further, an agent cannot use the information gained or the offers available to or by the principal to profit personally. For example, an agent hired to find a buyer for a new invention cannot interfere with the principal's possible sale by demonstrating his or her own product. Neither can an agent hired to find a piece of property buy the property and then sell it (secretly, of course) to the principal. *Lucini Italia Co.* v. *Grappolini* (Case 17.2) involves an issue of an agent's fiduciary duty in a sale transaction.

CASE 17.2

Lucini Italia Co. v. *Grappolini*
2003 W.L. 1989605 (N.D. Ill. 2003) (an unpublished opinion)

A SLICK DEAL BY THE OLIVE OIL AGENT

FACTS

Lucini Italia imports and sells premium extra virgin olive oil of Italy. Lucini was formed by Arthur Frigo, a Chicago entrepreneur and adjunct professor of management and strategy at Northwestern University's Kellogg Graduate School of Management. Giuseppe Grappolini and his company (defendants), from Loro Ciuffenna, Italy, served as a consultant to Lucini. Under his consulting contract, Mr. Grappolini was to develop Lucini Premium Select extra virgin olive oil. Mr. Frigo had discovered a market niche in the United States for high-end olive oil ($10 to $12 per bottle).

Mr. Frigo instructed Mr. Grappolini to negotiate an exclusive supply contract for Lucini with Vegetal, an Italian company with a unique olive oil that Mr. Frigo needed to develop an olive oil with lemon and garlic added (called the LEO project). Vegetal was the only company that could supply the type of olive oil Mr. Frigo needed. Mr. Grappolini led Mr. Frigo along with promises of a deal with the Vegetal company for nearly a year, through reports of meetings as well as with faxes and memos appearing to detail terms, conditions, and dates for delivery. Mr. Grappolini was meeting with Mr. Frigo almost daily as they discussed the plans for the new Lucini olive oil.

Nervous as he launched LPE, Mr. Frigo had Lucini's lawyer in Italy contact Vegetal directly for a copy of the contract he thought he had with Vegtal. The lawyer learned that Vegetal had a supply contract, but the contract was with Mr. Grappolini's company and that it was not transferable to Lucini. The officers at Vegetal said that Grappolini had been a "bad boy" in negotiating the contract for himself. Vegetal agreed to supply Lucini with olive oil, but could not deliver it in time for the launch of Lucini's new line. Mr. Frigo and Lucini sued against Mr. Grappolini and his company (defendants) for breach of fiduciary duty.

JUDICIAL OPINION

DENLOW, Magistrate

As agents, Defendants owed Lucini general duties of good faith, loyalty, and trust. In addition, Defendants owed Lucini "full disclosure of all relevant facts relating to the transaction or affecting the subject matter of the agency."

Defendants were Lucini's agents and owed Lucini a fiduciary duty to advance Lucini's interests, not their own. When Defendants obtained an exclusive supply agreement with Vegetal for the Grappolini Company instead of for Lucini, they were disloyal and breached their fiduciary duties. Lucini suffered substantial damages as a result of this breach.

Punitive damages are appropriate where the defendant has intentionally breached a fiduciary duty. Defendants' breach of their fiduciary duties was flagrant and intentional. Defendants deliberately usurped a corporate opportunity sought by Lucini, which Lucini had entrusted Defendants to secure on Lucini's behalf. Although Defendants explicitly accepted this trust and ensured Lucini that Mr. Grappolini and his company would do as Lucini requested, Defendants failed to do so and hid this fact from Lucini.

Defendants misappropriated Lucini's valuable trade secrets. Defendants acquired Lucini's trade secrets under circumstances giving rise to a duty to maintain their secrecy.

Lucini's decision to focus its LEO project around essential oils from Vegetal Progress was a closely guarded trade secret.

As a proximate result of Defendants' breach of their fiduciary duties, Lucini suffered lost profits damages of at least $4.17 million from selling its grocery line of LEO products from 2000 through 2003. The Court will award Lucini its lost profits of $4,170,000,

CONTINUED

together with its $800,000 of development costs for LEO project. Defendants engaged in willful and malicious misappropriation as evidenced by their use of the information for directly competitive purposes and their efforts to hide the misappropriation and, accordingly, the Court will award $1,000,000 in exemplary damages. Such an award is necessary to discourage Defendants from engaging in such conduct in the future.

CASE QUESTIONS

1. What lessons can you learn about contracts, suppliers, and product launches from the case?

2. Explain why the court decided to award both lost profits and punitive damages.

3. Evaluate the ethics of Mr. Grappolini's conduct. Why did Vegetal's officers refer to Mr. Grappolini as a "bad boy"?

Duty of Loyalty: Postemployment   Many companies have their employees sign contracts that include covenants not to compete or covenants not to disclose information about their former employers should they leave their jobs or be terminated from their employment.

The laws on noncompete agreements vary from state to state, with California's being the most protective of employees. California's statute in essence prohibits employers from enforcing agreements that prohibit employees from working in their chosen fields. However, across all states, courts are clear that an underlying reason for the noncompete agreement must be evident, such as an employee having had access to the company's proprietary information.

Employees' signatures on these agreements must be voluntary. California has provided protection for employees who refuse to sign noncompete agreements, punishing employers with punitive damages when employees are terminated following their refusals to sign.

ethical *issues*

FAO Schwarz filed suit against its former chairman and CEO, John Eyler, because Mr. Eyler left his position at FAO Schwarz and joined Toys "R" Us in January 2000. The suit was one for breach of contract that alleged specifically that Mr. Eyler violated a clause in his employment agreement that required him to give one year's notice of his departure and also prevents him from working for a competitor for two years after his departure.

Mr. Eyler was hired at FAO Schwarz in 1992 and was paid a $2.4 million bonus in 1999.

Toys "R" Us, also named as a defendant in the suit, issued a response denying any wrongdoing and explaining that it would "vigorously defend" against the lawsuit. Toys "R" Us and FAO Schwarz had been in merger discussions last year, and Toys "R" Us had signed an agreement that it would not recruit FAO Schwarz employees for two

years following the merger discussions if those discussions failed (they did not, in fact, result in a merger).

The suit also alleges that Mr. Eyler took with him trade secrets and that FAO is entitled to protection against their use by Mr. Eyler.

What kinds of trade secrets do you think Mr. Eyler might have? What kinds of covenants not to compete are enforceable? Do you think this covenant should be enforced against Mr. Eyler? Evaluate the ethics of Toys "R" Us and Mr. Eyler.

Aftermath: FAO Schwarz entered Chapter 11 bankruptcy in 2002. It was purchased by a group of investors in 2005.

Source: Dana Canedy, "Schwarz Sues Chief for Move to Toys "R" Us," *New York Times*, February 18, 2000, pp. C1, C20.

Duty of Obedience   An agent has the duty to obey reasonable instructions from the principal. The agent is not required to do anything criminally wrong or commit torts, of course, but is required to operate according to the principal's standards and instructions.

Duty of Care   Agents have a duty to use as much care and to act as prudently as they would if managing their own affairs. Agents must take the time and effort to perform their principals' assigned tasks. For example, officers of corporations must base their decisions on information, not guesses, and must ensure that their decisions are carried out by employees.

An agent who does not use reasonable care is liable to the principal for any damages resulting from a lack of care. When an agent does not make adequate travel arrangements for a speaker, the agent is liable to the speaker for damages that result from the speaker's nonappearance at an engagement.

The Principal's Rights and Responsibilities

The first obligation of a principal is that of compensation, which can take various forms. Some agents work for a fee on a contingency basis. A real estate agent, for example, may agree to receive compensation only if a buyer for the property is found.

Principals also have an obligation to indemnify agents for expenses the agents incur in carrying out the principal's orders. Corporate officers, for example, are entitled to travel compensation; sales agents are entitled to compensation for ads to sell goods, realty, or services.

Liability of Principals for Agents' Conduct: The Relationship with Third Parties

Contract Liability   Although the types of authority an agent has and the terms of the agency agreement define the authority of the agent, the contract liability of a principal is not determined by either what the principal intended or by the limitations agreed to privately by the agent and the principal. In other words, third parties have certain contract enforcement rights depending on the nature of the agent's work and the authority given by the principal.

The Disclosed Principal   In a situation in which a third party is aware a principal is involved and also knows who the principal is, the principal is liable to the third party, but the agent is not, regardless of whether the agent has express, implied, or apparent authority. If the agent has no authority, however, then the agent, not the principal, is liable. For example, most title insurers and escrow companies require corporations selling or buying real property to have board authorization in the form of a resolution. If a corporate officer signed to buy land and did not have a resolution, the officer would have no express authority, and without implied or apparent authority would be liable for the land contract. (See Chapter 13 for more discussion of board resolutions and officers' authority.)

The Partially Disclosed Principal   In this situation, the third party knows that the agent is acting for someone else, but the identity of the principal is not disclosed. For example, an agent might be used to purchase land for development purposes when the developer does not want to be disclosed because disclosure of a major developer's involvement might drive up land prices. In this situation, the third-party seller of the land can hold either the principal or the agent liable on the contract. The agent assumes some risk of personal liability by not disclosing the identity of the principal.

The Undisclosed Principal   In this situation, an agent acts without disclosing either the existence of a principal or the principal's identity. Again, such an arrangement might be undertaken to avoid speculation, or it could be intended simply to protect someone's privacy, such as when a famous person purchases a home and does not want any advance disclosure of the purchase or its location. Here, the agent is directly liable to the third party. If the third party discovers the identity of the principal, the third party could hold either the principal or the agent liable. Exhibits 17.1 and 17.2 provide summaries of the liability of agents and principals under the three forms of disclosure.

EXHIBIT   17.1   Contract Liability of Disclosed Principal

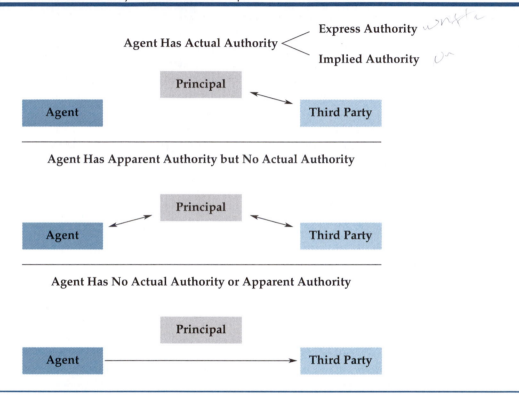

EXHIBIT   17.2   Contract Liability of Undisclosed or Partially Disclosed Principal

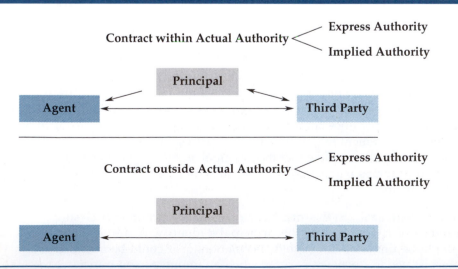

Liability of Principals for Agents' Torts

As for the liability of principals for torts committed by agents, two types of agents must be considered: servants and independent contractors. The amount of liability a principal has for an agent's torts depends first on the status of the agent.

Master–Servant Relationship   The principal is liable for the torts of the servant—an agent whose work, assignments, and time are controlled by the principal.

Scope of Employment   Employers (principals) are liable for the conduct of employees (agents/servants) while those employees are acting in the **scope of employment**. Scope of employment means that an employee is doing work for an employer at the time a tort occurs. Suppose a florist delivery driver, while delivering flowers, has an auto accident that is the delivery driver's fault. In addition to the driver's responsibility for the negligence in the accident, the florist is also liable to injured parties under the doctrine of *respondeat superior*.

Scope of employment has been defined broadly by the courts. Negligent torts committed while an employee is driving to a sales call or delivery are clearly within the scope of employment.

An employee who takes the afternoon off is not within the scope of employment, and the principal is not liable if an accident occurs during that time. An employee who uses the lunch hour to shop is not within the scope of employment. When an employee is acting on personal business, the scope of employment ends.

consider 17.2

Matt Theurer was an 18-year-old high school senior with many extracurricular activities, including being a member of the National Guard. Mr. Theurer was employed by a McDonald's restaurant in Portland, Oregon, on a part-time basis. While his employer called Mr. Theurer an enthusiastic worker, his friends and family felt that he was doing too much and getting too little sleep.

McDonald's employed many high school students on a part-time basis, and their restaurants closed at 11:00 p.m., with clean-up and other procedures taking up another hour until midnight. McDonald's informal policy did not permit high school students to work more than one midnight shift per week or allow the students to work split shifts. Split shifts forced the students to work in the morning and then evening. McDonald's felt the commuting time between the shifts prevented "people from getting their rest." Despite these policies, high school employees frequently complained about being tired, and at least two of McDonald's employees had accidents while driving home after working the closing shift.

A few times each year, McDonald's scheduled special cleanup projects at the restaurant that required employees to work after the midnight closing until 5 a.m. Student workers were to be used for cleanup shifts only on weekends or during spring break. However, for one scheduled cleanup project, there were not enough regular employees, and the manager asked for volunteers for a midnight to 5 a.m. cleanup shift. Mr. Theurer volunteered; the manager knew that Mr. Theurer had to drive about 20 minutes to and from work.

During the week of the scheduled special cleanup, Mr. Theurer had worked five nights. One night he worked until midnight, another until 11:30 p.m., two until 9 p.m., and another until 11 p.m. On Monday, April 4, 1988, Mr. Theurer worked his regular shift from 3:30 until 7:30 p.m., followed by a cleanup shift beginning at midnight until 5 a.m. on April 5, and then worked another shift from 5 a.m. until 8:21 a.m. During that shift Mr. Theurer told his manager that he was tired and asked to be excused from his next regular shift. The manager excused him, and Mr. Theurer began his drive home.

Mr. Theurer was driving 45 miles per hour on a two-lane road when he became drowsy or fell asleep, crossed the dividing line into oncoming traffic, crashed into the van of Frederic Faverty, and was killed. Mr. Faverty was seriously injured. Mr. Faverty settled his claims with Mr. Theurer's estate and then filed suit against McDonald's. Is McDonald's liable? (Analysis appears at the end of the chapter.) [*Faverty* v. *McDonald's Restaurants of Oregon, Inc.*, 892 P.2d 703 (Ct. App. Or. 1995)]

. . . .

Generally, intentional acts not authorized by employers do not result in liability. However, as *Lange* v. *National Biscuit Co.* (Case 17.3) discusses, employers may have potential liability for intentional acts that occur during work for the employer. This case also provides the answer for the chapter's opening Consider.

CASE 17.3

Lange v. *National Biscuit Co.*
211 N.W.2D 783 (MINN. 1973)

SHELF SPACE IS MY LIFE: FLIPPING OUT OVER OREOS

FACTS

Jerome Lange (plaintiff) was the manager of a small grocery store in Minnesota that carried Nabisco (defendant) products. Ronnell Lynch had been hired by Nabisco as a cookie salesman-trainee in October 1968. On March 1, 1969, Mr. Lynch was assigned his own territory, which included Mr. Lange's store.

Between March 1 and May 1, 1969, Nabisco received numerous complaints from grocers about Mr. Lynch being overly aggressive and taking shelf space in the stores reserved for competing cookie companies.

On May 1, 1969, Mr. Lynch came to Mr. Lange's store to place Nabisco merchandise on the shelves. An argument developed between the two over Mr. Lynch's service to the store. Mr. Lynch became very angry and started swearing. Mr. Lange told him to either stop swearing or leave the store because children were present. Mr. Lynch then became uncontrollably angry and said, "I ought to break your neck." He then went behind the counter and dared Mr. Lange to fight. When Mr. Lange refused, Mr. Lynch viciously assaulted him, after which he threw cookies around the store and left.

Mr. Lange filed suit against Nabisco and was awarded damages based on the jury's finding that although the acts of Mr. Lynch were outside the scope of employment, Nabisco was negligent in hiring and retaining him. The judge granted Nabisco's motion for judgment notwithstanding the verdict, and Mr. Lange appealed.

JUDICIAL OPINION

TODD, Justice

There is no dispute with the general principle that in order to impose liability on the employer under the doctrine of *respondeat superior* it is necessary to show that the employee was acting within the scope of his employment. Unfortunately, there is a wide disparity in the case law in the application of the "scope of employment" test to those factual situations involving intentional torts.

In developing a test for the application of *respondeat superior* when an employee assaults a third person, we believe that the focus should be on the basis of the assault rather than the motivation of the employee. We reject as the basis for imposing liability the arbitrary determination of when, and at what point, the argument and assault leave the sphere of the employer's business and become motivated by personal animosity. Rather, we believe the better approach is to view both the argument and assault as an indistinguishable event for purposes of vicarious liability.

We hold that an employer is liable for an assault by his employee when the source of the attack is related to the duties of the employee and the assault occurs within work-related limits of time and place. The assault in this case obviously occurred within work-related limits of time and place, since it took place on authorized premises during working hours. The precipitating cause of the initial argument concerned the employee's conduct of his work. In addition, the employee originally was motivated to become argumentative in furtherance of his employer's business. Consequently, under the facts of this case we hold as a matter of law that the employee was acting within the scope of employment at the time of the aggression and that plaintiff's posttrial motion for judgment notwithstanding the verdict on that ground should have been granted under the rule we herein adopt. To the extent that our former decisions are inconsistent with the rule now adopted, they are overruled.

Plaintiff may recover damages under either the theory of *respondeat superior* or negligence. Having disposed of the matter on the former issue, we need not undertake the questions raised by defendant's asserted negligence in the hiring or retention of the employee.

Reversed and remanded.

CASE QUESTIONS

1. What previous indications did Nabisco have that Mr. Lynch might cause some problems?

2. Was the attack of Mr. Lange within the scope of employment?

3. What test does the court give for determining scope of employment?

Negligent Hiring and Supervision   A rapidly evolving area of tort liability relates to one part of the discussion in the *Lange* case and is referred to as the tort of negligent hiring and/or supervision of employees. Negligent hiring requires proof that the principal/employer hired an agent/employee whose background made her ill-suited for the position. For example, a school district that does not check the background of a bus driver or teacher for, particularly, past charges or history of child abuse and molestation, has committed the tort of negligent hiring. Negligent supervision liability results when an employer has been put on notice that an employee has engaged in behavior that is harmful to others but the employer takes no steps to manage the employee's harmful conduct. An example is a college or university leaving a professor in the classroom after having received complaints regarding his inappropriate conduct in class and with students. If the professor then harms one of his students, the college or university would be liable to the student for the failure to make a timely termination, suspension, or other action to remove the professor from student contact or at least provide appropriate monitoring of the professor with the students.

Independent Contractors   Principals are not generally liable for the torts of independent contractors, but three exceptions apply to this general no-liability rule. The first exception covers **inherently dangerous activities**, which are those that cannot be made safe. For example, using dynamite to demolish old buildings is an inherently dangerous activity. Without this liability exception, a principal could hire an independent contractor to perform the task and then assume no responsibility for the damages or injuries that might result.

The second exception to the no-liability rule occurs when a principal negligently hires an independent contractor. A landlord who hires a security guard, therefore, must check that guard's background because if a tenant's property is stolen by a guard with a criminal record, the landlord is responsible. Also, a business that hires a collection agency to collect past-due accounts, knowing that agency's reputation for violence, is liable for the agency's torts even though they are independent contractors.

The third exception is the situation in which the principal has provided the specifications for the independent contractor's procedures or process.

TERMINATION OF THE AGENCY RELATIONSHIP

An agency relationship can end in several different ways. First, the parties can have a definite duration for the agency relationship. A listing agreement for the sale of real property usually ends after 90 days. An agency can also end because the agent quits or the principal fires the agent. When the principal dies or is incapacitated, an agency ends automatically because the agent no longer has anyone to contract on behalf of.

Although the agency ends easily when an agent is fired or quits, the authority of the agent does not end so abruptly or easily. An agent can still have **lingering apparent authority** that exists beyond the termination of the agency in relation to third parties who are unaware of the agency termination. For example, if the purchasing agent for a corporation retires after 25 years, the agency relationship between the agent and corporation has ended. However, many customers are used to dealing with the agent and may not be aware of the end of the agency. That purchasing agent could still bind the principal corporation even though actual authority has ended. The principal corporation can end lingering apparent authority by giving public or **constructive notice** and private or **actual notice**. Public notice is publication of the resignation, which also provides constructive notice. Many trade magazines and business newspapers publish announcements and personal columns about business associate changes and other personnel news. The principal must also give private notice to those firms that have dealt with the agent or have been creditors in the past. This notice is accomplished by a letter to each firm or individual who has dealt with the agent.

TERMINATION OF AGENTS UNDER EMPLOYMENT AT WILL

Most employees do not have written contracts that specify the start and duration of their employment. Rather, most employees work at the discretion of their employers, which is to say that they have **employment at will**. Recent cases have placed some restrictions on this employer freedom to hire and fire at will. Employees have based their protection rights on several theories, including implied contract and public policy.

The Implied Contract

Many courts have implied the existence of a contract because of the presence of promises, procedures, and policies in an employee personnel manual. Personnel manuals have been held to constitute, both expressly and impliedly, employee contracts or to become part of the employee contracts when they are given to employees at the outset. One of the factors that determines whether a personnel manual and its terms constitute a contract is reliance by employees on its procedures and terms.

The Public Policy Exception

In a second group of employment-at-will cases, the courts have afforded protection to those employees called *whistle-blowers* who report illegal conduct and to those who refuse to participate in conduct that is illegal or that violates public policy. For example, an employee was found to be wrongfully discharged when fired after supplying information to police who were investigating alleged criminal violations by a co-employee [*Palmateer* v. *International Harvester Co.*, 421 N.E.2d 876

(Ill. 1981)]. Other cases in which courts have found a wrongful discharge involve a refusal by an employee to commit perjury, a refusal by an employee to participate in price fixing, and an employee-reported violation of the Food, Drug, and Cosmetic Act.

In *Gardner* v. *Loomis Armored, Inc.* (Case 17.4), a court deals with the issue of an employer firing an employee who has taken action in an area not directly related to his employment.

CASE 17.4

Gardner v. *Loomis Armored, Inc.*
913 P.2d 377 (Wash. 1996)

TERMINATION FOR HELPING DURING A KNIFE ATTACK

FACTS

Kevin Gardner is a driver with Loomis Armored, Inc., which is a company that supplies armored truck delivery services to banks, businesses, and others requiring secure transport of funds and other valuables. Because of the safety and liability issues surrounding armored truck deliveries, Loomis has adopted a policy for all drivers that their trucks cannot be left unattended. The policy is provided in the employee handbook and the penalty for violation of the rule is as follows:

Violations of this rule will be grounds for termination.

While Mr. Gardner was making a scheduled stop at a bank for a pickup of funds, he noticed a woman being threatened with a knife by an obviously agitated man. Mr. Gardner left his truck unattended as he went to the aid of the woman. The woman was saved and her assailant apprehended, and Mr. Gardner was then fired by Loomis for violating the company policy of not leaving the truck unattended. Mr. Gardner filed suit for wrongful termination in violation of public policy.

JUDICIAL OPINION

DOLLIVER, Justice
The narrow public policy encouraging citizens to rescue persons from life threatening situations clearly evinces [demonstrates] a fundamental societal interest. . . . The value attached to such acts of heroism is plainly demonstrated by the fact that society has waived most criminal and tort penalties stemming from conduct necessarily committed in the course of saving a life. If our society has placed the rescue of a life above constitutional rights and above the criminal code, then such conduct clearly rises above a company's work rule. Loomis' work rule

does not provide an overriding justification for firing Gardner when his conduct directly served the public policy encouraging citizens to save persons from serious bodily injury or death.

We find that Gardner's discharge for leaving the truck and saving a woman from an imminent life threatening situation violates the public policy encouraging such heroic conduct. This holding does not create an affirmative legal duty requiring citizens to intervene in dangerous life threatening situations. We simply observe that society values and encourages voluntary rescuers when a life is in danger. Additionally, our adherence to this public policy does nothing to invalidate Loomis' work rule regarding drivers' leaving the trucks. . . . Our holding merely forbids Loomis from firing Gardner when he broke the rule because he saw a woman who faced imminent life threatening harm, and he reasonably believed his intervention was necessary to save her life. Finally, by focusing on the narrow public policy encouraging citizens to save human lives from life threatening situations, we continue to protect employers from frivolous lawsuits.

CASE QUESTIONS

1. Why is this case different from one in which an employee "rescues" a member of the public from fraud in bids or injury from defective products?

2. Did Mr. Gardner do the right thing in leaving his truck unattended? What were his ethical obligations under the circumstances? What would you have done?

3. Does this case create any affirmative legal duty for helping those in danger?

Many companies, in the interest of maintaining fairness and saving expenses, have adopted a peer review policy. **Peer review** is a formal grievance procedure for nonunion employees. Employee cases are presented to a panel of fellow employees and managers (three employees, two managers is the general configuration). Panel members listen to the presentation, can ask for more information, vote on the issue, and issue a written opinion with an explanation.

The Antiretaliation Statutes: Protections for Whistle-Blowers

All states as well as the federal government have passed whistle-blower protections statutes, which prevent employers from firing employees who report violations, note safety concerns, or in some way take action that benefits the public but does not help or reflect well on their employers.

Two generic federal statutes afford protection for federal employees: the Civil Service Reform Act of 1978 and the Whistleblower Protection Act of 1989. The statutes protect federal employees who report wrongdoing and permit them to recover both back pay and their attorney's fees in the event they litigate or protest a termination for their disclosure of possible violations of the law. The False Claims Act permits employees of government contractors whose tips and disclosures to federal investigators and agencies result in fines and penalties to collect 25 percent of those fines and penalties. Many employees of the health care providers involved in Medicare/Medicaid fraud cases have collected under this act (an employee in one case recovered $17.5 million after a $70 million fine was paid).

The Sarbanes-Oxley (SOX) Act also provides antiretaliation protections for employees who raise concerns about the financial reports or internal controls of their companies. The protections apply to employees who help with an audit, employees who join in a shareholder suit against the company, employees who report financial issues to a government agency, and employees who use internal reporting systems to raise a financial concern or compliance issue. The SOX protections are unique because they are the first whistle-blower protections that go beyond those for employees who raise public safety concerns. The protections cover not only employees of companies, but also analysts who raise concerns about companies they study. The research firms or investment houses the analysts work for cannot take retaliatory action against the analysts for issuing negative reports on companies that might also be clients of the analyst's employer. Companies that retaliate face criminal penalties or fines as well as imprisonment for those within the company who take action against the whistle-blower. The individual penalties for SOX retaliation are up to 10 years in prison. For the employee, damages for retaliation include back pay, actual damages, and a right to reinstatement.[2]

The Statutory Rights and Protections in the Employment Relationship

WAGES AND HOURS PROTECTION: THE FAIR LABOR STANDARDS ACT

Exhibit 17.3 summarizes the series of laws affecting employee rights over the past 50 years, which are discussed in this chapter.

The **Fair Labor Standards Act** (FLSA) is commonly called by workers the "minimum wage law" or the wage and hour law. This act does establish a minimum

EXIIIBIT	17.3 Statutory Scheme for Employee Welfare

STATUTE	DATE	PROVISIONS
Worker's Compensation	1900	Absolute liability of employers for employee injury; no common law tort suits by employees against employers
Social Security Act 42 U.S.C. § 301	1935	FICA contributions; unemployment compensation; retirement benefits
Fair Labor Standards Act 29 U.S.C. § 201	1938	Minimum wages; child labor restrictions; overtime pay
Equal Pay Act 29 U.S.C. § 206	1963	Amendment to FLSA; equal pay for equal work
Occupational Safety and Health Act 29 U.S.C. § 651	1970	Safety in the workplace; employee rights; employer reporting; inspections
Employment Retirement Income Security Act 29 U.S.C. § 441	1974	Disclosure of contributions, investments, loans; employee vesting; employee statements
Family and Medical Leave Act 29 U.S.C. § 2601	1993	Protection of job after family leave (for pregnancy, child care, adult illness, elderly care)
Pension Protection Act 29 U.S.C. §§ 302 *et seq.*	2006	Amends ERISA to require higher funding levels as well as limits on officer stock sales during blackout periods

wage, but it also includes provisions regulating child labor, overtime pay requirements, and equal pay provisions. The FLSA was originally introduced in the Senate by Hugo L. Black when he was a senator from Alabama. His 1937 appointment to the U.S. Supreme Court may have helped it pass the high court's scrutiny. Having been amended several times, the FLSA is an enabling statute that sets up various administrative agencies to handle the regulations and necessary enforcement.

Coverage of FLSA
The FLSA applies to all businesses that affect interstate commerce. As discussed in Chapter 4, "affecting" interstate commerce is a broad standard.

FLSA Minimum Wage and Overtime Regulations
Under FLSA, all covered employees must be paid a **minimum wage**. The minimum wage is established by Congress and is increased through legislation, with the latest increase taking effect in 2007. The FLSA also includes an hours protection for covered employees in the form of time-and-one-half pay for hours worked above 40 hours per week. Regardless of the pay period for covered employees (monthly, weekly, or biweekly), overtime is computed on the basis of 40 hours per week. For example, if a covered employee worked 38, 42, 35, and 47 hours in four consecutive weeks and is paid on a monthly basis, that employee is entitled to 9 hours of **overtime pay**.

The definition of covered employees is provided in the FLSA. Some categories of employees are covered for purposes of minimum wage protections but not for overtime pay. For example, professionals, executives, and others who exercise discretion and judgment in their positions may be covered for purposes of minimum wage protections but not for purposes of overtime protections.[3] The reason for this exemption is that these employees, often referred to as "white-collar" workers, possess sufficient training, knowledge, and experience to counter employer unfairness. Under new FLSA rules passed in 2004, the Department of Labor has specific salary and job requirements for employees to be covered under the overtime exemption.

FLSA and Child Labor Provisions

The child labor provisions of the FLSA were created to keep children in school for at least a minimum number of years. The provisions of the act govern particular ages and restrict the types of employment those age groups can hold.

Among the exemptions to the laws are those for young actors and actresses, for example. But even in this field, many states require approval of their contracts and also require that some of the earnings be put in trust for use by the child when the child becomes an adult. Other exemptions apply to work-study programs and farm work.

Enforcement of FLSA

Enforcement of the FLSA requirements may begin in several different ways. Employees can initiate the process by filing a complaint with the U.S. Department of Labor. In some cases, employers make the laws self-enforcing by requesting interpretations from the Labor Department that are then published in the *Code of Federal Regulations.*

In a final type of case, the Labor Department initiates its own investigation of a firm for possible violations. For example, in 1999, the Labor Department focused on the car dealership programs that had high-school-age vocational students working in service departments. Although the mechanical work was permissible, using the under-18 students as car jockeys to bring the customers' cars around to them following service was a violation of the age restrictions in the labor laws on certain types of work.

The FLSA carries both civil and criminal penalties for violations. Employees have the right to recover from an employer any wages that were not paid or any overtime compensation that was denied, plus reasonable attorney fees required to bring the action to recover. In addition to the employees' rights, the U.S. Department of Labor's Wage and Hour Division has enforcement power for violations. A willful violation of FLSA carries a maximum $10,000 fine and possible imprisonment of up to six months.

To help employees pursue their rights, the FLSA makes it a violation for any employer to fire an employee for filing an FLSA complaint or for participating in any FLSA proceeding.

Officers of a corporation can be held individually liable for the corporation's violations. The FLSA imposes fines on both corporations and officers involved in managing employees. These personal penalties are particularly likely in cases in which the company has not kept accurate records of the wages and hours worked of its employees, a requirement of the FLSA. Case 17.5, *Chao* v. *Hotel Oasis, Inc.,* indicates the new enforcement standards and policies of the Department of Labor.

CASE 17.5

Chao v. Hotel Oasis, Inc.
493 F.3D 26, (1ST CIR. 2007)

TWO SETS OF BOOKS, ONE BIG PENALTY

FACTS

Hotel Oasis, Inc., operates a hotel and restaurant in southwestern Puerto Rico. Dr. Lionel Lugo-Rodríguez (Defendant-appellant) (Lugo) is the president of the corporation, runs the hotel, and manages its employees. Oasis's records show that between October 3, 1990, and June 30, 1993, employees were paid less than minimum wage, were not paid for training time or meetings held during non-working hours, were paid in cash "off the books," and were not paid correctly for overtime. Oasis also maintained two sets of payroll records for the same employees, covering the same time periods, one showing fewer hours at a higher rate, and the other showing more hours at a sub-minimum wage rate. Lugo maintains that the two sets of books were necessary, one for temporary employees and one for permanent employees.

On April 5, 1994, the Secretary of Labor (the "Secretary") filed a complaint in the United States District Court for the District of Puerto Rico against Oasis and Lugo ("Defendants"), alleging violations of the minimum wage, overtime, and recordkeeping provisions of the Fair Labor Standards Act ("FLSA"). The Secretary also sought liquidated damages.

After years of litigation, the district court ordered Oasis to pay $141,270.64 in back wages and an equal amount in liquidated damages to 282 current and former employees. The court also found Lugo personally liable for the back wages and penalties. Lugo and Oasis appealed.

JUDICIAL OPINION

Torruella, Circuit Judge

"[T]he overwhelming weight of authority is that a corporate officer with operational control of a corporation's covered enterprise is an employer along with the corporation, jointly and severally liable under the FLSA for unpaid wages."

. . . [Because] not every corporate employee who exercised supervisory control should be held personally liable, we identified several factors that were important to the personal liability analysis, including the individual's ownership interest, degree of control over the corporation's financial affairs and compensation practices, and role in "caus[ing] the corporation to compensate (or not to compensate) employees in accordance with the FLSA."

Based on the above considerations, we affirm the district court's judgment holding Lugo personally liable for Oasis's compensation decisions. Lugo was not just any employee with some supervisory control over other employees. He was the president of the corporation, and he had ultimate control over the business's day-to-day operations. In particular, it is undisputed that Lugo was the corporate officer principally in charge of directing employment practices, such as hiring and firing employees, requiring employees to attend meetings unpaid, and setting employees' wages and schedules. He was thus instrumental in "causing" the corporation to violate the FLSA. The FLSA contemplates, at least in certain circumstances, holding officers with such personal responsibility for statutory compliance jointly and severally liable along with the corporation. The FLSA authorizes the Secretary of Labor to recover on behalf of employees unpaid wages and overtime compensation plus an equal amount in liquidated damages.

Oasis's failure to keep adequate payroll records and its intentional manipulation of the records it did keep are sufficient grounds for concluding that Oasis did not act in good faith or with a reasonable belief that it was in compliance with the FLSA. "[T]he fact that an employer knowingly under-reported its employee's work hours could suggest to a [fact finder] that the employer was attempting to conceal its failure to pay overtime from regulators, or was acting to eliminate evidence that might later be used against it in a suit by one of its employees."

[I]t is the *employer's* burden to show good faith and objective reasonableness, and therefore the Secretary's alleged failure to offer evidence of willfulness is not an impediment to the court's decision to refrain from awarding liquidated damages.

Affirmed.

CASE QUESTIONS

1. What shows willfulness of a violation?
2. What are the standards for holding an officer liable for FLSA violations?
3. Explain what liquidated damages are and when they are available for recovery.

WAGES PROTECTION: THE EQUAL PAY ACT OF 1963

The **Equal Pay Act of 1963** is an amendment to the FLSA that makes it illegal to pay different wages based on gender to men and women who are doing substantially the same work. If the jobs involve equal responsibility, training, or skill, men and women must have equal pay. Merit systems and seniority systems instituted in good faith do not violate the Equal Pay Act even though they may result in different pay rates for the same jobs. As long as the disparate pay is based on length of employment or a merit-raise system, the disparity is not a violation of the act.

The Equal Pay Act is not an act that requires the application of comparable worth. Comparable worth requires that men and women be paid on the same scale, not just for the same jobs but when they are doing different jobs that require equal skill, effort, and responsibility.

Laws on Workplace Safety: The Occupational Safety and Health Act

One of the worker welfare concerns of Congress has been safety in the workplace. In the past, the economic concerns of employers often overshadowed their concern for proper safety precautions. To ensure worker safety, Congress passed the **Occupational Safety and Health Act of 1970**, which created the **Occupational Safety and Health Administration** (OSHA). OSHA's enforcement powers include investigations, record-keeping requirements, and research.

OSHA coverage is broad: Every employer with one or more employees who is in a business affecting commerce is covered by OSHA. OSHA is responsible for promulgating rules and regulations for safety standards and procedures.

OSHA inspections are an enforcement tool. Inspectors can enter the workplace "without delay and at a reasonable time" to inspect. They can check the workplace and the records and can question employees.

If an inspection is the result of an employee complaint, the employer cannot take any retaliatory action against that employee. An employee who is fired, demoted, or discriminated against for registering an OSHA complaint can file a complaint, and the Department of Labor can pursue the employee's rights in federal district court.

Although most businesses voluntarily permit OSHA inspections, employers do have the right to refuse access. In *Marshall* v. *Barlows, Inc.*, 436 U.S. 307 (1978), the U.S. Supreme Court ruled that OSHA inspectors must obtain warrants if employers refuse access.

OSHA penalties are listed in Exhibit 17.4.

EMPLOYEE PENSIONS, RETIREMENT, AND SOCIAL SECURITY

One of the concerns of workers is what happens to them when they retire: Will they have an income? Other concerns are whether they will have a source of income in the event of disability, or whether their survivors will have income in the event of their death. Finally, what if no work is available? What income will they have until they find another job? These issues are the social issues of employment

EXHIBIT	17.4 OSHA Penalties	
TYPE OF OFFENSE	**DESCRIPTION**	**PENALTY**
Willful	Employer aware of danger or a repeat violator	Up to $70,000 (not less than $5,000) and/or six months imprisonment
Serious	Violation is a threat to life or could cause serious injury	$7,000
Nonserious	No threat of serious injury	Up to $7,000
De minimis	Failure to post rights	Up to $7,000 per violation
Failure to correct	Citation not followed	$7,000 per day

law—providing for those who, because of age, disability, or unemployment, are unable to provide for themselves.

Social Security

The **Social Security Act of 1935** was a key component of the massive reforms in federal government during Franklin Roosevelt's presidency.

The idea of the Social Security system was to have those who could work shoulder the social burden of providing for those who could not. Every employer and employee is required to contribute to the Social Security programs under the **Federal Insurance Contributions Act** (FICA). The amount employees contribute is based on their annual wage, with a maximum wage amount for contributions. FICA contributions are paid one-half by employers and one-half by employees. Independent contractors pay their own FICA contributions. Social Security includes provision of death benefits for spouses and children, as well as disability and retirement benefits.

The benefits paid to retired and disabled people are based on formulas. The amount depends on how long an individual worked and within what salary range. Surviving spouse and children's benefits are likewise tied to work and salary history.

Private Retirement Plans

Many retirement and pension plans are set up by employers, who enjoy tax benefits from some plans. However, when evidence revealed that employees' funds in plans were being misused, not invested wisely, and in some cases embezzled, Congress enacted the **Employee Retirement Income Security Act of 1974** (ERISA), which was amended by the **Pension Protection Act of 2006**. ERISA does not require employers to have pension plans, but if an employer chooses to have a pension plan, the employer is subject to funding, accounting, and disclosure requirements imposed by federal law, including the new provisions under the Pension Protection Act. As part of its 2006 Chapter 11 bankruptcy, United Airlines was relieved of its pension liabilities. Many lawmakers were taken aback when a company was able to renege on pension benefits when so many protections were built into the law under ERISA. Further, many former Enron employees lost their pensions because it was funded with Enron stock. Congressional hearings discovered that loopholes in the accounting processes for pension fund reporting had permitted United, and many others, to report pension numbers that made the health of the fund look better than it actually was.

Under the Pension Protection Act of 2006, these financial reporting accounting loopholes for general financial reports were changed. The changes require companies to fund their pension plans according to the numbers reported to the SEC in their financials. Under a 2008 U.S. Supreme Court decision, employees may bring suit against their employers for failure to honor their fiduciary duties in managing employee pension accounts [*LaRue* v. *DeWolff, Boberg & Associates, Inc.* 128 S.Ct. 1020 (2008)].

Unemployment Compensation

State laws provide for the amount of **unemployment compensation** that will be paid. The amount is tied to the average amount earned by an individual during the months preceding employment termination. The benefits are usually paid on a weekly or biweekly basis. Most states also have a minimum and maximum amount that can be collected regardless of average earnings during the base period. Further, benefit payments in most states are limited to 26 weeks.

Each state has its own standards for payment of benefits. Generally, eligibility requirements demand that an individual be (1) involuntarily terminated from a job, (2) able and available for work, and (3) involved in seeking employment.

Workers' Compensation Laws

The purpose of **workers' compensation** laws is to provide wage benefits and medical care to victims of work-related injuries. Although each state has its own system of workers' compensation, several general principles remain consistent throughout the states:

1. An employee who is injured in the scope of employment is automatically entitled to certain benefits (a discussion of work-related injuries and the scope of employment follows).
2. Fault is immaterial. Employees' contributory negligence does not lessen their right to compensation. Employers' care and precaution do not lessen their responsibility.
3. Coverage is limited to employees and does not extend to independent contractors.
4. Benefits include partial wages, hospital and medical expenses, and death benefits.
5. In exchange for these benefits, employees, their families, and dependents give up their common-law right to sue an employer for damages.
6. If third parties (e.g., equipment manufacturers) are responsible for an accident, recovery from the third party goes first to the employer for reimbursement.
7. Each state has some administrative agency responsible for administration of workers' compensation.
8. Every employer who is subject to workers' compensation regulation is required to provide some security for liability (such as insurance).

Over the years, the term *accident* has been interpreted broadly. Most injuries are those that result suddenly, such as broken arms, injured backs caused by falls, burns, and lacerations. But workers' compensation has been extended to cover injuries that develop over time. For example, workers involved in lifting heavy objects might eventually develop back problems. Even such medical problems as high blood pressure, heart attacks, and nervous breakdowns have in some cases been classified as work related and compensable.

The fact that an injury occurs or gets worse in the workplace is enough for recovery. Employee negligence, employer precautions, contributory negligence, and assumption of risk are generally not issues in workers' compensation cases.

Workers' benefits can be grouped into three different categories: medical, disability, and death. Medical benefits include typical insurance-covered costs such as hospital costs, physician and nursing fees, therapy fees, and rental costs for equipment needed for recovery.

Disability benefits are payments made to compensate employees for wages lost because of a disability injury. The amount of benefits is based on state statutory figures. Most states base disability benefits on an employee's average monthly wage, and they also specify a maximum amount. State statutes also generally have a list of **scheduled injuries**, which will carry a percentage disability figure. Total disability is also defined by statute. Workers who have total disability are generally entitled to two-thirds of their average monthly salary for the period of the disability.

Some injuries suffered by workers are not listed in statutes. Those not specifically described in statutes are called **unscheduled injuries**. The amount allowed for unscheduled injuries is discretionary and an area of frequent litigation.

Death benefits are paid to the family of a deceased employee and generally include burial expenses. The amount of death benefits is generally some percentage of the average monthly salary; for example, a surviving spouse might be entitled to a 35 percent benefit.

Forfeiture of the Right of Suit

The majority of states require employees to forfeit all other lawsuit rights in exchange for workers' compensation benefits. Employees receive automatic benefits but lose the right to sue their employers for covered incidents.

If an employee is injured by a machine malfunction while on the job, the employee is covered by workers' compensation. However, product liability may also be at issue in the accident. If suit is brought against the machine's manufacturer for product liability, any recovery goes first to the employer to compensate for the cost of the employee's benefits. In other words, third-party recovery is first used to reimburse the employer.

STATUTORY PROTECTIONS OF EMPLOYEES THROUGH LABOR UNIONS

The Norris-LaGuardia Act of 1932

The **Norris-LaGuardia Act** prohibits the use of injunctions as a remedy in labor disputes. Violent strikes can still be enjoined, provided evidence shows that violence did or would have occurred and that public officers could not control the violence and any resulting damage. Injunctions cannot be issued without first holding a hearing.

The Wagner Act

The **Wagner Act**, also known as the **National Labor Relations Act** (NLRA) of 1935, gave employees the right to organize and choose representatives to bargain collectively with their employers. Further, it established the **National Labor Relations Board** (NLRB), which had two functions: to conduct union elections and to investigate and remedy unfair labor practices.

The Taft-Hartley Act: The Labor-Management Relations Act of 1947

Over President Truman's veto, Congress passed the **Taft-Hartley Act**, which was a response to the public's concern about too many strikes, secondary boycotts, and the unrestrained power of union officials. Strikes to force employers to discharge nonunion employees, secondary boycotts, and strikes over work assignments are prohibited as unfair labor practices. Employees were also given the right to remove a union they no longer wanted as their representative. The act also contains provisions that allow the president to invoke a **cooling-off period** of bargaining before a strike that threatens to imperil the public health and safety can begin. This power has been used by presidents in transportation and coal strikes.

The Landrum-Griffin Act: The Labor-Management Reporting and Disclosure Act of 1959

The **Landrum-Griffin Act** provides employee protection within union organizations. The act gave union members a bill of rights, required certain procedures for election of officers, prescribed financial reporting requirements for union funds, and established criminal and civil penalties for union misconduct.

Union Organizing Efforts

Employees make the decision as to whether a union will represent them and, if so, which will serve as their representative. This process is called selecting a bargaining representative, and the NLRB has strict procedures for such selection. The NLRB carefully chooses how employees will be grouped together so that they share common interests.

The first step in union organization is the establishment of a collective bargaining unit. The **collective bargaining unit** is a group of employees recognized by the NLRB as appropriate for exclusive representation of all employees in that group. Collective bargaining units are determined by the NLRB. The standard for a collective bargaining unit is that it must consist of homogeneous employees.

Some bargaining units consist of entire plants of workers, whereas others are specialized units within a plant, such as the maintenance staff or the line workers in an assembly plant. For some national companies, the bargaining unit is all employees, whereas for other national firms the bargaining unit is one particular plant or store.

The NLRB monitors closely the conduct of both employer and union as the election approaches. Employers can prohibit oral campaigning during work hours and can restrict literature distribution both during and, to a degree, before and after work hours. Employers cannot make threats about relocation or make speeches to captive audiences (employees on their shifts) in the 24 hours before an election.

If a majority of employees vote for the union in a secret ballot process administered by the NLRB, the union has completed its **certification**. An employer who refuses to deal with the certified union can be forced to by an injunction obtained by the NLRB.

After a union has been certified, an election for a new union cannot be held for 12 months from the time of certification. If the union signs a collective bargaining agreement, no union certification election can be held until the collective bargaining agreement expires. These limitations on elections and certifications prevent chaos in the workplace that would result from constant changeovers in union representation.

Although the NLRA gave unions the right to exist, it also gave workers the right to a choice. Workers are not required to join unions and cannot be coerced into supporting union action. Attempts by a union to force its members to participate in strikes and other union activities are considered unfair labor practices.

Union Contract Negotiations

Once a union is certified as the employees' representative, one of its major roles is to obtain a contract or **collective bargaining agreement** between employer and employees. Both sides must engage in **good-faith bargaining**, which the NLRB defines as a mutual obligation of employer and union to meet at reasonable times, confer in good faith on employment issues, and execute a written agreement reflecting their oral agreement. Both parties must bargain with an open mind and the sincere intent of reaching an agreement.

Two types of subject matters can be discussed during bargaining: (1) mandatory or compulsory subject matter and (2) permissive subject matter. As to the former, the NLRA describes **mandatory bargaining terms** as those dealing with "wages, hours, and other terms and conditions of employment." Obviously, the amount to be paid as wages is included but so also are related issues, such as merit pay, vacations, overtime, work hours, leaves, and pay days.

Some subjects are "unbargainable." Employers and employees cannot bargain to give away statutory rights—for example, bargaining on the procedures for certifying a union would violate the law. Nor can employees bargain about having a **closed shop**, which requires employees to be union members before they can be hired. Such shops are illegal under the Taft-Hartley Act.

Failure to bargain on mandatory subject matter is an **unfair labor practice**, which is conduct prohibited by statute or NLRB decision. When an employer or union fails to bargain on a mandatory topic, a charge can be brought and the NLRB can proceed with a complaint.

Right-to-Work Laws

Section 14(b) of the Taft-Hartley Act is in some ways a protection for employers as well as for employees. This section outlaws the closed shop, which is a company that requires all employees to be union members. Based on this section of

Taft-Hartley, states can pass **right-to-work laws** that give people the right to work without having to join a union. About half the states have right-to-work statutes.

Federal plant-closing legislation is called the **Worker Adjustment and Retraining Notification Act of 1988** (WARN). Under this act, employers with 100 or more workers are required to give workers 60 days' advance notice of plant shutdowns that would affect at least 50 workers and of layoffs that would last more than six months and affect one-third of the workers at the site. There are some exceptions to the 60-day notice requirement, such as unforeseeable circumstances and seasonal, agricultural, and construction businesses. Penalties for violations include back pay and benefits for employees for each day of violation and up to $500 per day for each day notice was not given. The closing of Arthur Andersen following Enron has been the subject of WARN litigation [*Roquet* v. *Arthur Andersen LLP,* 398 F.3d 585 (7th Cir. 2005)].

International Issues in Employment Law

Today's labor market is considerably different from the market that existed at the time of the enactment of federal labor legislation. Both operations within the United States and operations in other countries are affected by a new international labor force. Domestic operations must be certain that all employees from other countries are documented workers. International operations present numerous ethical and public policy issues in the conditions and operations of plants in other countries with different labor standards.

IMMIGRATION LAWS

The **Immigration and Naturalization Act** (INA), the **Immigration Reform and Control Act of 1986** (IRCA), and the **Immigration Act of 1990** (8 U.S.C. § 11101 *et seq.*) are the federal laws that apply to immigrants in the United States and impose requirements on employers in the United States that employ immigrants. In 1996, two federal statutes changed dramatically the issues of immigration, deportation, and penalties for hiring illegal immigrants: the **Illegal Immigration Reform and Immigrant Responsibility Act of 1996** and the **Antiterrorism and Effective Death Penalty Act** (18 U.S.C. § 1). The statutes served to increase the types and numbers of crimes that rendered illegal immigrants deportable from the United States and denied them entry from other countries. The statutes also decreased the defenses to deportation as well as the procedural protections for opposing deportation. The enforcement of the immigration laws is now under a cabinet-level agency known as the **U.S. Department of Homeland Security** (DHS). DHS has Immigration and Customs Enforcement (ICE) as one of its reporting agencies. This reorganization and the creation and elevation of DHS to a cabinet-level position was the result of the **Uniting and Strengthening America by Providing Appropriate Tools Required to Intercept and Obstruct Terrorism Act (USA Patriot Act**; 18 U.S.C. § 1) and the Homeland Security Act of 2002. The Immigration and Naturalization Service (INS), originally housed within the U.S. Department of Justice, was abolished. INS's responsibilities have been divided into three separate bureaus under the DHS. In addition, the USA Patriot Act toughened security clearances and background checks for nonimmigrant and immigrant admittance into the United States, tightened coordination between immigration-related government agencies, and increased the U.S. government's ability to track foreign nationals in the United States. These agencies have programs to check employers' records for their verification of employees' citizenship or proper documentation for working in the United States. Many employers now use contractors to help them with documentation of employee status.

Red Flags FOR MANAGERS

- Principles of agency law make your company liable for what your employees do. Give employees guidelines on their conduct and correct them when they make mistakes so that your company is not liable for their conduct or your lack of supervision.

- You are responsible for who you hire. Check potential employees' background before employing them because, if they have criminal violations you do not discover, your company is liable if they harm one of your customers.

- You must know federal and state OSHA requirements for safety in the workplace. If employees find a violation, you must correct the problem.

- Always stay current on employer FICA and unemployment taxes because there is personal liability for not paying these wage taxes.

- Employees need to have the opportunity to raise issues, and there are statutes that protect employees and fine your company if you retaliate against them.

- If your work force is unionized or wants to become unionized, follow federal laws on employee rights.

- You will need to be able to establish that your employees are either citizens or in the country legally. Most companies use third-party vendors who are experienced and knowledgeable about checking citizenship and documentation on potential employees.

Summary

When is an employee acting on behalf of an employer?

- Principal—employer; responsible party

- Agent—party hired to act on another's behalf

- *Restatement of Agency*—common law view of agent–principal relationship

- Unincorporated association—nonlegal entity; no legal existence as natural or fictitious person

How much authority does an employee hold?

- Express authority—written or stated authority

- Implied authority—authority by custom

- Apparent authority—authority by perceptions of third parties

- Lingering apparent authority—authority left with terminated agent because others are not told of termination

- Actual notice—receipt of notice of termination

- Constructive notice—publication of notice of termination

- Ratification—after-the-fact recognition of agent's authority by principal

- Disclosed principal—existence and identity of principal are known

- Partially disclosed principal—existence but not identity of principal is known

- Undisclosed principal—neither existence nor identity of principal is known

When is a business liable for an employee's acts?

- Master–servant relationship—principal-agent relationship in which principal exercises great degree of control over agent
- Independent contractor—principal-agent relationship in which principal exercises little day-to-day control over agent
- Scope of employment—time when agent is doing work for the principal
- Inherently dangerous activities—activities for which, even if performed by independent contractor, principal is liable

What duties and obligations do employees owe employers?

- Fiduciary—one who has utmost duty of trust, care, loyalty, and obedience to another

How is an agency relationship terminated?

- Employment at will—right of employer to terminate noncontract employees at any time
- Protections for employees through express contract (manuals), implied contracts, and public policy
- Whistle-blowers protected by antiretaliation statutes

What happens when a worker is injured in the workplace?

- Workers' compensation—state-by-state system of employer strict liability for injuries of workers on the job; the few exceptions to recovery include self-inflicted injuries

What is the Social Security system, and what benefits does it provide?

- Social Security Act—federal law establishing disability, beneficiary, and retirement benefits
- Federal Insurance Contributions Act (FICA)—statute establishing system for withholding contributions for Social Security benefits

Are workers entitled to pensions, and are they regulated?

- Employment Retirement Income Security Act (ERISA)—federal law regulating employer-sponsored pension plans
- Pension Protection Plan of 2006

What rights do unemployed workers have?

- Unemployment compensation—federal program handled by states to provide temporary support for displaced workers

- Workers' compensation—system of no-fault liability for employees injured on the job

How are labor unions formed, and what is their relationship with employees?

- Norris-LaGuardia Act—federal law prohibiting injunctions to halt strikes
- National Labor Relations Act (Wagner Act)—federal law authorizing employee unionization
- Labor Management Relations Act (Taft-Hartley Act)—federal law limiting union economic weapons
- Labor-Management Reporting and Disclosure Act (Landrum-Griffin Act)—federal law regulating union membership and organizations
- National Labor Relations Board (NLRB)—federal agency responsible for enforcing labor laws
- Collective bargaining unit—group of employees recognized as exclusive bargaining agent
- Certification—recognition of union as exclusive bargaining agent
- Collective bargaining agreement—exclusive rights agreement between employer and employee
- Good-faith bargaining—requirement that parties negotiate terms in earnest
- Unfair labor practice—conduct by labor or management prohibited by statute
- Right-to-work laws—right to work at a company without being required to join a union
- Worker Adjustment and Retraining Notification Act (WARN)—federal law requiring employers to give 60 days' notice of plant shutdowns

What are the laws and procedures related to immigrants and employment?

- Immigration and Naturalization Act (INA)
- Immigration Reform and Control Act of 1986 (IRCA)
- Immigration Act of 1990
- Illegal Immigration Reform and Immigrant Responsibility Act of 1996
- Antiterrorism and Effective Death Penalty Act
- Uniting and Strengthening America by Proving Appropriate Tools Required to Intercept and Obstruct Terrorism Act (USA Patriot Act)
- The Homeland Security Act

Key Terms

Questions and Problems

1. On September 29, 1984, Wilton Whitlow was taken to Good Samaritan Hospital's emergency room in Montgomery County, Ohio, because he had suffered a seizure and a blackout. He was examined by Dr. Dennis Aumentado, who prescribed the anti-epileptic medication Dilantin. Mr. Whitlow experienced no further seizures and was monitored as an outpatient at Good Samaritan over the next few weeks.

Mr. Whitlow complained to Dr. Aumentado of warm and dry eyes, and his Dilantin dose was reduced. On October 20, 1984, he was again admitted to the emergency room with symptoms that were eventually determined to be from Stevens-Johnson syndrome, a condition believed to be caused by a variety of medications. Mr. Whitlow sued Dr. Aumentado and Good Samaritan for malpractice and Parke-Davis, the manufacturer of Dilantin, for breach of warranty.

The hospital maintains it is not liable because Dr. Aumentado was an independent contractor. Is the hospital correct? [*Whitlow* v. *Good Samaritan Hosp.*, 536 N.E.2d 659 (Ohio 1987)]

2. Nineteen-year-old Lee J. Norris was employed by Burger Chef Systems as an assistant manager of one of its restaurants. On a day when he was in charge and change was needed, Mr. Norris left to get change but also decided to get Kentucky Fried Chicken at a nearby store for his lunch to take back to Burger Chef. The bank where Mr. Norris usually got change is 1.6 miles from Burger Chef, and the Kentucky Fried Chicken outlet is 2.5 miles from Burger Chef. After Mr. Norris left the bank and was on his way to the Kentucky Fried Chicken restaurant, he negligently injured Lee J. Govro in an accident. Is Burger Chef liable for the accident? [*Burger Chef Systems* v. *Govro*, 407 F.2d 921 (8th Cir. 1969)]

3. Lennen & Newell, Inc. (L&N), is an advertising agency hired by Stokely-Van Camp to do its advertising. L&N contracted for the purchase of ad time from CBS, but no Stokely representative's signature is on the contract. If L&N does not pay for the ad time, is Stokely liable? [*CBS, Inc. v. Stokely-Van Camp, Inc.*, 456 F. Supp. 539 (E.D.N.Y. 1977)]

4. Whirlpool is a manufacturer of household appliances. In its plant in Marion, Ohio, Whirlpool uses a system of overhead conveyor belts to send a constant stream of parts to employees on the line throughout the plant. Beneath the conveyor belt is a netting or mesh screen to catch any parts or other objects that might fall from the conveyor belt.

Some items did fall to the mesh screen, located some 20 feet above the plant floor. Maintenance employees had the responsibility for removing the parts and other debris from the screen. They usually stood on the iron frames of the mesh screen, but occasionally they found it necessary to go onto the screen itself. While one maintenance employee was standing on the mesh, it broke, and he fell the 20 feet to his death on the floor below. After this fatal accident, maintenance employees were prohibited from standing on the mesh screen or the iron frames. A mobile platform and long hooks were used to remove objects.

Two maintenance employees, Virgil Deemer and Thomas Cornwell, complained about the screen and its safety problems. When the plant foreman refused to make corrections, Mr. Deemer and Mr. Cornwell asked for the name of an OSHA inspector, and Mr. Deemer contacted an OSHA official on July 7, 1974.

On July 8, 1974, Mr. Deemer and Mr. Cornwell reported for work and were told to do their maintenance work on the screen in the usual manner. Both refused on safety grounds, so the plant foreman sent them to the personnel office. They were then forced to punch out and were not paid for the six hours left on their shift.

Explain Mr. Deemer's and Mr. Cornwall's rights under OSHA. [*Whirlpool Corporation v. Marshall*, 445 U.S. 1 (1980)]

5. OSHA requires vehicles with an obstructed rear view to be equipped with a reverse signal alarm. Mr. Knight, an independent contractor working for Clarkson Construction, operated a Clarkson dump truck that had no warning signal but had an obstructed rear view. If an injury resulted to a pedestrian when Mr. Knight backed onto the highway, what liability would there be? What could OSHA do? What could the pedestrian do? What effect does Mr. Knight's being an independent contractor have? If Mr. Knight were also injured, could he recover? [*Clarkson Constr. Co. v. OSHA*, 531 F.2d 451 (10th Cir. 1980)]

Understanding "Consider" Problems

17.1

THINK: The *Grease Monkey* case held that a principal is liable for the acts of an agent that a third party would perceive are within the scope of the authority of the agent.

APPLY: When an agent is hired as a bouncer, battery and assault could be within the agent's apparent scope of authority.

ANSWER: The bar owner is liable for the bouncer's conduct because of the implied authority or the failure to take action when the bouncer does use physical force to remove customers.

17.2

THINK: Principals are liable for the injuries caused by agents when there is a master–servant relationship and the servant/agent commits the tort (causes injury) in the scope of employment. Employers/principals are not liable for torts of employees/servants when they occur while the employees are on their way to work.

APPLY: Theurer would fall under a master–servant relationship. He was on his way home from work. However, he was driving home after a double shift.

ANSWER: In the case the court held that McDonald's was liable because of its demands on the employee that made him tired. Some courts have declined to follow the decision in this case. In *Behrens* v. *Harrah's Illinois Corp.* 852 N.E.2d 553 (Ill. 2006), the court did not allow the family of an employee to recover from the employer when she experienced catastrophic injuries following a rollover accident that occurred when she was driving home from work after being required to work overtime at the casino. A hospital is not liable for injuries caused by a sleep-deprived doctor working extra hours at the hospital [*Brewster* v. *Rush-Presbyterian-St. Luke's Medical Center*, 836 N.E.2d 635 (Ill. App. 2005)]. However, other courts have followed the decision. In *Bussard* v. *Minimed, Inc.*, 105 Cal.App.4th 798, 129

Cal.Rptr.2d 675 (2003), an employer was held liable to a third party under *respondeat superior* theory where an employee became dizzy and light-headed after being exposed to pesticides at work and, while driving home, struck a car driven by the third party.

Note

1. The terminology of master and servant has its roots in the historical nature of the employment relationship of indentured servants and slaves. For more information, see the book's companion Web site.

2. Whistleblowers have not fared well under the SOX protections because their claim must relate to financial fraud, not other forms of misdeeds, even those that lead to financial fraud. Calls for reform for greater protection have resulted in Congressional attention and promises for action.

3. In *Long Island Care at Home, Ltd. v. Coke*, 127 S.Ct. 2339 (2007), the U.S. Supreme Court held that those who provide companionship services in a private home were properly exemption from minimum wage standards under Department of Labor regulations.

18

Employment Discrimination

update ▶

For up-to-date legal news, click on "Author Updates" at

www.cengage.com/blaw/jennings

Few employers have remained unaffected by the impact of antidiscrimination laws and cases. This chapter answers the following questions: What laws governing employment discrimination exist? What types of discrimination exist? Are there any defenses to discrimination? What penalties or damages can be imposed for violations? ■

Nature of Complaint	Number of Complaints
Total Charges	82,792
Race	30,510
Retaliation	26,663
Sex	24,826
Age	23,371
Disability	19,103
National origin	9,396
Religion	2,880
Equal pay	818

A total of 362 suits were filed from the complaints received.

EEOC 2007 data on employment discrimination cases

I have a dream that one day this nation will rise up and live out the true meaning of its creed: "We hold these truths to be self-evident; that all men are created equal." I have a dream. . . . I have a dream that my four little children will one day live in a nation where they will not be judged by the color of their skin but by the content of their character. I have a dream. . . .

DR. MARTIN LUTHER KING JR.

consider...

Kimberly Ellerth's supervisor, Ted Slowik, was interviewing her for a promotion. He said that she was not "loose enough," and then reached over and touched her knee. In a conversation between them in which Mr. Slowik told Ms. Ellerth she got the job, he commented that the men in the factories she would be working with "certainly like women with pretty legs." Ms. Ellerth complained to no one but then quit and filed suit for sexual harassment. Can she recover?

History of Employment Discrimination Law

Protections against employment discrimination are strictly statutory. Common law afforded employees no protection against discrimination. Indeed, common law viewed the entire employment relationship as a private contractual matter that should be subject to judicial interference.[1]

The first federal legislation to deal directly with the issue of discrimination was the **Equal Pay Act of 1963** (see Chapter 17 for more details). The statutory right to equality was expanded beyond the issue of pay less than a year later by **Title VII** of the **Civil Rights Act of 1964**. Title VII is the basis for discrimination law and judicial decisions in such matters. Although it has been amended many times, its basic purpose is to prohibit discrimination in employment on the basis of race, color, religion, sex, or national origin.

Title VII was first amended by the **Equal Employment Opportunity Act of 1972**. This amendment gave the act's enforcer, the **Equal Employment Opportunity Commission** (EEOC), greater powers—for example, the right to file suits in federal district court. In 1975, Title VII was again amended with the **Pregnancy Discrimination Act**, which defined sex discrimination to include discrimination on the basis of pregnancy and childbirth.

Laws have also been enacted to protect against discrimination because of age or handicap. Discrimination on the basis of age was prohibited by the **Age Discrimination in Employment Act of 1967** (discussed later in this chapter). Under the **Rehabilitation Act of 1973**, federal contractors are prohibited from discriminating against certain employees in performing their contracts. With the **Americans with Disabilities Act**, passed in 1990, employers of 15 or more employees are prohibited from discriminating against employees with disabilities and are required to make reasonable accommodations for qualified employees with disabilities. Although the substance of the existing antidiscrimination laws remains, the **Civil Rights Act of 1991** made significant changes in procedural aspects of Title VII litigation. Exhibit 18.1 provides a summary of federal antidiscrimination legislation to date.

EXHIBIT	18.1	Employment Discrimination Statutory Scheme

STATUTE	DATE	PROVISIONS
Civil Rights Acts of 1866 and 1870 42 U.S.C. § 1981	1866 1870	Prohibited intentional discrimination based on race, color, national origin, or ethnicity; permit lawsuits
Equal Pay Act 29 U.S.C. § 206	1963	Prohibits paying workers of one sex different wages from the other when the jobs involve substantially similar skill, effort, and responsibility; Wage and Hour Division of Department of Labor enforces; private lawsuits permitted; double damage recovery for up to three years' wages plus attorney fees
Civil Rights Act of 1964 42 U.S.C. § 1981	1964	Outlaws all employment discrimination on the basis of race, color, religion, sex, or national origin; applies to hiring, pay, work conditions, promotions, discipline, and discharge; EEOC enforces; private lawsuits permitted; costs and attorney fees recoverable
Age Discrimination in Employment Act 42 U.S.C. § 6101	1967	Prohibits employment discrimination because of age against employees over 40 and mandatory retirement restrictions; EEOC enforces; private lawsuits permitted; attorney fees and costs recoverable
Equal Employment Opportunity Act 42 U.S.C. § 2000	1972	Expanded enforcement power of EEOC
Rehabilitation Act 29 U.S.C. § 701	1973	Prohibits employment discrimination on the basis of handicaps
Pregnancy Discrimination Act 42 U.S.C. § 2000e	1975	Prohibits discrimination on the basis of pregnancy and childbirth
Americans with Disabilities Act 42 U.S.C. § 12101	1990	Prohibits discrimination against those with covered disabilities
Civil Rights Act of 1991 42 U.S.C. § 1981	1991	Clarifies disparate impact suit requirements; clarifies the meaning of "business necessity" and "job related"; changes some Supreme Court decisions (*Wards Cove*); punitive damage recovery
Glass Ceiling Act 42 U.S.C. § 2000e	1991	Creates commission to study barriers to women entering management and decision-making positions
Family and Medical Leave Act 29 U.S.C. § 2601	1993	Establishes 12 weeks of unpaid leave for medical or family reasons

Employment Discrimination: Title VII of the Civil Rights Act

APPLICATION OF TITLE VII

Groups Covered

Title VII does not apply to all employers but is limited to the following groups:

1. Employers with at least 15 workers during each working day in each of 20 or more calendar weeks in the current or preceding year (state antidiscrimination statutes may apply to employers with fewer than 15 employees)

2. Labor unions that have 15 members or more or operate a hiring hall that refers workers to covered employers

3. Employment agencies that procure workers for an employer who is covered by the law

4. Any labor union or employment agency, provided it has 15 or more employees

5. State and local agencies

Employment Procedures Covered

Every step in the employment process is covered by Title VII. Hiring, compensation, training programs, promotion, demotion, transfer, fringe benefits, employer rules, working conditions, and dismissals are all covered. In the case of an employment agency, the system for the agency's job referrals is also covered.

Theories of Discrimination Under Title VII

Three basic but not mutually exclusive theories of discrimination under Title VII include **disparate treatment**, **disparate impact**, and **pattern or practice of discrimination**.

DISPARATE TREATMENT

The most common form of discrimination at the time Title VII was passed was treating employees of one race or sex differently from employees of another race or sex. This different, or disparate, treatment results in unlawful discrimination when an individual is treated less favorably than other employees because of race, color, religion, national origin, or sex. The U.S. Supreme Court established the elements required to be shown to establish disparate treatment under Title VII in *McDonnell Douglas Corp.* v. *Green*, 411 U.S. 792 (1973), a case involving discrimination on the basis of race. For a *prima facie* case for discrimination these elements are:

1. The plaintiff belongs to a protected class (identified groups under Title VII).

2. The plaintiff applied for and was qualified for a job with the employee.

3. The plaintiff, despite job qualifications, was rejected.

4. After the plaintiff's rejection, the job remained open and the employer continued to seek applicants.

The employer has the burden of proof in showing that it had a nondiscriminatory reason for its employment decision. *Chescheir* v. *Liberty Mutual Ins. Co.* (Case 18.1) deals with an issue of disparate treatment and proof of discrimination in an employment decision.

CASE 18.1

Chescheir v. *Liberty Mutual Ins. Co.*
713 F.2D 1142 (5TH CIR. 1983)

WHY CAN HE GO TO LAW SCHOOL BUT I CAN'T? THE CASE OF THE LAW STUDENT CLAIMS ADJUSTOR

FACTS

Liberty Mutual Insurance Company has a rule prohibiting its adjustors and first-year supervisors from attending law school. This "law school rule" was proposed and implemented on a national basis by Edmund Carr, a vice president and general claims manager, in November 1972.

Joan Chescheir (plaintiff) was hired by Liberty Mutual's Dallas office in March 1973 as a claims adjustor.

In August 1976, Wyatt Trainer, the claims manager at the Houston office, received an anonymous letter informing him that Ms. Chescheir was attending law school. After consulting with his assistants and superior, Mr. Trainer fired her after she admitted she was attending law school.

Charity O'Connell also worked in the Houston office as a claims adjustor during the same period as Ms. Chescheir. During a coffee break with a new employee, Timothy Schwirtz (also an adjustor), Ms. O'Connell relayed the story of Ms. Chescheir's firing. Mr. Schwirtz then said, "Oh, that's strange, because when I was hired, when Wells [Southwest Division claims manager] interviewed me, he told me that I could go to law school and in fact if I came down to the Houston office, there were law schools in Houston." Ms. O'Connell then went to her supervisor and told him she also was attending law school. She refused to quit law school and was fired.

William McCarthy, Liberty's house counsel in its Houston office, attended law school while working as an adjustor and was retained as house counsel upon his graduation. Mr. McCarthy's supervisors were aware of his contemporaneous law school career. Alvin Dwayne White was employed as an adjustor in Liberty's Fort Worth office and asked for a transfer to Houston so he could attend law school. He was given the transfer and attended law school in Houston. James Ballard worked as an adjustor in Houston, attended law school, and was promoted to supervisor while in law school. Supervisors and employees were aware of his law school attendance, but the law school rule was not enforced against him.

Ms. Chescheir and Ms. O'Connell both filed complaints with the EEOC, were given right of suit letters, and filed suit in federal district court. After a lengthy trial, the court found that Liberty Mutual had violated Title VII. Both women were given back pay. Liberty Mutual appealed.

JUDICIAL OPINION

GOLDBERG, Circuit Judge

Title VII applies . . . not only to the more blatant forms of discrimination, but also to subtler forms, such as discriminatory enforcement of work rules.

The district court made multitudinous findings of subsidiary facts and concluded in a finding of ultimate fact: "The defendant applied its law school rule differently to male and female employees."

It is clear that the plaintiffs are members of a protected group and that there was a company policy or practice concerning the activity for which the plaintiffs were discharged; thus the first two elements of the test are met. It is also clear that minority employees were disciplined without the application of a lenient policy, and in conformity with a strict policy. All women known to violate the law school rule were immediately discharged. Furthermore, even potential violations of the rule by women were investigated promptly. An anonymous letter was sufficient to trigger an investigation of Chescheir, and the fact that Chescheir was attending law school moved the company to interrogate another woman.

The only remaining element of the *prima facie* case is a finding that male employees either were given the benefit of a lenient company practice or were not held to compliance with a strict company policy. This is the element upon which Liberty Mutual focuses its attack. Recasting Liberty Mutual's argument slightly, it claims that other males were strictly disciplined in accord with the law school rule, and that Liberty Mutual never knew that McCarthy, White, and Ballard were attending law school. Thus, claims Liberty Mutual, the third element was not met.

We are not persuaded. First, our review of the record does not disclose any males in the Southwest Division who were discharged because of the law school rule. Second, even were we to accept Liberty Mutual's contention that it did not actually know that McCarthy, White, and Ballard were attending law school, we would still affirm the judgment. The operative question is merely whether Liberty Mutual applied a more liberal standard to male employees. The district court found that there were widespread rumors that McCarthy and Ballard were attending law school.

That Liberty Mutual applied its law school rule discriminatorily finds firm support in the record; all four elements of the *prima facie* case are present.

Once Chescheir and O'Connell established a *prima facie* case of discrimination, the burden shifted to Liberty Mutual to present a justification. The district court found that Liberty Mutual offered no justification.

Accordingly, the judgment of the district court is affirmed.

Case Questions

1. What employer rule is at issue?
2. How were the plaintiffs fired using the rule?
3. What would Liberty have to offer as evidence to establish it did not discriminate?

consider 18.1

White employees at A. J. Gerrard Manufacturing were warned about their excessive absenteeism before they were discharged, but black employees were simply discharged for excessive absenteeism without warning. Is such a policy discriminatory? (Analysis appears at the end of the chapter.) [*Brown v. A. J. Gerrard Mfg. Co.,* 643 F.2d 273, 25 Fair Empl. Prac. Cas. (BNA) 1089, 25 Empl. Prac.Dec. (CCH) ¶31758 (5th Cir. 1981)]

· ·

Disparate Impact

Many employment hiring, promoting, and firing practices are not intentionally discriminatory. In fact, the basis for such decisions may be quite rational. Even so, the effect or impact of many employment standards is to discriminate against particular races or on the basis of sex.

In one case, the Alabama prison system had a minimum height requirement of 5′2″ and a minimum weight requirement of 120 pounds for all of its "correctional counselors" (prison guards). The impact of the rule was to exclude many females and very few males [*Dothard v. Rawlinson,* 433 U.S. 321 (1977)]. Although the rule had a purpose other than one of discrimination, namely, making sure guards were large enough to perform their jobs, the effect of the rule was to exclude women from the job position.

Pattern or Practice of Discrimination

The "pattern or practice" theory involves discrimination not against one person but, rather, against a group or class of persons (e.g., women or African-Americans). Generally, a party bringing a pattern or practice suit tries to show that a particular minority group is underrepresented in an employer's workforce as compared with that group's representation in the population base. For example, percentages are often compared. An employer's workforce may consist of 6 percent African-Americans, whereas the city's population consists of 30 percent African-Americans.

The standards for establishing a pattern or practice of discrimination are affected by the 1991 amendments to the Civil Rights Act; with a "reasonable justification" defense for employers. The plaintiff must show causation between the practice of the employer and the disparate impact. For example, in one case that immediately preceded the 1991 amendments, the Seventh Circuit found that a company's low percentage of African-Americans in its workforce was due to its location in a Hispanic neighborhood and not because of its practice of hiring by word of mouth [*EEOC v. Chicago Miniature Lamp Works,* 947 F. 2d 292 (7th Cir. 1991)].

Specific Applications of Title VII

The various theories of Title VII discrimination apply to specific types of discrimination. The following sections cover these types of discrimination and Title VII's application to them.

SEX DISCRIMINATION

A *prima facie* case of sex discrimination by an employer requires proof of the same elements established in the *Green* case. The only difference is that the issue of rejection, firing, or demotion is based on sex rather than race.

Other more subtle forms of discrimination have slowly been eliminated from every area of employment. Even job listings in classified ads cannot carry any sexual preference. For example, an employer cannot advertise for just a "waitress"; the ad must be for a "waiter/waitress." Further, state laws and company policies that prohibit women from working during certain hours if they have school-age children are violations of Title VII.

Sexual Harassment

Sexual harassment is a violation of Title VII of the Civil Rights Act. Company policies on this issue should attempt to make it clear that an environment of harassment is not appropriate for any employee. Companies should also enforce policies uniformly.

Sexual harassment cases take two forms. In *quid pro quo* cases, an employee is required to submit to sexual advances in order to remain employed, secure a promotion, or obtain a raise. In the other—*atmosphere of harassment* cases—the invitations, language, pictures, or suggestions become so pervasive as to create a hostile work environment.

Employers are held liable for the conduct of employees that amounts to sexual harassment, as illustrated by *Burlington Industries, Inc. v. Ellerth* (Case 18.2), which answers the chapter's opening Consider.

Business Planning Tip

Office Romances

New York lawyer Sidney Siller, who defends sexual harassment suits, offers this advice for office etiquette to avoid litigation.

1. Leave your office door open during meetings.

2. Don't go out to lunch with opposite sex coworkers.

3. Don't offer rides home (even in inclement weather).

4. Avoid physical contact in the office.

Some companies have adopted a policy of no fraternization among employees.

CASE 18.2

Burlington Industries, Inc. v. Ellerth
524 U.S. 742 (1998)

THE BOORISH SUPERVISOR MEETS VICARIOUS LIABILITY

FACTS

Kimberly Ellerth (respondent) worked as a salesperson in one of Burlington's divisions from March 1993 to May 1994. During her employment, she reported to a mid-level manager, Ted Slowik. Ms. Ellerth worked in a two-person office in Chicago and was one of Burlington's 22,000 employees. Mr. Slowik was based in New York but was responsible for Ms. Ellerth's office.

The following incidents of boorish and offensive behavior occurred during Ms. Ellerth's employment.

Summer 1993   While on a business trip, Ms. Ellerth accepted Mr. Slowik's invitation to the hotel lounge. Mr. Slowik made remarks about Ms. Ellerth's breasts, told her to "loosen up," and said, "You know, Kim,

	I could make your life very hard or very easy at Burlington."
March 1994	Ms. Ellerth was being considered for a promotion, and Mr. Slowik expressed concern during the interview that she was not "loose enough." Mr. Slowik then reached out and rubbed her knee.
March 1994	Mr. Slowik called Ms. Ellerth to give her the promotion and said, "You're gonna be out there with men who work in factories, and they certainly like women with pretty butts/legs."
May 1994	Ms. Ellerth called Mr. Slowik for permission to insert a logo into a fabric sample. Mr. Slowik said, "I don't have time for you right now, Kim—unless you want to tell me what you're wearing." Ms. Ellerth ended the call.
May 1994	Ms. Ellerth called again for permission, and Mr. Slowik said, "Are you wearing shorter skirts yet, Kim, because it would make your job a whole heck of a lot easier."

In May 1994, the supervisor in the Chicago office cautioned Ms. Ellerth about returning phone calls. Ms. Ellerth quit and faxed a letter giving reasons for her decision unrelated to the alleged sexual harassment. Three weeks later, however, she sent another letter complaining of Mr. Slowik's behavior.

During her employment at Burlington, Ms. Ellerth did not tell anyone about Mr. Slowik's behavior. She chose not to tell her supervisor in the Chicago office because, "It would be his duty as my supervisor to report any incidents of sexual harassment."

Ms. Ellerth filed suit against Burlington for violation of Title VII in that the sexual harassment forced her constructive discharge. The District Court found Mr. Slowik's behavior created a hostile work environment but found that Burlington neither knew nor should have known about the conduct. The Court of Appeals reversed, with eight separate opinions imposing vicarious liability on Burlington. Burlington appealed.

JUDICIAL OPINION

KENNEDY, Justice
We must decide, then, whether an employer has vicarious liability when a supervisor creates a hostile work environment by making explicit threats to alter a subordinate's terms or conditions of employment, based on sex, but does not fulfill the threat.

The concept of scope of employment has not always been construed to require a motive to serve the employer.

The general rule is that sexual harassment by a supervisor is not conduct within the scope of employment.

Scope of employment does not define the only basis for employer liability under agency principles. In limited circumstances, agency principles impose liability on employers even where employees commit torts outside the scope of employment.

An employer is subject to vicarious liability to a victimized employee for an actionable hostile environment created by a supervisor with immediate (or successively higher) authority over the employee. When no tangible employment action is taken, a defending employer may raise an affirmative defense to liability or damages, subject to proof by a preponderance of the evidence. The defense comprises two necessary elements: (a) that the employer exercised reasonable care to prevent and correct promptly any sexually harassing behavior, and (b) that the plaintiff employee unreasonably failed to take advantage of any preventive or corrective opportunities provided by the employer or to avoid harm otherwise. While proof that an employer had promulgated an anti-harassment policy with complaint procedure is not necessary in every instance as a matter of law, the need for a stated policy suitable to the employment circumstances may appropriately be addressed in any case when litigating the first element of the defense. And while proof that an employee failed to fulfill the corresponding obligation of reasonable care to avoid harm is not limited to showing any unreasonable failure to use any complaint procedure provided by the employer, a demonstration of such failure will normally suffice to satisfy the employer's burden under the second element of the defense. No affirmative defense is available, however, when the supervisor's harassment culminates in a tangible employment action, such as discharge, demotion, or undesirable reassignment.

Affirmed.

DISSENTING OPINION

Justice THOMAS, with whom Justice SCALIA joins, dissenting
The Court today manufactures a rule that employers are vicariously liable if supervisors create a sexually hostile work environment, subject to an affirmative defense that the Court barely attempts to define. . . .

The Court's holding does guarantee one result: There will be more and more litigation to clarify applicable legal rules in an area in which both practitioners and the courts have long been begging for guidance. . . .

Popular misconceptions notwithstanding, sexual harassment is not a freestanding federal tort, but a form of employment discrimination. As such, it should be treated no differently (and certainly no better) than the other forms of harassment that are illegal under Title VII. I would restore parallel treatment of employer liability for

CONTINUED

racial and sexual harassment and hold an employer liable for a hostile work environment only if the employer is truly at fault. I therefore respectfully dissent.

CASE QUESTIONS

1. What is vicarious liability?
2. When will an employer be held liable for sexual harassment despite a lack of actual knowledge?

3. What is the liability of a company for harassment of an employee by an immediate supervisor?
4. Does it matter that the company is unaware of the harassment?

consider 18.2

Determine whether the following would constitute sexual harassment (either *quid pro quo* or atmosphere of harassment) under Title VII.

1. A manager who referred to female customers as "bitchy" or "dumb," flirted with an employee's female relatives, and told of spending a weekend at a nudist camp [*Gleason* v. *Mesirow Financial, Inc.*, 118 F. 3d 1134 (7th Cir. 1997)]
2. A supervisor who referred to the architecture of a shopping mall as looking like "two hooters" and a "bra bazaar," while having dinner with an employee on a business trip [*Penry* v. *Federal Home Loan Bank of Topeka*, 970 F. Supp. 833 (D. Kan. 1997)]

(Analysis appears at the end of the chapter.)

. . . .

Sex Discrimination and Pensions

It is a statistical fact that women live longer than men. Employers have higher costs for a female employee's pension than for a male employee because she will likely live longer after retirement. In *City of Los Angeles Department of Water* v. *Manhart*, 435 U.S. 702 (1978), the Supreme Court held that employers could not require female employees to contribute more to their pension plans than males. If the Supreme Court had sanctioned the disparity in pension plan payments, the higher cost of having female employees could have been cited by employers as the reason for their hiring practices. Insurers and employers are required to treat employees as a group and not to break them down by their age, sex, or other characteristics.

THE PREGNANCY DISCRIMINATION ACT

This act, which revolutionized maternity issues in the employment world, prohibits the following specific acts:

1. Forcing a resignation due to pregnancy
2. Demoting or limiting an employee's job upon her return to work
3. Refusing to allow a mother to return to work after pregnancy
4. Providing different sick leave rules for pregnancy and other medical ailments
5. Providing different medical insurance benefits or disability leave for pregnancy and other ailments
6. Refusing to hire or promote on the basis of pregnancy or family plans

The landmark case, *International Union* v. *Johnson Controls, Inc.* (Case 18.3), focuses on some nuances in sex discrimination.

CASE 18.3

International Union v. *Johnson Controls, Inc.*
499 U.S. 187 (1991)

THE ACID TEST FOR WOMEN: THE RIGHT TO CHOOSE HIGH-RISK JOBS

FACTS

Johnson Controls, Inc. (respondent), manufactures batteries, a process in which lead is a primary ingredient. Occupational exposure to lead entails health risks, including the risk of harm to any fetus carried by a female employee.

Before the Civil Rights Act of 1964 became law, Johnson Controls did not employ any woman in a battery-manufacturing job. In June 1977, however, it announced its first official policy concerning its employment of women in jobs with lead exposure risk:

[P]rotection of the health of the unborn child is the immediate and direct responsibility of the prospective parents. While the medical profession and the company can support them in the exercise of this responsibility, it cannot assume it for them without simultaneously infringing their rights as persons. . . .

Since not all women who can become mothers wish to become mothers (or will become mothers), it would appear to be illegal discrimination to treat all who are capable of pregnancy as though they will become pregnant.

The company also required a woman who wished to be considered for employment to sign a statement indicating that she had been advised of the risk of having a child while she was exposed to lead. The statement informed the woman that although there was evidence "that women exposed to lead have a higher rate of abortion," this evidence was "not as clear . . . as the relationship between cigarette smoking and cancer," but that it was, "medically speaking, just good sense not to run that risk if you want children and do not want to expose the unborn child to risk, however small. . . ."

In 1982, Johnson Controls shifted from a policy of warning to a policy of exclusion. Between 1979 and 1983, eight employees became pregnant while maintaining lead levels in excess of 30 micrograms per deciliter of blood. The company responded by announcing a broad exclusion of women from jobs that exposed them to lead.

Several employees (petitioners) and their unions filed suit alleging that Johnson Controls' fetal protection policy violated Title VII of the Civil Rights Act. Included in the group were:

- Mary Craig—sterilized to avoid losing her job
- Elsie Nason—50-year-old divorcee who lost compensation when transferred out of lead exposure job
- Donald Penney—denied request for leave of absence to lower his lead level before becoming a father

The district court entered summary judgment for Johnson Controls. The court of appeals affirmed, and the employees appealed.

JUDICIAL OPINION

BLACKMUN, Justice

First, Johnson Controls' policy classifies on the basis of gender and childbearing capacity, rather than fertility alone. Respondent does not seek to protect the unconceived children of all its employees. Despite evidence in the record about the debilitating effect of lead exposure on the male reproductive system, Johnson Controls is concerned only with the harms that may befall the unborn offspring of its female employees. . . .

The Pregnancy Discrimination Act has now made clear that, for all Title VII purposes, discrimination based on a woman's pregnancy is, on its face, discrimination because of her sex. In its use of the words "capable of bearing children" in the 1982 policy statement as the criterion for exclusion, Johnson Controls explicitly classifies on the basis of potential for pregnancy.

We concluded above that Johnson Controls' policy is not neutral because it does not apply to the reproductive capacity of the company's male employees in the same way as it applies to that of the females. Whether an employment practice involves disparate treatment through explicit facial discrimination does not depend on why the employer discriminates but rather on the explicit terms of the discrimination.

We therefore turn to the question whether Johnson Controls' fetal-protection policy is one of those "certain instances" that come within the BFOQ exception.

Johnson Controls argues that its fetal-protection policy falls within the so-called safety exception to the BFOQ. Our cases have stressed that discrimination on the basis of sex because of safety concerns is allowed only in narrow circumstances.

The unconceived fetuses of Johnson Controls' female employees, however, are neither customers nor third parties whose safety is essential to the business of

CONTINUED

battery manufacturing. No one can disregard the possibility of injury to future children; the BFOQ, however, is not so broad that it transforms this deep social concern into an essential aspect of battery making.

A word about tort liability and the increased cost of fertile women in the workplace is perhaps necessary. One of the dissenting judges in this case expressed concern about an employer's tort liability and concluded that liability for a potential injury to a fetus is a social cost that Title VII does not require a company to ignore. It is correct to say that Title VII does not prevent the employer from having a conscience. The statute, however, does prevent sex-specific fetal-protection policies.

Although the issue is not before us, the concurrence observes that "it is far from clear that compliance with Title VII will preempt state tort liability."

Concern for a woman's existing or potential offspring historically has been the excuse for denying women equal employment opportunities.

It is no more appropriate for the courts than it is for individual employers to decide whether a woman's reproductive role is more important to herself and her family than her economic role. Congress has left this choice to the woman as hers to make.

The judgment of the Court of Appeals is reversed and the case is remanded for further proceedings consistent with this opinion.

CASE QUESTIONS

1. Describe Johnson Controls' evolving policy on lead exposure.

2. List the plaintiffs who brought suit in the case. Why is the exclusion of men from the policy important to the court?

3. What is the court's position on tort liability of the company with respect to the fetus?

RELIGIOUS DISCRIMINATION

Employers are required to make reasonable efforts to accommodate an employee's religious practices, holidays, and observances. Not all religious or church activities, however, are protected; for example, the observance of a religion's Sabbath is a protected activity, but taking time to prepare for a church bake sale or pageant is an unprotected activity. The 1972 amendments to Title VII defined religion to include "all aspects of religious observance and practice, as well as belief." The accommodation of religion is required unless an employer is able to establish that allowing the employee such an accommodation would result in "undue hardship on the conduct of the employer's business."

In *Trans World Airlines, Inc.* v. *Hardison*, 432 U.S. 63 (1977), the Supreme Court confirmed the clear language of the 1972 act that requires an employer to demonstrate inability to accommodate an employee's religious needs. As a member of a church that worshiped on Saturdays, Larry G. Hardison expressed a desire not to work that day. TWA worked through several alternatives to afford Mr. Hardison the opportunity for Saturdays off, including asking the union to waive a seniority rule that limited substitutes for him and looking for an alternative job that would not require Saturday work. The union would not waive its rule, and no managers were available to take the shift. When Mr. Hardison refused to work on Saturdays, he was dismissed and filed suit, but the Court found for TWA because of its extensive efforts and the constraints that prevented shifting of workers without substantial interference in TWA's operations.

Title VII requires only reasonable accommodation. Employees are not necessarily entitled to the accommodation they desire. Further, employees are expected to cooperate with their employers in making an accommodation, such as finding a fellow employee to take a shift. In *TWA* v. *Hardison,* the Court noted, "The statute is not to be construed to require an employer to discriminate against some employees in order for others to observe their Sabbath."

consider 18.3

Kimberly Cloutier was a member of the Church of Body Modification. Ms. Cloutier wore an eyebrow ring as a symbol of her religion. Ms. Cloutier also worked for Costco. Costco had a policy that prohibited employees from wearing any visible facial or tongue jewelry. When Ms. Cloutier objected because of religious discrimination, Costco indicated that she could wear a Band-Aid or plastic retainer over the jewelry as an accommodation. When she refused, Costco would not allow her to return to work. Costco says that its policy was developed and enforced to create an atmosphere of professionalism in its stores. Ms. Cloutier filed suit seeking an exemption on the basis of religious beliefs from the Costco policy. Should she be entitled to the exemption? (Analysis appears at the end of the chapter.) [*Cloutier* v. *Costco*, 390 F.3d 126 (1st Cir. 2004)]

. . . .

Antidiscrimination Laws and Affirmative Action

Some employers, either voluntarily or through the EEOC, have instituted **affirmative action** programs. Nothing prohibits such programs under Title VII, and the Supreme Court has sanctioned them as methods for remedying all the past years of discrimination. Although Title VII does not mandate such programs, employers may legally institute them.

WHAT IS AFFIRMATIVE ACTION?

Affirmative action is a remedial step taken to ensure that those who have been victims of discrimination in the past are given the opportunity to work in positions they would have attained had there not been discrimination. Affirmative action plans cannot be **quotas,** or actual percentage figures that mandate hiring certain numbers of protected class members.

WHO IS REQUIRED TO HAVE AFFIRMATIVE ACTION PROGRAMS?

Some federal funding laws, such as those for education and state and local governments, mandate affirmative action programs.

The following types of employers are obligated to undertake affirmative action programs:

1. Employers who, pursuant to consent decree or court order, must implement plans to compensate for past wrongs

2. State and local agencies, colleges, and universities that receive federal funds

3. Government contractors

4. Businesses that work on federal projects (10 percent of their subcontract work must employ minority businesses)

AFFIRMATIVE ACTION BACKLASH: THE THEORY OF REVERSE DISCRIMINATION

Currently, some legislative movements and grassroots referenda mandate the elimination of affirmative action programs. The U.S. Supreme Court continues to grapple with the issue of affirmative action. In two landmark decisions on affirmative action in admissions programs issued in the same day, the Court found that the University of Michigan's undergraduate admissions process was too much like a quota to be upheld under the U.S. Constitution's protections on equal protections. However, the Court also upheld the University of Michigan's law school admissions process on the grounds that race was but one factor in a group of many other non-racial factors the law school considered in its attempt to gain diversity in its law school classes [*Gratz* v. *Bollinger,* 539 U.S. 244 (2003) and *Grutter* v. *Bollinger,* 539 U.S. 306 (2003)]. However, the U.S. Supreme Court placed a limit of 25 years on the use of race in the school's admission process.

The Defenses to a Title VII Charge

Title VII is not a strict liability statute. The act provides some defenses that employers can use to defend against a charge of discrimination.

BONA FIDE OCCUPATIONAL QUALIFICATION

A **bona fide occupational qualification** (BFOQ) is a job qualification based on sex, religion, or national origin that is necessary for the operation of business. A particular religious belief is a BFOQ for a pastor of a church. Similarly, an actor, to qualify for a role, may need to be a certain sex for purposes of realism and thus sex is a BFOQ for such employment.

The BFOQ exception has been applied narrowly, however. For a discriminatory qualification for employment to fall within the BFOQ exception, the employer must be able to establish that the job qualification is carefully formulated to respond to public safety, privacy, or other public needs; and the formulation of the policy must not be broader than is reasonably necessary to preserve the safety or privacy of individuals involved. For example, a restriction on hiring male employees for work in a nursing home occupied by women is excessive if male employees can work in jobs not involved with the personal care of the residents. Nor is personal preference a justification for a BFOQ; for example, many airlines have argued that there is a customer preference for female as opposed to male flight attendants. But customer preference is not a basis for a BFOQ; it is not a business necessity. English-only policies in the workplace have become the fastest-growing area of EEOC challenges as well as litigation under Title VII. In 1996, the EEOC had 30 discrimination complaints related to English-only policies of employers. In 2007, that number had risen to 200. Lawyers offer the following guidelines for enforceable English-only policies:

1. Such policies are permitted if they are needed to promote safe or efficient operations (hospitals where emergencies mean that translators and time may not be available).

2. Such policies are permitted where communication with customers, coworkers, and supervisors (who speak only English) is also important.

3. Such policies are necessary in situations in which cooperation and close working relationships demand a common language and some workers speak only English.

SENIORITY OR MERIT SYSTEMS

The goals and objectives of Title VII are often inconsistent with labor union rules of operation. Although matters of discrimination and union supervision are both covered by federal law, the two statutory schemes conflict on some points. Which controls the other: the remedial effect of Title VII or the long-standing history of seniority and other union rules? The EEOC has rules and standards for determining whether a merit or seniority system is valid and can be used.

APTITUDE AND OTHER TESTS

Any employer charged with Title VII discrimination because of employee aptitude testing must be able to show that the tests used are valid. Validity means that the tests are related to successful job performance and that a test does not have the effect of eliminating certain races from the employment market.

MISCONDUCT

For many years, an absolute defense to discrimination was employee misconduct. If an employee violated company rules, the case did not involve discrimination. The defense was so broad that even evidence the employer acquired *after* the termination and charge of discrimination could be used as a defense. In *McKennon* v. *Nashville Banner Publishing Co.* 524 U.S. 742 (1995), the Supreme Court limited this defense by requiring the employer to show that the misconduct is not a cover for action that violates Title VII.

ethical *issues*

Consider the following circumstances and decide whether there has been a violation of Title VII. Consider the ethical implications of the conduct along with the legal.

1. An employee must be dismissed. Two women, one white and the other black, have been with the company for the same amount of time and have the same rate of absenteeism. Their performance evaluations are about the same. Can the black employee be dismissed without violating Title VII?

2. Company B has had a significant problem with absenteeism, tardiness, and failure to follow through on job assignments among the employees who are of a certain race. The personnel director is concerned about company productivity, the costs of training, and the costs of constant turnover. The personnel director is also aware of the constraints of Title VII. The director instructs those staffing the front office to tell members of that particular race who apply for a job that the company is not accepting applications. The director's theory is that his applicant pool will be prescreened and he will not have to make discriminatory hiring decisions. Is the director correct?

Enforcement of Title VII

Title VII is an enabling act that created the Equal Employment Opportunity Commission for the purpose of administration and enforcement. The EEOC is a five-member commission whose members are appointed by the president with the approval of the Senate.

STEPS IN AN EEOC CASE

The Complaint

An EEOC complaint can be filed by an employee or by the EEOC. An employee has 180 days (in some cases, up to 300 days) from the time of the alleged violation to file a complaint. In *Ledbetter* v. *Goodyear,* 550 U.S. 618 (2007), the U.S. Supreme Court clarified the 180-day rule for individual suits. Lilly Ledbetter filed suit against Goodyear after her retirement in 1999, following 19 years of employment at the company's plant in Gadsden, Alabama. While she filed suit within 180 days after receiving her last paycheck, the court held that she must have brought her pay discrimination suit within 180 days from when the alleged discrimination in pay occurred. The suit was dismissed with the high court noting that employers must have current enough allegations so that they can defend the suit with their records, which may not be available after 19 years. The court held that each paycheck was not an act of discrimination. Rather, the conduct that led to the paychecks was the discrimination that required suit within the six-month time frame.

The complaint is filed with either the EEOC or the state administrative agency set up for employment discrimination issues. For the state agency to continue handling the complaint, it must be an EEOC-approved program. If it is not, the EEOC handles the complaint. The EEOC has special forms that can be filled out by any employee wishing to file such a complaint.

Notification of the Employer

Once a complaint has been filed, the EEOC has 10 days to notify the employer of the charges. Employers are prohibited from the time of notification from taking any retaliatory action against the charging employee.

EEOC Action

After the complaint is filed, the EEOC has 180 days from that time to take action in the case before the complaining party can file suit on the matter. During this time, the EEOC can use its investigatory powers to explore the merits of the charges. In the case of *University of Pennsylvania* v. *EEOC,* 493 U.S. 182 (1990), the Supreme Court ruled that the EEOC could have access to all information in an employee's file—even evaluation letters in which evaluators were promised confidentiality. During this conciliation period the EEOC may also try to work out a settlement between the employer and the employee.

The Right-to-Sue Letter

If the EEOC has not settled its complaint within 180 days from the time of its filing, the employee has the right to demand a **right-to-sue letter** from the EEOC, which is a certification that the employee has exhausted available administrative remedies. If a state agency is involved, the time for its settlement of the matter must also expire before the employee can take the matter to court.

The employee has the right to this letter regardless of the EEOC's findings. Even if the EEOC has investigated and determined the charges have no merit, the employee can still pursue the case in court. Under *EEOC* v. *Waffle House,* 534 U.S. 279 (2002), the U.S. Supreme Court held that the EEOC, as an agency, has the right to proceed with its remedies even if the private remedies are dismissed or not available to the affected employee.

REMEDIES AVAILABLE UNDER TITLE VII

Remedies available under Title VII include injunctions, back pay, punitive damages, and attorneys' fees. If a court finds a violation, it may order that corrective or affirmative action be taken to compensate for past wrongs. An injunction usually requires the employer to stop the illegal discrimination and then institute a plan to hire or promote minorities. Back-pay awards are limited to two years under Title VII. Section 706(b) of the act permits successful parties to recover "reasonable attorneys' fees."

An employer cannot take retaliatory action against employees who file charges or who are successful in a suit; Title VII makes such action unlawful.

Title VII originally allowed damages for back pay for all forms of discrimination. Punitive and compensatory damages are now permitted in racial and ethnic discrimination cases. The 1991 amendments extend the recovery of punitive and compensatory damages to cases involving sex, religion, or disability.

Other Antidiscrimination Laws

AGE DISCRIMINATION IN EMPLOYMENT ACT OF 1967

Title VII does not cover age discrimination, which generally involves companies' hiring preference for younger people. To correct this loophole, the Age Discrimination in Employment Act (ADEA) was passed in 1967, and the EEOC was given responsibility for its enforcement. The act covers all employers with 20 or more employees and prohibits age discrimination in the hiring, firing, and compensation of employees. All employment agencies are covered. The act protects workforce members above age 40.

The elements in an age discrimination case are similar to those in other discrimination cases—simply substitute that the terminated employee was replaced with a younger employee. The replacement need not be below the age of 40 [*O'Connor* v. *Consolidated Coin Caterers Corp.*, 517 U.S. 308 (1996)].

EQUAL PAY ACT OF 1963

The Equal Pay Act of 1963 is an amendment to the Fair Labor Standards Act. (The details of its coverage are outlined in Chapter 17.)

COMMUNICABLE DISEASES IN THE WORKPLACE

Whether employees can be fired because they may carry a communicable disease has recently become a crucial issue. Court decisions on the treatment of infected employees have varied, but the Supreme Court decision *School Board of Nassau County* v. *Arline*, 480 U.S. 273 (1987), has been touted as a protectionist measure as a result of its finding that a school board could not discriminate against a teacher because she had tuberculosis (a contagious disease). The Americans with Disabilities Act will provide new issues and remedies with regard to communicable diseases (see the following discussion).

REHABILITATION ACT OF 1973

Congress enacted the Rehabilitation Act to prohibit discrimination in employment against handicapped persons by persons and organizations that receive federal contracts or assistance. The Labor Department is responsible for enforcing the act. The Rehabilitation Act laid the groundwork for the Americans with Disabilities Act, but is limited in application to employers who have federal contracts and requires the same reasonable accommodation standards now required under ADA.

AMERICANS WITH DISABILITIES ACT

The intent of the Americans with Disabilities Act (ADA) was to eliminate discrimination against individuals with disabilities. The ADA has been called the "Emancipation Proclamation" for disabled U.S. citizens.

Portions of the ADA apply to employment discrimination issues while other sections ensure that those with disabilities have access to public streets, walkways, buildings, and transportation.

Under the ADA, employers of 15 or more employees cannot discriminate in hiring, promotion, and selection criteria against a "qualified individual with a disability." "Qualified" means that the individual, with reasonable accommodation, can perform all "essential functions" of the job. Impairments such as gambling, kleptomania, pyromania, illegal drugs, and sexual disorders are excluded from protection.

A disability is defined by the ADA as a physical or mental impairment that substantially limits one or more major life activities such as seeing, hearing, speaking, walking, breathing, learning, or self-care. The ADA also includes as a disability having a record of impairment or having something others regard as a disability. Pursuant to a U.S. Supreme Court case [*Bragdon* v. *Abbott*, 524 U.S. 624 (1998)], human immunodeficiency virus (HIV) is considered a physical impairment for purposes of the ADA. In that case, a dentist's refusal to treat an HIV-positive patient who needed a cavity filled violated the ADA public accommodation provisions.

Preemployment medical examinations are prohibited under the ADA, as are specific questions about a protected individual's disabilities. However, an employer may inquire about the ability of the applicant to perform job-related functions. "Can you carry 50 pounds of mail?" is an appropriate question; "Do you have the use of both arms?" is not.

Employers must make "reasonable accommodations" for disabled individuals to enable them to perform essential functions. Included in reasonable accommodations are providing employee facilities that are readily accessible to and usable by disabled individuals, job restructuring, allowing part-time or modified work schedules, reassigning disabled individuals to vacant positions, acquiring or modifying equipment, and providing qualified readers or interpreters. Perhaps the accommodation best known to the public is the right golfer Casey Martin won in *PGA Tour, Inc.* v. *Martin* (Case 18.4) to use a cart in PGA tournaments because of his circulatory ailment.

CASE 18.4

PGA Tour, Inc. v. *Martin*
531 U.S. 1049 (2001)

A STROKE OF GENIUS FOR AN ADA IN FULL SWING

FACTS

Casey Martin (respondent) is a talented golfer. Mr. Martin is also an individual with a disability as defined in the Americans with Disabilities Act of 1990 (ADA). Since birth he has been afflicted with Klippel-Trenaunay-Weber Syndrome, a degenerative circulatory disorder that obstructs the flow of blood from his right leg back to his heart. The disease is progressive; it causes severe pain and has atrophied his right leg. During the latter part of his college career, the Pacific 10 Conference and the NCAA waived for Mr. Martin their rules requiring players to walk and carry their own clubs.

The PGA Tour, Inc. (petitioner), a nonprofit entity formed in 1968, sponsors and cosponsors professional golf tournaments. The basic rules of golf apply equally to all players in PGA competitions. The PGA interpretation of its rules was that Mr. Martin's use of a cart for participation in the four-day, 72-hole event would be an unfair advantage. The PGA would not allow him to use a cart.

The lower court and the court of appeals found that the hard cards (that contain the PGA rule on no carts) violated the ADA and required the PGA to permit Mr. Martin to use a cart pursuant to the act's rules on reasonable accommodation. The PGA appealed.

JUDICIAL OPINION

STEVENS, Justice
This case raises two questions concerning the application of the Americans with Disabilities Act of 1990, to a gifted athlete: first, whether the Act protects access to

professional golf tournaments by a qualified entrant with a disability; and second, whether a disabled contestant may be denied the use of a golf cart because it would "fundamentally alter the nature" of the tournaments, § 12182(b)(2)(A)(ii), to allow him to ride when all other contestants must walk. . . .

Petitioner does not contest that a golf cart is a reasonable modification that is necessary if Martin is to play in its tournaments. Martin's claim thus differs from one that might be asserted by players with less serious afflictions that make walking the course uncomfortable or difficult, but not beyond their capacity. In such cases, an accommodation might be reasonable but not necessary. In this case, however, the narrow dispute is whether allowing Martin to use a golf cart, despite the walking requirement that applies to the PGA TOUR, the NIKE TOUR, and the third stage of the Q-School, is a modification that would "fundamentally alter the nature" of those events.

We are not persuaded that a waiver of the walking rule for Martin would work a fundamental alteration in either sense.

As an initial matter, we observe that the use of carts is not itself inconsistent with the fundamental character of the game of golf. From early on, the essence of the game has been shot-making—using clubs to cause a ball to progress from the teeing ground to a hole some distance away with as few strokes as possible. The walking rule that is contained in petitioner's hard cards, based on an optional condition buried in an appendix to the Rules of Golf, is not an essential attribute of the game itself.

. . . [T]he ADA was enacted to eliminate discrimination against "individuals" with disabilities, and to that end Title III of the Act requires without exception that any "policies, practices, or procedures" of a public accommodation be reasonably modified for disabled "individuals" as necessary to afford access unless doing so would fundamentally alter what is offered. To comply with this command, an individualized inquiry must be made to determine whether a specific modification for a particular person's disability would be reasonable under the circumstances as well as necessary for that person, and yet at the same time not work a fundamental alteration.

The judgment of the Court of Appeals is affirmed.

DISSENTING OPINION

Justices SCALIA and THOMAS
The Court, for its part, pronounces respondent to be a "customer" of the PGA TOUR or of the golf courses on which it is played. That seems to me quite incredible. The professional golfers on the tour are no more "enjoying" (the statutory term) the entertainment that the tour provides, or the facilities of the golf courses on which it is held, than professional baseball players "enjoy" the baseball games in which they play or the facilities of Yankee Stadium. To be sure, professional ballplayers participate in the games, and use the ballfields, but no one in his right mind would think that they are customers of the American League or of Yankee Stadium. They are themselves the entertainment that the customers pay to watch. . . .

Why cannot the PGA TOUR, if it wishes, promote a new game, with distinctive rules (much as the American League promotes a game of baseball in which the pitcher's turn at the plate can be taken by a "designated hitter")? If members of the public do not like the new rules—if they feel that these rules do not truly test the individual's skill at "real golf" (or the team's skill at "real baseball") they can withdraw their patronage. But the rules are the rules. They are (as in all games) entirely arbitrary, and there is no basis on which anyone—not even the Supreme Court of the United States—can pronounce one or another of them to be "nonessential" if the rulemaker (here the PGA TOUR) deems it to be essential.

. . . [W]e Justices must confront what is indeed an awesome responsibility. It has been rendered the solemn duty of the Supreme Court of the United States, laid upon it by Congress in pursuance of the Federal Government's power "[t]o regulate Commerce with foreign Nations, and among the several States," U.S. Const., Art. I, § 8, cl. 3, to decide What Is Golf. I am sure that the Framers of the Constitution, aware of the 1457 edict of King James II of Scotland prohibiting golf because it interfered with the practice of archery, fully expected that sooner or later the paths of golf and government, the law and the links, would once again cross, and that the judges of this august Court would some day have to wrestle with that age-old jurisprudential question, for which their years of study in the law have so well prepared them: Is someone riding around a golf course from shot to shot really a golfer? The answer, we learn, is yes. . . . it will henceforth be the Law of the Land, that walking is not a "fundamental" aspect of golf.

Either out of humility or out of self-respect (one or the other) the Court should decline to answer this incredibly difficult and incredibly silly question.

CASE QUESTIONS

1. Does the use of a cart fundamentally alter the game of golf?

2. Is Mr. Martin seeking a public accommodation or an employee accommodation?

3. Do the dissenting justices believe that the court must define the essential elements of the game of golf?

Employers can refuse employment if an ADA-protected individual cannot perform necessary job functions. Also, employers can refuse to hire individuals who pose a direct threat to the health and safety of others in the workplace (assuming the risk cannot be minimized through accommodation).

The ADA is enforced through the EEOC and carries the same rights and remedies provided under Title VII. Exhibit 18.2 provides a list of items to help employers comply with ADA. Exhibit 18.3 examines proper and improper questions for job interviews under ADA.

THE FAMILY AND MEDICAL LEAVE ACT

Passed in 1993, the Family and Medical Leave Act (FMLA) requires companies with 50 or more employees to provide 12 weeks' leave each year for medical or family reasons, including the birth or adoption of a child or the serious health condition or illness of a spouse, parent, or child. Although pay is not required during the leave, medical benefits of the employee must continue, and the same or an equivalent job must be available for the employee upon return.

EXHIBIT   18.2   Compliance Tips for ADA

MINIMIZING AN EMPLOYER'S ADA RISKS

1. Post notices describing the provisions of the ADA in your workplace.

2. Review job requirements to ensure that they bear a direct relationship to the ability to perform the essential functions of the job in question.

3. Identify, in writing, the "essential functions" of a job before advertising for or interviewing potential candidates.

4. Before rejecting an otherwise qualified applicant or terminating an employee on the basis of a disability, first determine that (a) the individual cannot perform the essential duties of the position, or (b) the individual cannot perform the essential duties of the position without imminent and substantial risk of injury to self or others, and (c) the employer cannot reasonably accommodate the disability.

5. Articulate factors, other than an individual's disability, that are the basis of an adverse employment decision. Document your findings and the tangible evidence on which a decision to reject or terminate was based; make notes of accommodations considered.

6. Ask the disabled individual for advice on accommodations. This shows the employer's good faith and a willingness to consider such proposals.

7. Institute programs of benefits and consultation to assist disabled employees in effectively managing health, leave, and other benefits.

8. Check with insurance carrier regarding coverage of disabled employees and attempt (within economic reason) to maintain provided coverage or arrange for separate coverage.

9. Keep disabled individuals in mind when making structural alterations or purchasing office furniture and equipment.

10. Document all adverse employment actions, including reasons for the employment action with respect to disabled employees; focus on the employee's inability to do the job effectively rather than any relation to the employee's disability.

Source: EEOC Enforcement Guidance, http://www.eeoc.gov.

EXHIBIT	18.3	Legal and Illegal Versions of Similar Job Interview Questions

LEGAL	ILLEGAL
1. Do you have 20/20 corrected vision?	What is your corrected vision?
2. How well can you handle stress?	Does stress ever affect your ability to be productive?
3. Can you perform this function with or without reasonable accommodation?	Would you need reasonable accommodation in this job?
4. How many days were you absent from work last year?	How many days were you sick last year?
5. Are you currently illegally using drugs?	What medications are you currently taking?
6. Do you regularly eat three meals per day?	Do you need to eat a number of small snacks at regular intervals throughout the day in order to maintain your energy level?
7. Do you drink alcohol?	How much alcohol do you drink per week?

Source: EEOC's "Enforcement Guidance on Pre-Employment Disability-Related Inquiries," May 12, 1994.

The Global Workforce

Currently 2,000 U.S. companies have 21,000 subsidiary operations in 21 countries throughout the world. With the free trade agreements (see Chapter 6), those numbers will increase, as will the sizes of global operations. One of the many employment issues that arise with respect to employees in the subsidiary operations is whether the protections of Title VII apply to workers in these foreign operations. In *EEOC v. Arabian American Oil Co.,* 499 U.S. 244 (1991), the U.S. Supreme Court was faced with the issue of whether U.S. companies could engage in employment discrimination against U.S. citizens when they are working in countries outside the United States. The Court held that the companies are governed by the employment laws of the country of operations and not the provisions of U.S. legislation.

Congress responded to the Supreme Court's ruling in *Arabian American Oil* by adding a section to the Civil Rights Act of 1991 addressing the issue of foreign operations. The statutory provision on foreign operations and civil rights protections is neither universal nor automatic. The amendment provides basically that in a case of conflict between U.S. employment discrimination laws and those of a host country, a company should follow the laws of the host country. An example is a law in the host country that prohibits the employment of women in management. The company would be required to follow that prohibition for operations located in the host country. If the host country has no laws on employment discrimination, the company is then required to follow all U.S. antidiscrimination laws.

Several multilateral treaties govern the rights of workers. In 1948, the United Nations adopted its Universal Declaration of Human Rights. The declaration supports, among other things, equality of pay and nondiscriminatory employment policies. Also, the Helsinki Final Act of 1973 supports nondiscriminatory employment policies. In 1977, the International Labor Office issued its Tripartite Declaration of Principles Concerning Multinational Enterprises, which supports equal pay and nondiscriminatory payment policies. The EU has adopted all of these treaties and policies for their implementation.

Red Flags FOR MANAGERS

Employment discrimination, governed by Title VII and enforced by the EEOC, is complex and the litigation is frequent. Here are some simple guidelines for managers:

- Always hire, discipline, promote, fire, and compensate solely on the basis of qualifications and performance.
- Document employees' rules violations and disciplinary steps that you take against them.
- Observe and supervise your managers and supervisors to be sure that they are not harassing or discriminating against employees. Watch the language they use.
- Apply all of your employment policies, rules, and procedures consistently.
- Be sure your job requirements and qualifications do not use discriminatory terms.
- Accommodate employees' religious needs and physical disabilities as best you can.

Summary

What laws govern employment discrimination?

- Civil Rights Acts of 1866, 1964, 1991—federal statutes prohibiting discrimination in various aspects of life (employment, voting)
- Equal Pay Act—equal pay for the same work regardless of gender
- Equal Employment Opportunity Act—antidiscrimination employment amendment to Civil Rights Act
- Pregnancy Discrimination Act—prohibits refusing to hire, refusing to promote, or firing because of pregnancy
- Age Discrimination in Employment Act (ADEA)—prohibits hiring, firing, promotion, benefits, raises based on age
- Rehabilitation Act of 1973—federal statute prohibiting discrimination on basis of disability by federal agencies and contractors
- Americans with Disabilities Act (ADA)—federal law prohibiting discrimination on basis of disability by certain employees
- Family and Medical Leave Act (FMLA)—federal law providing for 12 weeks of leave for childbirth, adoption, or family illness

What types of discrimination exist?

- Disparate treatment—form of discrimination in which members of different races/sexes are treated differently
- Disparate impact—test or screening device that affects one group more than another
- Pattern or practice of discrimination—theory for establishing discrimination that compares population percentages with workplace percentages
- Sexual harassment—form of discrimination that involves a *quid pro quo* related to sexual favors or an atmosphere of harassment

What are the defenses to discrimination?

- Bona fide occupational qualification (BFOQ)—job qualification of sex, religion, or national origin that is necessary for the operation of a business, such as religious affiliation for the pastor of a church
- Affirmative action—programs created to remedy past wrongs that permit choices on the basis of race, sex, or national origin

Key Terms

Questions and Problems

1. Patricia Lorance is an hourly wage employee at the Montgomery Works AT&T electronics products plant. She had been employed there since the early 1970s and under union rules accrued seniority through her years of service at the plant. In 1979, the union entered into a new collective bargaining agreement providing that seniority would be determined by department and not on a plantwide basis. The effect of the change was to put Ms. Lorance at the bottom of the seniority ladder in the testing areas despite her longevity in the plant. When layoffs became necessary, she and the other female testers were laid off because of the new seniority rule. Without the new rule, Ms. Lorance and the other women would not have been victims of the cutbacks. Does the seniority system violate Title VII? [*Lorance v. AT&T Technologies, Inc.*, 490 U.S. 900 (1989)]

2. Vivian Martyszenko was working as a cashier at a Safeway grocery store in Ogallala, Nebraska, when she received a call from the police informing her that her two children might have been molested. Ms. Martyszenko's supervisor gave her two weeks' vacation leave to care for her children.

The psychiatrist's exam of the children was inconclusive, and Ms. Martyszenko was told it would take time for their recovery. She asked for leave under the FMLA, which Safeway denied. She then filed suit, alleging Safeway had violated FMLA. Was the boys' condition a serious health condition covered under FMLA? [*Martyszenko v. Safeway, Inc.*, 120 F.3d 120 (8th Cir. 1997)]

3. On August 11, 1980, Shelby Memorial Hospital hired Sylvia Hayes, a certified X-ray technician, to work the 3–11 P.M. shift in the hospital's radiology department. Two months later, she was fired after she informed her supervisor that she was pregnant. The supervisor fired Ms. Hayes because Dr. Cecil Eiland, the hospital's radiology director and director of radiation safety, recommended that Ms. Hayes be removed from all areas using ionizing radiation, and the hospital could not find alternative work for her. After her dismissal, Ms. Hayes filed suit for violation of the Pregnancy Discrimination Act and Title VII. Should she recover? [*Hayes v. Shelby Memorial Hosp.*, 726 F.2d 1543 (11th Cir. 1984)]

4. The Masonic nursing home has mostly female occupants and hires fewer male attendants than female ones. Home administrators maintain that the female occupants (for privacy reasons) would not consent to intimate personal care by males and would, in fact, leave the home. A substantial portion of the women at the home are "total care" patients who require assistance in performing virtually all activities, including bathing, dressing, and using toilets, catheters, and bedpans. In a suit brought by a male nurse's aide who was denied employment, who would win? [*Fessel v. Masonic Home*, 17 FEP Cases 330 (Del. 1978)]

5. Between 1985 and 1990, while attending college, Beth Ann Faragher worked part time and during the summers as an ocean lifeguard for the Parks and Recreation Department of the City of Boca Raton. Ms. Faragher worked for three immediate supervisors during this period: Bill Terry, David Silverman, and Robert Gordon. Ms. Faragher resigned in June 1990 and brought a Title VII sexual harassment suit against the City in 1992. She alleged a sexually hostile atmosphere because of "uninvited and offensive touching," lewd remarks, and Mr. Silverman's comment, "Date me or clean the toilets for a year."

Ms. Faragher had not complained to higher management, and the lifeguards had no significant contact with higher city officials. Two months before Ms. Faragher's resignation, a former lifeguard, Nancy E. Wanchew, wrote to the City's personnel director complaining about Mr. Terry and Mr. Silverman's harassment of female lifeguards. Should the City be held liable? Does it matter that Ms. Faragher asked only for nominal damages, attorney's fees, and costs? [*Faragher v. City of Boca Raton*, 524 U.S. 775 (1998)]

Understanding "Consider" Problems

18.1

THINK: The rulings in *Green* and *Chescheir* are that employers cannot treat those who are members of different groups or protected classes (race, gender, religion) using different standards or rules, with the result being that the members of the nonprotected group are hired or retained while those in the protected class are not.

APPLY: A. J. Gerrard did not apply the same standard to all employees. White employees were warned; black employees were not. The result was that white employees were retained, and black employees were not.

ANSWER: The treatment was disparate and constituted discrimination.

18.2

THINK: Under Title VII, sexual harassment is established when there is an atmosphere of harassment created by propositions, suggestive language, or sexual innuendo.

APPLY: In both situations, there were no propositions, but there was sexual language used.

ANSWER: Both situations would constitute sexual harassment through the creation of an atmosphere of harassment. Avoid sexually directed or suggestive language in the workplace. Employers are liable under Title VII for not curbing such language.

18.3

THINK: Under Title VII, employers cannot discriminate on the basis of religion. An employer's responsibility to its employees with religious issues is to make a reasonable accommodation.

APPLY: The employee here wore her jewelry as a religious commitment. However, Costco's policy was universal and applied to all employees. There was a reasonable accommodation offer of allowing her to wear the jewelry but covering it with a Band-Aid or some alternative.

ANSWER: Costco had a legitimate policy of requiring its employees to present a professional appearance. The court found that it would be undue hardship to require Costco to allow the cashier to wear facial jewelry even though the cashier claimed that her religion required her to wear facial jewelry.

Note

1. See this text's companion Web site for additional background on the history of employment discrimination law.

19

Environmental Regulation

update

For up-to-date legal news, click on "Author Updates" at **www.cengage.com/blaw/jennings**

Keeping a clean environment is a long-range goal for society and citizens that benefit from a healthy environment. This chapter answers the following questions: What are the public and private environmental laws? What protections and requirements are present in environmental laws? Who enforces environmental laws? What are the penalties for violations?

By the shores of Gitche Gumee,

By the shining Big-Sea-Water, . . .

How they built their nests in summer,

Where they hid themselves in winter,

How the beavers built their lodges,

Where the squirrels hid their acorns,

How the reindeer ran so swiftly,

Why the rabbit was so timid . . .

HENRY WADSWORTH LONGFELLOW

"Hiawatha's Childhood"

consider...

Sullivan's Ledge, once a popular swimming and hiking area located near New Bedford, Massachusetts, has become little more than an industrial dumping ground for scrap rubber, waste oils, gas, combustion ash, and old telephone poles. The sludge became so toxic, the refuse so thick, and the stench so overwhelming, that the city closed down the area in the 1970s.

The EPA eventually identified a number of business entities as responsible for the cleanup of the area. Following lengthy negotiations, those businesses entered into a consent decree in 1992 that required them to shoulder the costs of that plan for

returning Sullivan's Ledge to a nonhazardous site.

Following the agreement, Acushnet Company and others challenged their assessment of liability for the cost of cleanup because there were only very small amounts of substances at Sullivan's Ledge that could be traced to them. They were being held as liable as those companies that had dumped substances there. Is this a defense to liability under environmental cleanup requirements?

Common Law Remedies and the Environment

From earliest times, landowners have enjoyed the protections of the courts and various doctrines to prevent bad smells, noises, and emissions.

NUISANCES

Common law affords relief to adjoining landowners and communities when activities rise to the level of a **nuisance**. A nuisance exists when the activities of one landowner interfere with the use and enjoyment of their properties by other landowners or by members of the community in which the nuisance occurs. Bad smells, ongoing damage to paint on buildings, excessive noise, polluted air, and the operation of facilities that present health problems can all be enjoined as nuisances. The courts have the power to issue **injunctions** against nuisances. Courts grant injunctions only after careful review and balancing of interests. In *Spur Industries, Inc. v. Del E. Webb Dev. Co.* (Case 19.1), the Arizona Supreme Court was faced with an issue of bad smells and flies.

CASE 19.1

Spur Industries, Inc. v. Del E. Webb Dev. Co.
494 P.2D 700 (ARIZ. 1972)

CATTLE AND FLIES AND RETIREES, OH, MY!

FACTS

Spur Industries operated a cattle feedlot near Youngtown and Sun City, Arizona (communities 14 to 15 miles west of Phoenix). Spur had been operating the feedlot since 1956, and the area had been agricultural since 1911.

In 1959 Del E. Webb began development of the Sun City area, a retirement community. Webb purchased the 20,000 acres of land for about $750 per acre.

CONTINUED

In 1960 Spur began an expansion program in which it grew from an operation of 5 acres to 115 acres.

At the time of the suit, Spur was feeding between 20,000 and 30,000 head of cattle, which produced 35 to 40 pounds of wet manure per head per day, or over one million pounds per day, and that despite the admittedly good feedlot management and good housekeeping practices by Spur, the resulting odor and flies produced an annoying if not unhealthy situation as far as the senior citizens of southern Sun City were concerned. There is no doubt that some of the citizens of Sun City were unable to enjoy the outdoor living which Del Webb had advertised. Del Webb was faced with sales resistance from prospective purchasers as well as strong and persistent complaints from the people who had purchased homes in that area. Nearly 1,300 lots could not be sold. Webb then filed suit alleging Spur's operation was a nuisance because of flies and odors constantly drifting over Sun City. The trial court enjoined Spur's operations and Spur appealed.

JUDICIAL OPINION

CAMERON, Vice Chief Justice

In the so-called "coming to the nuisance" cases, the courts have held that the residential landowner may not have relief if he knowingly came into a neighborhood reserved for industrial or agricultural endeavors and has been damaged thereby:

"[People] desire to get away from the congestion of traffic, smoke, noise, foul air and the many other annoyances of city life. But with all these advantages in going beyond the area which is zoned and restricted to protect them in their homes, they must be prepared to take the disadvantages."

"The law of nuisance affords no rigid rule to be applied in all instances. It is elastic."

There was no indication in the instant case at the time Spur and its predecessors located in western Maricopa County that a new city would spring up, full-blown, alongside the feeding operation and that the developer of that city would ask the court to order Spur to move because of the new city. Spur is required to move not because of any wrongdoing on the part of Spur, but because of a proper and legitimate regard of the courts for the rights and interests of the public.

Del Webb, on the other hand, is entitled to the relief prayed for (a permanent injunction), not because Webb is blameless, but because of the damage to the people who have been encouraged to purchase homes in Sun City. It does not equitable or legally follow, however, that Webb, being entitled to the injunction, is then free of any liability to Spur if Webb has in fact been the cause of the damage Spur has sustained. It does not seem harsh to require a developer, who has taken advantage of the lesser land values in a rural area as well as the availability of large tracts of land on which to build and develop a new town or city in the area, to indemnify those who are forced to leave as a result.

Having brought people to the nuisance to the foreseeable detriment of Spur, Webb must indemnify Spur for a reasonable amount of the cost of moving or shutting down. It should be noted that this relief to Spur is limited to a case wherein a developer has, with foreseeability, brought into a previously agricultural or industrial area the population which makes necessary the granting of an injunction against a lawful business and for which the business has no adequate relief.

It is therefore the decision of this court that the matter be remanded to the trial court for a hearing upon the damages sustained by the defendant Spur as a reasonable and direct result of the granting of the permanent injunction. Since the result of the appeal may appear novel and both sides have obtained a measure of relief, it is ordered that each side will bear its own costs.

Affirmed in part, reversed in part, and remanded for further proceedings consistent with this opinion.

CASE QUESTIONS

1. Did Spur create a nuisance?
2. Should it make any difference that Spur was there first?
3. How does the court balance retirement communities and beef production being two of Arizona's biggest industries?

EMF AND NUISANCES

Because any electrical current sets up a magnetic field, computers and wire transmissions to and from computers set up magnetic fields that might affect electrical equipment in buildings on neighboring land; the stronger the current, the greater the magnetic field. Also, if a loose or broken circuit sparks, the interference with neighbors increases. If that interference rises to an unreasonable level, it may be stopped as a nuisance and damages recovered for the harm. The issue of electromagnetic fields (EMF) has produced litigation against electric utilities for their placement of overheads wires, transformers, and power plants. The litigation has focused on many legal theories, including trespass and nuisance.

For example, the Meridian Data Processing Center was an independent contractor that performed all the data processing for a large number of banks and stockbrokers within the state. Because of the large number of computers and direct wire lines to its customers, the center's operation set up a substantial magnetic field that interfered with some of the electronic display equipment in several neighboring stores. The stores sued the data processing center to obtain an injunction against it for nuisance.

Because of the social utility of the activity, it is unlikely a court would enjoin this form of activity. It might, however, impose some limitations on hours of operation or require investment in technology to find a means around the problem.[1]

NIMBYS AND NUISANCES

Environmental activists that rely on nuisance theories and local zoning laws have emerged as powerful forces in community development. Groups sometimes referred to as NIMBYs (Not In My Back Yard) challenge the placement of everything from power plants to refineries to cell phone towers to Wal-Marts as nuisances, backing their protests with data on traffic, crime, health and safety, and risk. Another group is called the BANANAs (Build Absolutely Nothing Anywhere Near Anything) who deal with the more generic issues of preventing urban sprawl and urban redevelopment.

> **Business Planning Tip**
>
> The groups that protest location of factories, cell towers, plants, and other development efforts are political and public relations issues that require businesses to do advance planning and work with local authorities so that proposed projects are not derailed or can perhaps be tailored to address concerns of those activists.

Statutory Environmental Laws

At the federal level, most environmental laws can be placed in one of three categories: those regulating air pollution, those regulating water pollution, and those regulating solid waste disposal on land. Specialized areas of regulation are also covered in this subsection.

AIR POLLUTION REGULATION

Early Legislation

The first legislation dealing with the problem of air pollution, the Air Pollution Control Act, was passed in 1955, but it lacked enforcement teeth. Federal regulation in this area continued to be ineffective in the 1960s. However, under the Air Quality Act of 1967, the-then Department of Health, Education, and Welfare was authorized to oversee the states' adoption of air quality standards and the implementation of those plans. Still, by 1970 no state had adopted a comprehensive plan.

1970 Amendments to the Clean Air Act: New Standards

Because the states did not take action concerning air pollution, Congress passed the 1970 amendments to the original but ineffective 1963 **Clean Air Act** (42 U.S.C. § 7401); these amendments constituted the first federal legislation with any real authority for enforcement. Under the act, the **Environmental Protection Agency** (EPA) was authorized to establish air quality standards; once those standards were developed, states were required to adopt implementation plans to achieve the federally developed standards. These **state implementation plans** (SIPs) had to be approved by the EPA, and adoption and enforcement of the plans were no longer discretionary but mandatory. To obtain EPA approval, the SIPs had to meet deadlines for compliance with the EPA air quality standards, and thus the Clean Air Act established time periods for achieving air quality. The EPA required that those state standards also mandate the development of air pollution devices. Lack of technology could not be used as a defense to air pollution.

1977 and 1990 Amendments

With the 1977 amendments came authority for the EPA to regulate business growth in an attempt to achieve air quality standards. With this authority, the EPA classified two types of areas in which business growth could be contained. **Nonattainment areas**, as originally defined under these amendments, included those areas with existing, significant air quality problems, the so-called dirty areas. Today, the number of nonattainment areas has been reduced significantly. In some categories, nonattainment areas have been eliminated. Clean areas designated under the amendments were labeled **prevention of significant deterioration (PSD) areas**.

New Forms of Control: EPA Uses Economic Forces

For nonattainment areas, the EPA developed its **emissions offset policy**, which requires three elements before a new facility can begin operation in a nonattainment area: (1) The new plant must have the greatest possible emissions controls; (2) the proposed plant operator must have all its other operations in compliance with standards; and (3) the new plant's emissions must be offset by reductions from other facilities in the area.

In applying these elements, the EPA follows the **bubble concept**, which examines all the air pollutants in the area as if they came from a single source. If it can be shown that a new plant will have no net effect on the air in the area (after offsets from other plants), the new facility will not be subject to a veto.

Although the EPA initially did not regulate the construction of plants in areas that already meet air quality standards, environmentalists' protests and suits brought about the application of EPA regulations to prevention of significant deterioration (PSD) areas. Basically, the purpose of PSD regulations is to permit the EPA to have the right to review proposed plant constructions prior to their construction. In their submissions for EPA review, the plant operators are required to establish that air quality will not experience any significant effects and that emissions will be controlled with appropriate devices.

The impact of the 1990 amendments was more substantial on smaller businesses, such as dry cleaners, paint shops, and bakeries, because the definition of a major source of pollution was changed from those businesses emitting 100 tons or more a year to those emitting 50 tons or more per year.

One of the effects of the Clean Air Act Amendments of 1990 has been the buying and selling of EPA permits for sulfur dioxide emissions. If, for example, a utility has an EPA permit to discharge one ton of sulfur dioxide per year, but its equipment permits it to run "cleaner" so that it discharges less than the one ton, the utility can sell the emissions savings portion of its permit to another utility.

Plants that are major sources of toxic emissions must use **maximum achievable control technology** (MACT), or the best available methods for limiting emissions, regardless of cost.

The EPA is authorized under the 1990 amendments to pay $10,000 rewards to people who provide information leading to criminal convictions or civil penalties. The penalties for violations, as noted in Exhibit 19-1, are now substantial.

WATER POLLUTION REGULATION

Early Legislation

In 1965, the first federal legislation on water quality standards was passed—the **Water Quality Act**. The act established a separate enforcement agency—the **Federal Water Pollution Control Administration** (FWPCA)—and required states to establish quality levels for the waters within their boundaries. Because the act contained few expeditious enforcement procedures, only about half of the states had developed their zones and standards by 1970, and none of the states were engaged in active enforcement of those standards with their implementation plans.

The **Rivers and Harbors Act of 1899** prohibited the release of "any refuse matter of any kind or description" into navigable waters in the United States without a permit from the Army Corps of Engineers. For a time, the act was used to prosecute industrial polluters that were discharging without permit.

Present Legislation

Not until 1972 was meaningful and enforceable federal legislation enacted with the passage of the **Federal Water Pollution Control Act of 1972** (33 U.S.C. § 1401). The act was amended in 1977 to allow extensions and flexibility in meeting the goals and was renamed the **Clean Water Act**. One of the major changes brought about by the act was the move of water pollution regulation from local to federal control. Federal standards for water discharges were established on an industry-wide basis, and all industries, regardless of state location, are required to comply.

The ranges of discharges permitted per industrial group are referred to as **effluent guidelines**. In addition, the EPA has established within each industrial group a specific amount of discharge for each plant, which is the effluent limitation. Finally, for a plant to be able to discharge wastes into waterways, it must obtain from the EPA a **National Pollution Discharge Elimination System** (NPDES) permit. This type of permit is required only for direct dischargers, or **point sources**, and is not required of plants that discharge into sewer systems (although these secondary dischargers may still be required to pretreat their discharges). Obtaining a permit is a complicated process that requires not only EPA approval but also state approval, public hearings, and an opportunity for the proposed plant owners to obtain judicial review of a permit decision.

In issuing permits, the EPA may still prescribe standards for release. Generally, the standards set depend on the type of substance the discharger proposes to release. For setting standards, the EPA has developed three categories of pollutants: **conventional**, **nonconventional**, and **toxic pollutants**. If a discharger is going to release a conventional pollutant, the EPA can require it to pretreat the substance with the **best conventional treatment** (BCT). If the pollutant to be discharged is either toxic or nonconventional, the EPA can require the **best available treatment** (BAT), which is the highest standard imposed. In issuing permits and requiring these various levels of treatment, the EPA need only consider environmental effects and not the economic effects on the applicant discharger.

In 1986, Congress passed the **Safe Drinking Water Act** (42 U.S.C. §300f), which provides for the EPA to establish national standards for contaminant levels in drinking water. The states are primarily responsible for enforcement and can have higher standards than the federal standards, but they must at least enforce the federal standards for their drinking water systems.

In 1990, Congress passed the **Oil Pollution Act** (OPA; 33 U.S.C. §1251). The act was passed in response to large oil tanker spills, such as the one resulting from the grounding of the *Exxon Valdez* in Prince William Sound, Alaska, that resulted in a spill of 11 million gallons of crude oil that coated 1,000 miles of Alaskan coastline. Another example was the 1990 explosion aboard the *Mega Borg* in Galveston Bay that resulted in a 4-million-gallon spill and a fire that burned for more than a week.

The OPA applies to all navigable waters up to 200 miles offshore and places the federal government in charge of all oil spills. Once full liability for cleanup is imposed on the company responsible for the spill, the federal government may step in and clean up a spill and then demand compensation for the costs incurred. The Oil Spill Liability Trust Fund, established by a five-cent-per-barrel tax, covers cleanup costs when the party responsible is financially unable to do the cleanup.

Those responsible for spills are liable for penalties, both individual and corporate, noted in Exhibit 19.1 on p. 455.

SOLID WASTE DISPOSAL REGULATION

Early Regulation

During the 1970s, two major toxic waste debacles resulted in a new federal regulatory scheme of toxic waste disposal. In 1978, "Love Canal," as it came to be called, made national news as 80,000 tons of hazardous waste were found in the ground in an area that was primarily residential and included an elementary school. Epidemiological studies of cancer and illness rates in the area led to the discovery and eventual cleanup. Also, in Sheppardsville, Kentucky, an area that came to be called "Valley of the Drums," 17,000 drums of hazardous waste leaked tons of chemicals into the ground and water supply before their removal.

The emotional reaction to these two problem areas and the public outcry resulted in the passage of legislation that provided the federal government with some enforcement power for improper solid waste disposal. The **Toxic Substances Control Act** (TOSCA; 15 U.S.C. § 601) was passed in 1976 and authorized the EPA to control the manufacture, use, and disposal of toxic substances. Under the act, the EPA is authorized to prevent the manufacture of dangerous substances and stop the manufacture of substances subsequently found to be dangerous.

Also passed by Congress in reaction to dangerous dumping practices was the **Resource Conservation and Recovery Act of 1976** (RCRA; 42 U.S.C. § 6901). The two goals of the act are to control the disposal of potentially harmful substances and to encourage resource conservation and recovery. A critical part of the act's control is a manifest or permit system that requires manufacturers to obtain a permit for the storage or transfer of hazardous wastes so that the location of such wastes can be traced through an examination of the permits issued.

The Superfund

In 1980, Congress passed the **Comprehensive Environmental Response, Compensation, and Liability Act** (CERCLA; 42 U.S.C. § 9601), which authorized the president to issue funds for the cleanup of areas that were once disposal sites for hazardous wastes. Under the act, a **Hazardous Substance Response Trust Fund** was set up to provide funding for cleanup. If funds are expended in such a cleanup, then, under the provisions of the act, the company responsible for the disposal of the hazardous wastes can be sued by the federal government and required to repay the amounts expended from the trust fund. Often called the **Superfund**, the funds are available for governmental use but cannot be obtained through suit by private citizens affected by the hazardous disposals. Under the **Superfund Amendment and Reauthorization Act**, the EPA can recover cleanup funds from those responsible for the release of hazardous substances. Approximately 700 hazardous substances are now covered. (They are listed at 40 C.F.R. § 302.)

CERCLA Lender Liability   One of the more intriguing issues that resulted from CERCLA liability was whether a lender has the responsibility of cleanup because it was back in possession of the property due to a foreclosure sale or a deed in lieu of foreclosure. The **Asset Conservation, Lender Liability, and Deposit Insurance Protection Act of 1996** provides a specific exclusion for lenders in that the definition of "owner/operator" does not include someone who "holds indicia of ownership primarily to protect his security interest." This provision has been called the "secured lender exemption" from CERCLA liability. However, the new act does provide that a lender can lose its status if it "actually participate[s] in the management or operational affairs of a vessel or facility." A lender can do the following and still not be subject to environmental liability:

- Monitor or enforce terms of the security agreement
- Monitor or inspect the premises or facility
- Mandate that the debtor take action on hazardous materials
- Provide financial advice or counseling
- Restructure or renegotiate the loan terms
- Exercise any remedies available at law
- Foreclose on the property
- Sell the property
- Lease the property

CERCLA—Four Classes of Liability Rules   Four classes of parties can be held liable under CERCLA. The present owners and operators of a contaminated piece of property comprise one group. While *owner* is self-explanatory, *operator* includes those who lease property and then contaminate it, such as those who lease factories, operate storage facilities, and so forth. The owners and operators at the time the property was contaminated form the second group. This group brings under CERCLA jurisdiction those who were responsible for the property contamination, as opposed to present owners who had the problem deeded to them. For example, many gas stations have been converted to other businesses. Suppose that one of the underground gas tanks once used by the gas station has been leaking hazardous materials into the surrounding soil. Not only would the present owners be liable; so also would be all those who owned the gasoline station previously.

The final two groups consist of those who transport hazardous materials and those who arrange for the transportation of hazardous materials. Virtually no liability exemptions are available to those who fit into these four groups. Case 19.2 about *Acushnet Company* v. *Mohasco* deals with a corporation's CERCLA liability and provides the answer to the chapter opening Consider.

CASE 19.2

Acushnet Company v. Mohasco
191 F.3d 69 (1st Cir. 1999)

SWIMMING IN SLUDGE AND MAYBE LIABILITY

FACTS

Sullivan's Ledge, once a popular swimming and hiking area located near New Bedford, Massachusetts, has become little more than an industrial dumping ground for scrap rubber, waste oils, gas, combustion ash, and old telephone poles. The sludge became so toxic, the refuse so thick, and the stench so overwhelming that the city closed the area in the 1970s.

The EPA eventually identified a number of business entities and their successors as responsible for the cleanup of the area. Following lengthy negotiations, those businesses entered into a consent decree in 1992 that required them to implement a remediation plan and shoulder the costs of that plan for returning Sullivan's Ledge to a nonhazardous site.

Following the agreement, Acushnet Company and others in the consent decree group (plaintiffs) filed suit seeking financial contribution from Mohasco Corporation and others including American Flexible Conduit (AFC), New England Telephone & Telegraph Company (NETT), and Ottaway Newspapers, Inc.

The trial court found that there was insufficient evidence to find these companies liable under CERCLA and granted them summary judgment. The plaintiffs appealed.

JUDICIAL OPINION

BOWNES, Senior Circuit Judge.
We have strong reservations about interpreting the statute's causation element to require that a defendant be responsible for a minimum quantity of hazardous waste before liability may be imposed. The text of the statute does not support such a construction—CERCLA itself does not expressly distinguish between releases (or threats of releases) by the quantity of hazardous waste attributable to a particular party. At least on its face; any reasonable danger of release, however insignificant, would seem to give rise to liability. On this point the courts of appeals are in unison.

To read a quantitative threshold into the language "causes the incurrence of response costs" would cast the plaintiff in the impossible role of tracing chemical waste to particular sources in particular amounts, a task that is often technologically infeasible due to the fluctuating quantity and varied nature of the pollution at a site over the course of many years.

Moreover, it would be extremely difficult, if not impossible, to articulate a workable numerical threshold in defining causation. How low would a polluter's contribution to the mix have to be before a judge could find, with equanimity, that the polluter was not a but-for "cause" of the clean up efforts? Less than 0.5 percent or 1 percent? We do not see how much a line, based on the quantity or concentration of the hazardous substance at issue, can be drawn on a principled basis in defining causation. To even begin down that path, we feel, is to invite endless confusion.

This does not mean, however, that the *de minimis* polluter must necessarily be held liable for all response costs.

We therefore hold that a defendant may avoid joint and several liability for response costs in a contribution action under §9613(f) if it demonstrates that its share of hazardous waste deposited at the site constitutes no more than background amounts of such substances in the environment and cannot concentrate with other wastes to produce higher amounts.

On the whole, the costs and inherent unfairness in saddling a party who has contributed only trace amounts of hazardous waste with joint and several liability for all costs incurred outweigh the public interest in requiring full contribution from *de minimis* polluters.

The ultimate failure of a contribution claim because someone did only a negligible amount of harm does not impede enforcement by the EPA or frustrate any of CERCLA's objectives.

Affirmed.

CASE QUESTIONS

1. Explain why companies are litigating against each other under CERCLA.

2. What is a *de minimis* violation of CERCLA?

3. Will the decision excusing companies from cleanup costs defeat the purposes of CERCLA? Why or why not?

consider..19.1

Grand Auto Parts Stores receives used automotive batteries from customers as trade-ins. Grand Auto drives a screwdriver through spent batteries and then sells them to Morris Kirk & Sons, a battery-cracking plant that extracts and smelts leads. Tons of crushed battery casings were found on Kirk's land. The EPA sought to hold Grand Auto liable for cleanup. Can Grand Auto be held liable? (Analysis appears at the end of the chapter.) [*Catellus Dev. Corp. v. United States*, 34 F.3d 748 (9th Cir. 1994)]

CERCLA and Corporate Liability   CERCLA liability has also extended to corporate board members and corporate successors and officers in cases where a company is purchased by another firm. Those who merge or buy corporations also buy into CERCLA liability—liability under CERCLA continues after a transfer of ownership. The U.S. Supreme Court has ruled in *United States* v. *Bestfoods,* 528 U.S. 810 (1999) that a parent corporation is not automatically liable under CERCLA for a subsidiary corporation's conduct, but may be responsible if the subsidiary is simply a shell. In other words, CERCLA liability of parent corporations for the actions of their subsidiaries is governed by corporate law on piercing the corporate veil (see Chapter 13). Under the *Bestfoods* case, liability of the parent corporation for actions of a subsidiary results if the parent operates or controls the operation of the subsidiary.[2]

CERCLA and Buying Land   The best safeguard for lenders against CERCLA liability is screening the property carefully before accepting it as collateral. The lender's sale to another is not covered, and the lender is in the position of trying to sell property with a CERCLA problem. The value of the collateral is reduced substantially. The lender and any purchaser of a piece of property should conduct a *due diligence review* of the property. A due diligence review has three phases. Phase I consists of a search to determine whether evidence of past or current environmental problems is present on the property. Evidence reviewed in a Phase I search would be private and public records, aerial photographs, and a site inspection. If Phase I reveals some concerns, the parties proceed to Phase II, which consists of chemical analysis of soil, structures, and water from the property. If Phase II finds the presence of contaminants, the report for Phase II estimates the cost of cleanup. Phase III is the actual cleanup plan.

New Developments under CERCLA

Judicial Developments   One issue that courts continue to face with respect to CERCLA cleanup efforts is whether insurance policies for comprehensive general liability apply to a company's cost of cleanup. The wording of individual policies and intent of the parties are controlling in these cases.

Another basis for CERCLA challenges has been one grounded in the basic administrative law principle of an arbitrary and capricious challenge to an EPA demand for cleanup of a site when the demand for cleanup is not linked to any danger. The EPA order for cleanup was upheld in *U.S.* v. *Broderick Investment Co.,* 200 F.3d 679 (10th Cir. 1999), despite the cleanup being very costly, because the EPA ordered a cleanup to the point that the cancer rate in the area would be reduced to 1 in 100,000, a rate higher than in non-Superfund sites. However, because a day-care center was planned for the land, the court held that the cleanup level was not arbitrary or capricious.

These types of challenges to CERCLA, including causation and the application of administrative law, such as challenges to arbitrary and capricious action, represent the first constraints on EPA actions regarding solid waste cleanup.

The Self-Audit   Companies have been responding to CERCLA liability with voluntary disclosures through the EPA's self-audit procedures. The EPA encourages companies to self-identify problem lands and areas in exchange for reduced fines. Companies have hired executive-level managers such as vice presidents for environment or vice presidents for health, safety, and environment to manage a staff of in-house professionals who do everything from supervising a company's current activities to investigating past activities to determine environmental problems. These problems are then reported to the EPA, and the company and agency work together to solve the problem and be certain cleanup is done where warranted. These self-audits and disclosures also help the companies to be more accurate in their disclosures to shareholders and analysts.

The EPA has established a program called Incentives for Self-Policing, Disclosure, Correction, and Prevention of Violations. Under the program, those companies that come forward voluntarily, having met certain conditions, will have their penalties reduced for any violations uncovered. The conditions for reduced penalties are:

1. The violations were uncovered as part of a self-audit or due diligence done on property.

2. The violations were uncovered voluntarily.

3. The violations were reported to the EPA within 10 days.

4. The violations were discovered independently and disclosed independently, not because someone else was reporting or threatening to report.

5. There is correction of the violation within 60 days.

6. There is a written agreement that the conduct will not recur.

7. There can be no repeat violations or patterns of violations.

8. There is no serious harm to anyone as a result of the violation.

9. The company cooperates completely with the EPA.

The EPA will reduce fines and penalties by 75 percent if substantially all the conditions are met. If a company falls into the 75 percent mitigation category, the EPA will not recommend criminal prosecution to the Department of Justice. The documents related to the audit can be protected by the attorney/client privilege, even those that are disclosed to the EPA. The clarification of the privilege has resulted in most companies taking advantage of the EPA's self-reporting protections.

CERCLA and Brownfields

CERCLA has been so effective that designated Superfund sites, as of 2002, that remained undeveloped totaled 450,000. Called "**brownfields**," these sites are defined by the EPA as "real property, the expansion, redevelopment, or reuse of which may be complicated by the presence or potential presence of a hazardous substance, pollutant, or contaminant." Brownfields often contribute to urban blight and are barriers to economic development and revitalization.[3]

As a result, the Small Business Liability Relief and Brownfields Revitalization Act was passed to allow 75 federal agencies to work together in the *Federal Partnership Action Agenda* to provide funding for proposals to clean up and use these brownfields (42 U.S.C.A. § 9601). EPA rules now provide a process for application to become an "innocent landowner," someone who seeks to develop the brownfield but wants an exemption from CERCLA exposure. That designation then allows the applicant to obtain federal funding for purposes of cleaning up and developing the brownfield.

update

Check the book's Web site updates for new approaches to environmental management by companies.

ENVIRONMENTAL QUALITY REGULATION

Environmental controls of air, water, and waste are directed at private parties in the use of their land. However, as part of the environmental control scheme, Congress also passed an act that regulates what governmental entities can do in the use of their properties. The **National Environmental Policy Act** (NEPA) of 1969 (42 U.S.C. § 4321) was passed to require federal agencies to take into account the environmental impact of their proposed actions and to prepare an **environmental impact statement** (EIS) before taking any proposed action.

An EIS must be prepared and filed with the EPA whenever an agency sends a proposed law to Congress and whenever an agency will take major federal action significantly affecting the quality of the environment. The information required in an EIS is as follows:

1. The proposed action's environmental impact
2. Adverse environmental effects (if any)
3. Alternative methods
4. Short-term effects versus long-term maintenance, enhancement, and productivity
5. Irreversible and irretrievable resource uses

Examples of federal agency actions that have faced the issue of preparation of EISs include the Alaskan oil pipeline, the extermination of wild horses on federal lands, the construction of government buildings, the NAFTA treaty, and highway construction.

OTHER FEDERAL ENVIRONMENTAL REGULATIONS

In addition to the previously discussed major environmental laws, many other specific federal statutes protect the environment.

Surface Mining

The **Surface Mining and Reclamation Act of 1977** (42 U.S.C. § 6907) requires those mining coal to restore land surfaces to their original conditions and prohibits surface coal mining without a permit.

Noise Control

Under the **Noise Control Act of 1972** (42 U.S.C. § 4901), the EPA, along with the FAA, can control the amount of noise emissions from low-flying aircraft for the protection of landowners in flight paths.

Pesticide Control

Under the **Federal Environmental Pesticide Control Act**, the use of pesticides is controlled. All pesticides must be registered with the EPA before they can be sold, shipped, distributed, or received. Also under the act, the EPA administrator is given the authority to classify pesticides according to their effects and dangers.

OSHA

The **Occupational Safety and Health Administration** (OSHA) is responsible for workers' environments. OSHA controls the levels of exposure to toxic substances and requires safety precautions for exposure to such dangerous substances as asbestos, benzene, and chloride.

Asbestos

Buildings that contain asbestos materials remain a problem for buyers, sellers, and occupants. The **Asbestos Hazard Emergency Response Act** (AHERA), passed in 1986, required all public and private schools to arrange for the inspection of their facilities to determine whether their buildings had asbestos-containing materials. Schools are required to develop plans for containment, but other buildings are not regulated. Questions such as the impact of the release of asbestos from the walls when tenants, employees, and others hang photos and other objects by nailing them into the walls remain. The issues of the degree of harm and the cost of replacement continue to be debated among property owners.

Endangered Species

In 1973, Congress passed the **Endangered Species Act** (ESA), a law that has been a powerful tool for environmentalists in protecting certain species through their advocacy of restrictions on commercial use and development when the habitats of certain species are interfered with. Under the act, the secretary of the interior is responsible for identifying endangered terrestrial species, and the secretary of commerce identifies endangered marine species. In addition, these cabinet members must designate habitats considered crucial for these species if they are to thrive. In many instances, litigation deals with which species should or should not be on the list. Once a species is on the list, its critical habitat cannot be disturbed by development, noise, or destruction. *Babbitt* v. *Sweet Home Chapter of Communities for a Great Oregon* (Case 19.3) has given federal agencies broad authority in protecting endangered species.

CASE 19.3

Babbitt v. *Sweet Home Chapter of Communities for a Great Oregon*
515 U.S. 687 (1995)

JOBS VERSUS OWLS: LUMBER VERSUS ENDANGERED SPECIES

FACTS

Two U.S. agencies halted logging in the Pacific Northwest because it endangered the habitat of the northern spotted owl and the red-cockaded woodpecker, both endangered species. Sweet Home Chapter (respondents) is a group of landowners, logging companies, and families dependent on the forest products industries in the Pacific Northwest. They brought suit, seeking clarification of the authority of the secretary of the interior and the director of the Fish and Wildlife Service (petitioners) to include habitation modification as a harm covered by the ESA.

The federal district court found for the secretary and director and held that they had the authority to protect the northern spotted owl through a halt to logging. The court of appeals reversed. Bruce Babbitt, the secretary of the interior, appealed.

JUDICIAL OPINION

STEVENS, Justice

The Court of Appeals made three errors in asserting that "harm" must refer to a direct application of force because the words around it do. First, the court's premise was flawed. Several of the words that accompany "harm" in the § 3 definition of "take," especially "harass," "pursue," "wound," and "kill," refer to actions or effects that do not require direct applications of force. Second, to the extent the court read a requirement of intent or purpose into the words used to define "take," it ignored § 9's express provision that a "knowing" action is enough to violate the Act. Third, the court employed *noscitur a sociis* to give "harm" essentially the same function as other words in the definition, thereby denying it independent meaning. The canon, to the contrary, counsels that a word "gathers meaning from the words around it." The statutory context of "harm" suggests that Congress meant that term to serve a particular function in the ESA, consistent with but distinct from the functions of the other verbs used to define "take." The Secretary's interpretation of "harm" to include indirectly injuring endangered animals through habitat modification permissibly interprets "harm" to have "a character of its own not to be submerged by its association."

When it enacted the ESA, Congress delegated broad administrative and interpretive power to the Secretary. See 16 U.S.C. §§ 1533, 1540(f). The task of defining and listing endangered and threatened species requires an expertise and attention to detail that exceeds the normal province of Congress. Fashioning appropriate standards for issuing permits under § 10 for takings that would otherwise violate § 9 necessarily requires the exercise of broad discretion. The proper interpretation of a term such as "harm" involves a complex policy choice. When Congress has entrusted the Secretary with broad discretion, we are especially reluctant to substitute our views of wise policy for his. In this case, that reluctance accords with our conclusion, based on the text, structure, and legislative history of the ESA, that the Secretary reasonably construed the intent of Congress when he defined "harm" to include "significant habitat modification or degradation that actually kills or injures wildlife."

In the elaboration and enforcement of the ESA, the Secretary and all persons who must comply with the law will confront difficult questions of proximity and degree; for, as all recognize, the Act encompasses a vast range of economic and social enterprises and endeavors. These questions must be addressed in the usual course of the law, through case-by-case resolution and adjudication.

The judgment of the Court of Appeals is reversed.

CASE QUESTIONS

1. Is habitat modification harming endangered species?

2. Is logging prevented now?

3. What ethical issues arise from this case?

Aftermath: In August 1995, Congress passed, as a rider to a budget-reduction bill, a provision that suspended environmental laws in some national forest areas in Washington and Oregon through 1996.

ethical *issues*

Asia Pacific Resources International Holdings, Ltd. (called April) is about to sign a landmark agreement with the World Wildlife Fund, an environmental activist group. April has agreed to curb timber-cutting areas in Sumatra, Indonesia, to preserve a natural rainforest with great biodiversity. Over the past 20 years, more than half of the forest has been cut down for lumber.

April's customers, such as Procter & Gamble (makers of Charmin and Bounty paper towels), were shunning April as a supplier because of its damage in Indonesia. While April complied with Indonesian law (leaving 20% of the forest untouched), it left long ribbon strips that could not support the local wildlife.

Terms of the deal include the following:

- April will not allow other loggers to use its transportation system (barges and roads).

- April will verify the source of all logs it purchases.

- April will plant tree plantations and expects to be able to sell only plantation-grown wood by 2009.

Local residents resent these agreements with environmental groups because their livelihoods have been blocked as April closes its road and prohibits use by illegal loggers.

What advantages do you see in these private contract promises on environmental policy? What disadvantages do you see? What ethical issues exist for April?

Source: Steve Stecklow, "Environmentalists, Loggers Near Deal on Asian Rainforest," *Wall Street Journal,* February 23, 2006, pp. A1, A14.

In *Bennett* v. *Spear,* 520 U.S. 154 (1997), the U.S. Supreme Court interpreted the ESA as also permitting lawsuits by landowners affected by the statute's application. Landowners have equal rights along with environmental groups to challenge ESA applications and restrictions.

consider 19.2

Arizona Cattle Growers' Association and Jeff Menges, a rancher seeking a grazing permit on the lands at issue (together called "ACGA"), sued the Fish and Wildlife Service and the Bureau of Land Management to challenge Incidental Take Statements (ITSs) issued by the Fish and Wildlife Service in a biological opinion for certain grazing lands. Mr. Menges sought livestock grazing permits for land within the area supervised by the Bureau of Land Management's Saffold and Tucson, Arizona, field offices, and the Association represented members who claimed to be harmed by the government action. The Fish and Wildlife Service's biological opinion, issued on September 26, 1997, analyzed 20 species of plants and animals and concluded that the livestock grazing program was not likely to jeopardize the continued existence of the species affected, nor was it likely to result in destruction or adverse modification of the designated or proposed critical habitat. The Fish and Wildlife Service did, however, issue ITSs for various species of fish and wildlife listed or proposed as endangered.

ACGA's suit challenged both the ITSs and their terms and conditions. The challenge was based on the fact that the razorback sucker and the cactus ferruginous pygmy-owl were in abundance and not endangered. The environmental groups challenged ACGA's right to challenge the conclusions of the agency. Who is correct? (Analysis appears at the end of the chapter.)

. . . .

State Environmental Laws

In addition to federal law, all the states have enacted some form of environmental regulation and have established their own environmental policies and agencies. Some states may require new industrial businesses to obtain a state permit along with the required federal permits for the operation of their plants. Some states regulate the types of fuels that can be used in vehicles and offer incentives for carpooling.

All states have some sort of CERCLA statute. The statutes are creative in their fines and remedies. For example, Oregon imposes a fine for each animal destroyed as a result of hazardous waste dumping and the failure to clean up in a timely manner. The death of one mountain goat due to hazardous waste carries a $3,500 fine under the Oregon statute. Other states require property sellers to disclose to buyers the history of the property's use. The purpose of these disclosure statutes is to provide buyers with a history of activity. For example, a buyer who learns through disclosure that the land was used at one time for chemical production or storage will do due diligence of Phases II and III.

Enforcement of Environmental Laws

Federal environmental laws can be enforced through criminal sanctions, penalties, injunctions, and suits by private citizens. In addition to federal enforcement rights, certain common-law remedies, such as nuisance or trespass, exist for the protection of property rights.

PARTIES RESPONSIBLE FOR ENFORCEMENT

Although many federal agencies are involved with environmental issues, the EPA, established in 1970, is the agency responsible for the major environmental problems of air and water pollution, solid waste disposal, toxic substance management, and noise pollution. The EPA promulgates specific standards and enforces those standards with the use of the remedies discussed in the following subsections. The federal EPA may work in conjunction with state EPAs in the development and enforcement of state programs.

The **Council on Environmental Quality** (CEQ) was established in 1966 under the National Environment Act and is part of the executive branch of government. Its role in the environment regulatory scheme is that of policymaker. The CEQ is responsible for formulating national policies on the quality of the environment and then making recommendations to lawmakers regarding its policy statements.

CRIMINAL SANCTIONS FOR VIOLATIONS

Most of the federal statutes previously discussed carry criminal sanctions for violations. Exhibit 19.1 summarizes the various penalties provided under each of the discussed acts. In exercising its enforcement power, the EPA may require businesses to maintain records or to install equipment necessary for monitoring the amounts of pollutants being released into the air or water.

GROUP SUITS: THE EFFECT OF ENVIRONMENTALISTS

In many circumstances, private suits have had the most effect either in terms of obtaining compliance with environmental regulations or in terms of abating existing

---

EXHIBIT   19.1 Penalties for Violation of Federal Environmental Laws

ACT	PENALTIES	PRIVATE SUIT
Clean Air Act	$25,000 per day, up to one year imprisonment; fifteen years for willful or repeat violations; $10,000 rewards	Citizen suits; authorized EPA suit for injunctive relief
Clean Water Act	$25,000 per day, up to one year imprisonment, or both; $50,000/three years for violations with knowledge; $100,000/six years for subsequent violations	Citizen suits; authorized EPA suit for injunctive relief
Resource Conservation and Recovery Act (Solid Waste Disposal Act)	$250,000 and/or fifteen years for intentional; $1,000,000 for corps; $50,000 and/or five years for others	Citizen and negligence suits after EPA refuses to handle
Oil Pollution Act	$25,000 per day, or $1,000 per barrel; $3,000 per barrel if willful or negligent; $250,000 and/or five years for failure to report	Hazardous Substance/Response Trust Fund for cleanup; EPA suit for injunctive relief and reimbursement of trust funds; private actions in negligence

nuisances affecting environmental quality. The reason for the success of these suits may be the ultimate outcome of the litigation—possible business shutdowns and, at the least, tremendous damages and costs.

Private suits have been brought by environmental groups that have both the organizational structure and sufficient funding to initiate and complete such suits. In some cases, environmental groups are formed to protest one specific action, as is the case of Citizens Against the Squaw Peak Parkway; other groups are national organizations that take on environmental issues and litigation in all parts of the country. Examples of these national groups include the Sierra Club, the Environmental Defense Fund, Inc., the National Resources Defense Council, and the League of Conservation Voters. Some environmental groups represent business interests in environmental issues, as does the Mountain States Legal Foundation, which becomes involved in presenting business issues when private organizations and individuals file environmental suits.

These environmental groups have been successful not only in bringing private damage and injunctive relief suits but also in forcing agencies to promulgate regulations and to enjoin projects when EISs should have been filed but were not.

International Environmental Issues

THE EU AND ENVIRONMENTALISM

By the end of 1992, the European Union (EU) had passed more than 200 environmental directives that focus on noise restrictions; protection of endangered species; energy efficiency; recycling; and air, land, and water quality. The view of the EU is that environmental planning is to be conducted by member states as part of their economic development plans and processes. In 1990, the EU created the European Environment Agency to serve as a clearinghouse for environmental information; eventually the agency will operate for members in a manner similar to the EPA.

Many EU directives are designed to eliminate the need for regulation by encouraging different business choices and educating consumers. One directive required manufacturers to make 90 percent of all packaging materials recyclable by the year 2000. Another directive awards companies the use of an "eco-audit" sticker on their labels and stationeries if they comply with an annual environmental audit of their manufacturing, waste management, materials use, and energy choices. The audits can be done in-house or conducted by registered eco-auditors, but results must be released to the public. An innovative directive of the EU created an EU-wide "eco-label" to be placed on all consumer goods to provide information about the environmental impact of a product's production, distribution, life, and disposal. Germany has had such a label, called the "Blue Angel," for a number of years, and the EU adopted the concept for its continental marketplace.

ISO 14000

The International Organization for Standardization (ISO) has developed its ISO 14000 series of international environmental standards. Some environmental scholars have predicted that the ISO standards will become the model for regulators and prosecutors in their enforcement and sentencing activities for environmental violations.

Under ISO 14000, companies can become ISO certified, which will permit them to place special insignias on their materials, correspondence, and products to indicate their ISO standing. ISO standards emphasize not only compliance but also self-audits and self-correction. Genuine dedication to improvement is a key standard for this environmental certification.

THE KYOTO PROTOCOL

At the Kyoto meeting of the United Nations Framework Convention for Climate Change (UNFCCC), the delegates adopted the *Kyoto Protocol*, a plan for reducing six greenhouse gases, primarily in the United States and other industrial nations. Under the Protocol, signatory countries will reduce their carbon dioxide levels to less than their 1990 levels, a reduction that will require transfer of industries to other countries. The Protocol took effect in 2005, and as of July 2008 had 180 signatory countries. The United States has not adopted the Kyoto Protocol. It faces strong opposition from businesses that believe the goal is the transfer of wealth from developed nations to undeveloped nations as well as strong support from environmental groups.

THE PRECAUTIONARY PRINCIPLE

The **precautionary principle** has become a dominant force in environmental regulation in Canada, Australia, and Europe. The precautionary principle requires those who propose change to demonstrate that their proposed actions will not cause serious or irreversible harm to the environment. The standard is used, for example, in Australia as the burden of proof for anyone who seeks to obtain a permit to dump hazardous waste. The government will not issue the permit unless and until the applicant demonstrates that the action will not cause serious or irreversible harm. It has been used in applications for logging permits and building construction.

Red Flags FOR MANAGERS

Environmental law does not just apply to factories and chemical plants. Even drycleaners have limits on what amounts of steam their facilities can release and what solvents they can use. Managers should remember the following:

- When in doubt, ask, and get a permit to discharge into air or water.
- If your company has made an unlawful discharge or dumped waste, voluntarily report the actions to the EPA.

- Do your due diligence before you buy property.
- Be careful who you hire for waste disposal. If your contractors don't follow the law, you are liable under CERCLA.
- Work closely with community groups on their environmental concerns.
- Supervise your employees and contractors to be sure they comply with the law.

Summary

What are the public and private environmental laws? What protections and requirements are present in environmental laws?

- Nuisance—bad smells, noises, or dirt from one property that interferes with another's use and enjoyment of their own property
- Nonattainment areas—areas with significant air pollution problems
- Emissions offset policy—new plants not built until new emissions are offset by reductions elsewhere
- Bubble concept—EPA policy of maximum air emissions in one area
- Clean Air Act—federal law that controls air emissions
- Maximum Achievable Control Technology (MACT)—best means for controlling emissions
- Clean Water Act—federal law that regulates emissions in various water sources
- Effluent guidelines—EPA maximum allowances for discharges into water
- Safe Drinking Water Act—federal law establishing standards for contaminants
- Oil Pollution Act (OPA)—federal law imposing civil and criminal liability for oil spills
- Resource Conservation and Recovery Act (RCRA)—federal law controlling disposal

of hazardous waste through a permit system

- Superfund—funds available for government to use to clean up toxic waste sites
- Comprehensive Environmental Response, Compensation, and Liability Act (CERCLA)—federal law providing funds and authority for hazardous waste site cleanups
- Endangered Species Act (ESA)—powerful federal law that can curb economic activity if it presents harm to endangered species or their habitat

Who enforces environmental laws?

- Environmental Protection Agency (EPA)—federal agency responsible for enforcement of environmental laws at the federal level
- National Environmental Policy Act (NEPA)—federal law that requires federal agencies to assess environmental issues before taking actions
- Environmental impact statement (EIS)—report by federal agency on study of proposed action's effect on the environment

What are the penalties for violations?

- Injunction—judicial order halting an activity
- Fines and criminal penalties

Key Terms

Asbestos Hazard Emergency Response Act 452
Asset Conservation, Lender Liability, and Deposit Insurance Protection Act of 1996 447
best available treatment 445
best conventional treatment 445
brownfields 450
bubble concept 444
Clean Air Act 443
Clean Water Act 445
Comprehensive Environmental Response, Compensation, and Liability Act 446
conventional pollutants 445
Council on Environmental Quality 455
effluent guidelines 445
emissions offset policy 444
Endangered Species Act 452

environmental impact statement 451
Environmental Protection Agency 443
Federal Environmental Pesticide Control Act 452
Federal Water Pollution Control Act of 1972 445
Federal Water Pollution Control Administration 445
Hazardous Substance Response Trust Fund 446
injunctions 441
maximum achievable control technology 444
National Environmental Policy Act 451
National Pollution Discharge Elimination System 445
Noise Control Act of 1972 451
nonattainment areas 444
nonconventional pollutants 445
nuisance 441

Occupational Safety and Health Administration 452
Oil Pollution Act 446
point sources 445
precautionary principle 457
prevention of significant deterioration (PSD) areas 444
Resource Conservation and Recovery Act of 1976 446
Rivers and Harbors Act of 1899 445
Safe Drinking Water Act 445
state implementation plans 444
Superfund 447
Superfund Amendment and Reauthorization Act 447
Surface Mining and Reclamation Act of 1977 451
toxic pollutants 445
Toxic Substances Control Act 446
Water Quality Act 445

Questions and Problems

1. In 1985, Manufacturers National Bank of Detroit issued a letter of credit for Z&Z Leasing, Inc., an industrial firm, in order to enable Z&Z to obtain bond financing from Canton Township, Michigan.

After six years of operation, Z&Z was not doing well and had defaulted on its bond obligations. A consultant for the bank found underground storage tanks on Z&Z's site. The tanks contained a yellowish liquid that was found to be a solvent and a hazardous substance. The bank paid off the Canton township bond obligation and foreclosed on the Z&Z property. By 1993, Z&Z had still not sold the property, and the EPA sought to hold the bank liable as an operator for the costs of cleaning up the tanks.

Can the bank be held liable? [*Z&Z Leasing, Inc.* v. *Graying Reel, Inc.*, 873 F. Supp. 51 (E.D. Mich. 1995)]

2. Kelley Technical Coatings is an industrial paint manufacturing company that operates two plants in Louisville, Kentucky. Arthur Sumner was the vice president in charge of manufacturing operations for Kelley. Sumner oversaw the manufacturing process at both plants, including the storage and disposal of hazardous wastes. He was also responsible for environmental regulatory compliance.

Kelley generated hazardous wastes in its manufacturing process including paint ingredients that contained, among other things, toxic heavy metals such as chromium, lead, cadmium, and nickel; and paint sludge. Kelley accumulated hundreds of drums of these waste materials and stored them in drums behind one of its plants. Kelley never applied for a permit to store or dispose of its hazardous wastes on-site.

Between 1986 and 1989, Sumner had arranged for a licensed hazardous waste disposal company to remove and dispose of some of the drums containing hazardous wastes. From late 1989 to July 1992, however, no drums of hazardous waste were shipped off-site. Instead, in an effort to save money, Kelley contracted with a hazardous waste disposal company to come on site and drain the liquids from the drums. After the bulk of the hazardous wastes were drained off, employees were directed to pour off any rainwater that had collected into the drums onto the ground and to consolidate the remaining residue into one drum. The consolidation process resulted in the spilling of hazardous substances onto the ground.

Both Kelley and Sumner were convicted under the RCRA. They appealed their convictions on the grounds that they did not have the *mens rea* required for conviction under the RCRA statute. Are they correct? Are they criminally responsible? [*U.S.* v. *Kelley Technical Coatings, Inc.*, 157 F.3d 432 (C.A. 6th 1998)]

3. Peabody Mine No. 47 was located one-fourth mile from Walter Patterson's land. Mr. Patterson used his land for farming and operated on a low-maintenance schedule. His house had never been painted. Mr. Patterson said that gas, smoke, fumes, and dust traveled to his property, and he complained his clothes turned black, his bedclothes were dusty, his food was covered in coal dust, and his throat and nostrils were affected. Mr. Patterson said he was forced to sleep with the windows closed, even in the summer, to avoid blowing coal dust. The coal mine facilities operated 24 hours a day, six days each week. Does Mr. Patterson have any remedy? [*Patterson* v. *Peabody Coal Co.*, 122 N.E.2d 48 (Ill. 1954)]

4. A federal regulation promulgated by the EPA restricts the amount of water than can flow from shower heads to a rate of 2.5 gallons per minute. When the regulation took effect, many hotel chains had complaints from their guests about the slow water flow and the difficulty they had in bathing. Westin Hotels and Resorts announced that it would install two showerheads in the baths and showers of its hotel rooms to accommodate its guests. Each showerhead will meet federal requirements, but if the two are both turned on, the guests will have water at a rate of 5 gallons per minute. Westin maintains that it is in compliance with the law. A federal employee responded, "But we didn't anticipate the loophole of 2 shower heads per shower."[4] Discuss the Westin approach to compliance with the law.

5. The Tennessee Valley Authority (TVA) proposed the construction of Tellico Dam. If the dam is constructed, the known population of snail darters will be eradicated. A snail darter is a three-inch-long fish protected by the Endangered Species Act, which requires all federal agencies (such as the TVA) not to fund, authorize, or carry out projects that would jeopardize the continued existence of an endangered species. At the time an environmental group brought the issue to light, the TVA had already expended $100 million in the construction of the dam, which would bring great economic benefits to the area. What factors are important in resolving such a dispute? Is it a matter of the significance of the species? Should an EIS have discussed this problem? [*Tennessee Valley Authority* v. *Hill*, 437 U.S. 153 (1978)]

Understanding "Consider" Problems

19.1

THINK: Under CERCLA, those who own the land, lease the land, dump on land, or hire others to dump on the land are liable for cleanup.

APPLY: Kirk & Sons was a contractor Grand Auto used to dispose of its spent batteries. Grand Auto sold the batteries to Kirk & Sons.

ANSWER: Kirk & Sons does not fit into the category of hauling toxic materials away, but Grand Auto did, through it sales, dispose of the toxic batteries. Grand Auto was part of the chain of transfer that resulted in the toxic substances in the soil. Grand Auto has liability under CERCLA for the Kirk cleanup.

19.2

THINK: The conclusion in the *Bennett* case was that those who sought to protect the species as well as those who were harmed by the protection had the right to challenge the agency's determination. Chapter 5 described the basis for challenging administrative agency actions, including that the action taken was not based on study and information but was arbitrary and capricious.

APPLY: The cattle growers here are the equivalent of Mr. Bennett in that case and therefore have standing to challenge the determination of endangered species status and the resulting impact on grazing lands. If the ACGA can show that the species are not endangered and challenge the factual findings of the agency, the rule can be set aside.

ANSWER: The federal district court found that the Fish and Wildlife Service's issuance of an ITS for both the razorback sucker and the pygmy-owl was arbitrary and capricious, reasoning that the Fish and Wildlife Service "failed to provide sufficient reason to believe that listed species exist in the allotments in question." [*Arizona Cattle Growers' Ass'n v. U.S. Fish and Wildlife, Bureau of Land Management*, 273 F.3d 1229 (9th Cir. 2001)]

Notes

1. E-commerce selection reprinted with permission from David Twomey, Marianne Jennings, and Ivan Fox, *Anderson's Business Law and the Legal Environment* (St. Paul, MN: West, 2002), p. 1011.

2. The work of Professors Cindy A. Schipani and Lynda J. Oswald is an excellent resource for discussions on parent liability for CERCLA violations as well as a history of the development and scope of CERCLA. See, for example, Oswald and Schipani, "CERCLA and the 'Erosion' of Traditional Corporate Law Doctrine," 86 *Northwestern Law Review* 259 (1990). Their work was referred to in the *Bestfoods* case.

3. For more information, about brownfields, go to http://www.epa.gov/brownfields/about.htm.

4. Chris Woodyard, "Dual Shower Heads Land Hotel in Hot Water," *USA Today*, May 22, 2001, p. 1B.

Appendix

The United States Constitution

We the People of the United States, in Order to form a more perfect Union, establish Justice, insure domestic Tranquility, provide for the common defence, promote the general Welfare, and secure the Blessings of Liberty to ourselves and our Posterity, do ordain and establish this Constitution for the United States of America.

Article I

Section 1

All legislative Powers herein granted shall be vested in a Congress of the United States, which shall consist of a Senate and House of Representatives.

Section 2

The House of Representatives shall be composed of Members chosen every second Year by the People of the several States, and the Electors in each State shall have the Qualifications requisite for Electors of the most numerous Branch of the State Legislature.

No Person shall be a Representative who shall not have attained to the Age of twenty five Years, and been seven Years a Citizen of the United States, and who shall not, when elected, be an Inhabitant of that State in which he shall be chosen.

Representatives and direct Taxes shall be apportioned among the several States which may be included within this Union, according to their respective Numbers, which shall be determined by adding to the whole Number of free Persons, including those bound to Service for a Term of Years, and excluding Indians not taxed, three fifths of all other Persons. The actual Enumeration shall be made within three Years after the first Meeting of the Congress of the United States, and within every subsequent Term of ten Years, in which Manner as they shall by Law direct. The Number of Representatives shall not exceed one for every thirty Thousand, but each State shall have at Least one Representative; and until such enumeration shall be made, the State of New Hampshire shall

be entitled to choose three, Massachusetts eight, Rhode Island and Providence Plantations one, Connecticut five, New York six, New Jersey four, Pennsylvania eight, Delaware one, Maryland six, Virginia ten, North Carolina five, South Carolina five, and Georgia three.

When vacancies happen in the Representation from any State, the Executive Authority thereof shall issue Writs of Election to fill such Vacancies.

The House of Representatives shall chuse their Speaker and other Officers; and shall have the sole Power of Impeachment.

Section 3

The Senate of the United States shall be composed of two Senators from each State, chosen by the Legislature thereof, for six Years; and each Senator shall have one Vote.

Immediately after they shall be assembled in Consequence of the first Election, they shall be divided as equally as may be into three Classes. The Seats of the Senators of the first Class shall be vacated at the Expiration of the second Year, of the second Class at the Expiration of the fourth Year, and of the third Class at the Expiration of the sixth Year, so that one third may be chosen every second Year; and if Vacancies happen by Resignation, or otherwise, during the Recess of the Legislature of any State, the Executive thereof may make temporary Appointments until the next Meeting of the Legislature, which shall then fill such Vacancies.

No Person shall be a Senator who shall not have attained to the Age of thirty Years, and been nine Years a Citizen of the United States, and who shall not, when elected, be an Inhabitant of that State for which he shall be chosen.

The Vice President of the United States shall be President of the Senate, but shall have no Vote, unless they be equally divided.

The Senate shall chuse their other Officers, and also a President pro tempore, in the Absence of the Vice President, or when he shall exercise the Office of President of the United States.

The Senate shall have the sole Power to try all Impeachments. When sitting for that Purpose, they shall be on Oath or Affirmation. When the President of the United States is tried the Chief Justice shall preside: And no Person shall be convicted without the Concurrence of two thirds of the Members present.

Judgment in Cases of Impeachment shall not extend further than to removal from Office, and disqualification to hold and enjoy any Office of honor, Trust or Profit under the United States: but the Party convicted shall nevertheless be liable and subject to Indictment, Trial, Judgment and Punishment, according to Law.

Section 4

The Times, Places and Manner of holding Elections for Senators and Representatives, shall be prescribed in each State by the Legislature thereof; but the Congress may at any time by Law make or alter such Regulations, except as to the Places of chusing Senators.

The Congress shall assemble at Least once in every Year, and such Meeting shall be on the first Monday in December, unless they shall by Law appoint a different Day.

Section 5

Each House shall be the Judge of the Elections, Returns and Qualifications of its own Members, and a Majority of each shall constitute a Quorum to do Business; but a smaller Number may adjourn from day to day, and may be authorized to compel the Attendance of absent Members, in such Manner, and under such Penalties as each House may provide.

Each House may determine the Rules in its Proceedings, punish its Members for disorderly Behaviour, and, with the Concurrence of two thirds, expel a Member.

Each House shall keep a Journal of its Proceedings, and from time to time publish the same, excepting such Parts as may in their Judgment require Secrecy; and the Yeas and Nays of the Members of either House on any question shall, at the Desire of one fifth of those Present, be entered on the Journal.

Neither House, during the Session of Congress, shall, without the Consent of the other, adjourn for more than three days, nor to any other Place than that in which the two Houses shall be sitting.

Section 6

The Senators and Representatives shall receive a Compensation for their Services, to be ascertained by Law, and paid out of the Treasury of the United States. They shall in all Cases, except Treason, Felony and Breach of the Peace, be privileged from Arrest during their Attendance at the Session of their respective Houses, and in going to and returning from the same; and for any Speech or Debate in either House, they shall not be questioned in any other Place.

No Senator or Representative shall, during the Time for which he was elected, be appointed to any civil Office under the Authority of the United States, which shall have been created, or the Emoluments whereof shall have been encreased during such time; and no Person holding any Office under the United States, shall be a Member of either House during his Continuance in Office.

Section 7

All Bills for raising Revenue shall originate in the House of Representatives; but the Senate may propose or concur with amendments as on other Bills.

Every Bill which shall have passed the House of Representatives and the Senate, shall, before it become a Law, be presented to the President of the United States; If he approve he shall sign it, but if not he shall return it, with his Objections to that House in which it shall have originated, who shall enter the Objections at large on their Journal, and proceed to reconsider it. If after such Reconsideration two thirds of that House shall agree to pass the Bill, it shall be sent, together with the Objections, to the other House, by which it shall like wise be reconsidered, and if approved by two thirds of that House, it shall become a Law. But in all such Cases the Votes of both Houses shall be determined by Yeas and Nays, and the names of the Persons voting for and against the Bill shall be entered on the Journal of each House respectively. If any Bill shall not be returned by the President within ten Days (Sundays excepted) after it shall have been presented to him, the Same shall be a Law, in like Manner as if he had signed it, unless the Congress by their Adjournment prevent its Return, in which Case it shall not be a Law.

Every Order, Resolution, or Vote to which the Concurrence of the Senate and House of Representatives may be necessary (except on a question of Adjournment) shall be presented to the President of the United States; and before the Same shall take Effect, shall be approved by him, or being disapproved by him, shall be repassed by two thirds of the Senate and House of Representatives, according to the Rules and Limitations prescribed in the Case of a Bill.

Section 8

The Congress shall have Power To lay and collect Taxes, Duties, Imposts and Excises, to pay the Debts and provide for the common Defense and general Welfare of the United States; but all Duties, Imposts and Excises shall be uniform throughout the United States;

To borrow Money on the credit of the United States;

To regulate Commerce with foreign Nations, and among the several States, and with the Indian Tribes;

To establish an uniform Rule of Naturalization, and uniform Laws on the subject of Bankruptcies throughout the United States;

To coin Money, regulate the Value thereof, and of foreign Coin, and fix the Standard of Weights and Measures;

To provide for the Punishment of counterfeiting the Securities and current Coin of the United States;

To establish Post Offices and post Roads;

To promote the Progress of Science and useful Arts, by securing for limited Times to Authors and Inventors the exclusive Right to their respective Writings and Discoveries;

To constitute Tribunals inferior to the supreme Court;

To define and punish Piracies and Felonies committed on the high Seas, and Offenses against the Law of Nations;

To declare War, grant Letters of Marque and Reprisal, and make Rules concerning Captures on Land and Water;

To raise and support Armies, but no Appropriation of Money to that Use shall be for a longer Term than two Years;

To provide and maintain a Navy;

To make Rules for the Government and Regulation of the land and naval Forces;

To provide for calling forth the Militia to execute the Laws of the Union, suppress Insurrections and repel Invasions;

To provide for organizing, arming, and disciplining, the Militia, and for governing such Part of them as may be employed in the Service of the United States, reserving to the States respectively, the Appointment of the Officers, and the Authority of training the Militia according to the discipline prescribed by Congress;

To exercise exclusive Legislation in all Cases whatsoever, over such District (not exceeding ten Miles square) as may, by Cession of particular States, and the Acceptance of Congress, become the Seat of the Government of the United States, and to exercise like Authority over all Places purchased by the Consent of the Legislature of the State in which the Same shall be, for the Erection of Forts, Magazines, Arsenals, dock-Yards, and other needful Buildings;—And

To make all Laws which shall be necessary and proper for carrying into Execution the foregoing Powers, and all other Powers vested by this Constitution in the Government of the United States, or in any Department or Officer thereof.

Section 9

The Migration or Importation of such Persons as any of the States now existing shall think proper to admit, shall not be prohibited by the Congress prior to the Year one thousand eight hundred and eight, but a Tax or duty may be imposed on such Importation, not exceeding ten dollars for each Person.

The Privilege of the Writ of Habeas Corpus shall not be suspended, unless when in Cases of Rebellion or Invasion the public Safety may require it.

No Bill of Attainder or ex post facto Law shall be passed.

No Capitation, or other direct, Tax shall be laid, unless in Proportion to the Census or Enumeration herein before directed to be taken.

No Tax or Duty shall be laid on Articles exported from any State.

No Preference shall be given to any Regulation of Commerce or Revenue to the Ports of one State over those of another; nor shall Vessels bound to, or from, one State, be obliged to enter, clear or pay Duties in another.

No Money shall be drawn from the Treasury, but in Consequence of Appropriations made by Law; and a regular Statement and Account of the

Receipts and Expenditures of all public Money shall be published from time to time.

No Title of Nobility shall be granted by the United States: And no Person holding any Office of Profit or Trust under them, shall, without the Consent of the Congress, accept of any present, Emolument, Office, or Title, of any kind whatever, from any King, Prince or foreign State.

Section 10

No State shall enter into any Treaty, Alliance, or Confederation; grant Letters of Marque and Reprisal; coin Money; emit Bills of Credit; make any Thing but gold and silver Coin a Tender in Payment of Debts; pass any Bill of Attainder, ex post facto Law or law impairing the Obligation of Contracts, or grant any Title of Nobility.

No State shall, without the Consent of the Congress, lay any Imposts or Duties on Imports or Exports, except what may be absolutely necessary for executing its inspection Laws: and the net Produce of all Duties and Imposts, laid by any State on Imports or Exports, shall be for the Use of the Treasury of the United States; and all such Laws shall be subject to the Revision and Control of the Congress.

No State shall, without the Consent of Congress, lay any Duty on Tonnage, keep Troops, or Ships of War in time of Peace, enter into any Agreement or Compact with another State, or with a foreign Power, or engage in War, unless actually invaded, or in such imminent Danger as will not admit of delay.

Article II

Section 1

The executive Power shall be vested in a President of the United States of America. He shall hold his Office during the Term of four Years, and, together with the Vice President, chosen for the same Term, be elected, as follows:

Each State shall appoint, in such Manner as the Legislature thereof may direct, a Number of Electors, equal to the whole Number of Senators and Representatives to which the State may be entitled in the Congress: but no Senator or Representative, or Person holding an Office of Trust or Profit under the United States, shall be appointed an Elector.

The Electors shall meet in their respective States, and vote by Ballot for two Persons, of whom one at least shall not be an Inhabitant of the same State with themselves. And they shall make a List of all the Persons voted for, and of the Number of Votes for each; which List they shall sign and certify, and transmit sealed to the Seat of the Government of the United States, directed to the President of the Senate. The President of the Senate shall, in the Presence of the Senate and House of Representatives, open all the Certificates, and the Votes shall then be counted. The Person having the greatest Number of Votes shall be the President, if such Number be a Majority of the whole Number of Electors appointed; and if there be more than one who have such Majority, and have an equal Number of Votes, then the House of Representatives shall immediately chuse by Ballot one of them for President; and if no Person have a Majority, then from the five highest on the List the said House shall in like Manner chuse the President. But in chusing the President, the Votes shall be taken by States, the Representation from each State having one Vote; a quorum for this Purpose shall consist of a Member or Members from two thirds of the States, and a Majority of all the States shall be necessary to a Choice. In every Case, after the Choice of the President, the Person having the greatest Number of Votes of the Electors shall be the Vice President. But if there should remain two or more who have equal Votes, the Senate shall chuse from them by Ballot the Vice President.

The Congress may determine the Time of chusing the Electors, and the Day on which they shall give their Votes; which Day shall be the same throughout the United States.

No Person except a natural born Citizen, or a Citizen of the United States, at the time of the Adoption of this Constitution, shall be eligible to the Office of President; neither shall any Person be eligible to that Office who shall not have attained to the Age of thirty-five Years, and been fourteen years a Resident within the United States.

In Case of the Removal of the President from Office, or of his Death, Resignation, or Inability to discharge the Powers and Duties of the said Office, the Same shall devolve on the Vice President, and the Congress may by Law provide for the Case of Removal, Death, Resignation, or Inability, both of the President and Vice President, declaring what Officer shall then act as President, and such Officer shall act accordingly, until the Disability be removed, or a President shall be elected.

The President shall, at stated Times, receive for his Services, a Compensation, which shall neither be encreased nor diminished during the Period for which he shall have been elected, and he shall not receive within that Period any other Emolument from the United States, or any of them.

Before he enter on the Execution of his Office, he shall take the following Oath or Affirmation:—"I do solemnly swear (or affirm) that I will faithfully execute the Office of President of the United States, and will to the best of my Ability, preserve, protect, and defend the Constitution of the United States."

Section 2

The President shall be Commander in Chief of the Army and Navy of the United States, and of the Militia of the several States, when called into the actual Service of the United States; he may require the Opinion, in writing, of the principal Officer in each of the executive Departments, upon any Subject relating to the Duties of their respective Offices, and he shall have Power to grant Reprieves and Pardons for Offenses against the United States, except in Cases of Impeachment.

He shall have Power, by and with the Advice and Consent of the Senate, to make Treaties, provided two thirds of the Senators present concur; and he shall nominate, and by and with the Advice and Consent of the Senate, shall appoint Ambassadors, other public Ministers and Consuls, Judges of the supreme Court, and all other Officers of the United States, whose Appointments are not herein otherwise provided for, and which shall be established by Law: but the Congress may by Law vest the Appointment of such inferior Officers, as they think proper, in the President alone, in the Courts of Law, or in the Heads of Departments.

The President shall have Power to fill up all Vacancies that may happen during the Recess of the Senate, by granting Commissions which shall expire at the End of their next Session.

Section 3

He shall from time to time give to the Congress Information of the State of the Union, and recommend to their Consideration such Measures as he shall judge necessary and expedient; he may, on extraordinary Occasions, convene both Houses, or either of them, and in Case of Disagreement between them, with Respect to the Time of Adjournment, he may adjourn them to such Time as he shall think proper; he shall receive Ambassadors and other public Ministers; he shall take Care that the Laws be faithfully executed, and shall Commission all the Officers of the United States.

Section 4

The President, Vice President and all Civil Officers of the United States, shall be removed from Office on Impeachment for, and Conviction of, Treason, Bribery, or other high Crimes and Misdemeanors.

Article III

Section 1

The judicial Power of the United States, shall be vested in one supreme Court, and in such inferior Courts as the Congress may from time to time ordain and establish. The Judges, both of the supreme and inferior Courts, shall hold their Offices during good Behaviour, and shall, at stated Times, receive for their Services, a Compensation, which shall not be diminished during their Continuance in Office.

Section 2

The judicial Power shall extend to all Cases, in Law and Equity, arising under this Constitution, the Laws of the United States, and Treaties made, or which shall be made, under their Authority;—to all Cases affecting Ambassadors, other public Ministers and Consuls;—to all Cases of admiralty and maritime Jurisdiction;—to Controversies to which the United States shall be a Party;—to Controversies between two or more States;—between a State and Citizens of another State;—between Citizens of different States,—between Citizens of the same State claiming Lands under Grants of different States, and between a State, or the Citizens thereof, and foreign States, Citizens or Subjects.

In all Cases affecting Ambassadors, other public Ministers and Consuls, and those in which a State shall be Party, the Supreme Court shall have original Jurisdiction. In all the other Cases before mentioned, the supreme Court shall have appellate Jurisdiction, both as to Law and Fact, with such Exceptions, and under such Regulations as the Congress shall make.

The Trial of all Crimes, except in Cases of Impeachment, shall be by Jury; and such Trial shall be held in the State where the said Crimes shall have been committed; but when not committed within any State, the Trial shall be at such Place or Places as the Congress may by Law have directed.

Section 3

Treason against the United States, shall consist only in levying War against them, or in adhering to their Enemies, giving them Aid and Comfort. No Person shall be convicted of Treason unless on the Testimony of two Witnesses to the same overt Act, or on Confession in open Court.

The Congress shall have Power to declare the Punishment of Treason, but no Attainder of Treason shall work Corruption of Blood, or Forfeiture except during the Life of the Person attainted.

Article IV

Section 1

Full Faith and Credit shall be given in each State to the public Arts, Records, and judicial Proceedings of every other State. And the Congress may by general Laws prescribe the Manner in which such Acts, Records and Proceedings shall be proved, and the Effect thereof.

Section 2

The Citizens of each State shall be entitled to all Privileges and Immunities of Citizens in the several States.

A Person charged in any State with Treason, Felony, or other Crime, who shall flee from Justice, and be found in another State, shall on Demand of the executive Authority of the State from which he fled, be delivered up, to be removed to the State having Jurisdiction of the Crime.

No Person held to Service or Labour in one State, under the Laws thereof, escaping into another, shall, in Consequence of any Law or Regulation therein, be discharged from such Service or Labour, but shall be delivered up on Claim of the Party to whom such Service or Labour may be due.

Section 3

New States may be admitted by the Congress into this Union; but no new State shall be formed or erected within the Jurisdiction of any other State; nor any State be formed by the Junction of two or more States, or Parts of States, without the Consent of the Legislatures of the States concerned as well as of the Congress.

The Congress shall have Power to dispose of and make all needful Rules and Regulations respecting the Territory or other Property belonging to the United States; and nothing in this Constitution shall be so construed as to Prejudice any Claims of the United States, or of any particular State.

Section 4

The United States shall guarantee to every State in this Union a Republican Form of Government, and shall protect each of them against Invasion; and on Application of the Legislature, or of the Executive (when the Legislature cannot be convened) against domestic Violence.

Article V

The Congress, whenever two thirds of both Houses shall deem it necessary, shall propose Amendments to this Constitution, or, on the Application of the Legislatures of two thirds of the several States, shall call a Convention for proposing Amendments, which, in either Case, shall be valid to all Intents and Purposes, as Part of this Constitution, when ratified by the Legislatures of three fourths of the several States, or by Conventions in three fourths thereof, as the one or the other Mode of Ratification may be proposed by the Congress; Provided that no Amendment which may be made prior to the Year One thousand eight hundred and eight shall in any Manner affect the first and fourth Clauses in the Ninth Section of the first Article; and that no State, without its Consent, shall be deprived of its equal Suffrage in the Senate.

Article VI

All Debts contracted and Engagements entered into, before the Adoption of this Constitution, shall be as valid against the United States under this Constitution, as under the Confederation.

This Constitution, and the Laws of the United States which shall be made in Pursuance thereof; and all Treaties made, or which shall be made, under the Authority of the United States, shall be the supreme Law of the Land; and the judges in every State shall be bound thereby, any Thing in the Constitution or Laws of any State to the Contrary notwithstanding.

The Senators and Representatives before mentioned, and the Members of the several State Legislatures, and all executive and judicial Officers, both of the United States and of the several States, shall be bound by Oath or Affirmation, to support this Constitution; but no religious Test shall ever be required as a Qualification to any Office or public Trust under the United States.

Article VII

The Ratification of the Conventions of nine States, shall be sufficient for the Establishment of this Constitution between the States so ratifying the Same.

Amendment I (1791)

Congress shall make no law respecting an establishment of religion, or prohibiting the free exercise thereof; or abridging the freedom of speech, or of the press; or the right of the people peaceably to assemble, and to petition the Government for a redress of grievances.

Amendment II (1791)

A well regulated Militia, being necessary to the security of a free State, the right of the people to keep and bear Arms, shall not be infringed.

Amendment III (1791)

No Soldier shall, in time of peace be quartered in any house, without the consent of the Owner, nor in time of war, but in a manner to be prescribed by law.

Amendment IV (1791)

The right of the people to be secure in their persons, houses, papers, and effects, against unreasonable searches and seizures, shall not be violated, and no Warrants shall issue, but upon probable cause, supported by Oath or affirmation, and particularly describing the place to be searched, and the persons or things to be seized.

Amendment V (1791)

No person shall be held to answer for a capital or otherwise infamous crime, unless on a presentment or indictment of a Grand Jury, except in cases arising in the land or naval forces, or in the Militia, when in actual service in time of War or public danger; nor shall any person be subject for the same offense to be twice put in jeopardy of life or limb; nor shall be compelled in any criminal case to be a witness against himself, nor be deprived of life, liberty, or property, without due process of law; nor shall private property be taken for public use, with out just compensation.

Amendment VI (1791)

In all criminal prosecutions, the accused shall enjoy the right to a speedy and public trial, by an impartial jury of the State and district wherein the crime shall have been committed, which district shall have been previously ascertained by law, and to be informed of the nature and cause of the accusation; to be confronted with the witnesses against him; to have compulsory process for obtaining Witnesses in his favor, and to have the Assistance of Counsel for his defense.

Amendment VII (1791)

In Suits at common law, where the value in controversy shall exceed twenty dollars, the right of trial by jury shall be preserved, and no fact tried by a jury, shall be otherwise reexamined in any Court of the United States, than according to the rules of the common law.

Amendment VIII (1791)

Excessive bail shall not be required nor excessive fines imposed, nor cruel and unusual punishments inflicted.

Amendment IX (1791)

The enumeration in the Constitution, of certain rights, shall not be construed to deny or disparage others retained by the people.

Amendment X (1791)

The powers not delegated to the United States by the Constitution, nor prohibited by it to the States, are reserved to the States respectively, or to the people.

Amendment XI (1798)

The Judicial power of the United States shall not be construed to extend to any suit in law or equity, commenced or prosecuted against one of the United States by Citizens of another State, or by Citizens or Subjects of any Foreign State.

Amendment XII (1804)

The Electors shall meet in their respective states and vote by ballot for President and Vice President, one of whom, at least, shall not be an inhabitant of the same state with themselves; they shall name in their ballots the person voted for as President, and in distinct ballots the person voted for as Vice-President, and they shall make distinct lists of all persons voted for as President, and of all persons voted for as Vice-President, and of the number of votes for each, which lists they shall sign and certify, and transmit sealed to the seat of the government of the United States, directed to the President of the Senate;—The President of the Senate shall, in the presence of the Senate and House of Representatives, open all the certificates and the votes shall then be counted;—The person having the greatest number of votes for President, shall be the President, if such number be a majority of the whole number of Electors appointed; and if no person have such majority, then from the persons having the highest numbers not exceeding three on the list of those voted for as President, the House of Representatives shall choose immediately, by ballot, the President. But in choosing the President, the votes shall be taken by states, the representation from each state having one vote; a quorum for this purpose shall consist of a member or members from two-thirds of the states, and a majority of all the states shall be necessary to a choice. And if the House of Representatives shall not choose a President whenever the right of choice shall devolve upon them, before the fourth day of March next following, then the Vice-President shall act as President, as in the case of the death or other constitutional disability of the President—The person having the greatest number of votes as Vice-President, shall be the Vice-President, if such number be a majority of the whole number of Electors appointed, and if no person have a majority, then from the two highest numbers on the list, the Senate shall choose the Vice-President; a quorum for the purpose shall consist of two-thirds of the whole numbers of Senators, and a majority of the whole number shall be necessary to a choice. But no person constitutionally ineligible to the office of President shall be eligible to that of Vice President of the United States.

Amendment XIII (1865)

Section 1

Neither slavery nor involuntary servitude, except as a punishment for crime whereof the party shall have been duly convicted, shall exist within the United States, or any place subject to their jurisdiction.

Section 2

Congress shall have power to enforce this article by appropriate legislation.

Amendment XIV (1868)

Section 1

All persons born or naturalized in the United States and subject to the jurisdiction thereof, are citizens of the United States and of the State wherein they reside. No State shall make or enforce any law which shall abridge the privileges or immunities of citizens of the United States; nor shall any State deprive any person of life, liberty, or property, without due process of law; nor deny to any person within its jurisdiction the equal protection of the laws.

Section 2

Representatives shall be apportioned among the several States according to their respective numbers, counting the whole number of persons in each State, excluding Indians not taxed. But when the right to vote at any election for the choice of electors for President and Vice President of the United States, Representatives in Congress, the Executive and Judicial officers of a State, or the members of the Legislature thereof, is denied to any of the male inhabitants of such State, being twenty-one years of age, and citizens of the United States, or in any way abridged, except for participation in rebellion, or other crime, the basis of representation therein shall be reduced in the proportion which the number of such male citizens shall bear to the whole number of male citizens twenty-one years of age in such State.

Section 3

No person shall be a Senator or Representative in Congress, or elector of President and Vice President, or hold any office, civil or military, under the United States, or under any State, who, having previously taken an oath, as a member of Congress, or as an officer of the United States, or as a member of any State legislature, or as an executive or judicial officer of any State, to support the Constitution of the United States, shall have engaged in insurrection or rebellion against the same, or given aid or comfort to the enemies thereof. But Congress may by a vote of two-thirds of each House, remove such disability.

Section 4

The validity of the public debt of the United States, authorized by law, including debts incurred for payment of pensions and bounties for services in suppressing insurrection or rebellion, shall not be questioned. But neither the United States nor any State shall assume or pay any debt or obligation incurred in aid of insurrection or rebellion against the United States, or any claim for the loss or emancipation of any slave; but all such debts, obligations and claims shall be held illegal and void.

Section 5

The Congress shall have power to enforce, by appropriate legislation, the provisions of this article.

Amendment XV (1870)

Section 1

The right of citizens of the United States to vote shall not be denied or abridged by the United States or by any State on account of race, color, or previous condition of servitude.

Section 2

The Congress shall have power to enforce this article by appropriate legislation.

Amendment XVI (1913)

The Congress shall have power to lay and collect taxes on incomes, from whatever source derived, without apportionment among the several States, and without regard to any census or enumeration.

Amendment XVII (1913)

The Senate of the United States shall be composed of two Senators from each State, elected by the people thereof, for six years; and each Senator shall have one vote. The electors in each State shall have the qualifications requisite for electors of the most numerous branch of the State legislatures.

When vacancies happen in the representation of any State in the Senate, the executive authority of such State shall issue writs of election to fill such vacancies: *Provided*, That the legislature of any State may empower the executive thereof to make temporary appointments until the people fill the vacancies by election as the legislature may direct.

This amendment shall not be so construed as to affect the election or term of any Senator chosen before it becomes valid as part of the Constitution.

Amendment XVIII (1919)

Section 1

After one year from the ratification of this article the manufacture, sale, or transportation of intoxicating liquors within, the importation thereof into, or the exportation thereof from the United States and all territory subject to the jurisdiction thereof for beverage purposes is hereby prohibited.

Section 2

The Congress and the several States shall have concurrent power to enforce this article by appropriate legislation.

Section 3

This article shall be inoperative unless it shall have been ratified as an amendment to the Constitution by the legislatures of the several States, as provided in the Constitution, within seven years from the date of the submission hereof to the States by the Congress.

Amendment XIX (1920)

The right of citizens of the United States to vote shall not be denied or abridged by the United States or by any State on account of sex.

Congress shall have power to enforce this article by appropriate legislation.

Amendment XX (1933)

Section 1

The terms of the President and Vice President shall end at noon on the 20th day of January, and the terms of Senators and Representatives at noon on the 3d day of January, of the years in which such terms would have ended if this article had not been ratified; and the terms of their successors shall then begin.

Section 2

The Congress shall assemble at least once in every year, and such meeting shall begin at noon on the 3d day of January, unless they shall by law appoint a different day.

Section 3

If, at the time fixed for the beginning of the term of the President, the President elect shall have died, the Vice President elect shall become President. If a President shall not have been chosen before the time fixed for the beginning of his term, or if the President elect shall have failed to qualify, then the Vice President elect shall act as President until a President shall have qualified; and the Congress may by law provide for the case wherein neither a President elect nor a Vice President elect shall have qualified, declaring who shall then act as President, or the manner in which one who is to act shall be selected, and such person shall act accordingly? until a President or Vice President shall have qualified.

Section 4

The Congress may by law provide for the case of the death of any of the persons from whom the House of Representatives may choose a President whenever the right of choice shall have devolved upon them, and for the case of the death of any of the persons from whom the Senate may choose a Vice President whenever the right of choice shall have devolved upon them.

Section 5

Sections 1 and 2 shall take effect on the 15th day of October following the ratification of this article.

Section 6

This article shall be inoperative unless it shall have been ratified as an amendment to the Constitution by the legislatures of three fourths of the several States within seven years from the date of its submission.

Amendment XXI (1933)

Section 1

The eighteenth article of amendment to the Constitution of the United States is hereby repealed.

Section 2

The transportation or importation into any State, Territory, or possession of the United States for delivery or use therein of intoxicating liquors, in violation of the laws thereof, is hereby prohibited.

Section 3

This article shall be inoperative unless it shall have been ratified as an amendment to the Constitution by conventions in the several States, as provided in the Constitution, within seven years from the date of the submission hereof to the States by the Congress.

Amendment XXII (1951)

Section 1

No person shall be elected to the office of the President more than twice, and no person, who has held the office of President, or acted as President, for more than two years of a term to which some other person was elected President shall be elected to the Office of the President more than once. But this Article shall not apply to any person holding the office of President when this Article was proposed by the Congress, and shall not prevent any person who may be holding the office of President, or acting as President, during the term within which this Article becomes operative from holding the Office of President or acting as President during the remainder of such term.

Section 2

This article shall be inoperative unless it shall have been ratified as an amendment to the Constitution by the legislatures of three fourths of the several States within seven years from the date of its submission to the States by the Congress.

Amendment XXIII (1961)

Section 1

The District constituting the seat of Government of the United States shall appoint in such manner as the Congress may direct:

A number of electors of President and Vice President equal to the whole number of Senators and Representatives in Congress to which the District would be entitled if it were a State, but in no event more than the least populous State; they shall be in addition to those appointed by the States, but they shall be considered, for the purposes of the election of President and Vice President, to be electors appointed by a State; and they shall meet in the District and perform such duties as provided by the twelfth article of amendment.

Section 2
The Congress shall have power to enforce this article by appropriate legislation.

Amendment XXIV (1964)

Section 1
The right of citizens of the United States to vote in any primary or other election for President or Vice President, for electors for President or Vice President, or for Senator or Representative in Congress, shall not be denied or abridged by the United States or any State by reason of failure to pay any poll tax or other tax.

Section 2
The Congress shall have power to enforce this article by appropriate legislation.

Amendment XXV (1967)

Section 1
In case of the removal of the President from office or of his death or resignation, the Vice President shall become President.

Section 2
Whenever there is a vacancy in the office of the Vice President, the President shall nominate a Vice President who shall take office upon confirmation by a majority vote of both Houses of Congress.

Section 3
Whenever the President transmits to the President pro tempore of the Senate and the Speaker of the House of Representatives his written declaration that he is unable to discharge the powers and duties of his office, and until he transmits to them a written declaration to the contrary, such powers and duties shall be discharged by the Vice President as Acting President.

Section 4
Whenever the Vice President and a majority of either the principal officers of the executive departments or of such other body as Congress may by law provide, transmit to the President pro tempore of the Senate and the Speaker of the House of Representatives their written declaration that the President is unable to discharge the powers and duties of his office, the Vice President shall immediately assume the powers and duties of the office as Acting President.

Thereafter, when the President transmits to the President pro tempore of the Senate and the Speaker of the House of Representatives his written declaration that no inability exists, he shall resume the powers and duties of his Office unless the Vice President and a majority of either the principal officers of the executive department or of such other body as Congress may by law provide, transmit within four days to the President pro tempore of the Senate and the Speaker of the House of Representatives their written declaration that the President is unable to discharge the powers and duties of his office. Thereupon Congress shall decide the issue, assembling within forty-eight hours for that purpose if not in session. If the Congress, within twenty-one days after receipt of the latter written declaration, or, if Congress is not in session, within twenty-one days after Congress is required to assemble, determines by two-thirds vote of both Houses that the President is unable to discharge the powers and duties of his office, the Vice President shall continue to discharge the same as Acting President; otherwise, the President shall resume the powers and duties of his office.

Amendment XXVI (1971)

Section 1
The right of citizens of the United States, who are eighteen years of age or older, to vote shall not be denied or abridged by the United States or by any State on account of age.

Section 2
The Congress shall have power to enforce this article by appropriate legislation.

Amendment XXVII (1992)

No law varying the compensation for services of the Senators and Representatives shall take effect until an election of representatives shall have intervened.

A

absolute privilege A defense to defamation; a protection given to legislators and courtroom participants for statements made relating to the proceedings; encourages people to come forward and speak without fear of liability.

acceptance Offeree's positive response to offeror's proposed contract.

accord and satisfaction An agreement (accord) to pay a certain amount, the payment of which constitutes full payment (satisfaction) of that debt.

accredited investor For purposes of Regulation D, an investor with certain financial stability who is not counted in the number of purchaser limitations for Rules 505 and 506.

act of state doctrine In international law, a theory that each country's governmental actions are autonomous and not subject to judicial review by the courts in other countries.

actual notice Private or individual notice sent directly to affected parties; this type of notice is effective only if the party actually receives it, as compared to constructive notice, for which publication is sufficient.

actus reus Latin term for the criminal act or conduct required for proof of a crime.

administrative agency Governmental unit created by the legislative body for the purposes of administering and enforcing the laws.

administrative law judge (ALJ) Special category of judicial official who presides over agency enforcement hearings.

Administrative Procedures Act (APA) Basic federal law governing the creation, operation, and reporting of federal administrative agencies.

affirm Action taken by an appellate court on an appealed case; the effect is that the court upholds the lower court's decision.

affirmative action Label given to employment processes and programs designed to help underrepresented groups obtain jobs and promotions.

Age Discrimination in Employment Act of 1967 (ADEA) Federal law that prohibits job discrimination on the basis of age; prohibits the consideration of age in an employment decision.

agency by estoppel Theory for creation of an agency relationship that holds the principal liable because the principal has allowed the agent to represent him as his principal.

agent One who acts on behalf of and at the direction of another.

alter ego theory Theory used for disregarding the corporate protection of limited liability for shareholders; results when individuals treat the corporation's properties and accounts as their own and fail to follow corporate formalities.

alternative dispute resolution (ADR) Means other than litigation used to resolve disputes and claims; includes arbitration, mediation, and negotiated settlements.

Alternative Fines Act (AFA) Under this act, the Justice Department can obtain two times the benefit that the bribe attempted to gain, known as disgorgement.

Americans with Disabilities Act (ADA) A 1991 federal law that prohibits discrimination in the workplace against persons with disabilities and requires employers to make reasonable accommodations for employees with disabilities who are otherwise qualified to perform a job.

annual percentage rate (APR) A financing term representing the annual debt cost and a required disclosure under Regulation Z.

answer Pleading filed by the defendant in a lawsuit; contains the defendant's version of the basis of the suit, counterclaims, and denials.

Antiterrorism and Effective Death Penalty Act One of several post 9/11/2001 federal statutes passed to increase grounds for deportation and penalties for criminal conduct for terrorist activities.

apparent authority Authority of an agent to act on behalf of a principal that results from the appearance of the agent's authority to third parties.

appellant The name on appeal for the party who appeals a lower court's decision.

appellate brief Lawyer's summation of issues of law and/or error for appellate court to consider.

appellate court A court of appeals or a court of review; a court whose function is to review the decision and actions of a trial court; does not hear witnesses; only reviews the transcript and studies the arguments and briefs of the parties.

appellee The name on appeal for the party who won a lower court's decision—that is, the party who does not appeal the lower court decision.

appraisal rights Rights of dissenting shareholders after a merger or takeover to be paid the value of their shares before the takeover or merger.

appropriation In international law, the taking of private property by a government; also known as expropriation; in torts, use of the name, likeness, or image of another for commercial purposes.

arbitrary and capricious Standard for challenging administrative agency rules; used to show decisions or rules were not based on sufficient facts.

arbitration Alternative form of dispute resolution in which parties submit evidence to a third party who is a member of the American Arbitration Association and who makes a decision after listening to the case.

arraignment Hearing in criminal procedure held after an indictment or information is returned; trial date is set and plea is entered.

articles of incorporation Organizational papers of a corporation; list the company's structure, capitalization, board structure, and so on.

articles of limited partnership Contract governing the rights and relations of limited partners.

articles of organization A document filed with a centralized state agency to form an LLC.

Asbestos Hazard Emergency Response Act (AHERA) Federal environmental legislation that requires removal of asbestos from public schools and other facilities where exposure is particularly dangerous (where young children are present).

Asset Conservation, Lender Liability, and Deposit Insurance Protection Act of 1996 Federal law that clarified the liability of lenders for CERCLA violations and clean-up upon their foreclosure and repossession of debtor's property.

assumption of risk Defense in negligence cases that prevents an injured party from recovering if it can be established that the injured party realized the risk and engaged in the conduct anyway.

attorney-client privilege Protection of client's disclosures to her attorney; attorney cannot disclose information client offers (with some exceptions, such as the client telling the attorney he is going to commit a crime); the confession of a crime already committed cannot be disclosed by the lawyer.

audit committee Committee of the board responsible for oversight of company financial statements.

B

bait and switch Term given to advertising technique in which a low-price product is advertised and then the customer is told that the product is unavailable or is talked into a higher-priced product; prohibited by the FTC.

Bankruptcy Abuse Prevention and Consumer Protection Act of 2005 The bankruptcy reform act that

changed the requirements for declaring bankruptcy and limited the exemptions for debtor property.

bargain and sale deed A special warranty deed.

bargained-for exchange The mutual exchange of detriment as the consideration element in a contract.

battle of the forms Term used to describe the problem of merchants using their purchase orders and invoices with conflicting terms as their contractual understanding; problem is remedied by § 2–207 of the UCC.

Berne Convention Implementation Act of 1988 Federal law that changed U.S. copyright law to comply with international agreement at Berne Convention.

best available treatment (BAT) In environmental law, the most advanced and effective technology for preventing pollution; a higher standard than the best conventional treatment.

best conventional treatment (BCT) Requirement imposed by EPA on point source pollution that requires firms to use the best existing treatments for water pollution.

bilateral contract Contract in which both parties make promises to perform.

bilateral treaties In international law, a treaty between two nations.

bill of lading Receipt for goods issued by a carrier; used as a means of transferring title in exchange for payment or a draw on a line of credit.

Bill of Rights Portion of the U.S. Constitution that consists of the first ten amendments and includes such rights as freedom of speech, right to privacy, the protections afforded in criminal procedures under the Fourth Amendment search and seizure, and the Fifth Amendment protections against self-incrimination.

bill of sale Informal document or contract that serves to prove and transfer title to tangible personal property.

binding arbitration Arbitration from which there is no judicial appeal.

Blanchard Peale Model A model for resolution of ethical dilemma that asserts that any proposed conduct must first be in compliance with the law.

blue sky laws State laws regulating the sale of securities.

board of directors Policy-setting governing group of a corporation.

bona fide occupational qualification (BFOQ) A justification for discrimination on the basis of sex if it can be established that gender is a requirement for a job; also applies to discrimination on the basis of religion, national origin, and so on.

brief Document prepared by lawyers on the appeal of a case to provide the appellate court with a summary of the case and the issues involved.

bubble concept Tactic employed by the EPA in determining levels of air pollution that determines appropriate levels of release by assuming that all the pollution in an area comes from one source.

burden of proof The responsibility of the party for proving the facts needed to recover in a lawsuit.

business judgment rule Duty of care imposed upon members of corporate boards that requires adequate review of issues and information, devotion of adequate time to deliberations, and hiring of outside consultants as necessary for making decisions; the standard does not require foolproof judgment, only reasonable care in making the judgment.

"but for" test In negligence, the standard used for determining whether the defendant's negligence caused the plaintiff's injury; "but for" the fact that the defendant was negligent, the plaintiff would not have been injured.

bylaws Operating rules of a corporation and its board; usually describe the officers and their roles and authority, along with meeting procedures and notices.

C

capacity Legal term for the ability to enter legally into a contract; for example, age capacity (minors do not have capacity).

categorical imperative A resolution of ethical dilemma proposed by Immanuel Kant that is similar to the Golden Rule: "Do unto others as you would have them do unto you."

causation In negligence, an element that requires the plaintiff to show that the defendant's lack of care caused the plaintiff's injury.

caveat emptor Latin term for "Let the buyer beware"; summarizes an attitude that once prevailed in contract law of a lack of protection for a buyer of defective goods.

celebrity endorsements Public figures advertising products on the basis of their personal use.

certification Process of authorizing a union to represent exclusively a group of workers.

charitable subscription A promise to make payment to a charitable organization; a pledge; it is enforceable even though the charity gives nothing in exchange.

checks and balances Term describing our tripartite system of government, in which each branch has some check mechanism to control abuses of powers by the other branches.

citation Name given to abbreviated description of a court case or statute; for example, 355 F. Supp. 291.

cite *See* **citation.**

civil law Laws affecting the private rights of individuals.

Civil Rights Act of 1964 Cornerstone of the antidiscrimination statutes; the original statute passed to prevent discrimination in housing, education, and employment.

Civil Rights Act of 1991 Amendments to original civil rights laws that changed damages, burden of proof, and claims standards for private suits for discrimination.

class action suit In civil law, a suit by a group of plaintiffs with the same claims; generally used in antitrust and securities lawsuits.

Clayton Act One of the major antitrust laws; governs the control of business through mergers, acquisitions, and interlocking directorates.

Clean Air Act The first effective anti-air-pollution act and the cornerstone of air pollution legislation.

Clean Water Act The first effective anti-water-pollution act and the cornerstone of water pollution legislation.

close corporation A type of corporation created by statute that allows limited liability with direct tax benefits.

closed-end transaction Term used in Regulation Z to describe credit transactions with definite times for and amounts of repayment that are not ongoing; for example, retail installment contracts.

closed shop A place of employment restricting hirees to union members only.

closing argument The summary attorneys give to the jury before it deliberates and after all the evidence has been presented.

Code of Federal Regulations (C.F.R.) Series of volumes carrying the enactments of all federal agencies.

collective bargaining agreement Contract between management and labor represented by one union for a collective bargaining unit.

collective bargaining unit NLRB term for a group of employees represented by one bargaining agent and agreement; can be a plant, a national group, or a subpart of a plant.

comment letter SEC response to registration filing; requires additional information or clarification on proposed offering.

Commerce Clause Provision in the U.S. Constitution controlling the regulation of intrastate, interstate, and foreign commerce and delineating authority for such regulation.

commercial impracticability Contract defense for nonperformance under the UCC that excuses a party when performance has become impossible or will involve much more than what was anticipated in the contract negotiations.

commercial speech The speech of business in the form of advertising, political endorsements, or comments on social issues.

common law Originally, the law of England made uniform after William the Conqueror; today, the nonstatutory law and the law found in judicial precedent.

common stock Type of shares in a corporation; the voting shares of the corporation and generally the bulk of ownership.

comparative negligence In negligence, a defense that allocates responsibility for an accident between the plaintiff and defendant when both were negligent and determines liability accordingly.

compensatory damages Damages to put nonbreaching party in the same position he would have been in had the breach not occurred.

complaint The first pleading in a lawsuit; the document that outlines the plaintiff's allegations against the defendant and specifies the remedies sought; with respect to federal agencies, can also be a formal change of rules or statutory violations by a company or individual.

Comprehensive Environmental Response, Compensation, and Liability Act (CERCLA) Federal law that authorized federal funds to clean up hazardous waste disposal.

computer crime Theft, espionage, and other illegal activities accomplished through the use of a computer.

Computer Software Copyright Act of 1980 Provides copyright protection for software.

concurrent jurisidiction Authority of more than one court to hear a case.

condition precedent In contracts, an event or action that must take place before a contract is required to be performed; for example, qualifying for financing is a condition precedent for a lender's performance on a mortgage loan.

conditions Events that must occur before contract performance is due.

conditions concurrent (conditions contemporaneous) In contracts, the conditions that must occur simultaneously for contract performance to be required; for example, in an escrow closing in real property, an agent collects title, insurance, funds, and other documents and sees that all the exchanges under the contract occur at the same time; the parties perform their part of the agreement at the same time.

confidential relationship A relationship of trust and reliance; necessary to establish the defense to undue influence.

confiscation In international law, the taking of private property by a government.

consent decree For administrative agencies, a type of plea bargain; a settlement document for an administrative agency's charges.

consequential damages Damages resulting from a contract breach, such as penalties or lost profits.

consideration In contracts, what each party gives to the other as part of the contract performance.

constitution Document that contains the basic rights in a society and the structure of its government; cannot be changed without the approval of the society's members.

constructive notice Notice given in a public place or published notice, as opposed to actual notice.

Consumer Credit Protection Act Act that provides disclosure requirements for lenders and protections for debtors; more commonly referred to as the Truth in Lending Act.

Consumer Leasing Act Act that provides for disclosure protection for consumers who are leasing goods.

Consumer Product Safety Commission Federal agency that establishes safety standards for consumer goods.

contentious jurisdiction Consensual jurisdiction of a court that is consented to when the parties have a dispute; for example, UN courts.

contract Binding agreement between two parties for the exchange of goods, real estate, or services.

contract defense Situation, term, or event that makes an otherwise valid contract invalid.

contract interference Tort involving a third party's actions resulting in a valid contract being lost or invalidated; an unfair method of competition.

contributory negligence Negligence defense that results when the injured party acted in a negligent way and contributed to her own injuries.

Controlling the Assault of Non-Solicited Pornography and Marketing (CAN-SPAM) Federal law that deals with those who use unsolicited e-mails for purposes of advertising.

Covenants not to compete Included in some contracts as long as they are reasonable in time and geographic scope.

conventional pollutant EPA classification of water pollutant that must be treated prior to its release into waterways.

cooling-off period Under the Taft-Hartley Act, a provision that can be invoked by the president to require laborers threatening to strike in an industry that affects the health and safety of the nation to continue to work during a negotiation period.

copyright Under federal law, a right given to protect the exclusive use of books, music, and other creative works.

Corporate Integrity Agreement (CIA) A form of corporate punishment that does not include an admission of guilt but provides a way to defer prosecution through the payment of a fine and a period of probation (usually 3 to 5 years) and agreeing to have monitors present in their companies.

corporate opportunity doctrine A business proposition or investment opportunity that a corporation would have an interest in pursuing; precludes directors from taking a profit opportunity when the corporation would have an interest.

corporate political speech *See* **political speech.**

corporate veil The personal liability shield; the corporate protection that en titles shareholders, directors, and officers to limited liability; can be pierced for improper conduct of business or fraud.

corporation Business entity created by statute that provides limited liability for its owners.

corrective advertising Potential FTC remedy required when ads run by a firm have been deceptive; requires company to run ads explaining previous ads or run a new statement in future ads.

Council on Environmental Quality (CEQ) Agency under the executive branch created in 1966 to formulate environmental policy and make recommendations for legislation.

counterclaim Pleading in a lawsuit in which the defendant makes allegations against the plaintiff in response to the plaintiff's complaint.

counteroffer Response by offeree to offer or when offeree changes terms of offer.

county courts Lesser trial courts that hear smaller disputes and misdemeanor cases; like justice of the peace courts in many states.

Court of Justice of European Communities The court of dispute settlement for the nations of the European Community.

covenants not to compete Promises to protect employers and buyers from loss of goodwill through employee or seller competition.

crime A wrong against society that carries penalties of imprisonment and/or fines.

criminal fraud A crime in which the victim is defrauded by an intentional act of the perpetrator.

criminal law As opposed to civil law, the law on wrongs against society.

cross-elasticity Economic term describing the willingness of customers to substitute various goods; for example, waxed paper for plastic wrap.

cross-examination Questioning by opposing parties of a witness in court; that is, defendant cross-examines plaintiff's witnesses and plaintiff cross-examines defendant's witnesses.

cumulative preferred stock Type of ownership in a corporation that gives the stock owners preference in the distribution of dividends and also guarantees earnings each year; in the event those earnings are not paid, they are carried over or accumulate until they can be paid.

customer and territorial restrictions Manufacturer's restrictions on retail sales locations and customers.

cyberbullying The use of any electronic communication device to harass, intimidate, or bully.

cybersquatting Process of registering sites and domain names that are deceptively or confusingly similar to existing names, trade names, and trademarks.

D

defamation Tort of making untrue statements about another that cause damage to his reputation or character.

default Judgment entered when the defendant fails to file an answer in a lawsuit.

defendant The party who is alleged to have committed a wrong in a civil lawsuit; the charged party in a criminal prosecution.

deficiency letter *See* **comment letter**.

delegation Transfer of obligations under a contract; generally accompanied by assignment of benefits.

deposition Form of discovery in which witnesses or parties can be questioned under oath in recorded testimony outside the courtroom.

derivative suit Lawsuit brought on behalf of another through the other's rights; for example, a shareholder suing to enforce corporation's rights.

Digital Millennium Copyright Act (DMCA) 1998 amendment to federal copyright laws that includes use of computer technology to copy music and other copyrighted materials as infringement.

direct examination Term that describes a party's questioning of her own witness.

directed verdict Verdict entered by judge upon motion of a party after the presentation of either side's case; can be entered if the plaintiff has not met his burden of proof or if the defendant fails to rebut the plaintiff's case.

disclaimer A provision in a contract that eliminates liability such as a warranty disclaimer or a disclaimer of tort liability.

discovery Process occurring before a trial that involves each side's investigation of the case, the evidence, and the witnesses; consists of depositions, interrogatories, requests for admissions and productions, and so on.

disparagement Form of unfair competition in which a business, its trademark, or its name is maligned; business defamation.

disparate impact Theory for establishing discrimination; involves using statistical analysis to demonstrate that a particular practice or an employer's hiring practices have a greater impact on protected classes.

disparate treatment In discrimination law, the application of different rules or standards to people of different races, genders, or national origins.

dissenting opinion In an appellate court's review of a case, an opinion written by a judge who disagrees with the decision of the majority of the court.

dissenting shareholder Shareholder who has objected to a merger or consolidation and votes against it; is entitled to receive the value of her shares before the merger or consolidation.

dissolution In partnerships, occurs when one partner ceases to be associated with the business; in corporations, the termination of the corporate existence.

diversity of citizenship A term referring to a requirement for federal court jurisdiction that plaintiff and defendant must be citizens of different states.

documents of title Formal legal document that serves to prove and transfer title to tangible personal property.

domain registration Public filing for ownership of the name for a Web site.

domestic corporation A term used to describe a corporation in the state in which it is incorporated.

due diligence Under the Securities Act of 1933, a defense for filing a false registration statement that requires proof that the individuals involved did all they could to uncover the truth and could not have discovered the false statements despite their due diligence.

due process Constitutional protection ensuring notice and a fair trial or hearing in all judicial proceedings.

duress In contract law, a defense that permits nonperformance of a contract if the party can show that physical or mental force was used to obtain the agreement to enter into the contract.

E

8-K form A filing required by the SEC under the 1934 Securities Act; an 8-K is filed by a registered company within ten days of a significant or material event affecting the company (e.g., a dividend being suspended).

effluent guidelines In environmental law, the standards for release of nonnatural substances into natural waters.

Electronic Signatures in Global and National Commerce Act of 2000 (E-sign) A federal law that recognizes digital signatures as authentic for purposes of contract formation; E-sign puts electronic signatures on equal footing with paper contracts.

elements The requirements for proof of a crime.

embezzlement Name for the crime of an employee stealing funds, property, or services from his employer.

eminent domain In constitutional law, the taking of private property by a government entity for a public purpose, with compensation paid to the owner.

emissions offset policy EPA procedure for approval of new facilities in nonattainment areas.

employment at will Doctrine that gives the employer the right to fire an employee at any time with or without cause; the doctrine and its protection for employers have been eroded by judicial decisions over recent years.

Employment Retirement Income Security Act of 1974 (ERISA) Congressional act establishing requirements for disclosure and other procedures with relation to employees' retirement plans.

enabling act Act of a legislative body establishing an administrative agency and providing it with guidelines and authority for the enforcement of the law.

Endangered Species Act (ESA) Federal environmental law that requires federal agencies to disclose the impact of proposed projects on species listed as protected under the act.

enlightened self-interest Theory of corporate social responsibility under which managers believe that by serving society they best serve their shareholders.

environmental impact statement (EIS) Report required to be filed when a federal agency is taking action that will affect land, water, or air; an analysis of the effect of a project on the environment.

Environmental Protection Agency (EPA) The main federal agency responsible for the enforcement of all the federal environmental laws.

Equal Credit Opportunity Act (ECOA) Federal law that prohibits discrimination on the basis of race, sex, national origin, marital status, or ethnicity in the decision to extend credit.

Equal Employment Opportunity Act of 1972 Congressional act that established the EEOC and provided strong enforcement powers for Title VII provisions.

Equal Employment Opportunity Commission (EEOC) Federal agency responsible for the enforcement of Title VII and other federal antidiscrimination laws.

Equal Pay Act of 1963 Act prohibiting wage discrimination on the basis of age, race, sex, ethnicity, and so on.

equitable remedy A remedy other than money damages, such as specific performance, injunction, and so on.

equity That portion of the law that originated to afford remedies when money damages were not appropriate; currently, remedies of law and equity have merged and courts can award either or both.

ethical culture The ethical tone of a company that can be enhanced by factors such as having a code of ethics, a means for employees to report misconduct anonymously, and sanctions and terminations for those employees and officers who violate the law and company rules.

European Court of Human Rights A noncommercial court dealing with disputes over the treatment of a country's citizens.

exclusionary conduct Monopolistic behavior that attempts to prevent market entry and exclude competition.

exclusive distributorship *See* **sole outlet**.

exclusive jurisdiction Authority granted to only one court for particular types of cases.

exculpatory clause Clause that attempts to hold a party harmless in the event of damage or injury to another's property.

executive branch That portion of the federal government that consists of the president and the administrative agencies; often referred to as the enforcement branch.

executive order Law of the executive branch; sets policies for administrative workers and contracts.

exempt securities Securities not required to be registered with the SEC under the 1933 Securities Act.

exempt transactions Under the 1933 Securities Act, sales of securities not required to be registered, such as shares issued under a Chapter 11 bankruptcy court reorganization.

exemptions Under the Securities Act of 1933, the securities and transactions that need not be registered with the SEC.

exhausting administrative remedies Requirement that all procedures internal to an administrative body be exhausted before an individual pursues a remedy in court.

express contract Contract agreed to orally or in writing.

express warranty Expressed promise by seller as to the quality, abilities, or performance of a product.

expropriation The taking of private property by a government for government use, also known as appropriation.

F

facilitation Steps to get officials to do their normal jobs and in a timely manner.

failing-company doctrine Under the Clayton Act, a justification for a generally illegal merger on the basis that the firm being merged is in financial difficulty and would not survive alone.

Fair Credit Billing Act Federal law governing credit card bills and requiring monthly statements, disclosure of dispute rights, and so on.

Fair Credit and Charge Card Disclosure Act of 1988 Amendment to the Truth in Lending Act that requires disclosure of terms in credit card solicitations.

Fair Credit Reporting Act (FCRA) Federal law governing the disclosure of credit information to consumers and the content of those credit reports.

Fair Debt Collections Practices Act (FDCPA) Federal law controlling the methods debt collectors may use in collecting consumer debts and also requiring disclosures to consumers when the debt collection process begins.

Fair Labor Standards Act (FLSA) Federal law on minimum wages, maximum hours, overtime, and compensatory time.

fair trade contracts Agreements requiring retailers not to sell products below a certain price; permitted in some states.

fair use One of the exceptions to copyright protection; permits limited use of copyright material; for example, an excerpt from a poem.

"fair-diclosure rule" (Regulations FD) An act promulgated by the SEC that requires that material information about the company be made available to everyone at the same time.

false imprisonment The intentional tort of retaining someone against that person's will.

federal circuits Geographic groupings of the federal district courts for purposes of appellate jurisdiction.

federal district court The trial court of the federal system.

Federal Environmental Pesticide Control Act Federal law that requires registration of all pesticides with the EPA.

Federal Insurance Contributions Act (FICA) Federal law that requires the joint contribution by employers and employees of the funds used for the SocialSecurity system.

Federal Privacy Act Federal law that prohibits exchange of information about individuals among agencies with out request and notification, unless for law enforcement purposes.

Federal Register A daily federal publication that reports the day-to-day actions of administrative agencies.

Federal Register Act Federal law that establishes all the publications and reporting mechanisms for federal administrative law, such as the *Federal Register* and the *Code of Federal Regulations.*

Federal Register System Part of the federal government responsible for the publication of government notices and rules.

Federal Trade Commission (FTC) Federal agency responsible for regulation of unfair and deceptive trade practices, including deceptive advertisements.

Federal Trade Commission Act Federal law establishing the FTC and its regulatory role.

Federal Trademark Dilution Act Federal law that permits litigation to halt the use of a trademark that results in the loss of unique appeal for its owner.

Federal Water Pollution Control Act of 1972 Federal law that set goals of swimmable and fishable waters by 1983 and zero pollution discharge by 1985.

Federal Water Pollution Control Administration (FWPCA) Separate federal agency established to monitor water quality standards.

fiduciary Position of trust and confidence.

Fifth Amendment Portion of the Bill of Rights of the U.S. Constitution providing protection against self-fincrimination and ensuring due process.

finance charges For credit cards, the interest paid each month on outstanding balances.

FOIA request Request to a government agency for information retained in that agency's files.

force majeure Clause in a contract that excuses performance in the event of war, embargo, or other generally unforeseeable event.

foreign corporation A corporation in any state except the state in which it is incorporated.

Foreign Corrupt Practices Act (FCPA) Federal law prohibiting bribes in foreign countries and requiring the maintenance of internal controls on accounting for firms registered under the Securities Exchange Act of 1934.

formal rulemaking Process for developing rules in an administrative agency; involves hearings and public comment period.

Fourteenth Amendment Provision of the U.S. Constitution that provides for equal protection and due process.

Fourth Amendment Part of the Bill of Rights of the U.S. Constitution that provides protection and assurance of privacy; the search and seizure amendment.

fraud Term for deception or intentional misrepresentation in contract negotiation.

Freedom of Information Act (FOIA) Federal law that permits access to information held by federal administrative agencies.

Front page-of-the Newspaper Test A simple ethical model that requires only that a decision maker envision how a reporter would describe a decision on the front page of a local or national newspaper.

full-disclosure standard SEC standard for registration; materiality disclosure requirements; not a merit standard.

G

garnishment Judicial process of taking funds or wages for satisfaction of a judgment.

general partner Partner in a general or limited partnership whose personal assets are subject to partnership creditors in the event of nonpayment of partnership debts.

general warranty deed Deed that transfers title with highest guarantees of title.

geographic market Relevant geographic location for a firm's market; used as a basis for determining monopoly power and market share.

good-faith bargaining Mutual obligation of employer and union to meet at reasonable times, confer in good faith on employment issues, and execute a written agreement.

government corporation Corporation created by a government agency to achieve a social goal.

Government in the Sunshine Act Federal law that requires advance notice and open meetings of agency heads.

grand jury Special group of jurors established as a review board for potential criminal prosecutions; generally established for a year to eighteen months.

gray market Market in which trade name goods are sold through unauthorized dealers or without authorization from the owner of the trade name.

grease payments Payments to any foreign official for facilitation. Examples of such payments include obtaining permits, licenses, or other official documents; processing governmental papers, such as visas and work orders; and providing police protection and mail pickup and delivery

group boycotts A practice, prohibited by federal antitrust laws, in which several firms agree not to sell or buy from one or several other firms.

H

Hazardous Substance Response Trust Fund Fund set up by CERCLA for waste site cleanup that is funded by the responsible company.

Health Insurance Portability and Accountability Act of 1996 (HIPAA) Federal law that provides protections and procedures for patient privacy.

hearing examiner *or* **hearing officer** Quasi-judicial figure for agency hearings.

hearsay Testimony about the statements of another; often inadmissible evidence in a trial.

Home Equity Loan Consumer Protection Act of 1988 Amendment to the Truth in Lending Act that requires disclosures in home equity loan documents, including the possibility of foreclosure, and allows three-day rescission period for home equity loans.

Home Ownership and Equity Protection Act of 1994 (HOEPA) An act that requires additional disclosures for those transactions in which consumers use their homes as security for the credit.

home solicitation sales Sales originated in the home of the buyer.

horizontal restraint of trade Anticompetitive activity among competitors; for example, price fixing among competitors.

hung jury Term used to describe a jury unable to come to a verdict.

hybrid rulemaking Process by which agency promulgates rules with some hearings but relies mostly on public comments.

I

Illegal Immigration Reform and Immigrant Responsibility Act of 1996 Federal statute that increased employer responsibility for use of illegal immigrants in their workforces.

Immigration Act of 1990 Federal law that requires an I-9 form for every employee who is an immigrant.

Immigration and Naturalization Act (INA) Original federal act governing employer obligations on employing immigrants.

Immigration Reform and Control Act of 1986 (IRCA) Federal law imposing additional requirements on employers for lawful employment of immigrants.

implied authortiy Authority of an agent that exists because of business custom in the principal's operation and in industry.

implied contract A contract that arises from circumstances and is not expressed by the parties.

implied warranty of fitness for a particular purpose Warranty given by seller to buyer that promises goods will meet the buyer's specified needs.

implied warranty of merchantability Under the Uniform Commercial Code, Article 2, Sales, a warranty that the goods are of average quality; given in every sale of goods by a merchant.

implied-in-fact contract A contract deemed to exist because of the way the parties have interacted (e.g., accepting treatment at a doctor's office).

implied-in-law contract *See* **quasi-contract**.

impossibility Contract defense that excuses performance when there is no objective way to complete the contract.

in personam **jurisdiction** Jurisdiction over the person; type of jurisdiction court must have to require a party to appear before it.

in rem **jurisdiction** Jurisdiction over the thing; a method whereby a court obtains jurisdiction by having property or money located within its geographic jurisdiction.

incidental damages Damages suffered by the non-breaching party to a contract as a result of the breach; for example, late performance fees on a buyer's contract because the seller failed to deliver on time.

incorporators Individuals who sign the incorporation papers for a newly formed corporation.

independent contractor Person who works for another but is not controlled in her day-to-day conduct.

indictment Formal criminal charges issued by the grand jury.

infant A minor; a person below the age of majority, in most states below the age of 18.

informal rulemaking Process by which an agency promulgates rules without formal public hearings.

information Formal criminal charges issued by a judge after a preliminary hearing.

infringement The use of a copyright, patent, trademark, or trade name without permission.

inherence Theory of corporate social responsibility under which managers serve shareholders only.

inherently dangerous activities In agency law, those activities that carry a high risk and for which the party hiring an independent contractor cannot disclaim liability; for example, dynamiting a building to demolish it.

initial appearance In criminal procedure, the first appearance of the accused before a judicial figure; must take place shortly after arrest.

initial meeting First meeting of a corporation's organizers after the state provides certification that the corporation exists.

injunction Equitable remedy in which courts order or enjoin a particular activity.

insider A corporate officer or director or other executive with access to corporate information not available to the public.

instructions Explanation of the law applicable in a case given to the jury at the end of the evidence and arguments.

intangible property Intellectual property, such as patents and copyrights.

intellectual property Forms of intangible property that include patents, copyrights, trademarks, trade names, and trade dress; protected by federal, international, and common law.

intentional infliction of emotional distress Intentional tort in which the defendant engages in outrageous conduct that is psychologically damaging to the plaintiff.

intentional torts Civil wrongs against individuals that are committed with a requisite state of mind and intent to harm; includes defamation, false imprisonment, battery, assault, and intentional infliction of emotional distress.

Inter-American Court of Human Rights In international law, the court for resolution of noncommercial issues or the violation of human rights by a particular nation in North or South America.

interbrand competition Competition among like products; for example, competition between Pepsi and Coke.

International Court of Justice (ICJ) Voluntary court in the international system of law; nonbinding decisions.

Internet Corporation for Assigned Names and Numbers (ICANN) Organization that registers domain names for purposes of protection of those names as intellectual property.

intervenors Interested parties who are permitted to participate in agency hearings even though they are not parties to the case.

intrabrand competition Competition among products made by the same manufacturer; for example, competition between Coke and Diet Coke.

invisible hand Theory of corporate social responsibility under which managers believe they serve society but do so in the best way by being accountable to shareholders.

J

joint venture A partnership for one activity or business venture.

judge Elected or appointed government official responsible for supervising trials, hearing appeals, and ruling on motions.

judgment The final decision of a court; formal entry of the decision or verdict.

judgment NOV Judgment *non obstante veredicto*; a judgment notwithstanding the verdict; a judgment issued by the judge after the jury has rendered a verdict; a trial court's reversal of a jury's decision on the grounds that the verdict was against the weight of the evidence.

judicial branch The one (of three) branches of the federal government that consists of all levels of federal courts.

judicial review Review by appellate court of decisions and actions of a lower court to determine whether reversible errors in procedure or law were made.

jurisdiction The concept of authority of a court to settle disputes.

jurisprudence The philosophy of law.

jury instructions Explanation to the jury of the law applicable in the case.

just compensation Principle in eminent domain that requires the government entity taking private property to pay the owner a fair amount.

justice of the peace courts Lower courts generally handling traffic citations and other lesser civil matters.

justice theory A theory of jurisprudence that allows only those laws that serve to offer fairness, equality, and opportunity.

K

knock-off goods Goods manufactured by someone other than the trademark or trade name holder without authorization and not according to the standards of the owner.

L

Landrum-Griffin Act Labor-Management Reporting and Disclosure Act; legislation passed to regulate unions and their governance.

Lanham Act Federal law dealing with trademark and trade name protection.

lawyer Licensed professional who serves as a representative for another in private negotiations and in judicial and other types of legal proceedings.

legislative branch One of the three branches of government; at the federal level, consists of the Congress (the Senate and the House of Representatives) and is the branch responsible for making laws.

letter of credit Generally used in international transactions; an assurance by a bank of the seller's right to draw on a line of credit established for the buyer.

libel Written defamation; defamation in a newspaper or magazine or, in some states, on television.

like grade or quality Under Robinson-Patman Act, this means that there are no differences in the physical product.

limited jurisdiction Specialty courts that have only limited authority over certain types of cases with distinct subject matter; probate courts have limited jurisdiction over probate matters only.

limited liability company (LLC) A business entity with limited liability but management participation permitted by all; statutory creature.

limited liability partnership (LLP) Partnership in which *all* partners have limited liability; statutory creature with strict formation requirements.

limited partner Partner in a limited partnership who has no personal liability and can only lose his investment in the partnership; must be formed according to statutory requirements; cannot use name in partnership name and cannot participate in the firm's management.

limited partnership Type of partnership in which some partners have unlimited liability (general partners) and other partners have only their investments at risk in the business (limited partners); must follow statutory procedures to properly create a limited partnership.

limited partnership agreement Contract governing the rights and relations of limited partners.

liquidated damages Damages agreed to in advance and provided for in the contract; usually appropriate when it is difficult to know how much the damages will be.

long arm statutes Statutes in each state that allow the state courts to bring in defendants from outside the state so long as they have some "minimum contact" with the state.

M

Madrid Agreement Trademark protection that provides for the Madrid System of International Registration of Marks (the Madrid Protocol), which is central registration through the International Bureau, which is part of the World Intellectual Property Organization (WIPO) in Geneva, Switzerland.

mailbox rule Timing rule in contract acceptances that provides that acceptance is effective upon mailing if properly done.

mandatory bargaining terms In collective bargaining, the terms both sides are required to discuss, such as wages, hours, and so on.

market power The ability of a firm to control prices and product demand.

master-servant relationship Type of agency relationship in which the principal directly controls the agent; for example, principal controls hours and supervises work directly.

material fact (*or* material misstatement) A statement of fact that would influence an individual's decision to buy or sell.

maximum achievable control technology (MACT) Under the 1990 Clean Air Act, the standard required for factories in controlling air emissions; replaced the old, less-stringent standard of best available technology (BAT).

mediation Alternative dispute resolution mechanism in which a third party is brought in to find a common ground between two disputing parties.

meeting the competition Defense to price discrimination that allows the defense of price reduction when competition in the area dictates that price.

mens rea Mental intent or state of mind necessary for the commission of a crime.

merchant's confirmation memoranda Memos between merchants, signed by one of them, that will satisfy the statute of frauds requirements and create an enforceable contract against both parties.

merchants' firm offer Under § 2–205 of the UCC, an offer required to be held open if made in writing by a merchant, even though no consideration is given.

merit review Process at the state level of reviewing securities registrations for their merit, as opposed to the federal review for full disclosure.

minimum contacts Standard used for determining *in personam* jurisdiction over residents outside the state of the court of litigation; nonresident defendants must have some contact with the state to justify a court taking jurisdiction.

minimum wage Part of the FLSA that requires all employees to be paid a minimum wage.

minitrial Alternative dispute resolution method in which the officers of two firms in a dispute listen to the key evidence in a case to see if a settlement can be determined.

minor An infant; an individual under the age of majority; generally someone under the age of 18.

Miranda **warnings** Statement required to be given to individuals when taken into custody to alert them to their right to remain silent, the fact that statements can be used against them, their right to an attorney, and the right to an appointed attorney if they cannot afford one.

misappropriation Intentional tort of using someone's name, likeness, voice, or image without permission.

misrepresentation In contract formation, misstatements of materials facts.

misuse In product liability, a defense based on the plaintiff's failure to follow instructions or use of a product for improper purposes.

Model Business Corporation Act (MBCA) Uniform law on corporations.

modify An option for an appellate court in its review of a lower court case; an action that is something less than reversing a decision but something more than simply affirming it; for example, an appellate court could agree with the verdict but modify the judgment amount or the remedy.

monopolization Controlling a product or geographic market.

monopsony The ability to control the market through the control of a supplier and/or supplier's prices.

moral relativism Ethical theory holding that there is no absolute right and wrong and that right and wrong vary according to circumstances, often referred to as "situational ethics."

moral standards Ethical standards, as opposed to legal standards.

motion for judgment on the pleadings A motion made to dismiss a suit for failure by the plaintiff to establish a cause of action in the pleadings.

motion for summary judgment A motion made for final disposition of a case in which there is no dispute of facts and only a dispute of law and its application.

multilateral treaties A treaty agreed to by several nations.

N

Nash Model A series of questions, developed by business ethicist Laura Nash, that business managers should ask themselves as they evaluate their ethical dilemmas; this model model forces managers to seek additional perspectives as decisions are evaluated and implemented.

National Environmental Policy Act (NEPA) The federal legislation on environmental impact statements.

National Labor Relations Act (Wagner Act 1935) (NLRA) First universal federal legislation that gave employees the right to organize and choose representatives for collective bargaining.

National Labor Relations Board (NLRB) Federal agency charged with supervising union elections and handling unfair labor practice complaints.

National Pollution Discharge Elimination System (NPDES) A system established by the EPA that requires those who discharge pollutants to obtain a permit, the granting of which is based on limits and pretreatments.

nationalization The taking of private property by a government for governmental use.

natural law theory Law or principles of behavior that exist without being written; supreme laws that cannot be circumvented.

necessaries With regard to minors, items for which minors can be held responsible.

negligence Tort of accidental wrong committed by oversight or failure to take precautions or corrective action.

nexus Connection; a term used in constitutional analysis of the authority to tax; there must be a sufficient connection between the business and the taxing state.

NLRB National Labor Relations Board.

Noise Control Act of 1972 Federal statute controlling noise levels and requiring product labels.

nolo contendere A "no contest" plea; the charges are neither denied nor admitted.

nonattainment area In federal air pollution regulation, an area unable to meet federal clean air goals and guidelines.

nonbinding arbitration   Arbitration in which the decision is not final, that is, the parties can still take the matter to court.

nonconventional pollutant   EPA classification of pollutant that requires the highest level of treatment prior to release into waterways.

nonprofit corporations   Those corporations performing a function that covers cost but does not provide a return on investment.

normative standard   Ethical standards as the generally accepted rules of conduct that govern society.

Norris-LaGuardia Act   The anti-injunction act; one of the first federal labor acts passed to prevent courts from issuing injunctions to stop labor strikes except in dangerous or emergency situations.

novation   Process of reworking a contract to substitute parties or terms, so that the old contract is abandoned and the new contract becomes the only valid contract.

nuisance   Civil wrong of creating a situation (noise, dust, smell) that interferes with others' ability to enjoy the use of their properties.

O

Occupational Safety and Health Act   Worker safety statute passed by Congress in 1970 that established OSHA and directs the development of safety standards in the workplace as well as systems for record keeping and compliance.

Occupational Safety and Health Administration (OSHA)   Federal agency responsible for the enforcement of federal health and safety standards in business and industry.

offer   Indication of present intent to contract; the first step in making a contract.

offeree   In contract negotiations, the person to whom the offer is made.

offeror   In contract negotiations, the person who makes the offer.

Oil Pollution Act (OPA)   Federal law providing penalties for oil spills and authorizing federal cleanup when private companies' cleanup efforts fail; also authorizes federal government to collect for costs of cleanup when firm or firms responsible for the spill fail to do so.

omnibus hearing   In criminal procedure, a hearing held before the trial to determine the admissibility of evidence.

open-end credit transaction   Under Regulation Z, credit transactions without a definite beginning and ending balance; for example, credit cards.

open meeting law   Law (at either state or federal level) requiring that notice be given of meetings of agency heads and that they be open to the public.

opening statement   In a trial, each side's overview of the case and the evidence that will be presented.

opposition proceedings   In non-U.S. countries, the patent process that allows third parties to appear and object to a patent application.

option   A contract for time on an offer; an agreement to hold an offer open for a period of time in exchange for consideration.

oral argument   Upon appeal of a case, the attorneys' presentation of their points on appeal to the panel of appellate judges.

order theory   A theory of jurisprudence that provides that only those laws that serve to create and preserve order are valid. Order theorists allow laws that control behavior or provide conduct guidelines.

ordinances   Laws at the city, town, or country level.

ordinary and reasonably prudent person   In negligence, standard used for determining the level of care required in any given situation.

Organization for Economic Cooperation and Development (OECD)   International organization of countries committed to developing trade, initially through the elimination of corruption.

overtime pay   Pay rate required for work beyond the maximum forty-hour work week.

P

palming off   Unfair trade practice of passing off mock goods as the goods of another.

parol evidence   Extrinsic evidence regarding a contract.

partnership   Voluntary association of two or more persons, co-owners in a business for profit.

partnership by estoppel   *See* **estoppel**.

partnership by implication   A partnership that exists because of the conduct of the parties rather than by agreement.

party autonomy   The right of parties to determine privately their choice of law.

patent   Government license or protection for a process, product, or ser vice.

pattern or practice of discrimination   In employment discrimination, a theory for establishing discrimination based on a pattern of dealing with minorities, women, and certain ethnic groups.

peer review   Method of dispute resolution in which peers of the party making a claim decide on its merits; for example, employee peer review of claims against the employer.

Pension Protection Act of 2006   Federal law that imposes additional funding and disclosure requirements on employers who have employee pension plans.

per curiam   A judicial opinion of the full court with no judge or justice claiming authorship.

peremptory challenge   Right to strike jurors with or without cause; lawyer's discretionary tool in selecting a jury; number of peremptory challenges is usually limited.

per se "On its face"; "without further proof."

petition Often the first document in a case.

petitioner Party filing a petition; or in the case of an appeal, the party filing the appeal of a lower court decision.

plaintiff Party filing suit, who is alleging a wrong committed by the defendant.

plea bargain A negotiated settlement of a criminal case prior to trial.

pleadings The complaint, answer, and counterclaim filed in a lawsuit.

point sources In environmental law, direct discharges of effluents.

police power Constitutional term describing the authority given to the states to regulate the health, safety, and welfare of their citizens.

political speech Term given to speech of businesses related to political candidates or issues; given First Amendment protection.

pooling agreement Agreement among shareholders to vote their stock a certain way.

positive law Codified law; law created and enforced by governmental entities.

power theory A theory of jurisprudence that the law is whatever those who are in charge say the law should be, that law comes from power.

precautionary principle A principle used to guide regulations in the area of the environment and product liability; the principle mandates regulation as a prevention measure even when data are not clear as to whether harm results from product or practice (in environmental context).

precedent Prior judicial decisions; the law as it exists; *see also* **stare decisis**.

predatory bidding Company with market power using high-bid pricing to drive its competitors from the market place by inflating the cost of supplies.

predatory pricing Discount pricing below cost for a short period of time in an attempt to drive new competition out of the market.

preemption Constitutional term from the Supremacy Clause, which provides that the federal government preempts state law where such preemption was intended or where the federal regulation is so pervasive that it prevents state regulation.

preferred stock Nonvoting shares of a corporation entitling its holders to dividend preference above the common shareholders.

Pregnancy Discrimination Act Federal law prohibiting discrimination in hiring or promotion decisions on the basis of pregnancy or plans for pregnancy.

preliminary hearing In criminal procedure, the hearing in which the prosecution establishes there is sufficient evidence to bind the defendant over for trial.

prevention of significant deterioration (PSD) areas Clean air areas given special protection by the EPA regarding the maintenance of air quality.

price discrimination Charging a different price for different customers on a basis other than different marginal costs.

prima facie **case** A case establishing all the necessary elements; without rebuttal evidence from the defendant, en titles the plaintiff to a verdict.

primary offering In securities, the initial offering of the security for sale.

principal The employer or master in the principal agent relationship.

private law The law of contracts and the intrabusiness laws such as personnel rules.

privity Direct contractual relationship.

procedural due process Constitutional protection that gives litigants in civil cases and defendants in criminal cases the right to notice in all steps in the process and the right of participation.

procedural laws Laws that provide the means for enforcing rights.

process servers Individuals licensed by a state to deliver summonses and subpoenas to individuals.

product disparagement Defamation of a product.

product market Relevant product market for a firm; used as a basis for determining monopoly power.

professional corporation A statutory entity that permits professionals such as lawyers and doctors to incorporate and enjoy limited personal liability on all debts except for those arising from malpractice.

profit corporations Those corporations seeking to earn a return for their investors.

promissory estoppel A promise that causes another to act in reliance upon it; if the reliance is substantial, the promise is enforceable.

proper purpose A shareholder's legitimate interest in accessing a corporation's books and records.

prospectus A formal document describing the nature of securities and the company offering them; an ad or other description of securities.

proxy Right (given in written form) to vote another's shares.

proxy solicitation The process of seeking voting rights from shareholders.

public comment period In administrative rulemaking, the period during which any member of the public can comment on the rule, its content, and potential efficacy.

public law Law passed by some governmental agency.

publicly held corporation A corporation owned by shareholders outside the officers and employees of the firm.

puffing Offering opinion about the quality of goods and products; not a basis for misrepresentation; not a material statement of fact.

Q

qualified privilege A defense to defamation available to the media that permits retraction and no liability so long as the information is not printed or given with malice or with reckless disregard for whether it is true.

quasi-contract A theory used to prevent unjust enrichment when no contract is formed; the court acts as if a contract had been formed and awards damages accordingly.

quotas Affirmative action plans that dictate a specific number of minority or female applicants be accepted for jobs, graduate school, and so on. Outlawed by U.S. Supreme Court; can only have affirmative action goals, not specific quotas.

R

ratification A principal's recognition of a contract entered into by an unauthorized agent.

record Expanded form of documentation that qualifies as a "writing" for purposes of contracts under the UCC.

red herring prospectus A prospectus issued in advance of the effective date of a securities registration statement; permissible to release these before the registration statement is effective so long as a disclaimer that it is not an offer to sell securities is noted in red on the prospectus.

redirect examination Plaintiff's questioning of his own witness after defendant's cross-examination is complete; or vice versa when defendant's witness is involved.

regional reporter Series of volumes reporting the appeals and supreme court decisions of state courts; grouped by geographic region; for example, Pacific Reporter for the western states.

registration statement (S-1) Requirement under the 1933 Securities Act; a filing with the SEC that discloses all the necessary information about a securities offering and the offeror.

Regulation A Short form offering regulation under 1933 Securities Act.

Regulation D A regulation of the SEC governing the small offering exemptions under the 1933 Securities Act.

Regulation Z The Federal Reserve Board's regulation for the Truth in Lending Act; specifies disclosure requirements and offers examples of required forms.

Regulatory Flexibility Act Reform act for federal agency rules promulgation; requires publication of proposed rules in trade magazines so that industries and individuals affected can properly respond during the public comment period.

Rehabilitation Act of 1973 Federal law prohibiting discrimination by federal contractors on the basis of a handicapping condition.

relevant market Term used to describe the market studied to determine whether a particular seller has a monopoly.

remand Term used to describe the action an appellate court takes when a case is sent down to a lower court for a retrial or other proceeding on the basis of the appellate court decision.

rent-a-judge Means of alternative dispute resolution in which the parties hire a former judge and a private hearing room and have the judge determine liability.

repatriation Reaffiliating as a citizen of a country after having renounced that citizenship through expatriation.

Reporting or "hot" line Anonymous phone access for employees to report legal and ethical violations in an organization.

request for admissions Discovery tool in which one side asks the other to admit certain facts as proven in a case.

request for production Discovery tool in which one side asks the other side to produce documents relevant to the case.

resale price maintenance Practice of manufacturer attempting to control the price at which a product is sold at retail level.

rescission Process of rescinding a contract.

Resource Conservation and Recovery Act of 1976 (RCRA) Federal law governing the transportation of hazardous materials; requires a permit for such transportation; also encourages environmental cleanup.

respondeat superior "Let the master answer"; doctrine holds principal responsible for torts of agent in scope of employment.

respondent On appeal of a case, the party who is not appealing; in a petition for a divorce, the party against whom the petition is filed.

Restatement of Agency A summary of the majority view of the states of the law of agency followed by courts in resolving agency issues and disputes.

Restatement (Second) of Contracts General summary of the nature of common law contracts in the United States.

reverse Action of an appellate court in changing the decision of a lower court because a reversible error has been made.

reversible error Mistake made in lower court proceedings that is ruled as improper by an appellate court and that requires a reversal of the case and possible retrial.

Revised Uniform Limited Partnership Act (RULPA) New version of the Uniform Limited Partnership Act that includes changes in the rights of limited partners and distributions on liquidation.

Revised Uniform Partnership Act (RUPA) Newest uniform revision of law on limited partnerships.

revocation In contract law, the retraction by the offeror of an outstanding offer.

right-to-sue letter Letter issued by the EEOC to a complainant after all necessary administrative steps have been taken in the case; permits the complainant to pursue court action.

right-to-work laws State laws providing employees with the right to work even though they are not union members.

Rivers and Harbors Act of 1899 A federal law revitalized during the 1960s and 1970s (prior to the enactment of specific federal legislation controlling emissions) to control water pollution.

Robinson-Patman Act Federal law that prohibits price discrimination.

Rule 10b-5 SEC antifraud rule.

rule of reason Standard for evaluation of antitrust activity that allows the court to consider various factors and does not require an automatic finding of a violation of antitrust laws.

Rules 504, 505, and 506 *See* **Regulation D;** the rules governing small offering exemptions under the 1933 Securities Act.

S

S Corporation A form of corporation that benefits from having shareholders' income and losses treated like those of partners yet the shareholders enjoy the protection of limited liability behind a corporate veil. The income earned and losses incurred by an S corporation are reported on the shareholders' individual returns, but the shareholders' personal assets are protected from creditors of the business.

Safe Drinking Water Act Federal law passed in 1986 that sets standards for drinking water systems and requires states to enforce them.

Sarbanes-Oxley Act of 2002 An act passed by Congress to restore public confidence and trust in the financial statements of companies.

scheduled injuries Under workers' compensation systems, listed injury for which certain payments are to be made to the injured worker.

scienter Mental intent; under 10(b) of the Securities Exchange Act of 1934, a requirement of intent to defraud as opposed to a standard of negligence.

scope of employment Phrase used to describe the liability limits of the principal for the agent; an act must be committed within this scope for the imposition of liability on the principal.

search warrant Judicially authorized document allowing the search of individuals' or businesses' premises.

Section 10(b) Antifraud provision of the Securities Exchange Act of 1934.

Section 16 Section of the Securities Exchange Act of 1934 that regulates sales and purchases of shares by directors, officers, and 10 percent shareholders.

securities Investments in a common enterprise with profits to come largely from the efforts of others.

Securities Act of 1933 The federal law governing the initial issuance and sale of securities to the public.

Securities Exchange Act of 1934 The federal law governing secondary sales of securities, the markets, and the firms dealing with securities.

Securities Exchange Commission (SEC) Federal agency responsible for enforcement of federal securities laws.

security agreement Contract that creates a security interest.

security interest Lien in personal property; created under Article IX of the UCC.

self-incrimination Protection provided under the Fifth Amendment of not being required to be a witness against oneself.

separation of powers Principle of U.S. Constitution that divides authority for various governmental functions among the three branches of government.

sexual harassment Unlawful suggestions, contact, or other advances in the workplace; prohibited under federal law.

shopkeeper's privilege A defense to the tort of false imprisonment for storeowners; allows reasonable detention of shoppers upon reasonable suspicion of shoplifting.

short-swing profits Profits made by corporate insiders during a period of less than six months between purchase and sale.

Sixth Amendment Amendment to U.S. Constitution that guarantees the right to a jury trial in criminal cases.

slander Tort of oral defamation.

slander of title Slander of business.

small claims court Specialized court designed to allow the hearing of claims of limited monetary amounts without the complexities of litigation and without attorneys.

small-company doctrine Exemption from merger prohibitions that permits two smaller firms to merge in order to compete better against other, larger firms in the market.

social responsibility Theory of corporate social responsibility under which managers serve society by being accountable to society, not shareholders.

sole outlet Manufacturer's only designated seller in a particular area.

sole proprietorship Method of business ownership; one person owns business, receives all profits, and is personally liable for all debts.

Sonny Bono Copyright Term Extension Act (CTEA) Federal law that amends copyright law to extend period of protection for copyrighted works.

sovereign immunity Doctrine that provides that courts in one country are that country's law and cannot be reversed by decisions of courts in other countries; for example, a U.S. court cannot reverse a finding of not guilty by a court in Germany.

stare decisis Latin term for "Let the decision stand"; the doctrine of following or distinguishing case precedent.

state codes State laws passed by legislatures.

state implementation plans (SIPs) State plans for attaining federal air quality standards.

statute of frauds Generic term referring to statutes requiring certain contracts to be in writing.

statute of limitations Generic term referring to various state statutes controlling the time periods in which suits must be brought by plaintiffs; time varies accordingto the nature of the suit; for example, contract statutes of limitations are generally four years.

statutory law Law codified and written; passed by some governmental entity.

stipulated means In contracts, a method of acceptance specified or stipulated in the offer; if followed by the offeree, the mailbox rule applies for the timing of the acceptance.

strict liability Degree of liability for conduct; an absolute standard of liability.

strict tort liability Standard established under the *Restatement of Torts* that holds product manufacturers and sellers liable for injuries resulting from their products regardless of whether they knew of the danger that caused the injury.

subject matter jurisdiction The right of a court to hear disputes involving certain areas of law and/or amounts.

submarket In antitrust law, a segment of a market examined for purposes of determining either the impact on competition of a merger or the market strength of a competitor (e.g., tennis court shoes as a submarket of the tennis shoe market).

substantial performance Contract defense for performing a contract slightly differently from what was agreed upon; justification for substitute but equal performance; generally applicable in construction contracts.

substantive due process Constitutional protection that requires laws to apply equally to all and not to deny property or rights without prior notice.

substantive laws Laws that give rights and responsibilities to individuals.

summary judgment Method for terminating a case at the trial court level when there are no issues of fact and only a decision on the application of law needs to be made.

summary jury trial A private method of alternative dispute resolution in which the parties present a summary of their evidence to a private jury and then agree to abide by their decision or settle, depending on what the jury concludes; held privately and can often save the cost of going to court for a real trial.

summons Court document issued to the defendant in a lawsuit that explains the requirement of filing an answer and the time period in which it must be done.

Superfund Federal fund used to clean up toxic waste disposal areas.

Superfund Amendment and Reauthorization Act Federal legislation extending CERCLA's authority and the liability of property owners and waste handlers for the cleanup of polluted lands.

superior skill, foresight, and industry Defense to monopolization based on "building a better mousetrap" and customers flocking to your door.

Supremacy Clause Constitutional provision allowing federal laws to preempt state laws where Congress intended or where the regulation is pervasive.

Supreme Court Reporter Series of volumes reporting the decisions of the U.S. Supreme Court.

Surface Mining and Reclamation Act of 1977 Federal law that requires restoration of surface coal mining land.

T

Taft-Hartley Act Labor Management Relations Act; federal law governing management in union relations.

tangible property Form of personal property that includes goods, but not intellectual property such as stocks, bonds, patents, trademarks, and copyright.

10-K form Annual report filed with the SEC; required of all 1934 Act firms.

10-Q form Quarterly report filed with the SEC; required of all 1934 Act firms.

theft Crime of taking property away from another permanently.

three-day cooling-off period Under Regulation Z, the period a buyer has to change his mind about a transaction initiated in the home.

tippee Party who is privy to inside information about a corporation or its securities and uses the information to trade securities profitably.

Title VII Portion of the Civil Rights Act of 1964 prohibiting employment discrimination.

tombstone ad Ad run in newspapers announcing an upcoming securities offering; permissible after the registration statement is filed but not yet effective; must indicate it is not an offer for sale.

Tone at the top A tone of ethical culture set by actions of officers and executives that show they "walk the talk" about ethics.

tort Private intentional or negligent wrong against an individual.

tortious interference with contracts Conduct by one party that results in another's breaching her contract with a third person (applies also to corporations).

toxic pollutant EPA classification of pollutant that requires the highest level of treatment prior to release.

Toxic Substances Control Act (TOSCA) Federal statute governing the control of the release of toxic substances into the environment.

trade dress The look, color, and decorative design of a business.

trade libel Libel of a business.

trade name Name of a firm or product; entitled to federal protection for exclusive use.

trade restraints Obstacles to free and open competition.

trade secret A protected method for doing business or an item crucial to a business's success (such as a customer list).

trademark The symbol of a firm; entitled to federal protection for exclusive use.

traffic court Lesser trial court, in which traffic cases and violations of other city ordinances are tried.

transfer restrictions Limitations on the resale of shares of a corporation.

treaty In international law, an agreement between two or more nations.

treble damages In antitrust law and securities law, a civil remedy that permits successful claimants to recover three times the amount of their actual damages.

trial Process in a court of presenting evidence for a determination of guilt, innocence, or liability.

trial *de novo* Latin for "trial again" or "trial anew."

Truth in Lending Act (TILA) The Consumer Credit Protection Act; affords disclosure protection for consumer debt.

tying sales Anticompetitive behavior requiring the purchase of another product in order to get the product actually needed.

U

ultra vires Action taken beyond the scope of authority; with federal agencies, action taken that is beyond the congressional authority given in the enabling statute.

unauthorized appropriation The use of someone's name, likeness, or voice without permission for commercial advantage.

unconscionable Term used to describe contracts that are grossly unfair to one side in the contract; a defense to an otherwise valid contract.

undue influence Contract defense based on one party taking advantage of a relationship of trust and confidence.

unenforceable contract A contract that cannot be enforced because of a procedural error.

Uniform Commercial Code (UCC) Uniform law adopted in forty-nine states governing sales contracts for goods, commercial paper, security interests, documents of title, and securities transfers.

Uniform Computer Information Transactions Act (UCITA) Uniform law that governs sales of software, databases, and other products used on computers.

Uniform Durable Power of Attorney Act Act that allows individuals to set up a power of attorney that takes effect only if they are incapacitated.

Uniform Electronic Transactions Act (UETA) Uniform law for states that provides the rule for formation of electronic contracts.

uniform laws Series of laws drafted by groups of business people, law professors, and lawyers; adopted and codified by states to help attain a more uniform commercial environment for transactions.

Uniform Partnership Act (UPA) Uniform law adopted in 49 states governing the creation, operation, and termination of general partnerships.

unincorporated association A group of individuals that acts as an entity but has no legal existence.

United Nations Convention on Contracts for the International Sale of Goods (CISG) U.N. version of Article II on sales of goods for international transactions.

United States Code (U.S.C.) Statutory volumes of congressional enactments.

Uniting and Strengthening America by Proving Appropriate Tools Required to Intercept and Obstruct Terrorism Act (USA Patriot Act) Federal law that permits expanded warrant and investigation techniques for federal agencies as well as the sharing of information about suspected terrorists; also imposes control on large cash transactions for banks, real property, and vehicles.

universal treaty A treaty accepted and recognized by all countries; for example, the Warsaw Convention on air travel.

unscheduled injuries Workplace injuries without specific award amounts covered in the workers' compensation statutes.

U.S. Constitution The cornerstone of the federal government's structure and the basis of private citizens' rights and protections.

U.S. Department of Homeland Security Federal agency that is an umbrella for several existing agencies that was designed to bring together all the functions related to emergencies, immigration, border security, and antiterrorism efforts.

U.S. Government Manual Book published by the U.S. government that includes descriptions and organizational charts for all federal agencies.

U.S. Supreme Court The highest appellate court in the federal system and also the highest appellate court for state appeals.

usury Charging interest above the statutory maximum.

V

verdict The outcome or decision in a trial.

vertical merger Merger between a manufacturer and a retailer; a merger between two companies in the chain of vertical distribution.

void contract In contracts, a contract that neither side is required to perform; for example, an illegal contract is void.

voidable contract In contracts, a contract one side can choose not to perform; for example, a minor can choose not to perform his contract.

voir dire Process of questioning jurors to screen for bias and determine whether a lawyer wishes to exercise her peremptory challenge.

voting trust Arrangement among shareholders to gain uniform voting and some power by signing over voting rights on shares to a trustee; shareholders still get dividends, but trustee votes the shares; must be in writing and recorded with the corporation.

W

Wagner Act National Labor Relations Act; federal law governing the rights of unions and establishing the NLRB.

Wall Street Journal Model A resolution of ethical dilemmas that consists of compliance, contribution, and consequences.

warrant Court document authorizing an arrest or a search.

Water Quality Act (1965) First federal law to set water quality standards.

watered shares Shares for which par value was not paid; shareholder is liable for the difference between what was paid and the par value per share.

Wheeler-Lea Act Amendment to the FTC Act that permits prosecution under Section 5 if a consumer is injured, even though there is no injury to a competitor.

white-collar crime Crimes committed in business administration and/or professional capacity; the socalled paperwork crimes.

work product An attorney's thoughts, research, and strategy in a case; nondiscoverable.

workers' compensation State system of providing for payment for workers injured on the job to avoid having liability suits by employees against employers.

working requirements Non-U.S. countries' patent requirement that the process or product be placed on the market within a certain time after the patent is granted, or the patent protection is lost.

Y

Yield spread premium The difference between what the mortgage broker charges and the actual interest rate on the loan, which is the broker's fee.

yellow-dog contract Agreement by employee with employer whereby employee will not join a union.

Table of Cases

Table of Products, People and Companies

Index

www - funbrain . Com